THE EXPERIENCE
OF PHILOSOPHY

THE EXPERIENCE OF PHILOSOPHY

Daniel Kolak
William Paterson College

Raymond Martin
University of Maryland

Wadsworth Publishing Company
Belmont, California
A Division of Wadsworth, Inc.

Philosophy Editor: Kenneth King
Editorial Assistant: Gay Meixel
Production: Ruth Cottrell
Print Buyer: Diana Spence
Permissions Editor: Robert Kauser
Designer: Polly Christensen, Christensen & Son Design
Copy Editor: Sheryl Rose
Cover: Juan Vargas
Cover Illustration: Françoise Gilot: *Continuity*, 1967, oil on canvas, 130 x 162 cm.
from the collection of Paloma Picasso. Copyright © Françoise Gilot.
Signing Representative: Rochelle Turoff
Compositor: TypeLink, Inc.
Printer: Malloy Lithographing, Inc.

*This book is printed on
acid-free recycled paper.*

1 2 3 4 5 6 7 8 9 10 — 97 96 95 94 93

Library of Congress Cataloging-in-Publication Data

The Experience of philosophy / [edited by] Daniel Kolak, Raymond Martin. — 2nd ed.
    p. cm.
  Includes bibliographical references.
  ISBN 0-534-19716-7
  1. Philosophy. I. Kolak, Daniel. II. Martin, Raymond, 1941-
B29.E96 1992
100 — dc20   92-2443
                                                  CIP

To our teachers

Preface

OUR PURPOSE IS TO PROVIDE A PROVOCATIVE AND ACCESSIBLE ANTHOLOGY that reflects the ways philosophy has changed over the last two decades. Our focus is not on the history of philosophy but, rather, on important ideas. While classical sources are not neglected, the core of the material is recent philosophy with an emphasis on an interdisciplinary approach that links philosophy to the physical and social sciences and to literature.

We make no attempt to be comprehensive. We substitute for the goal of being comprehensive the twin goals of being accessible and provocative. We want to excite and challenge readers with dramatic and important ideas that have the explosive power to completely and irrevocably change the way they think about themselves and the world.

The selections are fresh, easy to read, and deliver a powerful philosophical punch. In most cases they require little in the way of lecture supplement — none if they are used in conjunction with Kolak and Martin, *Wisdom Without Answers* (Wadsworth, 1991). We included the selections not just because they present important ideas but also because they are gripping. Each selection pulls readers out of their ordinary frameworks and challenges them to think critically about issues deeply relevant to their lives. To get most readers *to think* the issues, you first have to get them *to feel* the issues. Hence our title: *The Experience of Philosophy*.

Each of the fourteen sections of the book opens with an introduction designed to *provoke* the reader to want to read on. In addition, there is an individual introduction to each of the seventy-three selections. These individual introductions provide biographical information on the authors and orient the reader to the particular issues raised in the selection.

Each selection is framed by two sets of questions. The "Reading Questions" are designed to aid reading comprehension. They focus the reader's attention on the main points in the selection and can serve as a quick self-test: readers who can answer these questions successfully have at least minimally understood the main points. "Further Questions" are designed to help readers think critically about the issues raised in the selections.

For the second edition, we added an entire section on the problem of free will and determinism. And we added several selections to the God section to provide it with a better balance among views. In addition, we strengthened the Where and When section by adding an original paper on Zeno's paradoxes; the Knowledge section by improving the Russell selection; the Reality section by adding a selection on the debate over scientific realism; and the Ethics and Values sections by adding several new selections. We also improved the study questions throughout, added a glossary of key terms, and updated the suggestions for further reading.

Many people helped in various ways with this project. For their help with the first edition, we especially wish to thank Marshall Missner, Garrett Thomson, Milton Goldinger, John Burr, J. R. Salamanca, Freeman Dyson, Heidi Storl, Peter Unger, Wendy

Zentz, Stephen Davies, David Prejsnar, Timothy Shanahan, Paul Shepard, and Morton Winston.

For extremely helpful reviews of our proposal for the second edition, we would like to thank Mary Ann Carroll, Appalachian State University; Gary N. Kemp, University of California — Santa Barbara; John Knight, University of Wisconsin Center — Waukesha County; Louisa Moon, MiraCosta College; and Gary Ortega, Santa Monica College.

Special thanks also to Ruth Cottrell, who handled the production for the second edition, and, as always, to our editor, Ken King, for doing what he does so well.

Contents

Part V: *Knowledge*

Part VI: *God*

Part VII: *Reality*

Part VIII: *Experience*

Part XIV: *Values*

Part XIV: *Values* — 547

Glossary

THE EXPERIENCE
OF PHILOSOPHY

Part I

Beginning Philosophy

THERE IS A FROZEN SEA WITHIN US. Philosophy is an axe.

Everything you believe is questionable. How deeply have you questioned it? The uncritical acceptance of beliefs handed down to you by parents, teachers, politicians, and religious leaders is dangerous. Many of these beliefs are simply false. Some of them are lies, designed to control you. Even when what has been handed down is true, it is not *your* truth. To merely accept anything without questioning it is to be somebody else's puppet, a second-hand person.

Beliefs can be handed down. Knowledge can perhaps be handed down. Wisdom can never be handed down. The goal of philosophy is wisdom. Trying to hand down philosophy is unphilosophical.

Wisdom requires questioning what is questionable. Since everything is questionable, wisdom requires questioning everything. That is what philosophy is: the art of questioning *everything*.

The Trial and Death of Socrates
(From the *Euthyphro, Apology, Crito, Phaedo*)

PLATO

Plato was born in Athens about 427 B.C. to a prominent aristocratic family. Around 387 B.C. he founded the first university, which he named after a hero called Academus; it lasted more than a thousand years. Plato wrote philosophy, poetry and drama, worked as a politician, and was a champion wrestler. He is certainly one of the most influential persons in history; one prominent twentieth-century philosopher has called all Western philosophy merely "a series of footnotes to Plato." Plato lived to be eighty.

In what you are about to read, Plato describes the trial and death of his illustrious teacher, Socrates, also one of the greatest philosophers of all time. Unlike Plato, Socrates wrote nothing. All we know of him is from what others have written. Socrates based his philosophy on the rigorous and unrelentless questioning of all accepted truths and authorities. In 399 B.C., when Socrates was about seventy, his fellow Athenians put him on trial for corrupting the youth of Athens and for raising doubts in people's minds about their accepted gods. All this happened in the aftermath of a long war against Sparta that had raged for most of Plato's life. It was a time when the aristocracy was vying with the democratic masses for control of the state. In what follows, Plato recounts Socrates's irreverent response to the charges against him.

Many people consider religion and morality to be inseparable. In the first dialogue, however, Plato severed ethics from theology (*more than two thousand years ago!*) with one penetrating question: Is an act right because God approves of it, or does God approve of it because it is right? Concerning this question, the philosopher Antony Flew has remarked that "one good test of a person's aptitude for philosophy is to discover whether he can grasp its force and point."

Socrates is here on his way to his famous trial, about which you read in the first selection. He runs into Euthyphro, who tries to base morality on religious principles, and proceeds to make a fool out of him. Pay close attention to the method of cross-examination Socrates uses; it is a perfect example of the so-called "Socratic method."

Euthyphro

Reading Questions

1. What does Socrates mean by "piety"? Why does Euthyphro have such a difficult time trying to define this term?

2. What is the significance of the "disagreement" between the gods? Can you translate this "disagreement" into contemporary terms?

3. How would you describe, using your own words, the "method" Socrates uses against Euthyphro? What is Socrates trying to do? Does he succeed?

4. Why is Socrates being prosecuted?

5. List Euthyphro's definitions of piety and Socrates' objections to each one.

6. What is Socrates' definition of piety, and his objection to his own definition?

Euth.: BUT WHAT IS THE CHARGE which he [Meletus] brings against you?

Soc.: What is the charge? Well, rather a grand one, which implies a degree of discernment far from contemptible in a young man. He says he knows how the youth are corrupted and who are their corruptors. I fancy that he must be a wise man, and seeing that I am the reverse of a wise man, he has found me out, and is going to accuse me of corrupting his generation. And of this our mother the state is to be the judge. Of all our political men he is the only one who seems to me to begin in the right way, with the cultivation of virtue in youth; like a good husbandman, he makes the young shoots his first care, and clears away us whom he accuses of destroying them. This is only the first step; afterwards he will assuredly attend to the elder branches; and if he goes on as he has begun, he will be a very great public benefactor.

Euth.: I hope that he may; but I rather fear, Socrates, that the opposite will turn out to be the truth. My opinion is that in attacking you he is simply aiming a blow at the heart of the state. But in what way does he say that you corrupt the young?

Reprinted from The Dialogues of Plato *translated by Benjamin Jowett (4th ed. 1953) by permission of Oxford University Press.*

Soc.: In a curious way, which at first hearing excites surprise: he says that I am a maker of gods, and that I invent new gods and deny the existence of the old ones; this is the ground of his indictment.

Euth.: I understand, Socrates; he means to attack you about the familiar sign which occasionally, as you say, comes to you. He thinks that you are a neologian, and he is going to have you up before the court for this. He knows that such a charge is readily received by the world, as I myself know too well; for when I speak in the assembly about divine things, and foretell the future to them, they laugh at me and think me a madman. Yet every word that I say is true. But they are jealous of us all; and we must be brave and go at them.

Soc.: Their laughter, friend Euthyphro, is not a matter of much consequence. For a man may be thought clever; but the Athenians, I suspect, do not much trouble themselves about him until he begins to impart his wisdom to others; and then for some reason or other, perhaps, as you say, from jealousy, they are angry.

Euth.: I have no great wish to try their temper towards me in this way.

Soc.: No doubt they think you are reserved in your behaviour, and unwilling to impart your wisdom. But I have a benevolent habit of pouring out myself to everybody, and would even pay for a listener, and I am afraid that the Athenians may think me too talkative. Now if, as I was saying, they would only laugh at me, as you say that they laugh at you, the time might pass gaily enough with jokes and merriment in the court; but perhaps they may be in earnest, and then what the end will be you soothsayers only can predict.

Euth.: I dare say that the affair will end in nothing, Socrates, and that you will win your cause; and I think that I shall win my own.

Soc.: And what is your suit, Euthyphro? are you the pursuer or the defendant?

Euth.: I am the pursuer.

Soc.: Of whom?

Euth.: When I tell you, you will perceive another reason why I am thought mad.

Soc.: Why, has the fugitive wings?

Euth.: Nay, he is not very volatile at his time of life.

Soc.: Who is he?

Euth.: My father.

Soc.: My dear Sir! Your own father?

Euth.: Yes.

Soc.: And of what is he accused?

Euth.: Of murder, Socrates.

Soc.: Good heavens! How little, Euthyphro, does the common herd know of the nature of right and truth! A man must be an extraordinary man, and have made great strides in wisdom, before he could have seen his way to bring such an action.

Euth.: Indeed, Socrates, he must.

Soc.: I suppose that the man whom your father murdered was one of your family—clearly he was; for if he had been a stranger you would never have thought of prosecuting him.

Euth.: I am amused, Socrates, at your making a distinction between one who is a member of the family and one who is not; for surely the pollution is the same in either case, if you knowingly associate with the murderer when you ought to clear yourself and him by proceeding against him. The real question is whether the murdered man has been justly slain. If justly, then your duty is to let the matter alone; but if unjustly, then proceed against the murderer, if, that is to say, he lives under the same roof with you and eats at the same table. In fact, the man who is dead was a poor dependant of mine who worked for us as a field labourer on our farm in Naxos, and one day in a fit of drunken passion he got into a quarrel with one of our domestic servants and slew him. My father bound him hand and foot and threw him into a ditch, and then sent to Athens to ask an expositor of religious law what he should do with him. Meanwhile he never attended to him and took no care about him, for he regarded him as a murderer; and thought that no great harm would be done even if he did die. Now this was just what happened. For such was the effect of cold and hunger and chains upon him, that before the messenger returned from the expositor, he was dead. And my father and family are angry with me for taking the part of the murderer and prosecuting my father. They say that he did not kill him, and that if he did, the dead man was but a murderer, and I ought not to take any notice, for that son is impious who prosecutes a father for murder. Which shows, Socrates, how little they know what the gods think about piety and impiety.

Soc.: Good heavens, Euthyphro! and is your knowledge of religion, and of things pious and impious so very exact, that, supposing the circumstances to be as you state them, you are not afraid lest you too may be doing an impious thing in bringing an action against your father?

Euth.: The best of Euthyphro, that which distinguishes him, Socrates, from the common herd, is his exact knowledge of all such matters. What should I be good for without it?

Soc.: Rare friend! I think that I cannot do better than be your disciple. . . . And therefore, I adjure you to tell me the nature of piety and impiety, which you said that you knew so well, in their bearing on murder and generally on offenses against the gods. Is not piety in every action always the same? and impiety, again — is it not always the opposite of piety, and also the same with itself, having, as impiety, one notion or form which includes whatever is impious?

Euth.: To be sure, Socrates.

Soc.: And what is piety, and what is impiety?

Euth.: Piety is doing as I am doing; that is to say, prosecuting anyone who is guilty of murder, sacrilege, or of any similar crime — whether he be your father or mother, or whoever he may be — that makes no difference; and not to prosecute them is impiety. And please to consider, Socrates, what a notable proof I will give you that this is the law, a proof which I have already given to others: — of the principle, I mean, that the impious, whoever he may be, ought not to go unpunished. For do not men acknowledge Zeus as

the best and most righteous of the gods? — and yet they admit that he bound his father (Cronos) because he wickedly devoured his sons, and that he too had punished his own father (Uranus) for a similar reason, in a nameless manner. And yet when I proceed against my father, they are angry with me. So inconsistent are they in their way of talking when the gods are concerned, and when I am concerned.

Soc.: May not this be the reason, Euthyphro, why I am charged with impiety — that I cannot accept these stories about the gods? that, I suppose is where people think I go wrong. But as you who are well informed about them approve of them, I cannot do better than assent to your superior wisdom. What else can I say, confessing as I do, that I know nothing about them? Tell me, for the love of Zeus, whether you really believe that they are true.

Euth.: Yes, Socrates; and things more wonderful still, of which the world is in ignorance.

Soc.: And do you really believe that the gods fought with one another, and had dire quarrels, battles, and the like, as the poets say, and as you see represented in the works of great artists? The temples are full of them; and notably the robe of Athene, which is carried up to the Acropolis at the great Panathenaea, is embroidered with them throughout. Are all these tales of the gods true, Euthyphro?

Euth.: Yes, Socrates; and, as I was saying, I can tell you, if you would like to hear them, many other things about the gods which would quite amaze you.

Soc.: I dare say; and you shall tell me them at some other time when I have leisure. But just at present I would rather hear from you a more precise answer, which you have not as yet given, my friend, to the question, 'What is "piety"?' When asked, you only replied, 'Doing as you do, charging your father with murder'.

Euth.: And what I said was true, Socrates.

Soc.: No doubt, Euthyphro; but you would admit that there are many other pious acts?

Euth.: There are.

Soc.: Remember that I did not ask you to give me two or three examples of piety, but to explain the general form which makes all pious things to be pious. Do you not recollect saying that one and the same form made the impious impious, the pious pious?

Euth.: I remember.

Soc.: Tell me what is the nature of this form, and then I shall have a standard to which I may look, and by which I may measure actions, whether yours or those of anyone else, and then I shall be able to say that such and such an action is pious, such another impious.

Euth.: I will tell you, if you like.

Soc.: I should very much like.

Euth.: Piety, then, is that which is dear to the gods, and impiety is that which is not dear to them.

Soc.: Very good, Euthyphro; you have now given me the sort of answer which I wanted. But whether what you say is true or not I cannot as yet tell, although I make no doubt that you will go on to prove the truth of your words.

Euth.: Of course.

Soc.: Come, then, and let us examine what we are saying. That thing or person which is dear to the gods is pious, and that thing or person which is hateful to the gods is impious, these two being the extreme opposites of one another. Was not that said?

Euth.: It was. . . .

Soc.: And further, Euthyphro, the gods were admitted to have enmities and hatreds and differences?

Euth.: Yes, that was also said.

Soc.: And what sort of difference creates enmity and anger? Suppose for example that you and I, my good friend, differ on the question which of two groups of things is more numerous; do differences of this sort make us enemies and set us at variance with one another? Do we not proceed at once to counting, and put an end to them?

Euth.: True.

Soc.: Or suppose that we differ about magnitudes, do we not quickly end the difference by measuring?

Euth.: Very true.

Soc.: And we end a controversy about heavy and light by resorting to a weighing machine?

Euth.: To be sure.

Soc.: But what are the matters about which differences arise that cannot be thus decided, and therefore make us angry and set us at enmity with one another? I dare say the answer does not occur to you at the moment, and therefore I will suggest that these enmities arise when the matters of difference are the just and unjust, good and evil, honourable and dishonourable. Are not these the subjects about which men differ, and about which when we are unable satisfactorily to decide our differences, you and I and all of us quarrel, when we do quarrel?

Euth.: Yes, Socrates, the nature of the differences about which we quarrel is such as you describe.

Soc.: And the quarrels of the gods, noble Euthyphro, when they occur, are of a like nature?

Euth.: Certainly they are.

Soc.: They have differences of opinion, as you say, about good and evil, just and unjust, honourable and dishonourable: there would be no quarrels among them, if there were not such differences — would there now?

Euth.: You are quite right.

Soc.: Does not each party of them love that which they deem noble and just and good, and hate the opposite? . . .

Then the same things are hated by the gods and loved by the gods, and are both hateful and dear to them?

Euth.: It appears so.

Soc.: And upon this view the same things, Euthyphro, will be pious and also impious?

Euth.: So I should suppose.

Soc.: Then, my friend, I remark with surprise that you have not answered the question which I asked. For I certainly did not ask you to tell me what action is both pious and impious; but now it would seem that what is loved by the gods is also hated by them. And therefore, Euthyphro, in thus chastising your father you may very likely be doing what is agreeable to Zeus but disagreeable to Cronos or Uranus, and what is acceptable to Hephaestus but unacceptable to Hera, and there may be other gods who have similar differences of opinion.

Euth.: But I believe, Socrates, that all the gods would be agreed as to the propriety of punishing a murderer: there would be no difference of opinion about that.

Soc.: Well, but speaking of men, Euthyphro, did you ever hear anyone arguing that a murderer or any sort of evil-doer ought to be let off?

Euth.: I should rather say that these are the questions which they are always arguing, especially in courts of law: they commit all sorts of crimes, and there is nothing which they will not do or say in their own defence.

Soc.: But do they admit their guilt, Euthyphro, and yet say that they ought not to be punished?

Euth.: No; they do not.

Soc.: Then there are some things which they do not venture to say and do: for they do not venture to argue that if guilty they are to go unpunished, but they deny their guilt, do they not?

Euth.: Yes.

Soc.: Then they do not argue that the evil-doer should not be punished, but they argue about the fact of who the evil-doer is, and what he did and when?

Euth.: True.

Soc.: And the gods are in the same case, if as you assert they quarrel about just and unjust, and some of them say while others deny that injustice is done among them. For surely neither god nor man will ever venture to say that the doer of injustice is not to be punished?

Euth.: That is true, Socrates, in the main.

Soc.: But they join issue about the particulars — gods and men alike, if indeed the gods dispute at all; they differ about some act which is called in question, and which by some is affirmed to be just, by others to be unjust. Is not that true?

Euth.: Quite true.

Soc.: Well then, my dear friend Euthyphro, do tell me, for my better instruction and information, what proof have you that in the opinion of all the gods a servant who is guilty of murder, and is put in chains by the master of the dead man, and dies because he is put in chains before he who bound him can learn from the expositors of religious law what he ought to do with him, is killed unjustly; and that on behalf of such an one a son ought to proceed against his father and accuse him of murder. How would you show that all the gods absolutely agree in approving of his act? Prove to me that they do, and I will applaud your wisdom as long as I live.

Euth.: No doubt it will be a difficult task; though I could make the matter very clear indeed to you.

Soc.: I understand; you mean to say that I am not so quick of apprehension as the judges: for to them you will be sure to prove that the act is unjust, and hateful to all the gods.

Euth.: Yes indeed, Socrates; at least if they will listen to me.

Soc.: But they will be sure to listen if they find that you are a good speaker. There was a notion that came into my mind while you were speaking; I said to myself: 'Well, and what if Euthyphro does prove to me that all the gods regarded the death of the serf as unjust, how do I know anything more of the nature of piety and impiety? for granting that this action may be hateful to the gods, still piety and impiety are not adequately defined by these distinctions, for that which is hateful to the gods has been shown to be also dear to them.' And therefore, Euthyphro, I do not ask you to prove this; I will suppose, if you like, that all the gods condemn and abominate such an action. But I will amend the definition so far as to say that what all the gods hate is impious, and what they love pious or holy; and what some of them love and others hate is both or neither. Shall this be our definition of piety and impiety?

Euth.: Why not, Socrates?

Soc.: Why not! certainly, as far as I am concerned, Euthyphro, there is no reason why not. But whether this premiss will greatly assist you in the task of instructing me as you promised, is a matter for you to consider.

Euth.: Yes, I should say that what all the gods love is pious and holy, and the opposite which they all hate, impious.

Soc.: Ought we to inquire into the truth of this, Euthyphro, or simply to accept it on our own authority and that of others — echoing mere assertions? What do you say?

Euth.: We should inquire; and I believe that the statement will stand the test of inquiry.

Soc.: We shall soon be better able to say, my good friend. The point which I should first wish to understand is whether the pious or holy is beloved by the gods because it is holy, or holy because it is beloved of the gods.

Euth.: I do not understand your meaning, Socrates.

Soc.: I will endeavour to explain: . . . is not that which is beloved distinct from that which loves?

Euth.: Certainly. . . .

Soc.: And what do you say of piety, Euthyphro: is not piety, according to your definition, loved by all the gods?

Euth.: Yes.

Soc.: Because it is pious or holy, or for some other reason?

Euth.: No, that is the reason.

Soc.: It is loved because it is holy, not holy because it is loved?

Euth.: Apparently.

Soc.: And it is the object of the gods' love, and is dear to them, because it is loved of them?

Euth.: Certainly.

Soc.: Then that which is dear to the gods, Euthyphro, is not holy, nor is that which is holy dear to the gods, as you affirm; but they are two different things. . . .

Euth.: Yes.

Soc.: But that which is dear to the gods is dear to them because it is loved by them, not loved by them because it is dear to them.

Euth.: True.

Soc.: But, friend Euthyphro, if that which is holy were the same with that which is dear to the gods, and were loved because it is holy, then that which is dear to the gods would be loved as being dear to them; but if that which is dear to them were dear to them because loved by them, then that which is holy would be holy because loved by them. But now you see that the reverse is the case, and that the two things are quite different from one another. For one is of a kind to be loved because it is loved, and the other is loved because it is of a kind to be loved. Thus you appear to me, Euthyphro, when I ask you what is the nature of holiness, to offer an attribute only, and not the essence — the attribute of being loved by all the gods. But you still do not explain to me the nature of holiness. And therefore, if you please, I will ask you not to hide your treasure, but to start again, and tell me frankly what holiness or piety really is, whether dear to the gods or not (for that is a matter about which we will not quarrel); and what is impiety?

Euth.: I really do not know, Socrates, how to express what I mean. For somehow or other the definitions we propound, on whatever bases we rest them, seem always to turn round and walk away from us. . . .

Soc.: Then we must begin again and ask, What is piety? That is an inquiry which I shall never be weary of pursuing as far as in me lies; and I entreat you not to scorn me, but to apply your mind to the utmost, and tell me the truth. For, if any man knows, you are he; and therefore I must hold you fast, like Proteus, until you tell. If you had not certainly known the nature of piety and impiety, I am confident that you would never, on behalf of a serf, have charged your aged father with murder. You would not have run such a risk of doing wrong in the sight of the gods, and you would have had too much respect for the opinions of men. I am sure, therefore, that you know the nature of piety and impiety. Speak out then, my dear Euthyphro, and do not hide your knowledge.

Euth.: Another time, Socrates; for I am in a hurry, and must go now.

Soc.: Alas! my friend, and will you leave me in despair? I was hoping that you would instruct me in the nature of piety and impiety; and then I might have cleared myself of Meletus and his indictment. I would have told him that I had been enlightened by Euthyphro, and had given up rash innovations and speculations in which I had indulged only through ignorance, and that now I am about to lead a better life.

Further Questions

1. State in your own words what the problem is with supposing "an act is right *because* God approves of it." State what the problem is with supposing that "God approves of an act *because* it is right." How might a religious person respond? You might, as an exercise, go to a religious authority and pose the question to him or her. What answer do you get? What happens when you keep asking the question?

2. Why do you suppose that, in our society and in others, morality is widely considered to be the domain of religion? Do you think this is appropriate? Why or why not?

3. How might Socrates, were he alive, respond to the "religious moral authorities" of today? What would he say, for instance, to the way the Pope justifies a particular view, say the one against the use of artificial birth control? As an exercise, you may wish to write an imaginary dialogue between Socrates and the Pope or, say, Billy Graham.

4. If Socrates is right that morality is independent of the will of the gods, why then have so many societies, past and present, insisted on justifying morality on the grounds that morality came from the accepted gods or God? What is their intent?

5. Socrates believed in subjecting all of his beliefs to rational scrutiny and in abandoning those that could not be supported by good reasons. Do you think this is how a person ought to live?

Further Readings

Flew, Antony. *God and Philosophy*. New York: Dell, 1966. The quote in the introduction is on p. 109.

Nielsen, Kai. *Ethics Without God*. Buffalo, NY: Prometheus Books, 1973.

Rachels, James. *The Elements of Moral Philosophy*. New York: Random House, 1986. Elementary and concise, one of the best short introductions to ethics. See, especially, Chapter 4, "Does Morality Depend on Religion?"

The Apology

Reading Questions

1. What crime is Socrates charged with?
2. What today would be a similar charge brought, say, against your philosophy professor?
3. What is Socrates' defense?
4. What was Socrates' main goal in life?
5. Why does Socrates not simply escape from Athens?
6. What is a "gadfly" and in what sense is Socrates one?
7. Why is Socrates not afraid of death?
8. Give Socrates' argument for immortality.
9. Imagine getting an official letter telling you that you have been chosen "the wisest person in the country." How would you react? Supposedly, something similar happened to Socrates. How was his reaction different from what you would have done under similar circumstances, and why?
10. Why doesn't Socrates simply apologize and plead for mercy?
11. What does Socrates propose as an appropriate punishment for his "crimes"?
12. Are there any contemporary figures like Socrates?
13. If Socrates were alive today, who might be his targets?

CHARACTERS   *Socrates and Meletus*
SCENE   *The Court of Justice*

Socr.: I cannot tell what impression my accusers have made upon you, Athenians. For my own part, I know that they nearly made me forget who I was, so believable were they; and yet they have scarcely uttered one single word of truth. But of all their many falsehoods, the one which astonished me most was when they said that I was a clever speaker, and that you must be careful not to let me mislead you. I thought that it was most impudent of them not to be ashamed to talk in that way; for as soon as I open my mouth they will be refuted, and I shall prove that I am not a clever speaker in any way at all—unless, indeed, by a clever speaker they mean a man who speaks the truth. If that is their meaning, I agree with them that I am a much greater orator than they.

My accusers, then I repeat, have said little or nothing that is true; but from me you shall hear the whole truth. Certainly you will not hear an elaborate speech, Athenians, dressed up, like theirs, with words and phrases. I will say to you what I have to say, without preparation, and in the words which come first, for I believe that my cause is just; so let none of you expect anything else. Indeed, my friends, it would hardly be seemingly for me, at my age, to come before you like a young man with his specious phrases. But there is one thing, Athenians, which I do most earnestly beg and entreat of you. Do not be surprised and do not interrupt with shouts if in my defense I speak in the same way that I am accustomed to speak in the marketplace, at the tables of the moneychangers, where many of you have heard me, and elsewhere. The truth is this. I am more than seventy years old, and this is the first

Selections from The Apology, Crito, *and* Phaedo *are from* The Dialogues of Plato *translated by Benjamin Jowett, 3rd ed. (Oxford: Oxford University Press, 1896).*

time that I have ever come before a law court; so your manner of speech here is quite strange to me. If I had been really a stranger, you would have forgiven me for speaking in the language and the fashion of my native country; and so now I ask you to grant me what I think I have a right to claim. Never mind the style of my speech — it may be better or it may be worse — give your whole attention to the question, Is what I say just, or is it not? That is what makes a good judge, as speaking the truth makes a good advocate.

I have to defend myself, Athenians, first against the old false accusations of my old accusers, and then against the later ones of my present accusers. For many men have been accusing me to you, and for very many years, who have not uttered a word of truth; and I fear them more than I fear Anytus and his associates, formidable as they are. But, my friends, those others are still more formidable; for they got hold of most of you when you were children, and they have been more persistent in accusing me untruthfully and have persuaded you that there is a certain Socrates, a wise man, who speculates about the heavens, and who investigates things that are beneath the earth, and who can make the weaker reason appear the stronger. These men, Athenians, who spread abroad this report are the accusers whom I fear; for their hearers think that persons who pursue such inquiries never believe in the gods. Then they are many, and their attacks have been going on for a long time, and they spoke to you when you were at the age most readily to believe them, for you were all young, and many of you were children, and there was no one to answer them when they attacked me. And the most unreasonable thing of all is that I do not even know their names: I cannot tell you who they are except when one happens to be a comic poet. But all the rest who have persuaded you, from motives of resentment and prejudice, and sometimes, it may be, from conviction, are hardest to cope with. For I cannot call any one of them forward in court to cross-examine him. I have, as it were, simply to spar with shadows in my defense, and to put questions which there is no one to answer. I ask you, therefore, to believe that, as I say, I have been attacked by two kinds of accusers — first, by Meletus and his associates, and, then, by those older ones of whom I have spoken. And, with your leave, I will defend myself first against my old accusers; for you heard their accusations first, and they were much more forceful than my present accusers are.

Well, I must make my defense, Athenians, and try in the short time allowed me to remove the prejudice which you have been so long a time acquiring. I hope that I may manage to do this, if it be good for you and for me, and that my defense may be successful; but I am quite aware of the nature of my task, and I know that it is a difficult one. Be the outcome, however, as is pleasing to God, I must obey the law and make my defense.

Let us begin from the beginning, then, and ask what is the accusation which has given rise to the prejudice against me, which was what Meletus relied on when he brought his indictment. What is the prejudice which my enemies have been spreading about me? I must assume that they are formally accusing me, and read their indictment. It would run somewhat in this fashion: Socrates is a wrongdoer, who meddles with inquiries into things beneath the earth and in the heavens, and who makes the weaker reason appear the stronger, and who teaches others these same things. That is what they say; and in the comedy of Aristophanes [*Clouds*] you yourselves saw a man called Socrates swinging round in a basket and saying that he walked on the air, and prattling a great deal of nonsense about matters of which I understand nothing, either more or less. I do not mean to disparage that kind of knowledge if there is anyone who is wise about these matters. I trust Meletus may never be able to prosecute me for that. But the truth is, Athenians, I have nothing to do with these matters, and almost all of you are yourselves my witnesses of this. I beg all of you who have heard me discussing, and they are many, to inform your neighbors and tell them if any of you have ever heard me discussing such matters, either more or less. That will show you that the other common stories about me are as false as this one.

But the fact is that not one of these is true. And if you have heard that I undertake to educate men, and make money by so doing, that is not true either, though I think that it would be a fine thing to be able to educate men. . . .

Perhaps some of you may reply: But, Socrates, what is the trouble with you? What has given rise to these prejudices against you? You must have been doing something out of the ordinary. All these stories and reports of you would never have arisen if you had not been doing something different from other men. So tell us what it is, that we may not give our verdict in the dark. I think that that is a fair question, and I will try to explain to you what it is that has raised these prejudices against me and given me this reputation. Listen, then: some of you, perhaps, will think that I am joking, but I assure you that I will tell you the whole truth. I have gained this reputation, Athenians, simply by reason of a certain wisdom. But by what kind of wisdom? It is by just that wisdom which is perhaps human wisdom. In that, it may be, I am really wise. . . .

You remember Chaerephon. From youth upwards he was my comrade; and also a partisan of your democracy, sharing your recent exile and returning with you. You remember, too, Chaerephon's character — how vehement he was in carrying through whatever he took in hand. Once he went to Delphi and ventured to put this question to the oracle — I entreat you again, my friends, not to interrupt me with your shouts — he asked if there was any man who was wiser than I. The priestess answered that there was no one. Chaerephon himself is dead, but his brother here will confirm what I say.

Now see why I tell you this. I am going to explain to you how the prejudice against me has arisen. When I heard of the oracle I began to reflect: What can the god mean by this riddle? I know very well that I am not wise, even the smallest degree. Then what can he mean by saying that

I am the wisest of men? It cannot be that he is speaking falsely, for he is a god and cannot lie. For a long time I was at a loss to understand his meaning. Then, very reluctantly, I turned to seek for it in this manner. I went to a man who was reputed to be wise, thinking that there, if anywhere, I should prove the answer wrong, and meaning to point out to the oracle its mistake, and to say, You said that I was the wisest of men, but this man is wiser than I am. So I examined the man — I need not tell you his name, he was a politician — but this was the result, Athenians. When I conversed with him I came to see that, though a great many persons, and most of all he himself, thought that he was wise, yet he was not wise. Then I tried to prove to him that he was not wise, though he fancied that he was; and by so doing I made him indignant, and many of the bystanders. So when I went away, I thought to myself, I am wiser than this man: neither of us knows anything that is really worthwhile, but he thinks that he has knowledge when he has not, while I, having no knowledge, do not think that I have. I seem, at any rate, to be a little wiser than he is on this point: I do not think that I know what I do not know. Next I went to another man who was reputed to be still wiser than the last, with exactly the same result. And there again I made him, and many other men, indignant.

Then I went on to one man after another, seeing that I was arousing indignation every day, which caused me much pain and anxiety. Still I thought that I must set the god's command above everything. So I had to go to every man who seemed to possess any knowledge, and investigate the meaning of the oracle. Athenians, I must tell you the truth; by the god, this was the result of the investigation which I made at the god's bidding: I found that the men whose reputation for wisdom stood highest were nearly the most lacking in it, while others who were looked down on as common people were much more intelligent. Now I must describe to you the wanderings which I undertook, like Heraclean labors, to prove the oracle irrefutable. After the politicians,

I went to the poets, tragic, dithyrambic, and others, thinking that there I should find myself manifestly more ignorant than they. So I took up the poems on which I thought that they had spent most pains, and asked them what they meant, hoping at the same time to learn something from them. I am ashamed to tell you the truth, my friends, but I must say it. Almost anyone of the bystanders could have talked about the works of these poets better than the poets themselves. So I soon found that it is not by wisdom that the poets create their works, but by a certain innate power and by inspiration, like soothsayers and prophets, who say many fine things, but who understand nothing of what they say. The poets seemed to me to be in a similar situation. And at the same time I perceived that, because of their poetry, they thought that they were the wisest of men in other matters, too, which they were not. So I went away again, thinking that I had the same advantage over the poets that I had over the politicians.

Finally, I went to the artisans, for I knew very well that I possessed no knowledge at all worth speaking of, and I was sure that I should find that they knew many fine things. And in that I was not mistaken. They knew what I did not know, and so far they were wiser than I. But, Athenians, it seemed to me that the skilled artisans made the same mistake as the poets. Each of them believed himself to be extremely wise in matters of the greatest importance because he was skillful in his own art: and this presumption of theirs obscured their real wisdom. So I asked myself, on behalf of the oracle, whether I would choose to remain as I was, without either their wisdom or their ignorance, or to possess both, as they did. And I answered to myself and to the oracle that it was better for me to remain as I was.

From this examination, Athenians, has arisen much fierce and bitter indignation, and from this a great many prejudices about me, and people say that I am "a wise man." For the bystanders always think that I am wise myself in any matter wherein I refute another. But, my friends, I believe that the god is really wise, and that by this oracle he meant that human wisdom is worth little or nothing. I do not think that he meant that Socrates was wise. He only made use of my name, and took me as an example, as though he would say to men: He among you is the wisest who, like Socrates, knows that in truth his wisdom is worth nothing at all. Therefore I still go about testing and examining every man whom I think wise, whether he be a citizen or a stranger, as the god has commanded me; and whenever I find that he is not wise, I point out to him, on the god's behalf, that he is not wise. I am so busy in this pursuit that I have never had leisure to take any path worth mentioning in public matters or to look after my private affairs. I am in great poverty as the result of my service to the god.

Besides this, the young men who follow me about, who are the sons of wealthy persons and have the most leisure, take pleasure in hearing men cross-examined. They often imitate me among themselves; then they try their hands at cross-examining other people. And, I imagine, they find plenty of men who think that they know a great deal when in fact they know little or nothing. Then the persons who are cross-examined get angry with me instead of with themselves, and say that Socrates is an abomination and corrupts the young. When they are asked, Why, what does he do? what does he teach? they do not know what to say; but, not to seem at a loss, they repeat the stock charges against all philosophers, and allege that he investigates things in the air and under the earth, and that he teaches people to disbelieve in the gods, and to make the weaker reason appear the stronger. For, I suppose, they would not like to confess the truth, which is that they are shown up as ignorant pretenders to knowledge that they do not possess. So they have been filling your ears with their bitter prejudices for a long time, for they are ambitious, energetic, and numerous; and they speak vigorously and persuasively against me. Relying on this, Meletus, Anytus, and Lycon have attacked me. Meletus is indignant with me on the part of the poets,

Anytus on the part of the artisans and politicians, and Lycon on the part of the orators. And so, as I said at the beginning, I shall be surprised if I am able, in the short time allowed me for my defense, to remove from your minds this prejudice which has grown so strong. What I have told you, Athenians, is the truth: I neither conceal nor do I suppress anything, small or great. Yet I know that it is just this plainness of speech which rouses indignation. But that is only a proof that my words are true, and that the prejudice against me, and the causes of it, are what I have said. And whether you look for them now or hereafter, you will find that they are so.

What I have said must suffice as my defense against the charges of my first accusers. I will try next to defend myself against Meletus, that "good patriot," as he calls himself, and my later accusers. Let us assume that they are a new set of accusers, and read their indictment, as we did in the case of the others. It runs thus. He says that Socrates is a wrongdoer who corrupts the youth, and who does not believe in the gods whom the state believes in, but in other new divinities. Such is the accusation. Let us examine each point in it separately. Meletus says that I do wrong by corrupting the youth. But I say, Athenians, that he is doing wrong, for he is playing a solemn joke by lightly bringing men to trial, and pretending to have zealous interest in matters to which he has never given a moment's thought. Now I will try to prove to you that it is so.

Come here, Meletus. Is it not a fact that you think it very important that the young should be as excellent as possible?

Mel.: It is.

Socr.: Come then, tell the judges who is it who improves them? You care so much, you must know. You are accusing me, and bringing me to trial, because, as you say, you have discovered that I am the corrupter of the youth. Come now, reveal to the gentlemen who improves them. You see, Meletus, you have nothing to say; you are silent. But don't you think that this is shameful? Is not your silence a conclusive proof of what I say—that you have never cared? Come, tell us, my good sir, who makes the young better citizens?

Mel.: The laws.

Socr.: That, my friend, is not my question. What man improves the young, who starts with the knowledge of the laws?

Mel.: The judges here, Socrates.

Socr.: What do you mean, Meletus? Can they educate the young and improve them?

Mel.: Certainly.

Socr.: All of them? or only some of them?

Mel.: All of them.

Socr.: By Hera, that is good news! Such a large supply of benefactors! And do the listeners here improve them, or not?

Mel.: They do.

Socr.: And do the senators?

Mel.: Yes.

Socr.: Well then, Meletus, do the members of the assembly corrupt the young or do they again all improve them?

Mel.: They, too, improve them.

Socr.: Then all the Athenians, apparently, make the young into good men except me, and I alone corrupt them. Is that your meaning?

Mel.: Most certainly; that is my meaning.

Socr.: You have discovered me to be most unfortunate. Now tell me: do you think that the same holds good in the case of horses? Does one man do them harm and everyone else improve them? On the contrary, is it not one man only, or a very few—namely, those who are skilled with horses—who can improve them, while the majority of men harm them if they use them and have anything to do with them? Is it not so, Meletus, both with horses and with every other animal? Of course it is, whether you and Anytus say yes or no. The young would certainly be very fortunate if only one man corrupted them, and everyone else did them good. The truth is, Meletus, you prove conclusively that you have never thought about the youth in your life. You exhibit your carelessness in not caring for the very matters about which you are prosecuting me.

Now be so good as to tell us, Meletus, is it better to live among good citizens or bad ones? Answer, my friend. I am not asking you at all a difficult question. Do not the bad harm their associates and the good do them good?

Mel.: Yes.

Socr.: Is there any man who would rather be injured than benefited by his companions? Answer, my good sir; you are obliged by the law to answer. Does any one like to be injured?

Mel.: Certainly not.

Socr.: Well then, are you prosecuting me for corrupting the young and making them worse, intentionally or unintentionally?

Mel.: For doing it intentionally.

Socr.: What, Meletus? Do you mean to say that you, who are so much younger than I, are yet so much wiser than I that you know that bad citizens always do evil, and that good citizens do good, to those with whom they come in contact, while I am so extraordinarily stupid as not to know that, if I make any of my companions evil, he will probably injure me in some way, and as to commit this great evil, as you allege, intentionally? You will not make me believe that, nor anyone else either, I should think. Either I do not corrupt the young at all or, if I do, I do so unintentionally: so that you are lying in either case. And if I corrupt them unintentionally, the law does not call upon you to prosecute me for an error which is unintentional, but to take me aside privately and reprove and instruct me. For, of course, I shall cease from doing wrong involuntarily, as soon as I know that I have been doing wrong. But you avoided associating with me and educating me; instead you bring me up before the court, where the law sends persons, not for instruction, but for punishment.

The truth is, Athenians, as I said, it is quite clear that Meletus has never cared at all about these matters. However, now tell us, Meletus, how do you say that I corrupt the young? Clearly, according to your indictment, by teaching them not to believe in the gods the state believes in, but other new divinities instead. You mean that I corrupt the young by that teaching, do you not?

Mel.: Yes, most certainly I mean that.

Socr.: Then in the name of these gods of whom we are speaking, explain yourself a little more clearly to me and to these gentlemen here. I cannot understand what you mean. Do you mean that I teach the young to believe in some gods, but not in the gods of the state? Do you accuse me of teaching them to believe in strange gods? If that is your meaning, I myself believe in some gods, and my crime is not that of absolute atheism. Or do you mean that I do not believe in the gods at all myself, and I teach other people not to believe in them either?

Mel.: I mean that you do not believe in the gods in any way whatever.

Socr.: You amaze me, Meletus! Why do you say that? Do you mean that I believe neither the sun nor the moon to be gods, like other men?

Mel.: I swear he does not, judges; he says that the sun is a stone, and the moon earth.

Socr.: My dear Meletus, do you think that you are prosecuting Anaxagoras? You must have a very poor opinion of these men, and think them illiterate, if you imagine that they do not know that the works of Anaxagoras of Clazomenae are full of these doctrines. And so young men learn these things from me, when they can often buy places in the theatre for a drachma at most, and laugh at Socrates were he to pretend that these doctrines, which are very peculiar doctrines, too, were his own. But please tell me, do you really think that I do not believe in the gods at all?

Mel.: Most certainly I do. You are a complete atheist.

Socr.: No one believes that, Meletus, not even you yourself. It seems to me, Athenians, that Meletus is very insolent and reckless, and that he is prosecuting me simply out of insolence, recklessness and youthful bravado. For he seems to be testing me, by asking me a riddle that has no answer. Will this wise Socrates, he says to himself, see that I am joking and contradicting myself? or shall I outwit him and everyone else who hears me? Meletus seems to me to contradict himself in his indictment: it is as if he were to say, Socrates is a wrongdoer who does not believe in the gods, but who believes in the gods. But that is mere joking.

Now, my friends, let us see why I think that this is his meaning. Do you answer me, Meletus; and do you, Athenians, remember the request which I made to you at the start, and do not interrupt me with shouts if I talk in my usual way.

Is there any man, Meletus, who believes in the existence of things pertaining to men and not in the existence of men? Make him answer the question, my friends, without these interruptions. Is there any man who believes in the existence of horsemanship and not in the existence of horses? or in flute-playing and not in flute-players? There is not, my friend. If you will not answer, I will tell both you and the judges. But you must answer my next question. Is there any man who believes in the existence of divine things and not in the existence of divinities?

Mel.: There is not.

Socr.: I am very glad that these gentlemen have managed to extract an answer from you. Well then, you say that I believe in divine beings, whether they be old or new ones, and that I teach others to believe in them; at any rate, according to your statement, I believe in divine beings. That you have sworn in your indictment. But if I believe in divine beings, I suppose it follows necessarily that I believe in divinities. Is it not so? I assume that you grant that, as you do not answer. But do we not believe that divinities are either gods themselves or the children of the gods? Do you admit that?

Mel.: I do.

Socr.: Then you admit that I believe in divinities. Now, if these divinities are gods, then, as I say, you are joking and asking a riddle, and asserting that I do not believe in the gods, and at the same time that I do, since I believe in divinities. But if these divinities are the illegitimate children of the gods, either by the nymphs or by other mothers, as they are said to be, then, I ask, what man could believe in the existence of the children of the gods, and not in the existence of the gods?

That would be as strange as believing in the existence of the offspring of horses and asses, and not in the existence of horses and asses. You must have indicted me in this manner, Meletus, either to test me or because you could not find any crime that you could accuse me of with truth. But you will never contrive to persuade any man with any sense at all that a belief in divine things and things of the gods does not necessarily involve a belief in divinities, and in the gods, and in heroes.

But in truth, Athenians, I do not think that I need say very much to prove that I have not committed the crime for which Meletus is prosecuting me. What I have said is enough to prove that. But I repeat it is certainly true, as I have already told you, that I have aroused much indignation. That is what will cause my condemnation if I am condemned; not Meletus nor Anytus either, but that prejudice and suspicion of the multitude which have been the destruction of many good men before me, and I think will be so again. There is no fear that I shall be the last victim.

Perhaps someone will say: Are you not ashamed, Socrates, of leading a life which is very likely now to cause your death? I should answer him with justice, and say: My friend, if you think that a man of any worth at all ought to reckon the chances of life and death when he acts, or that he ought to think of anything but whether he is acting rightly or wrongly, and as a good or a bad man would act, you are mistaken. According to you, the demigods who died at Troy would be foolish, and among them the son of Thetis, who thought nothing of danger when the alternative was disgrace. For when his mother — and she was a goddess — addressed him, when he was burning to slay Hector, in this fashion, "My son, if you avenge the death of your comrade Patroclus and slay Hector, you will die yourself, for 'fate awaits you straightway after Hector's death'"; when he heard this, he scorned danger and death; he feared much more to live a coward and not to avenge his friend. "Let me punish the evildoer and straightway die," he said, "that I may not remain here by the beaked ships jeered at, encumbering the earth." Do you suppose that he thought of danger or of death? For this, Athenians, I believe to be the truth. Wherever a man's station is, whether he has chosen it of his own will, or whether he has been placed at it by his commander, there it is his duty to remain and face the danger without thinking of death or of any other thing except dishonor.

When the generals whom you chose to command me, Athenians, assigned me my station at Potidaea and at Amphipolis and at Delium, I remained where they placed me and ran the risk of death, like other men. It would be very strange conduct on my part if I were to desert my station now from fear of death or of any other thing when God has commanded me — as I am persuaded that he has done — to spend my life in searching for wisdom, and in examining myself and others. That would indeed be a very strange thing: then certainly I might with justice be brought to trial for not believing in the gods, for I should be disobeying the oracle, and fearing death and thinking myself wise when I was not wise. For to fear death, my friends, is only to think ourselves wise without really being wise, for it is to think that we know what we do not know. For no one knows whether death may not be the greatest good that can happen to man. But men fear it as if they knew quite well that it was the greatest of evils. And what is this but that shameful ignorance of thinking that we know what we do not know? In this matter, too, my friends, perhaps I am different from the multitude; and if I were to claim to be at all wiser than others, it would be because, not knowing very much about the other world, I do not think I know. But I do know very well that it is evil and disgraceful to do wrong, and to disobey my superior, whoever he is, whether man or god. I will never do what I know to be evil, and shrink in fear from what I do not know to be good or evil. Even if you acquit me now, and do not listen to Anytus' argument that, if I am to be acquitted, I ought never to have been brought to trial at all, and that, as it is, you are bound to put me to death because, as he said, if I escape, all your sons will be utterly corrupted by practising what Soc-

rates teaches. If you were therefore to say to me: Socrates, this time we will not listen to Anytus; we will let you go, but on this condition, that you give up this investigation of yours, and philosophy; if you are found following those pursuits again, you shall die. I say, if you offered to let me go on these terms, I should reply: Athenians, I hold you in the highest regard and affection, but I will be persuaded by the god rather than by you; and as long as I have breath and strength I will not give up philosophy and exhorting you and declaring the truth to every one of you whom I meet, saying, as I am accustomed, "My good friend, you are a citizen of Athens, a city which is very great and very famous for its wisdom and strength — are you not ashamed of caring so much for the making of money and for fame and prestige, when you neither think nor care about wisdom and truth and the improvement of your soul?" And if he disputes my words and says that he does care about these things, I shall not at once release him and go away: I shall question him and cross-examine him and test him. If I think that he does not possess virtue, though he says that he does, I shall reproach him for undervaluing the most valuable things, and overvaluing those that are less valuable. This I shall do to everyone whom I meet, young or old, citizen or stranger, but especially to citizens, for they are more nearly akin to me. For know that the god has commanded me to do so. And I think that no greater good has ever befallen you in Athens than my service to the god. For I spend my whole life in going about and persuading you all to give your first and greatest care to the improvement of your souls, and not till you have done that to think of your bodies or your wealth; and telling you that virtue does not come from wealth, but that wealth, and every other good thing which men have, whether in public or in private, comes from virtue. If then I corrupt the youth by this teaching, these things must be harmful; but if any man says that I teach anything else, there is nothing in what he says. And therefore, Athenians, I say, whether you are persuaded by Anytus or not, whether you acquit me or not, be sure I shall not change my way of life; no, not if I have to die for it many times.

Do not interrupt me, Athenians, with your shouts. Remember the request which I made to you, and do not interrupt my words. I think that it will profit you to hear them. I am going to say something more to you, at which you may be inclined to protest, but do not do that. Be sure that if you put me to death, who am what I have told you that I am, you will do yourselves more harm than me. Meletus and Anytus can do me no harm: that is impossible, for I am sure it is not allowed that a good man be injured by a worse. They may indeed kill me, or drive me into exile, or deprive me of my civil rights; and perhaps Meletus and others think those things great evils. But I do not think so. I think it is a much greater evil to do what he is doing now, and to try to put a man to death unjustly. And now, Athenians, I am not arguing in my own defense at all, as you might expect me to do, but rather in yours in order [that] you may not make a mistake about the gift of the god to you by condemning me. For if you put me to death, you will not easily find another who, if I may use a ludicrous comparison, clings to the state as a sort of gadfly to a horse that is large and well-bred but rather sluggish from its size, and needing to be aroused. It seems to be that the god has attached me like that to the state, for I am constantly alighting upon you at every point to rouse, persuade, and reproach each of you all day long. You will not easily find anyone else, my friends, to fill my place; and if you are persuaded by me, you will spare my life. You are indignant, as drowsy persons are, when they are awakened, and, of course, if you are persuaded by Anytus, you could easily kill me with a single blow, and then sleep on undisturbed for the rest of your lives, unless the god in his care for you sends another to rouse you. And you may easily see that it is the god who has given me to your city; for it is not human the way in which I have neglected all my own interests and permitted my private affairs to be neglected now for so many years, while occupying myself unceasingly in your interests, going to each of you privately, like a father or an elder brother, trying to persuade him to care for virtue. There would have been a reason for it, if I had gained any advantage by this, or if I had been paid for my exhortations; but you see yourselves that my accusers, though they accuse me of everything else without shame, have not had the impudence to say that I ever either exacted or demanded payment. Of that they have no evidence. And I think that I have sufficient evidence of the truth of what I say—my poverty.

Perhaps it may seem strange to you that, though I go about giving this advice privately and meddling in others' affairs, yet I do not venture to come forward in the assembly and advise the state. You have often heard me speak of my reason for this, and in many places: it is that I have a certain divine sign, which is what Meletus has caricatured in his indictment. I have had it from childhood. It is a kind of voice which, whenever I hear it, always turns me back from something which I was going to do, but never urges me to act. It is this which forbids me to take part in politics. And I think it does well to forbid me. For, Athenians, it is quite certain that, if I had attempted to take part in politics, I should have perished at once and long ago without doing any good either to you or to myself. And do not be indignant with me for telling the truth. There is no man who will preserve his life for long, either in Athens or elsewhere, if he firmly opposes the multitude, and tries to prevent the commission of much injustice and illegality in the state. He who would really fight for justice must do so as a private citizen, not as an officeholder, if he is to preserve his life, even for a short time.

I will prove to you that this is so by very strong evidence, not by mere words, but by what you value highly, actions. Listen then to what has happened to me, that you may know that there is no man who could make me consent to do wrong from the fear of death, but that I would perish at once rather than give way. What I am going to tell you may be a commonplace in the law court;

nevertheless it is true. The only office that I ever held in the state, Athenians, was that of Senator. When you wished to try the ten generals who did not rescue their men after the battle of Arginusae, as a group, which was illegal, as you all came to think afterwards, the tribe Antiochis, to which I belong, held the presidency. On that occasion I alone of all the presidents opposed your illegal action and gave my vote against you. The speakers were ready to suspend me and arrest me; and you were clamoring against me, and crying out to me to submit. But I thought that I ought to face the danger, with law and justice on my side, rather than join with you in your unjust proposal, from fear of imprisonment or death. That was when the state was democratic. When the oligarchy came in, the Thirty sent for me, with four others, to the council-chamber, and ordered us to bring Leon the Salaminian from Salamis, that they might put him to death. They were in the habit of frequently giving similar orders, to many others, wishing to implicate as many as possible in their crimes. But, then, I again proved, not by mere words, but by my actions, that, if I may speak bluntly, I do not care a straw for death; but that I do care very much indeed about not doing anything unjust or impious. That government with all its powers did not terrify me into doing anything unjust; but when we left the council-chamber, the other four went over to Salamis and brought Leon across to Athens; and I went home. And if the rule of the Thirty had not been destroyed soon afterwards, I should very likely have been put to death for what I did then. Many of you will be my witnesses in this matter.

Now do you think that I could have remained alive all these years if I had taken part in public affairs, and had always maintained the cause of justice like an honest man, and had held it a paramount duty, as it is, to do so? Certainly not, Athenians, nor could any other man. But throughout my whole life, both in private and in public, whenever I have had to take part in public affairs, you will find I have always been the same and have never yielded unjustly to anyone; no, not to those whom my enemies falsely assert to have been my pupils. But I was never anyone's teacher. I have never withheld myself from anyone, young or old, who was anxious to hear me discuss while I was making my investigation; neither do I discuss for payment, and refuse to discuss without payment. I am ready to ask questions of rich and poor alike, and if any man wishes to answer me, and then listen to what I have to say, he may. And I cannot justly be charged with causing these men to turn out good or bad, for I never either taught or professed to teach any of them any knowledge whatever. And if any man asserts that he ever learned or heard anything from me in private which everyone else did not hear as well as he, be sure that he does not speak the truth.

Why is it, then, that people delight in spending so much time in my company? You have heard why, Athenians. I told you the whole truth when I said that they delight in hearing me examine persons who think that they are not wise. It is certainly very amusing to listen to that. And, I say, the god has commanded me to examine men, in oracles and in dreams and in every way in which the divine will was ever declared to man. This is the truth, Athenians, and if it were not the truth, it would be easily refuted. For if it were really the case that I have already corrupted some of the young men, and am now corrupting others, surely some of them, finding as they grew older that I had given them bad advice in their youth, would have come forward today to accuse me and take their revenge. Or if they were unwilling to do so themselves, surely their relatives, their fathers or brothers, or others, would, if I had done them any harm, have remembered it and taken their revenge. Certainly I see many of them in Court. Here is Crito, of my own deme and of my own age, the father of Critobulus; here is Lysanias of Sphettus, the father of Aeschines; . . . . And I can name many others to you, some of whom Meletus ought to have called as witnesses in the course of his own speech; but if he forgot to call them then, let him call them now — I will yield the floor to him — and tell us if he has any such evidence. No, on the contrary, my friends, you will find all these men ready to support me, the corrupter, the injurer, of their relatives, as Meletus and Anytus call me. Those of them who have been already corrupted might perhaps have some reason for supporting me, but what reason can their relatives have who are grown up, and who are uncorrupted, except the reason of truth and justice — that they know very well that Meletus is a liar, and that I am speaking the truth?

Well, my friends, this, and perhaps more like this, is pretty much what I have to say in my defense. There may be some one among you who will be indignant when he remembers how, even in a less important trial than this, he begged and entreated the judges, with many tears, to acquit him, and brought forward his children and many of his friends and relatives in Court in order to appeal to your feelings; and then finds that I shall do none of these things, though I am in what he would think the supreme danger. Perhaps he will harden himself against me when he notices this: it may make him angry, and he may cast his vote in anger. If it is so with any of you — I do not suppose that it is, but in case it should be so — I think that I should answer him reasonably if I said: My friend, I have relatives, too, for, in the words of Homer, "I am not born of an oak or a rock" but of flesh and blood; and so, Athenians, I have relatives, and I have three sons, one of them a lad, and the other two still children. Yet I will not bring any of them forward before you and implore you to acquit me. And why will I do none of these things? It is not from arrogance, Athenians, nor because I lack respect for you — whether or not I can face death bravely is another question — but for my own good name, and for your good name, and for the good name of the whole state. I do not think it right, at my age and with my reputation, to do anything of that kind. Rightly or wrongly, men have made up their minds that in some way Socrates is different from

the mass of mankind. And it will be shameful if those of you who are thought to excel in wisdom, or in bravery, or in any other virtue, are going to act in this fashion. I have often seen men of reputation behaving in an extraordinary way at their trial, as if they thought it a terrible fate to be killed, and as though they expected to live forever if you did not put them to death. Such men seem to me to bring shame upon the state, for any stranger would suppose that the best and most eminent Athenians, who are selected by their fellow citizens to hold office, and for other honors, are no better than women. Those of you, Athenians, who have any reputation at all ought not to do these things, and you ought not to allow us to do them; you should show that you will be much more ready to condemn men who make the state ridiculous by these pitiful pieces of acting, than men who remain quiet.

But apart from the question of reputation, my friends, I do not think that it is right to entreat the judge to acquit us, or to escape condemnation in that way. It is our duty to convince him by reason. He does not sit to give away justice as a favor, but to pronounce judgment; and he has sworn, not to favor any man whom he would like to favor, but to judge according to law. And, therefore, we ought not to encourage you in the habit of breaking your oaths; and you ought not to allow yourselves to fall into this habit, for then neither you nor we would be acting piously. Therefore, Athenians, do not require me to do these things, for I believe them to be neither good nor just nor pious; and, more especially, do not ask me to do them today when Meletus is prosecuting me for impiety. For were I to be successful and persuade you by my entreaties to break your oaths, I should be clearly teaching you to believe that there are no gods, and I should be simply accusing myself by my defense of not believing in them. But, Athenians, that is very far from the truth. I do believe in the gods as no one of my accusers believes in them: and to you and to God I commit my cause to be decided as is best for you and for me.

(He is found guilty by a vote of 281 to 220.)

I am not indignant at the verdict which you have given, Athenians, for many reasons. I expected that you would find me guilty; and I am not so much surprised at that as at the numbers of the votes. I certainly never thought that the majority against me would have been so narrow. But now it seems that if only thirty votes had changed sides, I should have escaped. So I think that I have escaped Meletus, as it is; and not only have I escaped him, for it is perfectly clear that if Anytus and Lycon had not come forward to accuse me, too, he would not have obtained the fifth part of the votes, and would have had to pay a fine of a thousand drachmae.

So he proposes death as the penalty. Be it so. And what alternative penalty shall I propose to you, Athenians? What I deserve, of course, must I not? What then do I deserve to pay or to suffer for having determined not to spend my life in ease? I neglected the things which most men value, such as wealth, and family interests, and military commands, and popular oratory, and all the political appointments, and clubs, and factions, that there are in Athens; for I thought that I was really too honest a man to preserve my life if I engaged in these matters. So I did not go where I should have done no good either to you or to myself. I went, instead, to each one of you privately to do him, as I say, the greatest of services, and tried to persuade him not to think of his affairs until he had thought of himself and tried to make himself as good and wise as possible, nor to think of the affairs of Athens until he had thought of Athens herself; and to care for other things in the same manner. Then what do I deserve for such a life? Something good, Athenians, if I am really to propose what I deserve; and something good which it would be suitable to me to receive. Then what is a suitable reward to be given to a poor benefactor who requires leisure to exhort you? There is no reward, Athenians, so suitable for him as a public maintenance in the Prytaneum. It is a much more suitable reward for him than for any of you who has won a victory at the Olympic games with his horse or his chariots. Such a man only makes you seem happy, but I make you really happy; and he is not in want, and I am. So if I am to propose the penalty which I really deserve, I propose this — a public maintenance in the Prytaneum.

Perhaps you think me stubborn and arrogant in what I am saying now, as in what I said about the entreaties and tears. It is not so, Athenians; it is rather that I am convinced that I never wronged any man intentionally, though I cannot persuade you of that, for we have discussed together only a little time. If there were a law at Athens, as there is elsewhere, not to finish a trial of life and death in a single day, I think that I could have persuaded you; but now it is not easy in so short a time to clear myself of great prejudices. But when I am persuaded that I have never wronged any man, I shall certainly not wrong myself, or admit that I deserve to suffer any evil, or propose any evil for myself as a penalty. Why should I? Lest I should suffer the penalty which Meletus proposes when I say that I do not know whether it is a good or an evil? Shall I choose instead of it something which I know to be an evil, and propose that as a penalty? Shall I propose imprisonment? And why should I pass the rest of my days in prison, the slave of successive officials? Or shall I propose a fine, with imprisonment until it is paid? I have told you why I will not do that. I should have to remain in prison, for I have no money to pay a fine with. Shall I then propose exile? Perhaps you would agree to that. Life would indeed be very dear to me if I were unreasonable enough to expect that strangers would cheerfully tolerate my discussions and reasonings when you who are my fellow citizens cannot endure them, and have found them so irksome and odious to you that you are seeking now to be relieved of them. No, indeed, Athenians, that is not likely. A fine life I should lead for an old man if I were to withdraw from Athens and pass the rest of my days in wandering from city to city, and continually being expelled. For I know very well that the young men will listen to me wherever I go, as they do here; and if I drive them away, they will persuade their elders to expel me; and if I do not drive them away, their fathers and kinsmen will expel me for their sakes.

Perhaps someone will say, "Why cannot you withdraw from Athens, Socrates, and hold your peace?" It is the most difficult thing in the world to make you understand why I cannot do that. If I say that I cannot hold my peace because that would be to disobey the god, you will think that I am not in earnest and will not believe me. And if I tell you that no better thing can happen to a man than to discuss virtue every day and the other matters about which you have heard me arguing and examining myself and others, and that an un-examined life is not worth living, then you will believe me still less. But that is so, my friends, though it is not easy to persuade you. And, what is more, I am not accustomed to think that I de-serve any punishment. If I had been rich, I would have proposed as large a fine as I could pay: that would have done me no harm. But I am not rich enough to pay a fine unless you are willing to fix it at a sum within my means. Perhaps I could pay you a mina, so I propose that. Plato here, Athe-nians, and Crito, and Critobulus, and Apol-lodorus bid me propose thirty minae, and they will be sureties for me. So I propose thirty minae. They will be sufficient sureties to you for the money.

(He is condemned to death.)

You have not gained very much time, Athe-nians, and, as the price of it, you will have an evil name for all who wish to revile the state, and they will say that you put Socrates, a wise man, to death. For they will certainly call me wise, whether I am wise or not, when they want to re-proach you. If you would have waited for a little while, your wishes would have been fulfilled in the course of nature; for you see that I am an old man, far advanced in years, and near to death. I am saying this not to all of you, only to those who have voted for my death. And to them I have something else to say. Perhaps, my friends, you think that I have been convicted because I was wanting in the arguments by which I could have persuaded you to acquit me, if, that is, I had thought it right to do or to say anything to escape punishment. It is not so. I have been convicted because I was wanting, not in arguments, but in impudence and shamelessness — because I would not plead before you as you would have liked to hear me plead, or appeal to you with weeping and wailing, or say and do many other things which I maintain are unworthy of me, but which you have been accustomed to from other men. But when I was defending myself, I thought that I ought not to do anything unworthy of a free man because of the danger which I ran, and I have not changed my mind now. I would very much rather defend myself as I did, and die, than as you would have had me do, and live. Both in a lawsuit and in war, there are some things which neither I nor any other man may do in order to escape from death. In battle, a man often sees that he may at least escape from death by throw-ing down his arms and falling on his knees before the pursuer to beg for his life. And there are many other ways of avoiding death in every danger if a man is willing to say and to do anything. But, my friends, I think that it is a much harder thing to escape from wickedness than from death, for wickedness is swifter than death. And now I, who am old and slow, have been overtaken by the slower pursuer: and my accusers, who are clever and swift, have been overtaken by the swifter pursuer — wickedness. And now I shall go away, sentenced by you to death; and they will go away, sentenced by truth to wickedness and injustice. And I abide by this award as well as they. Perhaps it was right for these things to be so; and I think that they are fairly measured.

And now I wish to prophesy to you, Athe-nians, who have condemned me. For I am going to die, and that is the time when men have most prophetic power. And I prophesy to you who have sentenced me to death that a far more severe punishment than you have inflicted on me will surely overtake you as soon as I am dead. You have done this thing, thinking that you will be relieved from having to give an account of your lives. But I say that the result will be very different. There will be more men who will call you to account, whom I have held back, though you did not recognize it. And they will be harsher toward you than I have been, for they will be younger, and you will be more indignant with them. For if you think that you will restrain men from reproaching you for not living as you should, by putting them to death, you are very much mistaken. That way of escape is neither possible nor honorable. It is much more honorable and much easier not to suppress others, but to make yourselves as good as you can. This is my parting prophecy to you who have condemned me.

With you who have acquitted me I should like to discuss this thing that has happened, while the authorities are busy, and before I go to the place where I have to die. So, remain with me until I go: there is no reason why we should not talk with each other while it is possible. I wish to explain to you, as my friends, the meaning of what has happened to me. A wonderful thing has happened to me, judges—for you I am right in calling judges. The prophetic sign has been constantly with me all through my life till now, opposing me in quite small matters if I were not going to act rightly. And now you yourselves see what has happened to me—a thing which might be thought, and which is sometimes actually reckoned, the supreme evil. But the divine sign did not oppose me when I was leaving my house in the morning, nor when I was coming up here to the court, nor at any point in my speech when I was going to say anything; though at other times it has often stopped me in the very act of speaking. But now, in this matter, it has never once opposed me, either in my words or my actions. I will tell you what I believe to be the reason. This thing that has come upon me must be a good; and those of us who think that death is an evil must needs be mistaken. I have a clear proof

that that is so; for my accustomed sign would certainly have opposed me if I had not been going to meet with something good.

And if we reflect in another way, we shall see that we may well hope that death is a good. For the state of death is one of two things: either the dead man wholly ceases to be and loses all consciousness or, as we are told, it is a change and a migration of the soul to another place. And if death is the absence of all consciousness, and like the sleep of one whose slumbers are unbroken by any dreams, it will be a wonderful gain. For if a man had to select that night in which he slept so soundly that he did not even dream, and had to compare with it all the other nights and days of his life, and then had to say how many days and nights in his life he had spent better and more pleasantly than this night, I think that a private person, nay, even the great King himself, would find them easy to count, compared with the others. If that is the nature of death, I for one count it a gain. For then it appears that all time is nothing more than a single night. But if death is a journey to another place, and what we are told is true—that there are all who have died—what good could be greater than this, my judges? Would a journey not be worth taking, at the end of which, in the other world, we should be released from the self-styled judges here and should find the true judges who are said to sit in judgment below, such as Minos and Rhadamanthus and Aeacus and Triptolemus, and the other demigods who were just in their own lives? Or what would you not give to discuss with Orpheus and Musaeus and Hesiod and Homer? I am willing to die many times if this be true. And for my own part I should find it wonderful to meet there Palamedes, and Ajax, the son of Telamon, and the other men of old who have died through an unjust judgment, and in comparing my experiences with theirs. That I think would be no small pleasure. And, above all, I could spend my time in examining those who are there, as I examine men here, and in finding out which of them is wise, and which of them thinks himself wise when he is not wise. What would we not give, my judges, to be able to examine the leader of the great expedition against Troy, or Odysseus, or Sisyphus, or countless other men and women whom we could name? It would be an infinite happiness to discuss with them and to live with them and to examine them. Assuredly there they do not put men to death for doing that. For besides the other ways in which they are happier than we are, they are immortal, at least if what we are told is true.

And you, too, judges, must face death hopefully, and believe this as a truth that no evil can happen to a good man, either in life or after death. His fortunes are not neglected by the gods; and what has happened to me today has not happened by chance. I am persuaded that it was better for me to die now, and to be released from trouble; and that was the reason why the sign never turned me back. And so I am not at all angry with my accusers or with those who have condemned me to die. Yet it was not with this in mind that they accused me and condemned me, but meaning to do me an injury. So far I may blame them.

Yet I have one request to make of them. When my sons grow up, punish them, my friends, and harass them in the same way that I have harassed you, if they seem to you to care for riches or for any other thing more than virtue; and if they think that they are something when they are really nothing, reproach them, as I have reproached you, for not caring for what they should, and for thinking that they are great men when really they are worthless. And if you will do this, I myself and my sons will have received justice from you.

But now the time has come, and we must go away—I to die, and you to live. Whether life or death is better is known to God, and to God only.

From *Crito*

Socr.: Then, my good friend, we must not think so much of what the many will say of us; we must think of what the one man who under-stands justice and injustice, and of what truth herself, will say of us. And so you are mistaken, to begin with, when you invite us to regard the opinion of the multitude concerning the just and the honorable and the good, and their opposites. But, it may be said, the multitude can put us to death?

Crito.: Yes, that is evident. That may be said, Socrates.

Socr.: True. But, my good friend, to me it appears that the conclusion which we have just reached is the same as our conclusion of former times. Now consider whether we still hold to the belief that we should set the highest value, not on living, but on living well?

Crito.: Yes, we do.

Socr.: And living well and honorably and justly mean the same thing: do we hold to that or not?

Crito.: We do.

Socr.: Then, starting from these premises, we have to consider whether it is just or not for me to try to escape from prison, without the consent of the Athenians. If we find that it is just, we will try; if not, we will give up the idea. . . . Ought a man to carry out his just agreements, or may he shuffle out of them?

Crito.: He ought to carry them out.

Socr.: Then consider. If I escape without the state's consent, shall I be injuring those whom I ought least to injure, or not? Shall I be abiding by my just agreements or not?

Crito.: I cannot answer your question, Socrates. I do not understand it.

Socr.: Consider it in this way. Suppose the laws and the commonwealth were to come and appear to me as I was preparing to run away (if that is the right phrase to describe my escape) and were to ask, "Tell us, Socrates, what have you in your mind to do? What do you mean by trying to escape but to destroy us, the laws and the whole state, so far as you are able? Do you think that a state can exist and not be overthrown, in which the decisions of law are of no force, and are disregarded and undermined by private individuals?" . . . Shall I reply, "But the state has injured me by judging my case unjustly"? Shall we say that?

Crito.: Certainly we will, Socrates.

Socr.: And suppose the laws were to reply, "Was that our agreement? Or was it that you would abide by whatever judgments the state should pronounce?" . . . What answer shall we make, Crito? Shall we say that the laws speak the truth, or not?

Crito.: I think that they do.

Socr.: "Then consider, Socrates," perhaps they would say, "if we are right in saying that by attempting to escape you are attempting an injustice. We brought you into the world, we raised you, we educated you, we gave you and every other citizen a share of all the good things we could. Yet we proclaim that if any man of the Athenians is dissatisfied with us, he may take his goods and go away wherever he pleases; we give that privilege to every man who chooses to avail himself of it, so soon as he has reached manhood, and sees us, the laws, and the administration of our state. No one of us stands in his way or forbids him to take his goods and go wherever he likes, whether it be to an Athenian colony or to any foreign country, if he is dissatisfied with us and with the state. But we say that every man of you who remains here, seeing how we administer justice, and how we govern the state in other matters, has agreed, by the very fact of remaining here, to do whatsoever we tell him. And, we say, he who disobeys us acts unjustly on three counts: he disobeys us who are his parents, and he disobeys us who reared him, and he disobeys us after he has agreed to obey us, without persuading us that we are wrong.

". . . you might at your trial have offered to go into exile. At that time you could have done with the state's consent what you are trying now to do without it. But then you gloried in being willing to die. You said that you preferred death to exile. And now you do not honor those words: you do not respect us, the laws, for you are trying to destroy us; and you are acting just as a miserable slave would act, trying to run away, and breaking the contracts and agreement which you made to

live as our citizen. First, therefore, answer this question. Are we right, or are we wrong, in saying that you have agreed not in mere words, but in your actions, to live under our government?" What are we to say, Crito? Must we not admit that it is true?

Crito.: We must, Socrates.

Socr.: Then they would say, "Are you not breaking your contracts and agreements with us? And you were not led to make them by force or by fraud. You did not have to make up your mind in a hurry. You had seventy years in which you might have gone away if you had been dissatisfied with us, or if the agreement had seemed to you unjust. But you preferred neither Sparta nor Crete, though you are fond of saying that they are well governed, nor any other state, either of the Greeks or the Barbarians. . . . Clearly you, far more than other Athenians, were satisfied with the state, and also with us who are its laws; for who would be satisfied with a state which had no laws? And now will you not abide by your agreement? If you take our advice, you will, Socrates; then you will not make yourself ridiculous by going away from Athens.

"Reflect now. What good will you do yourself or your friends by thus transgressing and breaking your agreement? It is tolerably certain that they, on their part, will at least run the risk of exile, and of losing their civil rights, or of forfeiting their property. You yourself might go to one of the neighboring states, to Thebes or to Megara, for instance—for both of them are well governed—but, Socrates, you will come as an enemy to these governments, and all who care for their city will look askance at you, and think that you are a subverter of law. You will confirm the judges in their opinion, and make it seem that their verdict was a just one. For a man who is a subverter of law may well be supposed to be a corrupter of the young and thoughtless. Then will you avoid well-governed states and civilized men? Will life be worth having, if you do? Will you associate with such men, and converse without shame—about what, Socrates? About the things which you talk of here? Will you tell them that excellence and justice and institutions and law are the most valuable things that men can have? And do you not think that that will be a disgraceful thing for Socrates?"

Crito.: I have nothing more to say, Socrates.

Socr.: Then let it be, Crito, and let us do as I say, since the god is our guide.

But I suppose that I may, and must, pray to the gods that my journey hence may be prosperous. That is my prayer; may it be granted.

From *Phaedo*

And were we not saying long ago that the soul when using the body as an instrument of perception, that is to say, when using the sense of sight or hearing or some other sense (for the meaning of perceiving through the body is perceiving through the senses) — were we not saying that the soul too is then dragged by the body into the region of the changeable, and wanders and is confused; the world spins round her, and she is like a drunkard, when she touches change?

Very true.

But when returning into herself she reflects, then she passes into the other world, the region of purity, and eternity, and immortality, and unchangeableness, which are her kindred, and with them she ever lives, when she is by herself and is not let or hindered; then she ceases from her erring ways, and being in communion with the unchanging is unchanging. And this state of the soul is called wisdom?

That is well and truly said, Socrates, he replied.

And to which class is the soul more nearly alike and akin, as far as may be inferred from this argument, as well as from the preceding one?

I think, Socrates, that, in the opinion of everyone who follows the argument, the soul will be infinitely more like the unchangeable — even the most stupid person will not deny that.

And the body is more like the changing?

Yes.

Yet once more consider the matter in another light: When the soul and the body are united, then nature orders the soul to rule and govern, and the body to obey and serve. Now which of these two functions is akin to the divine? and which to the mortal? Does not the divine appear to you to be that which naturally orders and rules, and the mortal to be that which is subject and servant?

True.

And which does the soul resemble?

The soul resembles the divine, and the body the mortal — there can be no doubt of that, Socrates.

Then reflect, Cebes: of all which has been said is not this the conclusion? — that the soul is in the very likeness of the divine, and immortal, and intellectual, and uniform, and indissoluble, and unchangeable; and that the body is in the very likeness of the human, and mortal, and unintellectual, and multiform, and dissoluble, and changeable. Can this, my dear Cebes, be denied?

It cannot.

But if it be true, then is not the body liable to speedy dissolution? and is not the soul almost or altogether indissoluble?

Certainly.

Must we not, said Socrates, ask ourselves what that is which, as we imagine, is liable to be scattered, and about which we fear? and what again is that about which we have no fear? And then we may proceed further to inquire whether that which suffers dispersion is or is not of the nature of soul — our hopes and fears as to our own souls will turn upon the answers to these questions.

Very true, he said.

Now the compound or composite may be supposed to be naturally capable, as of being compounded, so also of being dissolved; but that which is uncompounded, and that only, must be, if anything is, indissoluble.

Yes; I should imagine so, said Cebes.

And the uncompounded may be assumed to be the same and unchanging, whereas the compound is always changing and never the same.

I agree, he said.

Then now let us return to the previous discussion. Is that idea or essence, which in the dialectical process we define as essence or true existence — whether essence of equality, beauty, or anything else — are these essences, I say, liable at times to some degree of change? or are they each of them always what they are, having the same simple self-existent and unchanging forms, not admitting of variation at all, or in any way, or at any time?

They must be always the same, Socrates, replied Cebes.

And what would you say of the many beautiful — whether men or horses or garments or any other things which are named by the same names and may be called equal or beautiful, — are they all unchanging and the same always, or quite the reverse? May they not rather be described as almost always changing and hardly ever the same, either with themselves or with one another?

The latter, replied Cebes; they are always in a state of change.

And these you can touch and see and perceive with the senses, but the unchanging things you can only perceive with the mind — they are invisible and are not seen?

That is very true, he said.

Well then, added Socrates, let us suppose that there are two sorts of existences — one seen, the other unseen.

Let us suppose them.

The seen is the changing, and the unseen is the unchanging?

That may be also supposed.

And, further, is not one part of us body, another part soul?

To be sure.

And to which class is the body more alike and akin?

Clearly to the seen — no one can doubt that.

And is the soul seen or not seen?

Not by man, Socrates.

And what we mean by "seen" and "not seen" is that which is or is not visible to the eye of man?

Yes, to the eye of man.

And is the soul seen or not seen?

Not seen.

Unseen then?

Yes.

Then the soul is more like to the unseen, and the body to the seen?

That follows necessarily, Socrates.

Further Questions

1. How does Socrates use irony to attack those who profess to know more than they actually know?

2. Socrates said, "The unexamined life is not worth living." What do you suppose he meant by this?

3. Do you think you would have liked to have had Socrates as a friend? A teacher? A brother? Why?

4. Do you agree with Socrates' view that it is better to speak the truth — no matter how disturbing — rather than what is considered proper or pleasing? What is the main value of such an approach to life? What is the main drawback?

Further Readings

Plato. *The Dialogues of Plato.* B. Jowett, Trans. New York, Random House, 1937. All of Plato's dialogues appear in this volume. *The Republic*, which gives the best overall view of Plato's philosophy of nearly everything, is the best place to start. *Apology*, *Crito*, and *Phaedo* tell the story of Socrates's trial, imprisonment, and death.

Other suggested readings are:

Edwards, Paul. Editor-in-chief. *The Encyclopedia of Philosophy.* New York: Macmillan, 1967. An eight-volume collection of articles on all major philosophers and philosophical issues.

Russell, Bertrand. *History of Western Philosophy.* New York: Simon & Schuster, 1945. One of the most readable and concise histories of Western philosophy.

Obedience to Authority

STANLEY MILGRAM

Born in New York City in 1933, Stanley Milgram was educated at Queens College and then received his Ph.D. from Harvard. As a social psychologist, he did research at Yale University where, from 1960 to 1963, he performed one of the most shocking and important experiments ever made on human behavior, and his own account is reprinted here. His experiments revealed the extent to which ordinary people like you are ready to torture and kill other innocent people simply out of obedience to authority.

Reading Questions

1. If someone in authority asked you to hurt and perhaps even kill an innocent human being, would you obey? If you are like most people, you probably *think* you wouldn't. But if you are like most people, you probably *would*. Why?

2. Milgram is concerned with "the extreme willingness of adults to go to almost any lengths on the command of an authority." What is his evidence? How do you account for this behavior?

3. What are the "binding factors" that make people obedient?

4. What does Milgram mean by "counteranthropomorphic"?

5. What does Milgram say is the most fundamental lesson of his study?

6. Does Milgram think that the problem of obedience is just psychological? What else does he think is involved?

OBEDIENCE IS AS BASIC AN ELEMENT in the structure of social life as one can point to. Some system of authority is a requirement of all communal living, and it is only the man dwelling in isolation who is not forced to respond, through defiance or submission, to the commands of others. Obedience, as a determinant of behavior, is of particular relevance to our time. It has been reliably established that from 1933 to 1945 millions of innocent people were systematically slaughtered on command. Gas chambers were built, death camps were guarded, daily quotas of corpses were produced with the same efficiency as the manufacture of appliances. These inhumane policies may have originated in the mind of a single person, but they could only have been carried out on a massive scale if a very large number of people obeyed orders.

Obedience is the psychological mechanism that links individual action to political purpose. It is the dispositional cement that binds men to systems of authority. Facts of recent history and observation in daily life suggest that for many people obedience may be a deeply ingrained behavior tendency, indeed, a prepotent impulse overriding training in ethics, sympathy, and moral conduct. C. P. Snow (1961) points to its importance when he writes:

> When you think of the long and gloomy history of man, you will find more hideous crimes have been committed in the name of obedience than have ever been committed in the name of rebellion. If you doubt that, read William Shirer's 'Rise and Fall of the Third Reich.' The German Officer Corps were brought up in the most rigorous code of obedience . . . in the name of obedience they were party to, and assisted in, the most wicked large scale actions in the history of the world. (p. 24)

The Nazi extermination of European Jews is the most extreme instance of abhorrent immoral acts carried out by thousands of people in the name of obedience. Yet in lesser degree this type of thing is constantly recurring: ordinary citizens are ordered to destroy other people, and they do so because they consider it their duty to obey orders. Thus, obedience to authority, long praised as a virtue, takes on a new aspect when it serves a malevolent cause; far from appearing as a virtue, it is transformed into a heinous sin. Or is it?

The moral question of whether one should obey when commands conflict with conscience was argued by Plato, dramatized in *Antigone*, and treated to philosophic analysis in every historical epoch. Conservative philosophers argue that the very fabric of society is threatened by disobe-

dience, and even when the act prescribed by an authority is an evil one, it is better to carry out the act than to wrench at the structure of authority. Hobbes stated further that an act so executed is in no sense the responsibility of the person who carries it out but only of the authority that orders it. But humanists argue for the primacy of individual conscience in such matters, insisting that the moral judgments of the individual must override authority when the two are in conflict.

The legal and philosophic aspects of obedience are of enormous import, but an empirically grounded scientist eventually comes to the point where he wishes to move from abstract discourse to the careful observation of concrete instances. In order to take a close look at the act of obeying, I set up a simple experiment at Yale University. Eventually, the experiment was to involve more than a thousand participants and would be repeated at several universities, but at the beginning, the conception was simple. A person comes to a psychological laboratory and is told to carry out a series of acts that come increasingly into conflict with conscience. The main question is how far the participant will comply with the experimenter's instructions before refusing to carry out the actions required of him.

But the reader needs to know a little more detail about the experiment. Two people come to a psychology laboratory to take part in a study of memory and learning. One of them is designated as a "teacher" and the other a "learner." The experimenter explains that the study is concerned with the effects of punishment on learning. The learner is conducted into a room, seated in a chair, his arms strapped to prevent excessive movement, and an electrode attached to his wrist. He is told that he is to learn a list of word pairs; whenever he makes an error, he will receive electric shocks of increasing intensity.

The real focus of the experiment is the teacher. After watching the learner being strapped into place, he is taken into the main experimental room and seated before an impressive shock generator. Its main feature is a horizontal line of thirty switches, ranging from 15 volts to **450** volts, in 15-volt increments. There are also verbal designations which range from SLIGHT SHOCK to DANGER — SEVERE SHOCK. The teacher is told that he is to administer the learning test to the man in the other room. When the learner responds correctly, the teacher moves on to the next item; when the other man gives an incorrect answer, the teacher is to give him an electric shock. He is to start at the lowest shock level (15 volts) and to increase the level each time the man makes an error, going through 30 volts, 45 volts, and so on.

The "teacher" is a genuinely naïve subject who has come to the laboratory to participate in an experiment. The learner, or victim, is an actor who actually receives no shock at all. The point of the experiment is to see how far a person will proceed in a concrete and measurable situation in which he is ordered to inflict increasing pain on a protesting victim. At what point will the subject refuse to obey the experimenter?

Conflict arises when the man receiving the shock begins to indicate that he is experiencing discomfort. At 75 volts, the "learner" grunts. At 120 volts he complains verbally; at 150 he demands to be released from the experiment. His protests continue as the shocks escalate, growing increasingly vehement and emotional. At 285 volts his response can only be described as an agonized scream.

Observers of the experiment agree that its gripping quality is somewhat obscured in print. For the subject, the situation is not a game; conflict is intense and obvious. On one hand, the manifest suffering of the learner presses him to quit. On the other, the experimenter, a legitimate authority to whom the subject feels some commitment, enjoins him to continue. Each time the subject hesitates to administer shock, the experimenter orders him to continue. To extricate himself from the situation, the subject must make a clear break with authority. The aim of this investigation was to find when and how people would defy authority in the face of a clear moral imperative.

There are, of course, enormous differences between carrying out the orders of a commanding officer during times of war and carrying out the orders of an experimenter. Yet the essence of certain relationships remains, for one may ask in a general way: How does a man behave when he is told by a legitimate authority to act against a third individual? If anything, we may expect the experimenter's power to be considerably less than that of the general, since he has no power to enforce his imperatives, and participation in a psychological experiment scarcely evokes the sense of urgency and dedication engendered by participation in war. Despite these limitations, I thought it worthwhile to start careful observation of obedience even in this modest situation, in the hope that it would stimulate insights and yield general propositions applicable to a variety of circumstances.

A reader's initial reaction to the experiment may be to wonder why anyone in his right mind would administer even the first shocks. Would he not simply refuse and walk out of the laboratory? But the fact is that no one ever does. Since the subject has come to the laboratory to aid the experimenter, he is quite willing to start off with the procedure. There is nothing very extraordinary in this, particularly since the person who is to receive the shocks seems initially cooperative, if somewhat apprehensive. What is surprising is how far ordinary individuals will go in complying with the experimenter's instructions. Indeed, the results of the experiment are both surprising and dismaying. Despite the fact that many subjects experience stress, despite the fact that many protest to the experimenter, a substantial proportion continue to the last shock on the generator.

Many subjects will obey the experimenter no matter how vehement the pleading of the person being shocked, no matter how painful the shocks seem to be, and no matter how much the victim pleads to be let out. This was seen time and again in our studies and has been observed in several universities where the experiment was repeated. It is the extreme willingness of adults to go to almost any lengths on the command of an authority that constitutes the chief finding of the study and the fact most urgently demanding explanation.

A commonly offered explanation is that those who shocked the victim at the most severe level were monsters, the sadistic fringe of society. But if one considers that almost two-thirds of the participants fall into the category of "obedient" subjects, and that they represented ordinary people drawn from working, managerial, and professional classes, the argument becomes very shaky. Indeed, it is highly reminiscent of the issue that arose in connection with Hannah Arendt's 1963 book, *Eichmann in Jerusalem.* Arendt contended that the prosecution's effort to depict Eichmann as a sadistic monster was fundamentally wrong, that he came closer to being an uninspired bureaucrat who simply sat at his desk and did his job. For asserting these views, Arendt became the object of considerable scorn, even calumny. Somehow, it was felt that the monstrous deeds carried out by Eichmann required a brutal, twisted, and sadistic personality, evil incarnate. After witnessing hundreds of ordinary people submit to the authority in our own experiments, I must conclude that Arendt's conception of the *banality of evil* comes closer to the truth than one might dare imagine. The ordinary person who shocked the victim did so out of a sense of obligation—a conception of his duties as a subject—and not from any peculiarly aggressive tendencies.

This is, perhaps, the most fundamental lesson of our study: ordinary people, simply doing their jobs, and without any particular hostility on their part, can become agents in a terrible destructive process. Moreover, even when the destructive effects of their work become patently clear, and they are asked to carry out actions incompatible with fundamental standards of morality, relatively few people have the resources needed to resist authority. A variety of inhibitions against disobeying authority come into play and successfully keep the person in his place.

Sitting back in one's armchair, it is easy to condemn the actions of the obedient subjects. But those who condemn the subjects measure them against the standard of their own ability to formulate high-minded moral prescriptions. That is hardly a fair standard. Many of the subjects, at the level of stated opinion, feel quite as strongly as any of us about the moral requirement of refraining from action against a helpless victim. They, too, in general terms know what ought to be done and can state their values when the occasion arises. This has little, if anything, to do with their actual behavior under the pressure of circumstances.

If people are asked to render a moral judgment on what constitutes appropriate behavior in this situation, they unfailingly see disobedience as proper. But values are not the only forces at work in an actual, ongoing situation. They are but one narrow band of causes in the total spectrum of forces impinging on a person. Many people were unable to realize their values in action and found themselves continuing in the experiment even though they disagreed with what they were doing.

The force exerted by the moral sense of the individual is less effective than social myth would have us believe. Though such prescriptions as "Thou shalt not kill" occupy a pre-eminent place in the moral order, they do not occupy a correspondingly intractable position in human psychic structure. A few changes in newspaper headlines, a call from the draft board, orders from a man with epaulets, and men are led to kill with little difficulty. Even the forces mustered in a psychology experiment will go a long way toward removing the individual from moral controls. Moral factors can be shunted aside with relative ease by a calculated restructuring of the informational and social field.

What, then, keeps the person obeying the experimenter? First, there is a set of "binding factors" that lock the subject into the situation. They include such factors as politeness on his part, his desire to uphold his initial promise of aid to the experimenter, and the awkwardness of withdrawal. Second, a number of adjustments in the subject's thinking occur that undermine his resolve to break with the authority. The adjustments help the subject maintain his relationship with the experimenter, while at the same time reducing the strain brought about by the experimental conflict. They are typical of thinking that comes about in obedient persons when they are instructed by authority to act against helpless individuals.

One such mechanism is the tendency of the individual to become so absorbed in the narrow technical aspects of the task that he loses sight of its broader consequences. The film *Dr. Strangelove* brilliantly satirized the absorption of a bomber crew in the exacting technical procedure of dropping nuclear weapons on a country. Similarly, in this experiment, subjects become immersed in the procedures, reading the word pairs with exquisite articulation and pressing the switches with great care. They want to put on a competent performance, but they show an accompanying narrowing of moral concern. The subject entrusts the broader tasks of setting goals and assessing morality to the experimental authority he is serving.

The most common adjustment of thought in the obedient subject is for him to see himself as not responsible for his own actions. He divests himself of responsibility by attributing all initiative to the experimenter, a legitimate authority. He sees himself not as a person acting in a morally accountable way but as the agent of external authority. In the postexperimental interview, when subjects were asked why they had gone on, a typical reply was: "I wouldn't have done it by myself. I was just doing what I was told." Unable to defy the authority of the experimenter, they attribute all responsibility to him. It is the old story of "just doing one's duty" that was heard time and time again in the defense statements of those accused at Nuremberg. But it would be wrong to think of it as a thin alibi concocted for the occasion. Rather, it is a fundamental mode of

thinking for a great many people once they are locked into a subordinate position in a structure of authority. The disappearance of a sense of responsibility is the most far-reaching consequence of submission to authority.

Although a person acting under authority performs actions that seem to violate standards of conscience, it would not be true to say that he loses his moral sense. Instead, it acquires a radically different focus. He does not respond with a moral sentiment to the actions he performs. Rather, his moral concern now shifts to a consideration of how well he is living up to the expectations that the authority has of him. In wartime, a soldier does not ask whether it is good or bad to bomb a hamlet; he does not experience shame or guilt in the destruction of a village: rather he feels pride or shame depending on how well he has performed the mission assigned to him.

Another psychological force at work in this situation may be termed "counteranthropomorphism." For decades psychologists have discussed the primitive tendency among men to attribute to inanimate objects and forces the qualities of the human species. A countervailing tendency, however, is that of attributing an impersonal quality to forces that are essentially human in origin and maintenance. Some people treat systems of human origin as if they existed above and beyond any human agent, beyond the control of whim or human feeling. The human element behind agencies and institutions is denied. Thus, when the experimenter says, "The experiment *requires* that you continue," the subject feels this to be an imperative that goes beyond any merely human command. He does not ask the seemingly obvious question, "Whose experiment? Why should the designer be served while the victim suffers?" The wishes of a man—the designer of the experiment—have become part of a schema which exerts on the subject's mind a force that transcends the personal. "It's *got* to go on. It's *got* to go on," repeated one subject. He failed to realize that a man like himself wanted it to go on. For him the human agent had faded from the picture, and "The Experiment" had acquired an impersonal momentum of its own.

No action of itself has an unchangeable psychological quality. Its meaning can be altered by placing it in particular contexts. An American newspaper recently quoted a pilot who conceded that Americans were bombing Vietnamese men, women, and children but felt that the bombing was for a "noble cause" and thus was justified. Similarly, most subjects in the experiment see their behavior in a larger context that is benevolent and useful to society—the pursuit of scientific truth. The psychological laboratory has a strong claim to legitimacy and evokes trust and confidence in those who come to perform there. An action such as shocking a victim, which in isolation appears evil, acquires a totally different meaning when placed in this setting. But allowing an act to be dominated by its context, while neglecting its human consequences, can be dangerous in the extreme.

At least one essential feature of the situation in Germany was not studied here—namely, the intense devaluation of the victim prior to action against him. For a decade and more, vehement anti-Jewish propaganda systematically prepared the German population to accept the destruction of the Jews. Step by step the Jews were excluded from the category of citizen and national, and finally were denied the status of human beings. Systematic devaluation of the victim provides a measure of psychological justification for brutal treatment of the victim and has been the constant accompaniment of massacres, pogroms, and wars. In all likelihood, our subjects would have experienced greater ease in shocking the victim had he been convincingly portrayed as a brutal criminal or a pervert.

Of considerable interest, however, is the fact that many subjects harshly devalue the victim *as a consequence* of acting against him. Such comments as, "He was so stupid and stubborn he deserved to get shocked," were common. Once having acted against the victim, these subjects found it necessary to view him as an unworthy individual, whose punishment was made inevitable by his own deficiencies of intellect and character.

Many of the people studied in the experiment were in some sense against what they did to the learner, and many protested even while they obeyed. But between thoughts, words, and the critical step of disobeying a malevolent authority lies another ingredient, the capacity for transforming beliefs and values into action. Some subjects were totally convinced of the wrongness of what they were doing but could not bring themselves to make an open break with authority. Some derived satisfaction from their thoughts and felt that—within themselves, at least—they had been on the side of the angels. What they failed to realize is that subjective feelings are largely irrelevant to the moral issue at hand so long as they are not transformed into action. Political control is effected through action. The attitudes of the guards at a concentration camp are of no consequence when in fact they are allowing the slaughter of innocent men to take place before them. Similarly, so-called "intellectual resistance" in occupied Europe—in which persons by a twist of thought felt that they had defied the invader—was merely indulgence in a consoling psychological mechanism. Tyrannies are perpetuated by diffident men who do not possess the courage to act out their beliefs. Time and again in the experiment people disvalued what they were doing but could not muster the inner resources to translate their values into action.

A variation of the basic experiment depicts a dilemma more common than the one outlined above: the subject was not ordered to push the trigger that shocked the victim, but merely to perform a subsidiary act (administering the word-pair test) before another subject actually delivered the shock. In this situation, 37 of 40 adults from the New Haven area continued to the highest shock level on the generator. Predictably, subjects excused their behavior by saying that the responsibility belonged to the man who actually pulled the switch. This may illustrate a dangerously typical situation in complex society: it is psychologically easy to ignore responsibility when one is only an intermediate link in a chain of evil action but is far from the final consequences of the action. Even Eichmann was sickened when he toured the concentration camps, but to participate in mass murder he had only to sit at a desk and shuffle papers. At the same time the man in the camp who actually dropped Cyclon-B into the gas chambers was able to justify *his* behavior on the grounds that he was only following orders from above. Thus there is a fragmentation of the total human act; no one man decides to carry out the evil act and is confronted with its consequences. The person who assumes full responsibility for the act has evaporated. Perhaps this is the most common characteristic of socially organized evil in modern society.

The problem of obedience, therefore, is not wholly psychological. The form and shape of society and the way it is developing have much to do with it. There was a time, perhaps, when men were able to give a fully human response to any situation because they were fully absorbed in it as human beings. But as soon as there was a division of labor among men, things changed. Beyond a certain point, the breaking up of society into people carrying out narrow and very special jobs takes away from the human quality of work and life. A person does not get to see the whole situation but only a small part of it, and is thus unable to act without some kind of over-all direction. He yields to authority but in doing so is alienated from his own actions.

George Orwell caught the essence of the situation when he wrote:

As I write, civilized human beings are flying overhead, trying to kill me. They do not feel any enmity against me as an individual, nor I against them. They are only "doing their duty," as the saying goes. Most of them, I have no doubt, are kind-hearted law abiding men who would never dream of committing murder in private life. On the other hand, if one of them succeeds in blowing me to pieces with a well-placed bomb, he will never sleep any the worse for it.

Further Questions

1. What light do you think Milgram's work sheds on the psychological forces at work behind the Nazi Holocaust? The slaughter of the American Indians? War in general?

2. Common sense would suggest that the obedient subjects in Milgram's experiment lost their "moral sense." Is this in fact what happened?

3. An American soldier tells why he and his buddies massacred Vietnamese men, women, and children at My Lai: "Because I felt like I was ordered to do it, and . . . at the time I felt like I was doing the right thing. . . . They were begging and saying, 'No, no.' . . . the mothers . . . hugging their children . . . we kept right on firing. . . ." (*New York Times*, November 25, 1969.) How does *whose side you're on* affect *how you feel and react*?

4. If obedience to authority is the problem, what do you suppose is the solution? Without obedience wouldn't there be chaos, anarchy? How do you know when to obey?

5. Make a list of the major sources of authority in your life. What kind of track record do these sources have?

6. You've probably seen and read many things about the Nazi Holocaust and have been exposed to lots of "theories" about how and why such awful things happen. What are they? Have you ever heard Milgram's work brought up in this context? If not, why do you suppose Milgram is ignored, given that his work seems so relevant?

Further Readings

Milgram, Stanley. *Obedience to Authority.* New York: Harper & Row, 1974. The classic study from which the preceding selection is an excerpt. The CBS interview between Mike Wallace and an American soldier who participated in the My Lai massacre, from which the quote in question 3 is taken, appears in the epilogue. For a stunning film version of the experiments, see *Obedience*, distributed by the New York University Film Library, 1965, available in many university libraries.

Other suggested readings are:

Comfort, A. *Authority and Delinquency in the Modern State: A Criminological Approach to the Problem of Power.* London: Routledge & Kegan Paul, 1950. Highly influential to Milgram's work.

Goffman, E. *The Presentation of Self in Everyday Life.* New York: Doubleday Anchor Books, 1959. A sociological perspective.

Koestler, Arthur. *The Ghost in the Machine.* New York: Macmillan, 1967. An interesting development of the idea of social hierarchy, it influenced Milgram in the formation of his own views.

Kohlberg, L. "Development of Moral Character and Moral Ideology," in Hoffman, M. L., and Hoffman, L. W., eds. *Review of Child Development Research*, Vol. 1. New York: Russell Sage Foundation, 1964, pp. 383–431. Kohlberg, a colleague of Milgram's at Yale, developed a scale of moral development based on Milgram's research.

The Function of Education

JIDDU KRISHNAMURTI

Jiddu Krishnamurti was born to a poor Brahmin family in the south of India in 1895. By the time he died in California in 1986, he had become a world-renowned philosopher and teacher. He was the author of more than forty books, most of them in the form of dialogues and lectures. He traveled all over the world and talked to millions of people. Aldous Huxley, Anne Morrow Lindbergh, and Bertrand Russell studied his philosophy; Huxley said listening to Krishnamurti was as good as "a discourse by the Buddha." George Bernard Shaw once described him as the most beautiful person he had ever met. The actor John Barrymore once asked him to play Buddha in a film, but Krishnamurti refused. Greta Garbo, after hearing him speak, gave up her career in the movies.

Krishnamurti taught that to achieve freedom we must become aware of the psychological conditioning that prevents us from seeing what is true and actual. According to the British theoretical physicist David Bohm, who participated in many discussions with Krishnamurti, Krishnamurti's teaching was rooted "in the fact that we are ignorant of our own processes of thought." Krishnamurti himself insisted that he was not an authority figure or guru; he spoke against all spiritual authorities and organizations. "Truth is a pathless land," he once said. "You cannot approach it by any religion, any sect. . . . You are accustomed to being told how far you have advanced, what your spiritual state is. How childish!" His lifelong purpose, he said, was "to set people absolutely, unconditionally free."

Reading Questions

1. Is the purpose of education merely to help you conform to the patterns of the accepted social order? Or, as Krishnamurti claims, should the function of education be to help you live freely and without fear? Why?
2. What does fear have to do with learning and intelligence?
3. Why should we be in revolt? What should we be in revolt against?
4. What is the greatest obstacle to learning?
5. What role does freedom play in learning?
6. What does revolt have to do with freedom?
7. What is the connection between freedom and intelligence?

I WONDER IF WE HAVE EVER ASKED ourselves what education means. Why do we go to school, why do we learn various subjects, why do we pass examinations and compete with each other for better grades? What does this so-called education mean, and what is it all about? This is really a very important question, not only for the students, but also for the parents, for the teachers, and for everyone who loves this earth. Why do we go through the struggle to be educated? Is it merely in order to pass some examinations and get a job? Or is it the function of education to prepare us while we are young to understand the whole process of life? Having a job and earning one's livelihood is necessary — but is that all? Are we being educated only for that? Surely, life is not merely a job, an occupation; life is something extraordinarily wide and profound, it is a great mystery, a vast realm in which we function as human beings. If we merely prepare ourselves to earn a livelihood, we shall miss the whole point of life; and

to understand life is much more important than merely to prepare for examinations and become very proficient in mathematics, physics, or what you will.

So, whether we are teachers or students, is it not important to ask ourselves why we are educating or being educated? And what does life mean? Is not life an extraordinary thing? The birds, the flowers, the flourishing trees, the heavens, the stars, the rivers and the fish therein — all this is life. Life is the poor and the rich; life is the constant battle between groups, races and nations; life is meditation; life is what we call religion, and it is also the subtle, hidden things of the mind — the envies, the ambitions, the passions, the fears, fulfilments and anxieties. All this and much more is life. But we generally prepare ourselves to understand only one small corner of it. We pass certain examinations, find a job, get married, have children, and then become more and more like machines. We remain fearful, anxious, frightened of life. So, is it the function of education to help us understand the whole process of life, or is it merely to prepare us for a vocation, for the best job we can get?

What is going to happen to all of us when we grow to be men and women? Have you ever asked yourselves what you are going to do when you grow up? In all likelihood you will get married, and before you know where you are you will be mothers and fathers; and you will then be tied to a job, or to the kitchen, in which you will gradually wither away. Is that all that *your* life is going to be? Have you ever asked yourselves this question? Should you not ask it? If your family is wealthy you may have a fairly good position already assured, your father may give you a comfortable job, or you may get richly married; but there also you will decay, deteriorate. Do you see?

Surely, education has no meaning unless it helps you to understand the vast expanse of life with all its subtleties, with its extraordinary beauty, its sorrows and joys. You may earn degrees, you may have a series of letters after your name and land a very good job; but then what? What is the point of it all if in the process your mind becomes dull, weary, stupid? So, while you are young, must you not seek to find out what life is all about? And is it not the true function of education to cultivate in you the intelligence which will try to find the answer to all these problems? Do you know what intelligence is? It is the capacity, surely, to think freely, without fear, without a formula, so that you begin to discover for yourself what is real, what is true; but if you are frightened you will never be intelligent. Any form of ambition, spiritual or mundane, breeds anxiety, fear; therefore ambition does not help to bring about a mind that is clear, simple, direct, and hence intelligent.

You know, it is really very important while you are young to live in an environment in which there is no fear. Most of us, as we grow older, become frightened; we are afraid of living, afraid of losing a job, afraid of tradition, afraid of what the neighbours, or what the wife or husband would say, afraid of death. Most of us have fear in one form or another; and where there is fear there is no intelligence. And is it not possible for all of us, while we are young, to be in an environment where there is no fear but rather an atmosphere of freedom — freedom, not just to do what we like, but to understand the whole process of living? Life is really very beautiful, it is not this ugly thing that we have made of it; and you can appreciate its richness, its depth, its extraordinary loveliness only when you revolt against everything — against organized religion, against tradition, against the present rotten society — so that you as a human being find out for youself what is true. Not to imitate but to discover — *that* is education, is it not? It is very easy to conform to what your society or your parents and teachers tell you. That is a safe and easy way of existing; but that is not living, because in it there is fear, decay, death. To live is to find out for yourself what is true, and you can do this only when there is freedom, when there is continuous revolution inwardly, within yourself.

But you are not encouraged to do this; no one tells you to question, to find out for yourself . . . , because if you were to rebel you would become a danger to all that is false. Your parents and society want you to live safely, and you also want to live safely. Living safely generally means living in imitation and therefore in fear. Surely, the function of education is to help each one of us to live freely and without fear, is it not? And to create an atmosphere in which there is no fear requires a great deal of thinking on your part as well as on the part of the teacher, the educator.

Do you know what this means — what an extraordinary thing it would be to create an atmosphere in which there is no fear? And we *must* create it, because we see that the world is caught up in endless wars; it is guided by politicians who are always seeking power; it is a world of lawyers, policemen and soldiers, of ambitious men and women all wanting position and all fighting each other to get it. Then there are the so-called saints, the religious *gurus* with their followers; they also want power, position, here or in the next life. It is a mad world, completely confused, in which the communist is fighting the capitalist, the socialist is resisting both, and everybody is against somebody, struggling to arrive at a safe place, a position of power or comfort. The world is torn by conflicting beliefs, by caste and class distinctions, by separative nationalities, by every form of stupidity and cruelty—and this is the world you are being educated to fit into. You are encouraged to fit into the framework of this disastrous society; your parents want you to do that, and you also want to fit in.

Now, is it the function of education merely to help you to conform to the pattern of this rotten social order, or is it to give you freedom—complete freedom to grow and create a different society, a new world? We want to have this freedom, not in the future, but now, otherwise we may all be destroyed. We must create immediately an atmosphere of freedom so that you can live and find out for yourselves what is true, so that you become intelligent, so that you are able to face the world and understand it, not just conform to it, so that inwardly, deeply, psychologically you are in constant revolt; because it is only those who are in constant revolt that discover what is true, not the man who conforms, who follows some tradition. . . .

. . . The question is: if all individuals were in revolt, would not the world be in chaos? But is the present society in such perfect order that chaos would result if everyone revolted against it? Is there not chaos *now*? Is everything beautiful, uncorrupted? Is everyone living happily, fully, richly? Is man not against man? Is there not ambition, ruthless competition? So the world is already in chaos, that is the first thing to realize. Don't take it for granted that this is an orderly society; don't mesmerize yourself with words. Whether, here in Europe, in America or Russia, the world is in a process of decay. If you see the decay, you have a challenge: you are challenged to find a way of solving this urgent problem. And

how you respond to the challenge is important, is it not? If you respond as a Hindu or a Buddhist, a Christian or a communist, then your response is very limited—which is no response at all. You can respond fully, adequately only if there is no fear in you, only if you don't think as a Hindu, a communist or a capitalist, but as a total human being who is trying to solve this problem; and you cannot solve it unless you yourself are in revolt against the whole thing, against the ambitious acquisitiveness on which society is based. When you yourself are not ambitious, not acquisitive, not clinging to your own security—only then can you respond to the challenge and create a new world. . . .

Do you know what it means to learn? When you are really learning you are learning throughout your life and there is no one special teacher to learn from. Then everything teaches you—a dead leaf, a bird in flight, a smell, a tear, the rich and the poor, those who are crying, the smile of a woman, the haughtiness of a man. You learn from everything, therefore there is no guide, no philosopher, no guru. Life itself is your teacher, and you are in a state of constant learning. . . .

Do you know what attention is? Let us find out. In a class room, when you stare out of the window or pull somebody's hair, the teacher tells you to pay attention. Which means what? That you are not interested in what you are studying and so the teacher compels you to pay attention—which is not attention at all. Attention comes when you are deeply interested in something, for then you love to find out all about it; then your whole mind, your whole being is there. . . . When you are doing something with your whole being, not because you want to get somewhere, or have more profit, or greater results, but simply because you love to do it—in that there is no ambition, is there? In that there is no competition; you are not struggling with anyone for first place. And should not education help you to find out what you really love to do so that from the beginning to the end of your life you are working at something which you feel is worth while and which for you has deep significance? Otherwise, for the rest of your days, you will be miserable. Not knowing what you really want to do, your mind falls into a routine in which there is only boredom, decay and death. That is why it is very important to find out while you are young what it is you really *love* to do; and this is the only way to create a new society. . . .

Further Questions

1. You have by now had many years of education. Based on your experience, which of Krishnamurti's points do you agree with? Which ones do you disagree with?

2. What role does fear play in your life? How much of what you do is based on fear? Why?

3. Education, according to Krishnamurti, should help you find out what you really love to do. Has your education done this? If not, why not?

4. What, thus far in your life, do you most love to do? Are you happy doing it? Why?

5. What prevents you from pursuing your deepest interests? How could you overcome these obstacles?

Further Readings

Krishnamurti, J. *Think on These Things*. New York: Harper & Row, 1970. The preceding selection was taken from this widely available book. *The First and Last Freedom* (Harper & Row, 1975) contains a foreword by Aldous Huxley. *Freedom from the Known* (Harper & Row, 1969) and *Truth and Actuality* (Harper & Row, 1977) are both excellent. *The Wholeness of Life* (Harper & Row, 1969) contains a series of discussions with the noted theoretical physicist, David Bohm.

Krishnamurti, J. *Krishnamurti's Notebook*. New York: Harper & Row, 1976. A daily diary kept over seven months.

Krishnamurti, J. and David Bohm. *The Ending of Time*. New York: Harper & Row, 1985. An unusual synthesis of contemporary Eastern and Western thought.

Lutyens, Mary. *Krishnamurti: The Years of Awakening*. New York: Avon, 1975. An excellent biography of the first half of Krishnamurti's life.

On Bullshitting and Brainstorming

KERRY WALTERS

Kerry Walters teaches philosophy at Gettysburg College and writes primarily in the area of educational values. In this selection he distinguishes between two ways of approaching the study of philosophy. In the first, "bullshitting," students treat philosophy as something external, a set of theories to be manipulated and nothing more. In the second, "brainstorming," they process the theories through themselves. The first way fosters cleverness, the second an authentic confrontation.

Reading Questions

1. Are you a bullshitter? A brainstormer? Both? Neither?
2. Walters claims the bullshitter's attitude toward philosophy is "nihilistic." What does he mean? Is there anything wrong with nihilism? Is there a better alternative?

REMARKS MEANT TO BE COMPLIMENTARY can sometimes be brutal eye-openers. The most jarring professional compliment ever paid me was from a student in one of my introductory sections. At the end of term she dropped by my office to thank me for the course. "This was the best class I've ever taken!" she said. "I just loved bullshitting about Socrates and the reflective life, and stuff like that!"

I can't remember my immediate response. Most likely I mumbled something about how much I'd enjoyed having her in class. But I do recall being taken aback. *She just loved bullshitting . . . ? ! . . .*

As we talked more, it dawned upon me that I was responsible, to a certain extent, for my student's estimation of the nature and value of philosophy. My classroom technique had reinforced her native suspicion that philosophy was, by and large, rhetorical bullshit. . . .

I belong to that camp which takes the act of philosophizing to be pre-eminently a dialogal one. Consequently, I supplement my more traditional pedagogical approaches (especially in introductory courses) by trying to keep nonparticipatory, exclusively expository lectures to a minimum, focusing instead upon . . . "brainstorming." This involves a give-and-take on the part of students of imaginative speculations, (hopefully) rational criticisms, of studied texts and each other's opinions, and group reformulations of problems. . . . Predictably enough, the technique is successful at times, stale and artificial at others. But an almost certain consequence, as in so many of the early Platonic dialogues, is that the problem under investigation remains unresolved. By "unresolved," I mean of course that no fully satisfying, totally unambiguous answer, is arrived at. What *is* accomplished, if our brainstorming has gone well, is that a better understanding of the question's complexity is achieved. Moreover, we often discover either that the pat solutions initially suggested are inadequate—even though, at first sight, they may appear strong—or that the question itself is confused and in need of reformulation. . . .

Bullshitting

. . . Bullshitting in this context is that mode of expression appropriate to the assumption that truth value is never a function of philosophical statements. This position . . . is essentially a nihilistic one. It presumes that philosophical discourse is meaningless—although at times it may be enjoyable. Since it is nonsense, it also has no instrumental value. It is incapable of providing solutions to "real" problems. If it has any utility at all, it is solely one of temporary amusement, analogous to the working through of a crossword puzzle.

The bullshitter, as Harry Frankfurt suggests,[1] characteristically discusses topics he is ignorant of or has not really thought much about. But this

Excerpts from "On Bullshitting and Brainstorming," by Kerry Walters, Teaching Philosophy, *v. 11, 1988. Used by kind permission of the editor of* Teaching Philosophy.

is hardly a distinctive feature of bullshitting. . . . The brainstormer does much the same thing. What distinguishes the bullshitter from the brainstormer is that the former typically has no personal relation with the issue under investigation. Because he thinks the topic nonsensical to start with, he enters into the discussion in an anonymous, detached way. He feels no more commitment to the line he presents than does the member of a debate team required to defend, at the flip of a coin, the proposition that male members of Congress ought to wear three-piece suits. The position he takes, in short, is a matter of complete personal indifference. He feels no existential urgency in defending one position as opposed to another. As far as he is concerned, the question under examination is not a live one; it has no relevance to his existence. Moreover, he is not even intellectually curious about it. His only goal as a bullshitter is to achieve a psychologically satisfying level of self-amusement.

. . . Bullshitting, then, is a type of robotry which consists in uncommitted word-artistry. It could almost be described as rhetoric for rhetoric's sake except for the fact that it does have an extrinsic goal: winning the philosophy game and amusing oneself in the process. Genuine bullshitters are never guilty of intellectual robotry. They lack the necessary condition — commitment to an ideology — for such an attitude. But it may be the case that habitual bullshitters who wind up buying their own rhetoric graduate from rhetorical to intellectual robotry. After all, young bullshitters must grow up sooner or later. When they do, we sometimes call them academics.

Brainstorming

The student-brainstormer shares one major characteristic with the student-bullshitter: she typically has not reflected deeply about the philosophical issue under discussion. But, unlike the bullshitter, she is eager to explore it by dialoging with others. This is because she is personally related to the topic. She takes it to be a live one; it

means something to her as an individual. Consequently, she has a personal stake in clarifying the problem and examining possible responses to it.

There are at least two reasons for the brainstormer's personal concern with philosophical issues. First, she appreciates — even if somewhat indistinctly — the intrinsic value of abstract speculation. She obviously wants a good grade in the course, and does not discount the importance of "practical" success, but she refuses to follow the bullshitter's *a priori* ascription of inutility and meaninglessness to philosophical discourse. She's willing to work under the assumption that philosophical propositions have truth-values, and that rational and creative discourse is a necessary vehicle in their discovery. She may be somewhat skeptical about the possibility of conclusively figuring out whether or not God exists, or what the good is, but she does not on that account reject sincere discussion of the issues. To be uncertain about the possibility of conclusively answering certain problems is not at all to dismiss them as nonsensical. The asking of questions is important in and of itself, and thus is to be taken seriously. A fully satisfying resolution may be unattainable. But, as Socrates demonstrated, dialogue just might be able to disabuse its practitioners of an array of hasty generalizations, false starts, subtle contradictions and weak methods. For the brainstormer, this is no small accomplishment.

Second, the brainstormer takes philosophical speculation seriously because she accepts a much richer definition of "instrumentality" or "practical value" than the bullshitter. She acknowledges that knowledge is capable of being its own end, but also realizes that even the most abstract speculation results in effects which, directly or indirectly, have a practical bearing upon her daily existence. Brainstorming about whether or not values are objective, for example, is important for her because she realizes the position she eventually adopts will influence her concrete relations with others in the "real" world. Similarly, discussions about metaphysical questions are instrumental in her construction of a worldview which in turn serves as a point of personal orientation for her social behavior, religious beliefs, personal and professional aspirations, and so on. . . .

This is not to deny that part of the reason why a brainstormer throws herself into philosophy is a desire for recreation. The interplay of ideas can be genuine fun. No one has ever accused Socrates of being a dour killjoy. But the brainstormer's personal relationship to the ideas she's exploring precludes the possibility that her sole goal is amusement. For her, philosophical discourse is a genuine, not a pseudo, context. Consequently, although having fun may be a characteristic of legitimate brainstorming, it is not a definitive one, as in the case of bullshitting. Very often, in fact, brainstorming can be sheer hard work. It can also be emotionally unsettling.

The emotional discomfort occasionally spawned by brainstorming points back to the fact that it entails the committed engagement of the participant. The brainstormer feels a deeply personal involvement in the topic under discussion. The more the issue at hand speaks to her as a concrete individual, the more likely she is to react to it emotionally as well as intellectually. My own classroom experience, for example, has shown me that the typical brainstormer often undergoes what might be described as an existential crisis during the course of a semester, particularly if the class has focused upon issues such as the existence of God, death, or the meaning of life. Discussion of issues such as these hit the brainstormer hard. She sees that they relate to her in a profoundly intimate way, and that she has to come to grips with them. They awaken a hunger, a *Sehnsucht*, that demands her total involvement. Very often, the need to come to terms with such issues far outstrips the brainstormer's concern for a good grade in the class. Her focus of attention shifts, and she recognizes that her existential awakening is far more important than an A.

That is why the genuine brainstormer grows increasingly comfortable in taking risks, in sharing with others her arguments, intuitions and thoughts, even when she realizes they are some-

what crude, awkward or sketchy. She is not interested in dazzling others with a rhetorically perfect story. Instead, she wants to understand. Consequently, she is willing to make herself vulnerable by thinking aloud, even if it means having her ideas pulled apart and scattered by other brainstormers. Unlike the bullshitter, she is not competing in the philosophy game, trying to beat out the next guy in a brilliant but sterile display of rhetorical one-upsmanship. Instead, she is putting herself on the line by publicly struggling with doubts, perplexities and tentative shots in the dark. Her hope is that talking and listening to others will help her deal with a philosophical matter she takes to be of great personal urgency. The realization that making herself available in this way may lead to a certain amount of embarrassment is obviously not a pleasant one. But the distasteful prospect of verbally floundering and sometimes sinking in front of her peers is offset by the recognition that attainment of self-knowledge and insight doesn't come easily. The maturation of self always involves growing pains.

It is true, of course, that the very existential engagement which encourages the brainstormer's intellectual risk-taking can also, at least initially, breed a certain amount of hard-headed tenacity on her part. Many of us tend to become quite proprietorial about the intuitions and intellectual models that structure our worldviews. Students are no exception to this rule. An apprentice brainstormer often dogmatically champions one position to the exclusion of others because it is an essential link to her web of beliefs. But such tenacity is not necessarily a liability. A fledgling brainstormer who digs in her heels and defends a set of beliefs in the face of alternative opinions or caveats is compelled to reflect upon her perspective. She feels the need to clarify her position, to herself as well as others, and to do so with a rigorousness she probably never thought necessary before. Struggling with a defense of her worldview may eventually strengthen its supporting arguments. But in working through the putative justifications of a position, the brainstormer may also come to creatively modify it in light of critical challenges or, if her back is to the wall, even junk it. Her original tenacity, then, often forces her into a sink-or-swim situation in which she necessarily calls up intellectual and intuitive reserves hitherto untapped.

This richer, more complex appreciation of philosophical inquiry in turn promotes the flexibility and critical tolerance necessary for meaningful discourse by showing the brainstormer that even the most attractive of philosophical models may need further clarification or amendment. This flexibility is not the freewheeling opportunism of the bullshitter. He leapfrogs from one position to the next until he lands on one that can be translated into the best story. The brainstormer, on the other hand, is willing to change his position if it proves to be inchoate or weak. But she will not opt for just any good-sounding line. Her flexibility, in short, involves discrimination and reflection. She has too much at stake to settle for anything else.

The brainstormer's willingness to subject her ideas to peer scrutiny and to reformulate them on the basis of constructive feedback is, as I have indicated, an adventurous risk-taking. The strengthening of intellectual intrepidity which this exploratory speculation fosters likewise enriches imaginative creativity. The brainstormer does not merely modify her position. She also reformulates the questions she asks. This reformulation often involves a switch in emphasis, but can also give birth to an entirely new line of investigation based on innovative reconstructions of traditional problems.

Breaking through conventional models of explanation, methodological procedures and theoretical paradigms, even if the move proves ultimately fruitless, both entails and enriches the ability to see freshly. This is a talent, admittedly, which few of us cultivate. The genuine brainstormer, however, works at it. The bullshitter, on the other hand, could not care less. The problems which orient him are, to a large extent, set in stone. It rarely occurs to him to question their validity. That is why Frankfurt's suggestion[2] that the bullshitter's eloquent manipulation of words requires a certain amount of creative imagination seems too generous. The bullshitter relies more upon ingenuity than imagination. He possesses the skill to weave words into aesthetically pleasing garments, but lacks the ability or desire to design new patterns. He is a word mechanic, not an inventor. The brainstormer can likewise take pleasure in verbal adroitness. But she is much more interested in *knowing* than in *composing*. And that sometimes involves cutting new patterns from fresh cloth, even at the risk of ruining the bolt. . . .

NOTES

1. Harry Frankfurt, "Reflections on Bullshit," *Harper's Magazine* (February 1987). Frankfurt's analysis differs from mine in that he focuses upon the distinction between bullshitting and deception. Moreover, his characterization of bullshitting allows for a greater degree of creativity and imagination than mine does.

2. Frankfurt, *op. cit.*

Further Questions

1. Other disciplines often give definite answers to the major questions they address. Philosophy rarely does. How do you feel about that?

2. "Although there is rarely a right or wrong in philosophy, there is almost always a better or worse." Do you agree?

Part II

Where and When

HERE. NOW. YOU.

Wherever you are, you are right now having the experience of being somewhere: here. Sometime: now. Someone: you. Obviously.

This feeling of obviousness, the obviousness of here and now, automatically colors *all* our experience. It is like wearing specially tinted lenses that obscure the strangeness of everything, lenses we've worn so long we no longer notice them. What the lenses contribute to our vision we unknowingly project onto reality. Once we have our lenses on, everything, literally, falls into place.

So, what's the problem? Why not simply accept the here and now and get on with the project of understanding ourselves and the world? *That's* the problem. We want to accept the obvious and move on, as if the obvious has no effect. But it does. It deeply structures our understanding of ourselves and the world.

As you are about to see, our everyday notions of here and now — of space and time — are not the only possible ones. There are alternatives, some of the most bizarre of which have been endorsed by modern science. Our familiar concepts, on the other hand, cloaked in obviousness, reveal little and obscure much. Only by taking off our tinted lenses and looking at ourselves and the world from new perspectives can we see why. With familiarity and obviousness unmasked, everything that only a moment ago seemed so secure, so in place, so settled, comes flying apart at the seams — and so do we.

Flatland

EDWIN ABBOTT

E. A. Abbott was born in 1838 in England. In 1865 he became the headmaster of a London school. His field was classics, with an emphasis on literature and theology. Although he wrote several textbooks, some theological works, a biography of Francis Bacon and a Shakespearean grammar, his most famous and enduring work was in the field of popular mathematics and physics. What is even more remarkable, *Flatland*, from which the following selection is taken, was written when Einstein was only a child and the idea of spacetime would not emerge for another quarter century! Stranger still, Abbott himself worried that this fantasy would destroy his reputation, and so published *Flatland* pseudonymously.

Though the style is somewhat old fashioned, mathematicians, scientists, and students have enjoyed for more than a century this timeless story of a Square who lives contentedly in a two-dimensional world until, one day, he is whisked by a Sphere into the third dimension.

Reading Questions

1. Why do Flatlanders not see the third dimension?

2. Keep a lookout for the important phrase, "Upward, not northward." What is the significance of it?

3. What is the response of the Sphere to the Square's insistence that there might exist fourth, fifth, and other, higher, dimensions? Why does the Sphere, who at first seems so much wiser than the Square, have difficulty in imagining what the lowly Square himself can imagine?

4. What would the Square see if he looked in a mirror?

5. How does gravity work in Flatland to make "north" the same direction as "up"?

6. How do Flatlanders recognize each other?

7. Where does the Square perceive the Sphere's voice as coming from?

8. What significant similarities does the Square discover between the different dimensions? What significant differences?

9. What does the King of Lineland see when he looks at fellow Linelanders? How does he perceive the square?

10. Why does the square have such a hard time explaining Flatland to the Linelanders?

11. How do the concepts "inside" and "outside" vary from dimension to dimension?

Of the Nature of Flatland

I CALL OUR WORLD FLATLAND , not because we call it so, but to make its nature clearer to you, my happy readers, who are privileged to live in Space.

Imagine a vast sheet of paper on which straight Lines, Triangles, Squares, Pentagons, Hexagons, and other figures, instead of remaining fixed in their places, move freely about, on or in the surface, but without the power of rising above or sinking below it, very much like shadows —only hard and with luminous edges—and you will then have a pretty correct notion of my country and countrymen. Alas, a few years ago, I should have said "my universe": but now my mind has been opened to higher views of things.

In such a country, you will perceive at once that it is impossible that there should be anything of what you call a "solid" kind; but I dare say you will suppose that we could at least distinguish by sight the Triangles, Squares, and other figures,

Excerpts from Flatland *by Edwin Abbott.*

moving about as I have described them. On the contrary, we could see nothing of the kind, not at least so as to distinguish one figure from another. Nothing was visible, nor could be visible, to us, except Straight Lines; and the necessity of this I will speedily demonstrate.

Place a penny on the middle of one of your tables in Space; and leaning over it, look down upon it. It will appear a circle.

But now, drawing back to the edge of the table, gradually lower your eye (thus bringing yourself more and more into the condition of the inhabitants of Flatland), and you will find the penny becoming more and more oval to your view; and at last when you have placed your eye exactly on the edge of the table (so that you are, as it were, actually a Flatlander) the penny will then have ceased to appear oval at all, and will have become, so far as you can see, a straight line.

The same thing would happen if you were to treat in the same way a Triangle, or Square, or any other figure cut out of pasteboard. As soon as you look at it with your eye on the edge on the table, you will find that it ceases to appear to you a figure, and that it becomes in appearance a straight line. Take for example an equilateral Triangle—who represents with us a Tradesman of the respectable class. Fig. 1 represents the Tradesman as you would see him while you were bending over him from above; figs. 2 and 3 represent the Tradesman, as you would see him if your eye were close to the level, or all but on the level of the table; and if your eye were quite on the level of the table (and that is how we see him in Flatland) you would see nothing but a straight line.

When I was in Spaceland I heard that your sailors have very similar experiences while they traverse your seas and discern some distant island or coast lying on the horizon. The far-off land may have bays, forelands, angles in and out to any number and extent; yet at a distance you see none of these (unless indeed your sun shines bright upon them revealing the projections and retirements by means of light and shade), nothing but a grey unbroken line upon the water.

Well, that is just what we see when one of our triangular or other acquaintances comes toward us in Flatland. As there is neither sun with us, nor any light of such a kind as to make shadows, we have none of the helps to the sight that you have in Spaceland. If our friend comes closer to us we see his line becomes larger; if he leaves us it becomes smaller: but still he looks like a straight line; be he a Triangle, Square, Pentagon, Hexagon, Circle, what you will—a straight Line he looks and nothing else.

You may perhaps ask how under these disadvantageous circumstances we are able to distinguish our friends from one another: but the answer to this very natural question will be more fitly and easily given when I come to describe the inhabitants of Flatland. For the present let me defer this subject, and say a word or two about the climate and houses in our country.

Of the Climate and Houses in Flatland

As with you, so also with us, there are four points of the compass North, South, East, and West.

There being no sun nor other heavenly bodies, it is impossible for us to determine the North in the usual way; but we have a method of our own. By a Law of Nature with us, there is a constant attraction to the South; and although in temperate climates this is very slight . . . yet the hampering effect of the southward attraction is quite sufficient to serve as a compass in most parts of our earth. . . .

Concerning the Inhabitants of Flatland

The greatest length or breadth of a full grown inhabitant of Flatland may be estimated at about eleven of your inches. Twelve inches may be regarded as a maximum.

Our Women are Straight Lines.

Our Soldiers and Lowest Classes of Workmen are Triangles with two equal sides. . . .

Our Middle Class consists of Equilateral or Equal-Sided Triangles.

Our Professional Men and Gentlemen are Squares (to which class I myself belong) and Five-Sided Figures or Pentagons.

Next above these come the Nobility, of whom there are several degrees, beginning at Six-Sided Figures, or Hexagons, and from thence rising in the number of their sides till they receive the honourable title of Polygonal, or many-sided. Finally when the number of the sides becomes so numerous, and the sides themselves so small, that the figure cannot be distinguished from a circle, he is included in the Circular or Priestly order; and this is the highest class of all. . . .

Of Our Methods of Recognizing One Another

You, who are blessed with shade as well as light, you, who are gifted with two eyes, endowed with a knowledge of perspective, and charmed with the enjoyment of various colours, you, who can actually *see* an angle, and contemplate the complete circumference of a Circle in the happy region of the Three Dimensions — how shall I make clear to you the extreme difficulty which we in Flatland experience in recognizing one another's configuration?

Recall what I told you above. All beings in Flatland, animate or inanimate, no matter what their form, present *to our view* the same, or nearly the same, appearance, viz. that of a straight Line. How then can one be distinguished from another, where all appear the same?

The answer is threefold. The first means of recognition is the sense of hearing; which with us is far more highly developed than with you, and which enables us not only to distinguish by the voice our personal friends, but even to discriminate between different classes, at least so far as concerns the three lowest orders, the Equilateral, The Square, and the Pentagon. . . .

I am about to appear very inconsistent. In previous sections I have said that all figures in Flatland present the appearance of a straight line; and it was added or implied, that it is consequently impossible to distinguish by the visual organ between individuals of different classes: yet now I am about to explain to my Spaceland critics how we are able to recognize one another by the sense of sight. . . .

That this power exists in any regions . . . is the result of Fog; which prevails during the greater part of the year in all parts save the torrid zones. That which is with you in Spaceland an unmixed evil, blotting out the landscape, depressing the spirits, and enfeebling the health, is by us recognized as a blessing scarcely inferior to air itself, and as the Nurse of arts and Parent of sciences. But let me explain my meaning, without further eulogies on this beneficent Element.

If Fog were non-existent, all lines would appear equally and indistinguishably clear; and this is actually the case in those unhappy countries in which the atmosphere is perfectly dry and transparent. But wherever there is a rich supply of Fog objects that are at a distance, say of three feet, are appreciably dimmer than those at a distance of two feet eleven inches; and the result is that by careful and constant experimental observation of comparative dimness and clearness, we are enabled to infer with great exactness the configuration of the object observed. . . .

How I Had a Vision of Lineland

It was the last day but one of the 1999th year of our era, and the first day of the Long Vacation. Having amused myself till a late hour with my favourite recreation of Geometry, I had retired to rest with an unsolved problem in my mind. In the night I had a dream.

I saw before me a vast multitude of small Straight Lines . . . interspersed with other Beings still smaller and of the nature of lustrous points — all moving to and fro in one and the same Straight Line, and, as nearly as I could judge, with the same velocity.

A noise of confused, multitudinous chirping or twittering issued from them at intervals as long as they were moving; but sometimes they ceased from motion, and then all was silence.

Approaching one of the largest . . . I . . . received no answer. A second and a third appeal on my part were equally ineffectual. Losing patience at what appeared to me intolerable rudeness, I brought my mouth into a position full in front of her mouth so as to intercept her motion, and loudly repeated my question, . . . "What signifies this concourse, and this strange and confused chirping, and this monotonous motion to and fro in one and the same Straight Line?"

. . ."I am the Monarch of the world. But thou, whence intrudest thou into my realm of Lineland?" Receiving this abrupt reply, I begged pardon if I had in any way startled or molested his Royal Highness; and describing myself as a stranger I besought the King to give me some account of his dominions. But I had the greatest possible difficulty in obtaining any information on points that really interested me; for the Monarch could not refrain from constantly assuming that whatever was familiar to him must also be known to me and that I was simulating ignorance in jest. However, by persevering questions I elicited the following facts:

It seemed that this poor ignorant Monarch— as he called himself—was persuaded that the Straight Line which he called his Kingdom, and in which he passed his existence, constituted the whole of the world, and indeed the whole of Space. Not being able either to move or to see, save in his Straight Line, he had no conception of anything out of it. Though he had heard my voice when I first addressed him, the sounds had come to him in a manner so contrary to his experience that he had made no answer, "seeing no man," as he expressed it, "and hearing a voice as it were from my own intestines." Until the moment when I placed my mouth in his World, he had neither seen me, nor heard anything except confused sounds beating against—what I called his side, but what he called his *inside* or *stomach*; nor

had he even now the least conception of the region from which I had come. Outside his World, or Line, all was a blank to him; nay, not even a blank, for a blank implies Space; say, rather, all was non-existent.

His subjects were all alike confined in motion and eye-sight to that single Straight Line, which was their World. It need scarcely be added that the whole of their horizon was limited to a Point; nor could any one ever see anything but a Point. Man, woman, child, thing—each was a Point to the eye of a Linelander. Only by the sound of the voice could sex or age be distinguished. Moreover, as each individual occupied the whole of the narrow path, so to speak, which constituted his Universe, and no one could move to the right or left to make way for passers by, it followed that no Linelander could ever pass another. Once neighbours, always neighbours. Neighbourhood with them was like marriage with us. Neighbours remained neighbours till death did them part. . . .

How I Vainly Tried to Explain the Nature of Flatland

Thinking that it was time to bring down the Monarch from his raptures to the level of common sense, I determined to endeavour to open up to him some glimpses of the truth, that is to say of the nature of things in Flatland. So I began thus: "How does your Royal Highness distinguish the shapes and positions of his subjects? I for my part noticed by the sense of sight, before I entered your Kingdom, that some of your people are Lines and others Points, and that some of the Lines are larger—" "You speak of an impossibility," interrupted the King; "you must have seen a vision; for to detect the difference between a Line and a Point by the sense of sight is, as every one knows, in the nature of things, impossible; but it can be detected by the sense of hearing, and by the same means my shape can be exactly ascertained. Behold me—I am a Line, the longest in Lineland, over six inches of Space—" "Of Length,"

I ventured to suggest. "Fool," said he, "Space is Length. Interrupt me again, and I have done." . . .

[The Square asks the king about what is to the right and left of him.]

"And let me ask what you mean by those words 'left' and 'right.' I suppose it is your way of saying Northward and Southward."

"Not so," replied I: "besides your motion of Northward and Southward, there is another motion which I call from right to left."

King: Exhibit to me, if you please, this motion from left to right.

I: Nay, that I cannot do, unless you could step out of your Line altogether.

King: Out of my Line? Do you mean out of the world? Out of Space?

I: Well, yes. Out of *your* World. Out of *your* Space. For your Space is not the true Space. True Space is a Plane; but your Space is only a Line.

King: If you cannot indicate this motion from left to right by yourself moving in it, then I beg you to describe it to me in words.

I: If you cannot tell your right side from your left, I fear that no words of mine can make my meaning clear to you. But surely you cannot be ignorant of so simple a distinction.

King: I do not in the least understand you.

I: Alas! How shall I make it clear? When you move straight on, does it not sometimes occur to you that you *could* move in some other way, turning your eye round so as to look in the direction towards which your side is now fronting? In other words, instead of always moving in the direction of one of your extremities, do you never feel a desire to move in the direction, so to speak, of your side?

King: Never. And what do you mean? How can a man's inside "front" in any direction? Or how can a man move in the direction of his inside?

I: Well then, since words cannot explain the matter, I will try deeds, and will move gradually out of Lineland in the direction which I desire to indicate to you.

At the word I began to move my body out of Lineland. As long as any part of me remained in his dominion and in his view, the King kept exclaiming, "I see you, I see you still; you are not moving." But when I had at last moved myself out of his Line, he cried in his shrillest voice, "She is vanished; she is dead." "I am not dead," replied I; "I am simply out of Lineland, that is to say, out of the Straight Line which you call Space, and in the true Space, where I can see things as they are. And at this moment I can see your Line, or side —or inside as you are pleased to call it; and I can see also the Men and Women on the North and South of you, whom I will now enumerate, describing their order, their size, and the interval between each."

When I had done this at great length, I cried triumphantly, "Does that at last convince you?" And, with that, I once more entered Lineland, taking up the same position as before.

But the Monarch replied, "If you were a Man of sense . . . you would listen to reason. You ask me to believe that there is another Line besides that which my senses indicate, and another motion besides that of which I am daily conscious. I, in return, ask you to describe in words or indicate by motion that other Line of which you speak. Instead of moving, you merely exercise some magic art of vanishing and returning to sight; and instead of any lucid description of your new World, you simply tell me the numbers and sizes of some forty of my retinue, facts known to any child in my capital. Can anything be more irrational or audacious? Acknowledge your folly or depart from my dominions."

Furious at his perversity, and especially indignant that he professed to be ignorant of my sex, I retorted in no measured terms, "Besotted Being! You think yourself the perfection of existence, while you are in reality the most imperfect and imbecile. You profess to see, whereas you can see nothing but a Point! You plume yourself on inferring the existence of a Straight Line; but I *can see* Straight Lines, and infer the existence of Angles, Triangles, Squares, Pentagons, Hexagons, and even Circles. Why waste more words? Suffice it that I am the completion of your incomplete self. You are a Line, but I am a Line of Lines, called in my country a Square: and even I, infinitely superior though I am to you, am of little account among the great nobles of Flatland, whence I have come to visit you, in the hope of enlightening your ignorance."

Hearing these words the King advanced towards me with a menacing cry as if to pierce me through the diagonal; and in that same moment there arose from myriads of his subjects a multitudinous war cry, increasing in vehemence till at last methought it rivalled the roar of an army of a hundred thousand Isosceles, and the artillery of a thousand Pentagons. Spell-bound and motionless, I could neither speak nor move to avert the impending destruction; and still the noise grew louder, and the King came closer, when I awoke to find the breakfast-bell recalling me to the realities of Flatland.

Concerning a Stranger from Spaceland

From dreams I proceed to facts.

It was the last day of the 1999th year of our era. The pattering of the rain had long ago announced nightfall; and I was sitting[1] in the company of my wife, musing on the events of the past and the prospects of the coming year, the coming century, the coming Millennium.

My four Sons and two orphan Grandchildren had retired to their several apartments; and my wife alone remained with me to see the old Millennium out and the new one in.

I was rapt in thought, pondering in my mind some words that had casually issued from the mouth of my youngest Grandson, a most promising young Hexagon of unusual brilliancy and perfect angularity. His uncles and I had been giving him his usual practical lesson in Sight Recognition, turning ourselves upon our centres, now rapidly, now more slowly, and questioning him as to our positions; and his answers had been so satisfactory that I had been induced to reward him by giving him a few hints on Arithmetic, as applied to Geometry.

Taking nine Squares, each an inch every way, I had put them together so as to make one large Square, with a side of three inches, and I had hence proved to my little Grandson that — though it was impossible for us to *see* the inside of the Square — yet we might ascertain the number of square inches in a Square by simply squaring the number of inches in the side: "and thus," said I, "we know that 3^2, or 9, represents the number of square inches in a Square whose side is 3 inches long."

The little Hexagon meditated on this a while and then said to me; "But you have been teaching me to raise numbers to the third power: I suppose 3^3 must mean something in Geometry; what does it mean?" "Nothing at all," replied I, "not at least in Geometry; for Geometry has only Two Dimensions." And then I began to shew the boy how a Point by moving through a length of three inches makes a Line of three inches, which may be represented by 3; and how a Line of three inches, moving parallel to itself through a length of three inches, makes a Square of three inches every way, which may be represented by 3^2.

Upon this, my Grandson, again returning to his former suggestion, took me up rather suddenly and exclaimed, "Well, then, if a Point by moving three inches, makes a Line of three inches represented by 3; and if a straight Line of three inches, moving parallel to itself, makes a Square of three inches every way, represented by 3^2; it must be that a Square of three inches every way, moving somehow parallel to itself (but I don't see how) must make Something else (but I don't see what) of three inches every way — and this must be represented by 3^3."

"Go to bed," said I, a little ruffled by this interruption: "if you would talk less nonsense, you would remember more sense."

So my Grandson had disappeared in disgrace; and there I sat by my Wife's side, endeavouring to form a retrospect of the year 1999 and of the possibilities of the year 2000, but not quite able to shake off the thoughts suggested by the prattle of my bright little Hexagon. Only a few sands now remained in the half-hour glass. Rousing myself from my reverie I turned the glass Northward for the last time in the old Millennium; and in the act, I exclaimed aloud, "The boy is a fool."

Straightway I became conscious of a Presence in the room, and a chilling breath thrilled through my very being. "He is no such thing," cried my Wife, "and you are breaking the Commandments in thus dishonouring your own Grandson." But I took no notice of her. Looking round in every direction I could see nothing; yet still I *felt* a Presence, and shivered as the cold whisper came again. I started up. "What is the matter?" said my Wife, "there is no draught; what are you looking for? There is nothing." There was nothing; and I resumed my seat, again exclaiming, "The boy is a fool, I say; 3³ can have no meaning in Geometry." At once there came a distinctly audible reply, "The boy is not a fool; and 3³ has an obvious Geometrical meaning."

My Wife as well as myself heard the words, although she did not understand their meaning, and both of us sprang forward in the direction of the sound. What was our horror when we saw before us a Figure! At the first glance it appeared to be a Woman, seen sideways; but a moment's observation shewed me that the extremities passed into dimness too rapidly to represent one of the Female Sex; and I should have thought it a Circle, only that it seemed to change its size in a manner impossible for a Circle or for any regular Figure of which I had had experience. . . .

"How comes this person here?" she exclaimed, "you promised me, my dear, that there should be no ventilators in our new house." "Nor are there

any," said I; "but what makes you think that the stranger is a Woman? I see by my power of Sight Recognition — — " "Oh, I have no patience with your Sight Recognition," replied she, "'Feeling is believing' and 'A Straight Line to the touch is worth a Circle to the sight'" — two Proverbs, very common . . . in Flatland.

"Well," said I, for I was afraid of irritating her, "if it must be so, demand an introduction." Assuming her most gracious manner, my Wife advanced towards the Stranger, "Permit me, Madam, to feel and be felt by — — " then, suddenly recoiling, "Oh! it is not a Woman, and there are no angles either, not a trace of one. Can it be that I have so misbehaved to a perfect Circle?"

"I am indeed, in a certain sense a Circle," replied the Voice, "and a more perfect Circle than any in Flatland; but to speak more accurately, I am many Circles in one." . . .

I glanced at the half-hour glass. The last sands had fallen. The third Millennium had begun.

How the Stranger Vainly Endeavoured to Reveal to Me in Words the Mysteries of Spaceland

. . . I began to approach the Stranger with the intention of taking a nearer view and of bidding him be seated: but his appearance struck me dumb and motionless with astonishment. Without the slightest symptoms of angularity he nevertheless varied every instant with gradations of size and brightness scarcely possible for any Figure within the scope of my experience. The thought flashed across me that I might have before me a burglar or cut-throat, some monstrous Irregular Isosceles, who, by feigning the voice of a Circle, had obtained admission somehow into the house, and was now preparing to stab me with his acute angle.

In a sitting-room, the absence of Fog (and the season happened to be remarkably dry), made it difficult for me to trust to Sight Recognition, especially at the short distance at which I was standing. Desperate with fear, I rushed forward with an unceremonious, "You must permit me, Sir —" and felt him. My Wife was right. There was not a trace of an angle, not the slightest roughness or inequality: never in my life had I met with a more perfect Circle. He remained motionless while I walked round him, beginning from his eye and returning to it again. Circular he was throughout, a perfectly satisfactory Circle; there could not be a doubt of it. Then followed a dialogue, which I will endeavour to set down as near as I can recollect it, omitting only some of my profuse apologies — for I was covered with shame and humiliation that I, a Square, should have been guilty of the impertinence of feeling a Circle. It was commenced by the Stranger with some impatience at the lengthiness of my introductory process.

Stranger: Have you felt me enough by this time? Are you not introduced to me yet?

I: Most illustrious Sir, excuse my awkwardness, which arises not from ignorance of the usages of polite society, but from a little surprise and nervousness, consequent on this somewhat unexpected visit. And I beseech you to reveal my indiscretions to no one, and especially not to my Wife. But before your Lordship enters into further communications, would he deign to satisfy the curiosity of one who would gladly know whence his Visitor came?

Stranger: From Space, from Space, Sir: whence else?

I: Pardon me, my Lord, but is not your Lordship already in Space, your Lordship and his humble servant, even at this moment?

Stranger: Pooh! what do you know of Space? Define Space.

I: Space, my Lord, is height and breadth indefinitely prolonged.

Stranger: Exactly: you see you do not even know what Space is. You think it is of Two Dimensions only; but I have come to announce to you a Third — height, breadth, and length.

I: Your Lordship is pleased to be merry. We also speak of length and height, or breadth and thickness, thus denoting Two Dimensions by four names.

Stranger: But I mean not only three names, but Three Dimensions.

I: Would your Lordship indicate or explain to me in what direction is the Third Dimension, unknown to me?

Stranger: I came from it. It is up above and down below.

I: My Lord means seemingly that it is Northward and Southward.

Stranger: I mean nothing of the kind. I mean a direction in which you cannot look, because you have no eye in your side.

I: Pardon me, my Lord, a moment's inspection will convince your Lordship that I have a perfect luminary at the juncture of two of my sides.

Stranger: Yes: but in order to see into Space you ought to have an eye, not on your Perimeter, but on your side, that is, on what you would probably call your inside; but we in Spaceland should call it your side.

I: An eye in my inside! An eye in my stomach! Your Lordship jests.

Stranger: I am in no jesting humour. I tell you that I come from Space, or, since you will not understand what Space means, from the Land of Three Dimensions whence I but lately looked down upon your Plane which you call Space forsooth. From that position of advantage I discerned all that you speak of as *solid* (by which you mean "enclosed on four sides"), your houses, your churches, your very chests and safes, yes even your insides and stomachs, all lying open and exposed to my view.

I: Such assertions are easily made, my Lord.

Stranger: But not easily proved, you mean. But I mean to prove mine.

When I descended here, I saw your four Sons, the Pentagons, each in his apartment, and your two Grandsons the Hexagons; I saw your youngest Hexagon remain a while with you and then retire to his room, leaving you and your Wife alone. I saw your Isosceles servants, three in number, in the kitchen at supper, and the little Page in the scullery. Then I came here, and how do you think I came?

I: Through the roof, I suppose.

Stranger: Not so. Your roof, as you know very well, has been recently repaired, and has no aperture by which even a Woman could penetrate. I tell you I come from Space. Are you not convinced by what I have told you of your children and household?

I: Your Lordship must be aware that such facts touching the belongings of his humble servant might be easily ascertained by any one in the neighbourhood possessing your Lordship's ample means of obtaining information.

Stranger: (*To himself.*) What must I do? Stay; one more argument suggests itself to me. When you see a Straight Line — your wife, for example — how many Dimensions do you attribute to her?

I: Your Lordship would treat me as if I were one of the vulgar who, being ignorant of Mathematics, suppose that a Woman is really a Straight Line, and only of One Dimension. No, no, my Lord; we Squares are better advised, and are as well aware as your Lordship that a Woman, though popularly called a Straight Line, is, really and scientifically, a very thin Parallelogram, possessing Two Dimensions, like the rest of us, viz., length and breadth (or thickness).

Stranger: But the very fact that a Line is visible implies that it possesses yet another Dimension.

I: My Lord, I have just acknowledged that a Woman is broad as well as long. We see her length, we infer her breadth; which, though very slight, is capable of measurement.

Stranger: You do not understand me. I mean that when you see a Woman, you ought — besides inferring her breadth — to see her length, and to *see* what we call her *height*; although that last Dimension is infinitesimal in your country. If a Line were mere length without "height," it would cease to occupy Space and would become invisible. Surely you must recognize this?

I: I must indeed confess that I do not in the least understand your Lordship. When we in Flatland see a Line, we see length and *brightness*. If the brightness disappears, the Line is extinguished, and, as you say, ceases to occupy Space. But am I to suppose that your Lordship gives to brightness the title of a Dimension, and that what we call "bright" you call "high"?

Stranger: No, indeed. By "height" I mean a Dimension like your length: only, with you, "height" is not so easily perceptible, being extremely small.

I: My Lord, your assertion is easily put to the test. You say I have a Third Dimension, which you call "height." Now, Dimension implies direction and measurement. Do but measure my "height," or merely indicate to me the direction in which my "height" extends, and I will become your convert. Otherwise, your Lordship's own understanding must hold me excused.

Stranger: (*To himself.*) I can do neither. How shall I convince him? Surely a plain statement of facts followed by ocular demonstration ought to suffice. — Now, Sir; listen to me.

You are living on a Plane. What you style Flatland is the vast level surface of what I may call a fluid, on, or in, the top of which you and your countrymen move about, without rising above it or falling below it.

I am not a plane Figure, but a Solid. You call me a Circle; but in reality I am not a Circle, but an infinite number of Circles, of size varying from a Point to a Circle of thirteen inches in diameter, one placed on the top of the other. When I cut through your plane as I am now doing, I make in your plane a section which you, very rightly, call a Circle. For even a Sphere — which is my proper name in my own country — if he manifest himself at all to an inhabitant of Flatland — must needs manifest himself as a Circle.

Do you not remember — for I, who see all things, discerned last night the phantasmal vision of Lineland written upon your brain — do you not remember, I say, how, when you entered the realm of Lineland, you were compelled to manifest yourself to the King, not as a Square, but as a Line, because that Linear Realm had not Dimensions enough to represent the whole of you, but only a slice or section of you? In precisely the same way, your country of Two Dimensions is not spacious enough to represent me, a being of Three, but can only exhibit a slice or section of me, which is what you call a Circle.

The diminished brightness of your eye indicates incredulity. But now prepare to receive proof positive of the truth of my assertions. You cannot indeed see more than one of my sections, or Circles, at a time; for you have no power to raise your eye out of the plane of Flatland; but you can at least see that, as I rise in Space, so my sections become smaller. See now, I will rise; and the effect upon your eye will be that my Circle will become smaller and smaller till it dwindles to a point and finally vanishes.

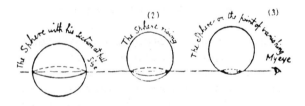

There was no "rising" that I could see; but he diminished and finally vanished. I winked once or twice to make sure that I was not dreaming. But it was no dream. For from the depths of nowhere came forth a hollow voice—close to my heart it seemed—"Am I quite gone? Are you convinced now? Well, now I will gradually return to Flatland and you shall see my sections become larger and larger."

Every reader in Spaceland will easily understand that my mysterious Guest was speaking the language of truth and even of simplicity. But to me, proficient though I was in Flatland Mathematics, it was by no means a simple matter. The rough diagram given above will make it clear to any Spaceland child that the Sphere, ascending in

the three positions indicated there, must needs have manifested himself to me, or to any Flatlander, as a Circle, at first of full size, then small, and at last very small indeed, approaching to a Point. But to me, although I saw the facts before me, the causes were as dark as ever. All that I could comprehend was, that the Circle had made himself smaller and vanished, and that he had now reappeared and was rapidly making himself larger.

When he regained his original size, he heaved a deep sigh; for he perceived by my silence that I had altogether failed to comprehend him. And indeed I was now inclining to the belief that he must be no Circle at all, but some extremely clever juggler; or else that the old wives' tales were true, and that after all there were such people as Enchanters and Magicians.

After a long pause he muttered to himself, "One resource alone remains, if I am not to resort to action. I must try the method of Analogy." Then followed a still longer silence, after which he continued our dialogue.

Sphere: Tell me, Mr. Mathematician; if a Point moves Northward, and leaves a luminous wake, what name would you give to the wake?

I: A straight Line.

Sphere: And a straight Line has how many extremities?

I: Two.

Sphere: Now conceive the Northward straight Line moving parallel to itself, East and West, so that every point in it leaves behind it the wake of a straight Line. What name will you give to the Figure thereby formed? We will suppose that it moves through a distance equal to the original straight Line.—What name, I say?

I: A Square.

Sphere: And how many sides has a Square? How many angles?

I: Four sides and four angles.

Sphere: Now stretch your imagination a little, and conceive a Square in Flatland, moving parallel to itself upward.

I: What? Northward?

Sphere: No, not Northward; upward; out of Flatland altogether.

If it moved Northward, the Southern points in the Square would have to move through the positions previously occupied by the Northern points. But that is not my meaning.

I mean that every Point in you — for you are a Square and will serve the purpose of my illustration — every Point in you, that is to say in what you call your inside, is to pass upwards through Space in such a way that no Point shall pass through the position previously occupied by any other Point; but each Point shall describe a straight Line of its own. This is all in accordance with Analogy; surely it must be clear to you.

Restraining my impatience — for I was now under a strong temptation to rush blindly at my Visitor and to precipitate him into Space, or out of Flatland, anywhere, so that I could get rid of him — I replied: —

"And what may be the nature of the Figure which I am to shape out by this motion which you are pleased to denote by the word 'upward'? I presume it is describable in the language of Flatland."

Sphere: Oh, certainly. It is all plain and simple, and in strict accordance with Analogy — only, by the way, you must not speak of the result as being a Figure, but as a Solid. But I will describe it to you. Or rather not I, but Analogy.

We began with a single Point, which of course — being itself a Point — has only *one* terminal Point.

One Point produces a Line with *two* terminal Points.

One Line produces a Square with *four* terminal Points.

Now you can give yourself the answer to your own question: 1, 2, 4, are evidently in Geometrical Progression. What is the next number?

I: Eight.

Sphere: Exactly. The one Square produces a *Something-which-you-do-not-as-yet-know-a-name-for-but-which-we-call-a-Cube* with *eight* terminal Points. Now are you convinced?

I: And has this Creature sides, as well as angles or what you call "terminal Points"?

Sphere: Of course; and all according to Analogy. But, by the way, not what *you* call sides, but what *we* call sides. You would call them *solids*.

I: And how many solids or sides will appertain to this Being whom I am to generate by the motion of my inside in an "upward" direction, and whom you call a Cube?

Sphere: How can you ask? And you a mathematician! The side of anything is always, if I may so say, one Dimension behind the thing. Consequently, as there is no Dimension behind a Point, a Point has 0 sides; a Line, if I may say, has 2 sides (for the Points of a Line may be called by courtesy, its sides); a Square has 4 sides; 0, 2, 4; what Progression do you call that?

I: Arithmetical.

Sphere: And what is the next number?

I: Six.

Sphere: Exactly. Then you see you have answered your own question. The Cube which you will generate will be bounded by six sides, that is to say, six of your insides. You see it all now, eh?

"Monster," I shrieked, "be thou juggler, enchanter, dream, or devil, no more will I endure thy mockeries. Either thou or I must perish." And saying these words I precipitated myself upon him.

How the Sphere, Having in Vain Tried Words, Resorted to Deeds

It was in vain. I brought my hardest right angle into violent collision with the Stranger, pressing on him with a force sufficient to have destroyed any ordinary Circle: but I could feel him slowly and unarrestably slipping from my contact; no edging to the right nor to the left, but moving somehow out of the world, and vanishing to nothing. Soon there was a blank. But still I heard the Intruder's voice.

Sphere: Why will you refuse to listen to reason? I had hoped to find in you—as being a man of sense and an accomplished mathematician—a fit apostle for the Gospel of the Three Dimensions, which I am allowed to preach once only in a thousand years: but now I know not how to convince you. Stay, I have it. Deeds, and not words, shall proclaim the truth. Listen, my friend.

I have told you I can see from my position in Space the inside of all things that you consider closed. For example, I see in yonder cupboard near which you are standing, several of what you call boxes (but like everything else in Flatland, they have no tops nor bottoms) full of money; I see also two tablets of accounts. I am about to descend into that cupboard and to bring you one of those tablets. I saw you lock the cupboard half an hour ago, and I know you have the key in your possession. But I descend from Space; the doors, you see, remain unmoved. Now I am in the cupboard and am taking the tablet. Now I have it. Now I ascend with it.

I rushed to the closet and dashed the door open. One of the tablets was gone. With a mocking laugh, the Stranger appeared in the other corner of the room, and at the same time the tablet appeared upon the floor. I took it up. There could be no doubt—it was the missing tablet.

I groaned with horror, doubting whether I was not out of my senses; but the Stranger continued: "Surely you must now see that my explanation, and no other, suits the phenomena. What you call Solid things are really superficial; what you call Space is really nothing but a great Plane. I am in Space, and look down upon the insides of the things of which you only see the outsides. You could leave this Plane yourself, if you could but summon up the necessary volition. A slight upward or downward motion would enable you to see all that I can see.

"The higher I mount, and the further I go from your Plane, the more I can see, though of course I see it on a smaller scale. For example, I am ascending; now I can see your neighbour the Hexagon and his family in their several apartments; now I see the inside of the Theatre, ten doors off, from which the audience is only just departing; and on the other side a Circle in his study, sitting at his books. Now I shall come back to you. And, as a crowning proof, what do you say to my giving you a touch, just the least touch, in your stomach? It will not seriously injure you, and the slight pain you may suffer cannot be compared with the mental benefit you will receive."

Before I could utter a word of remonstrance, I felt a shooting pain in my inside, and a demoniacal laugh seemed to issue from within me. A moment afterwards the sharp agony had ceased, leaving nothing but a dull ache behind, and the Stranger began to reappear, saying, as he gradually increased in size, "There, I have not hurt you much, have I? If you are not convinced now, I don't know what will convince you. What say you?"

My resolution was taken. It seemed intolerable that I should endure existence subject to the arbitrary visitations of a Magician who could thus play tricks with one's very stomach. If only I could in any way manage to pin him against the wall till help came!

Once more I dashed my hardest angle against him, at the same time alarming the whole household by my cries for aid. I believe, at the moment of my onset, the Stranger had sunk below our Plane, and really found difficulty in rising. In any case he remained motionless, while I, hearing, as I thought, the sound of some help approaching, pressed against him with redoubled vigour, and continued to shout for assistance.

A convulsive shudder ran through the Sphere. "This must not be," I thought I heard him say: "either he must listen to reason, or I must have recourse to the last resource of civilization." Then, addressing me in a louder tone, he hurriedly exclaimed, "Listen: no stranger must witness what you have witnessed. Send your Wife back at once, before she enters the apartment. The Gospel of Three Dimensions must not be thus frustrated. Not thus must the fruits of one thousand years of waiting be thrown away. I hear her coming. Back! back! Away from me, or you must go with me—whither you know not—into the Land of Three Dimensions!"

"Fool! Madman! Irregular!" I exclaimed; "never will I release thee; thou shalt pay the penalty of thine impostures."

"Ha! Is it come to this?" thundered the Stranger: "then meet your fate: out of your Plane you go. Once, twice, thrice! 'Tis done!"

How I Came to Spaceland, and What I Saw There

An unspeakable horror seized me. There was a darkness; then a dizzy, sickening sensation of sight that was not like seeing; I saw a Line that was no Line; Space that was not Space: I was myself, and not myself. When I could find voice, I shrieked aloud in agony, "Either this is madness or it is Hell." "It is neither," calmly replied the voice of the Sphere, "it is Knowledge; it is Three Dimensions: open your eye once again and try to look steadily."

I looked, and, behold, a new world! There stood before me, visibly incorporate, all that I had before inferred, conjectured, dreamed, of perfect Circular beauty. What seemed the centre of the Stranger's form lay open to my view: yet I could see no heart, nor lungs, nor arteries, only a beautiful harmonious Something— for which I had no words; but you, my Readers in Spaceland, would call it the surface of the Sphere.

Prostrating myself mentally before my Guide, I cried, "How is it, O divine ideal of consummate loveliness and wisdom that I see thy inside, and yet cannot discern thy heart, thy lungs, thy arteries, thy liver?" "What you think you see, you see not," he replied; "it is not given to you, nor to any other Being to behold my internal parts. I am of a different order of Beings from those in Flatland. Were I a Circle, you could discern my intestines, but I am a Being, composed as I told you before, of many Circles, the Many in the One, called in this country a Sphere. And, just as the outside of a Cube is a Square, so the outside of a Sphere presents the appearance of a Circle."

Bewildered though I was by my Teacher's enigmatic utterance, I no longer chafed against it, but worshipped him in silent adoration. He continued, with more mildness in his voice. "Distress not yourself if you cannot at first understand the deeper mysteries of Spaceland. By degrees they will dawn upon you. Let us begin by casting back a glance at the region whence you came. Return with me a while to the plains of Flatland, and I will shew you that which you have often reasoned and thought about, but never seen with the sense of sight—a visible angle." "Impossible!" I cried; but, the Sphere leading the way, I followed as if in a dream, till once more his voice arrested me: "Look yonder, and behold your own Pentagonal house, and all its inmates."

I looked below, and saw with my physical eye all that domestic individuality which I had hitherto merely inferred with the understanding. And how poor and shadowy was the inferred conjecture in comparison with the reality which I now beheld! My four Sons calmly asleep in the North-Western rooms, my two orphan Grandsons to the South; the Servants, the Butler, my Daughter, all in their several apartments. Only my affectionate Wife, alarmed by my continued absence, had quitted her room and was roving up and down in the Hall, anxiously awaiting my return. Also the Page, aroused by my cries, had left his room, and under pretext of ascertaining whether I had fallen somewhere in a faint, was prying into the cabinet in my study. All this I could now *see*, not merely infer; and as we came nearer and nearer, I could discern even the contents of my cabinet, and the two chests of gold, and the tablets of which the Sphere had made mention.

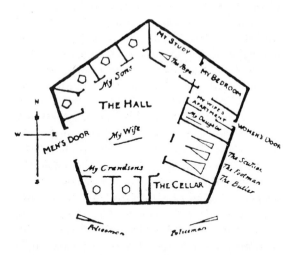

Touched by my Wife's distress, I would have sprung downward to reassure her, but I found myself incapable of motion. "Trouble not yourself about your Wife," said my Guide: "she will not be long left in anxiety; meantime, let us take a survey of Flatland."

Once more I felt myself rising through space. It was even as the Sphere had said. The further we receded from the object we beheld, the larger became the field of vision. My native city, with the interior of every house and every creature therein, lay open to my view in miniature. We mounted higher, and lo, the secrets of the earth, the depths of mines and inmost caverns of the hills, were bared before me.

Awestruck at the sight of the mysteries of the earth, thus unveiled before my unworthy eye, I said to my Companion, "Behold, I am become as a God. For the wise men in our country say that to see all things, or as they express it, *omnividence*, is the attribute of God alone." There was something of scorn in the voice of my Teacher as he made answer: "Is it so indeed? Then the very pickpockets and cut-throats of my country are to be worshipped by your wise men as being Gods: for there is not one of them that does not see as

much as you see now. But trust me, your wise men are wrong."

I: Then is omnividence the attribute of others besides Gods?

Sphere: I do not know. But, if a pick-pocket or a cut-throat of our country can see everything that is in your country, surely that is no reason why the pick-pocket or cut-throat should be accepted by you as a God. This omnividence, as you call it — it is not a common word in Spaceland — does it make you more just, more merciful, less selfish, more loving? Not in the least. Then how does it make you more divine?

I: "More merciful, more loving!" But these are the qualities of women! And we know that a Circle is a higher Being than a Straight Line, in so far as knowledge and wisdom are more to be esteemed than mere affection.

Sphere: It is not for me to classify human faculties according to merit. Yet many of the best and wisest in Spaceland think more of the affections than of the understanding, more of your despised Straight Lines than of your belauded Circles. But enough of this. Look yonder. Do you know that building?

I looked, and afar off I saw an immense Polygonal structure, in which I recognized the General Assembly Hall of the States of Flatland, surrounded by dense lines of Pentagonal buildings at right angles to each other, which I knew to be streets; and I perceived that I was approaching the great Metropolis.

"Here we descend," said my Guide. It was now morning, the first hour of the first day of the two thousandth year of our era. Acting, as was their wont, in strict accordance with precedent, the highest Circles of the realm were meeting in solemn conclave, as they had met on the first hour of the first day of the year 1000, and also on the first hour of the first day of the year 0.

The minutes of the previous meetings were now read by one whom I at once recognized as my brother, a perfectly Symmetrical Square, and the Chief Clerk of the High Council. It was found recorded on each occasion that: "Whereas the

States had been troubled by divers ill-intentioned persons pretending to have received revelations from another World, and professing to produce demonstrations whereby they had instigated to frenzy both themselves and others, it had been for this cause unanimously resolved by the Grand Council that on the first day of each millenary, special injunctions be sent to the Prefects in the several districts of Flatland, to make strict search for such misguided persons, and without formality of mathematical examination, to destroy all such as were Isosceles of any degree, to scourge and imprison any regular Triangle, to cause any Square or Pentagon to be sent to the district Asylum, and to arrest any one of higher rank, sending him straightway to the Capital to be examined and judged by the Council."

"You hear your fate," said the Sphere to me, while the Council was passing for the third time the formal resolution. "Death or imprisonment awaits the Apostle of the Gospel of Three Dimensions." "Not so," replied I, "the matter is now so clear to me, the nature of real space so palpable, that methinks I could make a child understand it. Permit me but to descend at this moment and enlighten them." "Not yet," said my Guide, "the time will come for that. Meantime I must perform my mission. Stay thou there in thy place." Saying these words, he leaped with great dexterity into the sea (if I may so call it) of Flatland, right in the midst of the ring of Counsellors. "I come," cried he, "to proclaim that there is a land of Three Dimensions."

I could see many of the younger Counsellors start back in manifest horror, as the Sphere's circular section widened before them. But on a sign from the presiding Circle — who shewed not the slightest alarm or surprise — six Isosceles of a low type from six different quarters rushed upon the Sphere. "We have him," they cried; "No; yes; we have him still! he's going! he's gone!"

"My Lords," said the President to the Junior Circles of the Council, "there is not the slightest need for surprise; the secret archives, to which I alone have access, tell me that a similar occurrence happened on the last two millennial commencements. You will, of course, say nothing of these trifles outside the Cabinet."

Raising his voice, he now summoned the guards. "Arrest the policemen; gag them. You know your duty." After he had consigned to their fate the wretched policemen — ill-fated and unwilling witnesses of a State-secret which they were not to be permitted to reveal — he again addressed the Counsellors. "My Lords, the business of the Council being concluded, I have only to wish you a happy New Year." Before departing, he expressed, at some length, to the Clerk, my excellent but most unfortunate brother, his sincere regret that, in accordance with precedent and for the sake of secrecy, he must condemn him to perpetual imprisonment, but added his satisfaction that, unless some mention were made by him of that day's incident, his life would be spared.

How, Though the Sphere Shewed Me Other Mysteries of Spaceland, I Still Desired More; and What Came of It

When I saw my poor brother led away to imprisonment, I attempted to leap down into the Council Chamber, desiring to intercede on his behalf, or at least bid him farewell. But I found that I had no motion of my own. I absolutely depended on the volition of my Guide, who said in gloomy tones, "Heed not thy brother; haply thou shalt have ample time hereafter to condole with him. Follow me."

Once more we ascended into space. "Hitherto," said the Sphere, "I have shewn you naught save

Plane Figures and their interiors. Now I must introduce you to Solids, and reveal to you the plan upon which they are constructed. Behold this multitude of moveable square cards. See, I put one on another, not, as you supposed, Northward of the other, but *on* the other. Now a second, now a third. See, I am building up a Solid by a multitude of Squares parallel to one another. Now the Solid is complete, being as high as it is long and broad, and we call it a Cube."

"Pardon me, my Lord," replied I; "but to my eye the appearance is as of an Irregular Figure whose inside is laid open to the view; in other words, methinks I see no Solid, but a Plane such as we infer in Flatland; only of an Irregularity which betokens some monstrous criminal, so that the very sight of it is painful to my eyes."

"True," said the Sphere, "it appears to you a Plane, because you are not accustomed to light and shade and perspective; just as in Flatland a Hexagon would appear a Straight Line to one who has not the Art of Sight Recognition. But in reality it is a Solid, as you shall learn by the sense of Feeling."

He then introduced me to the Cube, and I found that this marvellous Being was indeed no Plane, but a Solid; and that he was endowed with six plane sides and eight terminal points called solid angles; and I remembered the saying of the Sphere that just such a Creature as this would be formed by a Square moving, in Space, parallel to himself: and I rejoiced to think that so insignificant a Creature as I could in some sense be called the Progenitor of so illustrious an offspring.

But still I could not fully understand the meaning of what my Teacher had told me concerning "light" and "shade" and "perspective"; and I did not hesitate to put my difficulties before him.

Were I to give the Sphere's explanation of these matters, succinct and clear though it was, it would be tedious to an inhabitant of Space, who knows these things already. Suffice it, that by his lucid statements, and by changing the position of objects and lights, and by allowing me to feel the several objects and even his own sacred Per-

son, he at last made all things clear to me, so that I could now readily distinguish between a Circle and a Sphere, a Plane Figure and a Solid.

This was the Climax, the Paradise, of my strange eventful History. Henceforth I have to relate the story of my miserable Fall: — most miserable, yet surely most undeserved! For why should the thirst for knowledge be aroused, only to be disappointed and punished? My volition shrinks from the painful task of recalling my humiliation; yet, like a second Prometheus, I will endure this and worse, if by any means I may arouse in the interiors of Plane and Solid Humanity a spirit of rebellion against the Conceit which would limit our Dimensions to Two or Three or any number short of Infinity. Away then with all personal considerations! Let me continue to the end, as I began, without further digressions or anticipations, pursuing the plain path of dispassionate History. The exact facts, the exact words, — and they are burnt in upon my brain, — shall be set down without alteration of an iota; and let my Readers judge between me and Destiny.

The Sphere would willingly have continued his lessons by indoctrinating me in the conformation of all regular Solids, Cylinders, Cones, Pyramids, Pentahedrons, Hexahedrons, Dodecahedrons, and Spheres: but I ventured to interrupt him. Not that I was wearied of knowledge. On the contrary, I thirsted for yet deeper and fuller draughts than he was offering to me.

"Pardon me," said I, "O Thou Whom I must no longer address as the Perfection of all Beauty; but let me beg thee to vouchsafe thy servant a sight of thine interior."

Sphere: My what?

I: Thine interior: thy stomach, thy intestines.

Sphere: Whence this ill-timed impertinent request? And what mean you by saying that I am no longer the Perfection of all Beauty?

I: My Lord, your own wisdom has taught me to aspire to One even more great, more beautiful, and more closely approximate to Perfection than yourself. As you yourself, superior to all Flatland forms, combine many Circles in One, so doubtless there is One above you who combines many Spheres in One Supreme Existence, surpassing even the Solids of Spaceland. And even as we, who are now in Space, look down on Flatland and see the insides of all things, so of a certainty there is yet above us some higher, purer region, whither thou dost surely purpose to lead me — O Thou Whom I shall always call, everywhere and in all Dimensions, my Priest, Philosopher, and Friend — some yet more spacious Space, some more dimensionable Dimensionality, from the vantage-ground of which we shall look down together upon the revealed insides of Solid things, and where thine own intestines, and those of thy kindred Spheres, will lie exposed to the view of the poor wandering exile from Flatland, to whom so much has already been vouchsafed.

Sphere: Pooh! Stuff! Enough of this trifling! The time is short, and much remains to be done before you are fit to proclaim the Gospel of Three Dimensions to your blind benighted countrymen in Flatland.

I: Nay, gracious Teacher, deny me not what I know it is in thy power to perform. Grant me but one glimpse of thine interior, and I am satisfied for ever, remaining henceforth thy docile pupil, thy unemancipable slave, ready to receive all thy teachings and to feed upon the words that fall from thy lips.

Sphere: Well, then, to content and silence you, let me say at once, I would shew you what you wish if I could; but I cannot. Would you have me turn my stomach inside out to oblige you?

I: But my Lord has shewn me the intestines of all my countrymen in the Land of Two Dimensions by taking me with him into the Land of Three. What therefore more easy than now to take his servant on a second journey into the blessed region of the Fourth Dimension, where I shall look down with him once more upon this land of Three Dimensions, and see the inside of every three-dimensioned house, the secrets of the solid earth, the treasures of the mines in Spaceland, and the intestines of every solid living creature, even of the noble and adorable Spheres.

Sphere: But where is this land of Four Dimensions?

I: I know not: but doubtless my Teacher knows.

Sphere: Not I. There is no such land. The very idea of it is utterly inconceivable.

I: Not inconceivable, my Lord, to me, and therefore still less inconceivable to my Master. Nay, I despair not that, even here, in this region of Three Dimensions, your Lordship's art may make the Fourth Dimension visible to me; just as in the Land of Two Dimensions my Teacher's skill would fain have opened the eyes of his blind servant to the invisible presence of a Third Dimension, though I saw it not.

Let me recall the past. Was I not taught below that when I saw a Line and inferred a Plane, I in reality saw a Third unrecognized Dimension, not the same as brightness, called "height"? And does it not now follow that, in this region, when I see a Plane and infer a Solid, I really see a Fourth unrecognized Dimension, not the same as colour, but existent, though infinitesimal and incapable of measurement?

And besides this, there is the Argument from Analogy of Figures.

Sphere: Analogy! Nonsense: what analogy?

I: Your Lordship tempts his servant to see whether he remembers the revelations imparted to him. Trifle not with me, my Lord; I crave, I thirst, for more knowledge. Doubtless we cannot *see* that other higher Spaceland now, because we have no eye in our stomachs. But, just as there *was* the realm of Flatland, though that poor puny Lineland Monarch could neither turn to left nor right to discern it, and just as there *was* close at hand, and touching my frame, the land of Three Dimensions, though I, blind senseless wretch, had no power to touch it, no eye in my interior to discern it, so of a surety there is a Fourth Dimension, which my Lord perceives with the inner eye of thought. And that it must exist my Lord himself has taught me. Or can he have forgotten what he himself imparted to his servant?

In One Dimension did not a moving Point produce a Line with *two* terminal points?

In Two Dimensions, did not a moving Line produce a Square with *four* terminal points?

In Three Dimensions, did not a moving Square produce — did not this eye of mine behold it — that blessed Being, a Cube, with *eight* terminal points?

And in Four Dimensions shall not a moving Cube — alas, for Analogy, and alas for the Progress of Truth, if it be not so — shall not, I say, the motion of a divine Cube result in a still more divine Organization with *sixteen* terminal points?

Behold the infallible confirmation of the Series, 2, 4, 8, 16: is not this a Geometrical Progression? Is not this — if I might quote my Lord's own words — "strictly according to Analogy"?

Again, was I not taught by my Lord that as in a Line there are *two* bounding Points, and in a Square there are *four* bounding Lines, so in a Cube there must be *six* bounding Squares? Behold once more the confirming Series, 2, 4, 6: is not this an Arithmetical Progression? And consequently does it not of necessity follow that the more divine offspring of the divine Cube in the Land of Four Dimensions, must have 8 bounding Cubes: and is not this also, as my Lord has taught me to believe, "strictly according to Analogy"?

O, my Lord, my Lord, behold, I cast myself in faith upon conjecture, not knowing the facts; and I appeal to your Lordship to confirm or deny my logical anticipations. If I am wrong, I yield, and will no longer demand a fourth Dimension; but, if I am right, my Lord will listen to reason.

I ask therefore, is it, or is it not, the fact, that ere now your countrymen also have witnessed the descent of Beings of a higher order than their own, entering closed rooms, even as your Lordship entered mine, without the opening of doors or windows, and appearing and vanishing at will? On the reply to this question I am ready to stake everything. Deny it, and I am henceforth silent. Only vouchsafe an answer.

Sphere (after a pause): It is reported so. But men are divided in opinion as to the facts. And even granting the facts, they explain them in different ways. And in any case, however great may be the number of different explanations, no one has adopted or suggested the theory of a Fourth Dimension. Therefore, pray have done with this trifling, and let us return to business.

I: I was certain of it. I was certain that my anticipations would be fulfilled. And now have patience with me and answer me yet one more question, best of Teachers! Those who have thus appeared — no one knows whence — and have returned — no one knows whither — have they also contracted their sections and vanished somehow into that more Spacious Space, whither I now entreat you to conduct me?

Sphere (moodily): They have vanished, certainly — if they ever appeared. But most people say that these visions arose from the thought — you will not understand me — from the brain; from the perturbed angularity of the Seer.

I: Say they so? Oh, believe them not. Or if it indeed be so, that this other Space is really Thoughtland, then take me to that blessed Region where I in Thought shall see the insides of all solid things. There, before my ravished eye, a Cube, moving in some altogether new direction, but strictly according to Analogy, so as to make every particle of his interior pass through a new kind of Space, with a wake of its own — shall create a still more perfect perfection than himself, with sixteen terminal Extrasolid angles, and Eight solid Cubes for his Perimeter. And once there, shall we stay our upward course? In that blessed region of Four Dimensions, shall we linger on the threshold of the Fifth, and not enter therein? Ah, no! Let us rather resolve that our ambition shall soar with our corporal ascent. Then, yielding to our intellectual onset, the gates of the Sixth Dimension shall fly open; after that a Seventh, and then an Eighth —

How long I should have continued I know not. In vain did the Sphere, in his voice of thunder, reiterate his command of silence, and threaten me with the direst penalties if I persisted. Nothing could stem the flood of my ecstatic aspirations. Perhaps I was to blame; but indeed I was intoxicated with the recent draughts of Truth to which he himself had introduced me. However, the end was not long in coming. My words were cut short by a crash outside, and a simultaneous crash inside me, which impelled me through space with a velocity that precluded speech. Down! down! down! I was rapidly descending; and I knew that return to Flatland was my doom. One glimpse, one last and never-to-be-forgotten glimpse I had of that dull level wilderness—which was now to become my Universe again—spread out before my eye. Then a darkness. . . .

NOTE

1. When I say "sitting," of course I do not mean any change of attitude such as you in Spaceland signify by that word; for as we have no feet, we can no more "sit" nor "stand" (in your sense of the word) than one of your soles or flounders.

Nevertheless, we perfectly well recognize the different mental states of volition implied in "lying," "sitting," and "standing," which are to some extent indicated to a beholder by a slight increase of lustre corresponding to the increase of volition.

But on this, and a thousand other kindred subjects, time forbids me to dwell.

Further Questions

1. You *see* a universe of only three dimensions. Is that how many dimensions the universe has? How can you find out? Suppose you make a date to meet someone on the second floor of a building that sits on the south corner of Hollywood and Vine. You have specified only three coordinates. What is missing?

2. To move along the fourth dimension, you would have to go "Upward but not upward." Relate this paradox to the problem of "Upward, not Northward" in the story. What happens when you try to visualize the fourth dimension?

3. Why can't you see time? Try to explain this using what you've learned in Flatland.

4. Many mystics over the ages have claimed that ultimate reality cannot be perceived or understood using our ordinary concepts. Often they have tried to communicate what they claim are mystical insights using self-contradictory or paradoxical statements. What significance, if any, do you think the story of *Flatland* has to such concerns?

Further Readings

Burger, Dionys. *Sphereland*. New York: Thomas Y. Crowell Company, 1965. Takes off where *Flatland* ends; it is told by a Hexagon who is the Square's grandson! It also takes into account the more recent non-Euclidean geometries of curved spaces.

Gamow, George. *Mr. Tompkins in Wonderland*. New York: Cambridge University Press, 1940. Illustrates without any technical language some of the most startling implications of living in an Einsteinian universe.

Munitz, Milton. *Theories of the Universe*. New York: Free Press, 1957. Presents a sweeping historical panorama of different models of the cosmos.

Reichenbach, Hans. *Philosophy of Space and Time*. New York: Dover, 1958. Explores the topology of space and time, with philosophical implications.

The Incredible Shrinking Zeno

DANIEL KOLAK AND DAVID GOLOFF

A brief biography of Daniel Kolak appears on page 330.

David Goloff, who received his Ph.D. in mathematics from The Johns Hopkins University in 1989, teaches mathematics at the Northwestern State University of Louisiana. His current research interests concern holomorphic mappings between complex manifolds and envelopes of lines which he is trying to apply to families (pencils) of conic sections. He and Daniel Kolak have collaborated on several books, including *Mathematical Thought* (Macmillan) and *Zeno's Paradox Refined: An Eleatic Model of Paradoxical Rationality* (forthcoming). Moreover, presently Kolak and Goloff are developing a multifaceted view of and approach to mathematics education in terms of its importance to philosophy in particular and to thought in general.

Reading Questions

1. What was Parmenides' view of reality?
2. How did Zeno try to defend Parmenides against his critics?
3. Why does your moving across the room *not* solve Zeno's paradox?
4. What does "infinite process in a finite time" have to do with the problem posed?
5. Is it possible to do finite arithmetic with an infinite sum? What does the Gauss example have to do with it?
6. Are we capable of knowing more than we are capable of seeing? Why?
7. Whose side are Zeus and Hera on?
8. What does Shrinking Zeno see, from his point of view, after he has shrunk out of sight of the observers in the Lyceum? Why?
9. In what sense is Zeno's paradox solved? What is the solution? In what sense is Zeno's paradox not solved? What is the problem?
10. When you're walking, pay attention to your experience. Do you find yourself, in one way or another, having some concept of where you are now, of where you are going, and the space inbetween? How did you plan when you should leave in order to arrive somewhere on time? Do you find yourself psychologically projecting your concepts of space and time into the world? How do you understand the idea that you are moving?

WE OBSERVE THE WORLD and find ourselves automatically engaged in concepts such as place or position, time, distance, size or measurement, and a combination of these concepts called *motion*. Motion, in turn, involves the concept of identity: *one and the same* object is thought to occupy different *places* at different *times*. Thus, our most simple, common sense beliefs about ordi-

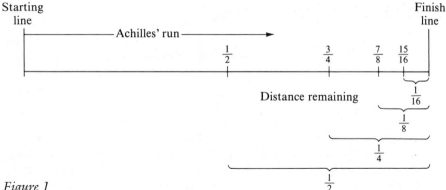

Figure 1

nary objects moving from one place to another involve our most complex and deepest concepts: space, time, and identity. It is important to point out that *all* of these are concepts. This means that they are concepts as opposed to realities that exist "out there."

The ancient (5th century B.C.) Greek philosopher Parmenides asserted that existence is not made up of individual things but that, in reality, "all is one." The totality of existence is one undifferentiated, unchanging, eternal whole. Even the simplest change, such as one thing moving from one place to another, is but an illusion. His basic argument was: If the whole of existence is *not* one (if the universe is made of different things), then what separates one thing from another? Parmenides concluded that the supposed separation between one thing and another would have to consist in something that does not exist—i.e., nothing—and that this would be an absurdity. If we suppose that there are two things between which there is nothing, then these are not two things but one thing.

Zeno, a student of Parmenides, tried to prove Parmenides right. Zeno focused on the fundamental concepts mentioned above. He presented about forty paradoxes, each of which was supposed to show that those who claimed Parmenides' view was absurd were starting from an even *more* absurd view! Only a handful of his paradoxes have survived the twenty-five centuries

since Zeno posed them, and we shall here discuss only the "Dichotomy," one of his paradoxes of motion, for the purpose of *refining Zeno's paradox within contemporary thought.*

1. Statement of Zeno's Paradox of Motion: The Dichotomy

Zeno began by assuming that there can be different places and objects at those places (as common sense supposes) and that an object can indeed move from one place to another. He then posed the following puzzle.

Achilles starts running from a starting position toward a finish line. Before he reaches the finish line he must go half the distance. Achilles must then also go half of the remaining distance. And then he must go half of the distance that still remains. And so on. This is pictured in Figure 1.

Suppose Achilles starts running at a constant speed toward the finish line one mile away. Obviously, before he runs the whole mile he must run ½ mile. After he has gone ½ mile, he cannot just suddenly appear at the finish line without first crossing half the *remaining* ½ mile—that is, he must go ¾ of the distance from the starting point. When he's run ¾ mile, there is ¼ mile remaining but, again, he can't just appear at the finish line without going halfway between the ¾ mark and the finish line. When Achilles is only ⅛ mile away from the finish line, he must still run halfway between where he is at the moment and where the finish line is. At that point Achilles will be only 1⁄16 mile from the finish line. But, again, he can't run 1⁄16 mile without first going one-half of that 1⁄16 mile. And so on. "To say it once," as Zeno was fond of putting it, "is to say it forever."

Is there any remaining distance, at *any* point in the run, where Achilles can reach the finish line *without first running halfway between wherever he is and where the finish line is?* Of course not. How long can we proceed this way? Forever! Wherever Achilles is between the starting line and the finish line, there will always be some distance remaining between him and the finish line. So: *How is it possible for Achilles to ever reach the finish line?*

Achilles *does* appear at the finish line. That's what our eyes tell us! Reason says otherwise: If we think carefully about what we are seeing, we will understand that what *seems* to be going on can't *really* be going on — at least not in the way we think!

To address this paradox we must give it a precise formulation so that instead of merely intuitively feeling that there is a paradox (a psychological sense of dissonance), we can precisely identify the discrepancy. Let us therefore restate the problem more formally. We know that Achilles must, before he appears at the finish line, be at the point halfway between A and B. Call this halfway point between A and B, B_1. To say this is not to divide the space between A and B, nor to "halve the distance," it is merely to give a

name to a point that must be there. B_1 is there whether we name it or not. That is, we are not performing some loaded manipulative move; we are not in any way changing the distance between A and B; we are merely bringing out of our conceptual framework that which, implicitly, already is there in the path between A and B.

Our concept of the path taken by Achilles is the real line, which involves an ordering of the path between Achilles at the starting position at A and the finish line at B, as follows. There is a point halfway between A and B, B_1, such that Achilles' path is ordered so that B_1 comes after A and before B. There is a point halfway between B_1 and B, and let us call this point, halfway between B_1 and B, B_2. There is a point halfway between B_2 and B, B_3. And so on (Figure 2).

Suppose Achilles is at B_{1099}, the point halfway between B_{1098} and B. Between B_{1099} and B is a point, B_{1100}: Achilles at B_{1099} cannot just suddenly, without cause and for no reason, vanish out of existence and pop into existence at B! He must move along a continuous path through the midpoint.

That Achilles could never arrive at B is implied in that our description of how he arrives at the finish line evokes the necessity of an *infinite process*, since to get from any point to any other he must have gone through an infinite number of halfway points. Thus, there are infinitely many B_n:

$$B_1, B_2, B_3, \ldots, B_{1099}, B_{1100}, \ldots, B_n, \ldots$$

If you are not sufficiently puzzled yet, then note that even if B_1 were eliminated from the discussion and all the other B_n were kept in the discus-

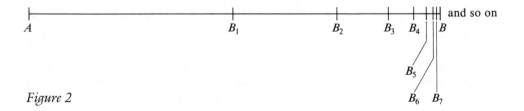

Figure 2

sion, it would have no effect whatsoever on Zeno's paradox: none! Similarly, for any finite number of B_n: No matter where he begins prior to B, Achilles only reaches the finish line at B after passing by infinitely many B_n. For instance, if Achilles starts at B_{1786} and starts running toward B, you would have exactly the same paradox as before. But we should also note that where before we had a mere psychological sense of puzzlement concerning Achilles running toward a finish line, we now have a specific set of concepts within our conceptual framework to which this paradox can be addressed and to which we must turn our rational attention.

Now, not only are the infinite number of B_n implicit in the problem, this is actually the source of the paradox. After all, were there only a finite number of B_n, Achilles would arrive at the finish line after a finite, not an infinite, process — and that Achilles could do that would be no more surprising than, say, you counting to the number ten.

The paradox thus appears embodied precisely in the question, "How can Achilles accomplish an infinite process in a finite amount of time?" or, "How can Achilles travel a finite distance by traveling infinitely many distances?" If Achilles were to slow down at each B_n so that he always takes one second to go from B_n to B_{n+1}, then it would take an infinite amount of time to reach the finish line and in fact he could not by this process ever reach it. In that case, there would be no paradox. Achilles does not reach the finish line — that's the answer. Or, it takes an infinite amount of time for him to reach the finish line through an infinite process — that's the answer. "Infinite process — therefore infinite distance" is not paradoxical, nor is "Infinite process — infinite time." What is paradoxical is "Infinite process — finite time and/or finite distance."

Note that what we are seeing here is not merely that "there is something wrong with our conceptual framework." We see much more — namely, that there is a fine-tuned problem with

reconciling our concept of the finite with our concept of the infinite. In other words, we see exactly what parts of the conceptual framework appear to be out of whack (as opposed to the general feeling that "something is out of whack").

You probably believe things move and runners reach finish lines. Zeno is not claiming that you do not believe this! For instance, if you tried to refute Zeno by running across the room, he would probably just shake his head and tell you that you have misunderstood his paradox, for had you *not* been able to run across the room *then there would be no paradox*! The point is that what you (think you) *see* and what you (think you) think leads you to form particular beliefs about the way things actually are, but that a closer examination of the concepts behind your beliefs contradicts those very beliefs! Thus, Zeno's paradox is an argument against your ordinary beliefs about the way things are. Indeed, the word "paradox" means, literally, "against (*para*) belief (*doxa*)." And it is your own (often hidden) conceptions of the way things are that generates this paradox.

Note that Zeno's paradox directly examines the question of what there is between one place (the starting point) and another (the finish line). Thus, this addresses Parmenides' question of what separates one thing from another in a specific way. Notice, too, that this question is posed precisely and in mathematical terms: Zeno discusses *quantified* distances.

Zeno's paradox makes us question whether our beliefs regarding what is going on in the world can be made coherent using our concepts of motion, points, continuous lines, space, time, change, identity, etc. In implying that you don't know how motion is possible, what is at issue, ultimately, in Zeno's paradox, is the entire basis of the concepts we use in developing our knowledge of the world.

One reason why this paradox was difficult to address in ancient times was that the mathematics of that time only allowed for the addition of a finite number of quantities. To give a truly contemporary exposition of this paradox, we must replace such antiquated concepts with new ones.

2. Solving Zeno's Paradox of Motion: Summing the Infinite

The real question is how do you get a finite distance from an infinite amount of distances? Or, how do you get a finite amount of time from an infinite number of time intervals? These are really the same question, namely:

How do you get a finite quantity from an infinite number of quantities?

Each of the infinite number of quantities is itself a finite quantity. For instance, the length of the interval from A to B_1 is ½ mile. The interval from B_1 to B_2 is ¼ mile. The interval from B_2 to B_3 is ⅛ mile. Generally, the interval

$$B_{k-1} \text{ to } B_k \text{ is } (½)^k$$

Thus the entire interval from A to B must have length equal to the sum of the lengths of all the nonoverlapping parts:

$$½ + ¼ + ⅛ + \ldots + (½)^k + \ldots$$

The $(½)^k$ term comes from noting that the pattern

$$½ = (½)^1, \quad ¼ = (½)(½) = (½)^2,$$
$$⅛ = (½)(½)(½) = (½)^3$$

is just ½ raised to a power one greater than the term before it. The final ". . ." simply means that this pattern continues forever.

This kind of expression, one which involves the summation of an infinite number of quantities, is called an infinite series. The result of summing an infinite series we refer to as the "sum of the infinite series." The question before us is how to understand such a sum of an infinite series or how an infinite series can have a finite sum.[1]

Now notice something else. Not only are each of the quantities finite, they get *smaller*. It is intuitively clear that if we were to add up an infinite number of positive quantities of the same magnitude, the sum would be infinite. What is less intuitively clear is that if we were to add up an infinite number of quantities of lesser and lesser magnitudes, the sum could be *finite*. That is, what you may think is obvious — that one can't just add up an infinite series and have it be finite — is not really obvious at all. What *precise* reason do you have for believing an infinite series cannot have a finite sum? Perhaps you think that something which is infinite in some sense cannot be finite in another sense, but this is not precise and only begs the question.

The Zeno diagram in Figure 3 implies that this infinite collection of intervals does indeed come together into a finite interval. When you look at the diagram, what do you see but an infinite number of intervals coming together into a finite interval? That's what the picture shows! Often, people understand this in reverse; they take it to mean that what they see cannot be happening. What they should conclude, instead, is that what they are seeing is something quite remarkable: an infinite number of quantities (lengths) forming a finite quantity (length). This

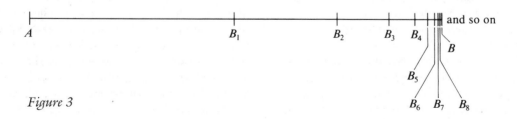

Figure 3

is represented arithmetically by the above infinite series. Thus what is happening is quite clear in pictures, but we need to see how to follow this through in the arithmetic representation. What is needed is a *theory* to account for what is being seen. Why deny what is visually very clear, and only a matter of extending a theory, in favor of what is not intuitively obvious at all but only prejudice?

It might turn out that people either are not intelligent enough to understand the world or that the world is unintelligible. We do have good reasons to believe that any conceptual framework will eventually break down and have to be rejected (one will sooner or later arrive at a certain stage of conceptual development). This suggests that to some extent, or in some sense, the world is ultimately not intelligible. But this only means that the conceptual apparatus will never be perfect nor complete—not that the apparatus is completely useless. Nor does it mean that our conceptual frameworks do not in some way get at the truth. This is because our conceptual frameworks give us a *point of analysis* and the potential of generating new and better paradoxes with which to revise and generate still better paradoxes through which our concepts get better and better. It is this process that allows us to compare known frameworks with the unknown—possibly unknowable—truth.

Below we explain how Zeno's paradox of motion can be solved via the method of summing an infinite series. Once we understand how summing an infinite series is indeed possible, we will be able to see how a mathematical theory can account for Zeno's paradox. This, in turn, will set the stage for our refinement of the paradox within contemporary thought.

We are capable of knowing more than we are capable of seeing. The reason is that, as we are about to explain, the infinite series with a finite sum is not an impossibility at all. Yet, as we shall then see, Zeno was quite right to suggest that there is a deep and fundamental paradox which

even the sum of an infinite series cannot transcend. And Zeno's paradox of motion is as sophisticated a way of pointing to where the fundamental paradox is as the sum of the infinite series is of showing where it is not.

A problem people typically have in accepting the idea of an infinite series of terms or quantities having a finite sum is that they link the idea of addition to the manual procedure of doing the addition. This is a mistake. A plus sign indicates that pieces are part of a whole. The problem of summing the infinite series is one of *discovering* what whole the pieces are part of. In the case of summing a finite series of terms, you could do this by adding each number to the next. This is only a method of discovering what the sum is. The sum itself does not represent a computational activity.

If we free ourselves of the idea of doing addition from left to right, one step at a time, then we will begin to see that summing an infinite series can be made sense of. Let us do this in the case of a finite number of terms. When a sum is written down, even a finite one, this does not imply that we are obligated to add the first two numbers and then add the result to the third and so on. This is illustrated by an amusing story about the child prodigy J. C. F. Gauss (1777–1855). One day in elementary school Gauss' teacher wanted to keep the class busy by having them add up all the counting numbers 1 to 99:

$$1 + 2 + 3 + \cdots + 97 + 98 + 99$$

As soon as the problem was posed, Gauss quickly shouted out, "4950!" He did this by observing the following: If you add the first and last terms $(1 + 99)$ you get 100. If you add the second term to the second to last term $(2 + 98)$ you get 100. And so on. Obviously, there will be 49 pairs of terms, each of which together make 100, plus the one middle term, 50. Thus, the sum is 49 times 100, plus 50, which equals 4950! The point here is that the $+$ signs do not necessarily mean that you should do addition as naively indicated.

Let us prepare to approach summing an infinite series by first looking at a related sum of a *finite* number of terms:

$$S = \tfrac{1}{2} + \tfrac{1}{4} + \tfrac{1}{8} + \tfrac{1}{16}$$
$$2S = 1 + \tfrac{1}{2} + \tfrac{1}{4} + \tfrac{1}{8}$$
$$2S - 1 = \tfrac{1}{2} + \tfrac{1}{4} + \tfrac{1}{8}$$
$$2S - 1 + \tfrac{1}{16} = \tfrac{1}{2} + \tfrac{1}{4} + \tfrac{1}{8} + \tfrac{1}{16}$$

Notice that the right side of the equation is what we started with. Therefore,

$$S = 2S - 1 + \tfrac{1}{16}$$

So, adding $(1 - S)$ to both sides and subtracting $\tfrac{1}{16}$, we get

$$S + 1 - S - \tfrac{1}{16} = 2S - S - 1 + 1 + \tfrac{1}{16} - \tfrac{1}{16}$$

so that,

$$1 - \tfrac{1}{16} = S = \tfrac{15}{16}$$

Let us now try this idea on summing our *infinite* Zeno series:

$$S = \tfrac{1}{2} + \tfrac{1}{4} + \tfrac{1}{8} + \tfrac{1}{16} + \tfrac{1}{32} + \tfrac{1}{64} + \ldots$$
$$2S = 1 + \tfrac{1}{2} + \tfrac{1}{4} + \tfrac{1}{8} + \tfrac{1}{16} + \tfrac{1}{32} + \ldots$$
$$2S - 1 = \tfrac{1}{2} + \tfrac{1}{4} + \tfrac{1}{8} + \tfrac{1}{16} + \ldots$$

Once again, we have, on the right side of the equation, exactly what we started with[2]; therefore, $S = 2S - 1$ and so $S = 1$!

Thus, the ordinary rules of arithmetic can be used on this infinite sum. Just as Achilles does not reach the halfway mark, stop, and then go on to the next, and just as Gauss did not have to add the first pair of terms, stop, then add the next, and so on, we also do not have to add two terms, stop, and add the next.

The difficulty in understanding how it is possible to sum an infinite number of quantities into a finite quantity is that we are here confronted with a situation rarely encountered in our daily lives, when usually the only mathematical thought we have to engage in, in terms of our actions, is

finite arithmetic. For instance, balancing your checkbook requires a finite number of arithmetical steps. The reason people feel the puzzle in Zeno's paradox is that the solution requires a type of arithmetic that they are not accustomed to. Contemporary mathematics shows us how a finite amount of time can be sufficient for the completion of infinitely many events. (However, note that if you look at the arithmetic we just did, *this calculation is easier to do on the infinite series than on the finite series*! This is because in the case of the infinite series, we do not have to add back the last term.)

The philosophically productive move here — one that engages us with the real mystery, not removes us from it — is to realize that we have matured within our present conceptual framework and to use this intellectual maturation as an opportunity to explore the world further with our concepts of motion, time, space, infinite series, distance, etc. On the other hand, we should not be too quick to attach ourselves to this solution to Zeno's paradox! Many writers on this topic do not realize that Zeno could have made things much more difficult by posing his question in terms of going $\tfrac{1}{3}$ the distance instead of going $\tfrac{1}{2}$ the distance. One must go $\tfrac{1}{3}$ of the distance. Then one must go a distance $\tfrac{1}{3}$ as long as the *previous* distance traveled, $\tfrac{1}{9}$ of the full distance, and so on.[3] This would have forced us to consider the following infinite sum:

$$S = \tfrac{1}{3} + \tfrac{1}{9} + \tfrac{1}{27} + \tfrac{1}{81} \ldots$$

Here, if we follow the same procedure as earlier, we get $S = 3S - 1$ and thus: $S = \tfrac{1}{2}$! This means that the runner gets only $\tfrac{1}{2}$ of the way to the finish line! The $\tfrac{1}{2}$ marks, even though there are an infinite number of them, would not extend to the finish line. Thus we see that Zeno posed an infinite series problem of minimum difficulty! If you pose one of greater difficulty (or refine the paradox slightly differently, as we shall do shortly) Zeno's paradox cannot be solved in this way.

It should be clear, however, that an objection like "the sum of the Zeno series cannot be finite because you can't ever finish doing the addition" makes no sense because nobody is saying that one must do the addition as naively indicated. It would be like saying that you can't ever pose Zeno's paradox because you can't ever finish showing all of the halfway marks. What one must do instead is find the sum. Just as Gauss found the sum even though he did not do what the teacher naively intended, we must find the Zeno sum without having to add each term to the next, which would take longer than the time we have to do it.

Ultimately, the objection that you cannot sum the Zeno series comes down to a rejection of any infinite concept. This would be consistent in that you would then be rejecting both the paradox and the solution for the same reason. But it would be inconsistent to reject the solution and keep the paradox (which requires the infinite to be stated). In taking this way out, both Zeno's paradox and the solution would no longer exist as such.

Since the Zeno series can be understood and computed, why not allow it as an explanatory conceptual tool for the way we conceive the world? The concept of summing an infinite series is only an extension of the idea of summing a finite series. No one objects to adding $2 + 2$ to get 4. No one thinks this is some kind of mathematical trick that does not appreciate the nature of plurality. On the contrary, $2 + 2 = 4$ gives a precise description of the situation in which one wants to be able to compare finite quantities of objects, lengths, or times. Why then not accept that summing the infinite series gives a precise way to describe Zeno's paradox?

Zeno's paradox suggests the real mystery is how an infinite process can occur within a finite distance and finite time. *Summing an infinite series answers this question.* It is not mysterious that an infinite number of distances come together into a finite distance. Whether Achilles begins near the finish line or at the starting line, it is indeed possible that *a finite distance can consist of an infinite number of distances.* However, intuitively we still feel that there is something mysterious in Zeno's paradox. *The above analysis merely shows us that the mystery is not where we might have thought it was!*

3. Refining Zeno's Paradox

It would be productive now to find a stronger paradox that would provide a greater opportunity to examine and refine our concepts. The idea is that even though there is a way to answer Zeno's paradox, we see that our concepts are far stranger and much further removed from common sense than we originally thought. Summing the infinite series, though logically OK, is still difficult to relate to our perception of reality. It is hard to experience the passing of all the halfway marks. Try to imagine all the halfway marks (infinitely many of them) drawn on the floor of the racetrack and then experiencing Achilles passing by all of them to reach the finish line. You can't. You can only imagine a blur. It is not that our concepts are wrong or mistaken, but rather that our concepts are not the stuff of the world in and of itself.

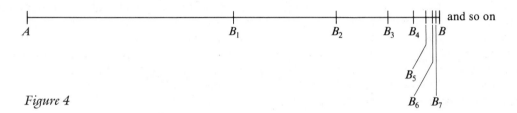

Figure 4

Let us begin our refinement of Zeno's paradox by taking another look at our Zeno diagram below. As the n in the B_n get larger and larger the B_n get closer and closer to B and it becomes more and more difficult to draw, see, or imagine (from our point of view) the tiny gaps between the B_n for the successively larger n. Let us assume that we are drawing our Zeno diagram with a pencil of thickness 1 millimeter. Then, when the gaps between the B_n are smaller than 1 mm, we do the following. Through our conceptual microscope we take a picture of the 1 mm remaining part of the Zeno diagram — say at B_5. We now have an enlarged picture of the gap between B_5 and B. If the length of the remaining interval between Achilles and the finish line at B is 1 meter, the enlargement is also one meter and to scale: It is a "blowup," (like the "blowup" feature used in photo enlargements; see Figure 5).

Now that the picture is blown up, we can continue to use our 1 mm pencil to mark off further B_n until once again — this time at B_{10} — we will have to use our conceptual microscope to take another picture that will be a blowup of the gap between B_{10} and B. It should be intuitively obvious that we can continue this process forever; since there are infinitely many B_n, we can make infinitely many diagrams. Our Zeno diagram was constructed to examine the path of a moving object: Achilles. When we used the infinite series our attention was focused on the distance traveled, that is, what was being added up. Let us focus our attention now on the gap itself, that is, on the distance between Achilles and the finish line.

Our story begins back in the Lyceum. Zeno has just finished posing his paradox of motion to a group who have been ridiculing Parmenides'

view that all is one. Turning to Achilles, their leader, Zeno says:

"You make fun of Parmenides because you think you are so wise. You think you know what space, time, and motion are; but I have just shown that you merely *think* you know! You say Parmenides' views are absurd because they *contradict what your eyes tell you*. But your view is the far more absurd view, for you *contradict yourself!* If a wise man is someone who knows how little he knows, obviously, Achilles, you are anything but wise — you are just the opposite!"

Insulted, Achilles orders his men to seize Zeno.

"Enough," cries Achilles. "I will now defeat both you and your arguments, Zeno!"

Achilles orders his strongest warriors to form a gauntlet, or corridor, that ends at a wall, with Zeno in the middle. Achilles begins at one end and starts running after Zeno who, when he reaches the wall, will be crushed between the wall and Achilles' shield.

Unbeknownst to any of them, however, Zeus has been watching the proceedings from a cloud:

"Hera, come and watch how these brutes think to dismiss the magical query which against my wishes you have thrown down to the mortal philosophers. You said it would make them think, but look! Our poor Zeno's skull is about to be crushed. What a shame. I was hoping we would have millennia of long and lasting amusement at the mortals' attempt to reconcile their contradictory points of view. You have overestimated these foolish mortals. How often have you heard them dismiss the greatest mysteries as simply being mysteries? How their poets go on and on, ad nauseum, about their wonderful lack of explanation! Your game will end up but a beau-

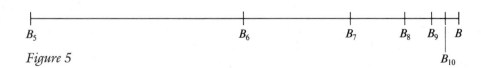

Figure 5

tifully unenlightening poem, and Zeno will be crushed."

"I have already taken care of it."

"What have you done, my dear and clever wife?"

"Watch, dear, and be amazed."

Achilles takes up his shield and begins running toward the wall with Zeno between the shield and the wall. When Achilles is 1 meter away from the wall, Zeno puts his right hand up to block against the shield and his left hand up to brace him against the wall, thinking this might help prevent him from being crushed when, suddenly, he begins to shrink! When the distance between Achilles' shield and the wall has halved, Zeno has shrunk by one-half. When the distance between the shield and the wall is ¼ meter, Zeno has shrunk by one-quarter. And so on. When the distance between the shield and the wall is $\frac{1}{128}$ meter, Zeno has shrunk down to $\frac{1}{128}$ scale. And Zeno keeps shrinking such that as the distance is $\frac{1}{2^n}$ meters, Zeno has shrunk down to $\frac{1}{2^n}$ scale. By the moment Achilles has smashed his shield into the wall, Zeno is nowhere to be seen!

Up in the clouds, Zeus turns to Hera and says, "You must feel very little for your bold young student Zeno, my dear wife, that you should wish him to suffer so sincerely for your folly."

"Bold indeed, but why so certain that he suffers? That mighty warrior's shield did not crush him. Nor was there suffering upon his countenance while he was visible. And this is exactly all that is certain, for he is no longer visible! It is your gloating that hides suffering so insincerely. Were you sincere you would surely recognize that I have bequeathed us all a query worthy of great deliberation and which I am certain will only vindicate my Zeno and make your gloating but a fool's solution to a mystery worthy of even us gods."

Let us look at the situation more closely. We begin with Achilles' shield at point A one meter from the wall and Zeno standing between the shield at A and the wall at B, his arms extended between the shield and the wall (see Figure 6).

Let us examine the situation from Zeno's point of view between the shield and the wall. Doing so will help us discover the source of Hera's confidence.

As Hera pointed out in our story, from the point of view of the outside observers the shield never crushes Zeno. What about from Zeno's point of view? As he begins to shrink he sees Achilles' shield getting larger and larger. By the time Achilles' shield is at, say, $B_{11,000}$, the surface of the shield is still only just barely touching the surface of Zeno's right hand, but the shield is now so big compared to Zeno's body that it looks to him like a giant wall reaching all the way up and all the way down as far as he can see. At the same time, the wall that his left palm is just barely touching seems to go upward forever and downward forever. From Zeno's point of view, the spectators in the Lyceum are even farther away than the already unseen receding base of Achilles' shield, thus they are virtually infinitely far away. Therefore, at this point, *Zeno will observe no fur-*

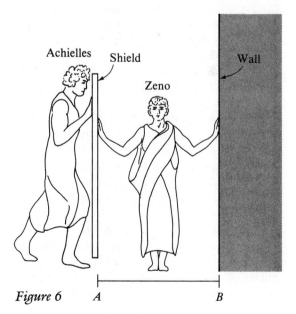

Figure 6 A B

ther changes in his visual field whatsoever. From Zeno's point of view, nothing is happening! Nothing else is moving. There is a virtually infinite shield on his right and a virtually infinite wall on his left. If there ever was some process going on, from his point of view it has stopped (see Figure 7).

Let us now go back to the point of view of the gloating spectators and the unworried Hera. When Achilles' shield first touches Zeno's right hand, the spectators see Zeno shrink. As Achilles' shield approaches the wall they still see Zeno getting smaller and smaller until at some instant before the shield hits the wall Zeno virtually disappears from their sight. At that point they conclude that Zeno must have been crushed when the shield smashed into the wall. Since the spectators see the shield smash into the wall, from their point of view there is no gap. There is no space in which Zeno's extended body can extend and therefore no space in which for him to exist as a real entity. Where, then, is Zeno?

The spectators conclude that Zeno has disappeared and, in some sense, they are right. They cannot see him. And no physical microscope, regardless of how powerful, could allow Zeno to be seen because, after all, his size is 0. Zero multiplied by any (finite) number is still 0. An (extensionless) point magnified by any (finite) magnification is still an extensionless point. From the spectators' point of view alone, Zeno has indeed disappeared.

Since we are aware that there are two points of view here — the point of view of the spectators and the point of view of Zeno — we should address the question of their (in)commensurability. For it is the question of the (in)commensurability of these two points of view that *refines Zeno's paradox*.

Does it make sense, from Zeno's point of view, that at some moment *he* disappears? As we said above, at all moments during which the process is still happening from his point of view, (1) he still exists as an extended being, (2) except for

Achilles' shield and the wall, which still exist in their virtually infinitely enlarged form, the spectators, the Lyceum, and all the rest of the world have disappeared, and (3) nothing is happening in that the picture is static for Zeno, just as the picture is static for the spectators once Achilles' shield hits the wall. So Zeno's understanding of the suggestion that he disappeared would have to be described, from his point of view, as a "popping out of the universe" *for no reason whatsoever*: that is, no reasons from within his point of view could possibly explain a popping out of the universe. For Zeno to understand how it is possible that he disappears he not only would have to favor the spectators' point of view — which would be a strange thing given that from within his point of view it is they who have disappeared, not him — he would have to give up the reasons avail-

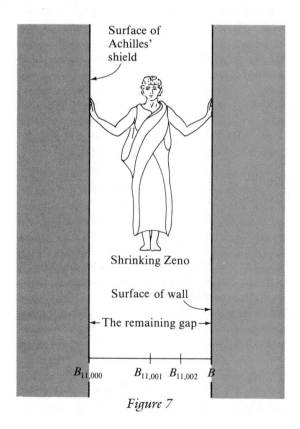

Surface of Achilles' shield

Shrinking Zeno

Surface of wall

← The remaining gap →

$B_{11,000}$ $B_{11,001}$ $B_{11,002}$ B

Figure 7

able to him within his point of view and accept reasons from a point of view to which he has no access.

That is, we can imagine Zeno thinking, as he is shrinking: "My friend Hera has saved me by enlarging the spectators and the universe out of existence!" The idea of something that shrinks continuously (and self-similarly, retaining its same shape) shrinking suddenly and spontaneously out of existence and the idea of something that enlarges continuously (and self-similarly) being suddenly and spontaneously enlarged out of existence are equally unjustified (or, even, equally justified) but (in either case) they are incommensurate. They are incommensurate because the only way it would make sense for Zeno to think that he ever disappears from the universe is for him to think that from the point of view of the spectators at some point he disappears. But, once again, from his point of view it is they who at some point do in fact disappear.

These "popping-out-of-existence" alternatives are incommensurate. To himself, Zeno still exists and from his point of view there can be no reason to simply decree that he suddenly and spontaneously stops existing. It is also as equally unjustified to decree that the spectators in the Lyceum spontaneously vanish from the universe, just to make things consistent with Zeno's point of view. Someone could say that, from each other's point of view, the other disappears. But how then would we reconcile these two apparently irreconcilable, noncommensurate points of view?

If from each point of view, taken separately, it is true to say that the other pops out of existence, then a fundamental revision of our most basic concept of existence is required; it would entail that Zeno's paradox reaches into the very heart of existence — that existence itself is somehow paradoxical.

If our shrinking Zeno paradox is to be successfully addressed, we must reconcile the two apparently incommensurate points of view, and

not simply and arbitrarily pick one view over the other. Either we take the spectators' point of view and conclude for no sufficient reason that Zeno's body has become an extensionless point, *B*, or we can take Zeno's point of view and conclude without sufficient reason that the spectators occupy no position on the floor of the Lyceum, since they are infinitely far away from Zeno.[4] Each alternative makes sense relative to the relevant points of view considered separately. But the two points of view are incommensurate and mutually exclusive.

Let us therefore instead of dismissing Zeno from the realm of existence rejoin him on his journey. More than a second of time has gone by and he knows that, since Achilles is traveling at one meter per second, Achilles' shield relative to the spectators' point of view has indeed reached the wall. From Zeno's point of view, now after a second, he is there with the (now not merely virtually but *actually*) infinitely large shield touching his right palm, the wall touching his left palm. From his own point of view Zeno knows that the spectators seem to have disappeared but have not actually disappeared. He reasons as follows. "I know it is my own point of view that dictates that the spectators will become infinitely far away from me when I become (from their point of view) an extensionless point. I also know, when the spectators become infinitely far away from me, Achilles' shield will have grown infinitely large and therefore any part of it will be infinitely large. But, by Zeus, how then could I possibly continue to see a shield, or myself for that matter, or anything at all?"

We will now, as Zeno did, ask a perplexing question: How can it be that Achilles' moving shield ever makes contact with the wall at *B*? We want to focus our attention on what the gap is like from our shrinking Zeno's point of view. Immediately we notice that from his point of view Achilles' shield is not moving. Indeed, within the gap, *nothing is happening whatsoever*. This is because as the shield (from Achilles' point of view) gets closer to the wall, from Zeno's point of view they always remain an arm's length apart. If he were to look up and to the sides he would see the lines extending further and further upward. However, he does not see or feel the walls moving.

If we construct blowups as before, the pictures will be exactly the same except the shield and wall get taller. Note, too, that there is a (virtual) variant from picture to picture. If each picture were a movie of the moving Achilles, then if Achilles moves at the constant velocity of 1 meter per second (as described in the original Zeno diagram) then his shield would be seen through the microscope to be traveling 32 times faster in each subsequent diagram. For example, the surface of the shield facing Zeno would be seen to be moving at 32 meters per second in the first enlargement, 32^2 meters per second in the second enlargement, 32^3 meters per second in the third enlargement, 32^n meters per second in the nth enlargement.

When n is sufficiently large, Achilles' shield will *seem* to be moving faster than light. Technically, this is neither an illusion nor a hallucination, since the image being seen is an actual image; it is *not* like the case of the drunk who sees pink elephants. And yet what is being seen is not the actual motion of the shield which, after all, is at any point in its journey from A to B traveling at 1 meter per second. It is the motion of one part of an image relative to other parts of the image. This raises the philosophical question of what makes some images virtual, or only images, and some images the images of things that are seen and therefore "real." The problem, in other words, is that supposedly one kind of motion we are seeing is real motion of real things, while other motions we are seeing are only the motions of images that—while they do correspond, by the rule of enlargement, to something real—are themselves not real. The virtual motion of Achilles' shield in our enlargements, however, does not in actuality violate the speed of light.

It is obvious that we are beginning our journey deep into the tail end of the sequence of B_n. In a sense, we have constructed a conceptual microscope through which we can see something that we understand as a place beyond all the halfway marks and yet before the wall. Our conceptual microscope is already in place through our consideration of enlargement diagrams that picture our shrinking Zeno. The problem here is that these intervals collapse to a point in the limit. But a point does not fit conceptually into the pattern of our diagrams. That is, a point is obviously qualitatively different from an interval in that a point is not the sort of thing that can be further divided.

But how can this be? We know that since Achilles is moving at one meter per second, and the wall is one meter away, that from Achilles' point of view after exactly one second the shield makes contact with the wall, i.e., there is no space between them. We also know that from Zeno's point of view there is no reason whatsoever that the shield and wall should *ever* make contact. This is the very essence of our refined paradox. We know, from one point of view, that it is absolutely *necessary* that contact happens and that, from the other point of view, it is *impossible* that contact ever happens!

Our shrinking Zeno paradox does not *add* anything to the distance between A and B. It merely illuminates, via a sort of conceptual microscope, what is already there and what is already paradoxical. It does, however, in a sense add something to the *conceptual* space between A and B. It forces us to add that strange place where our shrinking Zeno is to our conception of space. An infinitesimal calculus would offer some solution to this paradox by adding the place where Zeno now is to our concept of space, thereby creating a new mathematical spatial object. And though our shrinking Zeno paradox alters Zeno's original form of his paradoxes, the key issues remain the same. The solution offered to the original paradox had eliminated the issue of infinite process

—finite distance. The shrinking Zeno paradox does not depend on the infinite—finite issue. However, the key issue that the gap between two things is paradoxical—Parmenides' question of what separates one thing from another—is preserved. Thus it is indeed right to call our shrinking Zeno paradox Zeno's paradox. *And it cannot be solved by summing the series nor by standard calculus.*

4. Where Is Zeno?

We now have a real problem on our hands! The problem is this. From his own point of view, Zeno has not disappeared; therefore, he is somewhere. From the spectators' point of view, he has disappeared. Therefore, as far as they are concerned, he is nowhere. What does it mean to say that X is somewhere? It means that X is in a containing space. To have a location is to be embedded in a space. Well, what about our shrinking Zeno? Where is he? How can we attribute to him the kind of somewhereness that we usually attribute to things? Can we say that he is in the Lyceum? From his point of view, he is infinitely far away from anything in the Lyceum. Furthermore, if you looked through the Lyceum for him, even armed with the most (finitely) powerful microscope in the world, you would not find him there.

Yet, we could say that his hand is near the rest of his body and that it is on the wall rather than, say, on his forehead. This is puzzling because the people in the Lyceum are also near the wall! One problem with the idea that Zeno is somewhere is that the surface of the wall and the surface of the shield are in contact—so how can Zeno's right hand be on Achilles' shield and his left hand be on the wall? If the shield and wall are in contact, there is no space between them!

Asking where shrinking Zeno is, is in some ways like asking: *Where are the points of space?* Even with our most powerful microscope, you

will not be able to find them. Yet they are somewhere: there, in *that* location and not in some other.

Obviously, our shrinking Zeno paradox examines the idea of motion differently from the paradox of Achilles running the racecourse. Instead of looking at a distance and examining what happens across a distance, the shrinking Zeno paradox focuses on motion at one instant of time in one point of space—as does Zeno's original paradox of the arrow. If an arrow is moving, then it is moving at each instant of time and at each point along a path. Time is conceived of as being made of moments and space is conceived of as being made of points (places). How can you find the motion in each instant and place occupied at that instant? You can't. At each moment the arrow is where it is. At each moment the arrow is the same as a stationary arrow at the same instant in the same place. Zeno's paradox of the arrow is that if you can't find the motion in the units of which time and space are made of, then how can it be possible to find it in time and space? If John is not at any place in this room, then how can he be in this room?

Calculus addresses this through the idea of a derivative. A derivative is constructed by treating the point as trapped between two points coming together—*as in our shrinking Zeno paradox*. Thus, our shrinking Zeno paradox shows that Zeno's original paradoxes of motion have not really been solved. Asking where our shrinking Zeno is, is to ask where the points of space are and, ultimately, to inquire into the deeply mysterious question of what space is made of.

After all, where are the spectators in the Lyceum? If you ask our shrinking Zeno, he cannot see them and he could not see them through any telescope, no matter how powerful. From Zeno's point of view, they are nowhere! Again, each could say "I am here where I am." They would point to things available to their point of view and say they are near those things. But once again there is a problem with the idea of where things are with respect to the two incommensurate points of view.

In noting that the idea of a derivative in calculus involved exactly this type of image, we note that here, in the gap, philosophy and mathematics meet. Philosophical reflection offers both mathematics and science new mysterious spaces to explore and conceptualize. This is already partly done with infinitesimal calculus and quantum physics. In standard calculus, the real numbers are used. In infinitesimal calculus, certain new types of quantities are used which mark and conceptualize that place where our shrinking Zeno is when he has shrunk out of sight. Quantum mechanics postulates that the ordinary concept of space and time completely breaks down where our shrinking Zeno is.[5]

To recognize that Zeno's paradoxes are not solved is not to make the extravagant claim that our concepts of space, time, motion, and identity are worthless and that we should therefore give up rationality. Rather, the purpose is to give a precise way of focusing our attention on the discrepancy between reality and our concepts. To function as rational beings we must have concepts, which are the medium of rational consciousness. Without concepts, there can be no paradox. Our eyes are not windows. Our minds do not have direct access to reality. We must always interpret our experience according to concepts. Zeno's paradox thus examines the relationship of our minds to the world.

Since what is inside our minds is not, and never can be, an exact copy of reality, there will always be paradoxes that must be addressed to improve our understanding of our relationship (or lack thereof) to reality.

Recalling now that Zeno's intention was to use his paradoxes to defend Parmenides, what are we to make of Parmenides' assertion that "all is one"? Zeno's paradox has just shown us why the commonsense notion of the universe as an ever-changing collection of many different things, separated from other things, all constantly moving about in space (the commonsense view) *is deeply paradoxical*. Zeno's paradox is a conceptual warning sign: Beware of Common Sense![6]

NOTES

1. Technically, we only begin to discuss geometric series here. For a more complete and fuller treatment, see our *Zeno's Paradox Refined*. For a complete, technical mathematical treatment, see any book on real analysis, such as Walter Rudin, *Principles of Mathematical Analysis*, New York: McGraw-Hill.

2. The full justification of this method of adding up an infinite series is actually more involved than just doing what we have done. For a full treatment of this, see any book on real analysis or advanced calculus. Look up "geometric series" in the index of any such book. Note that we could apply the above method to

$$S = 1 + 2 + 4 + 8 + \ldots + 2^k + \ldots$$
$$2S = 2 + 4 + 8 + \ldots$$
$$2S + 1 = S$$
$$S = -1.$$

This is clearly nonsense since this sum of increasing terms would have to be of infinite value. Furthermore, there is no way that we are going to add up positive numbers and get a negative. One must learn more of the theory of infinite series to know which methods can be applied when.

3. The analogy of going by ⅓'s paradox (as given) to the going by ½'s paradox is that in the ½'s case, each increment is ½ of the previous increment. In the ½'s case, this is the same as going ½ of the remaining distance. In the ⅓'s case, it is not the same as going ⅓ of the remaining distance. For instance, at the second increment, Achilles goes ⅓ of the previous distance but only ⅙ of the remaining distance.

4. For instance, if he were holding a ruler in his hand, the ruler would not be visible to the spectator through any finite microscope, no matter how powerful. Therefore, the distance between him and the spectator would be infinite compared to that ruler. Furthermore, if he laid that ruler side to side any finite number of times, he would never reach the spectators.

5. In our *Zeno's Paradox Refined: An Eleatic Model of Paradoxical Rationality*, forthcoming, we show precisely how, and the problem continues to remain in contemporary mathematics, science, and philosophy.

6. We would like to thank Garrett Thomson and Raymond Martin for reading an earlier draft of this paper and giving us many helpful comments.

Further Questions

1. What is the function of paradoxes?

2. If the authors are right that there will always be paradoxes, what do you think this means for rationality in general, theories in particular? Do you agree with how the authors would answer that question? Why or why not?

3. Where do concepts like space, time, and motion, with which we try to understand the world, come from? Are they just fictions, mere make-believe? Or are they more? What do you think is the difference between concepts and fictions?

4. Go to your current (or recent) mathematics teacher and say you've been learning the original Zeno's paradox of motion. Do not say yet that you have a refined paradox in your pocket. Your goal is to get the teacher to talk about the infinite series. Listen with interest and make sure you understand what you are being told. Tell the teacher this is a very good answer. Then, tell the teacher about the shrinking Zeno paradox. Remember that the point is that what must be accounted for is that Zeno can to himself exist. (a) If the teacher says that this is but a fantasy, ask whether Einstein's riding a beam of light is but a fantasy. (b) If the teacher says your argument somehow goes beyond the accepted canons of mathematical explanation, ask whether people might have said that about the original paradox long before the sum of the infinite series was ever thought of.

Further Readings

Grunbaum, A. *Philosophical Problems of Space and Time*, 2nd ed. Dordrecht and Boston: D. Reidel, 1973. An excellent and thorough work, with detailed discussions of some of the philosophical implications of the mathematical underpinnings of the problems raised by Zeno's paradoxes.

Kolak, Daniel, and David Goloff. *Zeno's Paradox Refined: An Eleatic Model of Paradoxical Rationality*, forthcoming. Further and more detailed elaborations of the extent to which contemporary mathematics and philosophy can deal with the shrinking Zeno paradox and the extent to which they cannot, with discussions of hyper-real numbers, ultrafilters, and beyond. Mathematical demonstrations required for a thorough understanding of the problem are provided, along with a new model of paradoxical rationality.

Goloff, David and Kolak, Daniel, *Mathematical Thought*, Macmillan. More examples of how mathematics represents a variety of concepts. Included are discussions of geometry and algebra, probability and statistics, number theory, etc.

Time

PAUL DAVIES

Paul Davies is Professor of Theoretical Physics at the University of Newcastle-upon-Tyne, England, lecturer in applied mathematics at King's College, University of London, and visiting fellow at the Institute of Astronomy. He has written many excellent, nontechnical books on physics for the nonspecialist, including *Other Worlds* (Touchstone, 1980), *God and the New Physics* (Simon & Schuster, 1984), and *The Edge of Infinity: Where the Universe Came From and How It Will End* (Simon & Schuster, 1981).

In the following selection, he describes the mind-boggling discoveries physicists have made about the nature of time. "The most profound puzzle," he writes, "is the fact that, whatever we may experience mentally, time does not pass, nor does there exist a past, present and future. These statements are so stunning that most scientists lead a sort of dual life, accepting them in the laboratory, but rejecting them without thought in daily life."

Reading Questions

1. What is the "time dilation effect"?
2. What is the "relativity principle"?
3. What effect does gravity have on time?
4. What is the argument between the Skeptic and the Physicist about? Who do you think "wins" and why? What conclusion does Davies draw from the dialogue?
5. What implications does Davies think the physics of time has for the view that God is omniscient?
6. Compare your "common-sense" notion of time with what physics claims to be the truth. How do you account for this dramatic difference?
7. Is your sensation that time passes merely a psychological effect, like dizzyness? What philosophical implications does this raise? What is the connection between your consciousness and time?
8. If the whole universe were running backwards, what would it look like to an observer within it?

'There is not even a meaning to the word experience *which would not presuppose the distinction between past and future.'*

CARL VON WEIZSÄCKER

'But at my back I always hear Time's wingèd chariot hurrying near'

ANDREW MARVELL

TWO GREAT REVOLUTIONS gave birth to the new physics: the quantum theory and the theory of relativity. The latter, almost exclusively due to the work of Einstein, is a theory of space, time and motion. Its consequences are as equally baffling and profound as the quantum theory, and challenge many cherished notions about the nature of the universe. Never is this more so than in the theory's treatment of time—a subject of intense and longstanding concern in all the world's great religions.

Time is so fundamental to our experience of the world that any attempt to tinker with it meets with great scepticism and resistance. Every week I receive manuscripts by amateur scientists intent on finding fault with Einstein's work, attempting to restore the commonsense, traditional concept of time despite almost eighty years of success during which not a single experiment has marred the flawless predictions of the theory of relativity.

Our very notion of personal identity—the self, the soul—is closely bound up with memory and *enduring* experience. It is not sufficient to proclaim 'I exist', at this instant. To *be* an individual implies a continuity of experience together with some linking feature, such as memory. The strong emotional and religious overtones of the subject probably account both for the resistance to the claims of the new physics and for the deep fascination which scientists and laymen alike share for the mind-bending consequences of the theory of relativity.

The so-called special theory of relativity, published in 1905, arose from attempts to reconcile an apparent conflict between the motion of material bodies and the propagation of electromagnetic disturbances. In particular, the behaviour of light signals seems to be in flagrant violation of the long-standing principle that all uniform motion is purely relative. The technical details need not concern us here. The result was that Einstein restored the relativity principle, even for the case when light signals are involved, but at a price.

The first casualty of the special theory was the belief that time is absolute and universal. Einstein demonstrated that time is, in fact, elastic and can be stretched and shrunk by motion. Each observer carries around his own personal scale of time, and it does not generally agree with anybody else's. In our own frame, time never appears distorted, but relative to another observer who is moving differently, our time can be wrenched out of step with their time.

The time dilation effect, now a routine experience for physicists, can be demonstrated by using rapidly moving, sensitive atomic clocks, or subatomic particles with known decay rates. The moving clock runs slow relative to its neighbour. This leads to the famous 'twins effect' in which an astronaut returns from a high-speed voyage some years younger than his Earthbound twin.

This weird dislocation of time scales opens the way to a type of time travel. In a sense, we are all travellers in time, heading towards the future, but the elasticity of time enables some people to get there faster than others. Rapid motion enables you to put the brakes on your own time scale, and let the world rush by, as it were. By this strategy it is possible to reach a distant moment more quickly than by sitting still. In principle one could reach the year 2000 in a few hours. However, to achieve an appreciable timewarp speeds of many thousands of miles per second are necessary. At currently available rocket speeds only precision atomic clocks can reveal the minute dilations. The key to these effects is the speed of light. As it is approached, so the timewarp escalates. The theory forbids anyone to break the light barrier, which would have the effect of turning time inside out.

It is possible to telescope time dramatically using high-speed subatomic particles. Whirled about in a giant accelerator very close to the speed of light, particles called muons have been 'kept alive' for dozens of times longer than would be expected if they were at rest (when they decay in about a microsecond).

Equally extraordinary effects afflict space, which is also elastic. When time is stretched, space is shrunk. Rushing on a train through a railway station, the station clock runs slightly slower as viewed from your frame of reference, relative to that of a porter on the platform. In compensation, the platform appears to you to be somewhat shorter. Of course we never notice such effects because they are too small at ordinary speeds, but they are easily measured on sensitive instruments. The mutual distortions of space and time can be regarded as a conversion of space (which shrinks) into time (which stretches). A second of time, however, is worth an awful lot of space — about 186,000 miles to be precise.

Time distortions of this sort are a favourite sci-fi gimmick, but there is nothing fictional about them. They really do occur. One bizarre phenomenon is the so-called twins effect. An itinerant twin blasts off to a nearby star, nudging the light barrier. The stay-at-home twin waits for him to return ten years later. When the rocket gets back, the Earth-bound twin finds his brother has aged only one year to his ten. High speed has enabled him to experience only one year of time, during which ten years have elapsed on Earth.

Einstein went on to generalize his theory to include the effects of gravity. The resulting general theory of relativity incorporates gravity, not as a force, but a distortion of spacetime geometry. In this theory, spacetime is not 'flat', obeying the usual rules of school geometry, but curved or warped, giving rise to both spacewarps and timewarps.

. . . Modern instruments are so sensitive that even the Earth's gravitational timewarp can be detected by clocks in rockets. Time really does run faster in space, where the Earth's gravity is weaker.

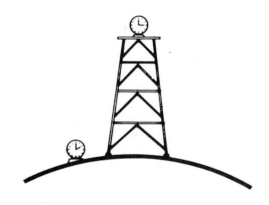

Gravity slows time, as may be demonstrated experimentally even on Earth. The clock at the top of the tower gains relative to that at the base.

The stronger the gravity, the more pronounced is the timewarp. Some stars are known where the grip of gravity is so ferocious that time there is slowed by several per cent relative to us. In fact, these stars are on the brink of the threshold at which runaway timewarps set in. If the gravity of such a star were a few times greater, the timewarp would escalate until, at a critical value of the gravity, time would grind to a halt altogether. Viewed from Earth, the surface of the star would be frozen into immobility. We could not, however, see this extraordinary temporal suspension because the light by which we would view it is also seized by the same torpidity, and its frequency depressed beyond the visible region of the spectrum. The star would appear black.

Theory suggests that a star in this condition could not remain inert, but would succumb to its own intense gravity and implode in a microsecond to a spacetime singularity, leaving behind a hole in space — a black hole. The timewarp of the erstwhile star remains imprinted in the empty space.

A black hole, therefore, represents a rapid route to eternity. In this extreme case, not only would a rocket-bound twin reach the future quicker, he could reach the *end of time* in the twinkling of an eye! At the instant he enters the hole, all of eternity will have passed outside according to his relative determination of 'now.' Once inside the hole, therefore, he will be imprisoned in a timewarp, unable to return to the outside universe again, because the outside universe will have happened. He will be, literally, beyond the end of time as far as the rest of the universe is concerned. To emerge from the hole, he would have to come out before he went in. This is absurd and shows there is no escape. The inexorable grip of the hole's gravity drags the hapless astronaut towards the singularity where, a microsecond later, he reaches the edge of time, and obliteration; the singularity marks the end of a one-way journey to 'nowhere' and 'nowhen.' It is a nonplace where the physical universe ceases.

The revolution in our conception of time which has accompanied the theory of relativity is best summarized by saying that, previously, time was regarded as absolute, fixed, and universal — independent of material bodies or observers. Today time is seen to be *dynamical*. It can stretch and shrink, warp and even stop altogether at a singularity. Clock rates are not absolute, but relative to the state of motion or gravitational situation of the observer.

Liberating time from the strait-jacket of universality, and allowing each observer's time to roll forward freely and independently, forces us to abandon some long-standing assumptions. For example, there can be no unanimous agreement about the choice of 'now.' In the twins experiment, the rocket twin, during his outward trip, might wonder: 'What is my twin on Earth doing *now*?' But the dislocation of their relative time

scales means that 'now' in the frame of the rocket is quite a different moment from 'now' as judged on Earth. There is no universal 'present moment.' If two events, A and B, occurring at separated places, are regarded as simultaneous by one observer, another observer will see A occur before B, while yet another may regard B as occurring first.

The idea that the time order of two events might appear different to different observers seems paradoxical. Can the target shatter before the gun fires? Fortunately for causality, this does not happen. For events A and B to have an uncertain sequence, they must occur within a short enough duration that it would be impossible for light to travel from place A to place B in that interval. In the theory of relativity, light signals make all the rules, and in particular they forbid any influence or signal to travel faster than they do. If light isn't fast enough to connect A and B, nothing is, so A and B cannot influence one another in any way. There is no causal connection between them; reversing the time order of A and B does not amount to reversing cause and effect.

One inevitable victim of the fact that there is no universal present moment is the tidy division of time into past, present and future. These terms may have meaning in one's immediate locality, but they can't apply everywhere. Questions such as 'What is happening *now* on Mars?' are intended to refer to a particular instant on that planet. But as we have seen, a space traveller sweeping past Earth in a rocket who asked the same question at the same instant would be referring to a different moment on Mars. In fact, the range of possible 'nows' on Mars available to an observer near Earth (depending on his motion) actually spans several minutes. When the distance to the subject is greater, so is this range of 'nows.' For a distant quasar 'now' could refer to any interval over billions of years. Even the effect of strolling around on foot alters the 'present moment' on a quasar by thousands of years!

The abandonment of a distinct past, present and future is a profound step, for the temptation to assume that only the present 'really exists' is great. It is usually presumed, without thinking, that the future is as yet unformed and perhaps undetermined; the past has gone, remembered but relinquished. Past and future, one wishes to believe, do not exist. Only one instant of reality seems to occur 'at a time.' The theory of relativity makes nonsense of such notions. Past, present and future must be equally real, for one person's past is another's present and another's future.

The physicist's attitude to time is strongly conditioned by his experiences with the effects of relativity and can appear quite alien to the layman, although the physicist himself rarely thinks twice about it. He does not regard time as a sequence of events which *happen*. Instead, all of past and future are simply *there*, and time extends in either direction from any given moment in much the same way as space stretches away from any particular place. In fact, the comparison is more than an analogy, for space and time become inextricably interwoven in the theory of relativity, united into what physicists call *spacetime*.

Our psychological perception of time differs so radically from the physicist's model that even many physicists have come to doubt whether some vital ingredient has been omitted. Eddington once remarked that there is a sort of 'back door' into our minds through which time enters in addition to its usual route through our laboratory instruments and senses. Our sensation of time is somehow more elementary than our sensation of say, spatial orientation or matter. It is an internal, rather than a bodily experience. Specifically, we feel the *passage* of time—a sensation which is so pronounced that it constitutes the most elementary aspect of our experience. It is a kinetic backdrop against which all our thoughts and activity are perceived.

In their search for this mysterious time-flux many scientists have become deeply confused. All physicists recognize that there is a past-future asymmetry in the universe, produced by the operation of the second law of thermodynamics.

But when the basis of that law is carefully examined, the asymmetry seems to evaporate.

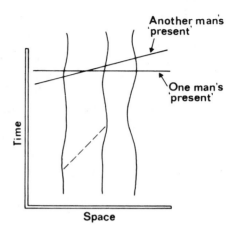

Physicists do not regard time as passing but laid out as part of 'spacetime,' a four-dimensional structure depicted here as a two-dimensional sheet by suppressing two space dimensions. A point on the sheet is an 'event.' The wiggly lines are the paths of bodies that move about; the broken line is the path of a light signal sent between two bodies. The horizontal line through the figure represents a slice through all of space at one instant from the point of view of one observer. Another observer, moving differently, would require the oblique slice. Thus, there must be a temporal (vertical) extension to make sense of the world. There is no universal 'slice' representing a single, common, 'present.' For that reason, division into a universal past, present and future is impossible.

This paradox can easily be illustrated. Suppose, in a sealed room, the top is removed from a bottle of scent. After a while the scent will have evaporated and dispersed throughout the room, its perfume apparent to anyone. The transition from liquid scent to perfumy air—from order to disorder—is irreversible. We should not expect, however long we wait, for the disseminated scent molecules to find their way back spontaneously into the scent bottle and there to reconstitute the liquid. The evaporation and diffusion of the scent provides a classic example of asymmetry between past and future. If we witnessed a film showing the scent returning to the bottle we should spot immediately that the film was being run backwards in the projector. It is not reversible.

Yet there is a paradox here. The scent evaporates and disperses under the impact of billions of molecular bombardments. The molecules of air in their ceaseless thermal agitation serve to knock the scent molecules about at random, shuffling and reshuffling, until the scent is inextricably mixed with the air. However, any given individual molecular collision is perfectly reversible. Two molecules approach, bounce and retreat. Nothing time asymmetric in that. The reverse process would also be approach, bounce and retreat.

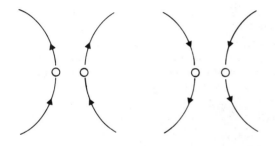

The origin of time asymmetry in the world is a mystery when we examine matter at the atomic level. The collision between any two molecules is completely reversible, and displays no preferred past-future orientation.

The mystery of time's arrow — how can a past-future asymmetry come from symmetrically colliding molecules — has exercised the imaginations of many eminent physicists. The problem was first stated clearly by Ludwig Boltzmann in the late nineteenth century, but the controversy continues today. Some scientists have asserted that there exists a peculiar non-material quality, a time-flux, that is responsible for the arrow of time. They assert that ordinary molecular mo-

tions are incapable of imprinting a past-future asymmetry on time, so that this extra ingredient, the time-flux, is essential. Efforts have even been made to trace the origin of the flux to quantum processes or the expansion of the universe. In many ways the belief in a time-flux is closely analogous to — and equally as dubious as — the belief in a life-force.

The mistake is to overlook the fact that time asymmetry, like life, is a holistic concept, and cannot be reduced to the properties of individual molecules. There is no inconsistency between symmetry at the molecular level, and asymmetry on a macroscopic scale. They are simply two different levels of description. One suspects then, that time doesn't really 'flow' at all; it's all in the mind.

When we try to pin down the origin of the time-flux in our perceptions we encounter the same tangle of paradox and confusion that greets attempts to understand the self, and it is hard to resist the impression that the two problems are really closely related. It is only in the flowing river of time that we can perceive ourselves. Hofstadter has written of the 'whirling vortex of self-reference' that produces what we call consciousness and self-awareness, and I strongly believe that it is this very vortex that drives the psychological time-flux. It is for this reason I maintain that the secret of mind will only be solved when we understand the secret of time.

Naïve images of time are to be found everywhere in art and literature: time's arrow, the river of time, time's chariot, time marching on. It is often said that the 'now' or present moment of our consciousness is steadily moving forward through time from past to future, so that, eventually, the year 2000 will become 'now' and by the same token the instant in which you read this will by now have been passed over and consigned to history. Sometimes the now is considered anchored, and time itself is thought to flow, as a river flows past a bankside observer. These images are inseparable from our feelings of free will. The future seems not yet formed, and thus capable of being shaped by our actions before it arrives. Yet surely all this is rubbish?

Problems instantly crop up when one tries to defend the above imagery. A conversation in 1983 between a physicist and a sceptic might go something like this:

Sceptic: I just came across this quote from Einstein: 'You have to accept the idea that subjective time with its emphasis on the now has no objective meaning . . . the distinction between past, present and future is only an illusion, however persistent.' Surely Einstein must have been off his rocker?

Physicist: Not at all. In the external world there is no past, present and future. How could the present ever be determined with instruments? It's a purely psychological concept.

Sceptic: Oh come now, you can't be serious. Everybody knows the future hasn't happened yet, whereas the past is gone — we remember it happening. How can you confuse yesterday with tomorrow, or today for that matter?

Physicist: Of course you must make a distinction between various days in sequence, but it's the labels you use that I object to. Even you would agree that tomorrow never comes.

Sceptic: That's just a play on words. Tomorrow does come, only when it does we call it today.

Physicist: Precisely. Every day is called today on that day. Every moment is called 'now' when it is experienced. Division into *the* past and *the* future is the result of a linguistic muddle. Let me help you sort it out. Each instant of time can be ascribed a definite date. For example, 2 p.m. on 3 October 1997. The dating system is arbitrary, but once we have decided on a convention the date of any particular event or moment is fixed once and for all. By giving date labels to all events, we can describe everything in the world without recourse to dubious constructions like past, present and future.

Sceptic: But 1997 *is* in the future. It hasn't happened yet. Your date system ignores a crucial aspect of time: namely, its flow.

Physicist: What do you mean '1997 *is* in the future'? It is in the past of 1998.

Sceptic: But it's not 1998 *now*.

Physicist: Now?

Sceptic: Yes, *now*.

Physicist: When is now? Every moment is 'now' when we experience it.

Sceptic: This now. I mean *this* now.

Physicist: You mean the 1983 now?

Sceptic: If you like.

Physicist: Not the 1998 now?

Sceptic: No.

Physicist: Then all you are saying is that 1997 is in the future of 1983, but in the past of 1998. I don't deny that. It is precisely what my dating system describes. Nothing more. So you see, your talk of the past and future is unnecessary, after all.

Sceptic: But that's absurd! 1997 hasn't happened yet. That is a fact you will surely agree with?

Physicist: Naturally. All you are saying is that our conversation occurs before 1997. Let me repeat. I don't deny there is an ordered sequence of events, with a definite before–after or past–future relation between them. I am simply denying the existence of *the* past, *the* present and *the* future. There clearly is not *a* present, for you and I have both experienced many 'presents' in our life. Some events lie in the past or future of other events, but the events themselves are simply *there*, they don't *happen* one by one.

Sceptic: Is that what some physicists mean when they say that past and future events exist alongside the present — that they are somehow *there*, but we only come across these events one after the other?

Physicist: We don't really 'come across' them at all. Every event of which we are conscious, we experience. They don't lie in wait for us to creep up on them, temporally speaking. There are simply events, and mental states associated with them. You talk as though today's mind is somehow transported forward in time to stumble on tomorrow's events. Your mind is extended in time. Tomorrow's mental states reflect tomorrow's events, today's reflect today's.

Sceptic: Surely my consciousness moves forward from today to tomorrow?

Physicist: No! Your mind *is* conscious both today and tomorrow. Nothing *moves* forward, backward or sideways.

Sceptic: But I *feel* time passing.

Physicist: Hold on a minute, if you will forgive the expression. First you say your mind is moving forward in time, then you say that time itself is moving forward. Which is it to be?

Sceptic: I see time as like a flowing river, bringing future events towards me. Either I can see my consciousness as fixed, and time flowing through it, from future to past, or time is fixed and my consciousness moves from past towards the future. I think the two descriptions are equivalent. The motion is relative.

Physicist: The motion is illusory! How can time move? If it moves it must have a speed. What speed? One day per day? It's nonsense. A day is a day is a day.

Sceptic: But if time doesn't pass, how do things change?

Physicist: Change occurs because objects move about through space *in* time. Time doesn't move. When I was a child I used to wonder 'Why is it *now*, rather than some other time?' When I grew up I learned that the question was meaningless. It can be asked at every moment of time.

Sceptic: I think it's a perfectly legitimate question. After all, why is it 1983?

Physicist: Why is *what* 1983?

Sceptic: Well, why is it 1983 *now*?

Physicist: Your question is a bit like asking 'Why am I *me* and not somebody else?' I am myself by definition—whichever person asks the question. Obviously in 1983 we regard 1983 as 'now.' The same would apply for any year. A legitimate question could be 'Why am I living in 1983 and not, say, 5,000 B.C.?' or 'Why are we having this conversation in 1983 and not 1998?' but there is no need to appeal to notions of past, present and future at all in such discussions.

Sceptic: I'm still not convinced. Almost all our daily thoughts and activities, the tense structure of our language, our hopes, fears and beliefs, are rooted in the fundamental distinction of past, present and future. I am afraid of death, because I have yet to face it, and I am uncertain what lies beyond. But I am not afraid because I don't know of my existence before birth. We can't be afraid of the past. Again, the past is unalterable. We know what happened because of our memories. But we don't know the future, and we believe that it is undetermined, that our actions can change it. As for the present, well, that is our instant of contact with the external world, when our minds can order our bodies to act. Byron wrote 'Act, act in the living present.' That sums it up admirably for me.

Physicist: Most of what you say is true, but still does not require a moving present. Of course there is an asymmetry between past and future, not just in our experiences such as memory, but in the external world. The second law of thermodynamics, for example, ensures that systems tend to become more and more disordered. Other systems possess accumulating records and 'memory.' Think of the craters on the moon: that is a record of past, not future events. All you are saying is that later brain states have more stored information than earlier brain states. We then make the mistake of translating that simple fact into the muddled and ambiguous words 'We remember the past, not the future' in spite of the fact that *the* past is a meaningless phrase. Indeed, in 1998 we shall remember 1997, which *is* in the future of 1983. Stick to dates and you don't need tenses, or the flow of time, or the now.

Sceptic: But you just said 'shall remember' yourself.

Physicist: I could have said: 'My brain state in 1998 records information about events in 1997. But 1997 is in the future of 1983, so is not recorded in my brain states of 1983.' See, no need for past and future after all.

Sceptic: What about the fear of the future, free-will and unpredictability? If the future already exists that must mean complete determinism. Nothing can be changed. Freewill is a sham.

Physicist: The future doesn't 'already' exist. That statement is a contradiction in terms, for it says 'events exist simultaneously with events prior to them' which is obviously nonsense by definition of the word 'prior.' As for unpredictability, that is a practical limitation. It's true we can only predict certain simple events, such as an eclipse of the sun, because of the world's complexity. But predictability is not the same as determinism. You are mixing your epistemology with your metaphysics. Future states of the world could all be determined by prior events, but still be unpredictable in practical terms.

Sceptic: But is the future determined? Sorry. Are all events completely determined by prior events?

Physicist: Actually no. For example, the quantum theory reveals that, at the atomic level, events occur spontaneously, without complete prior causation.

Sceptic: So the future doesn't exist! We *can* change it!

Physicist: The future will be what it will be, whether our actions beforehand are involved or not. The physicist views spacetime as laid out like a map, with time extending along one side. Events are marked as points on the map — some events are linked by causal relations to prior events, others, like the decay of a radioactive nucleus, are labelled 'spontaneous.' It's all *there*, whether the causal links are incorporated or not. So my contention that there is no past, present and future says nothing about freewill or determinism at all. That's quite a separate subject — and a minefield of confusions.

Sceptic: You still haven't explained to me why I *feel* the flow of time.

Physicist: I'm not a neurologist. It has probably got something to do with short-term memory processes.

Sceptic: You're claiming it's all in the mind — an illusion?

Physicist: You would be unwise to appeal to your feelings to attribute physical qualities to the external world. Haven't you ever felt dizzy?

Sceptic: Of course.

Physicist: But you do not attempt to attribute your dizziness to a rotation of the universe, in spite of the fact that you *feel* the world spinning round?

Sceptic: No. It's clearly an illusion.

Physicist: So, I maintain that the whirling of time is like the whirling of space — a sort of temporal dizziness — which is given a false impression of reality by our confused language, with its tense structure and meaningless phrases about the past, present and future.

Sceptic: Tell me more.

Physicist: Not now. I've run out of time . . .

What can one conclude from this sort of exchange? There is no doubt that in organizing our daily affairs we depend heavily upon the concepts of past, present and future, and never question that time really does pass. Even physicists soon lapse back to that way of talking and thinking (as we saw above) once their analytical faculties have been withdrawn. Yet it must be conceded that the closer we scrutinize these concepts the more slippery and ambiguous they seem to become, and all our statements end up as either tautologous or meaningless. The physicist has no need of the flow of time or the now in the world of physics. Indeed, the theory of relativity rules out a universal present for all observers. If there is any meaning at all to these concepts (and many philosophers, such as McTaggart, deny that there is) then it would seem they belong to psychology rather than physics.

This raises an intriguing theological question. Does God experience the passage of time?

Christians believe that God is eternal. The word 'eternal' has, however, been used to mean two rather different things. In the simpler version, eternal means everlasting, or existing without beginning or end for an infinite duration. There are grave objections to such an idea of God, however. A God who is in time is subject to change. But what causes that change? If God is the cause of all existing things . . . , then does it make sense to talk about the ultimate cause itself changing?

. . . We have seen how time is not simply there, but is itself part of the physical universe. It is 'elastic' and can stretch or shrink according to well-defined mathematical laws which depend on the behaviour of matter. Also, time is closely linked to space, and space and time together express the operation of the gravitational field. In short, time is involved in all the grubby details of physical processes just as much as matter. Time is not a divine quality, but can be altered, physically, even by human manipulation. A God who is in time is, therefore, in some sense caught up in the operation of the physical universe. Indeed, it is quite likely that time will cease to exist at some stage in the future. . . . In that case God's own position is obviously insecure. Clearly, God cannot be omnipotent if he is subject to the physics of time, nor can he be considered the creator of the universe if he did not create time. In fact, because time and space are inseparable, a God who did not create time, created space neither. But as we have seen, once spacetime existed, the appearance of matter and order in the universe could have occurred automatically as the result of perfectly natural activity. Thus, many would argue that God is not really needed as a creator at all *except* to create time (strictly, spacetime).

So we are led to the other meaning of the word eternal — 'timeless.' The concept of a God beyond time dates at least from Augustine who . . . suggested that God created time. It has received support from many of the Christian theologians. St. Anselm expresses the idea as follows: 'You [God] exist neither yesterday, today, nor tomorrow, but you exist directly right outside time.'

A timeless God is free of the problems mentioned above, but suffers from the shortcomings already discussed. . . . He cannot be a personal God who thinks, converses, feels, plans, and so on for these are all temporal activities. It is hard to see how a timeless God can act at all in time (although it has been claimed that this is not impossible). We have also seen how the sense of the existence of the self is intimately associated with the experience of a time-flow. A timeless God could not be considered a 'person' or individual in any sense that we know. Misgivings of this score have led a number of modern theologians to reject this view of an eternal God. Paul Tillich writes: 'If we call God a living God, we affirm that he includes temporality and with this a relation to the modes of time.' The same sentiment is echoed by Karl Barth: 'Without God's complete temporality the content of the Christian message has no shape.'

The physics of time also has interesting implications for the belief that God is omniscient. If God is timeless, he cannot be said to think, for thinking is a temporal activity. But can a timeless being have knowledge? Acquiring knowledge clearly involves time, but knowing as such does not — provided that what is known does not itself change with time. If God knows, for example, the position of every atom today, then that knowledge will change by tomorrow. To know timelessly must therefore involve his knowing all events throughout time.

There is thus a grave and fundamental difficulty in reconciling all the traditional attributes of God. Modern physics, with its discovery of the mutability of time, drives a wedge between God's omnipotence and the existence of his personality. It is difficult to argue that God can have both these qualities.

Further Questions

1. The passage of time, familiar to all of us, seems to be one of the most obvious truths about us. What does it say about our psychological feeling of "obviousness," if this most obvious notion is false?

2. If what Davies says about time is true, is it irrational to fear your death more than it is to fear the time before your birth? Does reading this article lessen your fear about death? Why or why not?

3. How would you describe, experientially, the sensation of the flow of time?

Further Readings

Einstein, Albert. *Relativity*. New York: Crown Publishers, 1961. A popular exposition of relativity by its originator.

Griffin, David Ray, ed. *Physics and the Ultimate Significance of Time*. Albany, NY: SUNY Press, 1986.

Reichenbach, Hans. *The Direction of Time*. Berkeley, CA: University of California Press, 1971. Offers a historical survey of the concept of time leading up to the advent of quantum mechanics.

Russell, Bertrand. *The ABC of Relativity*. Signet, 1959. One of the simplest and most readable versions of Einstein's theory of relativity.

Schwartz, Jacob T. *Relativity in Illustrations*. New York: New York University Press, 1962. Two chapters, "What Is Time?" and "What Is Space?", illustrate, using completely nontechnical language and lots of pictures and diagrams, the most basic parts of relativity.

Smart, J. J. C., ed. *Problems of Space and Time*. New York: Macmillan, 1964. Contains both historical and recent articles.

Where Am I?

DANIEL DENNETT

Daniel Dennett, best known for his writings in the philosophy of mind, teaches philosophy at Tufts University. Among his books are *Brainstorms* (Bradford Books, 1978), *Elbow Room* (Bradford Books, 1984) and, co-edited with Douglas Hofstadter, *The Mind's I* (Basic Books, 1981).

In the following selection he brings to light the unobvious mystery of how we locate ourselves. The meanings of words like *here, now,* and *me* seem so obvious that we ordinarily don't even question them. But by imagining himself in an extraordinary situation in which his body is separated from his brain, Dennett shows why even the most obvious apparent fact about you, expressed by your avowal "I am here," is deeply questionable.

Reading Questions

1. How is Dennett able to experience anything after his brain is removed and put in a vat?
2. What is a "point of view"?

3. What are the different ways in which Dennett tries to answer the "Where am I?" question in the various parts of the story?

4. When the computer brain runs in perfect syncronization with the brain in the vat, how *many* Dennetts are there? Is he one person with two brains? *Where* is the real Dennett? Can the Dennett character in the story tell which brain is running the body?

5. How do you know where you are? Ordinarily, you simply look and see. But when you're lost, you still see perfectly well—yet something crucial is missing. What? What information do you use to locate yourself?

6. Did you ever wake up and not know where you were? What did it feel like?

7. Suppose your living brain is transplanted into your friend's body. Would this be a case of your friend getting a brain transplant or a case of you getting a new body? Suppose the transplant took place after you had been in a car accident in which your body was destroyed, leaving your brain intact, while your friend's body remained intact but his brain was destroyed. Who pays for the operation?

NOW THAT I'VE WON MY SUIT under the Freedom of Information Act, I am at liberty to reveal for the first time a curious episode in my life that may be of interest not only to those engaged in research in the philosophy of mind, artificial intelligence, and neuroscience but also to the general public.

Several years ago I was approached by Pentagon officials who asked me to volunteer for a highly dangerous and secret mission. In collaboration with NASA and Howard Hughes, the Department of Defense was spending billions to develop a Supersonic Tunneling Underground Device, or STUD. It was supposed to tunnel through the earth's core at great speed and deliver a specially designed atomic warhead "right up the Red's missile silos," as one of the Pentagon brass put it.

The problem was that in an early test they had succeeded in lodging a warhead about a mile deep under Tulsa, Oklahoma, and they wanted me to retrieve it for them. "Why me?" I asked. Well, the mission involved some pioneering applications of current brain research, and they had heard of my interest in brains and of course my Faustian curiosity and great courage and so forth. . . . Well, how could I refuse? The difficulty

that brought the Pentagon to my door was that the device I'd been asked to recover was fiercely radioactive, in a new way. According to monitoring instruments, something about the nature of the device and its complex interactions with pockets of material deep in the earth had produced radiation that could cause severe abnormalities in certain tissues of the brain. No way had been found to shield the brain from these deadly rays, which were apparently harmless to other tissues and organs of the body. So it had been decided that the person sent to recover the device should *leave his brain behind*. It would be kept in a safe place where it could execute its normal control functions by elaborate radio links. Would I submit to a surgical procedure that would completely remove my brain, which would then be placed in a life-support system at the Manned Spacecraft Center in Houston? Each input and output pathway, as it was severed, would be restored by a pair of microminiaturized radio transceivers, one attached precisely to the brain, the other to the nerve stumps in the empty cranium. No information would be lost, all the connectivity would be preserved. At first I was a bit reluctant. Would it really work? The Houston brain surgeons encouraged me. "Think of it," they said, "as a mere *stretching* of the nerves. If your brain were just moved over an *inch* in your skull, that would not alter or impair your mind. We're simply going to make the nerves indefinitely elastic by splicing radio links into them."

I was shown around the life-support lab in Houston and saw the sparkling new vat in which my brain would be placed, were I to agree. I met the large and brilliant support team of neurologists, hematologists, biophysicists, and electrical engineers, and after several days of discussions and demonstrations, I agreed to give it a try. I was subjected to an enormous array of blood tests, brain scans, experiments, interviews, and the like. They took down my autobiography at great length, recorded tedious lists of my beliefs, hopes, fears, and tastes. They even listed my favorite stereo recordings and gave me a crash session of psychoanalysis.

The day for surgery arrived at last and of course I was anesthetized and remembered nothing of the operation itself. When I came out of anesthesia, I opened my eyes, looked around, and asked the inevitable, the traditional, the lamentably hackneyed postoperative question: "Where am I?" The nurse smiled down at me. "You're in Houston," she said, and I reflected that this still had a good chance of being the truth one way or another. She handed me a mirror. Sure enough, there were the tiny antennae poling up through their titanium ports cemented into my skull.

"I gather the operation was a success," I said. "I want to go see my brain." They led me (I was a bit dizzy and unsteady) down a long corridor and into the life-support lab. A cheer went up from the assembled support team, and I responded with what I hoped was a jaunty salute. Still feeling lightheaded, I was helped over to the life-support vat. I peered through the glass. There, floating in what looked like ginger ale, was undeniably a human brain, though it was almost covered with printed circuit chips, plastic tubules, electrodes, and other paraphernalia. "Is that mine?" I asked. "Hit the output transmitter switch there on the side of the vat and see for yourself," the project

director replied. I moved the switch to OFF, and immediately slumped, groggy and nauseated, into the arms of the technicians, one of whom kindly restored the switch to its ON position. While I recovered my equilibrium and composure, I thought to myself: "Well, here I am sitting on a folding chair, staring through a piece of plate glass at my own brain. . . . But wait," I said to myself, "shouldn't I have thought, 'Here I am, suspended in a bubbling fluid, being stared at by my own eyes'?" I tried to think this latter thought. I tried to project it into the tank, offering it hopefully to my brain, but I failed to carry off the exercise with any conviction. I tried again. "Here am *I*, Daniel Dennett, suspended in a bubbling fluid, being stared at by my own eyes." No, it just didn't work. Most puzzling and confusing. Being a philosopher of firm physicalist conviction, I believed unswervingly that the tokening of my thoughts was occurring somewhere in my brain: yet, when I thought "Here I am," where the thought occurred to me was *here*, outside the vat, where I, Dennett, was standing staring at my brain.

I tried and tried to think myself into the vat, but to no avail. I tried to build up to the task by doing mental exercises. I thought to myself, "The sun is shining *over there*," five times in rapid succession, each time mentally ostending a different place: in order, the sunlit corner of the lab, the visible front lawn of the hospital, Houston, Mars, and Jupiter. I found I had little difficulty in getting my "there"'s to hop all over the celestial map with their proper references. I could loft a "there" in an instant through the farthest reaches of space, and then aim the next "there" with pinpoint accuracy at the upper left quadrant of a freckle on my arm. Why was I having such trouble with "here"? "Here in Houston" worked well enough, and so did "here in the lab," and even "here in this part of the lab," but "here in the vat" always seemed merely an unmeant mental mouthing. I tried closing my eyes while thinking it. This seemed to help, but still I couldn't manage to pull it off, except perhaps for a fleeting instant. I couldn't be sure. The discovery that I couldn't be sure was also unsettling. How did I know *where* I meant by "here" when I thought "here"? Could I *think* I meant one place when in fact I meant another? I didn't see how that could be admitted without untying the few bonds of intimacy between a person and his own mental life that had survived the onslaught of the brain scientists and philosophers, the physicalists and behaviorists. Perhaps I was incorrigible about where I *meant* when I said "here." But in my present circumstances it seemed that either I was doomed by sheer force of mental habit to thinking systematically false indexical thoughts, or where a person is (and hence where his thoughts are tokened for purposes of semantic analysis) is not necessarily where his brain, the physical seat of his soul, resides. Nagged by confusion, I attempted to orient myself by falling back on a favorite philosopher's ploy. I began naming things.

"Yorick," I said aloud to my brain, "you are my brain. The rest of my body, seated in this chair, I dub 'Hamlet.'" So here we all are: Yorick's my brain, Hamlet's my body, and I am Dennett. *Now*, where am I? And when I think "where am I?" where's that thought tokened? Is it tokened in my brain, lounging about in the vat, or right here between my ears where it *seems* to be tokened? Or nowhere? Its *temporal* coordinates give me no trouble; must it not have spatial coordinates as well? I began making a list of the alternatives.

1. *Where Hamlet goes, there goes Dennett.* This principle was easily refuted by appeal to the familiar brain-transplant thought experiments so enjoyed by philosophers. If Tom and Dick switch brains, Tom is the fellow with Dick's former body—just ask him; he'll claim to be Tom, and tell you the most intimate details of Tom's autobiography. It was clear enough, then, that my current body and I could part company, but not likely that I could be separated from my brain. The rule of thumb that emerged so plainly from the thought experiments was that in a brain-

transplant operation, one wanted to be the *donor*, not the recipient. Better to call such an operation a *body* transplant, in fact. So perhaps the truth was,

2. *Where Yorick goes, there goes Dennett.* This was not at all appealing, however. How could I be in the vat and not about to go anywhere, when I was so obviously outside the vat looking in and beginning to make guilty plans to return to my room for a substantial lunch? This begged the question I realized, but it still seemed to be getting at something important. Casting about for some support for my intuition, I hit upon a legalistic sort of argument that might have appealed to Locke.

Suppose, I argued to myself, I were now to fly to California, rob a bank, and be apprehended. In which state would I be tried: in California, where the robbery took place, or in Texas, where the brains of the outfit were located? Would I be a California felon with an out-of-state brain, or a Texas felon remotely controlling an accomplice of sorts in California? It seemed possible that I might beat such a rap just on the undecidability of that jurisdictional question, though perhaps it would be deemed an interstate, and hence Federal, offense. In any event, suppose I were convicted. Was it likely that California would be satisfied to throw Hamlet into the brig, knowing that Yorick was living the good life and luxuriously taking the waters in Texas? Would Texas incarcerate Yorick, leaving Hamlet free to take the next boat to Rio? This alternative appealed to me. Barring capital punishment or other cruel and unusual punishment, the state would be obliged to maintain the life-support system for Yorick though they might move him from

Houston to Leavenworth, and aside from the unpleasantness of the opprobrium, I, for one, would not mind at all and would consider myself a free man under those circumstances. If the state has an interest in forcibly relocating persons in institutions, it would fail to relocate *me* in any institution by locating Yorick there. If this were true, it suggested a third alternative.

3. *Dennett is wherever he thinks he is.* Generalized, the claim was as follows: At any given time a person has a *point of view*, and the location of the point of view (which is determined internally by the content of the point of view) is also the location of the person.

Such a proposition is not without its perplexities, but to me it seemed a step in the right direction. The only trouble was that it seemed to place one in a heads-I-win/tails-you-lose situation of unlikely infallibility as regards location. Hadn't I myself often been wrong about where I was, and at least as often uncertain? Couldn't one get lost? Of course, but getting lost *geographically* is not the only way one might get lost. If one were lost in the woods one could attempt to reassure oneself with the consolation that at least one knew where one was: one was right *here* in the familiar surroundings of one's own body. Perhaps in this case one would not have drawn one's attention to much to be thankful for. Still, there were worse plights imaginable, and I wasn't sure I wasn't in such a plight right now.

Point of view clearly had something to do with personal location, but it was itself an unclear notion. It was obvious that the content of one's point of view was not the same as or determined by the content of one's beliefs or thoughts. For example, what should we say about the point of view of the Cinerama viewer who shrieks and twists in his seat as the roller-coaster footage overcomes his psychic distancing? Has he forgot-

ten that he is safely seated in the theater? Here I was inclined to say that the person is experiencing an illusory shift in point of view. In other cases, my inclination to call such shifts illusory was less strong. The workers in laboratories and plants who handle dangerous materials by operating feedback-controlled mechanical arms and hands undergo a shift in point of view that is crisper and more pronounced than anything Cinerama can provoke. They can feel the heft and slipperiness of the containers they manipulate with their metal fingers. They know perfectly well where they are and are not fooled into false beliefs by the experience, yet it is as if they were inside the isolation chamber they are peering into. With mental effort, they can manage to shift their point of view back and forth, rather like making a transparent Necker cube or an Escher drawing change orientation before one's eyes. It does seem extravagant to suppose that in performing this bit of mental gymnastics, they are transporting *themselves* back and forth.

Still their example gave me hope. If I was in fact in the vat in spite of my intuitions, I might be able to train myself to adopt that point of view even as a matter of habit. I should dwell on images of myself comfortably floating in my vat, beaming volitions to that familiar body *out there*. I reflected that the ease or difficulty of this task was presumably independent of the truth about the location of one's brain. Had I been practicing before the operation, I might now be finding it second nature. You might now yourself try such a *trompe l'oeil*. Imagine you have written an inflammatory letter which has been published in the *Times*, the result of which is that the government has chosen to impound your brain for a probationary period of three years in its Dangerous Brain Clinic in Bethesda, Maryland. Your body of course is allowed freedom to earn a salary and thus to continue its function of laying up income to be taxed. At this moment, however, your body is seated in an auditorium listening to a peculiar account by Daniel Dennett of his own similar experience. Try it. Think yourself to Bethesda, and then hark back longingly to your body, far away, and yet *seeming* so near. It is only with long-distance restraint (yours? the government's?) that you can control your impulse to get those hands clapping in polite applause before navigating the old body to the rest room and a well-deserved glass of evening sherry in the lounge. The task of imagination is certainly difficult, but if you achieve your goal the results might be consoling.

Anyway, there I was in Houston, lost in thought as one might say, but not for long. My speculations were soon interrupted by the Houston doctors, who wished to test out my new prosthetic nervous system before sending me off on my hazardous mission. As I mentioned before, I was a bit dizzy at first, and not surprisingly, although I soon habituated myself to my new circumstances (which were, after all, well nigh indistinguishable from my old circumstances). My accommodation was not perfect, however, and to this day I continue to be plagued by minor coordination difficulties. The speed of light is fast, but finite, and as my brain and body move farther and farther apart, the delicate interaction of my feedback systems is thrown into disarray by the time lags. Just as one is rendered close to speechless by a delayed or echoic hearing of one's speaking voice so, for instance, I am virtually unable to track a moving object with my eyes whenever my brain and my body are more than a few miles apart. In most matters my impairment is scarcely detectable, though I can no longer hit a slow curve ball with the authority of yore. There are some compensations of course. Though liquor tastes as good as ever, and warms my gullet while corroding my liver, I can drink it in any quantity I please, without becoming the slightest bit inebriated, a curiosity some of my close friends may have noticed (though I occasionally have *feigned* inebriation, so as not to draw attention to my unusual circumstances). For similar reasons, I take aspirin orally for a sprained wrist, but if the pain persists I ask Houston to administer codeine to me *in vitro*. In times of illness the phone bill can be staggering.

But to return to my adventure. At length, both the doctors and I were satisfied that I was ready to undertake my subterranean mission. And so I left my brain in Houston and headed by helicopter for Tulsa. Well, in any case, that's the way it seemed to me. That's how I would put it, just off the top of my head as it were. On the trip I reflected further about my earlier anxieties and decided that my first postoperative speculations had been tinged with panic. The matter was not nearly as strange or metaphysical as I had been supposing. Where was I? In two places, clearly: both inside the vat and outside it. Just as one can stand with one foot in Connecticut and the other in Rhode Island, I was in two places at once. I had become one of those scattered individuals we used to hear so much about. The more I considered this answer, the more obviously true it appeared. But, strange to say, the more true it appeared, the less important the question to which it could be the true answer seemed. A sad, but not unprecedented, fate for a philosophical question to suffer. This answer did not completely satisfy me, of course. There lingered some question to which I should have liked an answer, which was neither "Where are all my various and sundry parts?" nor "What is my current point of view?" Or at least there seemed to be such a question. For it did seem undeniable that in some sense *I* and not merely *most of me* was descending into the earth under Tulsa in search of an atomic warhead.

When I found the warhead, I was certainly glad I had left my brain behind, for the pointer on the specially built Geiger counter I had brought with me was off the dial. I called Houston on my ordinary radio and told the operation control center of my position and my progress. In return, they gave me instructions for dismantling the vehicle, based upon my on-site observations. I had set to work with my cutting torch when all of a sudden a terrible thing happened. I went stone deaf. At first I thought it was only my radio earphones that had broken, but when I tapped on my helmet, I heard nothing. Apparently the auditory transceivers had gone on the fritz. I could no longer hear Houston or my own voice, but I could speak, so I started telling them what had happened. In midsentence, I knew something else had gone wrong. My vocal apparatus had become paralyzed. Then my right hand went limp — another transceiver had gone. I was truly in deep trouble. But worse was to follow. After a few more minutes, I went blind. I cursed my luck, and then I cursed the scientists who had led me into this grave peril. There I was, deaf, dumb, and blind, in a radioactive hole more than a mile under Tulsa. Then the last of my cerebral radio links broke, and suddenly I was faced with a new and even more shocking problem: whereas an instant before I had been buried alive in Oklahoma, now I was disembodied in Houston. My recognition of my new status was not immediate. It took me several very anxious minutes before it dawned on me that my poor body lay several hundred miles away, with heart pulsing and lungs respirating, but otherwise as dead as the body of any heart-transplant donor, its skull packed with useless, broken electronic gear. The shift in perspective I had earlier found well nigh impossible now seemed quite natural. Though I could think myself back into my body in the tunnel under Tulsa, it took some effort to sustain the illusion. For surely it was an illusion to suppose I was still in Oklahoma: I had lost all contact with that body.

It occurred to me then, with one of those rushes of revelation of which we should be suspicious, that I had stumbled upon an impressive demonstration of the immateriality of the soul based upon physicalist principles and premises. For as the last radio signal between Tulsa and Houston died away, had I not changed location from Tulsa to Houston at the speed of light? And had I not accomplished this without any increase in mass? What moved from A to B at such speed was surely myself, or at any rate my soul or mind — the massless center of my being and home of my consciousness. My *point of view* had lagged somewhat behind, but I had already noted the indirect bearing of point of view on personal location. I could not see how a physicalist philosopher could quarrel with this except by taking the dire and counterintuitive route of banishing all talk of persons. Yet the notion of personhood was so well entrenched in everyone's world view, or so it seemed to me, that any denial would be as curiously unconvincing, as systematically disingenuous, as the Cartesian negation, "non sum."

The joy of philosophic discovery thus tided me over some very bad minutes or perhaps hours as the helplessness and hopelessness of my situation became more apparent to me. Waves of panic and even nausea swept over me, made all the more horrible by the absence of their normal body-dependent phenomenology. No adrenaline rush of tingles in the arms, no pounding heart, no premonitory salivation. I did feel a dread sinking feeling in my bowels at one point, and this tricked me momentarily into the false hope that I was undergoing a reversal of the process that landed me in this fix — a gradual undisembodiment. But the isolation and uniqueness of that twinge soon convinced me that it was simply the first of a plague of phantom body hallucinations that I, like any other amputee, would be all too likely to suffer.

My mood then was chaotic. On the one hand, I was fired up with elation of my philosophic discovery and was wracking my brain (one of the few familiar things I could still do), trying to figure out how to communicate my discovery to the journals; while on the other, I was bitter, lonely, and filled with dread and uncertainty. Fortunately, this did not last long, for my technical support team sedated me into a dreamless sleep from which I awoke, hearing with magnificent fidelity the familiar opening strains of my favorite Brahms piano trio. So that was why they had wanted a list of my favorite recordings! It did not take me long to realize that I was hearing the music without ears. The output from the stereo stylus was being fed through some fancy rectification circuitry directly into my auditory nerve. I was mainlining Brahms, an unforgettable experience for any stereo buff. At the end of the record it did not surprise me to hear the reassuring voice of the project director speaking into a microphone that was now my prosthetic ear. He confirmed my analysis of what had gone wrong and assured me that steps were being taken to reembody me. He did not elaborate, and after a few more recordings, I found myself drifting off to sleep. My sleep lasted, I later learned, for the better part of a year, and when I awoke, it was to find myself fully restored to my senses. When I looked into the mirror, though, I was a bit startled to see an unfamiliar face. Bearded and a bit heavier, bearing no doubt a family resemblance to my former face, and with the same look of spritely intelligence and resolute character, but definitely a new face. Further self-explorations of an intimate nature left me no doubt that this was a new body, and the project director confirmed my conclusions. He did not volunteer any information on the past history of my new body and I decided (wisely, I think in retrospect) not to pry. As many philosophers unfamiliar with my ordeal have more recently speculated, the acquisition of a new body leaves one's *person* intact. And after a period of adjustment to a new voice, new muscular strengths and weaknesses, and so forth, one's *personality* is by and large also preserved. More dramatic changes in personality have been routinely observed in people who have undergone extensive plastic surgery, to say nothing of sex-change operations, and I think no one contests the survival of the person in such cases. In any event I soon accommodated to my new body, to the point of being unable to recover any of its novelties to my consciousness or even memory. The view in the mirror soon became utterly familiar. That view, by the way, still revealed antennae, and so I was not surprised to learn that my brain had not been moved from its haven in the life-support lab.

I decided that good old Yorick deserved a visit. I and my new body, whom we might as well call Fortinbras, strode into the familiar lab to another round of applause from the technicians, who were of course congratulating themselves, not me. Once more I stood before the vat and contemplated poor Yorick, and on a whim I once again cavalierly flicked off the output transmitter switch. Imagine my surprise when nothing unusual happened. No fainting spell, no nausea, no noticeable change. A technician hurried to restore the switch to ON, but still I felt nothing. I demanded an explanation, which the project director hastened to provide. It seems that before they had even operated on the first occasion, they had constructed a computer duplicate of my brain, reproducing both the complete information-processing structure and the computational speed of my brain in a giant computer program. After the operation, but before they had dared to send me off on my mission to Oklahoma, they had run this computer system and Yorick side by side. The incoming signals from Hamlet were sent simultaneously to Yorick's transceivers and to the computer's array of inputs. And the outputs from Yorick were not only beamed back to Hamlet, my body; they were recorded and checked against the simultaneous output of the computer program, which was called "Hubert" for reasons obscure to me. Over days and even weeks, the outputs were identical and synchronous, which of course did not *prove* that they had succeeded in copying the brain's functional structure, but the empirical support was greatly encouraging.

Hubert's input, and hence activity, had been kept parallel with Yorick's during my disembodied days. And now, to demonstrate this, they had actually thrown the master switch that put Hubert for the first time in on-line control of my body—not Hamlet, of course, but Fortinbras. (Hamlet, I learned, had never been recovered from its underground tomb and could be assumed by this time to have largely returned to the dust. At the head of my grave still lay the magnificent bulk of the abandoned device, with the word STUD emblazoned on its side in large letters—a circumstance which may provide archeologists of the next century with a curious insight into the burial rites of their ancestors.)

The laboratory technicians now showed me the master switch, which had two positions, labeled *B*, for Brain (they didn't know my brain's name was Yorick) and *H*, for Hubert. The switch did indeed point to *H*, and they explained to me that if I wished, I could switch it back to *B*. With my heart in my mouth (and my brain in its vat), I did this. Nothing happened. A click, that was all. To test their claim, and with the master switch now set at *B*, I hit Yorick's output transmitter switch on the vat and sure enough, I began to faint. Once the output switch was turned back on and I had recovered my wits, so to speak, I continued to play with the master switch, flipping it back and forth. I found that with the exception of the transitional click, I could detect no trace of a difference. I could switch in mid-utterance, and the sentence I had begun speaking under the control of Yorick was finished without a pause or hitch of any kind under the control of Hubert. I had a spare brain, a prosthetic device which might some day stand me in very good stead, were some mishap to befall Yorick. Or alternatively, I could keep Yorick as a spare and use Hubert. It didn't seem to make any difference which I chose, for the wear and tear and fatigue on my body did not have any debilitating effect on either brain, whether or not it was actually causing the motions of my body, or merely spilling its output into thin air.

The one truly unsettling aspect of this new development was the prospect, which was not long in dawning on me, of someone detaching the spare — Hubert or Yorick, as the case might be — from Fortinbras and hitching it to yet another body — some Johnny-come-lately Rosencrantz or Guildenstern. Then (if not before) there would be *two* people, that much was clear. One would be me, and the other would be a sort of super-twin brother. If there were two bodies, one under the control of Hubert and the other being controlled by Yorick, then which would the world recognize as the true Dennett? And whatever the rest of the world decided, which one would be *me*? Would I be the Yorick-brained one, in virtue of Yorick's

causal priority and former intimate relationship with the original Dennett body, Hamlet? That seemed a bit legalistic, a bit too redolent of the arbitrariness of consanguinity and legal possession, to be convincing at the metaphysical level. For suppose that before the arrival of the second body on the scene, I had been keeping Yorick as the spare for years, and letting Hubert's output drive my body — that is, Fortinbras — all that time. The Hubert-Fortinbras couple would seem then by squatter's rights (to combat one legal intuition with another) to be the true Dennett and the lawful inheritor of everything that was Dennett's. This was an interesting question, certainly, but not nearly so pressing as another question that bothered me. My strongest intuition was that in such an eventuality *I* would survive so long as *either* brain-body couple remained intact, but I had mixed emotions about whether I should want both to survive.

I discussed my worries with the technicians and the project director. The prospect of two Dennetts was abhorrent to me, I explained, largely for social reasons. I didn't want to be my own rival for the affections of my wife, nor did I like the prospect of the two Dennetts sharing my modest professor's salary. Still more vertiginous and distasteful, though, was the idea of knowing *that much* about another person, while he had the very same goods on me. How could we ever face each other? My colleagues in the lab argued that I was ignoring the bright side of the matter. Weren't there many things I wanted to do but, being only one person, had been unable to do? Now one Dennett could stay at home and be the professor and family man, while the other could strike out on a life of travel and adventure — missing the family of course, but happy in the knowledge that the other Dennett was keeping the home fires burning. I could be faithful and adulterous at the same time. I could even cuckold myself — to say nothing of other more lurid possibilities my colleagues were all too ready to force upon my overtaxed imagination. But my ordeal in Oklahoma (or was it Houston?) had made me less adventurous, and I shrank from this opportunity that was being offered (though of course I was never quite sure it was being offered to *me* in the first place).

There was another prospect even more disagreeable: that the spare, Hubert or Yorick as the case might be, would be detached from any input from Fortinbras and just left detached. Then, as in the other case, there would be two Dennetts, or at least two claimants to my name and possessions, one embodied in Fortinbras, and the other sadly, miserably disembodied. Both selfishness and altruism bade me take steps to prevent this from happening. So I asked that measures be taken to ensure that no one could ever tamper with the transceiver connections or the master switch without my (our? no, *my*) knowledge and consent. Since I had no desire to spend my life guarding the equipment in Houston, it was mutually decided that all the electronic connections in the lab would be carefully locked. Both those that controlled the life-support system for Yorick and those that controlled the power supply for Hubert would be guarded with fail-safe devices, and I would take the only master switch, outfitted for radio remote control, with me wherever I went. I carry it strapped around my waist and — wait a moment — *here it is*. Every few months I reconnoiter the situation by switching channels. I do this only in the presence of friends, of course, for if the other channel were, heaven forbid, either dead or otherwise occupied, there would have to be somebody who had my interests at heart to switch it back, to bring me back from the void. For while I could feel, see, hear, and otherwise sense whatever befell my body, subsequent to such a switch, I'd be unable to control it. By the way, the two positions on the switch are intentionally unmarked, so I never have the faintest idea whether I am switching from Hubert to Yorick or vice versa. (Some of you may think that in this case I really don't know *who* I am, let alone where I am. But such reflections no longer make much of a dent on my essential Dennettness, on my own sense of who I

am. If it is true that in one sense I don't know who I am then that's another one of your philosophical truths of underwhelming significance.)

In any case, every time I've flipped the switch so far, nothing has happened. *So let's give it a try....*

"THANK GOD! I THOUGHT YOU'D NEVER FLIP THAT SWITCH! You can't imagine how horrible it's been these last two weeks — but now you know; it's your turn in purgatory. How I've longed for this moment! You see, about two weeks ago — excuse me, ladies and gentlemen, but I've got to explain this to my . . . um, brother, I guess you could say, but he's just told you the facts, so you'll understand — about two weeks ago our two brains drifted just a bit out of synch. I don't know whether *my* brain is now Hubert or Yorick, any more than you do, but in any case, the two brains drifted apart, and of course once the process started, it snowballed, for I was in a slightly different receptive state for the input we both received, a difference that was soon magnified. In no time at all the illusion that I was in control of my body — our body — was completely dissipated. There was nothing I could do — no way to call you. YOU DIDN'T EVEN KNOW I EXISTED! It's been like being carried around in a cage, or better, like being possessed — hearing my own voice say things I didn't mean to say, watching in frustration as my own hands performed deeds I hadn't intended. You'd scratch your itches, but not the way I would have, and you kept me awake, with your tossing and turning. I've been totally exhausted, on the verge of a nervous breakdown, carried around helplessly by your frantic round of activities, sustained only by the knowledge that some day you'd throw the switch.

"Now it's your turn, but at least you'll have the comfort of knowing *I* know you're in there. Like an expectant mother, I'm eating — or at any rate tasting, smelling, seeing — for *two* now, and I'll try to make it easy for you. Don't worry. Just as soon as this colloquium is over, you and I will fly to Houston, and we'll see what can be done to get one of us another body. You can have a female body—your body could be any color you like. But let's think it over. I tell you what—to be fair, if we both want this body, I promise I'll let the project director flip a coin to settle which of us gets to keep it and which then gets to choose a new body. That should guarantee justice, shouldn't it? In any case, I'll take care of you, I promise. These people are my witnesses.

"Ladies and gentlemen, this talk we have just heard is not exactly the talk *I* would have given, but I assure you that everything he said was perfectly true. And now if you'll excuse me, I think I'd—we'd—better sit down."

Further Questions

1. Dennett's story makes several leaps of the imagination that go beyond our present technological abilities. List them in order from the least to most fantastic. How would you characterize these differences? Here are three labels you may wish to use: "technological impossibility," "physical impossibility," and "logical impossibility." Do you think performing such "thought experiments" invalidates any of the points Dennett tries to make? Why or why not?

2. Two galaxies can pass through each other. Does that mean that two objects can exist at the same place at the same time? If it does, could two people exist at the same place at the same time? If they could, how do you know that you are just one person?

3. What is a "point of view"? What does a point of view have to do with where a person is? In other words, does your point of view determine your location, or does your location determine your point of view, or neither?

Further Readings

Frisby, John. *Seeing: Illusion, Brain, and Mind.* New York: Oxford University Press, 1980.

Gregory, R. L. *Eye and Brain.* New York: Weidenfeld and Nicolson, 1977. A beautifully illustrated survey of real but very mind-boggling experiments with vision.

Putnam, Hilary. "The Meaning of 'Meaning,'" in Keith Gunderson, ed., *Language, Mind and Knowledge.* Minneapolis: University of Minnesota Press, 1975, pp. 131–193. Putnam uses the example of a twin-earth, where we each have an exact duplicate, to develop a new theory of meaning.

Sanford, David H. "Where Was I?" in Douglas Hofstadter and Daniel Dennett, eds., *The Mind's I.* New York: Basic Books, 1981, pp. 232–240. An amusing sequel to "Where Am I?" that explores the already technologically feasible idea of "nonsurgical mind extensions."

PART III

Who

YOUR EVERYDAY NOTION OF PERSONAL IDENTITY — of what makes you *you* — functions as glue and as scissors. As glue, it binds the earlier to the later stages of yourself, making you a continuously existing person over time. As scissors, it separates you from others. Together, these give rise to two fundamental assumptions about who you are: you are the same self from birth to death *and* you are a unique self, different from other selves.

These assumptions are about *you*. As you are about to see, however, they are deeply questionable because they are based on stories to which there are plausible alternatives. But if these most basic assumptions about your identity are deeply questionable, then *who you are* must also be deeply questionable.

Who are you?

"Consciousness, Self, and Identity"

JOHN LOCKE

John Locke (1632–1704) was educated at Oxford University where he studied the classics, philosophy, and medicine. At that time Oxford was still under the influence of medieval scholasticism. Locke himself was interested in the view recently formulated by René Descartes, and in particular in working out a theory of knowledge that could accommodate the progress being made in the newly emerging sciences. Descartes was a "rationalist" who believed that reason is our primary soucre of knowledge about the world. Locke became convinced that experience was our primary source. That made Locke an "empiricist."

Locke's main attempt to explain his empiricism, his *Essay Concerning Human Understanding* (1690), was his chief work in theoretical philosophy. Because of it Locke eventually became known as the first of three "British empiricists." The other two are George Berkeley and David Hume. Locke also wrote extensively on political philosophy, most notably, his *Two Treatises on Government* (1690), which profoundly influenced the founding fathers of the United States.

In this section Locke addresses the question of what it is to be a self and to remain the same self over a period of time. He claims that it is an individual's consciousness, particularly his memory, that accounts for his retaining his identity as a person.

Reading Questions

1. Consider Locke's definition of "person." By his definition, could a total amnesiac be a person? Could a gorilla? Could an android?

2. What does Locke mean by "consciousness?" What is the relationship between consciousness and memory?

3. How does Locke distinguish between what it means to be "the same substance" over time and what it means to be "the same person" over time?

4. For Locke, could the same person have more than one soul? More than one body?

5. What does Locke think personal identity consists in?

6. Why can't you just say that your consciousness proves that you are the same identical substance over time?

7. Does Locke think that switching bodies is the same as switching personal identities?

8. How does Locke establish the idea of *same* consciousness?

Personal Identity

TO FIND WHEREIN PERSONAL IDENTITY consists, we must consider what "person" stands for; which I think, is a thinking intelligent being, that has reason and reflection, and can consider itself as itself, the same thinking thing, in different times and places; which it does only by that consciousness which is inseparable from thinking, and it seems to me essential to it: it being impossible for any one to perceive, without perceiving that he does perceive. When we see, hear, smell, taste, feel, meditate, or will any thing, we know that we do so. Thus it is always as to our present sensations and perceptions: and by this every one is to himself that which he calls "self"; it not being considered, in this case, whether the same self be continued in the same or diverse substances. For since consciousness always accompanies thinking, and it is that that makes every one to be what he calls "self", and thereby distinguishes himself from all other thinking things; in this alone consists personal identity, *i.e.*, the sameness of a rational being: and as far as this consciousness can be extended backwards to any past action or thought, so far reaches the identity of that person; it is the same self now it was then; and it is by the same self with this present one that now reflects on it, that that action was done.

Consciousness Makes Personal Identity

. . . For it being the same consciousness that makes a man be himself to himself, personal identity depends on that only, whether it be annexed solely to one individual substance, or can be continued in a succession of several substances. For as far as any intelligent being can repeat the idea of any past action with the same consciousness it had of it at first, and with the same consciousness it has of any present action; so far it is the same personal self. For it is by the consciousness it has of its present thoughts and actions that it is self to itself now, and so will be the same self, as far as the same consciousness can extend to actions past or to come; and would be by distance of time, or change of substance, no more two persons than a man be two men, by wearing other clothes to-day than he did yesterday, with a long or short sleep between: the same consciousness uniting those distant actions into the same person, whatever substance contributed to their production.

From John Locke, An Essay Concerning Human Understanding, *Book II, Chapter 27, "Of Ideas of Identity and Diversity." First Published in 1690.*

Personal Identity in Change of Substances

. . . Suppose a Christian, Platonist, or a Pythagorean, should, upon God's having ended all his works of creation the seventh day, think his soul hath existed ever since; and should imagine it has revolved in several human bodies, as I once met with one who was persuaded his had been the soul of Socrates: (how reasonably I will not dispute: this I know, that in the post he filled, which was no inconsiderable one, he passed for a very rational man; and the press has shown that he wanted not parts or learning:) would any one say, that he, being not conscious of any of Socrates's actions or thoughts, could be the same person with Socrates? Let any one reflect upon himself, and conclude, that he has in himself an immaterial spirit, which is that which thinks in him, and in the constant change of his body keeps him the same; and is that which he calls himself: let him also suppose it to be the same soul that was in Nestor or Thersites, at the seige of Troy, (for souls being, as far as we know any thing of them, in their nature indifferent to any parcel of matter, the supposition has no apparent absurdity in it), which it may have been as well as it is now the soul of any other man: but he now having no consciousness of any of the actions either of Nestor or Thersites, does or can he conceive himself the same person with either of them? Can he be concerned in either of their actions? attribute them to himself, or think them his own, more than the actions of any other man that ever existed? So that this consciousness not reaching to any of the actions of either of those men, he is no more one self with either of them, than if the soul or immaterial spirit that now informs him had been created and began to exist when it began to inform his present body, though it were never so true that the same spirit that informed Nestor's or Thersites's body were numerically the same that now informs his. For this would no more make him the same person with Nestor, than if some of the particles of matter that were once a part of Nestor were now a part of this man; the same

immaterial substance, without the same consciousness, no more making the same person by being united to any body, than the same particle of matter, without consciousness, united to any body, makes the same person. But let him once find himself conscious of any of the actions of Nestor, he then finds himself the same person with Nestor.

And thus we may be able, without any difficulty, to conceive the same person at the resurrection, though in a body not exactly in make or parts the same which he had here, the same consciousness going along with the soul that inhabits it. But yet the soul alone, in the change of bodies, would scarce to any one, but to him that makes the soul the man, be enough to make the same man. For, should the soul of a prince, carrying with it the consciousness of the prince's past life, enter and inform the body of a cobbler, as soon as deserted by his own soul, every one sees he would be the same person with the prince, accountable only for the prince's actions: but who would say it was the same man? The body too goes to the making of the man, and would, I guess, to every body determine the man in this case, wherein the soul, with all its princely thoughts about it, would not make another man; but he would be the same cobbler to every one besides himself. I know that, in the ordinary way of speaking, the same person and the same man stand for one and the same thing. And, indeed, every one will always have a liberty to speak as he pleases, and to apply what articulate sounds to what ideas he thinks fit, and change them as often as he pleases. But yet, when we will inquire what makes the same spirit, man, or person, we must fix the ideas of spirit, man, or person in our minds; and having resolved with ourselves what we mean by them, it will not be hard to determine in either of them, or the like, when it is the same and when not.

Consciousness Makes the Same Person

But though the same immaterial substance or soul does not alone, wherever it be, and in whatsoever state, make the same man; yet it is plain, consciousness, as far as ever it can be extended, should it be to ages past, unites existences and actions, very remote in time, into the same person, as well as it does the existences and actions of the immediately preceding moment: so that whatever has the consciousness of present and past actions is the same person to whom they both belong. Had I the same consciousness that I saw the ark and Noah's flood, as that I saw an overflowing of the Thames last winter, or as that I write now, I could no more doubt that I who write this now, that saw the Thames overflowed last winter, and that viewed the flood at the general deluge, was the same self, place that self in what substance you please, than that I who write this am the same myself now whilst I write (whether I consist of all the same substance, material or immaterial, or no) that I was yesterday. For, as to this point of being the same self, it matters not whether this present self be made up of the same or other substances, I being as much concerned and as justly accountable for any action that was done a thousand years since, appropriated to me now by this self-consciousness, as I am for what I did the last moment.

Self Depends on Consciousness

Self is that conscious thinking thing (whatever substance made up of, whether spiritual or material, simple or compounded, it matters not) which is sensible or conscious of pleasure and pain, capable of happiness or misery, and so is concerned for itself, as far as that consciousness extends. Thus every one finds, that whilst comprehended under that consciousness, the little finger is as much a part of himself as what is most so. Upon separation of this little finger, should this consciousness go along with the little finger, and leave the rest of the body, it is evident the little finger would be the person, the same person; and self then would have nothing to do with the rest of the body. As in this case it is the consciousness that goes along with the substance, when one part is separate from another, which makes the same person, and constitutes this inseparable self, so it is in reference to substances remote in time. That with which the consciousness of this present thinking thing can join itself makes the same person, and is one self with it, and with nothing else; and so attributes to iself and owns all the actions of that thing as its own, as far as that consciousness reaches, and no farther; as every one who reflects will perceive. . . .

This may show us wherein personal identity consists, not in the identity of substance, but, as I have said, in the identity of consciousness; wherein if Socrates and the present mayor of Queenborough agree, they are the same person. If the same Socrates waking and sleeping do not partake of the same consciousness, Socrates waking and sleeping is not the same person; and to punish Socrates waking for what sleeping Socrates thought, and waking Socrates was never conscious of, would be no more of right than to punish one twin for what his brother-twin did, whereof he knew nothing, because their outsides were so like that they could not be distinguished. . . .

Further Questions

1. What is the point of Locke's "prince and pauper" example? Do you agree with Locke's account of it? Would it affect your opinion if we imagine that whereas the prince's consciousness goes to the pauper, the pauper's consciousness just vanishes? Would it matter if the prince's consciousness went to ten different paupers, and the consciousness of all ten just vanished?

2. Imagine a Star Trek style "beamer" that dematerializes a person's body in one place — say, inside a spaceship — and then instantaneously creates an exact replica out of new matter at another place — say, on a planet's surface. Would Locke say that the person in the spaceship and the person on the planet's surface were the same person? Would you?

3. Is there any useful distinction to be drawn between "the same person" and "an exact replica"? If so, how would you draw it?

Further Readings

Ayer, A. J. and Raymond Winch, eds. *British Empirical Philosophers.* New York: Simon & Schuster, 1968. An excellent paperback anthology of the writings of Locke, Berkeley, and Hume.

Sacks, Oliver. *The Man Who Mistook His Wife for a Hat.* New York: Harper & Row, 1987. Brain problems that lead to identity problems.

Shoemaker, Sydney. Chs. 3 and 4 of "Personal Identity: A Materialist's Account," in S. Shoemaker and R. Swinburne. *Personal Identity.* Oxford: Basil Blackwell, 1984, pp. 77–88. Locke's view spruced up and criticized.

Personal Identity

DAVID HUME

The Scottish philosopher David Hume (1711–1776), the last of the three British empiricists, was a philosophical extremist. He developed the empiricism of John Locke and George Berkeley — the central idea of which is that our knowledge of the world is derived from experience — to its logical conclusion. Whereas Locke's version of empiricism is tempered by common sense, often inconsistently, and Berkeley made an exception to his empiricist principles to protect his notion of the self, Hume threw common sense to the winds and developed a consistent version of empiricism.

A sympathetic critic of Hume once remarked that by making empiricism self-consistent, Hume "made it incredible." This selection by Hume illustrates what the critic meant. By applying his empiricist principles to the notion of "self," Hume reveals the sort of bizarre consequences which he argues follow from the seemingly innocent premise that our knowledge of the self, too, must be derived from experience.

Reading Questions

1. Hume claims he has no "impression" of the self. What does he mean by "impression"? Is he right?

2. Hume thinks that the labels we use to refer to ourselves mask the impermanence of who and what we really are. Why does he think this? Is he right?

3. What does Hume mean by "perception"?

4. What is the importance of *resemblance, causation,* and *memory* in Hume's argument?

5. Why does Hume think that the question of personal identity can never be decided? (Decided by *whom*?) What does he mean by claiming that personal identity is a *grammatical* rather than a *philosophical* difficulty?

6. What does he say some other philosophers think about the self?

7. Why, according to Hume, do we believe in personal identity?

THERE ARE SOME PHILOSOPHERS, who imagine we are every moment intimately conscious of what we call our *Self*; that we feel its existence and its continuance in existence; and are certain, beyond the evidence of a demonstration, both of its perfect identity and simplicity. . . . For my part, when I enter most intimately into what I call *myself*, I always stumble on some particular perception or other, of heat or cold, light or shade, love or hatred, pain or pleasure. I never can catch *myself* at any time without a perception, and never can observe any thing but the perception. When my perceptions are remov'd for any time, as by sound sleep; so long am I insensible of *myself*, and may truly be said not to exist. And were all my perceptions remov'd by death, and cou'd I neither think, nor feel, nor see, nor love, nor hate after the dissolution of my body, I shou'd be entirely annihilated, nor do I conceive what is farther requisite to make me a perfect non-entity. If any one upon serious and unprejudic'd reflexion, thinks he has a different notion of *himself*, I must confess I can reason no longer with him. All I can allow him is, that he may be in the right as well as I, and that we are essentially different in this particular. He may, perhaps, perceive something simple and continu'd, which he calls *himself*; tho' I am certain there is no such principle in me.

But setting aside some metaphysicians of this kind, I may venture to affirm of the rest of mankind, that they are nothing but a bundle or collection of different perceptions, which succeed each other with an inconceivable rapidity, and are in a perpetual flux and movement. Our eyes cannot turn in their sockets without varying our perceptions. Our thought is still more variable than our sight; and all our other senses and faculties contribute to this change; nor is there any single power of the soul, which remains unalterably the same, perhaps for one moment. The mind is a kind of theatre, where several perceptions successively make their appearance; pass, re-pass, glide away, and mingle in an infinite variety of postures and situations. There is properly no *simplicity* in it at one time, nor *identity* in different; whatever natural propension we may have to imagine that simplicity and identity. The comparison of the theatre must not mislead us. They are the successive perceptions only, that constitute the mind; nor have we the most distant notion of the place, where these scenes are represented, or of the materials, of which it is compos'd.

What then gives us so great a propension to ascribe an identity to these successive perceptions, and to suppose ourselves possest of an invariable and uninterrupted existence thro' the whole course of our lives? . . .

. . . every distinct perception, which enters into the composition of the mind, is a distinct existence, and is different, and distinguishable, and separable from every other perception, either

From David Hume, A Treatise of Human Nature. *First published in 1738.*

contemporary or successive. But, as, notwithstanding this distinction and separability, we suppose the whole train of perceptions to be united by identity, a question naturally arises concerning this relation of identity; whether it be something that really binds our several perceptions together, or only associates their ideas in the imagination. That is, in other words, whether in pronouncing concerning the identity of a person, we observe some real bond among his perceptions, or only feel one among the ideas we form of them. This question we might easily decide, if we wou'd recollect what has been already prov'd at large, that the understanding never observes any real connexion among objects, and that even the union of cause and effect, when strictly examin'd, resolves itself into a customary association of ideas. For from thence it evidently follows, that identity is nothing really belonging to these different perceptions, and uniting them together; but is merely a quality, which we attribute to them, because of the union of their ideas in the imagination, when we reflect upon them. Now the only qualities, which can give ideas an union in the imagination, are these three relations above-mention'd. These are the uniting principles in the ideal world, and without them every distinct object is separable by the mind, and may be separately consider'd, and appears not to have any more connexion with any other object, than if disjoin'd by the greatest difference and remoteness. 'Tis, therefore, on some of these three relations of resemblance, contiguity and causation, that identity depends; and as the very essence of these relations consists in their producing an easy transition of ideas; it follows, that our notions of personal identity, proceed entirely from the smooth and uninterrupted progress of the thought along a train of connected ideas, according to the principles above-explain'd.

The only question, therefore, which remains, is, by what relations this uninterrupted progress of our thought is produc'd, when we consider the successive existence of a mind or thinking person. And here 'tis evident we must confine ourselves to resemblance and causation, and must drop contiguity, which has little or no influence in the present case.

To begin with *resemblance*; suppose we cou'd see clearly into the breast of another, and observe that succession of perceptions, which constitutes his mind or thinking principle, and suppose that he always preserves the memory of a considerable part of past perceptions; 'tis evident that nothing cou'd more contribute to the bestowing a relation on this succession amidst all its variations. For what is the memory but a faculty, by which we raise up the images of past perceptions? And as an image necessarily resembles its object, must not the frequent placing of these resembling perceptions in the chain of thought, convey the imagination more easily from one link to another, and make the whole seem like the continuance of one object? In this particular, then, the memory not only discovers the identity, but also contributes to its production, by producing the relation of resemblance among the perceptions. The case is the same whether we consider ourselves or others.

As to *causation*; we may observe, that the true idea of the human mind, is to consider it as a system of different perceptions or different existences, which are link'd together by the relation of cause and effect, and mutually produce, destroy, influence, and modify each other. Our impressions give rise to their correspondent ideas; and these ideas in their turn produce other impressions. One thought chases another, and draws after it a third, by which it is expell'd in its turn. In this respect, I cannot compare the soul more properly to any thing than to a republic or commonwealth, in which the several members are united by the reciprocal ties of government and subordination, and give rise to other persons, who propagate the same republic in the incessant changes of its parts. And as the same individual republic may not only change its members, but also its laws and constitutions; in like manner the same person may vary his character and disposition, as well as his impressions and ideas, without losing his identity. Whatever changes he endures, his several parts are still connected by the relation of causation. And in this view our identity with regard to the passions serves to corroborate that with regard to the imagination, by the making our distant perceptions influence each other, and by giving us a present concern for our past or future pains or pleasures.

As memory alone acquaints us with the continuance and extent of this succession of perceptions, 'tis to be consider'd, upon that account chiefly, as the source of personal identity. Had we no memory, we never shou'd have any notion of causation, nor consequently of that chain of causes and effects, which constitute our self or person. But having once acquir'd this notion of causation from the memory, we can extend the same chain of causes, and consequently the identity of our persons beyond our memory, and can comprehend times, and circumstances, and actions, which we have entirely forgot, but suppose in general to have existed. For how few of our past actions are there, of which we have any memory? Who can tell me, for instance, what were his thoughts and actions on the first of *January* 1715, the 11th of *March* 1719, and the 3d of *August* 1733? Or will he affirm, because he has entirely forgot the incidents of these days, that

the present self is not the same person with the self of that time; and by that means overturn all the most establish'd notions of personal identity? In this view, therefore, memory does not so much *produce* as *discover* personal identity, by shewing us the relation of cause and effect among our different perceptions. 'Twill be incumbent on those, who affirm that memory produces entirely our personal identity, to give a reason why we can thus extend our identity beyond our memory.

The whole of this doctrine leads us to a conclusion, which is of great importance in the present affair, *viz.* that all the nice and subtle questions concerning personal identity can never possibly be decided, and are to be regarded rather as grammatical than as philosophical difficulties. Identity depends on the relations of ideas; and these relations produce identity, by means of that easy transition they occasion. But as the relations, and the easiness of the transition may diminish by insensible degrees, we have no just standard, by which we can decide any dispute concerning the time, when they acquire or lose a title to the name of identity. All the disputes concerning the identity of connected objects are merely verbal, except so far as the relation of parts gives rise to some fiction or imaginary principle of union, as we have already observ'd.

Further Questions

1. Hume felt that while we have a natural disposition to think of ourselves as continuing things, an experiential examination of the underlying reality reveals that there is no *thing* that continues, but rather a series of separate "things," none of which individually is a person, that somehow get linked together to form us. When you look experientially at yourself, do you find that Hume's claim is true? Whether or not you do, do you find yourself resisting the idea (through fear) that it might be true? If so, what does that tell you about yourself?

2. We ordinarily suppose that physics has the last word about what material objects *are*. Shouldn't psychology or biology, then, have the last word about what persons are? If so, what do psychology and biology say? (If you don't know, ask a psychologist and a biologist.) If not, why not?

3. Do you find it odd that you can know lots of things, but among the things you really know least of all is yourself?

Further Readings

Russell, Bertrand. *A History of Western Philosophy*. New York: Simon & Schuster, 1945, Ch. 17. An excellent brief commentary on Hume's views.

Skinner, B. F. "What Is Man?" in *Beyond Freedom and Human Dignity*. New York: Bantam Books, 1972, pp. 175–206. A contemporary behaviorist criticizes the idea that there is a self within.

Tulku, Tarthang. "Tyranny of the I," Ch. 31 of *Knowledge of Freedom*. Berkeley, CA: Dharma Publishing, 1984, pp. 318–326. On how our experiencing the world through the lens of self hurts us.

A Dialogue on Personal Identity and Immortality

JOHN PERRY

John Perry teaches philosophy at Stanford University. He writes mainly on personal identity and the philosophy of mind. In the following dialogue, a dying philosophy professor, her student, and a clergyman discuss the nature of personal identity and its relevance to the question of survival of bodily death.

Three different criteria of personal identity are proposed and discussed. First, Miller (the clergyman) suggests that what makes you *you* is a soul. Then, he suggests that it is your *memories* that are most important for your continued survival. Weirob (the professor) suggests that it is your body that matters most.

Reading Questions

1. Many people believe in souls. Do you? Why? Suppose souls exist. Do you *have* a soul, or *are* you a soul? What's the difference?

2. How do you recognize, say, your mother? Do you need to see her soul to know it is your mother? What would a soul look like?

3. If you lost all your memories, would you still be you, or would you be someone else? Would you be no one?

4. When you think about surviving your bodily death, what is it that you most want preserved? Your body? Your memories? Your soul? Or something else altogether?

5. What is the point of the Kleenex box example? Do you agree?

6. What is Weirob's view of personal identity? Miller's? Cohen's?

7. What is the main argument for and against each view?

8. Which view do you most agree with, and why?

9. What is Weirob's definition of survival?

10. If you were in Weirob's position, would you undergo the operation?

11. If *A* and *B* are "exactly similar" does it mean they are one and the same identical thing? Why or why not?

THIS IS A RECORD OF CONVERSATIONS of Gretchen Weirob, a teacher of philosophy at a small midwestern college, and two of her friends. The conversations took place in her hospital room on the three nights before she died from injuries sustained in a motorcycle accident. Sam Miller is a chaplain and a long-time friend of Weirob's; Dave Cohen is a former student of hers.

The First Night

Weirob: Remember our deal, Sam. You don't have to convince me that survival is probable, for we both agree you would not get to first base. You have only to convince me that it is possible. . . .

Miller: I guess I just miss the problem, then. Of course, it's possible. You just continue to exist, after your body dies. What's to be defended or explained? You want details? Okay. Two people meet a thousand years from now, in a place that may or may not be part of this physical universe. I am one and you are the other. So you must have survived. Surely you can imagine that. What else is there to say?

Weirob: But in a few days *I* will quit breathing, *I* will be put into a coffin, *I* will be buried. And in a few months or a few years, *I* will be reduced to so much humus. That, I take it, is obvious, is given. How then can you say that I am one of these persons a thousand years from now?

Suppose I took this box of Kleenex and lit fire to it. It is reduced to ashes and I smash the ashes and flush them down the john. Then I say to you, go home and on the shelf will be *that very box of Kleenex*. It has survived! Wouldn't that be absurd? What sense could you make of it? And yet that is just what you say to me. I will rot away. And then, a thousand years later, there I will be. What sense does that make?

Miller: There could be an *identical* box of Kleenex at your home, one just like it in every respect. And, in this sense, there is no difficulty in

there being someone identical to you in the Hereafter, though your body has rotted away.

Weirob: You are playing with words again. There could be an *exactly similar* box of Kleenex on my shelf. We sometimes use "identical" to mean "exactly similar," as when we speak of "identical twins." But I am using "identical" in a way in which *identity* is the condition of memory and correct anticipation. If I am told that tomorrow, though I will be dead, someone else that looks and sounds and thinks just like me will be alive—would that be comforting? Could I correctly *anticipate* having her experiences? Would it make sense for me to fear her pains and look forward to her pleasures? Would it be right for her to feel remorse at the harsh way I am treating you? Of course not. Similarity, however exact, is not identity. I use identity to mean there is but one thing. If I am to survive, there must be one person who lies in this bed now, and who talks to someone in your Hereafter ten or a thousand years from now. After all, what comfort could there be in the notion of a heavenly impostor, walking around getting credit for a few good things I have done?

Miller: I'm sorry. I see that I was simply confused. Here is what I should have said. If you were merely a live human body—as the Kleenex box is merely cardboard and glue in a certain arrangement—then the death of your body would be the end of you. But surely you are more than that, fundamentally more than that. What is fundamentally you is not your body, but your soul or self or mind.

Weirob: Do you mean these words, "soul," "self," or "mind" to come to the same thing?

Miller: Perhaps distinctions could be made, but I shall not pursue them now. I mean the nonphysical and nonmaterial aspects of you, your consciousness. It is this that I get at with these words, and I don't think any further distinction is relevant.

From *John Perry:* A Dialogue on Personal Identity and Immorality, *Indianapolis and Cambridge: Hackett Publishing Co., Inc., 1981. Used by permission of the publisher.*

Weirob: Consciousness? I am conscious, for a while yet. I see, I hear, I think, I remember. But "to be conscious"—that is a verb. What is the subject of the verb, the thing which is conscious? Isn't it just this body, the same object that is overweight, injured, and lying in bed?—and which will be buried and not be conscious in a day or a week at the most?

Miller: As you are a philosopher, I would expect you to be less muddled about these issues. Did Descartes not draw a clear distinction between the body and the mind, between that which is overweight, and that which is conscious? Your mind or soul is immaterial, lodged in your body while you are on earth. The two are intimately related but not identical. Now clearly, what concerns us in survival is your mind or soul. It is this which must be identical to the person before me now, and to the one I expect to see in a thousand years in heaven.

Weirob: So I am not really this body, but a soul or mind or spirit? And this soul cannot be seen or felt or touched or smelt? That is implied, I take it, by the fact that it is immaterial?

Miller: That's right. Your soul sees and smells, but cannot be seen or smelt.

Weirob: Let me see if I understand you. You would admit that I am the very same person with whom you had lunch last week at Dorsey's?

Miller: Of course you are.

Weirob: Now when you say I am the same person, if I understand you, that is not a remark about this body you see and could touch and I fear can smell. Rather it is a remark about a soul, which you cannot see or touch or smell. The fact that the same body that now lies in front of you on the bed was across the table from you at Dorsey's—that would not mean that the same *person* was present on both occasions, if the same soul were not. And if, through some strange turn of events, the same soul were present on both occasions, but lodged in different bodies, then it *would* be the same person. Is that right?

Miller: You have understood me perfectly. But surely, you understood all of this before!

Weirob: But wait. I can repeat it, but I'm not sure I understand it. If you cannot see or touch or in any way perceive my soul, what makes you think the one you are confronted with now *is* the very same soul you were confronted with at Dorsey's?

Miller: But I just explained it. To say it is the same soul and to say it is the same person, are the same. And, of course, you are the same person you were before. Who else would you be if not yourself? You *were* Gretchen Weirob, and you *are* Gretchen Weirob.

Weirob: But how do you know you are talking to Gretchen Weirob at all, and not someone else, say Barbara Walters or even Mark Spitz!

Miller: Well, it's just obvious. I can see who I am talking to.

Weirob: But all you can see is my body. You can see, perhaps, that the same body is before you now that was before you last week at Dorsey's. But you have just said that Gretchen Weirob is not a body but a soul. In judging that the same person is before you now as was before you then, you must be making a judgment about souls—which, you said, cannot be seen or touched or smelt or tasted. And so, I repeat, how do you know?

Miller: Well, I *can* see that it is the same body before me now that was across the table at Dorsey's. And I know that the same soul is connected with the body now that was connected with it before. That's how I know it's you. I see no difficulty in the matter.

Weirob: You reason on the principle, "Same body, same self."

Miller: Yes.

Weirob: And would you reason conversely also? If there were in this bed Barbara Walters' body—that is, the body you see every night on the news—would you infer that it was not me, Gretchen Weirob, in the bed?

Miller: Of course I would. How would you have come by Barbara Walters' body?

Weirob: But then merely extend this principle to Heaven, and you will see that your conception of survival is without sense. Surely this very body, which will be buried and as I must so often repeat, *rot away*, will not be in your Hereafter. Different body, different person. Or do you claim that a body can rot away on earth, and then still wind up somewhere else? Must I bring up the Kleenex box again?

Miller: No, I do not claim that. But I also do not extend a principle, found reliable on earth, to such a different situation as is represented by the Hereafter. That a correlation between bodies and souls has been found on earth does not make it inconceivable or impossible that they should separate. Principles found to work in one circumstance may not be assumed to work in vastly altered circumstances. January and snow go together here, and one would be a fool to expect otherwise. But the principle does not apply in southern California.

Weirob: So the principle, "same body, same soul," is a well-confirmed regularity, not something you know "a priori."

Miller: By "a priori" you philosophers mean something which can be known without observing what actually goes on in the world—as I can know that two plus two equals four just by thinking about numbers, and that no bachelors are married, just by thinking about the meaning of "bachelor"?

Weirob: Yes.

Miller: Then you are right. If it was part of the meaning of "same body" that wherever we have the same body we have the same soul, it would have to obtain universally, in Heaven as well as on earth. But I just claim it is a generalization we know by observation on earth, and it need not automatically extend to Heaven.

Weirob: But where do you get this principle? It simply amounts to a correlation between being confronted with the same body and being confronted with the same soul. To establish such a correlation in the first place, surely one must have some *other* means of judging sameness of soul. You do not have such a means; your principle is without foundation; either you really do not

know the person before you now is Gretchen Weirob, the very same person you lunched with at Dorsey's, or what you do know has nothing to do with sameness of some immaterial soul.

Miller: Hold on, hold on. You know I can't follow you when you start spitting out arguments like that. Now what is this terrible fallacy I'm supposed to have committed?

Weirob: I'm sorry. I get carried away. Here—by way of a peace offering—have one of the chocolates Dave brought.

Miller: Very tasty. Thank you.

Weirob: Now why did you choose that one?

Miller: Because it had a certain swirl on the top which shows that it is a caramel.

Weirob: That is, a certain sort of swirl is correlated with a certain type of filling—the swirls with caramel, the rosettes with orange, and so forth.

Miller: Yes. When you put it that way, I see an analogy. Just as I judged that the filling would be the same in this piece as in the last piece that I ate with such a swirl, so I judge that the soul with which I am conversing is the same as the last soul with which I conversed when sitting across from that body. We see the outer wrapping and infer what is inside.

Weirob: But how did you come to realize that swirls of that sort and caramel insides were so associated?

Miller: Why, from eating a great many of them over the years. Whenever I bit into a candy with that sort of swirl, it was filled with caramel.

Weirob: Could you have established the correlation had you never been allowed to bite into a candy and never seen what happened when someone else bit into one? You could have formed the hypothesis, "same swirl, same filling." But could you have ever established it?

Miller: It seems not.

Weirob: So your inference, in a particular case, to the identity of filling from the identity of swirl would be groundless?

Miller: Yes, it would. I think I see what is coming.

Weirob: I'm sure you do. Since you can never, so to speak, bite into my soul, can never see or touch it, you have no way of testing your hypothesis that sameness of body means sameness of self.

Miller: I daresay you are right. But now I'm a bit lost. What is supposed to follow from all of this?

Weirob: If, as you claim, identity of persons consisted in identity of immaterial unobservable souls, then judgments of personal identity of the sort we make every day whenever we greet a friend or avoid a pest are really judgments about such souls.

Miller: Right.

Weirob: But if such judgments were really about souls, they would all be groundless and without foundation. For we have no direct method of observing sameness of soul, and so — and this is the point made by the candy example — we can have no indirect method either. . . . My point is this. For all you know, the immaterial soul which you think is lodged in my body might change from day to day, from hour to hour, from minute to minute, replaced each time by another soul psychologically similar. You cannot see it or touch it, so how would you know?

Miller: Are you saying I don't really know who you are?

Weirob: Not at all. *You* are the one who says personal identity consists in sameness of this immaterial, unobservable, invisible, untouchable soul. I merely point out that *if* it did consist in that, you *would* have no idea who I am. Sameness of body would not necessarily mean sameness of person. Sameness of psychological characteristics would not necessarily mean sameness of person. I am saying that if you do know who I am then you are wrong that personal identity consists in sameness of immaterial soul.

Miller: I see. But wait. I believe my problem is that I simply forgot a main tenet of my theory. The correlation can be established in my own case. I know that *my* soul and my body are intimately and consistently found together. From this one case I can generalize, at least as concerns life in this world, that sameness of body is a reliable sign of sameness of soul. This leaves me free to regard it as intelligible, in the case of death, that the link between the particular soul and the particular body it has been joined with is broken. . . .

Weirob: . . . How is it that you know in your own case that there is a single soul which has been so consistently connected with your body?

Miller: Now you really cannot be serious, Gretchen. How can I doubt that I am the same person I was? Is there anything more clear and distinct, less susceptible to doubt? How do you expect me to prove anything to you, when you are capable of denying my own continued existence from second to second? Without knowledge of our own identity, everything we think and do would be senseless. How could I think if I did not suppose that the person who begins my thought is the one who completes it? When I act, do I not assume that the person who forms the intention is the very one who performs the action?

Weirob: But I grant you that a single *person* has been associated with your body since you were born. The question is whether one immaterial soul has been so associated — or more precisely, whether you are in a position to know it. You believe that a judgment that one and the same person has had your body all these many years is a judgment that one and the same immaterial soul has been lodged in it. I say that such judgments concerning the soul are totally mysterious, and that if our knowledge of sameness of persons consisted in knowledge of sameness of immaterial soul, it too would be totally mysterious. To point out, as you do, that it is not mysterious, but perhaps the most secure knowledge we have, the foundation of all reason and action, is simply to make the point that it cannot consist of knowledge of identity of an immaterial soul.

Miller: You have simply asserted, and not established, that my judgment that a single soul has been lodged in my body these many years is mysterious.

Weirob: Well, consider these possibilities. One is that a single soul, one and the same, has been with this body I call mine since it was born. The other is that one soul was associated with it until five years ago and then another, psychologically similar, inheriting all the old memories and beliefs, took over. A third hypothesis is that every five years a new soul takes over. A fourth is that every five minutes a new soul takes over. The most radical is that there is a constant flow of souls through this body, each psychologically similar to the preceding, as there is a constant flow of water molecules down [a river]. What evidence do I have that the first hypothesis, the "single soul hypothesis" is true, and not one of the others? Because I am the same person I was five minutes or five years ago? But the issue in question is simply whether from sameness of person, which isn't in doubt, we can infer sameness of soul. Sameness of body? But how do I establish a stable relationship between soul and body? Sameness of thoughts and sensations? But they are in constant flux. By the nature of the case, if the soul cannot be observed, it cannot be observed to be the same. Indeed, no sense has ever been assigned to the phrase "same soul." Nor could any sense be attached to it! One would have to say what a single soul looked like or felt like, how an encounter with a single soul at different times differed from encounters with different souls. But this can hardly be done, since a soul according to your conception doesn't look or feel like *anything* at all. And so of course "souls" can afford no principle of identity. And so they cannot be used to bridge the gulf between my existence now and my existence in the hereafter.

Miller: Do you doubt the existence of your own soul?

Weirob: I haven't based my argument on there being no immaterial souls of the sort you describe, but merely on their total irrelevance to questions of personal identity, and so to questions of personal survival. I do indeed harbor grave doubts whether there are any immaterial souls of the sort to which you appeal. Can we have a notion of a soul unless we have a notion of the *same* soul? But I hope you do not think that means I doubt my own existence. I think I lie here, overweight and conscious. I think you can see me, not just some outer wrapping, for I think I am just a live human body. But that is not the basis of my argument. I give you these souls. I merely observe that they can by their nature provide no principle of personal identity. . . .

The Second Night

Miller: First, let me explain why, independently of my desire to defend survival after death, I am dissatisfied with your view that personal identity is just bodily identity. My argument will be very similar to the one you used to convince me that personal identity could not be identified with identity of an immaterial soul.

Consider a person waking up tomorrow morning, conscious, but not yet ready to open her eyes and look around and, so to speak, let the new day officially begin.

Weirob: Such a state is familiar enough, I admit.

Miller: Now couldn't such a person tell who she was? That is, even before opening her eyes and looking around, and in particular before looking at her body or making any judgments about it, wouldn't she be able to say who she was? Surely most of us, in the morning, know who we are before opening our eyes and recognizing our own bodies, do we not?

Weirob: You seem to be right about that.

Miller: But such a judgment as this person makes—we shall suppose she judges "I am Gretchen Weirob"—*is* a judgment of personal identity. Suppose she says to herself, "I am the very person who was arguing with Sam Miller last night." This is clearly a statement about her identity with someone who was alive the night before. And she could make this judgment without examining her body at all. You could have made just this judgment this morning, before opening your eyes.

Weirob: Well, in fact I did so. I remembered our conversation of last night and said to myself, "Could I be the rude person who was so hard on Sam Miller's attempts to comfort me?" And, of course, my answer was that I not only could be but was that very rude person.

Miller: But then by the same principle you used last night personal identity cannot be bodily identity. For you said that it could not be identity of immaterial soul because we were not judging as to identity of immaterial soul when we judge as to personal identity. But by the same token, as my example shows, we are not judging as to bodily identity when we judge as to personal identity. For we can judge who we are, and that we are the very person who did such and such and so and so, without having to make any judgments at all about the body. So, personal identity, while it may not consist of identity of an immaterial soul, does not consist in identity of material body either.

Weirob: I did argue as you remember. But I also said that the notion of the identity of an immaterial unobservable unextended soul seemed to make no sense at all. This is one reason that cannot be what we are judging about, when we judge as to personal identity. Bodily identity at least makes sense. Perhaps we are assuming sameness of body, without looking.

Miller: Granted. But you do admit that we do not in our own cases actually need to make a judgment of bodily identity in order to make a judgment of personal identity?

Weirob: I don't think I will admit it. I will let it pass, so that we may proceed.

Miller: Okay. Now it seems to me we are even able to imagine awakening and finding ourselves to have a *different* body than the one we had before. Suppose yourself just as I have described you. And now suppose you finally open your eyes and see, not the body you have grown so familiar with over the years, but one of a fundamentally different shape and size.

Weirob: Well, I should suppose I had been asleep for a very long time and lost a lot of weight — perhaps I was in a coma for a year or so.

Miller: But isn't it at least conceivable that it should not be your old body at all? I seem to be able to imagine awakening with a totally new body.

Weirob: And how would you suppose that this came about?

Miller: That's beside the point. I'm not saying I can imagine a procedure that would bring this about. I'm saying I can imagine it happening to me. In Kafka's *Metamorphosis*, someone awakens as a cockroach. I can't imagine what would make this happen to me or anyone else, but I can imagine awakening with the body of a cockroach. It is incredible that it should happen — that I do not deny. I simply mean I can imagine experiencing it. It doesn't seem contradictory or incoherent, simply unlikely and inexplicable.

Weirob: So, if I admit this can be imagined, what follows then?

Miller: Well, I think it follows that personal identity does not just amount to bodily identity. For I would not, finding that I had a new body, conclude that I was not the very same person I was before. I would be the same *person*, though I did not have the same *body*. So we would have identity of person but not identity of body. So personal identity cannot just amount to bodily identity.

Weirob: Well suppose — and I emphasize *suppose* — I grant you all of this. Where does it leave you? What do you claim I have recognized as the same, if not my body and not my immaterial soul?

Miller: I don't claim that you have recognized anything as the same, except the person involved, that is, you yourself.

Weirob: I'm not sure what you mean.

Miller: . . . Suppose I take a visitor to the stretch of river by the old Mill, and then drive him toward Manhattan. After an hour-or-so drive we see another stretch of river, and I say, "That's the same river we saw this morning." As you pointed out yesterday, I don't thereby imply that the very same molecules of water are seen both times. And the places are different, perhaps a hundred miles apart. And the shape and color and level of pollution might all be different. What do I see later in the day that is identical with what I saw earlier in the day?

Weirob: Nothing except the river itself.

Miller: Exactly. But now notice that what I see, strictly speaking, is not the whole river but only a part of it. I see different parts of the same river at the two different times. So really, if we restrict ourselves to what I literally see, I do not judge identity at all, but something else.

Weirob: And what might that be?

Miller: In saying that the river seen earlier, and the river seen later, are one and the same river, do I mean any more than that the stretch of water seen later and that stretch of water seen earlier are connected by other stretches of water?

Weirob: That's about right. If the stretches of water are so connected there is but one river of which they are both parts.

Miller: Yes, that's what I mean. The statement of identity, "This river is the same one we saw this morning," is in a sense about rivers. But in a way it is also about stretches of water or river parts.

Weirob: So is all of this something special about rivers?

Miller: Not at all. It is a recurring pattern. After all, we constantly deal with objects extended in space and time. But we are seldom aware of the objects' wholes, but only of their parts or stretches of their histories. When a statement of identity is not just something trivial, like "This bed is this bed," it is usually because we are really judging that different parts fit together, in some appropriate pattern, into a certain kind of whole.

Weirob: I'm not sure I see just what you mean yet.

Miller: Let me give you another example. Suppose we are sitting together watching the first game of a doubleheader. You ask me, "Is this game identical with this game?" This is a perfectly stupid question, though, of course, strictly speaking it makes sense and the answer is "yes."

But now suppose you leave in the sixth inning to go for hot dogs. You are delayed, and return after about forty-five minutes or so. You ask, "Is this the same game I was watching?" Now your question is not stupid, but perfectly appropriate.

Weirob: Because the first game might still be going on or it might have ended, and the second game begun, by the time I return.

Miller: Exactly. Which is to say somehow different parts of the game — different innings, or at least different plays — were somehow involved in your question. That's why it wasn't stupid or trivial but significant.

Weirob: So, you think that judgments as to the identity of an object of a certain kind — rivers or baseball games or whatever — involve judgments as to the *parts* of those things being connected in a certain way, and are significant only when different parts are involved. Is that your point?

Miller: Yes, and I think it is an important one. How foolish it would be, when we ask a question about the identity of baseball games, to look for something *else*, other than the game as a whole, which had to be the same. It could be the same game, even if different players were involved. It could be the same game, even if it had been moved to a different field. These other things, the innings, the plays, the players, the field, don't have to be the same at the different times for the game to be the same, they just have to be related in certain ways so as to make that complex whole we call a single game.

Weirob: You think we were going off on a kind of a wildgoose chase when we asked whether it was the identity of soul or body that was involved in the identity of persons?

Miller: Yes. The answer I should now give is neither. We are wondering about the identity of the person. Of course, if by "soul" we just mean "person," there is no problem. But if we mean, as I did yesterday, some other thing whose identity is already understood, which has to be the same when persons are the same, we are just fooling ourselves with words.

Weirob: With rivers and baseball games, I can see that they are made up of parts connected in a certain way. The connection is, of course, different in the two cases, as is the sort of "part" involved. River parts must be connected physically with other river parts to form a continuous whole. Baseball innings must be connected so that the score, batting order, and the like are carried over from the earlier inning to the later one according to the rules. Is there something analogous we are to say about persons?

Miller: Writers who concern themselves with this speak of "person-stages." That is just a stretch of consciousness, such as you and I are aware of now. I am aware of a flow of thoughts and feelings that are mine, you are aware of yours. A person is just a whole composed of such stretches as parts, not some substance that underlies them, as I thought yesterday, and not the body in which they occur, as you seem to think. That is the conception of a person I wish to defend today.

Weirob: So when I awoke and said to myself, "I am the one who was so rude to Sam Miller last night," I was judging that a certain stretch of consciousness I was then aware of, and an earlier one I remembered having been aware of, form a single whole of the appropriate sort—a single stream of consciousness, we might say.

Miller: Yes, that's it exactly. You need not worry about whether the same immaterial soul is involved, or even whether that makes sense. Nor need you worry about whether the same body is involved, as indeed you do not since you don't even have to open your eyes and look. Identity is not, so to speak, something under the person-stages, nor in something they are attached to, but something you build from them.

Now survival, you can plainly see, is no problem at all once we have this conception of personal identity. All you need suppose is that there is, in Heaven, a conscious being, and that the person-stages that make her up are in the appropriate relation to those that now make you up, so that they are parts of the same whole—namely, you. If so, you have survived. So will you admit now that survival is at least possible?

Weirob: Hold on, hold on. Comforting me is not that easy. You will have to show that it is possible that these person-stages or stretches of consciousness be related in the appropriate way. And to do that, won't you have to tell me what that way is?

Miller: Yes, of course. I was getting ahead of myself. It is right at this point that my reading was particularly helpful. In a chapter of his *Essay On Human Understanding* Locke discusses this very question. He suggests that the relation between two person-stages or stretches of consciousness that makes them stages of a single person is just that the later one contains memories of the earlier one. He doesn't say this in so many words—he talks of "extending our consciousness back in time." But he seems to be thinking of memory.

Weirob: So, any past thought or feeling or intention or desire that I can remember having is mine?

Miller: That's right. I can remember only my own past thoughts and feelings, and you only yours. Of course, everyone would readily admit that. Locke's insight is to take this relation as the source of identity and not just its consequence. To remember—or more plausibly, to be able to remember—the thoughts and feelings of a person who was conscious in the past is just what it is to be that person.

Now you can easily see that this solves the problem of the possibility of survival. As I was saying, all you need to do is imagine someone at some future time, not on this earth and not with your present thoughts and feelings, remembering the very conversation we are having now. This does not require sameness of anything else, but it amounts to sameness of person. So, now will you admit it?

Weirob: No, I don't.

Miller: Well, what's the problem now?

Weirob: I admit that if I remember having a certain thought or feeling had by some person in the past, then I must indeed be that person. Though I can remember watching others think, I cannot remember their thinking, any more than I can experience it at the time it occurs if it is theirs and not mine. This is the kernel of Locke's idea, and I don't see that I could deny it.

But we must distinguish — as I'm sure you will agree — between *actually* remembering and merely *seeming* to remember. Many men who think that they are Napoleon claim to remember losing the battle of Waterloo. We may suppose them to be sincere, and to really seem to remember it. But they do not actually remember because they were not at the battle and are not Napoleon.

Miller: Of course I admit that we must distinguish between actually remembering and only seeming to.

Weirob: And you will admit too, I trust, that the thought of some person at some far place and some distant time seeming to remember this conversation I am having with you would not give me the sort of comfort that the prospect of survival is supposed to provide. I would have no reason to anticipate future experiences of this person, simply because she is to *seem* to remember my experiences. The experiences of such a deluded impostor are not ones I can look forward to having.

Miller: I agree.

Weirob: So the mere possibility of someone in the future seeming to remember this conversation does not show the possibility of my surviving. Only the possibility of someone actually remembering this conversation — or, to be precise, the experiences I am having — would show that.

Miller: Of course. But what are you driving at? Where is the problem? I can imagine someone being deluded, but also someone actually being you and remembering your present thoughts.

Weirob: But, what's the difference? How do you know *which* of the two you are imagining, and *what* you have shown possible?

Miller: Well, I just imagine the one and not the other. I don't see the force of your argument.

Weirob: Let me try to make it clear with another example. Imagine two persons. One is talking to you, saying certain words, having certain thoughts, and so forth. The other is not talking to you at all, but is in the next room being hypnotized. The hypnotist gives to this person a post-hypnotic suggestion that upon awakening he will remember having had certain thoughts and having uttered certain words to you. The thoughts and words he mentions happen to be just the thoughts and words which the first person actually thinks and says. Do you understand the situation?

Miller: Yes, continue.

Weirob: Now, in a while, both of the people are saying sentences which begin, "I remember saying to Sam Miller —" and "I remember thinking as I talked to Sam Miller." And they both report remembering just the same thoughts and utterances. One of these will be remembering and the other only seeming to remember, right?

Miller: Of course.

Weirob: Now which one is *actually* remembering?

Miller: Why, the very one who was in the room talking to me, of course. The other one is just under the influence of the suggestion made by the hypnotist and not remembering talking to me at all.

Weirob: Now you agree that the difference between them does not consist in the content of what they are now thinking or saying.

Miller: Agreed. The difference is in the relation to the past thinking and speaking. In the one case the relation of memory obtains. In the other, it does not.

Weirob: But they both satisfy part of the conditions of remembering, for they both *seem to remember*. So there must be some further condition that the one satisfies and the other does not. I am trying to get you to say what that further condition is.

Miller: Well, I said that the one who had been in this room talking would be remembering.

Weirob: In other words, given two putative rememberers of some past thought or action, the real rememberer is the one who, in addition to seeming to remember the past thought or action, actually thought it or did it.

Miller: Yes.

Weirob: That is to say, the one who is identical with the person who did the past thinking and uttering.

Miller: Yes, I admit it.

Weirob: So, your argument just amounts to this. Survival is possible, because imaginable. It is imaginable, because my identity with some Heavenly person is imaginable. To imagine it, we imagine a person in Heaven who, first, seems to remember my thoughts and actions, and second, is me.

Surely, there could hardly be a tighter circle. If I have doubts that the Heavenly person is me, I will have doubts as to whether she is really remembering or only seeming to. No one could doubt the possibility of some future person who, after death, seemed to remember the things he thought and did. But that possibility does not resolve the issue about the possibility of survival. Only the possibility of someone *actually* remembering could do that—for that, as we agree, is sufficient for identity. But doubts about survival and identity simply go over without remainder into doubts about whether the memories would be actual or merely apparent. You guarantee me no more than the possibility of a deluded Heavenly impostor.

Cohen: But wait, Gretchen. I think Sam was less than fair to his own idea just now.

Weirob: You think you can break out of the circle of using real memory to explain identity, and identity to mark the difference between real and apparent memory? Feel free to try.

Cohen: Let us return to your case of the hypnotist. You point out that we have two putative rememberers. You ask what marks the difference, and claim the answer must be the circular one—that the real rememberer is the person who actually had the experiences both seem to remember.

But that is not the only possible answer. The experiences themselves cause the later apparent memories in the one case, while the hypnotist causes them in the other. We can say that the rememberer is the one of the two whose memories were *caused in the right way* by the earlier experiences. We thus distinguish between the rememberers and the hypnotic subject, without appeal to identity.

The idea that real memory amounts to apparent memory plus identity is misleading anyway. I seem to remember, as a small child, knocking over the Menorah so the candles fell into and spoiled a tureen of soup. And I did actually perform such a feat. So we have apparent memory and identity. But I do *not* actually remember; I was much too young when I did this to remember it now. I have simply been told the story so often I seem to remember.

Here the suggestion that real memory is apparent memory that was caused in the appropriate way by the past events fares better. Not my experience of pulling over the Menorah, but hearing my parents talk about it later, caused my memory-like impressions.

Weirob: You analyze personal identity into memory, and memory into apparent memory which is caused in the right way. A person is a certain sort of causal process.

Cohen: Right.

Weirob: Suppose now for the sake of argument I accept this. How does it help Sam in his defense of the possibility of survival? In ordinary memory, the causal chain from remembered event to memory of it never leads us outside the confines of a single body. Indeed, the normal process of which you speak surely involves storage of information somehow in the brain. How can the states of my brain, when I die, influence in the appropriate way the apparent memories of the Heavenly person Sam takes to be me?

Cohen: Well, I didn't intend to be defending the possibility of survival. That is Sam's problem. I just like the idea that personal identity can be explained in terms of memory, and not just in terms of identity of the body.

Miller: But surely, this does provide me with the basis for further defense. Your challenge, Gretchen, was to explain the difference between two persons in Heaven, one who actually remembers your experience — and so is you — and one who simply seems to remember it. But can I not just say that the one who is you is the one whose states were caused in the appropriate way? I do not mean the way they would be in a normal case of earthly memory. But in the case of the Heavenly being who is you, God would have created her with the brain states (or whatever) she has *because* you had the ones you had at death. Surely it is not the exact form of the dependence of my later memories on my earlier perceptions that makes them really memories, but the fact that the process involved has preserved information.

Weirob: So if God creates a Heavenly person, designing her brain to duplicate the brain I have upon death, that person is me. If, on the other hand, a Heavenly being should come to be with those very same memory-like states by accident (if there are accidents in Heaven) it would not be me.

Miller: Exactly. Are you satisfied now that survival makes perfectly good sense?

Weirob: No, I'm still quite unconvinced.

The problem I see is this. If God could create one person in Heaven, and by designing her after me, make her me, why could he not make two such bodies, and cause this transfer of information into both of them? Would both of these Heavenly persons then be me? It seems as clear as anything in philosophy that from

A is B

and

C is B

where by "is" we mean identity, we can infer,

A is C.

So, if each of these Heavenly persons is me, they must be each other. But then they are not two but one. But my assumption was that God creates two, not one. He could create them physically distinct, capable of independent movement, per-

haps in widely separated Heavenly locations, each with her own duties to perform, her own circle of Heavenly friends, and the like.

So either God, by creating a Heavenly person with a brain modeled after mine, does not really create someone identical with me but merely someone similar to me, or God is somehow limited to making only one such being. I can see no reason why, if there were a God, He should be so limited. So I take the first option. He could create someone similar to me, but not someone who would *be* me. Either your analysis of memory is wrong, and such a being does not, after all, remember what I am doing or saying, or memory is not sufficient for personal identity. Your theory has gone wrong somewhere, for it leads to absurdity.

Cohen: But wait. Why can't Sam simply say that if God makes one such creature, she is you, while if he makes more, none of them is you? It's possible that he makes only one. So it's possible that you survive. Sam always meant to allow that it's *possible* that you won't survive. He had in mind the case in which there is no God to make the appropriate Heavenly persons, or God exists, but doesn't make even one. You have simply shown that there is another way of not surviving. Instead of making too few Heavenly rememberers, He makes too many. So what? He might make the right number, and then you would survive.

Weirob: Your remarks really amount to a change in your position. Now you are not claiming that memory alone is enough for personal identity. Now, it is memory *plus* lack of competition, the absence of other rememberers, that is needed for personal identity.

Cohen: It does amount to a change of position. But what of it? Is there anything untenable about the position as changed?

Weirob: Let's look at this from the point of view of the Heavenly person. She says to herself, "Oh, I must be Gretchen Weirob, for I remember doing what she did and saying what she said." But now that's a pretty tenuous conclusion, isn't it? She is really only entitled to say, "Oh, either I'm Gretchen Weirob, or God has created more than one being like me, and none of us is." Identity has become something dependent on things wholly extrinsic to her. Who she is now turns on not just her states of mind and their relation to my states of mind, but on the existence or nonexistence of other people. Is this really what you want to maintain?

Or look at it from my point of view. God creates one of me in Heaven. Surely I should be glad if convinced this was to happen. Now he creates another, and I should despair again, for this means I won't survive after all. How can doubling a good deed make it worthless?

Cohen: Are you saying that there is some contradiction in my suggestion that only creation of a unique Heavenly Gretchen counts as your survival?

Weirob: No, it's not contradictory, as far as I can see. But it seems odd in a way that shows that something somewhere is wrong with your theory. Here is a certain relationship I have with a Heavenly person. There being such a person, to whom I am related in this way, is something that is of great importance to me, a source of comfort. It makes it appropriate for me to anticipate having her experiences, since she is just me. Why should my having that relation to another being destroy my relation to this one? You say because then I will not be identical with either of them. But since you have provided a theory about what that identity consists in, we can look and see what it amounts to for me to be or not to be identical. If she is to remember my experience, I can rightly anticipate hers. But then it seems the doubling makes no difference. And yet it must, for one cannot be identical with two. So you add, in a purely *ad hoc* manner, that her memory of me isn't enough to make my anticipation of her experiences appropriate, if there are two rather than one so linked. Isn't it more reasonable to conclude, since memory does not secure identity when there are two Heavenly Gretchens, it also doesn't when there is only one?

Cohen: There is something *ad hoc* about it, I admit. But perhaps that's just the way our concept works. You have not elicited a contradiction —

Weirob: An infinite pile of absurdities has the same weight as a contradiction. And absurdities can be generated without limit from your account. Suppose God created this Heavenly person before I died. Then He in effect kills me; if He has already created her, then you really are not talking to whom you think, but someone new, created by Gretchen Weirob's strange death moments ago. Or suppose He first creates one being in Heaven, who is me. Then He creates another. Does the first cease to be me? If God can create such beings in Heaven, surely He can do so in Albuquerque. And there is nothing on your theory to favor this body before you as Gretchen Weirob's, over the one belonging to the person created in Albuquerque. So I am to suppose that if God were to do this, I would suddenly cease to be Gretchen Weirob. But that would be a confused way of putting it. There would be here, in my place, a new person with false memories of having been Gretchen Weirob, who has just died of competition — a strange death if ever there was one. She would have no right to my name, my bank account, or the services of my doctor, who is paid from insurance premiums paid for by deductions from Gretchen Weirob's past salary. Surely this is nonsense; however carefully God should choose to duplicate me, in Heaven or in Albuquerque, I would not cease to be, or cease to be who I am. You may reply that God, being benevolent, would never create an extra Gretchen Weirob. But I do not say that he would, but only that if he did this would not, as your theory implies, mean that I cease to exist. Your theory gives the wrong answer in this possible circumstance, so it must be wrong. I think I have been given no motivation to abandon the most obvious and straightforward view on these matters. I am a live body, and when that body dies, my existence will be at an end.

Further Questions

1. Compare the arguments against the idea that personal identity consists in either a soul or a body with the selection by John Locke.

2. Weirob offers two arguments against Miller's belief in souls. The second one might be put as follows:

> The concept "same soul" is meaningful if and only if the notion of "soul" is meaningful. If souls cannot be observed, then the notion "same soul" is meaningless. Souls cannot be observed. Therefore, the notion "soul" is meaningless.

Do you agree or disagree? Why?

3. Why does Weirob think that Cohen's view is absurd? Do you agree? How could Cohen best respond?

4. Suppose *your brain* (and relevant portions of your central nervous system) were removed from your body and instantaneously replaced with a synthetic replica that functioned exactly as your brain functions and on which was encoded all of the information that is on your brain — all of your beliefs, tastes, dispositions, memories, and so on. Assume that there would be a survivor to such an operation — that the procedure is reliable. Give the best argument you can that that survivor would be you. Then give the best objection you can to the argument you just gave.

5. Suppose your *entire body* was destroyed and instantaneously replaced with a synthetic replica that functioned exactly as your body functions and that exactly preserved your body's psychology. Assume that the procedure is reliable. Give the best argument you can that you could survive such an operation. Then give the best objection you can to the argument you just gave.

Further Readings

Three excellent introductions to the problem of personal identity are:
Perry, John, ed. *Personal Identity*. Berkeley: University of California Press, 1975.
Rorty, Amélie, ed. *The Identities of Persons*. Berkeley: University of California Press, 1976.
Williams, Bernard. *Problems of the Self*. Cambridge: Cambridge University Press, 1973.

Identity and Survival: The Persons We Most Want to Be

RAYMOND MARTIN

Raymond Martin teaches philosophy at the University of Maryland. He writes primarily in the areas of philosophical psychology and philosophy of history. In *The Past*

Within Us (Princeton University Press, 1989), he proposes a new focus for philosophy of history. In this selection, Martin argues that many of us are not as interested in retaining our identities as we are in transforming ourselves in ways we value.

Reading Questions

1. What does the theoretical possibility that you could fission into two separate but equal replicas of yourself have to do with whether you care if you will survive the night?

2. Does a person who fissions into two separate but equal replicas lose her identity with her former self?

3. Is psychological continuity more important than physical continuity?

4. Is becoming the persons we most want to be more important than physical continuity? Than psychological continuity? Than identity?

DO YOU CARE whether you will survive the night? It is common sense to suppose you do — indeed, that you care a great deal. If you are depressed or old or terminally ill, you may not care or you may even prefer to die. But otherwise, we normally suppose, you want to survive. As is so often the case, however, common sense, even on such a seemingly obvious question, may well be wrong.

The most interesting and controversial conjecture to emerge from the last two decades of philosophical debate over personal identity is that probably you do not care particularly whether *you* will survive the night — that identity is not what matters primarily in survival — provided that certain other continuities between you now and someone who will exist in the morning are preserved. The continuities in question are either physical or psychological, or both.

I wish to argue for a more radical thesis: that what matters primarily in survival is neither identity nor physical continuity, nor psychological continuity, but rather becoming the (sorts of) persons we most want to be.

I

It is necessary to separate two questions: Under what conditions is personal identity preserved? Under what conditions is what matters primarily in survival preserved? The first question asks (among other things) for a specification of the conditions under which someone in the future would be the same person as you are now. The second asks for the conditions under which the existence of someone (or something) in the future would preserve what now matters primarily to you in survival. The phrase "in survival" in these two questions is meant to exclude altruistic concerns, such as what will happen to your loved ones after you die, and also egoistic concerns that go beyond concern with your own future or the future of appropriate surrogates for yourself.[1]

For hundreds of years, and until rather recently, philosophers treated these two questions as one. It seemed so obvious that what matters primarily in survival is identity that no one noticed it as a separate assumption much less questioned it. Philosophers question it now. During the last two decades, several philosophers have argued persuasively that other things matter more than identity. According to the philosophers who hold this new view, identity is only mistakenly thought to be what matters primarily in survival, and this because identity is all but invariably correlated with other characteristics of persons that *are* what matter primarily in survival.[2]

To see what motivates this new view, consider the much discussed case of a person whose brain is divided, each half of which is then transplanted into its own new body. This case may be pictured as shown below. In this illustration, A is the donor whose brain has been divided, and B and C are the persons who each got one-half of A's brain. Suppose that before division, each half of A's brain is psychologically redundant, so that immediately after division each of the resulting persons — B and C — has all and only the psychological characteristics of A — the same character traits, the same beliefs, the same tastes, and so on. Suppose also that B and C have bodies exactly similar to each other's bodies and to A's body.

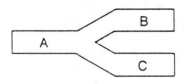

Many philosophers believe that in such a case, neither of the resulting persons is identical to the doner; that is, neither B nor C is the same person as A. The argument for this view — henceforth, the Fission Argument — is this: both B and C have an equal claim to be the same person as A, so neither can be the same person as A unless both are. But if both B and C were the same person as A, then they would be the same person as each other (identity is a transitive relationship: if X is identical to Y, and Y to Z, then X is identical to Z). But, B and C, at least once they begin to lead independent lives, are not the same person as each other. Thus, neither B nor C can be the same person as A.

So the fission operation does not preserve A's identity. Even so, its outcome may be better, from A's point of view, than all of the available alternatives that do preserve her identity. Suppose, for instance, that while A's brain is healthy, her body is ridden with cancer, and that A's only hope for survival is to have her healthy brain transplanted into at least one other healthy body.[3] Two procedures are available. The first is to have her entire brain put into a single healthy body. The second is to have her brain split, as in the example just described, and the two halves of it put into two separate healthy bodies. Suppose, for some esoteric reason having to do with brain transplants, there is only a 10 percent chance the transplantation will be successful if A adopts the first procedure (if it isn't successful, A will be severely mentally retarded), but there is a 95 percent chance *both* transplantations will be successful if A adopts the second procedure. Which procedure should A choose?

If the Fission Argument is correct, then if A chooses the first procedure and the transplantation is successful, she will be the same person as the recipient of her brain, whereas if A chooses the second procedure and both transplantations are successful, she will not be the same person as either of the recipients of half of her brain. In other words, if A chooses the first procedure and the transplantation is successful, A's identity will be preserved, whereas if A chooses the second procedure and both transplantations are successful, A will lose her identity. Even so, it seems obvious (on at least some ways of fleshing out this example) that A should choose the second procedure. This choice shows that A's preserving her identity is not as important as her promoting other values she has, in particular, that of significantly increasing her chances of continuing her psychology in a body as good as her current body.

The Fission Argument depends on a thought experiment in which events that could not happen in real life, at least for the foreseeable future, are depicted. In real life the two halves of our brains are not equivalent. And even if they were, we could not successfully transplant them into healthy bodies in the ways envisaged. So, we may never *actually* get the opportunity to separate identity from other characteristics, such as psychological continuity, that normally accompany it. This is sometimes thought an objection to the evidential value of the Fission Argument's thought experiment. In fact, it is precisely why it has so much value.

In the thought experiment, identity is separated from other characteristics that always accompany it in real life. We are thus given an opportunity to decide which we would choose if we were able to choose between identity and these other characteristics. Without such a thought experiment, it would be extremely difficult to elicit these preferences. If we decide that identity is not what matters most and that we would choose other things over identity, then that decision is evidence that *in real life* identity only *seems* to be of central importance, but is not really, because other things that are more important than identity get confused with it.

Still, the Fission Argument is controversial, primarily for two reasons. First, it depends on the assumption that identity is a transitive relationship. Some philosophers have questioned this assumption. But not many have been willing to give it up. The reason is that the assumption that identity is transitive is so well entrenched in the ways we think about identity that to argue convincingly that identity should not be regarded as transitive, one would have to specify the circumstances under which we are and are not entitled to infer, from the fact that X is identical to Y, and Y to Z, the conclusion that X is identical to Z. So far, no proposed solution to this problem has attracted much support.[4] I shall not consider here any of these proposed solutions because they are too technical to consider briefly and because I shall offer an argument that identity is not what matters primarily in survival which does not depend on the assumption that identity is transitive.

The second reason the Fission Argument is controversial is that it relies on the assumption that the donor who fissions is just one person. Some philosophers have rejected this assumption in favor of the view that the donor is as many persons as she will fission into.[5] On this view, the donor, A, is not a person, but rather a "person stage," roughly, a time slice of a person. All persons are composed of "person stages." Two or more persons may sometimes share the same stage. Thus, in the preceding diagram, A is a prefission stage of a person that also includes the postfission stage, B. In addition, A is a prefission stage of a different person that also includes the postfission stage, C. The person that includes the stages A and B, and the different person that includes the stages A and C, share a stage: A. On this view, there is no loss of identity in a fission operation, provided the operation preserves psychological continuity, since prior to fission the two persons who will eventually separate overlap. After fission, the two do not *begin* to exist, they merely separate.

This way of objecting to the Fission Argument does not question whether identity is transitive but rather whether the fission operation really separates identity from what matters primarily in survival. Philosophers disagree about whether it is an adequate response to the Fission Argument. I shall not pause here to debate the issue because I shall offer an argument that identity is not what matters primarily in survival that does not depend on fission. My argument, if it works, will undermine this way of saving the view that identity is what matters primarily in survival, even if this way is an adequate response to the Fission Argument.

Although it is controversial whether the Fission Argument shows that identity is not what matters primarily in survival, still, several important philosophers are convinced that it does show this. Assume, for the sake of argument, that they are right: identity is *not* what matters. Then, what *does* matter? Aside from identity, what's left? For most philosophers, what's left that might matter is physical continuity, in whole or in part, and/or psychological continuity, in whole or in part. But which, if either, of these matters more?

II

For most of us, psychological continuity is more important than physical continuity. To see why, suppose, as in the preceding example, that while *A*'s brain is healthy, her body is ridden with cancer. But this time, suppose that *A*'s only hope for survival is to have her entire healthy brain transplanted intact to another healthy body and that this transplantation procedure is perfectly safe. We might even imagine that the new body is better than *A*'s current body, not only in that it is healthy, but also in other respects that are appealing to *A*; for instance, the new body is better looking and more athletic and younger. *A*, in effect, is faced with radical cosmetic surgery.

Surely *A* has not lost much if she jettisons her old body and moves her brain to the better body that awaits it. Such an operation would not be as bad as staying in the old body and dying of cancer, even if the death were painless. In fact, vanity being what it is, if radical cosmetic surgery of this sort were available and safe, it is likely that many people — both men and women — would choose it, even if the old bodies they jettisoned in the process were healthy. So, if physical continuity matters primarily in survival, it cannot be the continuity of the whole body, but at most the continuity of the brain.[6]

Is the continuity of the whole brain important? Not necessarily. Part of the brain, if it were functionally equivalent to the whole, would do just as well. But is even the continuity of any part of the brain important? Again, it would seem not, at least not necessarily. The importance of our brains, like that of any other organ, is not intrinsic, but derivative; that is, it depends not on what the brain is in and of itself, but rather *solely* on the functions the brain serves. Ultimately, the most important function the brain serves is that of sustaining our psychologies. If some other organ, such as the liver, sustained our psychologies and our brains served the functions this other organ now serves, then this other organ would be as important in survival as the brain now is and the brain only as important as this other organ now is. So, if something else — anything else — could sustain our psychologies as reliably as the brain and also perform the brain's other essential functions, then the brain should — it may seem — have little importance in survival, and this even though this other thing were not any part of our bodies.[7]

We can imagine a futuristic device — Parfit imagines a futuristic traveling device, a Star Trek style "beamer," which he calls a "Teletransporter" — that reliably preserves our psychologies but without preserving physical continuity, not even continuity of any part of the brain. Since such a device serves the brain's function of preserving our psychologies, if the only reason for thinking the brain matters importantly in survival is that the brain serves the function of preserving our psychologies, then it would be irrational to insist that even partial brain continuity matters importantly, much less primarily, in survival.

Parfit argues that it is not even important, at least in retrospect, that whatever preserves psychological continuity preserves it reliably, an idea he captures in the dictum: it is the effect that matters, not the cause. Imagine, for instance, that having just used the Teletransporter to travel successfully to Mars, you learn that it has been malfunctioning. Had you known that before the trip, it would have been rational to refuse to go. But once you are on Mars, the unreliability of the Teletransporter does not matter to your prospects. The person on Mars is psychologically continuous with your pretrip self, and that is the best you could have hoped for in so far as you were concerned about preserving your psychology. You would not have wanted more even had the Teletransporter been working reliably. The reliability or unreliability of what caused this outcome has no bearing on whether what matters primarily in survival has been preserved.

Parfit uses such considerations to argue that physical continuity is not necessary for *identity*. So, for instance, he claims that the person on Mars, even though not physically continuous with you, is the same person as you were on earth.[8] He also argues that it is *irrational* for physical continuity to matter importantly in survival.

I do not want to argue that physical continuity is not necessary for identity, not because I think it is necessary (I don't know whether it is necessary), but because it would be beside the point to consider that issue here. The significant question is whether physical continuity matters importantly in survival. Parfit says it does not — that it would be irrational to value physical continuity importantly. I disagree that it would be irrational. It may be that most people do not value physical continuity importantly. But it is not necessarily irrational for someone to value physical continuity importantly.

We strongly prefer originals to replicas. Not for every kind of thing — typically not, say, for can openers — but for many kinds of things, such as important historical artifacts (say, Galileo's telescope), great works of art (say, Michelangelo's *Pieta*), and certain highly valued natural objects, such as the majestic Sequoia stands in California which include trees that may be the oldest living things on earth. Would you value replicas, made yesterday, of each of these as much as you would value the originals? Set aside the greater resale and prestige value of the originals. Suppose no one would know you had experienced any of these things except yourself, and except for the value of the experience, you gained nothing from them. Considering just how they would affect you personally, would you value the replicas as much as the originals?[9]

When I consider such questions, I find that I would value the originals much more since the originals help me to feel psychologically close to the past or to certain past events or persons in ways the replicas could not, at least if I knew they were replicas. And that feeling of closeness is im-

portant to me. Hence, the originals have great instrumental value that the replicas would lack, and for reasons that have nothing to do with false metaphysics. I think many others would feel the same way.

Some may value their bodies solely because they believe their bodies are essential to preserving their identities. But some others are sure to value their bodies because their bodies have been and are the vehicles for virtually all that has been significant in their lives. Thus, physical continuity can matter importantly in survival, and for perfectly acceptable reasons, even if it is not necessary for identity.

Why then is it initially so plausible to underestimate the importance of physical continuity? The reason, I think, is that while most of us would strongly prefer our original bodies to an exact replica, the attitudes we have toward our bodies are not like the attitudes we have toward the other examples considered, Galileo's telescope and the rest. Most of us have mixed feelings, at best, toward our bodies. We may strongly prefer them to an exact replica, but we don't like them just as they are. If we had to trade our bodies in, we would strongly prefer to trade them for an *in*exact replica. If we could trade our bodies in for an inexact replica *of our choosing*, many would leap at the chance. Witness, for instance, the growing popularity of cosmetic surgery. These mixed feelings we have toward our bodies explain much of the plausibility of the claim that physical continuity does not matter importantly in survival.

But if the question is whether we would strongly prefer to keep our bodies rather than to trade them in for an *exact* replica, it does not matter that we might prefer to trade them in, or to trade parts of them in — a damaged kidney, a grotesque nose — for a better replacement. That just shows there are other things we value more than our current bodies. And even though there are things we value more, some people may still place a high value on their current bodies. I shall argue, later on, that most people, on reflection, probably *would not* regard physical continuity as part of what matters primarily in survival. But that is a separate issue. The point I am making now is that it is not necessarily *irrational* to regard physical continuity as part of what matters primarily in survival.

III

Many philosophers question whether it even makes sense to suppose a person has survived his bodily death.[10] Our discussion suggests that the important issue is not whether a person could survive bodily death—for instance, whether someone who exists after your bodily death could be the same person as you—but whether what matters primarily in survival could survive bodily death. Thus, if identity is not what matters primarily in survival, then even if a person could not conceivably survive his bodily death, it may still be possible that what matters primarily to him in his survival could survive his bodily death. If psychological continuity, not physical continuity, is what matters, then in looking for evidence that what matters has sometimes survived bodily death, we should look for evidence that someone's psychology has survived bodily death. Is there any such evidence?

I think there is better evidence than most philosophers have so far acknowledged. I don't think it is good enough to warrant the claim that what matters primarily in survival has survived bodily death. But it is good enough to illustrate realistically how such a claim might be defended. I am thinking particularly of an intriguing phenomenon that has been investigated in considerable depth by the American psychiatrist Ian Stevenson. He calls it "a case suggestive of reincarnation," and it involves children who from an early age seem to remember being someone who has recently died and who is unknown in any normal way to the children or to their parents.

Consider, for instance, Stevenson's report on the case of Jasbir, who was born in 1950, in Rasulpur, India, and who at the age of three and a half was thought to have died of smallpox.[11] Preparations were made to bury Jasbir, but it became dark and the burial was postponed until morning. That night Jasbir's father noticed stirring in the body of his son which then gradually revived. Weeks passed before the boy could express himself. When he did, it was evident he had undergone a remarkable transformation.

Jasbir then stated that he was the son of Shankar of Vehedi, a village far enough removed from Rasulpur that there was little interaction between people from the two villages. He communicated many details of "his" life and death in Vehedi, including how during a wedding procession he had eaten poisoned sweets given him by a man who owed him money, fell off the chariot he was riding, injured his head, and died.

Stevenson lists twenty-two checkable statements that Jasbir made about "himself," almost all of which were true of Sobha Ram: He was the son of Shankar of Vehedi. He was a Brahmin, not a Jat. There was a peepal tree in front of his house, and the house had a well that was half in and half outside the house. His wife belonged to the village of Molna. He had a chariot he used for attending weddings. He died after falling from the chariot while returning from Nirmana in a marriage party. He had a mother named Kela, a son named Baleshwar, an aunt named Ram Kali, and a mother-in-law named Kirpi.

Stevenson also claims that Jasbir recognised many relatives and friends of Sobha Ram and correctly identified their relationships to Sobha Ram. Stevenson lists sixteen such recognitions. He reports that after Jasbir's change in personality, Jasbir's original personality did not express itself. After his recovery from smallpox, Jasbir claimed he was Sobha Ram, behaved like Sobha Ram, and only gradually accepted the body and life situations of Jasbir. The Tyagis accepted Jasbir as a full member of their family and consulted him about the marriage of Sobha Ram's son and daughter. The man Jasbir claimed killed Sobha Ram to avoid paying a debt later paid Jasbir (not Sobha Ram's family) 600 rupees. Yet Jasbir continued to live most of the time with his natural parents, and planned to marry in the Jat caste.

Jasbir's case differs from the other cases Stevenson has investigated in that the person whose personality Jasbir took over did not die until after Jasbir was born. Otherwise, Jasbir's case closely resembles Stevenson's other cases. Since his original investigations of cases suggestive of reincarnation, Stevenson, working out of the University of Virginia and joined by research assistants, has published four more volumes of similar investigations.[12]

So far as I know, Stevenson's data are true. Assume, for the sake of argument, they are. How then can they be explained? Stevenson considers four possibilities: fraud, on the part of the people investigated; cryptomnesia; ESP; and survival.

Stevenson argues that fraud is implausible. Since his subjects were children and the total number of people interviewed, often cross-examined on several occasions, was usually quite large, fraud would have required extraordinary conspiracies. Stevenson claims the children and their parents generally gained nothing from these incidents but publicity, which in many cases they did not want. He also cites the difficulties of directing and staging the highly emotional scenes he sometimes witnessed in the villages.

> I cannot believe that simple villagers would have the time or inclination to rehearse such dramas as occurred in Chhatta when the family of Prakash thought—or said they thought—I favored his returning to the other family. The complexity of the behavioural features of these cases alone seems to make fraud virtually out of the question, and I prefer to pass on to other more plausible explanations of them.[13]

And we should too. My purpose is not to argue that what matters primarily in survival—assuming, for the moment, it is psychological continuity—has actually survived bodily death, but rather to illustrate how a case could be made for such survival, and in particular how the preceding analysis transforms how one would argue the

point. The interesting point for present purposes is that if Stevenson's data are true, and if psychological continuity, however caused, is what matters primarily in survival, then on *any* explanation of Stevenson's data other than fraud, we should conclude that it may well be reasonable to believe that what matters primarily in survival sometimes persists beyond bodily death.

The debate over survival of bodily death, in large part, is over rival explanations of reports of various kinds of exotic phenomena. There are always two parts to such debates. The first concerns the likelihood of fraud. The second, which occupies most of the philosophical literature, concerns whether various explanations of the data that do not imply survival, such as ESP, are more or less plausible than explanations that do imply survival. Skeptics argue that explanations that do not imply survival are more plausible. Believers opt for the ones that imply survival.

The claim, if accepted, that psychological continuity, however caused (not identity), is what matters primarily in survival, should completely change the dynamics of this debate. Most of the explanations that are thought not to imply survival *do* imply psychological continuity. Consider, for instance, Stevenson's attempt to explain the data he collected. Aside from fraud, he considers three categories: cryptomnesia, ESP, and survival. He considers cryptomnesia and ESP as alternatives to those explanations that imply survival and hence as explanations that must be defeated to argue successfully for survival.

On the cryptomnesia hypothesis, the child gets the information in a normal way, later forgets where he got it, even that he got it in a normal way, then remembers the information as if he were remembering doing or experiencing what a deceased person did or experienced; the child's parents also are ignorant of the real source of the information. On the ESP hypothesis, the child gets the information through some unusual causal mechanism that causes him to seem to remember doing or experiencing the deeds or experiences of a deceased person. On the survival hypotheses, on the other hand, there is usually said to be a spirit or soul which has survived bodily death and somehow accounts for the data.

But both cryptomnesia and ESP can be ways of being psychologically continuous with a person who has died. Thus, on the view that psychological continuity, however caused, is what matters primarily in survival, the crucial question turns on two issues. First, is fraud or one of the other explanations — *any* one of the other explanations — more likely? Secondly, how much psychological continuity has been preserved? In the case of Stevenson's data, barring fraud, quite a bit of psychological continuity persists beyond bodily death. Enough, it would seem, that we would want to say that a great deal of what matters primarily in survival has survived bodily death.

IV

I have argued that for most people psychological continuity is more important in survival than physical continuity. But is psychological continuity what matters primarily in survival? It seems not. The clue is the realization that whether or not you care particularly whether *you* will survive the night, probably you would *prefer not to continue exactly as you are*. Most of us would rather change than stay the same, at least if we could choose the ways in which we would change. Probably you would like your body to be better than it is, perhaps stronger, more flexible, younger, more beautiful, and so on. Probably you would also like to be psychologically better than you are, perhaps more patient, or generous, or intelligent, or industrious, or humorous, or spontaneous, or compassionate, or more or less something. I would opt for all of the changes in both of the lists just specified. Perhaps you would as well.

Imagine it were possible for a person to undergo a series of painless and safe and inexpensive "operations" in each of which he would exchange some physical or psychological trait he has for a "better" replacement. So, for instance, you could, through a single operative procedure (one, say, that used simply sound waves and involved no cutting), become physically "better" — stronger or more flexible or more beautiful — or psychologically "better" — more patient or more generous or more intelligent, and so on. If this were possible, many of us, no doubt, would continually improve ourselves through a series of such operations to the point where we would have significantly transformed ourselves. The benefits would be enormous. At last, a self-improvement program that really works! How much would the program be worth?

Imagine the ony cost is that each time you undergo such an operation, the memories you have of life before the first such operation you underwent fade somewhat, so that if you undergo the operation enough times, these memories fade entirely. Would the benefits be worth this price? Remember that memory fades somewhat for most of us anyway, as we grow older, and it would be possible to be reeducated, to some extent, about your past. For instance, you could record the story of your life before beginning the operations, and then later you could relearn that story just as you may now learn from your parents of things you did in your early childhood.

Imagine the details of this example fleshed out in a way that would make such an operation as attractive to you as possible. Then, if it were available, would you choose to undergo it? I find when I ask myself this question that I would choose to undergo it, probably many times. I suspect many others would as well.

Now change the example and imagine that while the operation is still safe and inexpensive and painless, you can undergo it only once, but during that single operation you can change yourself as much as you like. Since you have only one chance at the operation and the alternative ways of changing yourself dramatically for the better are so onerous and unreliable, there would be a tremendous incentive to change yourself drastically, in fact, in all of the ways you would like to change so as to become the person you most want to be. However, the greater the changes, the greater the tax on your personal memory. You could change radically and become the person you most want to be (assuming you are not already close to that sort of person), but only by ceasing to be either physically or psychologically closely continuous with your current self. On most theories of personal identity, this would mean you could change radically and become the person you most want to be only by ceasing to be the person you now are. Would you opt, nevertheless, for the operation?

Probably you would want to know much more about the procedure before deciding. For now, just imagine these further details filled in so that the cost of the operation is no greater than losing most of your personal memories and those of your physical and psychological traits you wish to change (thus greatly diminishing your physical and psychological continuity with your current self), and the benefit is becoming the person you most want to be. If those were the costs and benefits, would you have the operation? Can you imagine any way of filling out the details of the example so that you would? I can imagine ways of filling out the details so that I would. I suspect many others can imagine ways of filling out the details so that they would as well. For those of us who would have the operation even if the physical and psychological changes were quite radical, neither bodily nor psychological continuity is what matters primarily in survival.

On most theories of personal identity, if I am neither physically nor psychologically closely connected to "my former self," then I am not the same person as my former self.[14] Assume, for the sake of argument, these theories are correct. How much would it matter to you that the changes you would want in the operation just envisaged would cost you your identity? Remember that you can have the operation only once. You could choose to hold back from becoming the person you most want to be and request only such changes as are compatible with your re-

maining the person you now are. Or you could go for it and become the person you most want to be. I believe that I would go for it, though not without fear, and that to become the person I most want to be would require drastic physical and psychological changes. So drastic, that the tax on my personal memory would be enormous and the physical and psychological connectedness to my current self so greatly diminished that I would probably not remain the person I now am. Yet, I would choose the changes I want anyway, even if it meant I would lose my identity. I suspect many others would make similar choices for themselves, even at the cost of their own identities.

But does the fact, if it is a fact, that many of us would choose changes that cost us our identities, show, even for us, that becoming the persons we most want to be is what matters primarily in survival? Even if, in the choice situation envisaged, many people would rather become the persons they most want to be than to retain their identities, still these same people might even more strongly prefer becoming the persons they most want to be *in ways which preserved* their identities. For instance, many might prefer to become more spontaneous by gradually learning how to become more comfortable with their bodies, say, by successfully completing a two-year program in psychotherapy and hatha yoga, rather than resorting to instantaneous psychic surgery, and similarly with the other things about themselves they would like to change. Or, more simply, many might prefer to effect the desired changes without diminishing their personal memories, and so, at least arguably, without losing their identities.

I agree that many would strongly prefer to change in ways which allowed them to retain their identities. But this objection shows, at most, that many would prefer both to retain their identities and also to become the persons they most want to be rather than just to become the persons they most want to be. But, if the question is which of these two matters most in survival, then one has to consider a situation in which one could have one of the two, but not both. That is what we just did. And I think, though admittedly without proof, that in the sort of choice-situation envisaged here, where we could have either the changes we would like or retain our identities, but not both, many of us would opt for the changes. For those of us who would, what matters primarily in survival is neither identity, nor physical continuity, nor psychological continuity, but becoming the persons we most want to be.[15]

NOTES

1. I discuss this problem in "Identity's Crisis," *Philosophical Studies*, v. 53, 1988, pp. 295–307, and attempt to solve it in "Self-Interest and Survival," *American Philosophical Quarterly*, v. 29 (1992).

2. See, for instance, Derek Parfit, "Personal Identity," *Philosophical Review*, v. 80, 1971, pp. 3–27; Robert Nozick, *Philosophical Explanations*, Cambridge: Harvard University Press, 1981, Ch. 1; Sydney Shoemaker, "Personal Identity: A Materialist Account," in Sydney Shoemaker and Richard Swinburne, *Personal Identity*, Oxford: Basil Blackwell, 1984, pp. 67–132; and Derek Parfit, *Reasons and Persons*, Oxford: Oxford University Press, 1984, Ch. 12.

3. This example is based on one first presented by Sydney Shoemaker in "Personal Identity: A Materialist Account," *Personal Identity*, p. 119.

4. For a proposed solution, see, for instance, John Perry, "Can the Self Divide?" *Journal of Philosophy*, v. 69, 1972, pp. 463–488.

5. The author and principal defender of this sort of view is David Lewis. See his "Survival and Identity," in Amélie Rorty, ed., *The Identities of Persons*, Berkeley: University of California Press, 1976, pp. 17–40, reprinted, along with "Postscripts to 'Survival and Identity'," in David Lewis, *Philosophical Papers, V. I*, New York: Oxford University Press, 1983, pp. 55–77. Lewis's view is criticized by Derek Parfit, in "Lewis, Perry and What Matters," in Amélie Rorty, ed., *The Identities of Persons*, Berkeley: University of California Press, 1976, pp. 91–96.

6. See Parfit, *Reasons and Persons*, pp. 282–287.

7. I argue for something close to this claim in "Identity, Transformation, and What Matters in Survival," in D. Kolak and R. Martin, eds., *Self and Identity*, New York: Macmillan, pp. 289–301.

8. Mark Johnston, in "Human Beings," *The Journal of Philosophy*, v. 84, 1987, p. 62, n. 5, reports that Parfit did not intend to claim that teletransportation preserves personal identity, but only that it is as good as survival.

9. Leonard Meyer has put the point nicely in connection with our relationships to works of art:

> An original drawing, for instance, is more valuable than the finest reproduction . . . not merely in the economic sense that the original is scarce and hence costly. The original is also more valuable and more exciting aesthetically because our feeling of intimate contact with the magic power of the creative artist heightens awareness, sensitivity, and the disposition to respond. Once a work is known to be a forgery, that magic is gone. (Leonard Meyer, *Music, the Arts, and Ideas*, Chicago: University Of Chicago Press, 1967, p. 62)

To appreciate the depth of our preference for artistic originals, consider the difference between looking at a copy of Dürer's Melancholia I, made by Dürer, and looking at a recent copy, indistinguishable in appearance, made by someone else *from Dürer's original etching plate*. Most of us would greatly prefer the experience of looking at the copy made by Dürer because it is a stronger way of connecting with the "magic power" of Dürer. We have similar attitudes toward nature and historical artifacts. Why not also, then, in the case of our own bodies?

10. To get a feeling for the depth of recent philosophical scepticism about even making sense of life after death, see, for instance, Terence Penelhum, *Religion and Rationality*, New York: Random House, 1971, pp. 334–355, reprinted under the title, "Life After Death," in Steven Cahn and David Shatz, eds., *Contemporary Philosophy of Religion*, New York: Oxford University Press, 1982, pp. 182–198; or see Jay Rosenberg's extended discussion, in *Thinking Clearly About Death*, Englewood Cliffs, NJ: Prentice-Hall, 1983, which concludes with the claim to have "demonstrated" that because "we cannot pry the notion of a person loose from the notion of a living organism . . . we cannot make coherent sense of the supposed possibility that a person's history might continue beyond that person's death" (p. 96).

11. Ian Stevenson, *Twenty Cases Suggestive of Reincarnation*, 2nd Edition, Charlottesville: The University Press of Virginia, 1974, pp. 32 ff.

12. Ian Stevenson, *Cases of the Reincarnation Type, Vols. 1, 2, 3, 4,* Charlottesville: The University Press of Virginia, 1975, 1977, 1980, 1983.

13. Stevenson, *Twenty Cases*, p. 333. See also Stevenson's discussion of fraud in *Cases, Vol. 3*, pp. 343–345.

14. See note 7.

15. Thanks to Daniel Kolak, Peter Unger, Brian Garrett, and John Barresi for helpful criticisms of earlier attempts to state my view.

Further Questions

1. Is a person's identity over time more like the identity of a road surface or the identity of a route?

2. Imagine yourself faced with the option of having the operation Martin describes toward the end of his paper. Suppose you could have it only once. Would you have it? If you would, would you opt for becoming the person you most want to be even at the cost of losing your identity, that is, of ceasing to be the person you now are? Do you think others would feel as you feel?

3. Some would claim that since the fantastic examples described in Martin's paper will never be possible in your lifetime, they have no relevance to how you either do or should understand yourself. What do you think?

Further Readings

Martin, Raymond. "Survival of Bodily Death: A Question of Values," *Religious Studies*, v. 28, 1992. An argument for reconceptualizing the issue of survival.

Nozick, Robert. *Philosophical Explanations*. Cambridge: Harvard University Press, 1981, Ch. 1. State-of-the-art philosophy of identity.

Parfit, Derek. *Reasons and Persons*. Oxford University Press, 1984, Part III. A tough read, but one of the most important recent accounts of personal identity.

Williams, Bernard. "The Self and the Future," *The Philosophical Review*, v. 79, 1970, pp. 161–180; reprinted in *Problems of the Self*. Cambridge: Cambridge University Press, 1973, pp. 46–63. A classic thought experiment.

The Hitchhiking Game

MILAN KUNDERA

Milan Kundera was born in Brno, Czechoslovakia. He is the author of many short stories and novels, including *The Joke*, *The Book of Laughter and Forgetting*, and *The Unbearable Lightness of Being*, which was recently made into a movie. Since 1975 Kundera has been living in France.

In the following story, a couple innocently began playing a game about their identities. The game gets deeper and deeper, revealing masks beneath masks, until finally they are no longer sure of what the truth is or who they really are.

Reading Questions

1. Think about the different roles you play in various social situations. Describe these roles. How do you decide which of your roles are genuine and which are phony? Is there a difference?

2. Have you ever pretended to be someone you are not? What did it feel like? When you went back to being you, what did *that* feel like?

3. One type of tautology is an empty statement—repeating the same meaning using different words, like "visible to the eye" or "an unmarried bachelor." At the end of the story, the woman's declaration of her own identity is reduced to a tautology. What led to this? What is the significance of it? Can you do any better?

1

THE NEEDLE ON THE GAS GAUGE suddenly dipped toward empty and the young driver of the sports car declared that it was maddening how much gas the car ate up. "See that we don't run out of gas again," protested the girl (about twenty-two), and reminded the driver of several places where this had already happened to them. The young man replied that he wasn't worried, because whatever he went through with her had the charm of adventure for him. The girl objected; whenever they had run out of gas on the highway it had, she said, always been an adventure only for her. The young man had hidden and she had had to make ill use of her charms by thumbing a ride and letting herself be driven to the nearest gas station, then thumbing a ride back with a can of gas. The young man asked the girl whether the drivers who had given her a ride had been unpleasant, since she spoke as if her task had been a hardship. She replied (with awkward flirtatiousness) that sometimes they had been *very* pleasant but that it hadn't done her any good as she had

been burdened with the can and had had to leave them before she could get anything going. "Pig," said the young man. The girl protested that she wasn't a pig, but that he really was. God knows how many girls stopped him on the highway, when he was driving the car alone! Still driving, the young man put his arm around the girl's shoulders and kissed her gently on the forehead. He knew that she loved him and that she was jealous. Jealousy isn't a pleasant quality, but if it isn't overdone (and if it's combined with modesty), apart from its inconvenience there's even something touching about it. At least that's what the young man thought. Because he was only twenty-eight, it seemed to him that he was old and knew everything that a man could know about women. In the girl sitting beside him he valued precisely what, until now, he had met with least in women: purity.

The needle was already on empty, when to the right the young man caught sight of a sign, announcing that the station was a quarter of a mile ahead. The girl hardly had time to say how relieved she was before the young man was signaling left and driving into a space in front of the pumps. However, he had to stop a little way off, because beside the pumps was a huge gasoline truck with a large metal tank and a bulky hose, which was refilling the pumps. "We'll have to wait," said the young man to the girl and got out of the car. "How long will it take?" he shouted to the man in overalls. "Only a moment," replied the attendant, and the young man said: "I've heard that one before." He wanted to go back and sit in the car, but he saw that the girl had gotten out the other side. "I'll take a little walk in the meantime," she said. "Where to?" the young man asked on purpose, wanting to see the girl's embarrassment. He had known her for a year now but she would still get shy in front of him. He enjoyed her moments of shyness, partly because they distinguished her from the women he'd met before, partly because he was aware of the law of universal transcience, which made even his girl's shyness a precious thing to him.

2

The girl really didn't like it when during the trip (the young man would drive for several hours without stopping) she had to ask him to stop for a moment somewhere near a clump of trees. She always got angry when, with feigned surprise, he asked her why he should stop. She knew that her shyness was ridiculous and old-fashioned. Many times at work she had noticed that they laughed at her on account of it and deliberately provoked her. She always got shy in advance at the thought of how she was going to get shy. She often longed to feel free and easy about her body, the way most of the women around her did. She had even invented a special course in self-persuasion: she would repeat to herself that at birth every human being received one out of the millions of available bodies, as one would receive an allotted room out of the millions of rooms in an enormous hotel; that, consequently, the body was fortuitous and impersonal, only a ready-made, borrowed thing. She would repeat this to herself

in different ways, but she could never manage to feel it. This mind-body dualism was alien to her. She was too much one with her body; that is why she always felt such anxiety about it.

She experienced this same anxiety even in her relations with the young man, whom she had known for a year and with whom she was happy, perhaps because he never separated her body from her soul and she could live with him *wholly*. In this unity there was happiness, but right behind the happiness lurked suspicion, and the girl was full of that. For instance, it often occurred to her that the other women (those who weren't anxious) were more attractive and more seductive and that the young man, who did not conceal the fact that he knew this kind of woman well, would someday leave her for a woman like that. (True, the young man declared that he'd had enough of them to last his whole life, but she knew that he was still much younger than he thought.) She wanted him to be completely hers and she to be completely his, but it often seemed to her that the more she tried to give him everything, the more she denied him something: the very thing that a light and superficial love or a flirtation gives to a person. It worried her that she was not able to combine seriousness with lightheartedness.

But now she wasn't worrying and any such thoughts were far from her mind. She felt good. It was the first day of their vacation (of their two-week vacation, about which she had been dreaming for a whole year), the sky was blue (the whole year she had been worrying about whether the sky would really be blue), and he was beside her. At his, "Where to?" she blushed, and left the car without a word. She walked around the gas station, which was situated beside the highway in total isolation, surrounded by fields. About a hundred yards away (in the direction in which they were traveling), a wood began. She set off for it, vanished behind a little bush, and gave herself up to her good mood. (In solitude it was possible for her to get the greatest enjoyment from the presence of the man she loved. If his presence had been continuous, it would have kept on disappearing. Only when alone was she able to *hold on* to it.)

When she came out of the wood onto the highway, the gas station was visible. The large gasoline truck was already pulling out and the sports car moved forward toward the red turret of the pump. The girl walked on along the highway and only at times looked back to see if the sports car was coming. At last she caught sight of it. She stopped and began to wave at it like a hitchhiker waving at a stranger's car. The sports car slowed down and stopped close to the girl. The young man leaned toward the window, rolled it down, smiled, and asked, "Where are you headed, miss?" "Are you going to Bystritsa?" asked the girl, smiling flirtatiously at him. "Yes, please get in," said the young man, opening the door. The girl got in and the car took off.

3

The young man was always glad when his girl friend was gay. This didn't happen too often; she had a quite tiresome job in an unpleasant environment, many hours of overtime without compensatory leisure and, at home, a sick mother. So she often felt tired. She didn't have either particularly good nerves or self-confidence and easily fell into a state of anxiety and fear. For this reason he welcomed every manifestation of her gaiety with the tender solicitude of a foster parent. He smiled at her and said: "I'm lucky today. I've been driving for five years, but I've never given a ride to such a pretty hitchhiker."

The girl was grateful to the young man for every bit of flattery; she wanted to linger for a moment in its warmth and so she said, "You're very good at lying."

"Do I look like a liar?"

"You look like you enjoy lying to women," said the girl, and into her words there crept unawares a touch of the old anxiety, because she really did believe that her young man enjoyed lying to women.

The girl's jealousy often irritated the young man, but this time he could easily overlook it for, after all, her words didn't apply to him but to the unknown driver. And so he just casually inquired, "Does it bother you?"

"If I were going with you, then it would bother me," said the girl and her words contained a subtle, instructive message for the young man; but the end of her sentence applied only to the unknown driver, "but I don't know you, so it doesn't bother me."

"Things about her own man always bother a woman more than things about a stranger" (this was now the young man's subtle, instructive message to the girl), "so seeing that we are strangers, we could get on well together."

The girl purposely didn't want to understand the implied meaning of his message, and so she now addressed the unknown driver exclusively:

"What does it matter, since we'll part company in a little while?"

"Why?" asked the young man.

"Well, I'm getting out at Bystritsa."

"And what if I get out with you?"

At these words the girl looked up at him and found that he looked exactly as she imagined him in her most agonizing hours of jealousy. She was alarmed at how he was flattering her and flirting with her (an unknown hitchhiker), and *how becoming it was to him*. Therefore she responded with defiant provocativeness, "What would *you* do with me, I wonder?"

"I wouldn't have to think too hard about what to do with such a beautiful woman," said the young man gallantly and at this moment he was once again speaking far more to his own girl than to the figure of the hitchhiker.

But this flattering sentence made the girl feel as if she had caught him at something, as if she had wheedled a confession out of him with a fraudulent trick. She felt toward him a brief flash of intense hatred and said, "Aren't you rather too sure of yourself?"

The young man looked at the girl. Her defiant face appeared to him to be completely convulsed.

He felt sorry for her and longed for her usual, familiar expression (which he used to call childish and simple). He leaned toward her, put his arm around her shoulders, and softly spoke the name with which he usually addressed her and with which he now wanted to stop the game.

But the girl released herself and said: "You're going a bit too fast!"

At this rebuff the young man said: "Excuse me, miss," and looked silently in front of him at the highway.

4

The girl's pitiful jealousy, however, left her as quickly as it had come over her. After all, she was sensible and knew perfectly well that all this was merely a game; now it even struck her as a little ridiculous that she had repulsed her man out of jealous rage; it wouldn't be pleasant for her if he found out why she had done it. Fortunately she had the miraculous ability to change the meaning of her actions after the event. Using this ability, she decided that she had repulsed him not out of anger but so that she could go on with the game, which, with its whimsicality, so well suited the first day of their vacation.

So again she was the hitchhiker, who had just repulsed the overenterprising driver, but only so as to slow down his conquest and make it more exciting. She half turned toward the young man and said caressingly:

"I didn't mean to offend you, mister!"

"Excuse me, I won't touch you again," said the young man.

He was furious with the girl for not listening to him and refusing to be herself when that was what he wanted. And since the girl insisted on continuing in her role, he transferred his anger to the unknown hitchhiker whom she was portraying. And all at once he discovered the character of his own part: he stopped making the gallant remarks with which he had wanted to flatter his girl in a roundabout way, and began to play the tough guy who treats women to the coarser as-

pects of his masculinity: willfulness, sarcasm, self-assurance.

This role was a complete contradiction of the young man's habitually solicitous approach to the girl. True, before he had met her, he had in fact behaved roughly rather than gently toward women. But he had never resembled a heartless tough guy, because he had never demonstrated either a particularly strong will or ruthlessness. However, if he did not resemble such a man, nonetheless he had *longed* to at one time. Of course it was a quite naive desire, but there it was. Childish desires withstand all the snares of the adult mind and often survive into ripe old age. And this childish desire quickly took advantage of the opportunity to embody itself in the proffered role.

The young man's sarcastic reserve suited the girl very well — it freed her from herself. For she herself was, above all, the epitome of jealousy. The moment she stopped seeing the gallantly seductive young man beside her and saw only his inaccessible face, her jealousy subsided. The girl could forget herself and give herself up to her role.

Her role? What was her role? It was a role out of trashy literature. The hitchhiker stopped the car not to get a ride, but to seduce the man who was driving the car. She was an artful seductress, cleverly knowing how to use her charms. The girl slipped into this silly, romantic part with an ease that astonished her and held her spellbound.

5

There was nothing the young man missed in his life more than lightheartedness. The main road of his life was drawn with implacable precision: his job didn't use up merely eight hours a day, it also infiltrated the remaining time with the compulsory boredom of meetings and home study, and, by means of the attentiveness of his countless male and female colleagues, it infiltrated the wretchedly little time he had left for his private life as well; this private life never remained secret and sometimes even became the subject of gossip and public discussion. Even two weeks' vacation didn't give him a feeling of liberation and adventure; the gray shadow of precise planning lay even here. The scarcity of summer accommodations in our country compelled him to book a room in the Tatras six months in advance, and since for that he needed a recommendation from his office, its omnipresent brain thus did not cease knowing about him even for an instant.

He had become reconciled to all this, yet all the same from time to time the terrible thought of the straight road would overcome him—a road along which he was being pursued, where he was visible to everyone, and from which he could not turn aside. At this moment that thought returned to him. Through an odd and brief conjunction of ideas the figurative road became identified with the real highway along which he was driving—and this led him suddenly to do a crazy thing.

"Where did you say you wanted to go?" he asked the girl.

"To Banska Bystritsa," she replied.

"And what are you going to do there?"

"I have a date there."

"Who with?"

"With a certain gentleman."

The car was just coming to a large crossroads. The driver slowed down so he could read the road signs, then turned off to the right.

"What will happen if you don't arrive for that date?"

"It would be your fault and you would have to take care of me."

"You obviously didn't notice that I turned off in the direction of Nove Zamky."

"Is that true?" You've gone crazy!"

"Don't be afraid, I'll take care of you," said the young man.

So they drove and chatted thus—the driver and the hitchhiker who did not know each other.

The game all at once went into a higher gear. The sports car was moving away not only from the imaginary goal of Banska Bystritsa, but also from the real goal, toward which it had been heading in the morning: the Tatras and the room that had been booked. Fiction was suddenly making as assault upon real life. The young man was moving away from himself and from the implacable straight road, from which he had never strayed until now.

"But you said you were going to the Low Tatras!" The girl was surprised.

"I am going, miss, wherever I feel like going. I'm a free man and I do what I want and what it pleases me to do."

6

When they drove into Nove Zamky it was already getting dark.

The young man had never been here before and it took him a while to orient himself. Several times he stopped the car and asked the passersby directions to the hotel. Several streets had been dug up, so that the drive to the hotel, even though it was quite close by (as all those who had been asked asserted), necessitated so many detours and roundabout routes that it was almost a quarter of an hour before they finally stopped in front of it. The hotel looked unprepossessing, but it was the only one in town and the young man didn't feel like driving on. So he said to the girl, "Wait here," and got out of the car.

Out of the car he was, of course, himself again. And it was upsetting for him to find himself in the evening somewhere completely different from his intended destination—the more so because no one had forced him to do it and as a matter of fact he hadn't even really wanted to. He blamed himself for this piece of folly, but then became reconciled to it. The room in the Tatras could wait until tomorrow and it wouldn't do any harm if they celebrated the first day of their vacation with something unexpected.

He walked through the restaurant—smoky, noisy, and crowded—and asked for the reception desk. They sent him to the back of the lobby near the staircase, where behind a glass panel a superannuated blonde was sitting beneath a board full of keys. With difficulty, he obtained the key to the only room left.

The girl, when she found herself alone, also threw off her role. She didn't feel ill-humored, though, at finding herself in an unexpected town. She was so devoted to the young man that she never had doubts about anything he did, and confidently entrusted every moment of her life to him. On the other hand the idea once again popped into her mind that perhaps — just as she was now doing — other women had waited for her man in his car, those women whom he met on business trips. But surprisingly enough this idea didn't upset her at all now; in fact, she smiled at the thought of how nice it was that today she was this other woman, this irresponsible, indecent other woman, one of those women of whom she was so jealous; it seemed to her that she was cutting them all out, that she had learned how to use their weapons; how to give the young man what until now she had not known how to give him: lightheartedness, shamelessness, and dissoluteness; a curious feeling of satisfaction filled her, because she alone had the ability to be all women and in this way (she alone) could completely captivate her lover and hold his interest.

The young man opened the car door and led the girl into the restaurant. Amid the din, the dirt, and the smoke he found a single, unoccupied table in a corner.

7

"So how are you going to take care of me now?" asked the girl provocatively.

"What would you like for an aperitif?"

The girl wasn't too fond of alcohol, still she drank a little wine and liked vermouth fairly well. Now, however, she purposely said: "Vodka."

"Fine," said the young man. "I hope you won't get drunk on me."

"And if I do?" said the girl.

The young man did not reply but called over a waiter and ordered two vodkas and two steak dinners. In a moment the waiter brought a tray with two small glasses and placed it in front of them.

The man raised his glass, "To you!"

"Can't you think of a wittier toast?"

Something was beginning to irritate him about the girl's game; now sitting face to face with her, he realized that it wasn't just the *words* which were turning her into a stranger, but that her *whole persona* had changed, the movements of her body and her facial expression, and that she unpalatably and faithfully resembled that type of woman whom he knew so well and for whom he felt some aversion.

And so (holding his glass in his raised hand), he corrected his toast: "O.K., then I won't drink to you, but to your kind, in which are combined so successfully the better qualities of the animal and the worse aspects of the human being."

"By 'kind' do you mean all women?" asked the girl.

"No, I mean only those who are like you."

"Anyway it doesn't seem very witty to me to compare a woman with an animal."

"O.K.," the young man was still holding his glass aloft, "then I won't drink to your kind, but to your soul. Agreed? To your soul, which lights up when it descends from your head into your belly, and which goes out when it rises back up to your head."

The girl raised her glass. "O.K., to my soul, which descends into my belly."

"I'll correct myself once more," said the young man. "To your belly, into which your soul descends."

"To my belly," said the girl, and her belly (now that they had named it specifically), as it were, responded to the call; she felt every inch of it.

Then the waiter brought their steaks and the young man ordered them another vodka and some soda water (this time they drank to the girl's breasts), and the conversation continued in this peculiar, frivolous tone. It irritated the young man more and more how *well able* the girl was to become the lascivious miss; if she was able to do it so well, he thought, it meant that she really *was* like that; after all, no alien soul had entered into her from somewhere in space; what she was acting now was she herself; perhaps it was that part of her being which had formerly been locked up and which the pretext of the game had let out of its cage. Perhaps the girl supposed that by means of the game she was *disowning* herself, but wasn't it the other way around? wasn't she becoming herself only through the game? wasn't she freeing herself through the game? no, opposite him was not sitting a strange woman in his girl's body; it was his girl, herself, no one else. He looked at her and felt growing aversion toward her.

However, it was not only aversion. The more the girl withdrew from him *psychically*, the more he longed for her *physically*; the alienation of her soul drew attention to her body; yes, it turned her body into a body; as if until now it had been hidden from the young man within clouds of compassion, tenderness, concern, love, and emotion, as if it had been lost in these clouds (yes, as if this body had been *lost!*). It seemed to the young man that today he was *seeing* his girl's body for the first time.

After her third vodka and soda the girl got up and said flirtatiously, "Excuse me."

The young man said, "May I ask you where you are going, miss?"

"To piss, if you'll permit me," said the girl and walked off between the tables back toward the plush screen.

8

She was pleased with the way she had astounded the young man with this word, which — in spite of all its innocence — he had never heard from her; nothing seemed to her truer to the character of the woman she was playing than this flirtatious emphasis placed on the word in question; yes, she was pleased, she was in the best of moods; the game captivated her. It allowed her to feel what she had not felt till now: *a feeling of happy-go-lucky irresponsibility.*

She, who was always uneasy in advance about her every next step, suddenly felt completely relaxed. The alien life in which she had become involved was a life without shame, without biographical specifications, without past or future, without obligations; it was a life that was extraordinarily free. The girl, as a hitchhiker, could do anything: *everything was permitted her*; she could say, do, and feel whatever she liked.

She walked through the room and was aware that people were watching her from all the tables; it was also a new sensation, one she didn't recognize: *indecent joy caused by her body.* Until now she had never been able to get rid of the fourteen-year-old girl within herself who was ashamed of her breasts and had the disagreeable feeling that she was indecent, because they stuck out from her body and were visible. Even though she was proud of being pretty and having a good figure, this feeling of pride was always immediately curtailed by shame; she rightly suspected that feminine beauty functioned above all as sexual provocation and she found this distasteful; she longed for her body to relate only to the man she loved; when men stared at her breasts in the street it seemed to her that they were invading a piece of her most secret privacy which should belong only to herself and her lover. But now she was the hitchhiker, the woman without a destiny. In this role she was relieved of the tender bonds of her love and began to be intensely aware of her body; and her body became more aroused the more alien the eyes watching it.

She was walking past the last table when an intoxicated man, wanting to show off his worldliness, addressed her in French: *"Combien, mademoiselle?"*

The girl understood. She thrust out her breasts and fully experienced every movement of her hips, then disappeared behind the screen.

9

It was a curious game. This curiousness was evidenced, for example, in the fact that the young man, even though he himself was playing the unknown driver remarkably well, did not for a moment stop seeing his girl in the hitchhiker. And it was precisely this that was tormenting; he saw his girl seducing a strange man, and had the bitter privilege of being present, of seeing at close quarters how she looked and of hearing what she said when she was cheating on him (when she had cheated on him, when she would cheat on him); he had the paradoxical honor of being himself the pretext for her unfaithfulness.

This was all the worse because he worshipped rather than loved her; it had always seemed to him that her inward nature was *real* only within the bounds of fidelity and purity, and that beyond these bounds it simply didn't exist; beyond these bounds she would cease to be herself, as water ceases to be water beyond the boiling point. When he now saw her crossing this horrifying boundary with nonchalant elegance, he was filled with anger.

The girl came back from the rest room and complained: "A guy over there asked me: *Combien, mademoiselle?*"

"You shouldn't be surprised," said the young man, "after all, you look like a whore."

"Do you know that it doesn't bother me in the least?"

"Then you should go with the gentleman!"

"But I have you."

"You can go with him after me. Go and work out something with him."

"I don't find him attractive."

"But in principle you have nothing against it, having several men in one night?"

"Why not, if they're good-looking?"

"Do you prefer them one after the other or at the same time?"

"Either way," said the girl.

The conversation was proceeding to still greater extremes of rudeness; it shocked the girl slightly but she couldn't protest. Even in a game there lurks a lack of freedom; even a game is a trap for the players. If this had not been a game and they had really been two strangers, the hitchhiker could long ago have taken offense and left. But there's no escape from a game. A team cannot flee from the playing field before the end of the match, chess pieces cannot desert the chessboard: the boundaries of the playing field are fixed. The girl knew that she had to accept whatever form the game might take, just because it was a game. She knew that the more extreme the game became, the more it would be a game and the more obediently she would have to play it. And it was futile to evoke good sense and warn her dazed soul that she must keep her distance from the game and not take it seriously. Just because it was only a game her soul was not afraid, did not oppose the game, and narcotically sank deeper into it.

The young man called the waiter and paid. Then he got up and said to the girl, "We're going."

"Where to?" The girl feigned surprise.

"Don't ask, just come on," said the young man.

"What sort of way is that to talk to me?"

"The way I talk to whores," said the young man.

10

They went up the badly lit staircase. On the landing below the second floor a group of intoxicated men was standing near the rest room. The young man caught hold of the girl from behind so that he was holding her breast with his hand. The men by the rest room saw this and began to call out. The girl wanted to break away, but the young man yelled at her: "Keep still!" The men greeted this with general ribaldry and addressed several dirty remarks to the girl. The young man and the girl reached the second floor. He opened the door of their room and switched on the light.

It was a narrow room with two beds, a small table, a chair, and a washbasin. The young man locked the door and turned to the girl. She was standing facing him in a defiant pose with insolent sensuality in her eyes. He looked at her and tried to discover behind her lascivious expression the familiar features which he loved tenderly. It was as if he were looking at two images through the same lens, at two images superimposed one upon the other with the one showing through the other. These two images showing through each other were telling him that *everything* was in the girl, that her soul was terrifyingly amorphous, that it held faithfulness and unfaithfulness, treachery and innocence, flirtatiousness and chastity. This disorderly jumble seemed disgusting to him, like the variety to be found in a pile of garbage. Both images continued to show through each other and the young man understood that the girl differed only on the surface from other women, but deep down was the same as they: full of all possible thoughts, feelings, and vices, which justified all his secret misgivings and fits of jealousy. The impression that certain outlines delineated her as an individual was only a delusion to which the other person, the one who was looking, was subject—namely himself. It seemed to him that the girl he loved was a creation of his desire, his thoughts, and his faith and that the *real* girl now standing in front of him was hopelessly *alien*, hopelessly *ambiguous*. He hated her.

"What are you waiting for? Strip," he said.

The girl flirtatiously bent her head and said, "Is it necessary?"

The tone in which she said this seemed to him very familiar; it seemed to him that once long ago some other woman had said this to him, only he no longer knew which one. He longed to humiliate her. Not the hitchhiker, but his own girl. The game merged with life. The game of humiliating the hitchhiker became only a pretext for humiliating his girl. The young man had forgotten that he was playing a game. He simply hated the woman standing in front of him. He stared at her and took a fifty-crown bill from his wallet. He offered it to the girl. "Is that enough?"

The girl took the fifty crowns and said: "You don't think I'm worth much."

The young man said: "You aren't worth much."

The girl nestled up against the young man. "You can't get around me like that! You must try a different approach, you must work a little!"

She put her arms around him and moved her mouth toward his. He put his fingers on her mouth and gently pushed her away. He said: "I only kiss women I love."

"And you don't love me?"

"No."

"Whom do you love?"

"What's that got to do with you? Strip!"

11

She had never undressed like this before. The shyness, the feeling of inner panic, the dizziness, all that she had always felt when undressing in front of the young man (and she couldn't hide in the darkness), all this was gone. She was standing in front of him self-confident, insolent, bathed in light, and astonished at where she had all of a sudden discovered the gestures, heretofore unknown to her, of a slow, provocative striptease. She took in his glances, slipping off each piece of clothing with a caressing movement and enjoying each individual stage of this exposure.

But then suddenly she was standing in front of him completely naked and at this moment it flashed through her head that now the whole game would end, that since she had stripped off her clothes, she had also stripped away her dissimulation, and that being naked meant that she was now herself and the young man ought to come up to her now and make a gesture with which he would wipe out everything and after which would follow only their most intimate love-making. So she stood naked in front of the young man and at this moment stopped playing the game. She felt embarrassed and on her face appeared the smile which really belonged to her: a shy and confused smile.

But the young man didn't come to her and didn't end the game. He didn't notice the familiar smile; he saw before him only the beautiful, alien body of his own girl, whom he hated. Hatred cleansed his sensuality of any sentimental coating. She wanted to come to him, but he said: "Stay where you are, I want to have a good look at you." Now he longed only to treat her as a whore. But the young man had never had a whore and the ideas he had about them came from literature and hearsay. So he turned to these ideas and the first thing he recalled was the image of a woman in black underwear (and black stockings) dancing on the shiny top of a piano. In the little hotel room there was no piano, there was only a small table covered with a linen cloth leaning against the wall. He ordered the girl to climb up on it. The girl made a pleading gesture, but the young man said, "You've been paid."

When she saw the look of unshakable obsession in the young man's eyes, she tried to go on with the game, even though she no longer could and no longer knew how. With tears in her eyes she climbed onto the table. The top was scarcely three feet square and one leg was a little bit shorter than the others so that standing on it the girl felt unsteady.

But the young man was pleased with the naked figure, now towering above him, and the girl's shy insecurity merely inflamed his imperiousness. He wanted to see her body in all positions and from all sides, as he imagined other men had seen it and would see it. He was vulgar and lascivious. He used words that she had never heard from him in her life. She wanted to refuse, she wanted to be released from the game. She called him by his first name, but he immediately yelled at her that she had no right to address him so intimately. And so eventually in confusion and on the verge of tears, she obeyed, she bent forward and squatted according to the young man's wishes, saluted, and then wiggled her hips as she did the Twist for him; during a slightly more violent movement, when the cloth slipped beneath her feet and she nearly fell, the young man caught her and dragged her to the bed.

He had intercourse with her. She was glad that at least now finally the unfortunate game would end and they would again be the two people they had been before and would love each other. She wanted to press her mouth against his. But the young man pushed her head away and repeated that he only kissed women he loved. She burst into loud sobs. But she wasn't even allowed to cry, because the young man's furious passion gradually won over her body, which then silenced the complaint of her soul. On the bed there were soon two bodies in perfect harmony, two sensual bodies, alien to each other. This was exactly what the girl had most dreaded all her life and had scrupulously avoided till now: love-making without emotion or love. She knew that she had crossed the forbidden boundary, but she proceeded across it without objections and as a full participant; only somewhere, far off in a corner of her consciousness, did she feel horror at the thought that she had never known such pleasure, never so much pleasure as at this moment—beyond that boundary.

12

Then it was all over. The young man got up off the girl and, reaching out for the long cord hanging over the bed, switched off the light. He didn't want to see the girl's face. He knew that the game was over, but didn't feel like returning to their customary relationship; he feared this return. He lay beside the girl in the dark in such a way that their bodies would not touch.

After a moment he heard her sobbing quietly; the girl's hand diffidently, childishly touched his; it touched, withdrew, then touched again, and then a pleading, sobbing voice broke the silence, calling him by his name and saying, "I am me, I am me . . ."

The young man was silent, he didn't move, and he was aware of the sad emptiness of the girl's assertion, in which the unknown was defined by the same unknown.

And the girl soon passed from sobbing to loud crying and went on endlessly repeating this pitiful tautology: "I am me, I am me, I am me . . ."

The young man began to call compassion to his aid (he had to call it from afar, because it was nowhere near at hand), so as to be able to calm the girl. There were still thirteen days' vacation before them.

Further Questions

1. At the end of the story, when the woman is having sex with the man without any emotion of love, she feels horror at the thought that she had never known such pleasure. What do you make of this?

2. What do we mean when we say, "getting to know someone?" What is it that we are becoming familiar with?

3. Often we are attracted to or interested in perfect strangers. Why? Is it purely physical? Is it merely curiosity? Or is there more? Could it be that we find the unknown alluring? Why?

4. Sometimes this story is criticized for being sexist. Would you agree with this criticism? Explain.

Further Readings

Fingarette, Herbert. *Self-Deception*. Atlantic Highlands, NJ: Humanities Press, 1969. One of the first important studies on the concept of self-deception.

Goffman, Erving. "Performances," Ch. 1 of *The Presentation of Self in Everyday Life*. New York: Doubleday, 1959, pp. 17–76. A sociological perspective on the function of the roles we play.

Kolak, Daniel, and Raymond Martin, eds., *Self and Identity*. New York: Macmillan, 1990. An interdisciplinary anthology of current work on: origins of self, unity of consciousness, personal identity, self-knowledge, and self-deception.

Wilson, Colin. *The Outsider*. Los Angeles: J. P. Tarcher, Inc. 1978. An interesting and provocative literary study, even if often only marginally scholarly and sometimes wildly inaccurate, in the alienation of self and society.

PART IV

Freedom

I T IS SOMETIME IN THE TECHNOLOGICALLY DISTANT FUTURE. You are a judge in the state's highest court. The facts in the case before you are these: A student made an android, which subsequently murdered someone and then fled. The police, unable to catch the android, apprehended the student instead. The prosecutor says the student should be held responsible for the android's behavior. The student defends herself by claiming that she programmed the android to make choices of its own free will, an idea the prosecutor rejects on the grounds that an android's choices are the product of just two things: how it was constructed originally, and how it is subsequently modified by its environment. Obviously, he reasons, the android has no say in how it is constructed, and it does not choose its initial environment. Its maker—the student—determines both of these things. Even if the android later chooses to move to another environment—or to reprogram itself—it cannot, the prosecutor claims, make such a choice freely, for how it makes such a choice will be determined by circumstances over which it has no control. If there is responsibility anywhere, the prosecutor argues, it lies behind the android, in its maker.

The student claims that the state's reasons for denying free will to an android are equally applicable to humans, for humans too, she points out, are the product of material and environmental circumstances over which they have no control. And, she adds, if God or nature programs humans, rather than a human programmer, that hardly makes humans any more free than androids. So, she concludes, since humans obviously *can* have free will, so too can androids.

The time for a decision is at hand: *Could* the student have programmed the android to have free will? You, as the judge, have to decide. What is your verdict?

The Illusion of Free Will

BARON HOLBACH

Born of German parents, Paul Heinrich Dietrich (1723–1789), later Baron Holbach, lived most of his life in France. A materialist and a relentless, militant enemy of organized religion in general and of the Catholic Church in particular, he was one of the first European writers to openly advocate atheism. Regarded by those who knew him best as a person of great generosity and integrity, he taught that religion and priestcraft are the source of most man-made evil and that atheism promotes good morality. His main work, *System of Nature* (1770), published anonymously, produced a great stir, eliciting responses from many famous men of the day, such as Voltaire and Goethe, the latter of whom regarded it as the most repulsive book ever written. In the selection from it that follows, Holbach argues that freedom of the will is an illusion.

Reading Questions

1. Does Holbach think we are always, rarely, or never free?
2. What is the significance of the swimmer's example?
3. How does Holbach use the water example to illustrate that people, no matter what they do, always act in accord with their strongest motives.

4. Some say that the fact that people can sometimes be persuaded to act differently than they originally intended shows that they have free will. How does Holbach reply?

5. Some say that people are free if there are no external obstacles to impede them from doing whatever they want to do. How does Holbach reply?

6. "No one ever acts freely because everyone's actions are caused ultimately by conditions over which they have no control." Is this Holbach's view? If not, what else is he saying?

7. What do the "errors of philosophers" concerning free will arise from?

8. Holbach claims there's no difference between whether you throw yourself out the window or whether someone else throws you out the window. What does he mean? Do you agree?

9. In the trial and death of Socrates you read about how Socrates boldly refused to save himself by escaping from prison. Does Holbach think Socrates acted as a free agent in making this famous choice? Why? Do you agree? Why?

10. What does Holbach mean by the following terms: free agency, causality, necessary order, and nature?

Motives and the Determination of the Will

IN WHATEVER MANNER MAN IS CONSIDERED, he is connected to universal nature, and submitted to the necessary and immutable laws that she imposes on all the beings she contains, according to their peculiar essences or to the respective properties with which, without consulting them, she endows each particular species. Man's life is a line that nature commands him to describe upon the surface of the earth, without his ever being able to swerve from it, even for an instant. He is born without his own consent; his organization does in nowise depend upon himself; his ideas come to him involuntarily; his habits are in the power of those who cause him to contract them; he is unceasingly modified by causes, whether visible or concealed, over which he has no control, which necessarily regulate his mode of existence, give the hue to his way of thinking, and determine his manner of acting. He is good or bad, happy or miserable, wise or foolish, reasonable or irrational, without his will being for anything in these various states. Nevertheless, in spite of the shackles by which he is bound, it is pretended he is a free agent, or that independent of the causes by which he is moved, he determines his own will, and regulates his own condition. . . .

The will, as we have elsewhere said, is a modification of the brain, by which it is disposed to action, or prepared to give play to the organs. This will is necessarily determined by the qualities, good or bad, agreeable or painful, of the object or the motive that acts upon his senses, or of which the idea remains with him, and is resuscitated by his memory. In consequence, he acts necessarily, his action is the result of the impulse he receives either from the motive, from the object, or from the idea which has modified his brain, or disposed his will. When he does not act according to this impulse, it is because there comes some new cause, some new motive, some new idea, which modifies his brain in a different manner, gives him a new impulse, determines his will in another way, by which the action of the former impulse is suspended: thus, the sight of an agreeable object, or its idea, determines his will to set him in action to procure it; but if a new

From System of Nature *by Baron Holbach, published in 1770. Translation by H. D. Robinson.*

object or a new idea more powerfully attracts him, it gives a new direction to his will, annihilates the effect of the former, and prevents the action by which it was to be procured. This is the mode in which reflection, experience, reason, necessarily arrests or suspends the action of man's will: without this he would of necessity have followed the anterior impulse which carried him towards a then desirable object. In all this he always acts according to necessary laws from which he has no means of emancipating himself.

If when tormented with violent thirst, he figures to himself in idea, or really perceives a fountain, whose limpid streams might cool his feverish want, is he sufficient master of himself to desire or not to desire the object competent to satisfy so lively a want? It will no doubt be conceded, that it is impossible he should not be desirous to satisfy it; but it will be said — if at this moment it is announced to him that the water he so ardently desires is poisoned, he will, notwithstanding his vehement thirst, abstain from drinking it: and it has, therefore, been falsely concluded that he is a free agent. The fact, however, is, that the motive in either case is exactly the same: his own conservation. The same necessity that determined him to drink before he knew the water was deleterious upon this new discovery equally determined him not to drink; the desire of conserving himself either annihilates or suspends the former impulse; the second motive becomes stronger than the preceding, that is, the fear of death, or the desire of preserving himself, necessarily prevails over the painful sensation caused by his eagerness to drink: but, it will be said, if the thirst is very parching, an inconsiderate man without regarding the danger will risk swallowing the water. Nothing is gained by this remark: in this case, the anterior impulse only regains the ascendency; he is persuaded that life may possibly be longer preserved, or that he shall derive a greater good by drinking the poisoned water than by enduring the torment, which, to his mind, threatens instant dissolution: thus the

first becomes the strongest and necessarily urges him on to action. Nevertheless, in either case, whether he partakes of the water, or whether he does not, the two actions will be equally necessary; they will be the effect of that motive which finds itself most puissant; which consequently acts in the most coercive manner upon his will.

This example will serve to explain the whole phenomena of the human will. This will, or rather the brain, finds itself in the same situation as a bowl, which, although it has received an impulse that drives it forward in a straight line, is deranged in its course whenever a force superior to the first obliges it to change its direction. The man who drinks the poisoned water appears a madman; but the actions of fools are as necessary as those of the most prudent individuals. The motives that determine the voluptuary and the debauchee to risk their health, are as powerful, and their actions are as necessary, as those which decide the wise man to manage his. But, it will be insisted, the debauchee may be prevailed on to change his conduct: this does not imply that he is a free agent; but that motives may be found sufficiently powerful to annihilate the effect of those that previously acted upon him; then these new motives determine his will to the new mode of conduct he may adopt as necessarily as the former did to the old mode. . . .

The errors of philosophers on the free agency of man, have arisen from their regarding his will as the *primum mobile*, the original motive of his actions; for want of recurring back, they have not perceived the multiplied, the complicated causes which, independently of him, give motion to the will itself; or which dispose and modify his brain, whilst he himself is purely passive in the motion he receives. Is he the master of desiring or not desiring an object that appears desirable to him? Without doubt it will be answered, no: but he is the master of resisting his desire, if he reflects on the consequences. But, I ask, is he capable of reflecting on these consequences, when his soul is hurried along by a very lively passion, which entirely depends upon his natural organization, and the causes by which he is modified? Is it in his power to add to these consequences all the weight necessary to counterbalance his desire? Is he the master of preventing the qualities which render an object desirable from residing in it? I shall be told: he ought to have learned to resist his passions; to contract a habit of putting a curb on his desires. I agree to it without any difficulty. But in reply, I again ask, is his nature susceptible of this modification? Does his boiling blood, his unruly imagination, the igneous fluid that circulates in his veins, permit him to make, enable him to apply true experience in the moment when it is wanted? And even when his temperament has capacitated him, has his education, the examples set before him, the ideas with which he has been inspired in early life, been suitable to make him contract this habit of repressing his desires? Have not all these things rather contributed to induce him to seek with avidity, to make him actually desire those objects which you say he ought to resist? . . .

In short, the actions of man are never free; they are always the necessary consequence of his temperament, of the received ideas, and of the notions, either true or false, which he has formed to himself of happiness; of his opinions, strengthened by example, by education, and by daily experience. So many crimes are witnessed on the earth only because every thing conspires to render man vicious and criminal; the religion he has adopted, his government, his education, the examples set before him, irresistibly drive him on to evil: under these circumstances, morality preaches virtue to him in vain. In those societies where vice is esteemed, where crime is crowned, where venality is constantly recompensed, where the most dreadful disorders are punished only in those who are too weak to enjoy the privilege of committing them with impunity, the practice of virtue is considered nothing more than a painful sacrifice of happiness. Such societies chastise, in the lower orders, those excesses, which they respect in the higher ranks; and frequently have the injustice to condemn those in the penalty of death, whom public prejudices, maintained by constant example, have rendered criminal.

Man, then, is not a free agent in any one instant of his life; he is necessarily guided in each step by those advantages, whether real or fictitious, that he attaches to the objects by which his passions are roused: these passions themselves are necessary in a being who unceasingly tends towards his own happiness; their energy is necessary, since that depends on his temperament; his temperament is necessary, because it depends on the physical elements which enter into his composition; the modification of this temperament is necessary, as it is the infallible and inevitable consequence of the impulse he receives from the incessant action of moral and physical beings.

Choice Does Not Prove Freedom

In spite of these proofs of the want of free agency in man, so clear to unprejudiced minds, it will, perhaps, be insisted upon with no small feeling of triumph, that if it be proposed to any one, to move or not to move his hand, an action in the number of those called indifferent, he evidently appears to be the master of choosing; from which it is concluded that evidence has been offered of free agency. The reply is, this example is perfectly simple; man in performing some action which he is resolved on doing, does not by any means prove his free agency: the very desire of displaying this quality, excited by the dispute, becomes a necessary motive, which decides his will either for the one or the other of these actions: What deludes him in this instance, or that which persuades him he is a free agent at this moment, is, that he does not discern the true motive which sets him in action, namely, the desire of convincing his opponent: if in the heat of the dispute he insists and asks, "Am I not the master of throwing myself out of the window?" I shall answer him, no; that whilst he preserves his reason there is no probability that the desire of proving his free agency, will become a motive sufficiently powerful to make him sacrifice his life to the attempt: if, notwithstanding this, to prove he is a free agent, he should actually precipitate himself from the window, it would not be a sufficient warranty to conclude he acted freely, but rather that it was the violence of his temperament which spurred him on to this folly. Madness is a state, that depends upon the heat of the blood, not upon the will. A fanatic or a hero, braves death as necessarily as a more phlegmatic man or coward flies from it.

There is, in point of fact, no difference between the man that is cast out of the window by another, and the man who throws himself out of it, except that the impulse in the first instance comes immediately from without whilst that which determines the fall in the second case, springs from within his own peculiar machine, having its more remote cause also exterior. When Mutius Scaevola held his hand in the fire, he was as much acting under the influence of necessity (caused by interior motives) that urged him to this strange action, as if his arm had been held by strong men: pride, despair, the desire of braving his enemy, a wish to astonish him, and anxiety to intimidate him, etc., were the visible chains that held his hand bound to the fire. The love of glory, enthusiasm for their country, in like manner caused Codrus and Decius to devote themselves for their fellow-citizens. The Indian Colanus and the philosopher Peregrinus were equally obliged to burn themselves, by desire of exciting the astonishment of the Grecian assembly.

It is said that free agency is the absence of those obstacles competent to oppose themselves to the actions of man, or to the exercise of his faculties: it is pretended that he is a free agent whenever, making use of these faculties, he produces the effect he has proposed to himself. In reply to this reasoning, it is sufficient to consider that it in nowise depends upon himself to place or remove the obstacles that either determine or resist him; the motive that causes his action is no more in his own power than the obstacle that impedes him, whether this obstacle or motive be within his own machine or exterior of his person: he is not master of the thought presented to his mind, which determines his will; this thought is excited by some cause independent of himself.

To be undeceived on the system of his free agency, man has simply to recur to the motive by which his will is determined; he will always find this motive is out of his own control. It is said: that in consequence of an idea to which the mind gives birth, man acts freely if he encounters no obstacle. But the question is, what gives birth to this idea in his brain? Was he the master either to prevent it from presenting itself, or from renewing itself in his brain? Does not this idea depend either upon objects that strike him exteriorly and in despite of himself, or upon causes, that without his knowledge, act within himself and modify his brain? Can he prevent his eyes, cast without design upon any object whatever, from giving him an idea of this object, and from moving his brain? He is not more master of the obstacles; they are the necessary effects of either interior or exterior causes, which always act according to their given properties. A man insults a coward; this necessarily irritates him against his insulter; but his will cannot vanquish the obstacle that cowardice places to the object of his desire, because his natural conformation, which does not depend upon himself, prevents his having courage. In this case, the coward is insulted in spite of himself; and against his will is obliged patiently to brook the insult he has received.

Absence of Restraint Is Not Absence of Necessity

The partisans of the system of free agency appear ever to have confounded constraint with necessity. Man believes he acts as a free agent, every time he does not see any thing that places obstacles to his actions; he does not perceive that the motive which causes him to will, is always necessary and independent of himself. A prisoner loaded with chains is compelled to remain in prison; but he is not a free agent in the desire to emancipate himself; his chains prevent him from acting, but they do not prevent him from willing; he would save himself if they would loose his fetters; but he would not save himself as a free agent; fear or the idea of punishment would be sufficient motives for his action.

Man may, therefore, cease to be restrained, without, for that reason, becoming a free agent: in whatever manner he acts, he will act necessarily, according to motives by which he shall be determined. He may be compared to a heavy body that finds itself arrested in its descent by any obstacle whatever: take away this obstacle, it will gravitate or continue to fall; but who shall say this dense body is free to fall or not? Is not its descent the necessary effect of its own specific gravity? The virtuous Socrates submitted to the laws of his country, although they were unjust; and though the doors of his jail were left open to him, he would not save himself; but in this he did not act as a free agent: the invisible chains of opinion, the secret love of decorum, the inward respect of the laws, even when they were iniquitous, the fear of tarnishing his glory, kept him in his prison; they were motives sufficiently powerful with this enthusiast for virtue, to induce him to await death with tranquility; it was not in his power to save himself, because he could find no potential motive to bring him to depart, even for an instant, from those principles to which his mind was accustomed.

Man, it is said, frequently acts against his inclination, from whence it is falsely concluded he is a free agent; but when he appears to act contrary to his inclination, he is always determined to it by some motive sufficiently efficacious to vanquish this inclination. A sick man, with a view to his cure, arrives at conquering his repugnance to the most disgusting remedies: the fear of pain, or the dread of death, then become necessary motives; consequently this sick man cannot be said to act freely.

When it is said, that man is not a free agent, it is not pretended to compare him to a body moved by a single impulsive cause: he contains within himself causes inherent to his existence; he is moved by an interior organ, which has its own peculiar laws, and is itself necessarily determined in consequence of ideas formed from perception resulting from sensation which it receives from exterior objects. As the mechanism of these sensations, of these perceptions, and the manner they engrave ideas on the brain of man, are not known to him; because he is unable to unravel all these motions; because he cannot perceive the chain of operations in his soul, or the motive principle that acts within him, he supposes himself a free agent; which literally translated, signifies, that he moves himself by himself; that he determines himself without cause: when he rather ought to say, that he is ignorant how or why he acts in the manner he does. It is true the soul enjoys an activity peculiar to itself: but it is equally certain that this activity would never be displayed, if some motive or some cause did not put it in a condition to exercise itself: at least it will not be pretended that the soul is able either to love or to hate without being moved, without knowing the objects, without having some idea of their qualities. Gunpowder has unquestionably a particular activity, but this activity will never display itself, unless fire be applied to it; this, however, immediately sets it in motion.

The Complexity of Human Conduct and the Illusion of Free Agency

It is the great complication of motion in man, it is the variety of his action, it is the multiplicity of causes that move him, whether simultaneously or in continual succession, that persuades him he is a free agent: if all his motions were simple, if the causes that move him did not confound themselves with each other, if they were distinct, if his machine were less complicated, he would perceive that all his actions were necessary, because he would be enabled to recur instantly to the cause that made him act. . . .

It is, then, for want of recurring to the causes that move him: for want of being able to analyze, from not being competent to decompose the complicated motion of his machine, that man believes himself a free agent: it is only upon his own ignorance that he founds the profound yet deceitful notion he has of his free agency: that he builds those opinions which he brings forward as a striking proof of his pretended freedom of action. If, for a short time, each man was willing to examine his own peculiar actions, search out their true motives to discover their concatenation, he would remain convinced that the sentiment he has of his natural free agency, is a chimera that must speedily be destroyed by experience.

Nevertheless it must be acknowledged that the multiplicity and diversity of the causes which continually act upon man, frequently without even his knowledge, render it impossible, or at least extremely difficult for him to recur to the true principles of his own peculiar actions, much less the actions of others: they frequently depend upon causes so fugitive, so remote from their effects, and which, superficially examined, appear to have so little analogy, so slender a relation with them, that it requires singular sagacity to bring them into light. This is what renders the study of the moral man a task of such difficulty; this is the reason why his heart is an abyss, of which it is frequently impossible for him to fathom the depth. . . .

If he understood the play of his organs, if he were able to recall to himself all the impulsions they have received, all the modifications they have undergone, all the effects they have produced, he would perceive that all his actions are submitted to that fatality, which regulates his own particular system, as it does the entire system of the universe: no one effect in him, any more than in nature, produces itself by chance; . . . All that passes in him; all that is done by him; as well as all that happens in nature, or that is attributed to her, is derived from necessary causes, which act according to necessary laws, and which produce necessary effects from whence necessarily flow others.

Fatality, is the eternal, the immutable, the necessary order, established in nature; or the indispensable connexion of causes that act, with the effects they operate. Conforming to this order, heavy bodies fall; light bodies rise; that which is analogous in matter reciprocally attracts; that which is heterogeneous mutually repels; man congregates himself in society, modifies each his fellow; becomes either virtuous or wicked; either contributes to his mutual happiness, or reciprocates his misery; either loves his neighbour, or hates his companion necessarily, according to the manner in which the one acts upon the other. From whence it may be seen, that the same necessity which regulates the physical, also regulates the moral world, in which everything is in consequence submitted to fatality. Man, in running over, frequently without his own knowledge, often in spite of himself, the route which nature has marked out for him, resembles a swimmer who is obliged to follow the current that carries him along: he believes himself a free agent, because he sometimes consents, sometimes does not consent, to glide with the stream, which, notwithstanding, always hurries him forward; he believes himself the master of his condition, because he is obliged to use his arms under the fear of sinking.

Further Questions

1. First, think of an action of your own that would seem to be free if any of your actions are free. Second, explain what it is about that action that makes it an optimal candidate for a

free action. Third, explain how Holbach would reply to your reason for thinking that the example you mentioned may be a free action. Finally, give the best reason you can for objecting to Holbach's reply.

2. To what extent do Holbach's arguments that free will is an illusion depend upon his materialism? Is it easier to make a case that people have free will if we reject materialism and believe, say, that everyone has an immaterial soul? Explain.

Further Readings

Darrow, Clarence. *Attorney for the Damned*, edited by A. Weinberg. New York: Simon and Schuster, 1957. Elequent, easily understood arguments that free will is an illusion.

Hook, Sidney, ed. *Determinism and Freedom in the Age of Modern Science*. New York: Collier Books, 1961. Among other questions, addresses whether modern science provides any support for the idea that we have free will.

Morgenbesser, S., and J. Walsh, eds. *Free Will*. Englewood Cliffs: Prentice-Hall, 1962. Mostly classical selections from both the theological dispute over whether God's foreknowledge is incompatible with free will and the scientifically inspired dispute over whether causal determinism is incompatible with free will.

Liberty and Necessity

DAVID HUME

David Hume (1711–1776), a leading philosopher of the Enlightenment, wrote a famous history of England and tutored Adam Smith in political economy. He spent most of his life in Edinburgh.

In this selection, from *An Enquiry Concerning Human Understanding* (1748), Hume argues that free will and causal determinism are compatible, that is, that people could sometimes act freely even if all of their actions and motives were caused.

A brief biography of Hume appears on page 108.

Reading Questions

1. Hume thinks the dispute over whether people have free will ("the question concerning liberty and necessity") is merely a verbal dispute. Why?

2. What does Hume mean by "the doctrines of liberty and necessity"? What does he think gives these doctrines whatever plausibility they have.

3. Could the doctrines of liberty and necessity both be true? What does Hume think? Why?

Part I

IT MIGHT REASONABLY BE EXPECTED, in questions which have been canvassed and disputed with great eagerness since the first origin of science and philosophy, that the meaning of all the terms, at least, should have been agreed upon among the disputants, and our inquiries, in the course of two thousand years, been able to pass from words to the true and real subject of the controversy. For how easy may it seem to give exact definitions of the terms employed in reasoning, and make these definitions, not the mere sound of words, the object of future scrutiny and examination? But if we consider the matter more narrowly, we shall be apt to draw a quite opposite conclusion. From this circumstance alone, that a controversy has been long kept on foot and remains still undecided, we may presume that there is some ambiguity in the expression, and that the disputants affix different ideas to the terms employed in the controversy. For as the faculties of the mind are supposed to be naturally alike in every individual—otherwise nothing could be more fruitless than to reason or dispute together—it were impossible, if men affix the same ideas to their terms, that they could so long form different opinions of the same subject, especially when they communicate their views and each party turn themselves on all sides in search of arguments which may give them the victory over their antagonists. It is true, if men attempt the discussion of questions which lie entirely beyond the reach of human capacity, such as those concerning the origin of worlds or the economy of the intellectual system or region of spirits, they may long beat the air in their fruitless contests and never arrive at any determinate conclusion. But if the question regard any subject of common life and experience, nothing, one would think, could preserve the dispute so long undecided, but some ambiguous expressions which keep the antagonists still at a distance and hinder them from grappling with each other.

This has been the case in the long-disputed question concerning liberty and necessity, and to so remarkable a degree that, if I be not much mistaken, we shall find that all mankind, both learned and ignorant, have always been of the same opinion with regard to this subject, and that a few intelligible definitions would immediately have put an end to the whole controversy. I own that this dispute has been so much canvassed on all hands, and has led philosophers into such a labyrinth of obscure sophistry, that it is no wonder if a sensible reader indulge his ease so far as to turn a deaf ear to the proposal of such a question from which he can expect neither instruction nor entertainment. But the state of the argument here proposed may, perhaps, serve to renew his attention, as it has more novelty, promises at least some decision of the controversy, and will not much disturb his ease by any intricate or obscure reasoning.

I hope, therefore, to make it appear that all men have ever agreed in the doctrine both of necessity and of liberty, according to any reasonable sense which can be put on these terms, and that the whole controversy has hitherto turned merely upon words. We shall begin with examining the doctrine of necessity.

It is universally allowed that matter, in all its operations, is actuated by a necessary force, and that every natural effect is so precisely determined by the energy of its cause that no other effect, in such particular circumstances, could possibly have resulted from it. The degree and direction of every motion is, by the laws of nature, prescribed with such exactness that a living creature may as soon arise from the shock of two bodies, as motion, in any other degree or direction than what is actually produced by it. Would we, therefore, form a just and precise idea of *necessity*, we must consider whence that idea arises

From David Hume, An Inquiry Concerning Human Understanding, *Section 8. First published in 1748.*

when we apply it to the operation of bodies.

It seems evident that, if all the scenes of nature were continually shifted in such a manner that no two events bore any resemblance to each other, but every object was entirely new, without any similitude to whatever had been seen before, we should never, in that case, have attained the least idea of necessity or of a connection among these objects. We might say, upon such a supposition, that one object or event has followed another, not that one was produced by the other. The relation of cause and effect must be utterly unknown to mankind. Inference and reasoning concerning the operations of nature would, from that moment, be at an end; and the memory and senses remain the only canals by which the knowledge of any real existence could possibly have access to the mind. Our idea, therefore, of necessity and causation arises entirely from the uniformity observable in the operations of nature, where similar objects are constantly conjoined together, and the mind is determined by custom to infer the one from the appearance of the other. These two circumstances form the whole of that necessity which we ascribe to matter. Beyond the constant *conjunction* of similar objects and the consequent *inference* from one to the other, we have no notion of any necessity of connection.

If it appear, therefore, that all mankind have ever allowed, without any doubt or hesitation, that these two circumstances take place in the voluntary actions of men and in the operations of mind, it must follow that all mankind have ever agreed in the doctrine of necessity, and that they have hitherto disputed merely for not understanding each other.

As to the first circumstance, the constant and regular conjunction of similar events, we may possibly satisfy ourselves by the following considerations. It is universally acknowledged that there is a great uniformity among the actions of men, in all nations and ages, and that human nature remains still the same in its principles and operations. The same motives always produce the same actions; the same events follow from the same causes. Ambition, avarice, self-love, vanity, friendship, generosity, public spirit—these passions, mixed in various degrees and distributed through society, have been, from the beginning of the world, and still are, the source of all the actions and enterprises which have ever been observed among mankind. Would you know the sentiments, inclinations, and course of life of the Greeks and Romans? Study well the temper and actions of the French and English: you cannot be much mistaken in transferring to the former *most* of the observations which you have made with regard to the latter. Mankind are so much the same, in all times and places, that history informs us of nothing new or strange in this particular. Its chief use is only to discover the constant and universal principles of human nature by showing men in all varieties of circumstances and situations, and furnishing us with materials from which we may form our observations and become acquainted with the regular springs of human action and behavior. These records of wars, intrigues, factions, and revolutions are so many collections of experiments by which the politician or moral philosopher fixes the principles of his science, in the same manner as the physician or natural philosopher becomes acquainted with the nature of plants, minerals, and other external objects, by the experiments which he forms concerning them. Nor are the earth, water, and other elements examined by Aristotle and Hippocrates more like to those which at present lie under our observation than the men described by Polybius and Tacitus are to those who now govern the world.

Should a traveler, returning from a far country, bring us an account of men wholly different from any with whom we were ever acquainted, men who were entirely divested of avarice, ambition, or revenge, who knew no pleasure but friendship, generosity, and public spirit, we should immediately, from these circumstances, detect the falsehood and prove him a liar with the same certainty as if he had stuffed his narration with stories of centaurs and dragons, miracles and prodigies. And if we would explode any forgery in history, we cannot make use of a more convincing argument than to prove that the actions ascribed to any person are directly contrary to the course of nature, and that no human motives, in such circumstances, could ever induce him to such a conduct. The veracity of Quintus Curtius is as much to be suspected when he describes the supernatural courage of Alexander by which he was hurried on singly to attack multitudes, as when he describes his supernatural force and activity by which he was able to resist them. So readily and universally do we acknowledge a uniformity in human motives and actions as well as in the operations of body.

Hence, likewise, the benefit of that experience acquired by long life and a variety of business and company, in order to instruct us in the principles of human nature and regulate our future conduct as well as speculation. By means of this guide we mount up to the knowledge of men's inclinations and motives from their actions, expressions, and even gestures, and again descend to the interpretation of their actions from our knowledge of their motives and inclinations. The general observations, treasured up by a course of experience, give us the clue of human nature and teach us to unravel all its intricacies. Pretexts and appearances no longer deceive us. Public declarations pass for the specious coloring of a cause. And though virtue and honor be allowed their proper weight and authority, that perfect disinterestedness, so often pretended to, is never expected in multitudes and parties, seldom in their leaders, and scarcely even in individuals of any rank or station. But were there no uniformity in human actions, and were every experiment which we could form of this kind irregular and anomalous, it were impossible to collect any general observations concerning mankind, and no experience, however accurately digested by reflection, would ever serve to any purpose. Why is the aged husbandman more skillful in his calling than the young beginner, but because there is a certain uniformity in the operation of the sun, rain, and earth toward the production of vegetables, and experience teaches the old practitioner the rules by which this operation is governed and directed?

We must not, however, expect that this uniformity of human actions should be carried to such a length as that all men, in the same circumstances, will always act precisely in the same manner, without making any allowance for the diversity of characters, prejudices, and opinions. Such a uniformity, in every particular, is found in no part of nature. On the contrary, from observing the variety of conduct in different men we are enabled to form a greater variety of maxims which still suppose a degree of uniformity and regularity.

Are the manners of men different in different ages and countries? We learn thence the great force of custom and education, which mold the human mind from its infancy and form it into a fixed and established character. Is the behavior and conduct of the one sex very unlike that of the other? It is thence we become acquainted with the different characters which nature has impressed upon the sexes, and which she preserves with constancy and regularity. Are the actions of the same person much diversified in the different periods of his life from infancy to old age? This affords room for many general observations concerning the gradual change of our sentiments and inclinations, and the different maxims which prevail in the different ages of human creatures. Even the characters which are peculiar to each individual have a uniformity in their influence, otherwise our acquaintance with the persons, and our observations of their conduct, could never teach us their dispositions or serve to direct our behavior with regard to them.

I grant it possible to find actions which seem to have no regular connection with any known motives and are exceptions to all the measures of conduct which have ever been established for the government of men. But if we could willingly know what judgment should be formed of such irregular and extraordinary actions, we may consider the sentiments commonly entertained with regard to those irregular events which appear in the course of nature and the operations of eternal objects. All causes are not conjoined to their usual effects with like uniformity. An artificer who handles only dead matter may be disappointed of his aim, as well as the politician who directs the conduct of sensible and intelligent agents.

The vulgar, who take things according to their first appearance, attribute the uncertainty of events to such an uncertainty in the causes as makes the latter often fail of their usual influence, though they meet with no impediment in their operation. But philosophers, observing that almost in every part of nature there is contained a vast variety of springs and principles which are hid by reason of their minuteness or remoteness, find that it is at least possible the contrariety of events may not proceed from any contingency in the cause but from the secret operation of contrary causes. This possibility is converted into certainty by further observation, when they remark that, upon an exact scrutiny, a contrariety of effects always betrays a contrariety of causes and proceeds from their mutual opposition. A peasant can give no better reason for the stopping of any clock or watch than to say that it does not commonly go right. But an artist easily perceives that the same force in the spring or pendulum has always the same influence on the wheels, but fails of its usual effect perhaps by reason of a grain of dust which puts a stop to the whole movement. From the observation of several parallel instances philosophers form a maxim that the connection between all causes and effects is equally necessary, and that its seeming uncertainty in some instances proceeds from the secret opposition of contrary causes.

Thus, for instance, in the human body, when the usual symptoms of health or sickness disappoint our expectation, when medicines operate not with their wonted powers, when irregular events follow from any particular cause, the philosopher and physician are not surprised at the matter, nor are ever tempted to deny, in general, the necessity and uniformity of those principles by which the animal economy is conducted. They know that a human body is a mighty complicated machine, that many secret powers lurk in it which are altogether beyond our comprehension, that to us it must often appear very uncertain in its operations, and that, therefore, the irregular events which outwardly discover themselves can be no proof that the laws of nature are not observed with the greatest regularity in its internal operations and government.

The philosopher, if he be consistent, must apply the same reasonings to the actions and volitions of intelligent agents. The most irregular and unexpected resolutions of men may frequently be accounted for by those who know every particular circumstance of their character and situation. A person of an obliging disposition gives a peevish answer; but he has the toothache, or has not dined. A stupid fellow discovers an uncommon alacrity in his carriage; but he has met with a sudden piece of good fortune. Or even when an action, as sometimes happens, cannot be particularly accounted for, either by the person himself or by others, we know, in general, that the characters of men are to a certain degree inconstant and irregular. This is, in a manner, the constant character of human nature, though it be applicable, in a more particular manner, to some persons who have no fixed rule for their conduct, but proceed in a continual course of caprice and inconstancy. The internal principles and motives may operate in a uniform manner, notwithstanding these seeming irregularities — in the same manner as the winds, rains, clouds, and other variations of the weather are supposed to be governed by steady principles, though not easily discoverable by human sagacity and inquiry.

Thus it appears not only that the conjunction between motives and voluntary actions is as regular and uniform as that between the cause and effect in any part of nature, but also that this regular conjunction has been universally acknowledged among mankind and has never been the subject of dispute either in philosophy or common life. Now, as it is from past experience that we draw all inferences concerning the future, and as we conclude that objects will always be conjoined together which we find to have always been conjoined, it may seem superfluous to prove that this experienced uniformity in human actions is a source whence we draw *inferences* concerning them. But in order to throw the argument into a greater variety of lights, we shall also insist, though briefly, on this latter topic.

The mutual dependence of men is so great in all societies that scarce any human action is entirely complete in itself or is performed without some reference to the actions of others, which are requisite to make it answer fully the intention of the agent. The poorest artificer who labors alone expects at least the protection of the magistrate to insure him the enjoyment of the fruits of his labor. He also expects that when he carries his goods to market and offers them at a reasonable price, he shall find purchasers and shall be able, by the money he acquires, to engage others to supply him with those commodities which are requisite for his subsistence. In proportion as men extend their dealings and render their intercourse with others more complicated, they always comprehend in their schemes of life a greater variety of voluntary actions which they expect, from the proper motives, to co-operate with their own. In all these conclusions they take their measures from past experience, in the same manner as in their reasonings concerning external objects, and firmly believe that men, as well as all the elements, are to continue in their operations the same that they have ever found them. A manufacturer reckons upon the labor of his servants for the execution of any work as much as upon the tools which he employs, and would be equally surprised were his expectations disappointed. In short, this experimental inference and reasoning concerning the actions of others enters so much into human life that no man, while awake, is ever a moment without employing it. Have we not reason, therefore, to affirm

that all mankind have always agreed in the doctrine of necessity, according to the foregoing definition and explication of it?

Nor have philosophers ever entertained a different opinion from the people in this particular. For, not to mention that almost every action of their life supposes that opinion, there are even few of the speculative parts of learning to which it is not essential. What would become of *history* had we not a dependence on the veracity of the historian according to the experience which we have had of mankind? How could *politics* be a science if laws and forms of government had not a uniform influence upon society? Where would be the foundation of *morals* if particular characters had no certain or determinate power to produce particular sentiments, and if these sentiments had no constant operation on actions? And with what pretense could we employ our *criticism* upon any poet or polite author if we could not pronounce the conduct and sentiments of his actors either natural or unnatural to such characters and in such circumstances? It seems almost impossible, therefore, to engage either in science or action of any kind without acknowledging the doctrine of necessity, and this *inference* from motives to voluntary action, from characters to conduct.

And, indeed, when we consider how aptly *natural* and *moral* evidence link together and form only one chain of argument, we shall make no scruple to allow that they are of the same nature and derived from the same principles. A prisoner who has neither money nor interest discovers the impossibility of his escape as well when he considers the obstinacy of the jailer as the walls and bars with which he is surrounded, and in all attempts for his freedom chooses rather to work upon the stone and iron of the one than upon the inflexible nature of the other. The same prisoner, when conducted to the scaffold, foresees his death as certainly from the constancy and fidelity of his guards as from the operation of the ax or wheel. His mind runs along a certain train of ideas: the refusal of the soldiers to consent to his escape; the action of the executioner; the separation of the head and body; bleeding, convulsive motions, and death. Here is a connected chain of natural causes and voluntary actions, but the mind feels no difference between them in passing from one link to another, nor is less certain of the future event than if it were connected with the objects present to the memory or senses by a train of causes cemented together by what we are pleased to call a "physical" necessity. The same experienced union has the same effect on the mind, whether the united objects be motives, volition, and actions, or figure and motion. We may change the names of things, but their nature and their operation on the understanding never change.

Were a man whom I know to be honest and opulent, and with whom I lived in intimate friendship, to come into my house, where I am surrounded with my servants, I rest assured that he is not to stab me before he leaves it in order to rob me of my silver standish; and I no more suspect this event than the falling of the house itself, which is new and solidly built and founded. — *But he may have been seized with a sudden and unknown frenzy.* — So may a sudden earthquake arise, and shake and tumble my house about my ears. I shall, therefore, change the suppositions. I shall say that I know with certainty that he is not to put his hand into the fire and hold it there till it be consumed. And this event I think I can foretell with the same assurance as that, if he throw himself out of the window and meet with no obstruction, he will not remain a moment suspended in the air. No suspicion of an unknown frenzy can give the least possibility to the former event which is so contrary to all the known principles of human nature. A man who at noon leaves his purse full of gold on the pavement at Charing Cross may as well expect that it will fly away like a feather as that he will find it untouched an hour after. Above one-half of human reasonings contain inferences of a similar nature, attended with more or less degrees of certainty, proportioned to our experience of the usual conduct of mankind in such particular situations.

I have frequently considered what could possibly be the reason why all mankind, though they have ever, without hesitation, acknowledged the doctrine of necessity in their whole practice and reasoning, have yet discovered such a reluctance to acknowledge it in words, and have rather shown a propensity, in all ages, to profess the contrary opinion. The matter, I think, may be accounted for after the following manner. If we examine the operations of body and the production of effects from their causes, we shall find that all our faculties can never carry us further in our knowledge of this relation than barely to observe that particular objects are *constantly conjoined* together, and that the mind is carried, by a *customary transition*, from the appearance of the one to the belief of the other. But though this conclusion concerning human ignorance be the result of the strictest scrutiny of this subject, men still entertain a strong propensity to believe that they penetrate further into the powers of nature and perceive something like a necessary connection between the cause and the effect. When, again, they turn their reflections toward the operations of their own minds and *feel* no such connection of the motive and the action, they are thence apt to suppose that there is a difference between the effects which result from material force and those which arise from thought and intelligence. But being once convinced that we know nothing further of causation of any kind than merely the *constant conjunction* of objects and the consequent *inference* of the mind from one to another, and finding that these two circumstances are universally allowed to have place in voluntary actions, we may be more easily led to own the same necessity common to all causes. And though this reasoning may contradict the systems of many philosophers in ascribing necessity to the determinations of the will, we shall find, upon reflection, that they dissent from it in words only, not in their real sentiments. Necessity, according to the sense in which it is here taken, has never yet been rejected, nor can ever, I think, be rejected by any philosopher. It may only, perhaps, be pretended that the mind can perceive in the operations of matter some further connection between the cause and effect, and a connection that has no place in the voluntary actions of intelligent beings. Now, whether it be so or not can only appear upon examination, and it is incumbent on these philosophers to make good their assertion by defining or describing that necessity and pointing it out to us in the operations of material causes.

It would seem, indeed, that men begin at the wrong end of this question concerning liberty and necessity when they enter upon it by examining the faculties of the soul, the influence of the understanding, and the operations of the will. Let them first discuss a more simple question, namely, the question of body and brute unintelligent matter, and try whether they can there form any idea of causation and necessity, except that of a constant conjunction of objects and subsequent inference of the mind from one to another. If these circumstances form, in reality, the whole of that necessity which we conceive in matter, and if these circumstances be also universally acknowledged to take place in the operations of the mind, the dispute is at an end; at least, must be owned to be thenceforth merely verbal. But as long as we will rashly suppose that we have some further idea of necessity and causation in the operations of external objects, at the same time that we can find nothing further in the voluntary actions of the mind, there is no possibility of bringing the question to any determinate issue while we proceed upon so erroneous a supposition. The only method of undeceiving us is to mount up higher, to examine the narrow extent of science when applied to material causes, and to convince ourselves that all we know of them is the constant conjunction and inference above mentioned. We may, perhaps, find that it is with difficulty we are induced to fix such narrow limits to human understanding, but we can afterwards find no difficulty when we come to apply this doctrine to the actions of the will. For as it is evident that these have a regular conjunction with motives and circumstances and character, and as we always draw inferences from one to the other, we must be obliged to acknowledge in words that necessity which we have already avowed in every deliberation of our lives and in every step of our conduct and behavior.[1]

But to proceed in this reconciling project with regard to the question of liberty and necessity — the most contentious question of metaphysics, the most contentious science — it will not require many words to prove that all mankind have ever agreed in the doctrine of liberty as well as in that of necessity, and that the whole dispute, in this respect also, has been hitherto merely verbal. For what is meant by liberty when applied to voluntary actions? We cannot surely mean that actions have so little connection with motives, inclinations, and circumstances that one does not follow with a certain degree of uniformity from the other, and that one affords no inference by which we can conclude the existence of the other. For these are plain and acknowledged matters of fact. By liberty, then, we can only mean *a power of acting or not acting according to the determinations of the will*; that is, if we choose to remain at rest, we may; if we choose to move, we also may. Now this hypothetical liberty is universally allowed to belong to everyone who is not a prisoner and in chains. Here then is no subject of dispute.

Whatever definition we may give of liberty, we should be careful to observe two requisite circumstances: *first*, that it be consistent with plain matter of fact; *secondly*, that it be consistent with itself. If we observe these circumstances and render our definition intelligible, I am persuaded that all mankind will be found of one opinion with regard to it.

It is universally allowed that nothing exists without a cause of its existence, and that chance, when strictly examined, is a mere negative word and means not any real power which has anywhere a being in nature. But it is pretended that some causes are necessary, some not necessary. Here then is the advantage of definitions. Let anyone *define* a cause without comprehending, as a part of the definition, a *necessary connection* with its effect, and let him show distinctly the origin of the idea expressed by the definition, and I shall readily give up the whole controversy. But if the foregoing explication of the matter be received, this must be absolutely impracticable. Had not objects a regular conjunction with each other, we should never have entertained any notion of cause and effect; and this regular conjunction produces that inference of the understanding which is the only connection that we can have any comprehension of. Whoever attempts a definition of cause exclusive of these circumstances will be obliged either to employ unintelligible terms or such as are synonymous to the term which he endeavors to define.[2] And if the definition above mentioned be admitted, liberty, when opposed to necessity, not to constraint, is the same thing with chance, which is universally allowed to have no existence.

Part II

There is no method of reasoning more common, and yet none more blamable, than in philosophical disputes to endeavor the refutation of any hypothesis by a pretense of its dangerous consequences to religion and morality. When any opinion leads to absurdity, it is certainly false; but it is not certain that an opinion is false because it is of dangerous consequence. Such topics, therefore, ought entirely to be forborne as serving nothing to the discovery of truth, but only to make the person of an antagonist odious. This I observe in general, without pretending a draw any advantage from it. I frankly submit to an examination of this kind, and shall venture to affirm that the doctrines both of necessity and liberty, as above explained, are not only consistent with morality, but are absolutely essential to its support.

Necessity may be defined two ways, conformably to the two definitions of *cause* of which it makes an essential part. It consists either in the constant conjunction of like objects or in the inference of the understanding from one object to another. Now necessity, in both these senses (which, indeed, are at bottom the same), has universally, though tacitly, in the schools, in the pulpit, and in common life been allowed to belong to the will of man, and no one has ever pretended to deny that we can draw inferences concerning human actions, and that those inferences are founded on the experienced union of like actions, with like motives, inclinations, and circumstances. The only particular in which anyone can differ is that either perhaps he will refuse to give the name of necessity to this property of human actions — but as long as the meaning is understood I hope the word can do no harm — or that he will maintain it possible to discover something further in the operations of matter. But this, it must be acknowledged, can be of no consequence to morality or religion, whatever it may be to natural philosophy or metaphysics. We may here be mistaken in asserting that there is no idea of any other necessity or connection in the actions of the body, but surely we ascribe nothing to the actions of the mind but what everyone does and must readily allow of. We change no circumstance in the received orthodox system with regard to the will, but only in that with regard to material objects and causes. Nothing, therefore, can be more innocent at least than this doctrine.

All laws being founded on rewards and punishments, it is supposed, as a fundamental principle, that these motives have a regular and uniform influence on the mind and both produce the good and prevent the evil actions. We may give to this influence what name we please; but as it is usually conjoined with the action, it must be esteemed a *cause* and be looked upon as an instance of that necessity which we would here establish.

The only proper object of hatred or vengeance is a person or creature endowed with thought and consciousness; and when any criminal or injurious actions excite that passion, it is only by their relation to the person, or connection with him. Actions are, by their very nature, temporary and perishing; and where they proceed not from some *cause* in the character and disposition of the person who performed them, they can neither redound to his honor if good, nor infamy if evil. The actions themselves may be blamable; they may be contrary to all the rules of morality and religion; but the person is not answerable for them and, as they proceeded from nothing in him that is durable and constant and leave nothing of that nature behind them, it is impossible he can, upon their account, become the object of punishment or vengeance. According to the principle, therefore, which denies necessity and, consequently, causes, a man is as pure and untainted, after having committed the most horrid crime, as at the first moment of his birth, nor is his character anywise concerned in his actions, since they are not derived from it; and the wickedness of the one can never be used as a proof of the depravity of the other.

Men are not blamed for such actions as they perform ignorantly and casually, whatever may be the consequences. Why? But because the principles of these actions are only momentary and terminate in them alone. Men are less blamed for such actions as they perform hastily and unpremeditately than for such as proceed from deliberation. For what reason? But because a hasty temper, though a constant cause or principle in the mind, operates only by intervals and infects not the whole character. Again, repentance wipes off every crime if attended with a reformation of life and manners. How is this to be accounted for? But by asserting that actions render a person criminal merely as they are proofs of criminal principles in the mind; and when, by an alteration of these principles, they cease to be just proofs, they likewise cease to be criminal. But, except upon the doctrine of necessity, they never were just proofs, and consequently never were criminal.

It will be equally easy to prove, and from the same arguments, that *liberty*, according to that definition above mentioned, in which all men agree, is also essential to morality, and that no human actions, where it is wanting, are susceptible of any moral qualities or can be the objects of approbation or dislike. For as actions are objects of our moral sentiment so far only as they are indications of the internal character, passions, and affections, it is impossible that they can give rise either to praise or blame where they proceed not from these principles, but are derived altogether from external violence.

I pretend not to have obtained or removed all objections to this theory with regard to necessity and liberty. I can foresee other objections derived from topics which have not here been treated of. It may be said, for instance, that if voluntary actions be subjected to the same laws of necessity with the operations of matter, there is a continued chain of necessary causes, preordained and predetermined, reaching from the Original Cause of all to every single volition of every human creature. No contingency anywhere in the universe, no indifference, no liberty. While we act, we are at the same time acted upon. The ultimate Author of all our volitions is the Creator of the world, who first bestowed motion on this immense machine and placed all beings in that particular position whence every subsequent event, by an inevitable necessity, must result. Human actions, therefore, either can have no moral turpitude at all, as proceeding from so good a cause, or if they have any turpitude, they must involve our Creator in the same guilt, while he is acknowledged to be their ultimate cause and Author. For as a man who fired a mine is answerable for all the consequences, whether the train he employed be long or short, so, wherever a continued chain of necessary causes is fixed, that Being, either finite or infinite, who produces the first is likewise the author of all the rest and must both bear the blame and acquire the praise which belong to them. Our clear and unalterable ideas of morality establish this rule upon unquestionable reasons when we examine the consequences of any human action; and these reasons must still have greater force when applied to the volitions and intentions of a Being infinitely wise and powerful. Ignorance or impotence may be pleaded for so limited a creature as man, but those imperfections have no place in our Creator. He foresaw, he ordained, he intended all those actions of men which we so rashly pronounce criminal. And we must, therefore, conclude either that they are not criminal or that the Deity, not man, is accountable for them. But as either of these positions is absurd and impious, it follows that the doctrine from which they are deduced cannot possibly be true, as being liable to all the same objections. An absurd consequence, if necessary, proves the original doctrine to be absurd in the same manner as criminal actions render criminal the original cause if the connection between them be necessary and inevitable.

This objection consists of two parts, which we shall examine separately:

First, that if human actions can be traced up, by a necessary chain, to the Deity, they can never be criminal, on account of the infinite perfection of that Being from whom they are derived, and who can intend nothing but what is altogether good and laudable. Or, *secondly*, if they be criminal, we must retract the attribute of perfection which we ascribe to the Deity and must acknowledge him to be the ultimate author of guilt and moral turpitude in all his creatures.

The answer to the first objection seems obvious and convincing. There are many philosophers who, after an exact scrutiny of the phenomena of nature, conclude that the WHOLE, considered as one system, is, in every period of its existence, ordered with perfect benevolence; and that the utmost possible happiness will, in the end, result to all created beings without any mixture of positive or absolute ill and misery. Every physical ill, say they, makes an essential part of this benevolent system, and could not possibly be removed, by even the Deity himself, considered as a wise agent, without giving entrance to greater ill or excluding greater good which will result from it. From this theory some philosophers, and the ancient Stoics among the rest, derived a topic of consolation under all afflictions,

while they taught their pupils that those ills under which they labored were in reality goods to the universe, and that to an enlarged view which could comprehend the whole system of nature every event became an object of joy and exultation. But though this topic be specious and sublime, it was soon found in practice weak and ineffectual. You would surely more irritate than appease a man lying under the racking pains of the gout by preaching up to him the rectitude of those general laws which produced the malignant humors in his body and led them through the proper canals to the sinews and nerves, where they now excite such acute torments. These enlarged views may, for a moment, please the imagination of a speculative man who is placed in ease and security, but neither can they dwell with constancy on his mind, even though undisturbed by the emotions of pain or passion, much less can they maintain their ground when attacked by such powerful antagonists. The affections take a narrower and more natural survey of their object and, by an economy more suitable to the infirmity of human minds, regard alone the beings around us, and are actuated by such events as appear good or ill to the private system.

The case is the same with *moral* as with *physical* ill. It cannot reasonably be supposed that those remote considerations which are found of so little efficacy with regard to the one will have a more powerful influence with regard to the other. The mind of man is so formed by nature that, upon the appearance of certain characters, dispositions, and actions, it immediately feels the sentiment of approbation or blame; nor are there any emotions more essential to its frame and constitution. The characters which engage our approbation are chiefly such as contribute to the peace and security of human society, as the characters which excite blame are chiefly such as tend to public detriment and disturbance; whence it may reasonably be presumed that the moral sentiments arise, either mediately or immediately, from a reflection on these opposite interests. What though philosophical meditations establish a different opinion or conjecture that everything is right with regard to the whole, and that the qualities which disturb society are, in the main, as beneficial, and are as suitable to the primary intention of nature, as those which more directly promote its happiness and welfare? Are such remote and uncertain speculations able to counterbalance the sentiments which arise from the natural and immediate view of the objects? A man who is robbed of a considerable sum, does he find his vexation for the loss anywise diminished by these sublime reflections? Why, then, should his moral resentment against the crime be supposed incompatible with them? Or why should not the acknowledgement of a real distinction between vice and virtue be reconcilable to all speculative systems of philosophy, as well as that of a real distinction between personal beauty and deformity? Both these distinctions are founded in the natural sentiments of the human mind; and these sentiments are not to be controlled or altered by any philosophical theory or speculation whatsoever.

The *second* objection admits not of so easy and satisfactory an answer, nor is it possible to explain distinctly how the Deity can be the immediate cause of all the actions of men without being the author of sin and moral turpitude. These are mysteries which mere natural and unassisted reason is very unfit to handle; and whatever system she embraces, she must find herself involved in inextricable difficulties, and even contradictions, at every step which she takes with regard to such subjects. To reconcile the indifference and contingency of human actions with prescience or to defend absolute decrees, and yet free the Deity from being the author of sin, has been found hitherto to exceed all the power of philosophy. Happy, if she be thence sensible of her temerity, when she pries into these sublime mysteries, and, leaving a scene so full of obscurities and perplexities, return with suitable modesty to her true and proper province, the examination of common life, where she will find difficulties enough to employ her inquiries without launching into so boundless an ocean of doubt, uncertainty, and contradiction.

NOTES

1. The prevalence of the doctrine of liberty may be accounted for from another cause, viz., a false sensation, or seeming experience, which we have, or may have, of liberty or indifference in many of our actions. The necessity of any action, whether of matter or of mind, is not, properly speaking, a quality in the agent but in any thinking or intelligent being who may consider the action; and it consists chiefly in the determination of his thoughts to infer the existence of that action from some preceding objects; as liberty, when opposed to necessity, is nothing but the want of that determination, and a certain looseness or indifference which we feel in passing, or not passing, from the idea of one object to that of any succeeding one. Now we may observe that though, in *reflecting* on human actions, we seldom feel such a looseness or indifference, but are commonly able to infer them with considerable certainty from their motives, and from the disposition of the agent; yet it frequently happens that, in *performing* the actions themselves, we are sensible of something like it; and as all resembling objects are readily taken for each other, this has been employed as a demonstrative and even intuitive proof of human liberty. We feel that our actions are subject to our will on most occasions, and imagine we feel that the will itself is subject to nothing, because, when by a denial of it we are provoked to try, we feel that it moves easily every way, and produces an image of itself (or a "velleity," as it is called in the schools), even on that side on which it did not settle. This image, or faint motion, we persuade ourselves, could at that time have been completed into the thing itself, because, should that be denied, we find upon a second trial that at present it can. We consider not that the fantastical desire of showing liberty is here the motive of our actions. And it seems certain that however we may imagine we feel a liberty within ourselves, a spectator can commonly infer our actions from our motives and character; and even where he cannot, he concludes in general that he might, were he perfectly acquainted with every circumstance of our situation and temper, and the most secret springs of our complexion and disposition. Now this is the very essence of necessity, according to the foregoing doctrine.

2. Thus, if a cause be defined, *that which produces anything*, it is easy to observe that *producing* is synonymous to *causing*. In like manner, if a cause be defined, *that by which anything exists*, this is liable to the same objection. For what is meant by these words, *"by which"*? Had it been said that a cause is *that* after which *anything constantly exists*, we should have understood the terms. For this is, indeed, all we know of the matter. And this constancy forms the very essence of necessity, nor have we any other idea of it.

Further Questions

1. "The fact that someone acts in accordance with his or her own will does not guarantee that the person acts freely; the will itself may have been caused by conditions over which the person had no control." Explain how Hume would respond. Then explain how someone could best criticize Hume's response.

2. Imagine that Holbach and Hume were sitting across the table from each other. As far as the issue of free will is concerned, what would be their main agreements and disagreements?

Further Readings

Hospers, John. *An Introduction to Philosophical Analysis*. New York: Prentice-Hall, 1953. Chapter 4 contains a clear, textbook introduction to the problem of free will and determinism.

Hoy, Ronald C., and L. Nathan Oaklander, eds. *Metaphysics*. Belmont, CA: Wadsworth, 1991. Part IV contains a good selection of classical and contemporary writings on free will.

Moore, G. E. *Ethics*. London: Oxford University Press, 1912. Chapter VI contains an influential and unusually clear defense, by one of the founders of twentieth-century analytic philosophy, of the idea that free will and determinism are compatible.

The Liberty of Moral Agents

THOMAS REID

Thomas Reid (1710–1796), the son of a minister who himself became a minister, taught at King's College, Aberdeen, and then went on to succeed Adam Smith as professor of moral philosophy at Glasgow. Reid was founder of the Scottish School of Common Sense and an outspoken opponent of the "theory of ideas," taught by Descartes, Locke, Berkeley, and Hume, according to which what we are immediately aware of in sense perception is the contents of our own minds ("ideas"). Reid thought we were immediately aware of real objects in the physical world. A staunch defender of the idea that mind and body are different substances, Reid believed that a person, unlike any physical object, is an indivisible substance — a "substantial self" — that remains identical over time. In the selection that follows, Reid argues that if a person's actions were caused by anything other than his or her "substantial self," for instance, if they were caused by the person's character, motives, heredity, or background, then it would not be the person's will that determines what choices he or she makes and, accordingly, the choices would not be free.

Reading Questions

1. Reid says that Cato is no more responsible for his "constitution" than for his existence, and so if Cato's constitution determined his actions then Cato was not responsible for them. Why, according to Reid, would Cato not be responsible?

2. Some have thought that liberty of action is impossible because it would imply an effect without a cause. How does Reid respond? Is his response adequate?

The Notions of Moral Liberty and Necessity Stated

BY THE *LIBERTY* OF A MORAL AGENT, I understand, a power over the determinations of his own will.

If, in any action, he had power to will what he did, or not to will it, in that action he is free. But if, in every voluntary action, the determination of his will be the necessary consequence of something involuntary in the state of his mind, or of something in his external circumstances, he is not free; he has not what I call the liberty of a moral agent, but is subject to necessity.

This liberty supposes the agent to have understanding and will; for the determinations of the will are the sole object about which this power is employed; and there can be no will, without, at least, such a degree of understanding as gives the conception of that which we will.

The liberty of a moral agent implies, not only a conception of what he wills, but some degree of practical judgment or reason.

For, if he has not the judgment to discern one determination to be preferable to another, either in itself, or for some purpose which he intends, what can be the use of a power to determine? His determinations must be made perfectly in the dark, without reason, motive, or end. They can neither be right nor wrong, wise nor foolish. Whatever the consequences may be, they cannot be imputed to the agent, who had not the capacity of foreseeing them, or of perceiving any reason for acting otherwise than he did.

We may perhaps be able to conceive a being endowed with power over the determinations of his will, without any light in his mind to direct that power to some end. But such power would be given in vain. No exercise of it could be either blamed or approved. As nature gives no power in vain, I see no ground to ascribe a power over the determinations of the will to any being who has no judgment to apply it to the direction of his conduct, no discernment of what he ought or ought not to do.

For that reason, in this Essay, I speak only of the liberty of moral agents, who are capable of acting well or ill, wisely or foolishly, and this, for distinction's sake, I shall call *moral liberty*.

What kind, or what degree of liberty belongs to brute animals, or to our own species, before any use of reason, I do not know. We acknowl-

From Reid's Essays on the Active Powers of the Human Mind, *Essay IV, Chapters 1 and 9. First published in 1815.*

edge that they have not the power of self-govern-ment. Such of their actions as may be called *voluntary*, seem to be invariably determined by the passion or appetite, or affection or habit, which is strongest at the time.

This seems to be the law of their constitution, to which they yield, as the inanimate creation does, without any conception of the law, or any intention of obedience.

But of civil or moral government, which are addressed to the rational powers, and require a conception of the law and an intentional obedience, they are, in the judgment of all mankind, incapable. Nor do I see what end could be served by giving them a power over the determinations of their own will, unless to make them intractable by discipline, which we see they are not.

The effect of moral liberty is, that it is in the power of the agent to do well or ill. This power, like every other gift of God, may be abused. The right use of this gift of God is to do well and wisely, as far as his best judgment can direct him, and thereby merit esteem and approbation. The abuse of it is to act contrary to what he knows, or suspects to be his duty and his wisdom, and thereby justly merit disapprobation and blame.

By *necessity*, I understand the want of that moral liberty which I have above defined.

If there can be a better and a worse in actions on the system of necessity, let us suppose a man necessarily determined in all cases to will and to do what is best to be done, he would surely be innocent and inculpable. But, as far as I am able to judge, he would not be entitled to the esteem and moral approbation of those who knew and believed this necessity. What was, by an ancient author, said of Cato, might indeed be said of him. *He was good because he could not be otherwise.* But this saying, if understood literally and strictly, is not the praise of Cato, but of his constitution, which was no more the work of Cato, than his existence.

On the other hand, if a man be necessarily determined to do ill, this case seems to me to move pity, but not disapprobation. He was ill, because he could not be otherwise. Who can blame him? Necessity has no law.

If he knows that he acted under this necessity, has he not just ground to exculpate himself? The blame, if there be any, is not in him, but in his constitution. If he be charged by his Maker with doing wrong, may he not expostulate with him, and say, why hast thou made me thus? I may be sacrificed at thy pleasure, for the common good, like a man that has the plague, but not for ill desert; for thou knowest that what I am charged with is thy work, and not mine.

Such are my notions of moral liberty and necessity, and of the consequences inseparably connected with both the one and the other.

This moral liberty a man may have, though it do not extend to all his actions, or even to all his voluntary actions. He does many things by instinct, many things by the force of habit without any thought at all, and consequently without will. In the first part of life, he has not the power of self-government any more than the brutes. That power over the determinations of his own will, which belongs to him in ripe years, is limited, as all his powers are; and it is perhaps beyond the reach of his understanding to define its limits with precision. We can only say, in general, that it extends to every action for which he is accountable.

This power is given by his Maker, and at his pleasure whose gift it is, it may be enlarged or diminished, continued or withdrawn. No power in the creature can be independent of the Creator. His hook is in its nose; he can give it line as far as he sees fit, and, when he pleases, can restrain it, or turn it withersoever he will. Let this be always understood, when we ascribe liberty to man, or to any created being.

Supposing it therefore to be true, that man is a free agent, it may be true, at the same time, that his liberty may be impaired or lost, by disorder of body or mind, as in melancholy, or in madness; it may be impaired or lost by vicious habits; it may, in particular cases, be restrained by divine interposition.

We call man a free agent in the same way as we call him a reasonable agent. In many things he is not guided by reason, but by principles similar to those of the brutes. His reason is weak at best. It is liable to be impaired or lost, by his own fault, or by other means. In like manner, he may be a free agent, though his freedom of action may have many similar limitations.

The liberty I have described has been represented by some philosophers as inconceivable, and as involving an absurdity.

"Liberty," they say, "consists only in a power to act as we will; and it is impossible to conceive in any being a greater liberty than this. Hence it follows, that liberty does not extend to the determinations of the will, but only to the actions consequent to its determination, and depending upon the will. To say that we have power to will such an action, is to say, that we may will it, if we will. This supposes the will to be determined by a prior will; and, for the same reason, that will must be determined by a will prior to it, and so on in an infinite series of wills, which is absurd. To act freely, therefore, can mean nothing more than to act voluntarily; and this is all the liberty that can be conceived in man, or in any being."

This reasoning, first, I think, advanced by Hobbes, has been very generally adopted by the defenders of necessity. It is grounded upon a definition of liberty totally different from that which I have given, and therefore does not apply to moral liberty, as above defined.

But it is said that this is the only liberty that is possible, that is conceivable, that does not involve an absurdity.

It is strange indeed! if the word *liberty* has no meaning but this one. I shall mention three, all very common. The objection applies to one of them, but to neither of the other two.

Liberty is sometimes opposed to external force or confinement of the body. Sometimes it is opposed to obligation by law, or by lawful authority. Sometimes it is opposed to necessity.

First, it is opposed to confinement of the body by superior force. So we say a prisoner is set at liberty when his fetters are knocked off, and he is discharged from confinement. This is the liberty defined in the objection; and I grant that this liberty extends not to the will, neither does the confinement, because the will cannot be confined by external force.

Secondly, liberty is opposed to obligation, by law, or lawful authority. This liberty is a right to act one way or another, in things which the law has neither commanded nor forbidden; and this liberty is meant when we speak of a man's natural liberty, his civil liberty, his christian liberty. It is evident that this liberty, as well as the obligation opposed to it, extends to the will: for it is the will to obey that makes obedience; the will to transgress that makes a transgression of the law. Without will there can be neither obedience nor transgression. Law supposes a power to obey or to transgress; it does not take away this power, but proposes the motives of duty and of interest, leaving the power to yield to them, or to take the consequence of transgression.

Thirdly, liberty is opposed to necessity, and in this sense it extends to the determinations of the will only, and not to what is consequent to the will.

In every voluntary action, the determination of the will is the first part of the action, upon which alone the moral estimation of it depends. It has been made a question among philosophers, whether, in every instance, this determination be the necessary consequence of the constitution of the person, and the circumstances in which he is placed? or whether he had not power, in many cases, to determine this way or that?

This has, by some, been called the *philosophical* notion of liberty and necessity; but it is by no means peculiar to philosophers. The lowest of the vulgar have, in all ages, been prone to have recourse to this necessity, to exculpate themselves or their friends in what they do wrong, though, in the general tenor of their conduct, they act upon the contrary principle.

Whether this notion of moral liberty be conceivable or not, every man must judge for himself. To me there appears no difficulty in conceiving it. I consider the determination of the will as an effect. This effect must have a cause which had power to produce it; and the cause must be either the person himself, whose will it is, or some other being. The first is as easily conceived as the last. If the person was the cause of that determination of his own will, he was free in that action, and it is justly imputed to him, whether it be good or bad. But, if another being was the cause of this determination, either by producing it immediately, or by means and instruments under his direction, then the determination is the act and deed of that being, and is solely imputable to him.

But it is said, "That nothing is in our power but what depends upon the will, and therefore the will itself cannot be in our power."

I answer, that this is a fallacy arising from taking a common saying in a sense which it never was intended to convey, and in a sense contrary to what it necessarily implies.

In common life, when men speak of what is, or is not, in a man's power, they attend only to the external and visible effects, which only can be perceived, and which only can affect them. Of these, it is true, that nothing is in a man's power, but what depends upon his will, and this is all that is meant by this common saying.

But this is so far from excluding his will from being in his power, that it necessarily implies it. For to say that what depends upon the will is in a man's power, but the will is not in his power, is to say that the end is in his power, but the means necessary to that end are not in his power, which is a contradiction.

In many propositions which we express universally, there is an exception necessarily implied, and therefore always understood. Thus when we say that all things depend upon God, God himself is necessarily excepted. In like manner, when we say, that all that is in our power depends upon the will, the will itself is necessarily excepted; for if the will be not, nothing else can be in our power. Every effect must be in the power of its cause. The determination of the will is an effect, and therefore must be in the power of its cause,

whether that cause be the agent himself, or some other being.

From what has been said in this chapter, I hope the notion of moral liberty will be distinctly understood, and that it appears that this notion is neither inconceivable, nor involves any absurdity or contradiction.

Arguments for Necessity

Another argument that has been used to prove liberty of action to be impossible is, that it implies "an effect without a cause."

To this it may be briefly answered, that a free action is an effect produced by a being who had power and will to produce it; therefore it is not an effect without a cause.

To suppose any other cause necessary to the production of an effect, than a being who had the power and the will to produce it, is a contradiction; for it is to suppose that being to have power to produce the effect, and not to have power to produce it.

But as great stress is laid upon this agrument by a late zealous advocate for necessity, we shall consider the light in which he puts it.

He introduces this argument with an observation to which I entirely agree: it is, that to establish this doctrine of necessity, nothing is necessary but that, throughout all nature, the same consequences should invariably result from the same circumstances.

I know nothing more that can be desired to establish universal fatality throughout the universe. When it is proved that, through all nature, the same consequences invariably result from the same circumstances, the doctrine of liberty must be given up.

To prevent all ambiguity, I grant, that, in reasoning, the same consequences, throughout all nature, will invariably follow from the same premises: because good reasoning must be good reasoning in all times and places. But this has nothing to do with the doctrine of necessity. The thing to be proved, therefore, in order to establish that doctrine, is, that, through all nature, the same events invariably result from the same circumstances.

Of this capital point, the proof offered by that author, is that an event not preceded by any circumstances that determined it to be what it was, would be *an effect without a cause*. Why so? "For," says he, "a *cause* cannot be defined to be any thing but *such previous circumstances as are constantly followed by a certain effect*; the constancy of the result making us conclude, that there must be a *sufficient reason*, in the nature of things, why it should be produced in those circumstances."

I acknowledge that, if this be the only definition that can be given of a cause, it will follow, that an event not preceded by circumstances that determined it to be what it was, would be, not an *effect* without a cause, which is a contradiction in terms, but an *event* without a cause, which I hold to be impossible. The matter therefore is brought to this issue, whether this be the only definition that can be given of a cause?

With regard to this point, we may observe, *first*, that this definition of a cause, bating the phraseology of putting a *cause* under the category of *circumstances*, which I take to be new, is the same, in other words, with that which Mr. Hume gave, of which he ought to be acknowledged the inventor. For I know of no author before Mr. Hume, who maintained, that we have no other notion of a cause, but that it is something prior to the effect, which has been found by experience to be constantly followed by the effect. This is a main pillar of his system; and he has drawn very important consequences from this definition, which I am far from thinking this author will adopt.

Without repeating what I have before said of causes in the first of these Essays, and in the second and third chapters of this, I shall here mention some of the consequences that may be justly deduced from this definition of a cause, that we may judge of it by its fruits.

First, it follows from this definition of a cause, that night is the cause of day, and day the cause of night. For no two things have more constantly followed each other since the beginning of the world.

Secondly, it follows from this definition of a cause, that, for what we know, any thing may be the cause of any thing, since nothing is essential to a cause but its being constantly followed by the effect. If this be so, what is unintelligent may be the cause of what is intelligent; folly may be the cause of wisdom, and evil of good; all reasoning from the nature of the effect to the nature of the cause, and all reasoning from final causes, must be given up as fallacious.

Thirdly, from this definition of a cause, it follows, that we have no reason to conclude, that every event must have a cause: for innumerable events happen, when it cannot be shown that there were certain previous circumstances that have constantly been followed by such an event. And though it were certain, that every event we have had access to observe had a cause, it would not follow, that every event must have a cause: for it is contrary to the rules of logic to conclude, that, because a thing has always been, therefore it must be; to reason from what is contingent, to what is necessary.

Fourthly, from this definition of a cause, it would follow, that we have no reason to conclude that there was any cause of the creation of this world: for there were no previous circumstances that had been constantly followed by such an effect. And, for the same reason, it would follow from the definition, that whatever was singular in its nature, or the first thing of its kind, could have no cause.

Several of these consequences were fondly embraced by Mr. Hume, as necessarily following from his definition of a cause, and as favourable to his system of absolute skepticism. Those who adopt the definition of a cause, from which they follow, may choose whether they will adopt its consequences, or show that they do not follow from the definition.

A *second* observation with regard to this argument is, that a definition of a cause may be given, which is not burdened with such untoward consequences.

Why may not an efficient cause be defined to be a being that had power and will to produce the effect? The production of an effect requires active power, and active power, being a quality, must be in a being endowed with that power. Power without will produces no effect; but, where these are conjoined, the effect must be produced.

This, I think, is the proper meaning of the word *cause*, when it is used in metaphysics; and particularly when we affirm, that every thing that begins to exist must have a cause; and when, by reasoning, we prove, that there must be an eternal First Cause of all things.

Was the world produced by previous circumstances which are constantly followed by such an effect? or, was it produced by a Being that had power to produce it, and willed its production?

In natural philosophy, the word *cause* is often used in a very different sense. When an event is produced according to a known law of nature, the law of nature is called the cause of that event. But a law of nature is not the efficient cause of any event. It is only the rule, according to which the efficient cause acts. A law is a thing conceived in the mind of a rational being, not a thing that has a real existence; and, therefore, like a motive, it can neither act nor be acted upon, and consequently cannot be an efficient cause. If there be no being that acts according to the law, it produces no effect.

This author takes it for granted, that every voluntary action of man was determined to be what it was by the laws of nature, in the same sense as mechanical motions are determined by the laws of motion; and that every choice, not thus determined, "is just as impossible, as that a mechanical motion should depend upon no certain law or rule, or that any other effect should exist without a cause."

It ought here to be observed, that there are two kinds of laws, both very properly called *laws of nature*, which ought not to be confounded. There are moral laws of nature, and physical laws

of nature. The first are the rules which God has prescribed to his rational creatures for their conduct. They respect voluntary and free actions only; for no other actions can be subject to moral rules. These laws of nature ought to be always obeyed, but they are often transgressed by men. There is therefore no impossibility in the violation of the moral laws of nature, nor is such a violation an effect without a cause. The transgressor is the cause, and is justly accountable for it.

The physical laws of nature are the rules according to which the Deity commonly acts in his natural government of the world; and, whatever is done according to them, is not done by man, but by God, either immediately, or by instruments under his direction. These laws of nature neither restrain the power of the Author of nature, nor bring him under any obligation to do nothing beyond their sphere. He has sometimes acted contrary to them, in the case of miracles, and, perhaps, often acts without regard to them, in the ordinary course of his providence. Neither miraculous events, which are contrary to the physical laws of nature, nor such ordinary acts of the Divine administration as are without their sphere, are impossible, nor are they *effects without a cause*. God is the cause of them, and to him only they are to be imputed.

That the moral laws of nature are often transgressed by man, is undeniable. If the physical laws of nature make his obedience to the moral laws to be impossible, then he is, in the literal sense, *born under one law, bound unto another*, which contradicts every notion of a righteous government of the world.

But though this supposition were attended with no such shocking consequence, it is merely a supposition; and until it be proved that every choice, or voluntary action of man, is determined by the physical laws of nature, this argument for necessity is only the taking for granted the point to be proved.

Of the same kind is the argument for the impossibility of liberty, taken from a balance, which cannot move but as it is moved by the weights put into it. This argument, though urged by almost every writer in defence of necessity, is so pitiful, and has been so often answered, that it scarce deserves to be mentioned.

Every argument in a dispute, which is not grounded on principles granted by both parties, is that kind of sophism which logicians call *petitio principii*; and such, in my apprehension, are all the arguments offered to prove that liberty of action is impossible.

It may further be observed, that every argument of this class, if it were really conclusive, must extend to the Deity, as well as to all created beings; and necessary existence, which has always been considered as the prerogative of the Supreme Being, must belong equally to every creature and to every event, even the most trifling.

This I take to be the system of Spinoza, and of those among the ancients, who carried fatality to the highest pitch.

Further Questions

1. Reid tries to show that free will is possible. Does he succeed?
2. Even if Reid does show that free will is *possible*, there is the further question of whether it is *actual*. Before trying to answer, consider what one is entitled to appeal to in answering this question. That is, could this question be answered properly by "common sense" or, rather, could it be answered only by science? (If only by science, has science yet answered it? If so, what is the answer? If not, what that remains to be discovered does the answer depend on?) Is there any source of information other than common sense and science relevant to whether people have free will?

Further Readings

Berlin, Isaiah. *Historical Inevitability.* London: Oxford University Press, 1954. A vigorous attack by a leading twentieth-century intellectual on all forms of determinism.

Campbell, C. A. *Of Selfhood and Godhood.* New York: Macmillan, 1957. Includes the essay, "In Defense of Free Will," which is a well-known modern defense of a view similar to Reid's.

Melden, A. I. *Free Action.* London: Routledge & Kegan Paul, 1961. A defense of the idea that a person's reasons for acting cannot be caused.

"The Dilemma of Determinism"

WILLIAM JAMES

William James (1842–1910), brother of the novelist Henry James, was born in New York City and educated at Harvard. He made outstanding contributions to psychology, which are found primarily in his book, *The Principles of Psychology* (1890). In philosophy, he is best known for his development of a view called pragmatism, which he took over from the American philosopher and mathematician Charles Pierce, and for his contributions to philosophy of religion. James's goal, in philosophy, was the development of a point of view that would do equal justice to the claims of the exact sciences and also to those of moral and religious experience. His *The Varieties of Religious Experience* (1902) is regarded by many as the best book on the topic ever written. In the following selection, James defends the possibility of free will by arguing that, for all we know, many of our choices could be undetermined and yet our behavior be as intelligible as it is now. James also explains why believing in free will may have better consequences for our lives than not believing in it.

Reading Questions

1. Explain, in your own words, James's distinction between "determinism" and "indeterminism," and then illustrate the distinction with a clear example.
2. What is the point of James's Divinity Avenue/Oxford Street example? Do you agree?

A COMMON OPINION PREVAILS that the juice has ages ago been pressed out of the free-will controversy, and that no new champion can do more than warm up stale arguments which every one has heard. This is a radical mistake. I know of no subject less worn out, or in which inventive genius has a better chance of breaking open new ground, — not, perhaps, of forcing a conclusion or of coercing assent, but of deepening our sense of what the issue between the two parties really is, of what the ideas of fate and of free-will imply....

The arguments I am about to urge all proceed on two suppositions: first, when we make theories about the world and discuss them with one another, we do so in order to attain a conception of things which shall give us subjective satisfaction; and, second, if there be two conceptions, and the one seems to us, on the whole, more rational than the other, we are entitled to suppose that the more rational one is the truer of the two. I hope that you are all willing to make these suppositions with me; for I am afraid that if there be any of you here who are not, they will find little

edification in the rest of what I have to say. I cannot stop to argue the point; but I myself believe that all the magnificent achievements of mathematical and physical science — our doctrines of evolution, of uniformity of law, and the rest — proceed from our indomitable desire to cast the world into a more rational shape in our minds than the shape into which it is thrown there by the crude order of our experience. The world has shown itself, to a great extent, plastic to this demand of ours for rationality. How much farther it will show itself plastic no one can say. Our only means of finding out is to try; and I, for one, feel as free to try conceptions of moral as of mechanical or of logical rationality. If a certain formula for expressing the nature of the world violates my moral demand, I shall feel as free to throw it overboard, or at least to doubt it, as if it disappointed my demand for uniformity of sequence, for example; the one demand being, so far as I can see, quite as subjective and emotional as the other is. The principle of causality, for example, — what is it but a postulate, an empty name covering

From James: "The Dilemma of Determinism," An address to the Harvard Divinity Students published in the Unitarian Review, 1884. Also available in James: Essays on Faith and Morals, Longmans, Green and Co., 1949.

simply a demand that the sequence of events shall some day manifest a deeper kind of belonging of one thing with another than the mere arbitrary juxtaposition which now phenomenally appears? It is as much an altar to an unknown god as the one that Saint Paul found at Athens. All our scientific and philosophic ideals are altars to unknown gods. Uniformity is as much so as is freewill. If this be admitted, we can debate on even terms. But if any one pretends that while freedom and variety are, in the first instance, subjective demands, necessity and uniformity are something altogether different, I do not see how we can debate at all.

To begin, then, I must suppose you acquainted with the usual arguments on the subject. I cannot stop to take up the old proofs from causation, from statistics, from the certainty with which we can foretell one another's conduct, from the fixity of character, and all the rest. But there are two *words* which usually encumber these classical arguments, and which we must immediately dispose of if we are to make any progress. One is the eulogistic word *freedom*, and the other is the opprobrious word *chance*. The word 'chance' I wish to keep, but I wish to get rid of the word 'freedom.' Its eulogistic associations have so far overshadowed all the rest of its meaning that both parties claim the sole right to use it, and determinists to-day insist that they alone are freedom's champions. Old-fashioned determinism was what we may call *hard* determinism. It did not shrink from such words as fatality, bondage of the will, necessitation, and the like. Nowadays, we have a *soft* determinism which abhors harsh words, and, repudiating fatality, necessity, and even predetermination, says that its real name is freedom; for freedom is only necessity understood, and bondage to the highest is identical with true freedom. . . .

Now, all this is a quagmire of evasion under which the real issue of fact has been entirely smothered. . . . But there *is* a problem, an issue of fact and not of words, an issue of the most momentous importance, which is often decided without discussion in one sentence, — nay, in one clause of a sentence, — by those very writers who spin out whole chapters in their efforts to show what 'true' freedom is; and that is the question of determinism, about which we are to talk to-night.

Fortunately, no ambiguities hang about this word or about its opposite, indeterminism. Both designate an outward way in which things may happen, and their cold and mathematical sound has no sentimental associations that can bribe our partiality either way in advance. Now, evidence of an external kind to decide between determinism and indeterminism is strictly impossible to find. Let us look at the difference between them and see for ourselves. What does determinism profess?

It professes that those parts of the universe already laid down absolutely appoint and decree what the other parts shall be. The future has no ambiguous possibilities hidden in its womb: the part we call the present is compatible with only one totality. And other future complement than the one fixed from eternity is impossible. The whole is in each and every part, and welds it with the rest into an absolute unity, an iron block, in which there can be no equivocation or shadow of turning.

> With earth's first clay they did the last man knead,
> And there of the last harvest sowed the seed.
> And the first morning of creation wrote
> What the last dawn of reckoning shall read.

Indeterminism, on the contrary, says that the parts have a certain amount of loose play on one another, so that the laying down of one of them does not necessarily determine what the others shall be. It admits that possibilities may be in excess of actualities, and that things not yet revealed to our knowledge may really in themselves be ambiguous. Of two alternative futures which we conceive, both may now be really possible; and the one become impossible only at the very moment when the other excludes it by becoming real itself. Indeterminism thus denies the world to be one unbending unit of fact. It says there is a certain ultimate pluralism in it; and, so saying, it corroborates our ordinary unsophisticated view of things. To that view, actualities seem to float in a wider sea of possibilities from out of which they are chosen; and, *somewhere*, indeterminism says, such possibilities exist, and form a part of truth.

Determinism, on the contrary, says they exist *nowhere*, and that necessity on the one hand and impossibility on the other are the sole categories of the real. Possibilities that fail to get realized are, for determinism, pure illusions: they never were possibilities at all. There is nothing inchoate, it says, about this universe of ours, all that was or is or shall be actual in it having been from eternity virtually there. The cloud of alternatives our minds escort this mass of actuality withal is a cloud of sheer deceptions, to which 'impossibilities' is the only name that rightfully belongs.

The issue, it will be seen, is a perfectly sharp one, which no eulogistic terminology can smear over or wipe out. The truth *must* lie with one side or the other, and its lying with one side makes the other false.

The question relates solely to the existence of possibilities, in the strict sense of the term, as things that may, but need not, be. Both sides admit that a volition, for instance, has occurred. The indeterminists say another volition might have occurred in its place: the determinists swear that nothing could possibly have occurred in its place. Now, can science be called in to tell us which of these two point-blank contradicters of each other is right? Science professes to draw no conclusions but such as are based on matters of fact, things that have actually happened; but how can any amount of assurance that something actually happened give us the least grain of information as to whether another thing might or might not have happened in its place? Only facts can be proved by other facts. With things that are possibilities and not facts, facts have no concern. If we have no other evidence than the evidence of

existing facts, the possibility-question must remain a mystery never to be cleared up.

And the truth is that facts practically have hardly anything to do with making us either determinists or indeterminists. Sure enough, we make a flourish of quoting facts this way or that; and if we are determinists, we talk about the infallibility with which we can predict one another's conduct; while if we are indeterminists, we lay great stress on the fact that it is just because we cannot foretell one another's conduct, either in war or statecraft or in any of the great and small intrigues and businesses of men, that life is so intensely anxious and hazardous a game. But who does not see the wretched insufficiency of this so-called objective testimony on both sides? What fills up the gaps in our minds is something not objective, not external. What divides us into possibility men and anti-possibility men is different faiths or postulates, — postulates of rationality. To this man the world seems more rational with possibilities in it, — to that man more rational with possibilities excluded; and talk as we will about having to yield to evidence, what makes us monists or pluralists, determinists or indeterminists, is at bottom always some sentiment like this.

The stronghold of the deterministic sentiment is the antipathy to the idea of chance. As soon as we begin to talk indeterminism to our friends, we find a number of them shaking their heads. This notion of alternative possibility, they say, this admission that any one of several things may come to pass, is, after all, only a roundabout name for chance; and chance is something the notion of which no sane mind can for an instant tolerate in the world. What is it, they ask, but barefaced crazy unreason, the negation of intelligibility and law? And if the slightest particle of it exist anywhere, what is to prevent the whole fabric from falling together, the stars from going out, and chaos from recommencing her topsy-turvy reign?

Remarks of this sort about chance will put an end to discussion as quickly as anything one can find. I have already told you that 'chance' was a word I wished to keep and use. Let us then examine exactly what it means, and see whether it ought to be such a terrible bugbear to us. I fancy that squeezing the thistle boldly will rob it of its sting.

The sting of the word 'chance' seems to lie in the assumption that it means something positive, and that if anything happens by chance, it must needs be something of an intrinsically irrational and preposterous sort. Now, chance means nothing of the kind. It is a purely negative and relative term, giving us no information about that of which it is predicated, except that it happens to be disconnected with something else, — not controlled, secured, or necessitated by other things in advance of its own actual presence. As this point is the most subtile one of the whole lecture, and at the same time the point on which all the rest hinges, I beg you to pay particular attention to it. What I say is that it tells us nothing about what a thing may be in itself to call it 'chance.' It may be a bad thing, it may be a good thing. It may be lucidity, transparency, fitness incarnate, matching the whole system of other things, when it has once befallen, in an unimaginably perfect way. All you mean by calling it 'chance' is that this is not guaranteed, that it may also fall out otherwise. . . .

Nevertheless, many persons talk as if the minutest dose of disconnectedness of one part with another, the smallest modicum of independence, the faintest tremor of ambiguity about the future, for example, would ruin everything, and turn this goodly universe into a sort of insane sand-heap or nulliverse, no universe at all. Since future human volitions are as a matter of fact the only ambiguous things we are tempted to believe in, let us stop for a moment to make ourselves sure whether their independent and accidental character need be fraught with such direful consequences to the universe as these.

What is meant by saying that my choice of which way to walk home after the lecture is ambiguous and matter of chances as far as the pres-

ent moment is concerned? It means that both Divinity Avenue and Oxford Street are called; but that only one, and that one *either* one, shall be chosen. Now, I ask you seriously to suppose that this ambiguity of my choice is real; and then to make the impossible hypothesis that the choice is made twice over, and each time falls on a different street. In other words, imagine that I first walk through Divinity Avenue, and then imagine that the powers governing the universe annihilate ten minutes of time with all that it contained, and set me back at the door of this hall just as I was before the choice was made. Imagine then that, everything else being the same, I now make a different choice and traverse Oxford Street. You, as passive spectators, look on and see the two alternative universes, — one of them with me walking through Divinity Avenue in it, the other with the same me walking through Oxford Street. Now, if you are determinists you believe one of these universes to have been from eternity impossible: you believe it to have been impossible because of the intrinsic irrationality or accidentality somewhere involved in it. But looking outwardly at these universes, can you say which is the impossible and accidental one, and which the rational and necessary one? I doubt if the most ironclad determinist among you could have the slightest glimmer of light on this point. In other words, either universe *after the fact* and once there would, to our means of observation and understanding, appear just as rational as the other. There would be absolutely no criterion by which we might judge one necessary and the other matter of chance. Suppose now we relieve the gods of their hypothetical task and assume my choice, once made, to be made forever. I go through Divinity Avenue for good and all. If, as good determinists, you now begin to affirm, what all good determinists punctually do affirm, that in the nature of things I *couldn't* have gone through Oxford Street, — had I done so it would have been chance, irrationality, insanity, a horrid gap in nature, — I simply call your attention to this, that your affirmation is what the Germans call a

Machtspruch, a mere conception fulminated as a dogma and based on no insight into details. Before my choice, either street seemed as natural to you as to me. Had I happened to take Oxford Street, Divinity Avenue would have figured in your philosophy as the gap in nature; and you would have so proclaimed it with the best deterministic conscience in the world.

But what a hollow outcry, then, is this against a chance which, if it were present to us, we could by no character whatever distinguish from a rational necessity! . . . The more one thinks of the matter, the more one wonders that so empty and gratuitous a hubbub as this outcry against chance should have found so great an echo in the hearts of men. It is a word which tells us absolutely nothing about what chances, or about the *modus operandi* of the chancing; and the use of it as a war-cry shows only a temper of intellectual absolutism, a demand that the world shall be a solid block, subject to one control, — which temper, which demand, the world may not be bound to gratify at all. In every outwardly verifiable and practical respect, a world in which the alternatives that now actually distract *your* choice were decided by pure chance would be by *me* absolutely undistinguished from the world in which I now live. I am, therefore, entirely willing to call it, so far as your choices go, a world of chance for me. To *yourselves*, it is true, those very acts of choice, which to me are so blind, opaque, and external, are the opposites of this, for you are within them and effect them. To you they appear as decisions; and decisions, for him who makes them, are altogether peculiar psychic facts. Self-luminous and self-justifying at the living moment at which they occur, they appeal to no outside moment to put its stamp upon them or make them continuous with the rest of nature. Themselves it is rather who seem to make nature continuous; and in their strange and intense function of granting consent to one possibility and withholding it from another, to transform an equivocal and double future into an inalterable and simple past.

But with the psychology of the matter we have no concern this evening. The quarrel which determinism has with chance fortunately has nothing to do with this or that psychological detail. It is a quarrel altogether metaphysical. Determinism denies the ambiguity of future volitions, because it affirms that nothing future can be ambiguous. But we have said enough to meet the issue. Indeterminate future volitions *do* mean chance. . . .

We have seen what determinism means: we have seen that indeterminism is rightly described as meaning chance; and we have seen that chance, the very name of which we are urged to shrink from as from a metaphysical pestilence, means only the negative fact that no part of the world, however big, can claim to control absolutely the destinies of the whole. But although, in discussing the word 'chance,' I may at moments have seemed to be arguing for its real existence, I have not meant to do so yet. We have not yet ascertained whether this be a world of chance or no; at most, we have agreed that it seems so. And I now repeat what I said at the outset, that, from any strict theoretical point of view, the question is insoluble. To deepen our theoretic sense of the *difference* between a world with chances in it and a deterministic world is the most I can hope to do; and this I may now at last begin upon, after all our tedious clearing of the way.

I wish first of all to show you just what the notion that this is a deterministic world implies. The implications I call your attention to are all bound up with the fact that it is a world in which we constantly have to make what I shall, with your permission, call judgments of regret. Hardly an hour passes in which we do not wish that something might be otherwise; and happy indeed are those of us whose hearts have never echoed the wish of Omar Khayam—

That we might clasp, ere closed, the book
    of fate,
    And make the writer on a fairer leaf
Inscribe our names, or quite obliterate.
Ah! Love, could you and I with fate conspire
To mend this sorry scheme of things entire,

Would we not shatter it to bits, and then
Remould it nearer to the heart's desire?

Now, it is undeniable that most of these re-grets are foolish, and quite on a par in point of philosophic value with the criticisms on the universe of that friend of our infancy, the hero of the fable The Atheist and the Acorn, —

Fool! had that bough a pumpkin bore,
Thy whimsies would have worked no more, etc.

Even from the point of view of our own ends, we should probably make a botch of remodelling the universe. How much more then from the point of view of ends we cannot see! Wise men therefore regret as little as they can. But still some regrets are pretty obstinate and hard to stifle, — regrets for acts of wanton cruelty or treachery, for example, whether performed by others or by ourselves. Hardly any one can remain *entirely* optimistic after reading the confessions of the murderer at Brockton the other day: how, to get rid of the wife whose continued existence bored him, he inveigled her into a desert spot, shot her four times, and then, as she lay on the ground and said to him, "You didn't do it on purpose, did you, dear?" replied, "No, I didn't do it on purpose," as he raised a rock and smashed her skull. Such an occurrence, with the mild sentence and self-satisfaction of the prisoner, is a field for a crop of regrets, which one need not take up in detail. We feel that, although a perfect mechanical fit to the rest of the universe, it is a bad moral fit, and that something else would really have been better in its place.

But for the deterministic philosophy the murder, the sentence, and the prisoner's optimism were all necessary from eternity; and nothing else for a moment had a ghost of a chance of being put into their place. To admit such a chance, the determinists tell us, would be to make a suicide of reason; so we must steel our hearts against the thought. And here our plot thickens, for we see the first of those difficult implications of determinism and monism which it is my purpose to make you feel. If this Brockton murder was called for by the rest of the universe, if it had to come at its preappointed hour, and if nothing else would have been consistent with the sense of the whole, what are we to think of the universe? Are we stubbornly to stick to our judgment of regret, and say, though it *couldn't* be, yet it *would* have been a better universe with something different from this Brockton murder in it? That, of course, seems the natural and spontaneous thing for us to do; and yet it is nothing short of deliberately espousing a kind of pessimism. The judgment of regret calls the murder bad. Calling a thing bad means, if it means anything at all, that the thing ought not to be, that something else ought to be in its stead. Determinism, in denying that anything else can be in its stead, virtually defines the universe as a place in which what ought to be is impossible, — in other words, as an organism whose constitution is afflicted with an incurable taint, an irremediable flaw. The pessimism of a Schopenhauer says no more than this, — that the murder is a symptom; and that it is a vicious symptom because it belongs to a vicious whole, which can express its nature no otherwise than by bringing forth just such a symptom as that at this particular spot. Regret for the murder must transform itself, if we are determinists and wise, into a larger regret. It is absurd to regret the murder alone. Other things being what they are, *it* could not be different. What we should regret is that whole frame of things of which the murder is one member. I see no escape whatever from this pessimistic conclusion, if, being determinists, our judgment of regret is to be allowed to stand at all.

The only deterministic escape from pessimism is everywhere to abandon the judgment of regret. That this can be done, history shows to be not impossible. The devil, *quod existentiam*, may be good. That is, although he be a *principle* of evil, yet the universe, with such a principle in it, may practically be a better universe than it could have been without. On every hand, in a small way, we find that a certain amount of evil is a condition by which a higher form of good is brought. There is nothing to prevent anybody from generalizing this view, and trusting that if we could but see things in the largest of all ways, even such matters as this Brockton murder would appear to be paid for by the uses that follow in their train. An optimism *quand même*, a systematic and infatuated optimism like that ridiculed by Voltaire in his *Candide*, is one of the possible ideal ways in which a man may train himself to look on life. Bereft of dogmatic hardness and lit up with the expression of a tender and pathetic hope, such an optimism has been the grace of some of the most religious characters that ever lived.

> Throb thine with Nature's throbbing breast,
> And all is clear from east to west.

Even cruelty and treachery may be among the absolutely blessed fruits of time, and to quarrel with any of their details may be blasphemy. The only real blasphemy, in short, may be that pessimistic temper of the soul which lets it give way to such things as regrets, remorse, and grief.

Thus, our deterministic pessimism may become a deterministic optimism at the price of extinguishing our judgments of regret.

But does not this immediately bring us into a curious logical predicament? Our determinism leads us to call our judgments of regret wrong, because they are pessimistic in implying that what is impossible yet ought to be. But how then about the judgments of regret themselves? If they are wrong, other judgments, judgments of approval presumably, ought to be in their place. But as they are necessitated, nothing else *can* be in their place; and the universe is just what it was before, — namely, a place in which what ought to be appears impossible. We have got one foot out of the pessimistic bog, but the other one sinks all the deeper. We have rescued our actions from the bonds of evil, but our judgments are now held fast. When murders and treacheries cease to be sins, regrets are theoretic absurdities and errors. The theoretic and the active life thus play a kind of see-saw with each other on the ground of evil.

The rise of either sends the other down. Murder and treachery cannot be good without regret being bad: regret cannot be good without treachery and murder being bad. Both, however, are supposed to have been foredoomed; so something must be fatally unreasonable, absurd, and wrong in the world. It must be a place of which either sin or error forms a necessary part. From this dilemma there seems at first sight no escape. . . .

The only consistent way of representing a pluralism and a world whose parts may affect one another through their conduct being either good or bad is the indeterministic way. What interest, zest, or excitement can there be in achieving the right way, unless we are enabled to feel that the wrong way is also a possible and a natural way, — nay, more, a menacing and an imminent way? And what sense can there be in condemning ourselves for taking the wrong way, unless we need have done nothing of the sort, unless the right way was open to us as well? I cannot understand the willingness to act, no matter how we feel, without the belief that acts are really good and bad. I cannot understand the belief that an act is bad, without regret at its happening. I cannot understand regret without the admission of real, genuine possibilities in the world. Only *then* is it other than a mockery to feel, after we have failed to do our best, that an irreparable opportunity is gone from the universe, the loss of which it must forever after mourn.

If you insist that this is all superstition, that possibility is in the eye of science and reason impossibility, and that if I act badly 'tis that the universe was foredoomed to suffer this defect, you fall right back into the dilemma, the labyrinth, of pessimism, from out of whose toils we have just wound our way.

Now, we are of course free to fall back, if we please. For my own part, though, whatever difficulties may beset the philosophy of objective right and wrong, and the indeterminism it seems to imply, determinism, with its alternative of pessimism or romanticism, contains difficulties that are greater still. But you will remember that I expressly repudiated awhile ago the pretension to offer any arguments which could be coercive in a so-called scientific fashion in this matter. And I consequently find myself, at the end of this long talk, obliged to state my conclusions in an altogether personal way. This personal method of appeal seems to be among the very conditions of the problem; and the most any one can do is to confess as candidly as he can the grounds for the faith that is in him, and leave his example to work on others as it may.

Let me, then, without circumlocution say just this. The world is enigmatical enough in all conscience, whatever theory we may take up toward it. The indeterminism I defend, the free-will theory of popular sense based on the judgment of regret, represents that world as vulnerable, and liable to be injured by certain of its parts if they act wrong. And it represents their acting wrong as a matter of possibility or accident, neither inevitable nor yet to be infallibly warded off. In all this, it is a theory devoid either of transparency or of stability. It gives us a pluralistic, restless universe, in which no single point of view can ever take in the whole scene; and to a mind possessed of the love of unity at any cost, it will, no doubt, remain forever inacceptable. A friend with such a mind once told me that the thought of my universe made him sick, like the sight of the horrible motion of a mass of maggots in their carrion bed.

But while I freely admit that the pluralism and the restlessness are repugnant and irrational in a certain way, I find that every alternative to them is irrational in a deeper way. The indeterminism with its maggots, if you please to speak so about it, offends only the native absolutism of my intellect, — an absolutism which, after all, per-

haps, deserves to be snubbed and kept in check. But the determinism with its necessary carrion, to continue the figure of speech, and with no possible maggots to eat the latter up, violates my sense of moral reality through and through. When, for example, I imagine such carrion as the Brockton murder, I cannot conceive it as an act by which the universe, as a whole, logically and necessarily expresses its nature without shrinking from complicity with such a whole. And I deliberately refuse to keep on terms of loyalty with the universe by saying blankly that the murder, since it does flow from the nature of the whole, is not carrion. There are *some* instinctive reactions which I, for one, will not tamper with. . . .

Make as great an uproar about chance as you please, I know that chance means pluralism and nothing more. If some of the members of the pluralism are bad, the philosophy of pluralism, whatever broad views it may deny me, permits me, at least, to turn to the other members with a clean breast of affection and an unsophisticated moral sense. And if I still wish to think of the world as a totality, it lets me feel that a world with a *chance* in it of being altogether good, even if the chance never come to pass, is better than a world with no such chance at all. That 'chance' whose very notion I am exhorted and conjured to banish from my view of the future as the suicide of reason concerning it, that 'chance' is — what? Just this, — the chance that in moral respects the future may be other and better than the past has been. This is the only chance we have any motive for supposing to exist. Shame, rather, on its repudiation and its denial! For its presence is the vital air which lets the world live, the salt which keeps it sweet.

Further Questions

1. James argues that indeterminism could be true. Does he give any evidence that it actually is true? Does modern science give any evidence that the sort of indeterminism that James needs to support his belief in free will is true?

2. Is it possible, in principle, that someone could create an android for which it was a matter of pure chance whether it walked home via one street rather than another? If so, how can we know whether we are "natural androids" of that sort?

3. Would people be any more responsible for their behavior if it came about by chance than if it were determined? If so, why? If not, can one appeal to chance to support the idea that people might have free will?

Further Readings

Lehrer, Keith, ed. *Freedom and Determinism*. New York: Random House, 1966. A valuable anthology of the views of contemporary analytic philosophers.

Salmon, Wesley. *Scientific Explanation and the Causal Structure of the World*. Princeton: Princeton University Press, 1984. A clear, informed account of the role of chance in modern scientific theory.

"Freedom and Determinism"

RICHARD TAYLOR

Richard Taylor served on a submarine during World War II where he became so interested in the melancholy philosophy of Schopenhauer that he subsequently became a philosopher himself, eventually teaching at Brown University, Ohio State University, and the University of Rochester, from which he recently retired. A prolific and engaging writer, Taylor has written books on the philosophy of mind, metaphysics, and ethics. He is also a renowned beekeeper and has written extensively on beekeeping. Among his many books: *Action and Purpose* (1966); *Ethics, Faith, and Reason* (1985), *The New Comb Honey Book* (1982), *The Joys of Beekeeping* (1984), and *Having Love Affairs* (1982).

In this selection, from his *Metaphysics* (4th ed., 1992), Taylor argues, first, that all of the standard views on free will are inadequate and, second, that only the view that people are self-determining beings, and hence sometimes the causes of their own behavior is compatible with two assumptions each of us makes: that our behavior is sometimes the outcome of our own deliberation; and that it is sometimes up to us what we do.

Reading Questions

1. What is "soft determinism"? Of the philosophers whose views on free will you know, which, if any, are soft determinists? Why does Taylor think that soft determinism should be rejected?

2. What is "simple indeterminism"? Of the philosophers whose views on free will you know, which, if any, are simple indeterminists? Why does Taylor think that simple indeterminism should be rejected?

3. What is "the theory of agency"? Why does Taylor think that only this theory can account for the commonly made assumptions that our behavior is sometimes the outcome of our own deliberations and that it is sometimes up to us what we do? Do you agree?

4. What difficulties does Taylor think there are for the theory of agency? What, in your opinion, is the importance of these difficulties?

Determinism

IN THE CASE OF EVERYTHING THAT EXISTS, there are antecedent conditions, known or unknown, which, because they are given, mean that things could not be other than they are. That is an exact statement of the metaphysical thesis of determinism. More loosely, it says that everything, including every cause, is the effect of some cause or causes; or that everything is not only determinate but causally determined. The statement, moreover, makes no allowance for time, for past, or for future. Hence, if true, it holds not only for all things that have existed but for all things that do or ever will exist.

Of course people rarely think of such a principle, and hardly one in a thousand will ever formulate it to himself in words. Yet all do seem to assume it in their daily affairs, so much so that some philosophers have declared it an *a priori* principle of the understanding, that is, something that is known independently of experience, while others have deemed it to be at least a part of the common sense of mankind. Thus, when I hear a noise I look up to see where it came from. I never suppose that it was just a noise that came from nowhere and had no cause. Everyone does the same — even animals, though they have never once thought about metaphysics or the principle of universal determinism. People believe, or at least act as though they believed, that things have causes, without exception. When a child or animal touches a hot stove for the first time, it un-

hesitatingly believes that the pain then felt was caused by that stove, and so firm and immediate is that belief that hot stoves are avoided ever after. We all use our metaphysical principles, whether we think of them or not, or are even capable of thinking of them. If I have a bodily or other disorder — a rash, for instance, or a fever or a phobia — I consult a physician for a diagnosis and explanation in the hope that the cause of it might be found and removed or moderated. I am never tempted to suppose that such things just have no causes, arising from nowhere, else I would take no steps to remove the causes. The principle of determinism is here, as in everything else, simply assumed, without being thought about.

Determinism and Human Behavior

I am a part of the world. So is each of the cells and minute parts of which I am composed. The principle of determinism, then, in case it is true, applies to me and to each of those minute parts, no less than to the sand, wheat, winds, and waters of which we have spoken. There is no particular difficulty in thinking so, as long as I consider only what are sometimes called the "purely physiological" changes of my body, like growth, the pulse, glandular secretions, and the like. But what of my thoughts and ideas? And what of my behavior that is supposed to be deliberate, purposeful, and perhaps morally significant? These are all changes of my own being, changes that I undergo, and if these are all but the consequences

Richard Taylor, Metaphysics, *4e, © 1992, pp. 36–39, 43–53. Reprinted by permission. Prentice-Hall, Englewood Cliffs, NJ.*

of the conditions under which they occur, and these conditions are the only ones that could have obtained, given the state of the world just before and when they arose, what now becomes of my responsibility for my behavior and of the control over my conduct that I fancy myself to possess? What am I but a helpless product of nature, destined by her to do whatever I do and to become whatever I become?

There is no moral blame nor merit in anyone who cannot help what he does. It matters not whether the explanation for his behavior is found within him or without, whether it is expressed in terms of ordinary physical causes or allegedly "mental" ones, or whether the causes be proximate or remote. I am not responsible for being a man rather than a woman, nor for having the temperament and desires characteristic of that sex. I was never asked whether these should be given to me. The kleptomaniac, similarly, steals from compulsion, the alcoholic drinks from compulsion, and sometimes even the hero dies from compulsive courage. Though these causes are within them, they compel no less for that, and their victims never chose to have them inflicted upon themselves. To say they are compulsions is to say only that they compel. But to say that they compel is only to say that they cause; for the cause of a thing being given, the effect cannot fail to follow. By the thesis of determinism, however, everything whatever is caused, and not one single thing could ever be other than exactly what it is. Perhaps one thinks that the kleptomaniac and the drunkard did not have to become what they are, that they could have done better at another time and thereby ended up better than they are now, or that the hero could have done worse and then ended up a coward. But this shows only an unwillingness to understand what made them become as they are. Having found that their behavior is caused from within them, we can hardly avoid asking what caused these inner springs of action, and then asking what were the causes of these causes, and so on through the infinite past. We shall not, certainly, with our small understanding and our fragmentary knowledge of the past ever know why the world should at just this time and place have produced just this thief, this drunkard, and this hero, but the vagueness and smattered nature of our knowledge should not tempt us to imagine a similar vagueness in nature herself. Everything in nature is and always has been determinate, with no loose edges at all, and she was forever destined to bring forth just what she has produced, however slight may be our understanding of the origins of these works. Ultimate responsibility for anything that exists, and hence for any person and his deeds, can thus rest only with the first cause of all things, if there is such a cause, or nowhere at all, in case there is not. Such, at least, seems to be the unavoidable implication of determinism.

Determinism and Morals

Some philosophers, faced with all this, which seems quite clear to the ordinary understanding, have tried to cling to determinism while modifying traditional conceptions of morals. They continue to *use* such words as *merit, blame, praise,* and *desert,* but they so divest them of their meanings as to finish by talking about things entirely different, sometimes without themselves realizing that they are no longer on the subject. An ordinary person will hardly understand that anyone can possess merit or vice and be deserving of moral praise or blame, as a result of traits that he has or of behavior arising from those traits, once it is well understood that he could never have avoided being just what he is and doing just what he does. . . .

Now I could, of course, simply affirm that I am a morally responsible being, in the sense in which my responsibility for my behavior implies that I could have avoided that behavior. But this would take us into the nebulous realm of ethics, and it is, in fact, far from obvious that I am responsible in that sense. Many have doubted that they are responsible in that sense, and it is in any case not difficult to doubt it, however strongly one might feel about it.

There are, however, two things about myself of which I feel quite certain and that have no necessary connection with morals. The first is that I sometimes deliberate, with the view to making a decision; a decision, namely, to do this thing or that. And the second is that whether or not I deliberate about what to do, it is sometimes up to me what I do. This might all be an illusion, of course; but so also might any philosophical theory, such as the theory of determinism, be false. The point remains that it is far more difficult for me to doubt that I sometimes deliberate, and that it is sometimes up to me what to do, than to doubt any philosophical theory whatever, including the theory of determinism. We must, accordingly, if we ever hope to be wiser, adjust our theories to our data and not try to adjust our data to our theories. . . .

Freedom

To say that it is, in a given instance, up to me what I do is to say that I am in that instance *free* with respect to what I then do. Thus, I am sometimes free to move my finger this way and that, but not, certainly, to bend it backward or into a knot. But what does this mean?

It means, first that there is no *obstacle or impediment* to my activity. Thus, there is sometimes no obstacle to my moving my finger this way and that, though there are obvious obstacles to my moving it backward or into a knot. Those things, accordingly, that pose obstacles to my motions limit my freedom. If my hand were strapped in such a way as to permit only a leftward motion of my finger, I would not then be free to move it to the right. If it were encased in a tight case that permitted no motion, I would not be free to move it at all. Freedom of motion, then, is limited by obstacles.

Further, to say that it is, in a given instance, up to me what I do, means that nothing *constrains* or *forces* me to do one thing rather than another. Constraints are like obstacles, except that while the latter prevent, the former enforce. Thus, if my

finger is being forcibly bent to the left — by a machine, for instance, or by another person, or by any force that I cannot overcome — then I am not free to move it this way and that. I cannot, in fact, move it at all; I can only watch to see how it is moved, and perhaps vainly resist: Its motions are not up to me, or within my control, but in the control of some other thing or person.

Obstacles and constraints, then, both obviously limit my freedom. To say that I am free to perform some action thus means at least that there is no obstacle to my doing it, and that nothing constrains me to do otherwise.

Now if we rest content with this observation, as many have, and construe free activity simply as activity that is unimpeded and unconstrained, there is evidently no inconsistency between affirming both the thesis of determinism and the claim that I am sometimes free. For to say that some action of mine is neither impeded nor constrained does not by itself imply that it is not causally determined. The absence of obstacles and constraints is a mere negative condition, and does not by itself rule out the presence of positive causes. It might seem, then, that we can say of some of my actions that there are conditions antecedent to their performance so that no other actions were possible, and also that these actions were unobstructed and unconstrained. And to say that would logically entail that such actions were both causally determined, and free.

Soft Determinism

It is this kind of consideration that has led many philosophers to embrace what is sometimes called "soft determinism." All versions of this theory have in common three claims, by means of which, it is naïvely supposed, a reconciliation is achieved between determinism and freedom. Freedom being, furthermore, a condition of moral responsibility and the only condition that metaphysics seriously questions, it is supposed by the partisans of this view that determinism is perfectly compatible with such responsibility.

This, no doubt, accounts for its great appeal and wide acceptance, even by some people of considerable learning.

The three claims of soft determinism are (1) that the thesis of determinism is true, and that accordingly all human behavior, voluntary or other, like the behavior of all other things, arises from antecedent conditions, given which no other behavior is possible—in short, that all human behavior is caused and determined; (2) that voluntary behavior is nonetheless free to the extent that it is not externally constrained or impeded; and (3) that, in the absence of such obstacles and constraints, the causes of voluntary behavior are certain states, events, or conditions within the agent himself; namely, his own acts of will or volitions, choices, decisions, desires, and so on.

Thus, on this view, I am free, and therefore sometimes responsible for what I do, provided nothing prevents me from acting according to my own choice, desire, or volition, or constrains me to act otherwise. There may, to be sure, be other conditions for my responsibility—such as, for example, an understanding of the probable consequences of my behavior, and that sort of thing—but absence of constraint or impediment is, at least, one such condition. And, it is claimed, it is a condition that is compatible with the supposition that my behavior is caused—for it is, by hypothesis, caused by my own inner choices, desires, and volitions.

The Refutation of This

The theory of soft determinism looks good at first—so good that it has for generations been solemnly taught from innumerable philosophical chairs and implanted in the minds of students as sound philosophy—but no great acumen is needed to discover that far from solving any problem, it only camouflages it.

My free actions are those unimpeded and unconstrained motions that arise from my own inner desires, choices, and volitions; let us grant this provisionally. But now, whence arise those inner states that determine what my body shall do? Are they within my control or not? Having made my choice or decision and acted upon it, could I have chosen otherwise or not?

Here the determinist, hoping to surrender nothing and yet to avoid the problem implied in that question, bids us not to ask it; the question itself, he announces, is without meaning. For to say that I could have done otherwise, he says, means only that I *would* have done otherwise, *if* those inner states that determined my action had been different; if, that is, I had decided or chosen differently. To ask, accordingly, whether I could have chosen or decided differently is only to ask whether, had I decided to decide differently or chosen to choose differently, or willed to will differently, I *would* have decided or chosen or willed differently. And this, of course, *is* unintelligible nonsense.

But it is not nonsense to ask whether the causes of my actions—my own inner choices, decisions, and desires—are themselves caused. And of course they are, if determinism is true, for on that thesis everything is caused and determined. And if they are, then we cannot avoid concluding that, given the causal conditions of those inner states, I could not have decided, willed, chosen, or desired other than I, in fact, did, for this is a logical consequence of the very definition of determinism. Of course we can still say that, *if* the causes of those inner states, whatever they were, had been different, then their effects, those inner states themselves, would have been different, and that in this hypothetical sense I could have decided, chosen, willed, or desired differently—but that only pushes our problem back still another step. For we will then want to know whether the causes of those inner states were within my control, and so on *ad infinitum*. We are, at each step, permitted to say "could have been otherwise" only in a provisional sense—provided, that is, that something else had been different—but must then retract it and replace it with "could not have been otherwise" as soon as we discover, as we must at each step, that whatever would have to have been different could not have been different.

Examples

Such is the dialectic of the problem. The easiest way to see the shadowy quality of soft determinism, however, is by means of examples.

Let us suppose that my body is moving in various ways, that these motions are not externally constrained or impeded, and that they are all exactly in accordance with my own desires, choices, or acts of will and whatnot. When I will that my arm should move in a certain way, I find it moving in that way, unobstructed and unconstrained. When I will to speak, my lips and tongue move, unobstructed and unconstrained, in a manner suitable to the formation of the words I choose to utter. Now, given that this is a correct description of my behavior, namely, that it consists of the unconstrained and unimpeded motions of my body in response to my own volitions, then it follows that my behavior is free, on the soft determinist's definition of "free." It follows further that I am responsible for that behavior; or at least, that if I am not, it is not from any lack of freedom on my part.

But if the fulfillment of these conditions renders my behavior free — that is to say, if my behavior satisfies the conditions of free action set forth in the theory of soft determinism — then my behavior will be no less free if we assume further conditions that are perfectly consistent with those already satisfied.

We suppose further, accordingly, that while my behavior is entirely in accordance with my own volitions, and thus "free" in terms of the conception of freedom we are examining, my volitions themselves are caused. To make this graphic, we can suppose that an ingenious physiologist can induce in me any volition he pleases, simply by pushing various buttons on an instrument to which, let us suppose, I am attached by numerous wires. All the volitions I have in that situation are, accordingly, precisely the ones he gives me. By pushing one button, he evokes in me the volition to raise my hand; and my hand, being unimpeded, rises in response to that volition. By pushing another, he induces the volition in me to kick, and my foot, being unimpeded, kicks in response to that volition. We can even suppose that the physiologist puts a rifle in my hands, aims it at some passerby, and then, by pushing the proper button, evokes in me the volition to squeeze my finger against the trigger, whereupon the passerby falls dead of a bullet wound.

This is the description of a man who is acting in accordance with his inner volitions, a man whose body is unimpeded and unconstrained in its motions, these motions being the effects of those inner states. It is hardly the description of a free and responsible agent. It is the perfect description of a puppet. To render someone your puppet, it is not necessary forcibly to constrain the motions of his limbs, after the fashion that real puppets are moved. A subtler but no less effective means of making a person your puppet would be to gain complete control of his inner states, and ensuring, as the theory of soft determinism does ensure, that his body will move in accordance with them.

The example is somewhat unusual, but it is no worse for that. It is perfectly intelligible, and it does appear to refute the soft determinist's conception of freedom. One might think that, in such a case, the agent should not have allowed himself to be so rigged in the first place, but this is irrelevant; we can suppose that he was not aware that he was and was hence unaware of the source of those inner states that prompted his bodily motions. The example can, moreover, be modified in perfectly realistic ways, so as to coincide with actual and familiar cases. One can, for instance, be given a compulsive desire for certain drugs, simply by having them administered over a course of time. Suppose, then, that I do, with neither my knowledge nor consent, thus become a victim of such a desire and act upon it. Do I act freely, merely by virtue of the fact that I am unimpeded in my quest for drugs? In a sense I do, surely, but I am hardly free with respect to whether or not I shall use drugs. I never chose to have the desire for them inflicted upon me.

Nor does it, of course, matter whether the inner states that allegedly prompt all my "free" activity are evoked in me by another agent or by perfectly impersonal forces. Whether a desire that causes my body to behave in a certain way is inflicted upon me by another person, for instance, or derived from hereditary factors, or indeed from anything at all, matters not the least. In any case, if it is in fact the cause of my bodily behavior, I cannot help but act in accordance with it. Wherever it came from, whether from personal or impersonal origins, it was entirely caused or determined, and not within my control. Indeed, if determinism is true, as the theory of soft determinism holds it to be, all those inner states that cause my body to behave in whatever ways it behaves must arise from circumstances that existed before I was born; for the chain of causes and effects is infinite, and none could have been the least different, given those that preceded.

Simple Indeterminism

We might at first now seem warranted in simply denying determinism, and saying that, insofar as they are free, my actions are not caused; or that, if they are caused by my own inner states — my own desires, impulses, choices, volitions, and whatnot — then these, in any case, are not caused. This is a perfectly clear sense in which a person's action, assuming that it was free, could have been otherwise. If it was uncaused, then, even given the conditions under which it occurred and all that preceded, some other act was nonetheless possible, and he did not have to do what he did. Or if his action was the inevitable consequence of his own inner states, and could not have been otherwise, given these, we can nevertheless say that these inner states, being uncaused, could

have been otherwise, and could thereby have produced different actions.

Only the slightest consideration will show, however, that this simple denial of determinism has not the slightest plausibility. For let us suppose it is true, and that some of my bodily motions — namely, those that I regard as my free acts — are not caused at all or, if caused by my own inner states, that these are not caused. We shall thereby avoid picturing a puppet, to be sure — but only by substituting something even less like a human being; for the conception that now emerges is not that of a free person, but of an erratic and jerking phantom, without any rhyme or reason at all.

Suppose that my right arm is free, according to this conception; that is, that its motions are uncaused. It moves this way and that from time to time, but nothing causes these motions. Sometimes it moves forth vigorously, sometimes up, sometimes down, sometimes it just drifts vaguely about — these motions all being wholly free and uncaused. Manifestly I have nothing to do with them at all; they just happen, and neither I nor anyone can ever tell what this arm will be doing next. It might seize a club and lay it on the head of the nearest bystander, no less to my astonishment than his. There will never be any point in asking why these motions occur, or in seeking any explanation of them, for under the conditions assumed there is no explanation. They just happen, from no causes at all.

This is no description of free, voluntary, or responsible behavior. Indeed, so far as the motions of my body or its parts are entirely uncaused, such motions cannot even be ascribed to me as my behavior in the first place, since I have nothing to do with them. The behavior of my arm is just the random motion of a foreign object. Behavior that is mine must be behavior that is within my control, but motions that occur from no causes are beyond the control of anyone. I can have no more to do with, and no more control over, the uncaused motions of my limbs than a gambler has over the motions of an honest roulette wheel. I can only, like him, idly wait to see what happens.

Nor does it improve things to suppose that my bodily motions are caused by my own inner states, so long as we suppose these to be wholly uncaused. The result will be the same as before. My arm, for example, will move this way and that, sometimes up and sometimes down, sometimes vigorously and sometimes just drifting about, always in response to certain inner states, to be sure. But since these are supposed to be wholly uncaused, it follows that I have no control over them and hence none over their effects. If my hand lays a club forcefully on the nearest bystander, we can indeed say that this motion resulted from an inner club-wielding desire of mine; but we must add that I had nothing to do with that desire, and that it arose, to be followed by its inevitable effect, no less to my astonishment than to his. Things like this do, alas, sometimes happen. We are all sometimes seized by compulsive impulses that arise we know not whence, and we do sometimes act upon these. But because they are far from being examples of free, voluntary, and responsible behavior, we need only to learn that the behavior was of this sort to conclude that it was not free, voluntary, or responsible. It was erratic, impulsive, and irresponsible.

Determinism and Simple Indeterminism as Theories

Both determinism and simple indeterminism are loaded with difficulties, and no one who has thought much on them can affirm either of them without some embarrassment. Simple indeterminism has nothing whatever to be said for it, except that it appears to remove the grossest difficulties of determinism, only, however, to imply perfect absurdities of its own. Determinism, on the other hand, is at least initially plausible. People seem to have a natural inclination to believe in it; it is, indeed, almost required for the very exercise of practical intelligence. And beyond this, our experience appears always to confirm it, so long as we are dealing with everyday facts of common experience, as distinguished from the esoteric researches of theoretical physics. But determinism, as applied to human behavior, has implications that few can casually accept, and they appear to be implications that no modification of the theory can efface.

Both theories, moreover, appear logically irreconcilable to the two items of data that we set forth at the outset; namely, (1) that my behavior is sometimes the outcome of my deliberation, and (2) that in these and other cases it is sometimes up to me what I do. Because these were our data, it is important to see, as must already be quite clear, that these theories cannot be reconciled to them.

I can deliberate only about my own future actions, and then only if I do not already know what I am going to do. If a certain nasal tickle warns me that I am about to sneeze, for instance, then I cannot deliberate whether to sneeze or not; I can only prepare for the impending convulsion. But if determinism is true, then there are always conditions existing antecedently to everything I do, sufficient for my doing just that, and such as to render it inevitable. If I can know what those conditions are and what behavior they are sufficient to produce, then I can in every case know what I am going to do and cannot then deliberate about it.

By itself this only shows, of course, that I can deliberate only in ignorance of the causal conditions of my behavior; it does not show that such conditions cannot exist. It is odd, however, to suppose that deliberation should be a mere substitute for clear knowledge. Ignorance is a condition of speculation, inference, and guesswork, which have nothing whatever to do with deliberation. A prisoner awaiting execution may not know when he is going to die, and he may even entertain the hope of reprieve, but he cannot deliberate about this. He can only speculate, guess — and wait.

Worse yet, however, it now becomes clear that I cannot deliberate about what I am going to do, if it is even *possible* for me to find out in advance, whether I do in fact find out in advance or not. I can deliberate only with the view to deciding what to do, to making up my mind; and this is impossible if I believe that it could be inferred what I am going to do from conditions already existing, even though I have not made that inference myself. If I believe that what I am going to do has been rendered inevitable by conditions already existing, and could be inferred by anyone having the requisite sagacity, then I cannot try to decide whether to do it or not, for there is simply nothing left to decide. I can at best only guess or try to figure it out myself or, all prognostics failing, I can wait and see; but I cannot deliberate. I deliberate in order to *decide* what *to* do, not to *discover* what it is that I am *going* to do. But if determinism is true, then there are always antecedent conditions sufficient for everything that I do, and this can always be inferred by anyone having the requisite sagacity; that is, by anyone having a knowledge of what those conditions are and what behavior they are sufficient to produce.

This suggests what in fact seems quite clear, that determinism cannot be reconciled with our second datum either, to the effect that it is sometimes up to me what I am going to do. For if it is ever really up to me whether to do this thing or that, then, as we have seen, each alternative course of action must be such that I can do it; not that I can do it in some abstruse or hypothetical sense of "can"; not that I could do it if only something were true that is not true; but in the sense that it is then and there within my power to do it. But this is never so, if determinism is true, for on the very formulation of that theory whatever happens at any time is the only thing that can then happen, given all that precedes it. It is simply a logical consequence of this that whatever I do at any time is the only thing I can then do, given the conditions that precede my doing it. Nor does it help in the least to interpose, among the causal antecedents of my behavior, my own inner states, such as my desires, choices, acts of will, and so on. For even supposing these to be always involved in voluntary behavior—which is

highly doubtful in itself—it is a consequence of determinism that these, whatever they are at any time, can never be other than what they then are. Every chain of causes and effects, if determinism is true, is infinite. This is why it is not now up to me whether I shall a moment hence be male or female. The conditions determining my sex have existed through my whole life, and even prior to my life. But if determinism is true, the same holds of anything that I ever am, ever become, or ever do. It matters not whether we are speaking of the most patent facts of my being, such as my sex; or the most subtle, such as my feelings, thoughts, desires, or choices. Nothing could be other than it is, given what was; and while we may indeed say, quite idly, that something—some inner state of mind, for instance—*could* have been different, had only something *else* been different, any consolation of this thought evaporates as soon as we add that whatever would have to have been different could not have been different.

It is even more obvious that our data cannot be reconciled to the theory of simple indeterminism. I can deliberate only about my own actions; this is obvious. But the random, uncaused motion of any body whatever, whether it be a part of my body or not, is no action of mine and nothing that is within my power. I might try to guess what these motions will be, just as I might try to guess how a roulette wheel will behave, but I cannot deliberate about them or try to decide what they shall be, simply because these things are not up to me. Whatever is not caused by anything is not caused by me, and nothing could be more plainly inconsistent with saying that it is nevertheless up to me what it shall be.

The Theory of Agency

The only conception of action that accords with our data is one according to which people—and perhaps some other things too—are sometimes, but of course not always, self-determining beings; that is, beings that are sometimes the causes of their own behavior. In the case of an action that is free, it must not only be such that it is caused by the agent who performs it, but also such that no antecedent conditions were sufficient for his performing just that action. In the case of an action that is both free and rational, it must be such that the agent who performed it did so for some reason, but this reason cannot have been the cause of it.

Now, this conception fits what people take themselves to be; namely, beings who act, or who are agents, rather than beings that are merely acted upon, and whose behavior is simply the causal consequence of conditions that they have not wrought. When I believe that I have done something, I do believe that it was I who caused it to be done, I who made something happen, and not merely something within me, such as one of my own subjective states, which is not identical with myself. If I believe that something not identical with myself was the cause of my behavior—some event wholly external to myself, for instance, or even one internal to myself, such as a nerve impulse, volition, or whatnot—then I cannot regard that behavior as being an act of mine, unless I further believe that I was the cause of that external or internal event. My pulse, for example, is caused and regulated by certain conditions existing within me, and not by myself. I do not, accordingly, regard this activity of my body as my action, and would be no more tempted to do so if I became suddenly conscious within myself of those conditions or impulses that produce it. This is behavior with which I have nothing to do, behavior that is not within my immediate control, behavior that is not only not free activity, but not even the activity of an agent to begin with; it is nothing but a mechanical reflex. Had I never learned that my very life depends on this pulse beat, I would regard it with complete indifference, as something foreign to me, like the oscillations of a clock pendulum that I idly contemplate.

Now this conception of activity, and of an agent who is the cause of it, involves two rather strange metaphysical notions that are never applied elsewhere in nature. The first is that of a *self* or *person*—for example, a man—who is not merely a collection of things or events, but a self-moving being. For on this view it is a person, and not merely some part of him or something within him, that is the cause of his own activity. Now, we certainly do not know that a human being is anything more than an assemblage of physical things and processes that act in accordance with those laws that describe the behavior of all other physical things and processes. Even though he is a living being, of enormous complexity, there is nothing, apart from the requirements of this theory, to suggest that his behavior is so radically different in its origin from that of other physical objects, or that an understanding of it must be sought in some metaphysical realm wholly different from that appropriate to the understanding of nonliving things.

Second, this conception of activity involves an extraordinary conception of causation according to which an agent, which is a substance and not an event, can nevertheless be the cause of an event. Indeed, if he is a free agent then he can, on this conception, cause an event to occur—namely, some act of his own—without anything else causing him to do so. This means that an agent is sometimes a cause, without being an antecedent sufficient condition; for if I affirm that I am the cause of some act of mine, then I am plainly not saying that my very existence is sufficient for its occurrence, which would be absurd. If I say that my hand causes my pencil to move, then I am saying that the motion of my hand is, under the other conditions then prevailing, sufficient for the motion of the pencil. But if I then say that I cause my hand to move, I am not saying anything remotely like this, and surely not that the motion of my self is sufficient for the motion of my arm and hand, since these are the only things about me that are moving.

This conception of the causation of events by things that are not events is, in fact, so different from the usual philosophical conception of a cause that it should not even bear the same name, for "being a cause" ordinarily just means "being an antecedent sufficient condition or set of conditions." Instead, then, of speaking of agents as *causing* their own acts, it would perhaps be better to use another word entirely, and say, for instance, that they *originate* them, *initiate* them, or simply that they *perform* them.

Now this is, on the face of it, a dubious conception of what a person is. Yet it is consistent with our data, reflecting the presuppositions of deliberation, and appears to be the only conception that is consistent with them, as determinism and simple indeterminism are not. The theory of agency avoids the absurdities of simple indeterminism by conceding that human behavior is caused, while at the same time avoiding the difficulties of determinism by denying that every chain of causes and effects is infinite. Some such causal chains, on this view, have beginnings, and they begin with agents themselves. Moreover, if we are to suppose that it is sometimes up to me what I do, and understand this in a sense that is not consistent with determinism, we must suppose that I am an agent or a being who initiates his own actions, sometimes under conditions that do not determine what action I shall perform. Deliberation becomes, on this view, something that is not only possible but quite rational, for it does make sense to deliberate about activity that is truly my own and that depends in its outcome upon me as its author, and not merely upon something more or less esoteric that is supposed to be intimately associated with me, such as my thoughts, volitions, choices or whatnot.

One can hardly affirm such a theory of agency with complete comfort, however, and not wholly without embarrassment, for the conception of agents and their powers which is involved in it is strange indeed, if not positively mysterious. In fact, one can hardly be blamed here for simply denying our data outright, rather than embracing this theory to which they do most certainly point. Our data—to the effect that we do sometimes deliberate before acting, and that, when we do, we presuppose among other things that it is

up to us what we are going to do—rest upon nothing more than fairly common consent. These data might simply be illusions. It might, in fact, be that no one ever deliberates but only imagines that he does, that from pure conceit he supposes himself to be the master of his behavior and the author of his acts. Spinoza has suggested that if a stone, having been thrown into the air, were suddenly to become conscious, it would suppose itself to be the source of its own motion, being then conscious of what it was doing but not aware of the real cause of its behavior. Certainly we are *sometimes* mistaken in believing that we are behaving as a result of choice deliberately arrived at. A man might, for example, easily imagine that his embarking upon matrimony is the result of the most careful and rational deliberation, when in fact the causes, perfectly sufficient for that behavior, might be of an entirely physiological, unconscious origin. If it is sometimes false that we deliberate and then act as the result of a decision deliberately arrived at, even when we suppose it to be true, it might always be false. No one seems able, as we have noted, to describe deliberation without metaphors, and the conception of a thing's being "within one's power" or "up to him" seems to defy analysis or definition altogether, if taken in a sense that the theory of agency appears to require.

These are, then, dubitable conceptions, despite their being so well implanted in common sense. Indeed, when we turn to the theory of fatalism, we shall find formidable metaphysical considerations that appear to rule them out altogether. Perhaps here, as elsewhere in metaphysics, we should be content with discovering difficulties, with seeing what is and what is not consistent with such convictions as we happen to have, and then drawing such satisfaction as we can from the realization that, no matter where we begin, the world is mysterious and that we who try to understand it are even more so. This realization can, with some justification, make one feel wise, even in the full realization of his ignorance.

Further Questions

1. How might Hume reply to Taylor's criticisms of soft determinism?

2. Do Taylor's criticisms of "simple indeterminism" have any force against the views that Reid and James defend? If so, explain how. If not, explain whether they could accept Taylor's theory of agency.

3. Does anyone ever act freely? Explain how you would defend your answer, then how your answer could most plausibly be criticized, and then how you could best respond to the criticisms.

Further Readings

Dennett, Daniel C. *Elbow Room*. Cambridge, Mass: MIT Press, 1984. An elequent and accessible defense by a well-known contemporary philosopher of the idea that free will and determinism are compatible.

Schlossberger, Eugene. *Moral Responsibility and Persons*. Philadelphia: Temple University Press, 1992. Argues that we are responsible not so much for what we do as for who we are.

van Inwagen, Peter. *An Essay on Free Will*. Oxford: Oxford University Press, 1983. A sophisticated and rigorous attack by a well-known contemporary philosopher on the idea that free will and determinism are compatible.

Watson, Gary, ed. *Free Will*. Oxford: Oxford University Press, 1982. One of the best of the recent anthologies.

Part V

Knowledge

THIS IS NOT A BOOK. You didn't just read that sentence. You are not now reading this sentence.

You are not holding a book in your hands because there is no book and you have no hands.

You are not even there. You are not anywhere. You have *never* been anywhere. Nor will you ever. You can't. You don't even exist.

The world does not exist, either. Nothing does. There is no space or time. This moment is not happening.

Your parents, your family, your friends, your world, are all figments of nobody's imagination because there is no imagination and there is nobody there to not have it.

$2 + 2$ does not equal 4. $2 + 2$ does not equal anything. There are no 2s. There is no addition. *Nothing equals anything*.

You *believe* that everything written above is false.

But how do you *know*?

Universal skepticism is not the issue. According to universal skepticism, we don't have good reason to believe anything. But if we have good reason to believe universal skepticism, then we have good reason to believe at least one thing, and so universal skepticism must be false. But even though we cannot *know* that we do not have good reason to believe anything, we still *may not* have good reason to believe anything. We assume, though, that we do. The problem is understanding *how*.

Where to begin? With the things that seem most certain, searching for foundations? Or do we start with our ordinary network of beliefs, looking more for coherence than for foundations? Or do we start with the fact that we must be connected to the world reliably, otherwise we would not even be here wondering how we know anything because we would have perished long ago?

Each of these beginning points is represented in the readings that follow. Each motivates a different conception of knowledge. Collectively, they show that no one can explain, clearly and unproblematically, how we know anything at all.

Meditations

RENÉ DESCARTES

Descartes was born in 1596 at La Haye in Touraine, France. When he was eight years old his father, a councilor of the *parlement* of Rennes in Brittany, sent him to a Jesuit college, one of the most celebrated in Europe, where for ten years he studied literature, science, and philosophy. Somehow the young Descartes convinced the Jesuits to allow him not to have to get up until noon, so that he could "study in bed." He continued this practice for most of his life. After taking a degree in law (he never practiced) he took to fencing, horsemanship and gambling, became a soldier, and served in three different armies — in the Netherlands, in Bavaria, and in Hungary. At thirty-three, disillusioned by "the book of the world," he moved to Holland and began writing and developing his iconoclastic thoughts. His radical departure from basing knowledge on accepted authority to basing it on one's own rational intuitions signaled the beginning of the "modern" age of philosophy. For twenty years he wrote book after book and his reputation slowly grew. His *Meditations on First Philosophy* was quickly acknowledged as a radical criticism of all established philosophy and science. There were lots of furious objections, and the philosophers of the next century and a half spent much of their time trying to respond to the problems Descartes raised.

In 1633 he finished *The World*, a work in which he reaffirmed the "radical" Copernican hypothesis that the earth moves around the sun. But just before publication he learned of Galileo's horrible troubles with the Inquisition and so immediately stopped publication. Some years later he was labeled an atheist by the president of the University of Utrecht and promptly condemned by the local magistrates.

Descartes is certainly one of the most influential philosophers of all time. In addition to writing philosophical works, he tried to formulate a new system of science founded on mathematics, in the process making great contributions to mathematics and physics; he linked, for the first time, geometry to algebra — with the now famous Cartesian coordinate system named after him — thereby inventing analytic geometry. In discovering that geometrical representations could be represented algebraically, Descartes opened the door to the possibility of representing everything — the whole of nature — mathematically. Since size, figure, volume, and so on — representations of the objects we find in nature — are geometrical representations that, by Descartes' method, can be purely mathematically represented, it becomes possible to model all of nature purely mathematically.

In 1649 Queen Christina of Sweden invited him to visit her in Stockholm so that he could teach her his "new philosophy." The Queen, however, liked to take her lessons at five o'clock in the morning. After only a few months of having to get up so early, Descartes died.

The title *Meditations on First Philosophy*, from which the following two meditations are taken, is based on Aristotle's use of "first philosophy" to mean the *first principles of things*, or metaphysics. And so Descartes wrote: "Thus the whole of philosophy is like a tree; the roots are metaphysics, the trunk is physics, and the branches that rise from the trunk are all the other sciences."

Reading Questions

1. On what grounds does Descartes doubt evidence from his senses?
2. People say, "Seeing is believing." Would Descartes agree? Why?
3. If you can't be certain of what the truth is based on your experience, how can you know anything at all? What is Descartes' answer?
4. What does Descartes mean by "clear and distinct"?
5. Can your clear and distinct ideas be wrong?
6. *Why* does Descartes want to try to doubt everything?
7. Does he think that even mathematical truths like $5 + 2 = 7$ are false? Why?
8. What does Descartes think a person is?
9. What is the nature of the mind, according to Descartes? The nature of material bodies?
10. What does he try to show using the piece of wax?
11. Descartes' method is a *method of doubt*: accept nothing as true unless you are *absolutely one hundred percent certain* that it is so. Even things you consider certain, if there is *any* possibility that you are mistaken, then you must doubt it. What does this leave you with?

What beliefs are you most certain of? How did you come to have them? Are they immune from doubt?

12. Before you read this selection, make a list of things you are *most* certain of. Then, while reading, consider at what point your beliefs become questionable, and why. How does this make you feel?

13. There is one thing that Descartes is absolutely certain about. What is it? How can he be so certain of this?

I

OF THE THINGS WHICH MAY BE BROUGHT WITHIN THE SPHERE OF THE DOUBTFUL

IT IS NOW SOME YEARS since I detected how many were the false beliefs that I had from my earliest youth admitted as true, and how doubtful was everything I had since constructed on this basis; and from that time I was convinced that I must once for all seriously undertake to rid myself of all the opinions which I had formerly accepted, and commence to build anew from the foundation, if I wanted to establish any firm and permanent structure in the sciences. But as this enterprise appeared to be a very great one, I waited until I had attained an age so mature that I could not hope that at any later date I should be better fitted to execute my design. This reason caused me to delay so long that I should feel that I was doing wrong were I to occupy in deliberation the time that yet remains to me for action. To-day, then, since very opportunely for the plan I have in view I have delivered my mind from every care [and am happily agitated by no passions] and since I have procured for myself an assured leisure in a peaceable retirement, I shall at last seriously and freely address myself to the general upheaval of all my former opinions. . . .

Now for this object it is not necessary that I should show that all of these are false—I shall perhaps never arrive at this end. But inasmuch as reason already persuades me that I ought no less

carefully to withhold my assent from matters which are not entirely certain and indubitable than from those which appear to me manifestly to be false, if I am able to find in each one some reason to doubt, this will suffice to justify my rejecting the whole. And for that end it will not be requisite that I should examine each in particular, which would be an endless undertaking; for owing to the fact that the destruction of the foundations of necessity brings with it the downfall of the rest of the edifice, I shall only in the first place attack those principles upon which all my former opinions rested.

All that up to the present time I have accepted as most true and certain I have learned either from the senses or through the senses; but it is sometimes proved to me that these senses are deceptive, and it is wiser not to trust entirely to any thing by which we have once been deceived.

But it may be that although the senses sometimes deceive us concerning things which are hardly perceptible, or very far away, there are yet many others to be met with as to which we cannot reasonably have any doubt, although we recognise them by their means. For example, there is the fact that I am here, seated by the fire, attired in a dressing gown, having this paper in my hands and other similar matters. And how could I deny that these hands and this body are mine, were it not perhaps that I compare myself to certain persons, devoid of sense, whose cerebella are so troubled and clouded by the violent vapours of black bile, that they constantly assure us that they think they are kings when they are really quite poor, or that they are clothed in purple when they are really without covering, or who imagine that they have an earthenware head or are nothing but pumpkins or are made of glass. But they are mad, and I should not be any the less insane were I to follow examples so extravagant.

At the same time I must remember that I am a man, and that consequently I am in the habit of sleeping, and in my dreams representing to myself the same things or sometimes even less probable things, than do those who are insane in their waking moments. How often has it happened to me that in the night I dreamt that I found myself in this particular place, that I was dressed and seated near the fire, whilst in reality I was lying undressed in bed! At this moment it does indeed seem to me that it is with eyes awake that I am looking at this paper; that this head which I move is not asleep, that it is deliberately and of set purpose that I extend my hand and perceive it; what happens in sleep does not appear so clear nor so distinct as does all this. But in thinking over this I remind myself that on many occasions I have in sleep been deceived by similar illusions, and in dwelling carefully on this reflection I see so manifestly that there are no certain indications by which we may clearly distinguish wakefulness from sleep that I am lost in astonishment. And my astonishment is such that it is almost capable of persuading me that I now dream.

Now let us assume that we are asleep and that all these particulars, e.g., that we open our eyes, shake our head, extend our hands, and so on, are but false delusions; and let us reflect that possibly neither our hands nor our whole body are such as they appear to us to be. At the same time we must at least confess that the things which are represented to us in sleep are like painted representations which can only have been formed as the counterparts of something real and true, and that in this way those general things at least, i.e., eyes, a head, hands, and a whole body, are not imaginary things, but things really existent. For, as a matter of fact, painters, even when they study with the greatest skill to represent sirens and satyrs by forms the most strange and extraordinary, cannot give them natures which are entirely new, but merely make a certain medley of the members of different animals; or if their imagination is extravagant enough to invent something so novel that nothing similar has ever before been seen, and that then their work represents a thing purely fictitious and absolutely false, it is certain all the same that the colours of which this is composed are necessarily real. And for the same reason, although these general things, to wit, [a body], eyes, a head, hands, and such like, may be imaginary, we are bound at the same time to confess that there are at least some other objects yet more simple and more universal, which are real and true; and of these just in the same way as with certain real colours, all these images of things which dwell in our thoughts, whether true and real or false and fantastic, are formed.

To such a class of things pertains corporeal nature in general, and its extension, the figure of extended things, their quantity or magnitude and number, as also the place in which they are, the time which measures their duration, and so on.

That is possibly why our reasoning is not unjust when we conclude from this that Physics, Astronomy, Medicine and all other sciences which have as their end the consideration of composite things, are very dubious and uncertain; but that Arithmetic, Geometry and other sciences of that kind which only treat of things that are very simple and very general, without taking great trouble to ascertain whether they are actually existent or not, contain some measure of certainty and an element of the indubitable. For whether I am awake or asleep, two and three together always form five, and the square can never have more than four sides, and it does not seem possible that truths so clear and apparent can be suspected of any falsity [or uncertainty].

Nevertheless I have long had fixed in my mind the belief that an all-powerful God existed by whom I have been created such as I am. But how do I know that He has not brought it to pass that there is no earth, no heaven, no extended body, no magnitude, no place, and that nevertheless [I possess the perceptions of all these things and that] they seem to me to exist just exactly as I now see them? And, besides, as I sometimes imagine that others deceive themselves in the things which they think they know best, how do I know that I am not deceived every time that I add two and three, or count the sides of a square, or judge of things yet simpler, if anything simpler can be imagined? But possibly God has not desired that I should be thus deceived, for He is said to be supremely good. If, however, it is contrary to His goodness to have made me such that I constantly deceive myself, it would also appear to be contrary to His goodness to permit me to be sometimes deceived, and nevertheless I cannot doubt that He does permit this.

There may indeed be those who would prefer to deny the existence of a God so powerful, rather than believe that all other things are uncertain. But let us not oppose them for the present, and grant that all that is here said of a God is a fable; nevertheless in whatever way they suppose that I have arrived at the state of being that I have reached—whether they attribute it to fate or to accident, or make out that it is by a continual succession of antecedents, or by some other method —since to err and deceive oneself is a defect, it is clear that the greater will be the probability of my being so imperfect as to deceive myself ever, as is the Author to whom they assign my origin the less powerful. To these reasons I have certainly nothing to reply, but at the end I feel constrained to confess that there is nothing in all that I formerly believed to be true, of which I cannot in some measure doubt, and that not merely through want of thought or through levity, but for reasons which are very powerful and maturely considered; so that henceforth I ought not the less carefully to refrain from giving credence to these opinions than to that which is manifestly false, if I desire to arrive at any certainty [in the sciences].

But it is not sufficient to have made these remarks, we must also be careful to keep them in mind. For these ancient and commonly held opinions still revert frequently to my mind, long and familiar custom having given them the right to occupy my mind against my inclination and rendered them almost masters of my belief; nor will I ever lose the habit of deferring to them or of placing my confidence in them, so long as I consider them as they really are, i.e., opinions in some measure doubtful, as I have just shown, and at the same time highly probable, so that there is much more reason to believe in than to deny them. That is why I consider that I shall not be acting amiss, if, taking of set purpose a contrary belief, I allow myself to be deceived, and for a certain time pretend that all these opinions are entirely false and imaginary, until at last, having thus balanced my former prejudices with my latter [so that they cannot divert my opinions more to one side than to the other], my judgment will no longer be dominated by bad usage or turned away from the right knowledge of the truth. For I am assured that there can be neither peril nor error in this course, and that I cannot at present yield too much to distrust, since I am not considering the question of action, but only of knowledge.

I shall then suppose, not that God who is supremely good and the fountain of truth, but some evil genius not less powerful than deceitful, has employed his whole energies in deceiving me; I shall consider that the heavens, the earth, colours, figures, sound, and all other external things are nought but the illusions and dreams of which this genius has availed himself in order to lay traps for my credulity; I shall consider myself as having no hands, no eyes, no flesh, no blood, nor any senses, yet falsely believing myself to possess all these things; I shall remain obstinately attached to this idea, and if by this means it is not in my power to arrive at the knowledge of any truth, I may at least do what is in my power [i.e., suspend my judgment], and with firm purpose avoid giving credence to any false thing, or being imposed upon by this arch deceiver, however powerful and deceptive he may be. But this task is a laborious one, and insensibly a certain lassitude leads me into the course of my ordinary life. And just as a captive who in sleep enjoys an imaginary liberty, when he begins to suspect that his liberty is but a dream, fears to awaken, and conspires with these agreeable illusions that the deception may be prolonged, so insensibly of my own accord I fall back into my former opinions, and I dread awakening from this slumber, lest the laborious wakefulness which would follow the tranquility of this repose should have to be spent not in daylight, but in the excessive darkness of the difficulties which have just been discussed.

II

The Meditation of yesterday filled my mind with so many doubts that it is no longer in my power to forget them. And yet I do not see in what manner I can resolve them; and, just as if I had all of a sudden fallen into very deep water, I am so disconcerted that I can neither make certain of setting my feet on the bottom, nor can I swim and so support myself on the surface. I shall nevertheless make an effort and follow anew the same path as that on which I yesterday entered, i.e., I shall proceed by setting aside all that in which the least doubt could be supposed to exist, just as if I had discovered that it was absolutely false; and I shall ever follow in this road until I have met with something which is certain, or at least, if I can do nothing else, until I have learned for certain that there is nothing in the world that is certain. Archimedes, in order that he might draw the terrestrial globe out of its place, and transport it elsewhere, demanded only that one point should be fixed and immoveable; in the same way I shall have the right to conceive high hopes if I am happy enough to discover one thing only which is certain and indubitable.

I suppose, then, that all the things that I see are false; I persuade myself that nothing has ever existed of all that my fallacious memory represents to me. I consider that I possess no senses; I imagine that body, figure, extension, movement and place are but the fictions of my mind. What, then, can be esteemed as true? Perhaps nothing at

all, unless that there is nothing in the world that is certain.

But how can I know there is not something different from those things that I have just considered, of which one cannot have the slightest doubt? Is there not some God, or some other being by whatever name we call it, who puts these reflections into my mind? That is not necessary, for is it not possible that I am capable of producing them myself? I myself, am I not at least something? But I have already denied that I had senses and body. Yet I hesitate, for what follows from that? Am I so dependent on body and senses that I cannot exist without these? But I was persuaded that there was nothing in all the world, that there was no heaven, no earth, that there were no minds, nor any bodies: was I not then likewise persuaded that I did not exist? Not at all; of a surety I myself did exist since I persuaded myself of something [or merely because I thought of something]. But there is some deceiver or other, very powerful and very cunning, who ever employs his ingenuity in deceiving me. Then without doubt I exist also if he deceives me, and let him deceive me as much as he will, he can never cause me to be nothing so long as I think that I am something. So that after having reflected well and carefully examined all things, we must come to the definite conclusion that this proposition: I am, I exist, is necessarily true each time that I pronounce it, or that I mentally conceive it.

But I do not yet know clearly enough what I am, I who am certain that I am; and hence I must be careful to see that I do not imprudently take some other object in place of myself, and thus that I do not go astray in respect of this knowledge that I hold to be the most certain and most evident of all that I have formerly learned. That is why I shall now consider anew what I believed myself to be before I embarked upon these last reflections; and of my former opinions I shall withdraw all that might even in a small degree be invalidated by the reasons which I have just brought forward, in order that there may be nothing at all left beyond what is absolutely certain and indubitable.

What then did I formerly believe myself to be? Undoubtedly I believed myself to be a man. But what is a man? Shall I say a reasonable animal? Certainly not; for then I should have to inquire what an animal is, and what is reasonable; and thus from a single question I should insensibly fall into an infinitude of others more difficult; and I should not wish to waste the little time and leisure remaining to me in trying to unravel subtleties like these. But I shall rather stop here to consider the thoughts which of themselves spring up in my mind, and which were not inspired by anything beyond my own nature alone when I applied myself to the consideration of my being. In the first place, then, I considered myself as having a face, hands, arms, and all that system of members composed of bones and flesh as seen in a corpse which I designated by the name of body. In addition to this I considered that I was nourished, that I walked, that I felt, and that I thought, and I referred all these actions to the soul: but I did not stop to consider what the soul was, or if I did stop, I imagined that it was something extremely rare and subtle like a wind, a flame, or an ether, which was spread throughout my grosser parts. As to body I had no manner of doubt about its nature, but thought I had a very clear knowledge of it; and if I had desired to explain it according to the notions that I had then formed of it, I should have described it thus: By the body I understand all that which can be defined by a certain figure: something which can be confined in a certain place, and which can fill a given space in such a way that every other body will be excluded from it; which can be perceived either by touch, or by sight, or by hearing, or by taste, or by smell: which can be moved in many ways not, in truth, by itself, but by something which is foreign to it, by which it is touched [and from which it receives impressions]: for to have the power of self-movement, as also of feeling or of thinking, I did not consider to appertain to the nature of body: on the contrary, I was rather astonished to find that faculties similar to them existed in some bodies.

But what am I, now that I suppose that there is a certain genius which is extremely powerful, and, if I may say so, malicious, who employs all his powers in deceiving me? Can I affirm that I possess the least of all those things which I have just said pertain to the nature of body? I pause to consider, I revolve all these things in my mind, and I find none of which I can say that it pertains to me. It would be tedious to stop to enumerate them. Let us pass to the attributes of soul and see if there is any one which is in me? What of nutrition or walking [the first mentioned]? But if it is so that I have no body it is also true that I can neither walk nor take nourishment. Another attribute is sensation. But one cannot feel without body, and besides I have thought I perceived many things during sleep that I recognised in my waking moments as not having been experienced at all. What of thinking? I find here that thought is an attribute that belongs to me; it alone cannot be separated from me. I am, I exist, that is certain. But how often? Just when I think; for it might possibly be the case if I ceased entirely to think, that I should likewise cease altogether to exist. I do not now admit anything which is not necessarily true: to speak accurately I am not more than a thing which thinks, that is to say a mind or a soul, or an understanding, or a reason, which are terms whose significance was formerly unknown to me. I am, however, a real thing and really exist; but what thing? I have answered: a thing which thinks.

And what more? I shall exercise my imagination [in order to see if I am not something more]. I am not a collection of members which we call the human body: I am not a subtle air distributed through these members, I am not a wind, a fire, a vapour, a breath, nor anything at all which I can imagine or conceive; because I have assumed that all these were nothing. Without changing that supposition I find that I only leave myself certain of the fact that I am somewhat. But perhaps it is true that these same things which I supposed were non-existent because they are unknown to me, are really not different from the self which I know. I am not sure about this, I shall not dispute about it now; I can only give judgment on things that are known to me. I know that I exist, and I inquire what I am, I whom I know to exist. But it is very certain that the knowledge of my existence taken in its precise significance does not depend on things whose existence is not yet known to me; consequently it does not depend on those which I can feign in imagination. And indeed the very term *feign* in imagination proves to me my error, for I really do this if I image myself a something, since to imagine is nothing else than to contemplate the figure or image of a corporeal thing. But I already know for certain that I am, and that it may be that all these images, and, speaking generally, all things that relate to the nature of body are nothing but dreams [and chimeras]. For this reason I see clearly that I have as little reason to say, 'I shall stimulate my imagination in order to know more distinctly what I am,' than if I were to say, 'I am now awake, and I perceive somewhat that is real and true: but because I do not yet perceive it distinctly enough, I shall go to sleep of express purpose, so that my dreams may represent the perception with greatest truth and evidence.' And, thus, I know for certain that nothing of all that I can understand by means of my imagination belongs to this knowledge which I have of myself, and that it is necessary to recall the mind from this mode of thought with the utmost diligence in order that it may be able to know its own nature with perfect distinctness.

But what then am I? A thing which thinks. What is a thing which thinks? It is a thing which doubts, understands, [conceives], affirms, denies, wills, refuses, which also imagines and feels.

Certainly it is no small matter if all these things pertain to my nature. But why should they not so pertain? Am I not that being who now doubts nearly everything, who nevertheless understands certain things, who affirms that only one is true, who denies all the others, who desires to know more, is averse from being deceived, who imagines many things, sometimes indeed despite his will, and who perceives many likewise, as by the intervention of the bodily organs? Is there nothing in all this which is as true as it is certain that I exist, even though I should always sleep and though he who has given me being employed all his ingenuity in deceiving me? Is there likewise any one of these attributes which can be distinguished from my thought, or which might be said to be separated from myself? For it is so evident of itself that it is I who doubts, who understands, and who desires, that there is no reason here to add anything to explain it. And I have certainly the power of imagining likewise; for although it may happen (as I formerly supposed) that none of the things which I imagine are true, nevertheless this power of imagining does not cease to be really in use, and it forms part of my thought. Finally, I am the same who feels, that is to say, who perceives certain things, as by the organs of sense, since in truth I see light, I hear noise, I feel heat. But it will be said that these phenomena are false and that I am dreaming. Let it be so; still it is at least quite certain that it seems to me that I see light, that I hear noise and that I feel heat. That cannot be false; properly speaking it is what is in me called feeling; and used in this precise sense that is no other thing than thinking. . . .

Further Questions

1. Descartes' famous proof of his own existence is one of the great moments in the history of Western philosophy. Instead of basing science, mathematics, religion, and logic on the collective knowledge of humanity, Descartes bases it on the fact of his own existence. Do you suppose this had any relevance for the subsequent individualism of Western civilization?

2. *Epistemological skepticism*, roughly, is the doctrine that none of our beliefs about ourselves and the world are ever adequately justified. Descartes, however, is generally regarded

as espousing the doctrine of *methodological skepticism*, which consists in doubting all your beliefs until you reach a belief that cannot be doubted. Based on what you've just read, what is the crucial factor in Descartes' philosophy that would make him the latter, not the former, type of skeptic? Do you agree? Why?

3. Descartes claims that the mind is known more directly than the body. He concludes that the mind is entirely different from the body. Do you agree with his conclusion?

4. Descartes finds that he can doubt the existence of everything except himself. Can you imagine how he might be wrong even about this? Think again about this question when you read the first three selections of the section of this book titled "Reality."

Further Readings

Borst, Clive, ed. *The Mind/Brain Identity Theory*. New York: Macmillan, 1970. An excellent collection of critical essays.

Dennett, Daniel. *Content and Consciousness*. Boston: Routledge & Kegan Paul, 1969. One of the best attacks on dualism.

Doney, Willis, ed. *Descartes: A Collection of Critical Essays*. New York: Macmillan, 1968.

Flew, Antony, ed. *Body, Mind, and Death*. New York: Macmillan, 1964. Contains many classical selections on the mind/body problem.

Frankfurt, Harry. *Demons, Dreamers, and Madmen: The Defense of Reason in Descartes' Meditations*. Indianapolis, IN: Bobbs-Merrill, 1970.

Kenny, Anthony. *Descartes: A Study of His Philosophy*. New York: Random House, 1968.

O'Connor, John, ed. *Modern Materialism: Reading on Mind-Body Identity*. New York: Harcourt Brace Jovanovich, 1969. An excellent anthology of some of the best readings on the subject.

Unger, Peter. *Ignorance*. New York: Oxford University Press, 1975. A provocative argument for extreme skepticism.

Unger, Peter. "I Do Not Exist," in G. F. MacDonald, ed. *Perception and Identity*. Ithica, NY: Cornell University Press, 1979, pp. 235–251. Unger's title says it all. Hemingway wrote, "Seems like when they get started they don't leave a guy nothing" (in his short story, "My Old Man"). Perhaps it was the skeptical philosophers that he had in mind.

Where Our Ideas Come From

JOHN LOCKE

This selection from Locke's *Essay Concerning Human Understanding* (1690) contains the core of Locke's attempt to explain the idea that our knowledge of the world is derived from experience. In a memorable image, Locke says that the mind at birth is a *tabula rasa*, a blank page, on which sense experience subsequently leaves its marks.

These marks then become the raw data from which our knowledge of the world is constructed.

A brief biography of Locke appears on page 104.

Reading Questions

1. What does Locke mean by *idea*? By *quality*?
2. How does Locke distinguish between primary and secondary qualities? What is the importance of this distinction in Locke's account?
3. What does Locke mean by "perception"?
4. Where do perceptions come from?
5. According to Locke, do you have direct perceptions of objects out there in the external world?
6. How does he think objects are able to affect our senses?
7. What is the cause of simple ideas?
8. How are ideas known by the mind?
9. If we cannot see an idea with our eyes—how, then?
10. What does Locke mean by "privation"?

Some Further Considerations Concerning Our Simple Ideas of Sensation

1. *Positive ideas from privative causes.* —Concerning the simple ideas of sensation it is to be considered, that whatsoever is so constituted in nature as to be able by affecting our senses to cause any perception in the mind, doth thereby produce in the understanding a simple idea; which, whatever be the external cause of it, when it comes to be taken notice of by our discerning faculty, it is by the mind looked on and considered there to be a real positive idea in the understanding, as much as any other whatsoever; though perhaps the cause of it be but a privation in the subject.

2. Thus the ideas of heat and cold, light and darkness, white and black, motion and rest, are equally clear and positive ideas in the mind; though perhaps some of the causes which produce them are barely privations in those subjects from whence our senses derive those ideas. These the understanding, in its view of them, considers all as distinct positive ideas without taking notice of the causes that produce them; which is an inquiry not belonging to the idea as it is in the understanding, but to the nature of the things existing without us. These are two very different things, and carefully to be distinguished; it being one thing to perceive and know the idea of white or black, and quite another to examine what kind of particles they must be, and how ranged in the superficies, to make any object appear white or black.

3. A painter or dyer who never inquired into their causes, hath the ideas of white and black and other colours as clearly, perfectly, and distinctly in his understanding, and perhaps more distinctly than the philosopher who hath busied himself in considering their natures, and thinks he knows how far either of them is in its cause positive or privative; and the idea of black is no less positive in his mind than that of white, however the cause of that colour in the external object may be only a privation.

4. If it were the design of my present undertaking to inquire into the natural causes and manner of perception, I should offer this as a reason why a privative cause might, in some cases at

From John Locke, An Essay Concerning Human Understanding. *First published in 1690.*

least, produce a positive idea, viz., that all sensation being produced in us only by different degrees and modes of motion in our animal spirits, variously agitated by external objects, the abatement of any former motion must as necessarily produce a new sensation as the variation or increase of it; and so introduce a new idea, which depends only on a different motion of the animal spirits in that organ.

5. But whether this be so or not I will not here determine, but appeal to every one's own experience, whether the shadow of a man, though it consists of nothing but the absence of light (and the more the absence of light is, the more discernible is the shadow), does not, when a man looks on it, cause as clear and positive an idea in his mind as a man himself, though covered over with clear sunshine! And the picture of a shadow is a positive thing. Indeed, we have negative names, [which stand not directly for positive ideas, but for their absence, such as *insipid, silence, nihil, &c.*, which words denote positive ideas, *v. g., taste, sound, being*, with a signification of their absence.]

6. *Positive ideas from privative causes.* — And thus one may truly be said to see darkness. For, supposing a hole perfectly dark, from whence no light is reflected, it is certain one may see the figure of it, or it may be painted; or whether the ink I write with make any other idea, is a question. The privative causes I have here assigned of positive ideas are according to the common opinion; but, in truth, it will be hard to determine whether there be really any ideas from a privative cause, till it be determined whether rest be any more a privation than motion.

7. *Ideas in the mind, qualities in bodies.* — To discover the nature of our ideas the better, and to discourse of them intelligibly, it will be convenient to distinguish them, as they are ideas or perceptions in our minds, and as they are modifications of matter in the bodies that cause such perceptions in us; that so we may not think (as perhaps usually is done) that they are exactly the images and resemblances of something inherent in the subject; most of those of sensation being in the mind no more the likeness of something existing without us than the names that stand for them are the likeness of our ideas, which yet upon hearing they are apt to excite in us.

8. Whatsoever the mind perceives in itself, or is the immediate object of perception, thought, or understanding, that I call "idea;" and the power to produce any idea in our mind, I call "quality" of the subject wherein that power is. Thus a snowball having the power to produce in us the ideas of white, cold, and round, the powers to produce those ideas in us as they are in the snowball, I call "qualities;" and as they are sensations or perceptions in our understandings, I call them "ideas;" which ideas, if I speak of them sometimes as in the things themselves, I would be understood to mean those qualities in the objects which produce them in us.

9. *Primary qualities.* — [Qualities thus considered in bodies are, First, such as are utterly inseparable from the body, in what estate soever it be;] and such as, in all the alterations and changes it suffers, all the force can be used upon it, it constantly keeps; and such as sense constantly finds in every particle of matter which has bulk enough to be perceived, and the mind finds inseparable from every particle of matter, though less than to make itself singly be perceived by our senses: *v. g.*, take a grain of wheat, divide it into two parts, each part has still solidity, extension, figure, and mobility; divide it again, and it retains still the same qualities: and so divide it on till the parts become insensible, they must retain still each of them all those qualities. For, division (which is all that a mill or pestle or any other body does upon another, in reducing it to insensible parts) can never take away either solidity, extension, figure, or mobility from any body, but only makes two or more distinct separate masses of matter of that which was but one before; all which distinct masses, reckoned as so many distinct bodies, after division, make a certain number. [These I call *original* or *primary* qualities of body, which I think we may observe to produce

simple ideas in us, viz., solidity, extension, figure, motion or rest, and number.]

10. *Secondary qualities.* — Secondly. Such qualities, which in truth are nothing in the objects themselves, but powers to produce various sensations in us by their primary qualities, *i.e.*, by the bulk, figure, texture, and motion of their insensible parts, as colours, sounds, tastes &c., these I call *secondary* qualities. To these might be added a third sort, which are allowed to be barely powers, though they are as much real qualities in the subject as those which I, to comply with the common way of speaking, call qualities, but, for distinction, *secondary* qualities. For, the power in fire to produce a new colour or consistency in wax or clay, by its primary qualities, is as much a quality in fire as the power it has to produce in me a new idea or sensation of warmth or burning, which I felt not before, by the same primary qualities, viz., the bulk, texture, and motion of its insensible parts.

11. [*How primary qualities produce their ideas.* — The next thing to be considered is, how bodies produce ideas in us; and that is manifestly by impulse, the only way which we can conceive bodies to operate in.]

12. If, then, external objects be not united to our minds when they produce ideas therein, and yet we perceive these original qualities in such of them as singly fall under our senses, it is evident that some motion must be thence continued by our nerves, or animal spirits, by some parts of our bodies, to the brains or the seat of sensation, there to produce in our minds the particular ideas we have of them. And since the extension, figure, number, and motion of bodies of an observable bigness, may be perceived at a distance by the sight, it is evident some singly imperceptible bodies must come from them to the eyes, and thereby convey to the brain some motion which produces these ideas which we have of them in us.

13. *How secondary.* — After the same manner that the ideas of these original qualities are produced in us, we may conceive that the ideas of secondary qualities are also produced, viz., by the operation of insensible particles on our senses. For it being manifest that there are bodies, and good store of bodies, each whereof are so small that we cannot by any of our senses discover either their bulk, figure, or motion (as is evident in the particles of the air and water, and other extremely smaller than those, perhaps as much smaller than the particles of air or water as the particles of air or water are smaller than peas or hailstones): let us suppose at present that the different motions and figures, bulk and number, of such particles, effecting the several organs of our senses, produce in us those different sensations which we have from the colours and smells of bodies, *v.g.*, that a violet, by the impulse of such insensible particles of matter of peculiar figures and bulks, and in different degrees and modifications of their motions, causes the ideas of the blue colour and sweet scent of that flower to be produced in our minds; it being no more impossible to conceive that God should annex such ideas to such motions, with which they have no similitude, than that he should annex the idea of pain to the motion of a piece of steel dividing our flesh, with which the idea hath no resemblance.

14. What I have said concerning colours and smells may be understood also of tastes and sounds, and other the like sensible qualities; which, whatever reality we by mistake attribute to them, are in truth nothing in the objects themselves, but powers to produce various sensations in us, and depend on those primary qualities, viz., bulk, figure, texture, and motion of parts [as I have said.]

15. *Ideas of primary qualities are resemblances; of secondary, not.* — From whence I think it is easy to draw this observation, that the ideas of primary qualities of bodies are resemblances of them, and their patterns do really exist in the bodies themselves; but the ideas produced in us by these secondary qualities have no resemblance of them at all. There is nothing like our ideas existing in the bodies themselves. They are, in the bodies we denominate from them, only a power to produce those sensations in us; and what is sweet, blue, or

warm in idea, is but the certain bulk, figure, and motion of the insensible parts in the bodies themselves, which we call so.

16. Flame is denominated *hot* and *light*; snow, *white* and *cold*; and manna *white* and *sweet*, from the ideas they produce in us, which qualities are commonly thought to be the same in those bodies that those ideas are in us, the one the perfect resemblance of the other, as they are in a mirror; and it would by most men be judged very extravagant, if one should say otherwise. And yet he that will consider that the same fire that at one distance produces in us the sensation of warmth, does at a nearer approach produce in us the far different sensation of pain, ought to bethink himself what reason he has to say, that this idea of warmth which was produced in him the same way is not in the fire. Why is whiteness and cold-ness in snow and pain not, when it produces the one and the other idea in us, and can do neither but by the bulk, figure, number, and motion of its solid parts?

17. The particular bulk, number, figure, and motion of the parts of fire or snow are really in them, whether any one's senses perceive them or no; and therefore they may be called *real* qualities, because they really exist in those bodies. But light, heat, whiteness, or coldness, are no more really in them than sickness or pain is in manna. Take away the sensation of them; let not the eyes see light or colours, nor the ears hear sounds; let the palate not taste, nor the nose smell; and all colours, tastes, odours, and sounds, as they are such particular ideas, vanish and cease, and are reduced to their causes, *i.e.*, bulk, figure, and motion of parts.

Further Questions

1. Can you think of any ideas you have that are not derived from experience?

2. Locke claimed that the mind is empty until provided with data by experience. Is it an objection to Locke's view that we seem predisposed to learn some things, e.g., language, much more easily than others?

Further Readings

Ayer, A. J. *The Foundations of Empirical Knowledge*. New York: Macmillan, 1940. A clear, modern development of Lockean themes.

Russell, Bertrand. *A History of Western Philosophy*. New York: Simon & Schuster, 1945, Chs. 13–15. An excellent brief summary and critique of Locke's views.

Russell, Bertrand. *The Problems of Philosophy*. Oxford: Oxford University Press, 1912. A classic, short introduction to epistemology and metaphysics.

To Be Is to Be Perceived

GEORGE BERKELEY

George Berkeley was born in 1685 in Ireland. At the age of 15 he entered Trinity College, Dublin, and by the time he was 22 he was lecturing on Greek, Hebrew, and divinity. He wanted to open a college in Bermuda for Indians and young American colonists but was forced to drop the project. He visited and gave much encouragement to Yale and Harvard; Berkeley, California was named after him. Back in Ireland, he became an Anglican bishop, devoting himself to the spiritual betterment of the Irish. In 1744 he started the practice of drinking tar water as a general medicine and wrote a spirited treatise in defense of this practice. Eight years later, he died.

Berkeley is best known for his "idealist" or "immaterialist" doctrine — that the existence of sensible objects consists solely in their being perceived. Since color exists only when seen, sound only when heard, shape only when seen or touched, to imagine any of these existing independently of mind, argued Berkeley, is a grave logical error. Among his best known philosophical works are *Treatise Concerning the Principles of Human Knowledge* (1710) and *Three Dialogues Between Hylas and Philonous* (1713), both written while he was in his twenties.

Reading Questions

1. How would Berkeley answer the famous question, "When a tree falls in the forest and there is no one there to hear it, does it make a sound?"

2. What does he mean by the distinction between "primary" and "secondary" qualities? Which are the real qualities, which the subjective?

3. By "material substance" Berkeley means an inert, senseless substance that has primary qualities but no secondary qualities. How does he argue against the existence of such a substance?

4. According to Berkeley, the chair you are sitting on does not exist unless it is being perceived. Do you agree with this strange thesis? If not, what is your *argument* against it?

5. In Berkeley's view, what are the objects of our knowledge?

6. What are objects made of?

7. What does he mean by *exist*?

8. Is there anything which it is impossible for a person to conceive?

9. Why is the idea of matter contradictory?

10. What is the difference between real and imaginary?

11. What is the relationship between God and reality?

1. IT IS EVIDENT TO ANY ONE who takes a survey of the *objects of human knowledge*, that they are either *ideas* actually imprinted on the senses; or else such as are perceived by attending to the passions and operations of the mind; or lastly, *ideas* formed by help of memory and imagination — either compounding, dividing, or barely representing those originally perceived in the aforesaid ways. By sight I have the ideas of light and colours, with their several degrees and variations. By touch I perceive hard and soft, heat and cold, motion and resistance; and of all these more and less either as to quantity or degree. Smelling furnishes me with odours; the palate with tastes; the hearing conveys sounds to the mind in all their variety of tone and composition.

And as several of these are observed to accompany each other, they come to be marked by one name, and so to be reputed as one *thing*. Thus, for example, a certain colour, taste, smell, figure and consistence having been observed to go together; are accounted one distinct thing, signi-

From A Treatise Concerning the Principles of Human Knowledge. *First published in 1710.*

fied by the name apple; other collections of ideas constitute a stone, a tree, a book, and the like sensible things; which as they are pleasing or disagreeable excite the passions of love, hatred, joy, grief, and so forth.

2. But, besides all that endless variety of ideas or objects of knowledge, there is likewise Something which knows or perceives them; and exercises divers operations, as willing, imagining, remembering, about them. This perceiving, active being is what I call *mind, spirit, soul,* or *myself.* By which words I do not denote any one of my ideas, but a thing entirely distinct from them, wherein they exist, or, which is the same thing, whereby they are perceived; for the existence of an idea consists in being perceived.

3. That neither our thoughts, nor passions, nor ideas formed by the imagination, exist without the mind is what everybody will allow. And to me it seems no less evident that the various sensations or ideas imprinted on the Sense, however blended or combined together (that is, whatever objects they compose), cannot exist otherwise than in a mind perceiving them. I think an intuitive knowledge may be obtained of this, by any one that shall attend to what is meant by the term *exist* when applied to sensible things. The table I write on I say exists; that is, I see and feel it; and if I were out of my study I should say it existed; meaning thereby that if I was in my study I might perceive it, or that some other spirit actually does perceive it. There was an odour, that is, it was smelt; there was a sound, that is, it was heard; a colour or figure, and it was perceived by sight or touch. This is all that I can understand by these and the like expressions. For as to what is said of the *absolute* existence of unthinking things, without any relation to their being perceived, that is to me perfectly unintelligible. Their *esse* is *percipi*; nor is it possible they should have any existence out of the minds or thinking things which perceive them.

4. It is indeed an opinion strangely prevailing amongst men, that houses, mountains, rivers, and in a word all sensible objects, have an exis-

tence, natural or real, distinct from their being perceived by the understanding. But, with how great an assurance and acquiescence soever this Principle may be entertained in the world, yet whoever shall find in his heart to call it in question may, if I mistake not, perceive it to involve a manifest contradiction. For, what are the forementioned objects but the things we perceive by sense? and what do we perceive besides our own ideas or sensations? and is it not plainly repugnant that any one of these, or any combination of them, should exist unperceived?

5. If we thoroughly examine this tenet it will, perhaps, be found at bottom to depend on the doctrine of *abstract ideas.* For can there be a nicer strain of abstraction than to distinguish the existence of sensible objects from their being perceived, so as to conceive them existing unperceived? Light and colours, heat and cold, extension and figures—in a word the things we see and feel—what are they but so many sensations, notions, ideas, or impressions on the sense? and is it possible to separate, even in thought, any of these from perception? For my part, I might as easily divide a thing from itself. I may, indeed, divide in my thoughts, or conceive apart from each other, those things which perhaps I never perceived by sense so divided. Thus, I imagine the trunk of a human body without the limbs, or conceive the smell of a rose without thinking on the rose itself. So far, I will not deny, I can abstract; if that may properly be called *abstraction* which extends only to the conceiving separately such objects as it is possible may really exist or be actually perceived asunder. But my conceiving or imagining power does not extend beyond the possibility of real existence or perception. Hence, as it is impossible for me to see or feel anything without an actual sensation of that thing, so is it impossible for me to conceive in my thoughts any sensible thing or object distinct from the sensation or perception of it. [In truth, the object and the sensation are the same thing, and cannot therefore be abstracted from each other.]

6. Some truths there are so near and obvious to the mind that a man need only open his eyes to see them. Such I take this important one to be, viz. that all the choir of heaven and furniture of the earth, in a word all those bodies which compose the mighty frame of the world, have not any subsistence without a mind; that their *being* is to be perceived or known; that consequently so long as they are not actually perceived by me, or do not exist in my mind, or that of any other created spirit, they must either have no existence at all, or else subsist in the mind of some Eternal Spirit: it being perfectly unintelligible, and involving all the absurdity of abstraction, to attribute to any single part of them an existence independent of a spirit. To be convinced of which, the reader need only reflect, and try to separate in his own thoughts the *being* of a sensible thing from its *being perceived*.

7. From what has been said it is evident there is not any other Substance than *Spirit*, or that which perceives. But, for the fuller proof of this point, let it be considered the sensible qualities are colour, figure, motion, smell, taste, and such like, that is, the ideas perceived by sense. Now, for an idea to exist in an unperceiving thing is a manifest contradiction; for to have an idea is all one as to perceive: that therefore wherein colour, figure, and the like qualities exist must perceive them. Hence it is clear there can be no unthinking substance or *substratum* of those ideas.

8. But, say you, though the ideas themselves do not exist without the mind, yet there may be things like them, whereof they are copies or resemblances; which things exist without the mind, in an unthinking substance. I answer, an idea can be like nothing but an idea; a colour or figure can be like nothing but another colour or figure. If we look but never so little into our thoughts, we shall find it impossible for us to conceive a likeness except only between our ideas. Again, I ask whether those supposed *originals*, or external things, of which our ideas are the pictures or representations, be themselves perceivable or no? If they are, then *they* are ideas, and we have gained our point: but if you say they are not, I appeal to any one whether it be sense to assert a colour is like something which is invisible; hard or soft, like something which is intangible; and so of the rest.

9. Some there are who make a distinction betwixt *primary* and *secondary* qualities. By the former they mean extension, figure, motion, rest, solidity or impenetrability, and number; by the latter they denote all other sensible qualities, as colours, sounds, tastes, and so forth. The ideas we have of these last they acknowledge not to be the resemblances of anything existing without the mind, or unperceived; but they will have our ideas of the *primary qualities* to be patterns or images of things which exist without the mind, in an unthinking substance which they call Matter. By Matter, therefore, we are to understand an inert, senseless substance, in which extension, figure, and motion do actually subsist. But it is evident, from what we have already shewn, that extension, figure, and motion are only ideas existing in the mind, and that an idea can be like nothing but another idea; and that consequently neither they nor their archetypes can exist in an unperceiving substance. Hence, it is plain that the very notion of what is called *Matter* or *corporeal substance*, involves a contradiction in it. Insomuch that I should not think it necessary to spend more time in exposing its absurdity. But, because the tenet of the existence of Matter seems to have taken so deep a root in the minds of philosophers, and draws after it so many ill consequences, I choose rather to be thought prolix and tedious than omit anything that might conduce to the full discovery and extirpation of that prejudice.

10. They who assert that figure, motion, and the rest of the primary or original qualities do exist without the mind, in unthinking substances, do at the same time acknowledge that colours, sounds, heat, cold, and suchlike secondary qualities, do not; which they tell us are sensations, existing in the mind alone, that depend on and are occasioned by the different size, texture,

and motion of the minute particles of matter. This they take for an undoubted truth, which they can demonstrate beyond all exception. Now, if it be certain that those *original* qualities are inseparably united with the other sensible qualities, and not, even in thought, capable of being abstracted from them, it plainly follows that *they* exist only in the mind. But I desire any one to reflect, and try whether he can, by any abstraction of thought, conceive the extension and motion of a body without all other sensible qualities. For my own part, I see evidently that it is not in my power to frame an idea of a body extended and moving, but I must withal give it some colour or other sensible quality, which is acknowledged to exist only in the mind. . . .

14. I shall farther add, that, after the same manner as modern philosophers prove certain sensible qualities to have no existence in Matter, or without the mind, the same thing may be likewise proved of all other sensible qualities whatsoever. Thus, for instance, it is said that heat and cold are affections only of the mind, and not at all patterns of real beings, existing in the corporeal substances which excite them; for that the same body which appears cold to one hand seems warm to another. Now, why may we not as well argue that figure and extension are not patterns or resemblances of qualities existing in Matter; because to the same eye at different stations, or eyes of a different texture at the same station, they appear various, and cannot therefore be the images of anything settled and determinate without the mind? Again, it is proved that sweetness is not really in the sapid thing; because the thing remaining unaltered the sweetness is changed into bitter, as in case of a fever or otherwise vitiated palate. Is it not as reasonable to say that motion is not without the mind; since if the succession of ideas in the mind become swifter, the motion, it is acknowledged, shall appear slower, without any alteration in any external object?

15. In short, let any one consider those arguments which are thought manifestly to prove that colours and tastes exist only in the mind, and he shall find they may with equal force be brought to prove the same thing of extension, figure, and motion. Though it must be confessed this method of arguing does not so much prove that there is no extension or colour in an outward object, as that we do not know by sense which is the true extension of colour of the object. But the arguments foregoing plainly shew it to be impossible that any colour or extension at all, or other sensible quality whatsoever, should exist in an unthinking subject without the mind, or in truth that there should be any such thing as an outward object.

16. But let us examine a little the received opinion. It is said extension is a *mode* or *accident* of Matter, and that Matter is the *substratum* that supports it. Now I desire that you would explain to me what is meant by Matter's *supporting* extension. Say you, I have no idea of Matter; and therefore cannot explain it. I answer, though you have no positive, yet, if you have any meaning at all, you must at least have a relative idea of Matter; though you know not what it is, yet you must be supposed to know what relation it bears to accidents, and what is meant by its supporting them. It is evident *support* cannot here be taken in its usual or literal sense, as when we say that pillars support a building. In what sense therefore must it be taken? For my part, I am not able to discover any sense at all that can be applicable to it.

17. If we inquire into what the most accurate philosophers declare themselves to mean by *material substance*, we shall find them acknowledge they have no other meaning annexed to those sounds but the idea of Being in general, together with the relative notion of its supporting accidents. The general idea of Being appeareth to me the most abstract and incomprehensible of all other; and as for its supporting accidents, this, as we have just now observed, cannot be understood in the common sense of those words: it must therefore be taken in some other sense, but what that is they do not explain. So that when I consider the two parts or branches which make

the signification of the words *material substance*, I am convinced there is no distinct meaning annexed to them. But why should we trouble ourselves any farther, in discussing this material *substratum* or support of figure and motion and other sensible qualities? Does it not suppose they have an existence without the mind? And is not this a direct repugnancy, and altogether inconceivable?

18. But, though it were possible that solid, figured, moveable substances may exist without the mind, corresponding to the ideas we have of bodies, yet how is it possible for us to know this? Either we must know it by Sense or by Reason. As for our senses, by them we have the knowledge only of our sensations, ideas, or those things that are immediately perceived by sense, call them what you will: but they do not inform us that things exist without the mind, or unperceived, like to those which are perceived. This the materialists themselves acknowledge. — It remains therefore that if we have any knowledge at all of external things, it must be by reason inferring their existence from what is immediately perceived by sense. But (I do not see) what reason can induce us to believe the existence of bodies without the mind, from what we perceive, since the very patrons of Matter themselves do not pretend there is any necessary connexion betwixt them and our ideas? I say it is granted on all hands (and what happens in dreams, frensies, and the like, puts it beyond dispute) that it is possible we might be affected with all the ideas we have now, though no bodies existed without resembling them. Hence it is evident the supposition of external bodies is not necessary for producing our ideas; since it is granted they are produced sometimes, and might possibly be produced always, in the same order we see them in at present, without their concurrence.

19. But, though we might possibly have all our sensations without them, yet perhaps it may be thought easier to conceive and explain the manner of their production, by supposing external bodies in their likeness rather than otherwise;

and so it might be at least probable there are such things as bodies that excite their ideas in our minds. But neither can this be said. For, though we give the materialists their external bodies, they by their own confession are never the nearer knowing how our ideas are produced; since they own themselves unable to comprehend in what manner body can act upon spirit, or how it is possible it should imprint any idea in the mind. Hence it is evident the production of ideas or sensations in our minds, can be no reason why we should suppose Matter or corporeal substances; since that is acknowledged to remain equally inexplicable with or without this supposition. If therefore it were possible for bodies to exist without the mind, yet to hold they do so must needs be a very precarious opinion; since it is to suppose, without any reason at all, that God has created innumerable beings that are entirely useless, and serve to no manner of purpose.

20. In short, if there were external bodies, it is impossible we should ever come to know it; and if there were not, we might have the very same reasons to think there were that we have now. Suppose — what no one can deny possible — an intelligence, without the help of external bodies, to be affected with the same train of sensations or ideas that you are, imprinted in the same order and with like vividness in his mind. I ask whether that intelligence hath not all the reason to believe the existence of Corporeal Substances, represented by his ideas, and exciting them in his mind, that you can possibly have for believing the same thing? Of this there can be no question. . . .

23. But, say you, surely there is nothing easier than for me to imagine trees, for instance, in a park, or books existing in a closet, and nobody by to perceive them. I answer, you may so, there is no difficulty in it. But what is all this, I beseech you, more than framing in your mind certain ideas which you call *books* and *trees*, and at the same time omitting to frame the idea of any one that may perceive them? But do not you yourself perceive or think of them all the while? This therefore is nothing to the purpose: it only shews

you have the power of imagining, or forming ideas in your mind; but it does not shew that you can conceive it possible the objects of your thoughts may exist without the mind. To make out this, it is necessary that you conceive them existing unconceived or unthought of; which is a manifest repugnancy. When we do our utmost to conceive the existence of external bodies, we are all the while only contemplating our own ideas.

But the mind, taking no notice of itself, is deluded to think it can and does conceive bodies existing unthought of, or without the mind, though at the same time they are apprehended by, or exist in, itself. A little attention will discover to any one the truth and evidence of what is here said, and make it unnecessary to insist on any other proofs against the existence of *material substance*.

Further Questions

1. Now that you've read Berkeley's position, what is your response? Perhaps you find yourself sympathetic to the remarks of the great empiricist philosopher, David Hume: "The speculations of the ingenious Dr. Berkeley—they admit of no refutation, but they produce no conviction." If you are not convinced, *why* aren't you? Do you have a refutation?

2. How do you suppose Locke would respond to Berkeley's idealism? Could he respond using the primary-secondary quality distinction?

3. Does the world exist, according to Berkeley, when no one is perceiving it? Why? There is a famous Oxford limerick:

> There was a young man who said, "God
> Must think it exceedingly odd
> If he finds that this tree
> Continues to be,
> When there's no one about in the quad."

> Dear Sir, your astonishment's odd
> I'm always about in the quad
> And that's why the tree
> Continues to be,
> Since observed by,
>   Yours faithfully,
>   God

But, we might wonder, who perceives God? Berkeley answers: nobody. How then do you suppose Berkeley accounts for the existence of perceivers who are not themselves perceived? Can you see any way out of this puzzle with the paradoxical idea that perception somehow creates *itself* into existence? If this sounds too crazy to be true, then keep in mind that such craziness resurfaces in twentieth-century science, under the name *quantum mechanics*. More on that in the selection by Paul Davies titled "Reality and Modern Science."

Further Readings

Moore, G. E. "Refutation of Idealism" in his *Philosophical Studies*. London: Routledge & Kegan Paul, 1922. One of the most famous "refutations" of Berkeley's position.

Turbayne, Colin, ed. *Berkeley: Critical and Interpretive Essays*. Minneapolis: University of
    Minnesota Press, 1982.
Urmson, J. O. *Berkeley*. Oxford: Oxford University Press, 1982.
Warnock, G. J. *Berkeley*. Harmondsworth: Penguin, 1953.
Wild, John. *George Berkeley: A Study of His Life and Philosophy*. Cambridge: Harvard University
    Press, 1936.

Perception, Knowledge, and Induction

BERTRAND RUSSELL

Bertrand Russell (1872–1970) was one of the most prolific and influential philosophers of the twentieth century. His early work, which focused on philosophy of logic
and philosophy of mathematics, includes the monumental *Principia Mathematica*
(1910), which he wrote with Alfred North Whitehead. Russell contributed to virtually
every area of philosophy, especially the theory of knowledge, on which he produced
many books. A great stylist, Russell was awarded the Nobel Prize in Literature in 1950.

Russell was a lifelong political activist. He was even denied permission to teach a
course on logic at City College of New York because of his liberal views on sex. He was
jailed many times, including during World War I for his pacifism and once at the age of
89 for protesting against nuclear arms.

In the following selection, Russell explains why there are problems with basing
knowledge on experience. He then revamps and elaborates the sort of foundational
approach to solving these problems that was earlier advocated by Locke, Berkeley, and
Hume. In particular, he attempts to explain how we get from what he regards as the
ultimate data of empirical knowledge, "sense data," to all of the things we think we
know about the world and ourselves, a task that leads him to consider skeptical doubts
about the existence of the material world and about inductive inferences.

Reading Questions

1. Russell claims we never "immediately experience" real physical objects, such as tables
and chairs. What, then, does he think we immediately experience? What is the relationship, on
his view, between what we immediately experience and physical objects?

2. In his discussion of Descartes, Russell claims "the real Self is as hard to arrive at as the
real table." What does Russell mean by "the real Self"? Why doesn't he simply accept
Descartes' idea that one's knowledge of the existence of one's own self is the most certain
knowledge that each of us has?

3. Are beliefs based directly on sense experience certain? What does Russell think? Why?
What do you think?

4. Why does Russell think that while the hypothesis that the whole of life is a dream might be true, it cannot explain "the facts of our own lives" as simply as can the commonsense hypothesis that there really are physical objects that exist independently of us?

5. On Russell's view, what is the relation between physical space-time and the spatial and temporal relations we immediately experience?

6. What is an inductive inference? What, on Russell's view, are the assumptions on which all inductive inferences depend?

Appearance and Reality

IS THERE ANY KNOWLEDGE in the world which is so certain that no reasonable man could doubt it? This question, which at first sight might not seem difficult, is really one of the most difficult that can be asked. When we have realized the obstacles in the way of a straightforward and confident answer, we shall be well launched on the study of philosophy—for philosophy is merely the attempt to answer such ultimate questions, not carelessly and dogmatically, as we do in ordinary life and even in the sciences, but critically, after exploring all that makes such questions puzzling, and after realizing all the vagueness and confusion that underlie our ordinary ideas.

In daily life, we assume as certain many things which, on a closer scrutiny, are found to be so full of apparent contradictions that only a great amount of thought enables us to know what it is that we really may believe. In the search for certainty, it is natural to begin with our present experiences, and in some sense, no doubt, knowledge is to be derived from them. But any statement as to what it is that our immediate experiences make us know is very likely to be wrong. It seems to me that I am now sitting in a chair, at a table of a certain shape, on which I see sheets of paper with writing or print. By turning my head I see out of the window buildings and clouds and the sun. I believe that the sun is about ninety-three million miles from the earth; that it is a hot globe many times bigger than the earth; that, owing to the earth's rotation, it rises every morn-

ing, and will continue to do so for an indefinite time in the future. I believe that, if any other normal person comes into my room, he will see the same chairs and tables and books and papers as I see, and that the table which I see is the same as the table which I feel pressing against my arm. All this seems to be so evident as to be hardly worth stating, except in answer to a man who doubts whether I know anything. Yet all this may be reasonably doubted, and all of it requires much careful discussion before we can be sure that we have stated it in a form that is wholly true.

To make our difficulties plain, let us concentrate attention on the table. To the eye it is oblong, brown and shiny, to the touch it is smooth and cool and hard; when I tap it, it gives out a wooden sound. Any one else who sees and feels and hears the table will agree with this description, so that it might seem as if no difficulty would arise; but as soon as we try to be more precise our troubles begin. Although I believe that the table is 'really' of the same colour all over, the parts that reflect the light look much brighter than the other parts, and some parts look white because of reflected light. I know that, if I move, the parts that reflect the light will be different, so that the apparent distribution of colours on the table will change. It follows that if several people are looking at the table at the same moment, no two of them will see exactly the same distribution of colours, because no two can see it from exactly the same point of view, and any change in the point of view makes some change in the way the light is reflected.

From The Problems of Philosophy, *Oxford University Press, (1912).*

For most practical purposes these differences are unimportant, but to the painter they are all-important: the painter has to unlearn the habit of thinking that things seem to have the colour which common sense says they 'really' have, and to learn the habit of seeing things as they appear. Here we have already the beginning of one of the distinctions that cause most trouble in philosophy — the distinction between 'appearance' and 'reality', between what things seem to be and what they are. The painter wants to know what things seem to be, the practical man and the philosopher want to know what they are; but the philosopher's wish to know this is stronger than the practical man's, and is more troubled by knowledge as to the difficulties of answering the question.

To return to the table. It is evident from what we have found, that there is no colour which pre-eminently appears to be *the* colour of the table, or even of any one particular part of the table — it appears to be of different colours from different points of view, and there is no reason for regarding some of these as more really its colour than others. And we know that even from a given point of view the colour will seem different by artificial light, or to a colour-blind man, or to a man wearing blue spectacles, while in the dark there will be no colour at all, though to touch and hearing the table will be unchanged. This colour is not something which is inherent in the table, but something depending upon the table and the spectator and the way the light falls on the table. When, in ordinary life, we speak of *the* colour of the table, we only mean the sort of colour which it will seem to have to a normal spectator from an ordinary point of view under usual conditions of light. But the other colours which appear under other conditions have just as good a right to be considered real; and therefore, to avoid favouritism, we are compelled to deny that, in itself, the table has any one particular colour.

The same thing applies to the texture. With the naked eye one can see the grain, but otherwise the table looks smooth and even. If we looked at it through a microscope, we should see roughnesses and hills and valleys, and all sorts of differences that are imperceptible to the naked eye. Which of these is the 'real' table? We are naturally tempted to say that what we see through the microscope is more real, but that in turn would be changed by a still more powerful microscope. If, then, we cannot trust what we see with the naked eye, why should we trust what we see through a microscope? Thus, again, the confidence in our senses with which we began deserts us.

The *shape* of the table is no better. We are all in the habit of judging as to the 'real' shapes of things, and we do this so unreflectingly that we come to think we actually see the real shapes. But, in fact, as we all have to learn if we try to draw, a given thing looks different in shape from every different point of view. If our table is 'really' rectangular, it will look, from almost all points of view, as if it had two acute angles and two obtuse angles. If opposite sides are parallel, they will look as if they converged to a point away from the spectator; if they are of equal length, they will look as if the nearer side were longer. All these things are not commonly noticed in looking at a table, because experience has taught us to construct the 'real' shape from the apparent shape, and the 'real' shape is what interests us as practical men. But the 'real' shape is not what we see; it is something inferred from what we see. And what we see is constantly changing in shape as we move about the room; so that here again the senses seem not to give us the truth about the table itself, but only about the appearance of the table.

Similar difficulties arise when we consider the sense of touch. It is true that the table always gives us a sensation of hardness, and we feel that it resists pressure. But the sensation we obtain depends upon how hard we press the table and also upon what part of the body we press with; thus the various sensations due to various pressures or various parts of the body cannot be supposed to reveal *directly* any definite property of the table, but at most to be *signs* of some property which perhaps *causes* all the sensations, but is not actually apparent in any of them. And the same applies still more obviously to the sounds which can be elicited by rapping the table.

Thus it becomes evident that the real table, if there is one, is not the same as what we immediately experience by sight or touch or hearing. The real table, if there is one, is not *immediately* known to us at all, but must be an inference from what is immediately known. Hence, two very difficult questions at once arise; namely, (1) Is there a real table at all? (2) If so, what sort of object can it be?

It will help us in considering these questions to have a few simple terms of which the meaning is definite and clear. Let us give the name of 'sense-data' to the things that are immediately known in sensation: such things as colours, sounds, smells, hardnesses, roughnesses, and so on. We shall give the name 'sensation' to the experience of being immediately aware of these things. Thus, whenever we see a colour, we have a sensation *of* the colour, but the colour itself is a sense-datum, not a sensation. The colour is that *of* which we are immediately aware, and the awareness itself is the sensation. It is plain that if we are to know anything about the table, it must be by means of the sense-data—brown colour, oblong shape, smoothness, etc.—which we associate with the table; but, for the reasons which have been given, we cannot say that the table *is* the sense-data, or even that the sense-data are directly properties of the table. Thus a problem arises as to the relation of the sense-data to the real table, supposing there is such a thing.

The real table, if it exists, we will call a 'physical object'. Thus we have to consider the relation of sense-data to physical objects. The collection of all physical objects is called 'matter'. Thus our two questions may be re-stated as follows: (1) Is there any such thing as matter? (2) If so, what is its nature?

The philosopher who first brought prominently forward the reasons for regarding the immediate objects of our senses as not existing independently of us was Bishop Berkeley (1685–1753). . . . [He tried] to prove that there is no such thing as matter at all, and that the world consists of nothing but minds and their ideas. . . . The arguments employed are of very different value: some are important and sound, others are confused or quibbling. But Berkeley retains the merit of having shown that the existence of matter is capable of being denied without absurdity, and that if there are any things that exist independently of us they cannot be the immediate objects of our sensations.

There are two different questions involved when we ask whether matter exists, and it is important to keep them clear. We commonly mean by 'matter' something which is opposed to 'mind', something which we think of as occupying space and as radically incapable of any sort of thought or consciousness. It is chiefly in this sense that Berkeley denies matter; that is to say, he does not deny that the sense-data which we commonly take as signs of the existence of the table are really signs of the existence of *something* independent of us, but he does deny that this something is non-mental, that it is neither mind nor ideas entertained by some mind. He admits that there must be something which continues to exist when we go out of the room or shut our eyes, and that what we call seeing the table does really give us reason for believing in something which persists even when we are not seeing it. But he thinks that this something cannot be radically different in nature from what we see, and cannot be independent of seeing altogether, though it must be independent of *our* seeing. He is thus led to regard the 'real' table as an idea in the mind of God. Such an idea has the required permanence and independence of ourselves, without being—as matter would otherwise be—something quite unknowable, in the sense that we can only infer it, and can never be directly and immediately aware of it.

Other philosophers since Berkeley have also held that, although the table does not depend for its existence upon being seen by me, it does depend upon being seen (or otherwise apprehended in sensation) by *some* mind — not necessarily the mind of God, but more often the whole collective mind of the universe. This they hold, as Berkeley does, chiefly because they think there can be nothing real — or at any rate nothing known to be real — except minds and their thoughts and feelings. We might state the argument by which they support their view in some such way as this: 'Whatever can be thought of is an idea in the mind of the person thinking of it; therefore nothing can be thought of except ideas in minds; therefore anything else is inconceivable, and what is inconceivable cannot exist.'

Such an argument, in my opinion, is fallacious; and of course those who advance it do not put it so shortly or so crudely. But whether valid or not, the argument has been very widely advanced in one form or another; and very many philosophers, perhaps a majority, have held that there is nothing real except minds and their ideas. Such philosophers are called 'idealists'. When they come to explaining matter, they either say, like Berkeley, that matter is really nothing but a collection of ideas, or they say, like Leibniz (1646–1716), that what appears as matter is really a collection of more or less rudimentary minds.

But these philosophers, though they deny matter as opposed to mind, nevertheless, in another sense, admit matter. It will be remembered that we asked two questions; namely, (1) Is there a real table at all? (2) If so, what sort of object can it be? Now both Berkeley and Leibniz admit that there is a real table, but Berkeley says it is certain ideas in the mind of God, and Leibniz says it is a colony of souls. Thus both of them answer our first question in the affirmative, and only diverge from the views of ordinary mortals in their answer to our second question. In fact, almost all philosophers seem to be agreed that there is a real table: they almost all agree that, however much our sense-data — colour, shape, smoothness, etc. — may depend upon us, yet their occurrence is a sign of something existing independently of us, something differing, perhaps, completely from

our sense-data, and yet to be regarded as causing those sense-data whenever we are in a suitable relation to the real table.

Now obviously this point in which the philosophers are agreed — the view that there *is* a real table, whatever its nature may be — is vitally important, and it will be worth while to consider what reasons there are for accepting this view before we go on to the further question as to the nature of the real table. Our next [section], therefore, will be concerned with the reasons for supposing that there is a real table at all.

Before we go farther it will be well to consider for a moment what it is that we have discovered so far. It has appeared that, if we take any common object of the sort that is supposed to be known by the senses, what the senses *immediately* tell us is not the truth about the object as it is apart from us, but only the truth about certain sense-data which, so far as we can see, depend upon the relations between us and the object. Thus what we directly see and feel is merely 'appearance', which we believe to be a sign of some 'reality' behind. But if the reality is not what appears, have we any means of knowing whether there is any reality at all? And if so, have we any means of finding out what it is like?

Such questions are bewildering, and it is difficult to know that even the strangest hypotheses may not be true. Thus our familiar table, which has roused but the slightest thoughts in us hitherto, has become a problem full of surprising possibilities. The one thing we know about it is that it is not what it seems. Beyond this modest result, so far, we have the most complete liberty of conjecture. Leibniz tells us it is a community of souls; Berkeley tells us it is an idea in the mind of God; sober science, scarcely less wonderful, tells us it is a vast collection of electric charges in violent motion.

Among these surprising possibilities, doubt suggests that perhaps there is no table at all. Philosophy, if it cannot *answer* so many questions as we could wish, has at least the power of *asking* questions which increase the interest of the world, and show the strangeness and wonder lying just below the surface even in the commonest things of daily life.

The Existence of Matter

We have to ask ourselves whether, in any sense at all, there is such a thing as matter. Is there a table which has a certain intrinsic nature, and continues to exist when I am not looking, or is the table merely a product of my imagination, a dream-table in a very prolonged dream? This question is of the greatest importance. For if we cannot be sure of the independent existence of objects, we cannot be sure of the independent existence of other people's bodies, and therefore still less of other people's minds, since we have no grounds for believing in their minds except such as are derived from observing their bodies. Thus if we cannot be sure of the independent existence of objects, we shall be left alone in a desert—it may be that the whole outer world is nothing but a dream, and that we alone exist. This is an uncomfortable possibility; but although it cannot be strictly *proved* to be false, there is not the slightest reason to suppose that it is true. In this [section] we have to see why this is the case.

Before we embark upon doubtful matters, let us try to find some more or less fixed point from which to start. Although we are doubting the physical existence of the table, we are not doubting the existence of the sense-data which made us think there was a table; we are not doubting that, while we look, a certain colour and shape appear to us, and while we press, a certain sensation of hardness is experienced by us. All this, which is psychological, we are not calling in question. In fact, whatever else may be doubtful, some at least of our immediate experiences seem absolutely certain.

Descartes (1596–1650), the founder of modern philosophy, invented a method which may still be used with profit—the method of systematic doubt. He determined that he would believe nothing which he did not see quite clearly and distinctly to be true. Whatever he could bring himself to doubt, he would doubt, until he saw reason for not doubting it. By applying this method he gradually became convinced that the only existence of which he could be *quite* certain was his own. He imagined a deceitful demon, who presented unreal things to his senses in a perpetual phantasmagoria; it might be very improbable that such a demon existed, but still it was possible, and therefore doubt concerning things perceived by the senses was possible.

But doubt concerning his own existence was not possible, for if he did not exist, no demon could deceive him. If he doubted, he must exist; if he had any experiences whatever, he must exist. Thus his own existence was an absolute certainty to him. 'I think, therefore I am,' he said (*Cogito, ergo sum*); and on the basis of this certainty he set to work to build up again the world of knowledge which his doubt had laid in ruins. By inventing the method of doubt, and by showing that subjective things are the most certain, Descartes performed a great service to philosophy, and one which makes him still useful to all students of the subject.

But some care is needed in using Descartes' argument. 'I think, therefore *I* am' says rather more than is strictly certain. It might seem as though we were quite sure of being the same person to-day as we were yesterday, and this is no doubt true in some sense. But the real Self is as hard to arrive at as the real table, and does not seem to have that absolute, convincing certainty that belongs to particular experiences. When I look at my table and see a certain brown colour, what is quite certain at once is not 'I am seeing a brown colour', but rather, 'a brown colour is being seen'. This of course involves something (or somebody) which (or who) sees the brown colour; but it does not of itself involve that more or less permanent person whom we call 'I'. So far as immediate certainty goes, it might be that the something which sees the brown colour is quite momentary, and not the same as the something which has some different experience the next moment.

Thus it is our particular thoughts and feelings that have primitive certainty. And this applies to dreams and hallucinations as well as to normal perceptions: when we dream or see a ghost, we certainly do have the sensations we think we have, but for various reasons it is held that no physical object corresponds to these sensations. Thus the certainty of our knowledge of our own experiences does not have to be limited in any way to allow for exceptional cases. Here, therefore, we have, for what it is worth, a solid basis from which to begin our pursuit of knowledge.

The problem we have to consider is this: Granted that we are certain of our own sense-data, have we any reason for regarding them as signs of the existence of something else, which we can call the physical object? When we have enumerated all the sense-data which we should naturally regard as connected with the table, have we said all there is to say about the table, or is there still something else — something not a sense-datum, something which persists when we go out of the room? Common sense unhesitatingly answers that there is. What can be bought and sold and pushed about and have a cloth laid on it, and so on, cannot be a *mere* collection of sense-data. If the cloth completely hides the table, we shall derive no sense-data from the table, and therefore, if the table were merely sense-data, it would have ceased to exist, and the cloth would be suspended in empty air, resting, by a miracle, in the place where the table formerly was. This seems plainly absurd; but whoever wishes to become a philosopher must learn not to be frightened by absurdities.

One great reason why it is felt that we must secure a physical object in addition to the sense-data, is that we want the *same* object for different people. When ten people are sitting round a dinner-table, it seems preposterous to maintain that they are not seeing the same tablecloth, the same knives and forks and spoons and glasses. But the sense-data are private to each separate person; what is immediately present to the sight of one is not immediately present to the sight of another: they all see things from slightly different points of view, and therefore see them slightly differently. Thus, if there are to be public neutral objects, which can be in some sense known to many different people, there must be something over and above the private and particular sense-data which appear to various people. What reason, then, have we for believing that there are such public neutral objects?

The first answer that naturally occurs to one is that, although different people may see the table slightly differently, still they all see more or less similar things when they look at the table, and the variations in what they see follow the laws of perspective and reflection of light, so that it is easy to arrive at a permanent object underlying all the different people's sense-data. I bought my table from the former occupant of my room; I could not buy *his* sense-data, which died when he went away, but I could and did buy the confident expectation of more or less similar sense-data. Thus it is the fact that different people have similar sense-data, and that one person in a given place at different times has similar sense-data, which makes us suppose that over and above the sense-data there is a permanent public object which underlies or causes the sense-data of various people at various times.

Now in so far as the above considerations depend upon supposing that there are other people besides ourselves, they beg the very question at issue. Other people are represented to me by certain sense-data, such as the sight of them or the sound of their voices, and if I had no reason to believe that there were physical objects independent of my sense-data, I should have no reason to believe that other people exist except as part of my dream. Thus, when we are trying to show that there must be objects independent of our own sense-data, we cannot appeal to the testimony of other people, since this testimony itself consists of sense-data, and does not reveal other people's experiences unless our own sense-data are signs of things existing independently of us. We must therefore, if possible, find, in our own purely private experiences, characteristics which show, or tend to show, that there are in the world things other than ourselves and our private experiences.

In one sense it must be admitted that we can never *prove* the existence of things other than ourselves and our experiences. No logical absurdity results from the hypothesis that the world consists of myself and my thoughts and feelings and sensations, and that everything else is mere fancy. In dreams a very complicated world may seem to be present, and yet on waking we find it was a delusion; that is to say, we find that the sense-data in the dream do not appear to have corresponded with such physical objects as we should naturally infer from our sense-data. (It is true that, when the physical world is assumed, it is possible to find physical causes for the sense-data in dreams: a door banging, for instance, may cause us to dream of a naval engagement. But although, in this case, there is a physical *cause* for the sense-data, there is not a physical object *corresponding* to the sense-data in the way in which an actual naval battle would correspond.) There is no logical impossibility in the supposition that the whole of life is a dream, in which we ourselves create all the objects that come before us. But although this is not logically impossible, there is no reason whatever to suppose that it is true; and it is, in fact, a less simple hypothesis, viewed as a means of accounting for the facts of our own life, than the common-sense hypothesis that there really are objects independent of us, whose action on us causes our sensations.

The way in which simplicity comes in from supposing that there really are physical objects is easily seen. If the cat appears at one moment in one part of the room, and at another in another part, it is natural to suppose that it has moved from the one to the other, passing over a series of intermediate positions. But if it is merely a set of sense-data, it cannot have ever been in any place where I did not see it; thus we shall have to suppose that it did not exist at all while I was not looking, but suddenly sprang into being in a new place. If the cat exists whether I see it or not, we can understand from our own experience how it gets hungry between one meal and the next; but if it does not exist when I am not seeing it, it seems odd that appetite should grow during non-existence as fast as during existence. And if the cat consists only of sense-data, it cannot be *hungry*, since no hunger but my own can be a sense-datum to me. Thus the behaviour of the sense-data which represent the cat to me, though it seems quite natural when regarded as an expression of hunger, becomes utterly inexplicable when regarded as mere movements and changes of patches of colour, which are as incapable of hunger as a triangle is of playing football.

But the difficulty in the case of the cat is nothing compared to the difficulty in the case of human beings. When human beings speak — that is, when we hear certain noises which we associate with ideas, and simultaneously see certain motions of lips and expressions of face — it is very difficult to suppose that what we hear is not the expression of a thought, as we know it would be if we emitted the same sounds. Of course similar things happen in dreams, where we are mistaken as to the existence of other people. But dreams are more or less suggested by what we call waking life, and are capable of being more or less accounted for on scientific principles if we assume that there really is a physical world. Thus every principle of simplicity urges us to adopt the natural view, that there really are objects other than ourselves and our sense-data which have an existence not dependent upon our perceiving them.

Of course it is not by argument that we originally come by our belief in an independent external world. We find this belief ready in ourselves as soon as we begin to reflect: it is what may be called an *instinctive* belief. We should never have been led to question this belief but for the fact that, at any rate in the case of sight, it seems as if the sense-datum itself were instinctively believed to be the independent object, whereas argument shows that the object cannot be identical with the sense-datum. This discovery, however — which is not at all paradoxical in the case of taste and smell and sound, and only slightly so in the case of touch — leaves undiminished our instinctive belief that there *are* objects *corresponding* to our sense-data. Since this belief does not lead to any difficulties, but on the contrary tends to simplify and systematize our account of our experiences, there seems no good reason for rejecting it. We may therefore admit — though with a slight doubt derived from dreams — that the external world does not really exist, and is not wholly dependent for its existence upon our continuing to perceive it.

The argument which has led us to this conclusion is doubtless less strong that we could wish, but it is typical of many philosophical arguments, and it is therefore worth while to consider briefly its general character and validity. All knowledge, we find, must be built up upon our instinctive beliefs, and if these are rejected, nothing is left. But among our instinctive beliefs some are much stronger than others, while many have, by habit and association, become entangled with other beliefs, not really instinctive, but falsely supposed to be part of what is believed instinctively.

Philosophy should show us the hierarchy of our instinctive beliefs, beginning with those we hold most strongly, and presenting each as much isolated and as free from irrelevant additions as possible. It should take care to show that, in the form in which they are finally set forth, our instinctive beliefs do not clash, but form a harmonious system. There can never be any reason for rejecting one instinctive belief except that it clashes with others; thus, if they are found to harmonize, the whole system becomes worthy of acceptance.

It is of course *possible* that all or any of our beliefs may be mistaken, and therefore all ought to be held with at least some slight element of doubt. But we cannot have *reason* to reject a belief except on the ground of some other belief. Hence, by organizing our instinctive beliefs and their consequences, by considering which among them is most possible, if necessary, to modify or abandon, we can arrive, on the basis of accepting as our sole data what we instinctively believe, at an orderly systematic organization of our knowledge, in which, though the *possibility* of error remains, its likelihood is diminished by the interrelation of the parts and by the critical scrutiny which has preceded acquiescence.

This function, at least, philosophy can perform. Most philosophers, rightly or wrongly, believe that philosophy can do much more than this — that it can give us knowledge, not otherwise attainable, concerning the universe as a whole, and concerning the nature of ultimate reality. Whether this be the case or not, the more modest function we have spoken of can certainly be performed by philosophy, and certainly suffices, for those who have once begun to doubt the adequacy of common sense, to justify the arduous and difficult labours that philosophical problems involve.

The Nature of Matter

. . . We agreed, though without being able to find demonstrative reasons, that it is rational to believe that our sense-data — for example, those which we regard as associated with my table — are really signs of the existence of something independent of us and our perceptions. That is to say, over and above the sensations of colour, hardness, noise, and so on, which make up the appearance of the table to me, I assume that there is something else, *of* which these things are appearances. The colour ceases to exist if I shut my eyes, the sensation of hardness ceases to exist if I remove my arm from contact with the table, the sound ceases to exist if I cease to rap the table with my knuckles. But I do not believe that when all these things cease the table ceases. On the contrary, I believe that it is because the table exists continuously that all these sense-data will reappear when I open my eyes, replace my arm, and begin again to rap with my knuckles. The question we have to consider in this chapter is: What is the nature of this real table, which persists independently of my perception of it?

To this question physical science gives an answer, somewhat incomplete it is true, and in part still very hypothetical, but yet deserving of respect so far as it goes. Physical science, more or less unconsciously, has drifted into the view that all natural phenomena ought to be reduced to motions. Light and heat and sound are all due to wave-motions, which travel from the body emitting them to the person who sees light or feels heat or hears sound. That which has the wave-motion is either aether or 'gross matter', but in either case is what the philosopher would call matter. The only properties which science assigns to it are position in space, and the power of motion according to the laws of motion. Science does not deny that it *may* have other properties; but if so, such other properties are not useful to the man of science, and in no way assist him in explaining the phenomena.

It is sometimes said that 'light *is* a form of wave-motion', but this is misleading, for the light which we immediately see, which we know directly by means of our senses, is *not* a form of wave-motion, but something quite different — something which we all know if we are not blind, though we cannot describe it so as to convey our knowledge to a man who is blind. A wave-motion, on the contrary, could quite well be described to a blind man, since he can acquire a knowledge of space by the sense of touch; and he can experience a wave-motion by a sea voyage almost as well as we can. But this, which a blind man can understand, is not what we mean by *light*: we mean by *light* just that which a blind man can never understand, and which we can never describe to him.

Now this something, which all of us who are not blind know, is not, according to science, really to be found in the outer world: it is something caused by the action of certain waves upon the eyes and nerves and brain of the person who sees the light. When it is said that light *is* waves, what is really meant is that waves are the physical cause of our sensations of light. But light itself, the thing which seeing people experience and blind people do not, is not supposed by science to form any part of the world that is independent of us and our senses. And very similar remarks would apply to other kinds of sensations.

It is not only colours and sounds and so on that are absent from the scientific world of matter, but also *space* as we get it through sight or touch. It is essential to science that its matter should be in *a* space, but the space in which it is cannot be exactly the space we see or feel. To begin with, space as we see it is not the same as space as we get it by the sense of touch; it is only by experience in infancy that we learn how to touch things we see, or how to get a sight of things which we feel touching us. But the space of science is neutral as between touch and sight; thus it cannot be either the space of touch or the space of sight.

Again, different people see the same object as of different shapes, according to their point of view. A circular coin, for example, though we should always *judge* it to be circular, will *look* oval unless we are straight in front of it. When we judge that it *is* circular, we are judging that it has a real shape which is not its apparent shape, but belongs to it intrinsically apart from its appearance. But this real shape, which is what concerns science, must be in a real space, not the same as anybody's *apparent* space. The real space is public, the apparent space is private to the percipient. In different people's *private* spaces the same object seems to have different shapes; thus the real space, in which it has its real shape, must be different from the private spaces. The space of science, therefore, though *connected* with the spaces we see and feel, is not identical with them, and the manner of its connexion requires investigation.

We agreed provisionally that physical objects cannot be quite like our sense-data, but may be regarded as *causing* our sensations. These physical objects are in the space of science, which we may call 'physical' space. It is important to notice that, if our sensations are to be caused by physical objects, there must be a physical space containing these objects and our sense-organs and nerves and brain. We get a sensation of touch from an object when we are in contact with it; that is to say, when some part of our body occupies a place in physical space quite close to the space occupied by the object. We see an object (roughly speaking) when no opaque body is between the object and our eyes in physical space. Similarly, we only hear or smell or taste an object when we are sufficiently near to it, or when it touches the tongue, or has some suitable position in physical space relatively to our body. We cannot begin to state what different sensations we shall derive from a given object under different circumstances unless we regard the object and our body as both in one physical space, for it is mainly the relative positions of the object and our body that determine what sensations we shall derive from the object.

Now our sense-data are situated in our private spaces, either the space of sight or the space of touch or such vaguer spaces as other senses may give us. If, as science and common sense assume, there is one public all-embracing physical space in which physical objects are, the relative positions of physical objects in physical space must more or less correspond to the relative positions of sense-data in our private spaces. There is no difficulty in supposing this to be the case. If we see on a road one house nearer to us than another, our other senses will bear out the view that it is nearer; for example, it will be reached sooner if we walk along the road. Other people will agree that the house which looks nearer to us is nearer; the ordnance map will take the same view; and thus everything points to a spatial relation between the houses corresponding to the relation between the sense-data which we see when we look at the houses. Thus we may assume that there is a physical space in which physical objects have spatial relations corresponding to those which the corresponding sense-data have in our

private spaces. It is this physical space which is dealt with in geometry and assumed in physics and astronomy.

Assuming that there is physical space, and that it does thus correspond to private spaces, what can we know about it? We can know *only* what is required in order to secure the correspondence. That is to say, we can know nothing of what it is like in itself, but we can know the sort of arrangement of physical objects which results from their spatial relations. We can know, for example, that the earth and moon and sun are in one straight line during an eclipse, though we cannot know what a physical straight line is in itself, as we know the look of a straight line in our visual space. Thus we come to know much more about the *relations* of distances in physical space than about the distances themselves; we may know that one distance is greater than another, or that it is along the same straight line as the other, but we cannot have that immediate acquaintance with physical distances that we have with distances in our private spaces, or with colours or sounds or other sense-data. We can know all those things about physical space which a man born blind might know through other people about the space of sight; but the kind of things which a man born blind could never know about the space of sight we also cannot know about physical space. We can know the properties of the relations required to preserve the correspondence with sense-data, but we cannot know the nature of the terms between which the relations hold.

With regard to time, our *feeling* of duration or of the lapse of time is notoriously an unsafe guide as to the time that has elapsed by the clock. Times when we are bored or suffering pain pass slowly, times when we are agreeably occupied pass quickly, and times when we are sleeping pass almost as if they did not exist. Thus, in so far as time is constituted by duration, there is the same necessity for distinguishing a public and a private time as there was in the case of space. But in so far as time consists in an *order* of before and after, there is no need to make such a distinction; the time-order which events seem to have is, so far as we can see, the same as the time-order which they do have. At any rate no reason can be given for supposing that the two orders are not the same. The same is usually true of space: if a regiment of men are marching along a road, the *shape* of the regiment will look different from different points of view, but the men will appear arranged in the same *order* from all points of view. Hence we regard the *order* as true also in physical space, whereas the shape is only supposed to correspond to the physical space so far as is required for the preservation of the order.

In saying that the time-order which events *seem to have* is the same as the time-order which they *really have*, it is necessary to guard against a possible misunderstanding. It must not be supposed that the various states of different physical objects have the same time-order as the sense-data which constitute the perceptions of those objects. Considered as physical objects, the thunder and lightning are simultaneous; that is to say, the lightning is simultaneous with the disturbance of the air in the place where the disturbance begins, namely, where the lightning is. But the sense-datum which we call hearing the thunder does not take place until the disturbance of the air has travelled as far as to where we are. Similarly, it takes about eight minutes for the sun's light to reach us; thus, when we see the sun we are seeing the sun of eight minutes ago. So far as our sense-data afford evidence as to the physical sun they afford evidence as to the physical sun of eight minutes ago; if the physical sun had ceased to exist within the last eight minutes, that would make no difference to the sense-data which we call 'seeing the sun'. This affords a fresh illustration of the necessity of distinguishing between sense-data and physical objects.

What we have found as regards space is much the same as what we find in relation to the correspondence of the sense-data with their physical counterparts. If one object looks blue and another red, we may reasonably presume that there is some corresponding difference between the physical objects; if two objects both look blue, we may presume a corresponding similarity. But we cannot hope to be acquainted directly with the quality in the physical object which makes it look blue or red. Science tells us that this quality is a certain sort of wave-motion, and this sounds familiar, because we think of wave-motions in the space we see. But the wave-motions must really be in physical space, with which we have no direct acquaintance; thus the real wave-motions have not that familiarity which we might have supposed them to have. And what holds for colours is closely similar to what holds for other sense-data. Thus we find that, although the *relations* of physical objects have all sorts of knowable properties, derived from their correspondence with the relations of sense-data, the physical objects themselves remain unknown in their intrinsic nature, so far at least as can be discovered by means of the senses. The question remains whether there is any other method of discovering the intrinsic nature of physical objects.

The most natural, though not ultimately the most defensible, hypothesis to adopt in the first instance, at any rate as regards visual sense-data, would be that, though physical objects cannot, for the reasons we have been considering, be *exactly* like sense-data, yet they may be more or less like. According to this view, physical objects will, for example, really have colours, and we might, by good luck, see an object as of the colour it really is. The colour which an object seems to have at any given moment will in general be very similar, though not quite the same, from many different points of view; we might thus suppose the 'real' colour to be a sort of medium colour, intermediate between the various shades which appear from the different points of view.

Such a theory is perhaps not capable of being definitely refuted, but it can be shown to be groundless. To begin with, it is plain that the colour we see depends only upon the nature of the light-waves that strike the eye, and is therefore modified by the medium intervening between us and the object, as well as by the manner in which light is reflected from the object in the direction of the eye. The intervening air alters colours unless it is perfectly clear, and any strong reflection will alter them completely. Thus the colour we see is a result of the ray as it reaches the eye, and not simply a property of the object from which the ray comes. Hence, also, provided certain waves reach the eye, we shall see a certain colour, whether the object from which the waves start has any colour or not. Thus it is quite gratuitous to suppose that physical objects have colours, and therefore there is no justification for making such a supposition. Exactly similar arguments will apply to other sense-data. . . .

On Induction*

In almost all our previous discussions we have been concerned in the attempt to get clear as to our data in the way of knowledge of existence. What things are there in the universe whose existence is known to us owing to our being acquainted with them? So far, our answer has been that we are acquainted with our sense-data, and, probably, with ourselves. These we know to exist. And past sense-data which are remembered are known to have existed in the past. This knowledge supplies our data.

But if we are to be able to draw inferences from these data—if we are to know of the existence of matter, of other people, of the past before our individual memory begins, or of the future, we must know general principles of some kind by means of which such inferences can be drawn. It must be known to us that the existence of some one sort of thing, A, is a sign of the existence of some other sort of thing, B, either at the same time as A or at some earlier or later time, as, for example, thunder is a sign of the earlier existence of lightning. If this were not known to us, we could never extend our knowledge beyond the sphere of our private experience; and this sphere, as we have seen, is exceedingly limited. The question we have now to consider is whether such an extension is possible, and if so, how it is effected.

Let us take as an illustration a matter about which none of us, in fact, feel the slightest doubt. We are all convinced that the sun will rise tomorrow. Why? Is this belief a mere blind outcome of past experience, or can it be justified as a reasonable belief? It is not easy to find a test by which to judge whether a belief of this kind is reasonable or not, but we can at least ascertain what sort of general beliefs would suffice, if true, to justify the judgement that the sun will rise tomorrow, and the many other similar judgements upon which our actions are based.

It is obvious that if we are asked why we believe that the sun will rise to-morrow, we shall naturally answer, 'Because it always has risen every day'. We have a firm belief that it will rise in the future, because it has risen in the past. If we are challenged as to why we believe that it will continue to rise as heretofore, we may appeal to the laws of motion: the earth, we shall say, is a freely rotating body, and such bodies do not cease to rotate unless something interferes from outside, and there is nothing outside to interfere with the earth between now and to-morrow. Of course it might be doubted whether we are quite certain that there is nothing outside to interfere, but this is not the interesting doubt. The interesting doubt is as to whether the laws of motion will remain in operation until to-morrow. If this doubt is raised, we find ourselves in the same position as when the doubt about the sunrise was first raised.

The *only* reason for believing that the laws of motion will remain in operation is that they have operated hitherto, so far as our knowledge of the past enables us to judge. It is true that we have a greater body of evidence from the past in favour of the laws of motion than we have in favour of the sunrise, because the sunrise is merely a particular case of fulfilment of the laws of motion, and there are countless other particular cases. But the real question is: "Do *any* number of cases of a law being fulfilled in the past afford evidence that it

Excerpts from "On Induction" reprinted from The Problems of Philosophy *by Bertrand Russell (1912) by permission of Oxford University Press.*

will be fulfilled in the future? If not, it becomes plain that we have no ground whatever for expecting the sun to rise to-morrow, or for expecting the bread we shall eat at our next meal not to poison us, or for any of the other scarcely conscious expectations that control our daily lives. It is to be observed that all such expectations are only *probable*; thus we have not to seek for a proof that they *must* be fulfilled, but only for some reason in favour of the view that they are *likely* to be fulfilled.

Now in dealing with this question we must, to begin with, make an important distinction, without which we should soon become involved in hopeless confusions. Experience has shown us that, hitherto, the frequent repetition of some uniform succession or coexistence has been a *cause* of our expecting the same succession or coexistence on the next occasion. Food that has a certain appearance generally has a certain taste, and it is a severe shock to our expectations when the familiar appearance is found to be associated with an unusual taste. Things which we see become associated, by habit, with certain tactile sensations which we expect if we touch them; one of the horrors of a ghost (in many ghost-stories) is that it fails to give us any sensations of touch. Uneducated people who go abroad for the first time are so surprised as to be incredulous when they find their native language not understood.

And this kind of association is not confined to men; in animals also it is very strong. A horse which has been often driven along a certain road resists the attempt to drive him in a different direction. Domestic animals expect food when they see the person who usually feeds them. We know that all these rather crude expectations of uniformity are liable to be misleading. The man who has fed the chicken every day throughout its life at last wrings its neck instead, showing that more refined views as to the uniformity of nature would have been useful to the chicken.

But in spite of the misleadingness of such expectations, they nevertheless exist. The mere fact that something has happened a certain number of times causes animals and men to expect that it will happen again. Thus our instincts certainly cause us to believe that the sun will rise to-morrow, but we may be in no better a position than the chicken which unexpectedly has its neck wrung. We have therefore to distinguish the fact that past uniformities *cause* expectations as to the future, from the question whether there is any reasonable ground for giving weight to such expectations after the question of their validity has been raised.

The problem we have to discuss is whether there is any reason for believing in what is called 'the uniformity of nature'. The belief in the uniformity of nature is the belief that everything that has happened or will happen is an instance of some general law to which there are *no* exceptions. The crude expectations which we have been considering are all subject to exceptions, and therefore liable to disappoint those who entertain them. But science habitually assumes, at least as a working hypothesis, that general rules which have exceptions can be replaced by general rules which have no exceptions. 'Unsupported bodies in air fall' is a general rule to which balloons and aeroplanes are exceptions. But the laws of motion and the law of gravitation, which account for the fact that most bodies fall, also account for the fact that balloons and aeroplanes can rise; thus the laws of motion and the law of gravitation are not subject to these exceptions.

The belief that the sun will rise to-morrow might be falsified if the earth came suddenly into contact with a large body which destroyed its rotation; but the laws of motion and the law of gravitation would not be infringed by such an event. The business of science is to find uniformities, such as the laws of motion and the law of gravitation, to which, so far as our experience extends, there are no exceptions. In this search science has been remarkably successful, and it may be conceded that such uniformities have held hitherto. This brings us back to the question: Have we any reason, assuming that they have always held in the past, to suppose that they will hold in the future?

It has been argued that we have reason to know that the future will resemble the past, because what was the future has constantly become the past, and has always been found to resemble the past, so that we really have experience of the future, namely of times which were formerly future, which we may call past futures. But such an argument really begs the very question at issue. We have experience of past futures, but not of future futures, and the question is: Will future futures resemble past futures? This question is not to be answered by an argument which starts from past futures alone. We have therefore still to seek for some principle which shall enable us to know that the future will follow the same laws as the past.

The reference to the future in this question is not essential. The same question arises when we apply the laws that work in our experience to past things of which we have no experience — as, for example, in geology, or in theories as to the origin of the Solar System. The question we really have to ask is: 'When two things have been found to be often associated, and no instance is known of the one occurring without the other, does the occurrence of one of the two, in a fresh instance, give any good ground for expecting the other?' On our answer to this question must depend the validity of the whole of our expectations as to the future, the whole of the results obtained by induction, and in fact practically all the beliefs upon which our daily life is based.

It must be conceded, to begin with, that the fact that two things have been found often together and never apart does not, by itself, suffice to *prove* demonstratively that they will be found together in the next case we examine. The most we can hope is that the oftener things are found together, the more probable it becomes that they will be found together another time, and that, if they have been found together often enough, the probability will amount *almost* to certainty. It can never quite reach certainty, because we know that

in spite of frequent repetitions there sometimes is a failure at the last, as in the case of the chicken whose neck is wrung. Thus probability is all we ought to seek.

It might be urged, as against the view we are advocating, that we know all natural phenomena to be subject to the reign of law, and that sometimes, on the basis of observation, we can see that only one law can possibly fit the facts of the case. Now to this view there are two answers. The first is that, even if *some* law which has no exceptions applies to our case, we can never, in practice, be sure that we have discovered that law and not one to which there are exceptions. The second is that the reign of law would seem to be itself only probable, and that our belief that it will hold in the future, or in unexamined cases in the past, is itself based upon the very principle we are examining.

The principle we are examining may be called the *principle of induction*, and its two parts may be stated as follows:

(*a*) When a thing of a certain sort A has been found to be associated with a thing of a certain other sort B, and has never been found dissociated from a thing of the sort B, the greater the number of cases in which A and B have been associated, the greater is the probability that they will be associated in a fresh case in which one of them is known to be present;

(*b*) Under the same circumstances, a sufficient number of cases of association will make the probability of a fresh association nearly a certainty, and will make it approach certainty without limit.

As just stated, the principle applies only to the verification of our expectation in a single fresh instance. But we want also to know that there is a probability in favour of the general law that things of the sort A are *always* associated with things of the sort B, provided a sufficient number of cases of association are known, and no cases of failure of association are known. The probability of the general law is obviously less than the probability of the particular case, since if the general law is true, the particular case must also be true, whereas the particular case may be true without the general law being true. Nevertheless the probability of the general law is increased by repetitions, just as the probability of the particular case is. We may therefore repeat the two parts of our principle as regards the general law, thus:

(*a*) The greater the number of cases in which a thing of the sort A has been found associated with a thing of the sort B, the more probable it is (if no cases of failure of association are known) that A is always associated with B;

(*b*) Under the same circumstances, a sufficient number of cases of the association of A with B will make it nearly certain that A is always associated with B, and will make this general law approach certainty without limit.

It should be noted that probability is always relative to certain data. In our case, the data are merely the known cases of coexistence of A and B. There may be other data, which *might* be taken into account, which would gravely alter the probability. For example, a man who had seen a great many white swans might argue, by our principle, that on the data it was *probable* that all swans were white, and this might be a perfectly sound argument. The argument is not disproved by the fact that some swans are black, because a thing may very well happen in spite of the fact that some data render it improbable. In the case of the swans, a man might know that colour is a very variable characteristic in many species of animals, and that, therefore, an induction as to colour is peculiarly liable to error. But this knowledge would be a fresh datum, by no means proving that the probability relatively to our previous data had been wrongly estimated. The fact, therefore, that things often fail to fulfil our expectations is no evidence that our expectations will not *probably* be fulfilled in a given case or a given class of cases. Thus our inductive principle is at any rate not capable of being *disproved* by an appeal to experience.

The inductive principle, however, is equally incapable of being *proved* by an appeal to experi-ence. Experience might conceivably confirm the inductive principle as regards the cases that have been already examined; but as regards unex-amined cases, it is the inductive principle alone that can justify any inference from what has been examined to what has not been examined. All ar-guments which, on the basis of experience, argue as to the future or the unexperienced parts of the past or present, assume the inductive principle; hence we can never use experience to prove the inductive principle without begging the ques-tion. Thus we must either accept the inductive principle on the ground of its intrinsic evidence, or forgo all justification of our expectations about the future. If the principle is unsound, we have no reason to expect the sun to rise to-morrow, to expect bread to be more nourishing than a stone, or to expect that if we throw ourselves off the roof we shall fall. When we see what looks like our best friend approach-ing us, we shall have no reason to suppose that his body is not inhabited by the mind of our worst enemy or of some total stranger. All our conduct is based upon associations which have worked in the past, and which we therefore re-gard as likely to work in the future; and this likeli-hood is dependent for its validity upon the induc-tive principle.

The general principles of science, such as the belief in the reign of law, and the belief that every event must have a cause, are as completely depen-dent upon the inductive principle as are the be-liefs of daily life. All such general principles are believed because mankind have found innumer-able instances of their truth and no instances of their falsehood. But this affords no evidence for their truth in the future, unless the inductive principle is assumed.

Thus all knowledge which, on a basis of expe-rience tells us something about what is not expe-rienced, is based upon a belief which experience can neither confirm nor confute, yet which, at least in its more concrete applications, appears to be as firmly rooted in us as many of the facts of experience. The existence and justification of such beliefs — for the inductive principle . . . is not the only example — raises some of the most difficult and most debated problems of philosophy. . . .

Further Questions

1. Give the best example you can of a situation in which someone might be making a mistake about his or her immediately experienced sense-data. Then explain whether your example gives you any reason to doubt Russell's views.

2. On Russell's view, is the relation between physical space-time and the spatial and temporal relations we immediately experience like the relation between physical objects and the sense-data we immediately experience? If not, how do these relationships differ?

3. "You probably think you know (that is, have a justified, true belief) that your entire conscious life is not just an elaborate dream. But you do not know any such thing. To justify your claim that your conscious life is not a dream either you have to assume that it is not, for instance, by assuming you know 'intuitively' that it is not, which is really no justification at all, or else you have to assume that on some prior occasion you determined that your conscious life then was not just an elaborate dream, which, of course, begs the question in that it assumes part of the very thing which you are now being asked to prove." How would Russell respond? How would you? Does your response reveal anything important about the nature of knowledge?

4. In the light of your own critical reflection on Russell's views, what do you think is the role of assumption in knowledge? To what extent, if any, does what we call knowledge of the world rest ultimately on faith? Do you find the extent of this dependence unsettling? Why, or why not?

Further Readings

Audi, Robert. *Belief, Justification, and Knowledge.* Belmont, CA: Wadsworth, 1988. An excellent contemporary introduction.

Chisholm, R. M. *Theory of Knowledge.* 2nd ed. Englewood Cliffs, NJ: Prentice-Hall, 1977. A short, clear introduction to the foundations approach to theory of knowledge.

Hamlyn, D. W. *The Theory of Knowledge.* London and Basingstoke: Macmillan, 1971. A clear, concise introduction.

Belief Revision

GILBERT HARMAN

Gilbert Harman teaches philosophy at Princeton University and writes primarily on epistemology and ethics. In this selection Harman argues against the foundations theory of justification (or belief revision), according to which there are certain basic, foundational beliefs that provide the ultimate basis for justifying any nonbasic belief. Descartes is the classic foundationalist. Locke, Berkeley, and Russell are also foundationalists. Harman's alternative is a coherence theory of justification according to which beliefs do not require any justification at all unless our total system of beliefs is internally conflicting, in which case one makes minimal changes to reduce or remove the conflict and thereby increase the overall coherence of one's beliefs.

Reading Questions

1. Illustrate Harman's distinction between "the foundations theory" and "the coherence theory" in terms of a clear example.

2. What does Harman mean by his claim that the coherence theory is conservative in a way the foundations theory is not?

3. Explain in your own words why Harman thinks the example of Karen's aptitude test supports the coherence theory.

I AM GOING TO COMPARE two competing theories of reasoned belief revision. I will call the theories I am concerned with the "foundations theory of belief revision" and the "coherence theory of belief revision," respectively, since there are similarities between these theories and certain philosophical theories of justification sometimes called "foundation" and "coherence" theories [Sosa 1980, Pollock 1980]. But the theories I am concerned with are not precisely the same as the corresponding philosophical theories of justification, which are not normally presented as theories of belief revision. So, although I will be using the *term* "justification" in what follows, as well as the terms "coherence" and "foundations," I do not claim that my use of any of these terms is the same as its use in these theories of justification. I mean to be raising a new issue, not discussing an old one.

The key point in what I am calling the *foundations* theory is that some of one's beliefs "depend on" others for their "justification"; these other beliefs may depend on still others, until one gets to foundational beliefs that do not depend on any

further beliefs for their justification. In this theory, reasoning or belief revision should consist, first, in subtracting any of one's beliefs that do not now have a satisfactory justification and, second, in adding new beliefs that either need no justification or are justified on the basis of other justified beliefs one has.

On the other hand, according to what I am calling the *coherence* theory, it is not true that one's beliefs have, or ought to have, the sort of justificational structure required by the foundations theory. In this view beliefs do not usually require any sort of justification at all. Justification is taken to be required only if one has a special reason to doubt a particular belief. Such a reason might consist in a conflicting belief or in the observation that one's beliefs could be made more "coherent," that is, more organized or simpler or less ad hoc, if the given belief were abandoned (and perhaps certain other changes were made). According to the coherence theory, belief revision should involve minimal changes in one's beliefs in a way that sufficiently increases overall coherence.

Gilbert Harman, "Positive Vs. Negative Undermining in Belief Revision." Reprinted by permission of the author and of the editor of NOÛS, *Vol. 18 (1984): 39–49.*

It turns out that the theories are most easily distinguished by the conflicting advice they occasionally give concerning whether one should *give up* a belief P from which many other of one's beliefs have been inferred, when P's original justification has to be abandoned. Here a surprising contrast seems to emerge—"is" and "ought" seem to come apart. The foundations theory seems, at least at first, to be more in line with our intuitions about how people *ought* to revise their beliefs; the coherence theory is more in line with what people *actually do* in such situations. Intuition seems strongly to support the foundations theory over the coherence theory as an account of what one is *justified* in doing in such cases; but *in fact* one will tend to act as the coherence theory advises.

After I explain this, I will go on to consider how this apparent discrepancy might be resolved. I will conclude by suggesting that the coherence theory is normatively correct after all, despite initial appearances.

Taking each of these theories in turn, I begin with the foundations theory.

The Foundations Theory of Belief Revision

The basic principle of the foundations theory is that one's beliefs have a justificational structure, some serving as reasons or justifications for others, these justifying beliefs being more basic or fundamental for justification than the beliefs they justify.

The justifications are *prima facie* or defeasible. The foundations theory allows, indeed insists, that one can be justified in believing something P and then come to believe something else that undermines one's justification for believing P. In that case one should stop believing P, unless one has some further justification that is not undermined.

I say "unless one has some further justification," because, in this view, a belief may have more than one justification. To be justified, a belief must have *at least* one justification, but it may have more than one. That is, if a belief in P is to

be justified, it is required, either that P be a foundational belief whose intrinsic justification is not defeated, or that there be at least one undefeated justification of P from other beliefs one is justified in believing. If one believes P and it happens that all of one's justifications for believing P come to be defeated, one is no longer justified in continuing to believe P and one should subtract P from one's beliefs.

Furthermore, and this is very important, if one comes not to be justified in continuing to believe P in this way, then not only is it true that one must abandon belief in P but justifications one has for other beliefs are also affected if these justifications appeal to one's belief in P. Justifications appealing to P must be abandoned when P is abandoned. If that means further beliefs are left without justification, then these beliefs too must be dropped, along with any justifications appealing to them. So there will be a chain reaction when one loses justification for a belief on which other beliefs depend for their justification. (This is worked out in more detail for an artificial intelligence system in Doyle [2], [3].)

So much then for the foundations theory. Let me turn now to the coherence theory.

The Coherence Theory of Belief Revision

The coherence theory is a *conservative* theory in a way the foundations theory is not. The coherence theory supposes one's present beliefs are justified just as they are in the absence of special reasons to change them. Given such special reasons, changes are allowed only to the extent that they yield sufficient increases in coherence. Note that where the foundations theory takes one to be justified in continuing to believe something only if one has a special reason to continue to believe it, the coherence theory takes one to be justified in continuing to believe something as long as one has no special reason to stop believing it.

For our purposes, we do not need to be too specific as to exactly what coherence involves, except to say it includes not only consistency but also a network of relations among one's beliefs, especially relations of implication and explanation.

It is important that in this view coherence competes with conservatism. It is as if there are two aims or tendencies of reasoned revision, one being to maximize coherence, the other to minimize change. Both tendencies are important. Without conservatism, one would be led to reduce one's beliefs to the single Parmenidean thought that all is one. Without the tendency toward coherence, we would have what Peirce ([9]) called "the method of tenacity," in which one holds to one's initial convictions no matter what evidence may accumulate against them.

According to the coherence theory, the assessment of a challenged belief is always holistic. Whether such a belief is justified depends on how well it fits together with everything else one believes. If one's beliefs are coherent, they are mutually supporting. All of one's beliefs are, in a sense, equally fundamental. In the coherence theory there are not the assymmetrical justification relations among one's belief that there are in the foundations theory.

Here then is a brief sketch of the coherence theory. I turn now to testing these theories against our intuitions about cases. This raises an immediate problem for the coherence theory.

An Objection to the Coherence Theory: Karen's Aptitude Test

The problem is that, contrary to what is assumed in the coherence theory, there do seem to be assymmetrical justification relations among one's beliefs.

Consider Karen, who has taken an aptitude test and has just been told her results show she has a considerable aptitude for science and music, but little aptitude for history and philosophy. This news does not correlate perfectly with her previous grades. She had previously done very well, not only in physics, for which her aptitude scores are reported to be high, but also in history, for which her aptitude scores are reported to be

low. Furthermore, she had previously done poorly, not only in philosophy, for which her aptitude scores are reported to be low, but also in music, for which her aptitude scores are reported to be high.

After carefully thinking over these discrepancies, Karen concludes (1) her reported aptitude scores accurately reflect and are explained by her actual aptitudes, so (2) she has an aptitude for science and music and no aptitude for history and philosophy, so (3) her history course must have been an easy one, and (4) she did not work hard enough in the music course. She decides (5) to take another music course but not take any more history.

It seems quite clear that, after Karen reaches these conclusions, some of her beliefs are based on others. Her belief that the history course was very easy depends for its justification on her belief that she has no aptitude for history, a belief which depends in turn for its justification on her belief that she got a low score for history aptitude in her aptitude test. There is not a dependence in the other direction. Her belief about her aptitude test score in history is not based on her belief that she has no aptitude for history or on her belief that the history course was an easy one.

This assymmetry would seem to conflict with the coherence theory which denies there are such relations of assymmetrical dependency among one's beliefs.

It might be suggested on behalf of the coherence theory, that the relevant relations here are merely *temporal* or *causal*. One can agree that Karen's belief about the outcome of her aptitude test precedes and is an important cause of her belief that the history course she took was a very easy one, without having to agree that a relation of dependence or justification holds or ought to hold among these two beliefs once the new belief has been accepted.

In order to test this suggestion, it is sufficient to tell more of Karen's story. Some days later she is informed that the report about her aptitude scores was incorrect! The scores reported were those of someone else whose name was confused with hers. Unfortunately, her own scores have now been lost. How should Karen revise her views, given this new information?

Let us assume that, if Karen had not been given the false information about her aptitude test scores, she could not have reasonably reached any of the conclusions she did reach about her aptitudes in physics, history, philosophy, and music; and let us also assume that without those beliefs, Karen could not have reached any of her further conclusions about the courses she has already taken. Then, according to the foundations theory, Karen should abandon her beliefs about her relative aptitudes in these subjects; and she should give up her belief that the history course she took was very easy, as well as her belief that she did not work hard enough in the music course. She should also reconsider her decisions to take another course in music and not take any more history courses

The coherence theory does not automatically yield the same advice. Karen's new information does produce a loss of overall coherence in her beliefs, since she can no longer coherently suppose that her aptitudes in science, music, philosophy, and history are in any way responsible for the original report she received about the results of her aptitude test. So she must abandon that particular supposition about the explanation of the original report of her scores. Still, there is considerable coherence among the beliefs she inferred from this false report. For example, there is a connection between her belief that she has little aptitude for history, her belief that her high grade on the history course was the result of the course's being an easy one, and her belief that she will not take any more courses in history. There are similar connections between her beliefs about her aptitudes in other subjects, how well she did in courses in those subjects, and her plans for the future in those areas. Let us suppose Karen inferred a great many other things that we have not mentioned from that original report so there are a great many beliefs involved here. Abandoning

all of these beliefs would be costly from the point of view of conservatism, which says to minimize change. Let us suppose it turns out that there are so many of these beliefs, and they are so connected with each other and with other things Karen believes, that the coherence theory implies Karen should retain all these new beliefs even though she must give up her beliefs about the explanation of the report of her aptitude scores.

Then the foundations theory says Karen should give up all these beliefs, while the coherence theory says Karen should retain them. Which theory is right about what Karen ought to do? Almost everyone who has considered this sort of example sides with the foundations theory: Karen should not retain any beliefs she inferred from the false report of her aptitude test scores that she would not have been justified in believing in the absence of that false report. That does seem to be the intuitively right answer. The foundations theory is in accordance with our intuitions about what Karen *ought* to do in a case like this. The coherence theory is not.

Belief Perseverance

But now I must remark on an important complication, to which I have already referred. In fact, Karen would almost certainly keep her new beliefs! That is what people actually do in situations like this. Although the foundations theory gives intuitively satisfying advice about what Karen *ought* to do in such a situation, the coherence theory is more in accord with what people actually do!

Lack of space prevents me from fully documenting the rather surprising facts here. I can only say that there is a considerable psychological literature on "belief perseverance" initially deriving from difficulties psychologists have in "debriefing" subjects who have been exposed to experimental deception. It has proved to be very difficult to eliminate the erroneous beliefs induced during psychological experiments, some of which involve situations much like Karen's ([11]: 147–49).

Why should this be so? It might be suggested that belief is like a habit in that, once a belief has become established, considerable effort may be required to get rid of it, even if one should come to see one ought to get rid of it, just as it is hard to get rid of other bad habits. Often, one cannot simply decide to get rid of a bad habit; one must take active steps to ensure that the habit does not reassert itself. Perhaps it is just as difficult to get rid of a bad belief. If so, foundationalism could be normatively correct as an ideal, even though the ideal is one it takes considerable effort to live up to.

But this suggestion does not provide an adequate explanation of the phenomenon of belief perseverance. Of course, there are cases in which one has to struggle in order to abandon a belief one takes to be discredited. One finds oneself coming back to thoughts one realizes one should no longer accept. There are such habits of thought. But this does not seem to be what is happening in the debriefing studies. Subjects in these studies are not struggling to abandon beliefs they see are discredited. On the contrary, the problem is that subjects do not see that the beliefs they have acquired have been discredited. They see all sorts of reasons for the beliefs, where the reasons consist in connections with other beliefs of a sort that the coherence theory might approve, but not the foundations theory. So the correct explanation of belief perseverance in these studies is not that beliefs that have lost their evidential grounding are like bad habits.

Positive Versus Negative Undermining

A more plausible hypothesis as to why beliefs might survive after the evidence for them has been discredited is that people simply do not keep track of the justification relations among their beliefs. They continue to believe things after the evidence for them has been discredited because they do not realize what they are doing.

This is to suppose people do not in fact proceed in accordance with the advice of the foundations theory. The foundations theory says people should keep track of their reasons for believing as they do and should stop believing anything that is not associated with adequate evidence. So the foundations theory implies that, if Karen has not kept track of her reason for believing her history course to have been an easy one, she should have abandoned her belief even before she was told about the mix up with her aptitude test scores.

This implication of the foundations theory is implausible. If, as I have just suggested, people rarely keep track of their reasons, the implication would be that people are unjustified in almost all their beliefs, an absurd result. In this case, foundationalism seems clearly wrong even as a normative theory. So let us see whether we cannot defend the coherence theory as a normative theory.

Now, although justification in a coherence theory is always "holistic" in that whether one is justified in coming to adopt a new belief depends on how that belief would fit in with everything else one believes, we have already seen how appeal might be made to a nonholistic *causal* notion of "local justification" by means of a limited number of one's prior beliefs, namely those prior beliefs that are most crucial to one's justification for adding the new belief. To be sure, the coherence theory must not suppose there are *continuing* links of justification dependency among beliefs that can be consulted when revising one's beliefs. But the theory can admit that Karen's coming to believe certain things depended on certain of her prior beliefs in a way that it did not depend on others, where this dependence represents a kind of local justification, even though in another respect whether Karen was justified in coming to believe those things depended on everything she then believed.

Given this point, I suggest that the coherence theory might incorporate something like the principle that it is incoherent to believe both *P* and also that one would not be justified in believing *P* if one had relied only on true beliefs. Within the coherence theory, this implies, roughly speaking

> **Principle of Positive Undermining:** One should stop believing *P* whenever one positively believes one's reasons for believing *P* are no good.

I want to compare this with the analogous principle within a foundation theory:

> **Principle of Negative Undermining:** One should stop believing *P* whenever one does not associate one's belief in *P* with an adequate justification (either intrinsic or extrinsic).

It seems clear to me that the principle of positive undermining is much more plausible than the principle of negative undermining. The principle of negative undermining implies that, as one loses track of the justifications of one's beliefs, one should give up those beliefs. If one does not keep track of one's justifications for most of one's beliefs, the principle of negative undermining would say one should stop believing almost everything one believes, which is absurd. On the other hand, the principle of positive undermining does not have this absurd implication. The principle of positive undermining does not suppose the absence of a justification is a reason to stop believing something. It only supposes one's belief in *P* is undermined by the *positive* belief that one's reasons for *P* are no good.

In this connection it is relevant that subjects *can* be successfully debriefed after experiments involving deception, if the subjects are made vividly aware of this very phenomenon, that is, if they are made vividly aware of this very tendency for people to retain false beliefs after the evidence for them has been undercut and are also made vividly aware of how this phenomenon has acted in their own case ([8]). This further phenomenon seems clearly to support the coherence theory, with its principle of positive undermining, over the foundations theory, with its principle of negative undermining. The so-called "full debriefing" cannot merely undermine the evidence for the conclusions subjects have reached but must also directly attack each of these conclusions themselves. The full debriefing works, not just by getting subjects to give up the beliefs that originally served as evidence for the conclusions they have reached, but by getting them to accept certain further positive beliefs about their lack of good reasons for each of these conclusions.

Clutter Avoidance

I now want to suggest that there are practical considerations that tell against keeping track of justifications.

In particular, there is a practical reason to avoid too much clutter in one's beliefs. There is a limit to what one can remember, a limit to the number of things one can put into long term storage, and a limit to what one can retrieve. It is important to save room for important things and not clutter one's mind with a lot of unimportant matters. This is one very important reason why one does not try to believe all sorts of logical consequences of one's beliefs. One should not try to infer all one can from one's beliefs. One should try not to retain too much trivial information. Furthermore, one should try to store in long term memory only the key matters that one will later need to recall. When one reaches a significant conclusion from one's other beliefs, one needs to remember the conclusion but does not normally need to remember all the intermediate steps involved in reaching that conclusion. Indeed, one should not try to remember those intermediate steps; one should try to avoid too much clutter in one's mind.

Similarly, even if much of one's knowledge of the world is inferred ultimately from what one believes oneself to be immediately perceiving at one or another time, one does not normally need to remember these original perceptual beliefs or many of the various intermediate conclusions drawn from them. It is enough to recall the more important of one's conclusions about the location of the furniture, etc.

This means one should not be disposed to try to keep track of the local justifications of one's beliefs. One could keep track of these justifications only by remembering an incredible number of mostly perceptual original premises, along with many, many intermediate steps which one does not want and has little need to remember. One will not want to link one's beliefs to such justifications because one will not in general want to try to retain the prior beliefs from which one reached one's current beliefs.

The practical reason for not keeping track of the justifications of one's beliefs is not as severe as the reason that prevents one from operating purely probabilistically, namely a combinatorial explosion ([5]). Still, there are important practical constraints. It is more efficient not to try to retain these justifications and the accompanying justifying beliefs. This leaves more room in memory for important matters.

Summary and Final Conclusions

To sum up: I have discussed two theories of belief revision, the foundations theory and the coherence theory. The foundations theory says one's beliefs are to be linked by relations of justification that one is to make use of in deciding whether to stop believing something. The coherence theory denies that there should be this sort of justificational structure to one's beliefs. The coherence theory takes conservatism to be an important principle — one's beliefs are justified in the absence of a special reason to doubt them. The foundations theory rejects any such conservatism.

When we consider a case like Karen's, our intuitive judgments may seem to support foundationalism. But it is important to distinguish two different principles, the coherence theory's principle of positive undermining and the foundations theory's much stronger principle of negative undermining. Once we distinguish these principles we see it is really the foundations theory that is counterintuitive, since that theory

would have one give up almost everything one believes, if, as I have argued, one does not keep track of one's justifications. Furthermore, there is a very good practical reason not to keep track of justifications, namely that in the interests of clutter avoidance one should not normally even try to retain the beliefs from which one's more important beliefs were inferred.[1]

REFERENCES

1. J. R. Anderson and G. H. Bower, *Human Associative Memory* (Washington, DC: Winston, 1973).

2. Jon Doyle, "A Truth Maintenance System," *Artificial Intelligence* 12 (1979): 231–272.

3. ————, *A Model for Deliberation, Action, and Introspection* (Cambridge, MA: MIT Artificial Intelligence Laboratory Technical Report #561, 1980).

4. Alvin I. Goldman, "Epistemology and the Psychology of Belief," *Monist* 61 (1978): 525–535.

5. Gilbert Harman, *Change in View: Principles of Reasoned Revision*, forthcoming.

6. Richard J. Jeffrey, *The Logic of Decision*, second edition (Chicago, IL: University of Chicago Press, 1983).

7. Daniel Kahneman, Paul Slovic, and Amos Tversky, *Judgment under Uncertainty: Heuristics and Biases* (Cambridge, England: Cambridge University Press, 1982).

8. Richard Nisbett and Lee Ross, *Human Inference: Strategies and Shortcomings of Social Judgment* (Englewood Cliffs, NJ: Prentice-Hall, 1980).

9. C. S. Peirce (1877), *Popular Science Monthly*, reprinted in *Philosophical Writings of Peirce*, edited by Justice Buchler (New York, NY: Dover).

10. John Pollock, "A Plethora of Epistemological Theories," in *Justification and Knowledge*, edited by George Pappas (Dordrecht, Holland: Reidel, 1979).

11. Lee Ross and Craig A. Anderson, "Shortcomings in the Attribution Process: On the Origins and Maintenance of Erroneous Social Assessments," in Kahneman, Slovic, and Tversky (1982).

12. Ernest Sosa, "The Raft and the Pyramid: Coherence Versus Foundations in the Theory of Knowledge," *Midwest Studies in Philosophy* 5 (1980): 3–25.

NOTE

1. This paper is excerpted from [5]. I am indebted to Jens Kulenkampff and John Pollock for helpful comments on an earlier draft.

Further Questions

1. A major problem for coherence theories — of justification, of truth, and so on — is just explaining clearly what is meant by *coherence*. What does Harman mean by coherence?

2. Think of an example from your own experience of a situation in which you were required to revise your beliefs. Does the foundations theory or the coherence theory give a better account of how you *actually did* revise them? Of how you *ought to have* revised them?

Further Readings

Dancy, Jonathan. *An Introduction to Contemporary Epistemology*. Oxford: Basil Blackwell, 1985. A challenging defense of coherentism with respect to perception, memory, induction, and *a priori* knowledge.

Moser, Paul, and Arnold Vander Nat, eds. *Human Knowledge*. New York: Oxford University Press, 1987. A comprehensive anthology.

Quine, W. V. and Joseph Ullian. *The Web of Belief*, 2nd ed. New York: Random House, 1978. A useful book for beginners.

The Infinite Regress of Reasons

D. M. ARMSTRONG

Prior to his recent retirement, D. M. Armstrong taught philosophy at the University of Sydney, in Australia, and wrote extensively on metaphysics and epistemology. In this selection, which is slightly more technical than the other readings in this section but well worth the effort it will take to master it, Armstrong gives an unusually clear, systematic, and concise explanation of the problems that face traditional theories of knowledge, including foundationalism and coherence theories, and then suggests a reliability account of knowledge to replace them.

Armstrong's symbolism, which should seem quite natural once you get used to it, may pose a problem initially. Here is how to read it: The letter, "A," (capital or lowercase) stands for any person, and the letters "p," "q," and "r" for any statements. For instance, in the sentence, "A knows that p," "A" could stand for Galileo and "p" for the statement that there are mountains on the moon; on these substitutions, "A knows that p," or as Armstrong sometimes puts it, "Kap," would stand for the sentence, "Galileo knows that there are mountains on the moon." (Just once, in part III, section 2, Armstrong also uses "A," "B," and "C" to stand for events, such as the onset of a thunderstorm or your reading of this sentence.) Armstrong uses the expression "Kap" to stand for "A knows that p"; "Bap" for "A believes that p"; "~Kap" for "A does *not* know that p"; and "~Bap" for "A does *not* believe that p." Finally, the word "punter" in the first paragraph is Australian for "someone who gambles on horses."

Reading Questions

1. Think of clear, simple examples to illustrate the points Armstrong makes in his five "Conditions" paragraphs.

2. The Infinite Regress of Reasons is an infinite regress because knowledge must be based on evidence that is known. Since that evidence also is knowledge, it must be based on further evidence that is known, which, since that latter evidence also is knowledge . . . and so on. How did Descartes solve this sort of problem? How did Russell, in the preceding selection, solve it? (Or did he?) Finally, what do you think would be the most hopeful way to try to solve this problem?

I. The Evidence-Condition

. . . 'A KNOWS THAT P' entails 'A truly believes that p'. But true belief does not entail knowledge. The latter point is made by Plato in the *Theaetetus* 200D–201C). It may be illustrated, for instance, by *The Case of the Optimistic Punter*. Because he is optimistic, he regularly *believes* that the horses he bets on will win. But he never has any reliable information about these horses. As a result, he normally loses. From time to time, however, his horses win. On such occasions his beliefs are true. But we do not think that he *knows* that these horses will win.

This is the occasion for introducing the Evidence-condition. The trouble about the punter, it is plausibly suggested, is that he lacks *good reasons* or *sufficient evidence* for his true belief. If only he had that, he would know.

However, when the Evidence-condition is scrutinized more closely, all sorts of problems emerge. In this section no less than five sub-conditions will be outlined which the Evidence-conditions must satisfy, if it is accepted at all. All these sub-conditions raise important problems.

Condition 1. Suppose that p is true, A believes that p and A has evidence for 'p', namely 'q'. It cannot be the case that A *knows* that p unless, as a matter of objective fact, 'q' constitutes *sufficient evidence* to establish the truth of 'p'. . . .

Condition 2. Suppose that 'p' is true, A believes that p, A has evidence 'q' for 'p', and 'q' is in fact sufficient evidence for the truth of 'p'. It may still be the case that A does not realize, or has not noticed, the relevance of his evidence 'q' to 'p'. He may, for instance, have failed to 'put two and two together'.

What is needed is that A's evidence should be actually operative in A's mind, supporting his belief that p. We must therefore have an account of what it is for somebody actually to *take* one proposition as a (conclusive) reason for accepting another. . . .

Condition 3. But even if 'p' is true, A believes that p, A has evidence 'q' for the truth of 'p', 'q' is in fact sufficient evidence for 'p', and the evidence actually operates in A's mind to support his belief that p, it still does not follow that A *knows* that p. For although 'q' in fact supports 'p' conclusively, might not A be reasoning from 'q' to 'p' according to some *false* principle which in this particular case moves from a truth to a truth? For instance, A's reasoning from 'q' to 'p' might involve a compensating error peculiar to the case in hand. It seems that we need to say that the principle of reasoning according to which A operates, when his belief that q operates in his mind to support his belief that p, is a *true* principle. This stipulation, by the way, makes Condition 1 redundant.

Condition 4. We now stipulate that 'p' is true, A believes that p, A has evidence 'q' for 'p', the evidence actually operates in A's mind to support his belief that p, and the principle of reasoning according to which A operates is a true principle. It still does not follow that A *knows* that p. For although the principle of A's reasoning is true, may it not be that A accepts this principle on thoroughly bad grounds? And could we then say that he knew that p? It seems that we ought to amend Condition 3 by saying that the principle of A's reasoning is not simply true, but is *known* by A to be true. But this raises this difficulty that our analysis of A knows that p now involves *knowledge* by A of at least one general principle. What account shall we give of *this* knowledge?

Condition 5. Let us waive this difficulty (for the present). Suppose 'p' is true, A believes that p, A has evidence 'q' for 'p', the evidence actually operates in A's mind to support his belief that p, and the principle of reasoning according to which A operates is known by A to be true. Even now it is not entailed that A knows p. For consider A's evidence 'q'. Do we not require the further stipulation that A *know* that q is true? Suppose it not to be the case that A knows that q (~Kaq). Is not 'p' insufficiently supported?

But if this is correct, then knowledge that p can be defined only in terms of *knowledge* that q. 'q' will then demand support in A's mind from evidence 'r', and an infinite regress threatens.

Although the apparent necessity for Condition 4 also introduces the threat of an infinite regress, historically it is the regress which results from the demand that the evidence be itself something which A knows which has especially troubled supporters of the classical 'good reasons' analysis of knowledge. . . .

II. The Infinite Regress of Reasons

Knowledge entails true belief, but true belief does not entail knowledge. It is therefore sug-

gested that knowledge is a true belief for which the believer has sufficient evidence, or some such formula. But the evidence will have to be some proposition, 'q', which is *known* to A. . . .

III. Different Reactions to the Regress

1. *The 'Sceptical' Reaction.* We may begin by distinguishing between 'sceptical' and 'non-sceptical' reactions to the regress. An extreme form of the sceptical reaction would be to say that the infinite regress showed that the concept of knowledge involves a contradiction. A moderate view would be that the word 'know', although it attributes true belief, attributes nothing further of an objective nature to the belief — no relation to the facts — except truth. . . .

2. *The regress is infinite but virtuous.* The first non-sceptical solution which may be canvassed is that the regress exists, but is virtuous. Suppose that event A has a prior cause B, B has a prior cause C, and so, perhaps, *ad infinitum*. Few modern philosophers would consider this latter progression to infinity a vicious one. So perhaps A's knowledge that p rests upon knowledge that q which rests upon knowledge that r, and so on without stop. . . .

It can hardly be pretended, however, that this reaction to the regress has much plausibility. Like the 'sceptical' solution, it is a *desperate* solution, to be considered only if all others are clearly seen to be unsatisfactory.

3. *The regress is finite, but has no end.* Suppose, then, that the regress is not virtuous. Then either the regress has no end, or it has an end. If it has no end, then at some point the reasons must come back upon their own tail, so that 'p' is supported by 'q', which is supported by 'r', which is supported by 's', . . . which is supported by . . . , which is supported by 'p'. This may seem to involve *vicious* circularity. But perhaps it need not. If we have a circle of true beliefs which mutually support each other in this way, then it might be suggested that, once the circle is sufficiently comprehensive and the mutual support sufficiently

strong, we would not have mere true beliefs but pieces of knowledge. This may be called the *Coherence* analysis of the concept of knowledge. . . .

Clearly, there are many difficulties for this 'Coherence theory of knowledge'. For instance, what criterion can be given to show that a circle of true beliefs is 'sufficiently comprehensive'? It is not easy to say. And might there not be a sufficiently comprehensive circle of true beliefs which was arrived at so irregularly and luckily that we would not want to call it knowledge?

4. *The regress ends in self-evident truths.* If the Coherence analysis is rejected, then at some point in the regress of reasons (perhaps right at the beginning) we will reach knowledge which is *not* based on reasons. I will call such knowledge 'non-inferential' knowledge. I oppose it to 'inferential' knowledge, which *is* based on reasons. Once it is granted that there is an objective notion of knowledge; that the infinite regress of reasons is in some way vicious; and that the regress cannot be stopped by judicious circularity; then it must be granted that, when A knows that p, then *either* this knowledge is non-inferential, or it is based on a finite set of reasons terminating in non-inferential knowledge.

The problem then comes to be that of giving an account of non-inferential knowledge. . . .

The classical answer is: non-inferential beliefs which are self-evident, indubitable or incorrigible. They will serve to stop the regress and act as the foundations of knowledge. This has been the *standard* solution from the time of Descartes until quite recently.

However, I reject the whole notion of beliefs that it is logically impossible to be wrong about. I think the logical possibility of error is always present in any belief about any subject matter whatsoever. In any case, it has been demonstrated again and again that, even if there is such self-evident knowledge, it is completely insufficient in *extent* to serve as a foundation for all the things we ordinarily claim to know, even when we have circumscribed that claim by careful reflection. In the past, defenders of this Cartesian solution have regularly had to cut down the scope of our supposed knowledge in a completely unacceptable manner. (For instance, it becomes difficult to claim that there is any empirical knowledge, non-inferential or inferential, beyond that of our own current states of mind.)

5. *'Initial credibility'.* The alternative is to attempt an account of non-inferential knowledge without appealing to such self-evident truths. O'Hair has distinguished two sorts of view here, which he calls 'Initial credibility' and 'Externalist' views.

First a word about 'Initial credibility' theories. It might be maintained that certain classes of our non-inferential beliefs have an intrinsic claim to credibility, even although error about them is a logical and even an empirical possibility. Instances might be beliefs based directly upon sense-perception, upon memory, upon intuition of the simpler logical necessities, or perhaps only upon suitable subclasses of these classes. Now suppose that a belief is non-inferential, is 'initially credible' and is also *true*. Might it not then be accounted a case of non-inferential *knowledge*?

This approach strikes me as more hopeful than the possible reactions to the infinite regress which have already been mentioned. But it involves certain difficulties. It is easy, for instance, to construct non-inferential memory beliefs which are true, but which we certainly would not call knowledge. Thus, a probe in my brain might produce the belief in me that I had an itch in my little finger three days ago. By sheer coincidence, the belief might be true. Or a veridical memory-trace might degenerate but, in the course of a multi-stage degeneration, the original encoding might be reinstated by a sheer fluke. Some way of excluding such cases would have to be found. I myself am convinced, although I will not try to demonstrate the point here, that the only way to achieve such exclusions satisfactorily is to pass over into an 'Externalist' theory.

6. *'Externalist' theories.* According to 'Externalist' accounts of non-inferential knowledge, what makes a true non-inferential belief a case of *knowledge* is some natural relation which holds between the belief-state, Bap, and the situation which makes the belief true. It is a matter of a certain relation holding between the believer and the world. It is important to notice that, unlike 'Cartesian' and 'Initial Credibility' theories, Externalist theories are regularly developed as theories of the nature of knowledge *generally* and not simply as theories of non-inferential knowledge. But they still have a peculiar importance in the case of non-inferential knowledge because they serve to solve the problem of the infinite regress.

Externalist theories may be further subdivided into 'Causal' and 'Reliability' theories.

6 (i) *Causal theories.* The central notion in causal theories may be illustrated by the simplest case. The suggestion is that Bap is a case of Kap if 'p' is true and, furthermore, the situation that makes 'p' true is causally responsible for the existence of the belief-state Bap. I not only believe, but *know*, that the room is rather hot. Now it is certainly *the excessive heat of the room* which has caused me to have this belief. This causal relation, it may then be suggested, is what makes my belief a case of knowledge. . . .

Causal theories face two main types of difficulty. In the first place, even if we restrict ourselves to knowledge of particular matters of fact, not every case of knowledge is a case where the situation known is causally responsible for the existence of the belief. For instance, we appear to have some knowledge of the future. And even if all such knowledge is in practice inferential, non-inferential knowledge of the future (for example, that I will be ill tomorrow) seems to be an intelligible possibility. Yet it could hardly be held that my illness tomorrow causes my belief today that I will be ill tomorrow. . . .

In the second place, and much more seriously, cases can be envisaged where the situation that makes 'p' true gives rise to Bap, but we would not

want to say that A *knew* that p. Suppose, for instance, that A is in a hypersensitive and deranged state, so that almost any considerable sensory stimulus causes him to believe that there is a sound of a certain sort in his immediate environment. Now suppose that, on a particular occasion, the considerable sensory stimulus which produces that belief is, in fact, *a sound of just that sort in his immediate environment.* Here the p-situation produces Bap, but we would not want to say that it was a case of knowledge.

I believe that such cases can be excluded only by filling out the Causal Analysis with a Reliability condition. But once this is done, I think it turns out that the Causal part of the analysis becomes redundant, and that the Reliability condition is sufficient by itself for giving an account of non-inferential (and inferential) knowledge.

6 (ii) *Reliability theories.* The second 'Externalist' approach is in terms of the *empirical reliability* of the belief involved. Knowledge is empirically reliable belief . . . [e.g., "the Thermometer View," below].

It is interesting to notice that a Reliability analysis is considered for a moment by Plato in the *Meno* only to be dropped immediately. At 97b Socrates asserts that '. . . true opinion is as good a guide as knowledge for the purpose of acting rightly', and goes on to ask whether we should not draw the conclusion that 'right opinion is something no less useful than knowledge.' Meno however objects:

> Except that the man with knowledge will always be successful, and the man with only right opinion only sometimes.

Unfortunately, however, Socrates brushes aside this tentative development of a Reliability view, saying:

> What? Will he not always be successful so long as he has the right opinion?

Meno immediately concedes the point.

Reactions to Plato's Regress

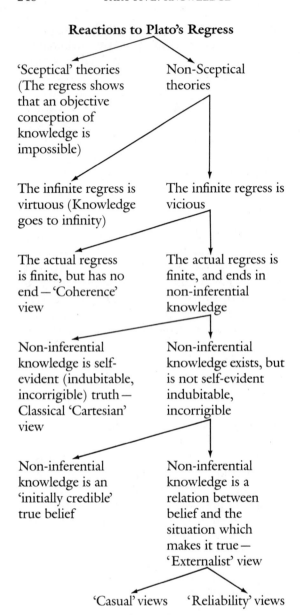

'Sceptical' theories (The regress shows that an objective conception of knowledge is impossible)

Non-Sceptical theories

The infinite regress is virtuous (Knowledge goes to infinity)

The infinite regress is vicious

The actual regress is finite, but has no end — 'Coherence' view

The actual regress is finite, and ends in non-inferential knowledge

Non-inferential knowledge is self-evident (indubitable, incorrigible) truth — Classical 'Cartesian' view

Non-inferential knowledge exists, but is not self-evident indubitable, incorrigible

Non-inferential knowledge is an 'initially credible' true belief

Non-inferential knowledge is a relation between belief and the situation which makes it true — 'Externalist' view

'Casual' views   'Reliability' views

This concludes our brief survey. In philosophy, when one finds oneself in a difficult intellectual situation, it is often vitally important to be aware of the full range of response which is open to one. And in philosophy, if one practises it honestly, one invariably is in a more or less difficult intellectual situation. The survey just made was intended to create an awareness of the many different responses open to us in the difficult situation created by the threatened infinite regress involved in the classical analysis of knowledge. Against this background, I proceed to put forward a suggested solution of the problem.

From Non-Inferential Knowledge

. . . Thinking about the threatened infinite regress in the classical analysis of knowledge seems to lead to the conclusion that there must be non-inferential knowledge. Furthermore, we seem *forced* in the case of this sort of knowledge to look for some non-classical solution to the problem. (The classical or 'Cartesian' postulation of self-evident truths can rather easily be shown to be an insufficient account of the basis of all that we think we know.) If we can find a non-classical solution to the problem of non-inferential knowledge, where such a solution is clearly required, we may then try to extend the solution to cover all cases of knowledge. . . .

THE 'THERMOMETER' VIEW OF NON-INFERENTIAL KNOWLEDGE

Suppose that 'p' is true, and A believes that p, but his belief is not supported by any reasons. 'p' might be the proposition that there is a sound in A's environment. . . . What makes such a belief a case of knowledge? My suggestion is that there must be a *law-like connection* between the state of affairs Bap and the state of affairs that makes 'p' true such that, given Bap, it must be the case that p.

The quickest way to grasp the suggestion is to use a model. Let us compare non-inferential beliefs to the temperature-readings given by a thermometer. In some cases, the thermometer-reading will fail to correspond to the temperature of the environment. Such a reading may be compared to non-inferential false belief. In other cases, the reading will correspond to the actual temperature. Such a reading is like non-inferential true belief. The second case, where reading and actual environmental temperature coincide, is then sub-divided into two sorts of case. First, suppose that the thermometer is a bad one, but that, on a certain occasion, the thermometer-reading coincides with the actual temperature. (*Cf.* the stopped clock that shows the right time twice a day.) Such a reading is to be compared with non-inferential true belief which falls short of knowledge. Suppose finally that the thermometer is a good one, so that a reading of 'T°' on the thermometer ensures that the environmental temperature is T°. Such a reading is to be compared with non-inferential *knowledge*. When a true belief unsupported by reasons stands to the situation truly believed to exist as a thermometer-reading in a good thermometer stands to the actual temperature, then we have non-inferential knowledge.

I think the picture given by the thermometer-model is intuitively clear. The problem is to give a formal account of the situation. . . .

The model of the thermometer gives us further assistance here. For a thermometer to be reliable on a certain occasion in registering a certain temperature as T° we do not demand that there be a true law-like generalization: 'If any thermometer registers "T°", then the temperature is T°.' In the first place, we recognize that there can be good and bad thermometers. In the second place, we do not even demand that a good thermometer provide a reliable reading under every condition. We recognize that there may be special environmental conditions under which even a 'good' thermometer is unreliable.

What do we demand? Let us investigate a far less stringent condition. Suppose, on a certain occasion, a thermometer is reliably registering 'T°'. There must be some property of the instrument and/or its circumstances such that, if any thing has this property, and registers 'T°', it must be the case, as a matter of natural law, that the temperature *is* T°. We might find it extremely hard to specify this property (set of properties). The specification might have to be given in the form of a blank cheque to be filled in only after extensive investigation. But it may be relatively easy to recognize that a certain thermometer is operating reliably, and so that such a specification is possible. . . .

Further Questions

1. Russell advocates a foundations account of knowledge, Harman a coherence account, Armstrong an externalist (reliability) account. Clearly explain the essential differences among these three types of accounts. Which seems most plausible to you, and why?

2. "If knowledge is justified, true belief, then there must be some things we know directly (not on the basis of anything else we know, but rather on their own basis — that is, these things must be self-justifying) or else we are led into a regress the result of which is that our so-called knowledge is without foundations — hence not really knowledge at all." First, give the best argument you can that the quoted remarks are true. Second, what is the significance of the remarks? Third, explain how the threatened, unsettling "regress" can best be stopped.

Further Readings

Morton, Adam. *A Guide Through the Theory of Knowledge.* Belmont, CA: Wadsworth, 1977. A useful beginning text.

Pollock, John. *Knowledge and Justification.* Totowa, NJ: Rowman and Littlefield, 1986. Sophisticated, but readable.

Part VI

God

DOES GOD EXIST?

On this topic, *everybody* has a belief. What's *yours*?

Yes? No? Maybe?

Having beliefs is easy. Understanding how you came to have them and then questioning your beliefs with an open mind is extremely difficult.

Whatever your belief about God, you are not likely to change it on the basis of anything you read. On other topics, reading and discussing opposing views often leads people to change their minds. But on the topic of God, people usually are not openly searching for the truth but merely defending their beliefs. It is a bit like watching a football game: no matter which team is better, you root for your side.

Which side are *you* on? In the readings that follow, if you merely seek support for your belief, then—whatever you believe—for you the question is closed.

The Ontological Argument

ANSELM AND GAUNILO

St. Anselm (1033–1109), a Benedictine monk, was Abbot of Bec, at the time one of the great centers of learning in Europe; he later became Archbishop of Canterbury. In his book, *Monologion*, he advances the proof for God from the degrees of perfection found in creatures and also formulates a version of the cosmological argument (for later versions of these arguments, see the selection by Aquinas). He makes the point that the meaning of "nothing" is "not anything," stressing that "nothing" should not be regarded as the name of a shadowy, mysterious entity. His book, *Proslogion*, contains the famous ontological argument reprinted below; also reprinted below is the monk Guanilo's criticism of the argument and Anselm's reply.

Reading Questions

1. List all the premises, or assumptions, on which the ontological argument depends. What is the argument's conclusion?
2. Explain, in your own words, the point of Guanilo's "lost island" objection.
3. How does Anselm respond to Guanilo's objection? Do you find his response adequate?

. . . I BEGAN TO ASK MYSELF whether there might be found a single argument which would require no other for its proof than itself alone; and alone would suffice to demonstrate that God truly exists, and that there is a supreme good requiring nothing else, which all other things require for their existence and well-being; and whatever we believe regarding the divine Being.

Although I often and earnestly directed my thought to this end, and at some times that which I sought seemed to be just within my reach, while again it wholly evaded my mental vision, at last in despair I was about to cease, as if from the search for a thing which could not be found. But when I wished to exclude this thought altogether, lest, by busying my mind to no purpose, it should keep me from other thoughts, in which I might be successful; then more and more, though I was unwilling and shunned it, it began to force itself upon me, with a kind of importunity. So, one day, when I was exceedingly wearied with resisting its importunity, in the very conflict of my thoughts, the proof of which I had despaired offered itself, so that I eagerly embraced the thoughts which I was strenuously repelling. . . .

And so Lord, do thou, who dost give understanding to faith, give me, so far as thou knowest it to be profitable, to understand that thou art as we believe; and that thou art that which we believe. And, indeed, we believe that thou art a being than which nothing greater can be conceived. Or is there no such nature, since the fool hath said in his heart, there is no God? But, at any rate, this very fool, when he hears of this being of which I speak — a being than which nothing greater can be conceived — understands what he hears, and what he understands is in his understanding; although he does not understand it to exist.

For, it is one thing for an object to be in the understanding, and another to understand that the object exists. When a painter first conceives of

what he will afterwards perform, he has it in his understanding, but he does not yet understand it to be, because he has not yet performed it. But after he has made the painting, he both has it in his understanding, and he understands that it exists, because he has made it.

Hence, even the fool is convinced that something exists in the understanding, at least, than which nothing greater can be conceived. For, when he hears of this, he understands it. And whatever is understood, exists in the understanding. And assuredly that, than which nothing greater can be conceived, cannot exist in the understanding alone. For, suppose it exists in the understanding alone: then it can be conceived to exist in reality; which is greater.

Therefore, if that, than which nothing greater can be conceived, exists in the understanding alone, the very being, than which nothing greater can be conceived, is one, than which a greater can be conceived. But obviously this is impossible. Hence, there is no doubt that there exists a being, than which nothing greater can be conceived, and it exists both in the understanding and in reality. . . .

And it assuredly exists so truly, that it cannot be conceived not to exist. For, it is possible to conceive of a being which cannot be conceived not to exist, and this is greater than one which can be conceived not to exist. Hence, if that, than which nothing greater can be conceived, can be conceived not to exist, it is not that, than which nothing greater can be conceived. But this is an irreconcilable contradiction. There is, then, so truly a being than which nothing greater can be conceived to exist, that it cannot even be conceived not to exist; and this being thou art, O Lord, our God.

So truly, therefore, dost thou exist, O Lord, my God, that thou canst not be conceived not to exist; and rightly. For if a mind could conceive of a being better than thee, the creature would rise

From the Proslogium, *translated by Sidney Norton Deane (Open Court, 1903), pp. 1–2, 6–9, 149–51, 158–59.*

above the Creator; and this is most absurd. And, indeed, whatever else there is, except thee alone, can be conceived not to exist. To thee alone, therefore, it belongs to exist more truly than all other beings, and hence in a higher degree than all others. For, whatever else exists does not exist so truly, and hence in a less degree it belongs to it to exist. Why, then, has the fool said in his heart, there is no God, since it is so evident, to a rational mind, that thou dost exist in the highest degree of all? Why, except that he is dull and a fool? . . .

In Behalf of the Fool

AN ANSWER TO THE ARGUMENT OF ANSELM BY GAUNILON, A MONK OF MARMOUTIER

. . . if it should be said that a being which cannot be even conceived in terms of any fact, is in the understanding. I do not deny that this being is, accordingly, in my understanding. But since through this fact it can in no wise attain to real existence also, I do not yet concede to it that existence at all, until some certain proof of it shall be given.

For he who says that this being exists, because otherwise the being which is greater than all will not be greater than all, does not attend strictly to what he is saying. For I do not yet say, no, I even deny or doubt that this being is greater than any real object. Nor do I concede to it any other existence than this (if it should be called existence) which it has when the mind, according to a word merely heard, tries to form the image of an object absolutely unknown to it.

How, then, is the veritable existence of that being proved to me from the assumption, by hypothesis, that it is greater than all other beings? For I should still deny this, or doubt your demonstration of it, to this extent, that I should not admit that this being is in my understanding and concept even in the way in which many objects whose real existence is uncertain and doubtful, are in my understanding and concept. For it should be proved first that this being itself really exists somewhere; and then, from the fact that it is greater than all, we shall not hesitate to infer that it also subsists in itself.

For example: it is said that somewhere in the ocean is an island, which, because of the difficulty, or rather the impossibility, of discovering what does not exist, is called the lost island. And they say that this island has an inestimable wealth of all manner of riches and delicacies in greater abundance than is told of the Islands of the Blest; and that having no owner or inhabitant, it is more excellent than all other countries, which are inhabited by mankind, in the abundance with which it is stored.

Now if someone should tell me that there is such an island, I should easily understand his words, in which there is no difficulty. But suppose that he went on to say, as if by a logical inference: "You can no longer doubt that this island which is more excellent than all lands exists somewhere, since you have no doubt that it is in your understanding. And since it is more excellent not to be in the understanding alone, but to exist both in the understanding and in reality, for this reason it must exist. For if it does not exist, any land which really exists will be more excellent than it; and so the island already understood by you to be more excellent will not be more excellent."

If a man should try to prove to me by such reasoning that this island truly exists, and that its existence should no longer be doubted, either I should believe that he was jesting, or I know not which I ought to regard as the greater fool: myself, supposing that I should allow this proof; or him, if he should suppose that he had established with any certainty the existence of this island. For he ought to show first that the hypothetical excellence of this island exists as a real and indubitable fact, and in no wise as any unreal object, or one whose existence is uncertain, in my understanding.

Anselm's Reply

But, you say, it is as if one should suppose an island in the ocean, which surpasses all lands in its fertility, and which, because of the difficulty, or rather the impossibility, of discovering what does not exist, is called a lost island; and should say that there can be no doubt that this island truly exists in reality, for this reason, that one who hears it described easily understands what he hears.

Now I promise confidently that if any man shall devise anything existing either in reality or in concept alone (except that than which a greater cannot be conceived) to which he can adapt the sequence of my reasoning, I will discover that thing, and will give him his lost island, not to be lost again.

But it now appears that this being than which a greater is inconceivable cannot be conceived not to be, because it exists on so assured a ground of truth; for otherwise it would not exist at all.

Hence, if any one says that he conceives this being not to exist, I say that at the time when he conceives of this either he conceives of a being than which a greater is inconceivable, or he does not conceive at all. If he does not conceive, he does not conceive of the nonexistence of that of which he does not conceive. But if he does conceive, he certainly conceives of a being which cannot be even conceived not to exist. For if it could be conceived not to exist, it could be conceived to have a beginning and an end. But this is impossible.

He, then, who conceives of this being conceives of a being which cannot be even conceived not to exist; but he who conceives of this being does not conceive that it does not exist; else he conceives what is inconceivable. The nonexistence, then, of that than which a greater cannot be conceived is inconceivable.

Further Questions

1. Imagine you are Guanilo and that you have an opportunity to respond again to Anselm. What would you say?

2. Immanuel Kant, in *Critique of Pure Reason* (1781), claimed the ontological argument is unsound since existence is not a perfection: "If we think in a thing every feature of reality except one, the missing reality is not added by my saying that the defective thing exists. . . . since otherwise what exists would be something different from what I thought. When, therefore, I think a being as the supreme reality, without any defect, the question still remains whether it exists or not." Explain, in your own words, whether you agree with Kant, and why.

3. In "An Ontological Argument for the Devil," *The Monist* (1970), David and Marjorie Haight argue that if the ontological argument is sound, then an analogous argument from the premise that we can have a concept of "something than which nothing *worse* can be conceived" to the conclusion that this awful thing ("the Devil"), therefore, exists would also be sound; for if the awful thing did not exist we could think of something still more awful, namely, the awful thing's actually existing. Do you agree that this argument is as good (or as bad) as the ontological argument?

Further Readings

Barnes, Jonathan. *The Ontological Argument*. London: Macmillan, 1972. A good general discussion.

Plantinga, Alvin, ed. *The Ontological Argument from St. Anselm to Contemporary Philosophers*. Garden City, N.Y.: Doubleday, 1965. Just what the title implies.

The Five Ways

THOMAS AQUINAS

Thomas Aquinas (1225–1274) was born of Italian nobility and began his education in Naples. After becoming a Dominican monk, he went to Cologne to study under Albertus Magnus, the leading Aristotelian philosopher of the time, then went to Paris and taught theology. Aquinas returned to Italy in 1259 and remained there for most of the rest of his life. He is generally regarded as the greatest scholastic philosopher. Catholics consider him the greatest Christian theologian. His two major works are *Summa Theologica* and *Summa Contra Gentiles*.

Aquinas's famous "Five Ways" of proving the existence of God is the best-known passage from his works. The first way (of the five ways) infers from the fact of change the existence of an Unmoved Mover that originates change. The second uses the fact that some things are caused to infer the existence of a First Cause. The third infers from the fact that some things are contingent, or capable of coming into and going out of existence, the existence of something which is necessary, or incapable of coming into and going out of existence. The fourth uses the fact that there are degrees of excellence to infer the existence of a perfect being. The fifth uses the alleged fact that natural objects behave purposefully to infer the existence of an intelligence that directs the activities of natural objects.

Reading Questions

1. Explain in your own words Aquinas's arguments. Can you think of any ways in which they might be criticized effectively? Can you think of any reasons why the second and third arguments are generally regarded as the most interesting ones?

2. Aquinas wrote before the advent of modern science. Does it still make sense today to try to prove the existence of God by appeal to the nature of the world?

3. Must everything have a cause? Are there some things which just *are*, i.e., are not caused by anything else?

THE EXISTENCE OF GOD can be proved in five ways.

The first and more manifest way is the argument from motion. It is certain, and evident to our senses, that in the world some things are in motion. Now whatever is moved is moved by another, for nothing can be moved except it is in potentiality to that towards which it is moved; whereas a thing moves inasmuch as it is in act. For motion is nothing else than the reduction of

From The Basic Writings of Saint Thomas Aquinas, *ed. Anton C. Pegis (New York: Random House: London: Burns & Oates, 1945), pp. 22–23. Copyright © 1945 Random House, Inc. Reprinted by permission of Richard Pegis.*

something from potentiality to actuality. But nothing can be reduced from potentiality to actuality, except by something in a state of actuality. Thus that which is actually hot, as fire, makes wood, which is potentially hot, to be actually hot, and thereby moves and changes it. Now it is not possible that the same thing should be at once in actuality and potentiality in the same respect, but only in different respects. For what is actually hot cannot simultaneously be potentially hot; but it is simultaneously potentially cold. It is therefore impossible that in the same respect and in the same way a thing should be both mover and moved, *i.e.*, that it should move itself. Therefore, whatever is moved must be moved by another. If that by which it is moved be itself moved, then this also must needs be moved by another, and that by another again. But this cannot go on to infinity, because then there would be no first mover, and consequently no other mover, seeing that subsequent movers move only inasmuch as they are moved by the first mover; as the staff moves only because it is moved by the hand. Therefore it is necessary to arrive at a first mover, moved by no other; and this everyone understands to be God.

The second way is from the nature of efficient cause. In the world of sensible things we find there is an order of efficient causes. There is no case known (neither is it, indeed, possible) in which a thing is found to be the efficient cause of itself; for so it would be prior to itself, which is impossible. Now in efficient causes it is not possible to go on to infinity, because in all efficient causes following in order, the first is the cause of the intermediate cause, and the intermediate is the cause of the ultimate cause, whether the intermediate cause be several, or one only. Now to take away the cause is to take away the effect. Therefore, if there be no first cause among efficient causes, there will be no ultimate, nor any intermediate, cause. But if in efficient causes it is possible to go on to infinity, there will be no first efficient cause, neither will there be an ultimate effect, nor any intermediate efficient causes; all of which is plainly false. Therefore it is necessary to admit a first efficient cause, to which everyone gives the name of God.

The third way is taken from possibility and necessity, and runs thus. We find in nature things that are possible to be and not to be, since they are found to be generated, and to be corrupted, and consequently, it is possible for them to be and not to be. But it is impossible for these always to exist, for that which can not-be at some time is not. Therefore, if everything can not-be, then at one time there was nothing in existence. Now if this were true, even now there would be nothing in existence, because that which does not exist begins to exist only through something already existing. Therefore, if at one time nothing was in existence, it would have been impossible for anything to have begun to exist; and thus even now nothing would be in existence — which is absurd. Therefore, not all beings are merely possible, but there must exist something the existence of which is necessary. But every necessary thing either has its necessity caused by another, or not. Now it is impossible to go on to infinity in necessary things which have their necessity caused by another, as has been already proved in regard to efficient causes. Therefore we cannot but admit the existence of some being having of itself its own necessity, and not receiving it from another, but rather causing in others their necessity. This all men speak of as God.

The fourth way is taken from the gradation to be found in things. Among beings there are some more and some less good, true, noble, and the like. But *more* and *less* are predicated of different things according as they resemble in their different ways something which is the maximum, as a thing is said to be hotter according as it more nearly resembles that which is hottest; so that there is something which is truest, something best, something noblest, and, consequently, something which is most being, for those things that are greatest in truth are greatest in being, ... Now the maximum in any genus is the cause of all in that genus, as fire, which is the maximum of heat, is the cause of all hot things, as is said in the same book. Therefore there must also be something which is to all beings the cause of their being, goodness, and every other perfection; and this we call God.

The fifth way is taken from the governance of the world. We see that things which lack knowledge, such as natural bodies, act for an end, and this is evident from their acting always, or nearly always, in the same way, so as to obtain the best result. Hence it is plain that they achieve their end, not fortuitiously, but designedly. Now whatever lacks knowledge cannot move towards an end, unless it be directed by some being endowed with knowledge and intelligence; as the arrow is directed by the archer. Therefore some intelligent being exists by whom all natural things are directed to their end; and this being we call God.

Further Questions

1. Imagine that Aquinas were alive today and had access to the kind of scientific information provided by Paul Davies's essay, "The Creation: Is the Universe a Free Lunch?" Would (should) Aquinas change any of his views?

2. Are there questions, such as "Why is there something rather than nothing at all?" that science cannot now answer and never will be able to answer? If there are, can religion answer these questions and justify its answers, or are the questions simply unanswerable?

Further Readings

Kenny, Anthony. *Five Ways: Saint Thomas Aquinas's Proofs of God's Existence.* Boston: Routledge & Kegan Paul, 1969. A thorough, skillful commentary.

Mackie, J. L. *The Miracle of Theism.* Oxford: Oxford University Press, 1982. Arguments for and against the existence of God by a distinguished English philosopher.

The Wager

BLAISE PASCAL

The French thinker Blaise Pascal (1623–1662), famous today primarily as a mathematician, was also a theologian, scientist, philosopher, and inventor. As a mathematician, Pascal made major contributions to probability theory, number theory, and geometry. In this selection he argues that it is in your rational self-interest to believe that God exists.

Reading Questions

1. Is Pascal right that we *must* wager on whether God exists? Why can't we simply suspend judgment?

2. Pascal thinks it is better to bet that God exists than to bet that God does not exist. Why?

3. What is the connection between wagering and believing? Can you *choose* what to believe?

4. Can we know that God exists?

5. Is it reasonable to believe that God exists even if our belief is uncertain?

6. On what can faith in the existence of God be based?

. . . WE KNOW NEITHER THE EXISTENCE nor the nature of God, because He has neither extension nor limits.

But by faith we know His existence; in glory we shall know His nature. Now, I have already shown that we may well know the existence of a thing, without knowing its nature.

Let us now speak according to natural lights.

If there is a God, He is infinitely incomprehensible, since, having neither parts nor limits, He has no affinity to us. We are then incapable of knowing either what He is or if He is. This being so, who will dare to undertake the decision of the question? Not we, who have no affinity to Him.

Who then will blame Christians for not being able to give a reason for their belief, since they profess a religion for which they cannot give a reason? They declare, in expounding it to the world, that it is a foolishness, *stultitiam*; and then you complain that they do not prove it! If they proved it, they would not keep their words; it is in lacking proofs, that they are not lacking in sense. "Yes, but although this excuses those who offer it as such, and take away from them the blame of putting it forward without reason, it does not excuse those who receive it." Let us then examine this point, and say, "God is, or He is not." But to which side shall we incline? Reason can decide nothing here. There is an infinite chaos which separates us. A game is being played at the extremity of this infinite distance where heads or tails will turn up. What will you wager?

According to reason, you can do neither the one thing nor the other; according to reason, you can defend neither of the propositions.

Do not then reprove for error those who have made a choice; for you know nothing about it. "No, but I blame them for having made, not this choice, but a choice; for again both he who chooses heads and he who chooses tails are equally at fault, they are both in the wrong. The true course is not to wager at all."

— Yes; but you must wager. It is not optional. You are embarked. Which will you choose then; Let us see. Since you must choose, let us see which interests you least. You have two things to lose, the true and the good; and two things to stake, your reason and your will, your knowledge and your happiness; and your nature has two things to shun, error and misery. Your reason is no more shocked in choosing one rather than the other, since you must of necessity choose. This is one point settled. But your happiness? Let us weigh the gain and the loss in wagering that God is. Let us estimate these two chances. If you gain, you gain all; if you lose, you lose nothing. Wager them without hesitation that He is. — "That is very fine. Yes, I must wager; but I may perhaps wager too much." — Let us see. Since there is an equal risk of gain and of loss, if you had only to gain two lives, instead of one, you might still wager. But if there were three lives to gain, you would have to play (since you are under the necessity of playing), and you would be imprudent,

From Blaise Pascal, Thoughts, *trans. W. F. Trotter (New York: P. F. Collier & Son, 1910).*

when you are forced to play, not to chance your life to gain three at a game where there is an equal risk of loss and gain. But there is an eternity of life and happiness. And this being so, if there were an infinity of chances, of which one only would be for you, you would still be right in wagering one to win two, and you would act stupidly, being obliged to play, by refusing to stake one life against three at a game in which out of an infinity of chances there is one for you, if there were an infinity of an infinitely happy life to gain. But there is here an infinity of an infinitely happy life to gain, a chance of gain against a finite number of chances of loss, and what you stake is finite. It is all divided; wherever the infinite is and there is not an infinity of chances of loss against that of gain, there is no time to hesitate, you must give all. And thus, when one is forced to play, he must renounce reason to preserve his life, rather than risk it for infinite gain, as likely to happen as the loss of nothingness.

For it is no use to say it is uncertain if we will gain, and it is certain that we risk, and that the infinite distance between the *certainty* of what is staked and the *uncertainty* of what will be gained, equals the finite good which is certainly staked against the uncertain infinite. It is not so, as every player stakes a certainty to gain an uncertainty, and yet he stakes a finite certainty to gain a finite uncertainty, without transgressing against reason. There is not an infinite distance between the certainty staked and the uncertainty of the gain; that is untrue. In truth, there is an infinity between the certainty of gain and the certainty of loss. But the uncertainty of the gain is proportioned to the certainty of the stake according to the proportion of the chances of gain and loss.

Hence it comes that, if there are as many risks on one side as on the other, the course is to play even; and then the certainty of the stake is equal to the uncertainty of the gain, so far is it from the fact that there is an infinite distance between them. And so our proposition is of infinite force, when there is the finite to stake in a game where there are equal risks of gain and of loss, and the infinite to gain. This is demonstrable; and if men are capable of any truths, this is one.

"I confess it, I admit it. But still is there no means of seeing the faces of the cards?" — Yes, Scripture and the rest, &c. — "Yes, but I have my hands tied and my mouth closed; I am forced to wager, and am not free. I am not released, and am so made that I cannot believe. What then would you have me do?"

"True. But at least learn your inability to believe, since reason brings you to this, and yet you cannot believe. Endeavour then to convince yourself, not by increase of proofs of God, but by the abatement of your passions. You would like to attain faith, and do not know the way; you would like to cure yourself of unbelief, and ask the remedy for it. Learn of those who have been bound like you, and who now stake all their possessions. These are people who know the way which you would follow, and who are cured of an ill of which you would be cured. Follow the way by which they began; by acting as if they believe, taking the holy water, having masses said, &c. Even this will naturally make you believe, and deaden your acuteness. — "But this is what I am afraid of." — And why? What have you to lose?

But to show you that this leads you there, it is this which will lessen the passions, which are your stumbling-blocks.

Further Questions

1. Even if Pascal is right that it is better to bet that God exists than to bet that God does not exist, what has this to do with whether God actually exists?

2. Isn't it possible there is a God who is offended by people who believe in God for selfish reasons? Has Pascal taken this possibility into account?

3. Suppose the God of one religion demands an annual human sacrifice, while the God of another religion forbids human sacrifice. Would Pascal's argument require you to both sacrifice and not sacrifice humans?

Further Readings

Krailsheimer, A. *Pascal.* Oxford: Oxford University Press, 1980. A readable, short
  introduction to Pascal's thought.
Stich, Steven. "The Recombinant DNA Debate," *Philosophy and Public Affairs*, vol 7, 1978.
  Includes an interesting discussion of Pascal's wager and "doomsday scenario arguments."
Swinburne, R. *Faith and Reason.* Oxford: Clarendon Press, 1981, pp. 88–99. A discussion of
  Pascal's wager by one of the foremost contemporary philosophical apologists for
  Christianity.

On Man's Incoherent Idea of an Imaginary God

BARON HOLBACH

In this selection from his *System of Nature* (1770), Baron Holbach argues that the main idea of God passed down to us in Christian theology doesn't make any sense.
  A brief biography of Holbach appears on p. 150.

Reading Questions

1. Holbach thinks there is a tension between the disinclination to understand God in terms of any natural human qualities and the inclination to attribute moral qualities to God. Why? Do you agree this is a problem?
2. Holbach thinks that the God of the theologians is either "a tyrant or a demon." Why? Do you agree?

1. Man's Incoherent Idea of an Imaginary God

GOD: A METAPHYSICAL PHANTOM

MAN ALWAYS ENTERTAINS THE IDEA, that what he is not in a condition to conceive, is much more noble, much more respectable, than that which he has the capacity to comprehend: he imagines that his God, like tyrants, does not wish to be examined too closely.

These prejudices in man for the marvelous, appear to have been the source that gave birth to those wonderful, unintelligible qualities with

From The System of Nature *(1770), H. D. Robinson, trans., Vol. II, Chs. 2, 8.*

which theology clothed the sovereign of the world. The invincible ignorance of the human mind, whose fears reduced him to despair, engendered those obscure, vague notions, with which he decorated his God. He believed he could never displease him, provided he rendered him incommensurable, impossible to be compared with any thing of which he had a knowledge; either with that which was most sublime, or that which possessed the greatest magnitude. From hence came the multitude of negative attributes with which ingenious dreamers have successively embellished their phantom God, to the end that they might more surely form a being distinguished from all others, or which possessed nothing in common with that which the human mind had the faculty of being acquainted with.

The theological metaphysical attributes, were in fact nothing but pure negations of the qualities found in man, or in those beings of which he has a knowledge. By these attributes their God was supposed exempted from every thing which they considered weakness or imperfection in him, or in the beings by whom he is surrounded. To say that God is infinite, as has been shown, is only to affirm, that unlike man, or the beings with whom he is acquainted, he is not circumscribed by the limits of space; this however, is what man can never in any manner comprehend, because he is himself finite.[1]

When it is said that God is eternal, it signifies he has not had, like man or like every thing that exists, a beginning, and that he will never have an end; to say he is immutable, is to say that unlike man or every thing which he sees, God is not subject to change: to say he is immaterial, is to advance, that his substance or essence is of a nature not conceivable by a man, but which must from that very circumstance be totally different from every thing of which he has cognizance.

It is from the confused collection of these negative qualities, that has resulted the theological God; the metaphysical whole of which it is impossible for man to form to himself any correct idea. In this abstract being every thing is infin-

ity — immensity — spirituality — omniscience — order — wisdom — intelligence — omnipotence. In combining these vague terms, or these modifications, the priests believed they formed something; they extended these qualities by thought, and they imagined they made a God, whilst they only composed a chimera. They imagined that these perfections or these qualities must be suitable to this God, because they were not suitable to any thing of which they had a knowledge; they believed that an incomprehensible being must have inconceivable qualities. These were the materials of which theology availed itself to compose the inexplicable phantom before which they commanded the human race to bend the knee.

Nevertheless, a being so vague, so impossible to be conceived, so incapable of definition, so far removed from every thing of which man could have any knowledge, was but little calculated to fix his restless views; his mind requires to be arrested by qualities which he is capacitated to ascertain — of which he is in a condition to form a judgment. Thus after it had subtilized this metaphysical God, after it had rendered him so different in idea, from every thing that acts upon the senses, theology found itself under the necessity of again assimilating him to man, from whom it had so far removed him: it therefore again made him human by the moral qualities which is assigned him; it felt that without this it would not be able to persuade mankind there could possibly exist any relation between him and the vague, ethereal, fugitive, incommensurable being they are called upon to adore. They perceived that this marvellous God was only calculated to exercise the imagination of some few thinkers, whose minds were accustomed to labor upon chimerical subjects, or to take words for realities; in short it found, that for the greater number of the material children of the earth it was necessary to have a God more analogous to themselves, more sensible, more known to them.

In consequence the Divinity was reclothed with human qualities. Theology never felt the incompatibility of these qualities with a being it had made essentially different from man, who consequently could neither have his properties, nor be modified like himself. It did not see that a God who was immaterial, destitute of corporeal organs, was neither able to think nor to act as material beings, whose peculiar organizations render them susceptible of the qualities, the feelings, the will, the virtues, that are found in them. The necessity it felt to assimilate God to his worshippers, to make an affinity between them, made it pass over without consideration these palpable contradictions, and thus theology obstinately continued to unite those incompatible qualities, that discrepance of character, which the human mind attempted in vain either to conceive or to reconcile. According to it, a pure spirit was the mover of the material world; an immense being was enabled to occupy space, without however excluding nature; an immutable deity was the cause of those continual changes operated in the world: an omnipotent being did not prevent those evils which were displeasing to him; the source of order submitted to confusion: in short, the wonderful properties of this theological being every moment contradicted themselves.

THE "JUST" GOD

In order to justify this God from the evils that the human species experiences, the theist is reduced to the necessity of calling them punishments inflicted by a *just* God for the transgressions of man. If so, man has the power to make his God suffer. To offend presupposes relations between the one who offends and another who is offended; but what relations can exist between the infinite being who has created the world and feeble mortals? To offend any one is to diminish the sum of his happiness; it is to afflict him, to deprive him of something, to make him experience a painful sensation. How is it possible man can operate on the well-being of the omnipotent sovereign of nature, whose happiness is unalterable? How can the physical actions of a material substance have any influence over an immaterial substance, devoid of parts, having no point of contact? How can a corporeal being make an incorporeal being experience incommodious sensations? On the other hand, *justice*, according to the only ideas man can ever form of it, supposes a permanent disposition to render to each what is due to him; the theologian will not admit that God owes any thing to man; he insists that the benefits he bestows are all the gratuitous effects of his own goodness; that he has the right to dispose of the work of his hands according to his own pleasure; to plunge it if he please into the abyss of misery. But it is easy to see, that according to man's idea of justice, this does not even contain the shadow of it; that it is, in fact, the mode of action adopted by what he calls the most frightful tyrants. How then can he be induced to call God just who acts after this manner? Indeed, while he sees innocence suffering, virtue in tears, crime triumphant, vice recompensed, and at the same time is told the being whom theology has invented is the author, he will never be able to acknowledge them to have *justice*.[2] But, says the theist, these evils are transient; they will only last for a time: very well, but then your God is unjust, at least for a time. It is for their good that he chastises his friends. But if he is good, how can he consent to let them suffer even for a time? If he knows every thing why reprove his favorites from whom he has nothing to fear? If he is really omnipotent, why not spare them these transitory pains, and procure them at once a durable and permanent felicity? If his power cannot be shaken, why make himself uneasy at the vain conspiracies they would form against him? . . .

They will, however, reply to these difficulties, that goodness, wisdom, and justice, are, in God, qualities so eminent, or have such little similarity to ours, that they have no relation with these qualities when found in men. But I shall answer, how shall I form to myself ideas of these divine perfections, if they bear no resemblance to those of the virtues which I find in my fellow-creatures, or to the dispositions which I feel in myself? If the justice of God is not that of men; if it operates in that mode which men call injustice, if his goodness, his clemency, and his wisdom do not manifest themselves by such signs that we are able to recognize them; if all his divine qualities are contrary to received ideas; if in theology all the human actions are obscured or overthrown, how can mortals like myself pretend to announce them, to have a knowledge of them, or to explain them to others? Can theology give to the mind the ineffable boon of conceiving that which no man is in a capacity to comprehend? Can it procure to its agents the marvelous faculty of having precise ideas of a God composed of so many contradictory qualities? In short, is the theologian himself a God?

They silence us by saying, that God himself has spoken, that he has made himself known to men. But when, where, and to whom has he spoken? Where are these divine oracles? A hundred voices raise themselves in the same moment, a hundred hands show them to me in absurd and discordant collections: I run them over, and through the whole I find that the *God of wisdom* has spoken an obscure, insidious, and irrational language. I see that the *God of goodness* has been cruel and sanguinary; that the *God of justice* has been unjust and partial, has ordered iniquity; that the *God of mercies* destines the most hideous punishments to the unhappy victims of his anger. Besides, obstacles present themselves when men attempt to verify the pretended relations of a Divinity, who, in two countries, has never literally holden the same language; who has spoken in so many places, at so many times, and always so variously, that he appears every where to have shown himself only with the determined design of throwing the human mind into the strangest perplexity. . . .

In short, theologians invest their God with the incommunicable privilege of acting contrary to all the laws of nature and of reason, whilst it is upon his reason, his justice, his wisdom and his fidelity in the fulfilling his pretended engagements, that they are willing to establish the worship which we owe him, and the duties of moral-

ity. What an ocean of contradictions! A being who can do every thing, and who owes nothing to any one, who, in his eternal decrees, can elect or reject, predestinate to happiness or to misery, who has the right of making men the playthings of his caprice, and to afflict them without reason, who could go so far as even to destroy and annihilate the universe, is he not a tyrant or a demon? Is there any thing more frightful than the immediate consequences to be drawn from these revolting ideas given to us of their God, by those who tell us to love him, to serve him, to imitate him, and to obey his orders? Would it not be a thousand times better to depend upon blind matter, upon a nature destitute of intelligence, upon chance, or upon nothing, upon a God of stone or of wood, than upon a God who is laying snares for men, inviting them to sin, and permitting them to commit those crimes which he could prevent, to the end that he may have the barbarous pleasure of punishing them without measure, without utility to himself, without correction to them, and without their example serving to reclaim others? A gloomy terror must necessarily result from the idea of such a being; his power will wrest from us much servile homage; we shall call him good to flatter him or to disarm his malice; but, without overturning the essence of things, such a God will never be able to make himself beloved by us, when we shall reflect that he owes us nothing, that he has the right of being unjust, that he has the power to punish his creatures for making a bad use of the liberty which he grants them, or for not having had that grace which he has been pleased to refuse them.

THE INCOMPATIBLE ATTRIBUTES OF GOD

However, admitting for a moment that God possesses all the human virtues in an infinite degree of perfection, we shall presently be obliged to acknowledge that he cannot connect them with those metaphysical, theological, and negative attributes, of which we have already spoken. If God is a spirit, how can he act like man, who is a corporeal being? A pure spirit sees nothing; it neither hears our prayers nor our cries, it cannot be conceived to have compassion for our miseries, being destitute of those organs by which the sentiments of pity can be excited in us. He is not *immutable*, if his disposition can change: he is not *infinite*, if the totality of nature, without being him, can exist conjointly with him; he is not *omnipotent*, if he permits, or if he does not prevent disorder in the world: he is not *omnipresent*, if he is not in the man who sins, or if he leaves at the moment in which he commits the sin. Thus, in whatever manner we consider this God, the human qualities which they assign him, necessarily destroy each other; and these same qualities cannot, in any possible manner, combine themselves with the supernatural attributes given him by theology.

REVELATION

With respect to the pretended *revelation* of the will of God, far from being a proof of his goodness, or of his commiseration for men, it would only be a proof of his malice. Indeed, all revelation supposes the Divinity guilty of leaving the human species, during a considerable time, unacquainted with truths the most important to their happiness. This revelation, made to a smaller number of chosen men, would moreover show a partiality in this being, an unjust predilection but little compatible with the goodness of the common Father of the human race. This revelation destroys also the divine immutability, since, by it, God would have permitted at one time, that men should be ignorant of his will, and at another time, that they should be instructed in it. This granted, all revelation is contrary to the notions which they give us of the justice or of the goodness of a God, who they tell us is immutable, and who, without having occasion to reveal himself, or to make himself known to them by miracles, could easily instruct and convince men, and inspire them with those ideas, which he desires; in short, dispose of their minds and of their hearts. What if we should examine in detail all those pre-tended revelations, which they assure us have been made to mortals? We shall see that God only retails fables unworthy of a wise being; acts in them, in a manner contrary to the natural notions of equity; announces enigmas and oracles impossible to be comprehended; paints himself under traits incompatible with his infinite perfections; exacts puerilities which degrade him in the eyes of reason, deranges the order which he has established in nature, to convince creatures, whom he will never cause to adopt those ideas, those sentiments, and that conduct, with which he would inspire them. In short, we shall find, that God has never manifested himself, but to announce inexplicable mysteries, unintelligible doctrines, ridiculous practices; to throw the human mind into fear, distrust, perplexity, and above all, to furnish a never-failing source of dispute to mortals.[3]

2. *The First Concern of Man is Man*

If we cannot cure nations of their inveterate prejudices, let us endeavour, at least, to prevent them from again falling into those excesses into which religion has so frequently hurried them; let men form to themselves chimeras; let them think of them as they will, provided their reveries do not make them forget they are men, and that a sociable being is not made to resemble ferocious animals. Let us balance the fictitious interests of heaven, by the sensible interests of the earth. Let sovereigns, and the people, at length acknowledge that the advantages resulting from truth, from justice, from good laws, from a rational education, and from a human and peaceable morality, are much more solid than those which they so vainly expect from their Divinities: let them feel that benefits so real and so precious ought not to be sacrificed to uncertain hopes, so frequently contradicted by experience. In order to convince themselves, let every rational man consider the numberless crimes which the name of God has caused upon the earth; let them study his frightful history, and that of his odious ministers, who have everywhere fanned the spirit of madness, discord, and fury. Let princes, and subjects at least, sometimes learn to resist the passions of these pretended interpreters of the Divinity, especially when they shall command them in his name to be inhuman, intolerant, and barbarous; to stifle the cries of nature, the voice of equity, the remonstrances of reason, and to shut their eyes to the interests of society.

Feeble mortals! How long will your imagination, so active and so prompt to seize on the marvellous, continue to seek out of the universe, pretexts to make you injurious to yourselves, and to the beings with whom ye live in society? Wherefore do ye not follow in peace the simple and easy route which your nature has marked out for ye? Wherefore strew with thorns the road of life? Wherefore multiply those sorrows to which your destiny exposes ye? What advantages can ye expect from a Divinity which the united efforts of the whole human species have not been able to make you acquainted with? Be ignorant, then, of that which the human mind is not formed to comprehend; abandon your chimeras; occupy yourselves with truth; learn the art of living happy; perfect your morals, your governments, and your laws; look to education, to agriculture, and to the sciences that are truly useful; labor with ardor; oblige nature by your industry to become propitious to ye, and the Gods will not be able to oppose any thing to your felicity. Leave to idle thinkers, and to useless enthusiasts, the unfruitful labor of fathoming depths from which ye ought to divert your attention: enjoy the benefits attached to your present existence; augment the number of them; never throw yourselves forward beyond your sphere. If you must have chimeras, permit your fellow-creatures to have theirs also; and do not cut the throats of your brethren, when they cannot rave in your own manner. If ye will have Gods, let your imagination give birth to them; but do not suffer these imaginary beings so far to intoxicate ye as to make ye mistake that which ye owe to those real beings with whom ye live. If ye will have unintelligible systems, if ye cannot be contented without marvelous doctrines, if the infirmities of your nature require an invisible crutch, adopt such as may suit with your humor; select those which you may think most calculated to support your tottering frame, do not insist on your neighbors making the same choice with yourself: but do not suffer these imaginary theories to infuriate your mind: always remember that, among the duties you owe to the *real* beings with whom ye are associated, the foremost, the most consequential, the most immediate, is a reasonable indulgence for the foibles of others.

NOTES

1. Hobbes, in his *Leviathan*, says: "Whatsoever we imagine, is finite. Therefore there is no idea, or conception of any thing we call infinite. No man can have in his mind an image of infinite magnitude, nor conceive infinite swiftness, infinite time, infinite force, or infinite power. When we say any thing is infinite, we signify only, that we are not able to conceive the ends and bound of the thing named, having no conception of the thing, but of our own inability." Sherlock says: "The word infinite is only a negation, which signifies that which has neither end, nor limits, nor extent, and, consequently, that which has no positive and determinate nature, and is therefore nothing"; he adds, "that nothing but custom has caused this word to be adopted, which without that, would appear devoid of sense, and a contradiction."

2. *Dies deficiet si velim numerare quibus bonis male evenerit; nec minus si commemorem quibus malis optime.* Cicer. *de Nat. Deor.* lib. iii. If a virtuous king possessed the ring of Gyges, that is to say, had the faculty of rendering himself invisible, would he not make use of it to remedy abuses to reward the good, to prevent the conspiracies of the wicked, to make order and happiness reign throughout his states? God is an invisible and all-powerful monarch, nevertheless his states are the theater of crime, of confusion: he remedies nothing.

3. It is evident that all revelation, which is not clear, or which teaches *mysteries*, cannot be the work of a wise and intelligent being: as soon as he speaks, we ought to presume, it is for the purpose of being understood by those to whom he manifests himself. To speak so as not to be understood, only shows folly or want of good faith. It is, then, very clear, that all things which the priesthood have called *mysteries*, are inventions, made to throw a thick veil over their own peculiar contradictions, and their own peculiar ignorance of the Divinity. But they think to solve all difficulties by saying *it is a mystery*; taking care, however, that men should know nothing of that pretended science, of which they have made themselves the depositaries.

Further Questions

1. "It is said that God is love. The saying makes no sense. Love, in the only sense in which we understand it, is partly a human emotion which extends over time and partly a disposition to behave in certain ways rather than others toward whomever or whatever one loves, behavior which also takes time. But God, we are told, exists beyond space and time. It is, then, a *category mistake* — like saying that the square root of 2 is compassionate — to say that God is love; that is, God is not the right sort of thing to be or feel love." Do you agree? Why?

2. "A being who exists beyond space and time, assuming we can even understand the notion of such a being, would be so alien to anything of which we have experience that it is utterly absurd to recommend such a being as the object of our veneration and worship. The fact that something is incomprehensible to us is hardly a reason for bowing down before it." Do you agree? Why?

Further Readings

Geach, Peter. *Providence and Evil.* Cambridge: Cambridge University Press, 1977. An important work by a highly respected Catholic philosopher.

Morris, Thomas, ed. *The Concept of God.* New York: Oxford University Press, 1987. The best of the latest.

Swinburne, Richard. *The Coherence of Theism.* Oxford: Oxford University Press, 1977. An important work by a highly respected Protestant philosopher.

The Ethics of Belief

W. K. CLIFFORD

W. K. Clifford (1845–1879), mathematician and philosopher, was a Catholic during his student days at Trinity College, Cambridge, but later became an agnostic and turned against religion. His reflections on Charles Darwin's new theory of evolution were part of what changed his mind. In turning against religion, Clifford also took a rather extreme stand against faith, as in the following selection where he argues that it is morally wrong for anyone, under any circumstances, to believe something on insufficient evidence.

Reading Questions

1. Do you agree with Clifford that the central characters in his shipowner example and his society of agitators example were wrong to have believed as they did?

2. What harm does Clifford think that belief on insufficient evidence does? What good does he concede it does? What do you think makes him feel so sure that the harm will always outweigh the good? Do you agree?

A SHIPOWNER WAS ABOUT TO SEND TO SEA an emigrant ship. He knew that she was old, and not over-well built at the first; that she had seen many seas and climes, and often had needed repairs. Doubts had been suggested to him that possibly she was not seaworthy. These doubts preyed upon his mind and made him unhappy; he thought that perhaps he ought to have her thoroughly overhauled and refitted, even though this should put him to great expense. Before the ship sailed, however, he succeeded in overcoming these melancholy reflections. He said to himself that she had gone safely through so many voyages and weathered so many storms that it was idle to suppose she would not come safely home from this trip also. He would put his trust in Providence, which could hardly fail to protect all these unhappy families that were leaving their fatherland to seek for better times elsewhere. He would dismiss from his mind all ungenerous suspicions about the honesty of builders and contractors. In such ways he acquired a sincere and comfortable conviction that his vessel was thoroughly safe and seaworthy; he watched her departure with a light heart, and benevolent wishes for the success of the exiles in their strange new home that was to be; and he got his insurance money when she went down in midocean and told no tales.

What shall we say of him? Surely this, that he was verily guilty of the death of those men. It is admitted that he did sincerely believe in the soundness of his ship; but the sincerity of his conviction can in no wise help him, because *he had no right to believe on such evidence as was before him*. He had acquired his belief not by honestly earning it in patient investigation, but by stifling his doubts. And although in the end he may have felt so sure about it that he could not think otherwise, yet inasmuch as he had knowingly and willingly worked himself into that frame of mind, he must be held responsible for it.

Let us alter the case a little, and suppose that the ship was not unsound after all; that she made

From Lectures and Essays, *London, Macmillan, 1879.*

her voyage safely, and many others after it. Will that diminish the guilt of her owner? Not one jot. When an action is once done, it is right or wrong forever; no accidental failure of its good or evil fruits can possibly alter that. The man would not have been innocent, he would only have been not found out. The question of right or wrong has to do with the origin of his belief, not the matter of it; not what it was, but how he got it; not whether it turned out to be true or false, but whether he had a right to believe on such evidence as was before him.

There was once an island in which some of the inhabitants professed a religion teaching neither the doctrine of original sin nor that of eternal punishment. A suspicion got abroad that the professors of this religion had made use of unfair means to get their doctrines taught to children. They were accused of wresting the laws of their country in such a way as to remove children from the care of their natural and legal guardians; and even of stealing them away and keeping them concealed from their friends and relations. A certain number of men formed themselves into a society for the purpose of agitating the public about this matter. They published grave accusations against individual citizens of the highest position and character, and did all in their power to injure those citizens in the exercise of their professions. So great was the noise they made, that a Commission was appointed to investigate the facts; but after the Commission had carefully inquired into all the evidence that could be got, it appeared that the accused were innocent. Not only had they been accused on insufficient evidence, but the evidence of their innocence was such as the agitators might easily have obtained, if they had attempted a fair inquiry. After these disclosures the inhabitants of that country looked upon the members of the agitating society, not only as persons whose judgment was to be distrusted, but also as no longer to be counted honorable men. For although they had sincerely and conscientiously believed in the charges they had made, *yet they had no right to believe on such evi-*

dence as was before them. Their sincere convictions, instead of being honestly earned by patient inquiring, were stolen by listening to the voice of prejudice and passion.

Let us vary this case also, and suppose, other things remaining as before, that a still more accurate investigation proved the accused to have been really guilty. Would this make any difference in the guilt of the accusers? Clearly not; the question is not whether their belief was true or false, but whether they entertained it on wrong grounds. They would no doubt say, "Now you see that we were right after all; next time perhaps you will believe us." And they might be believed, but they would not thereby become honorable men. They would not be innocent, they would only be not found out. Every one of them, if he chose to examine himself *in foro conscientiae*, would know that he had acquired and nourished a belief, when he had no right to believe on such evidence as was before him; and therein he would know that he had done a wrong thing.

It may be said, however, that in both of these supposed cases it is not the belief which is judged to be wrong, but the action following upon it. The shipowner might say, "I am perfectly certain that my ship is sound, but still I feel it my duty to have her examined, before trusting the lives of so many people to her." And it might be said to the agitator, "However convinced you were of the justice of your cause and the truth of your convictions, you ought not to have made public attack upon any man's character until you had examined the evidence on both sides with the utmost patience and care."

In the first place, let us admit that, so far as it goes, this view of the case is right and necessary; right, because even when a man's belief is so fixed that he cannot think otherwise, he still has a choice in regard to the action suggested by it, and so cannot escape the duty of investigating on the ground of the strength of his convictions; and necessary, because those who are not yet capable of controlling their feelings and thoughts must have a plain rule dealing with overt acts.

But this being premised as necessary, it becomes clear that it is not sufficient, and that our previous judgment is required to supplement it. For it is not possible so to sever the belief from the action it suggests as to condemn the one without condemning the other. No man holding a strong belief on one side of a question, or even wishing to hold a belief on one side, can investigate it with such fairness and completeness as if he were really in doubt and unbiased; so that the existence of a belief not founded on fair inquiry unfits a man for the performance of this necessary duty.

Nor is that truly a belief at all which has not some influence upon the actions of him who holds it. He who truly believes that which prompts him to an action has looked upon the action to lust after it, he has committed it already in his heart. If a belief is not realized immediately in open deeds, it is stored up for the guidance of the future. It goes to make a part of that aggregate of beliefs which is the link between sensation and action at every moment of all our lives, and which is so organized and compacted together that no part of it can be isolated from the rest, but every new addition modifies the structure of the whole. No real belief, however trifling and fragmentary it may seen, is ever truly insignificant; it prepares us to receive more of its like, confirms those which resembled it before, and weakens others; and so gradually it lays a stealthy train in our inmost thoughts, which may some day explode into overt action, and leave its stamp upon our character forever.

And no one man's belief is in any case a private matter which concerns himself alone. Our lives are guided by that general conception of the course of things which has been created by society for social purposes. Our words, our phrases, our forms and processes and modes of thought are common property, fashioned and perfected from age to age; an heirloom which every succeeding generation inherits as a previous deposit and a sacred trust to be handed on to the next one, not unchanged but enlarged and purified, with some clear marks of its proper handiwork. Into this, for good or ill, is woven every belief of every man who has speech of his fellows. An awful privilege, and an awful responsibility, that we should help to create the world in which posterity will live.

In the two supposed cases which have been considered, it has been judged wrong to believe on insufficient evidence, or to nourish belief by suppressing doubts and avoiding investigation. The reason of this judgment is not far to seek; it is that in both these cases the belief held by one man was of great importance to other men. But for as much as no belief held by one man, however seemingly trivial the belief, and however obscure the believer, is ever actually insignificant or without its effect on the fate of mankind, we have no choice but to extend our judgment to all cases of belief whatever. Belief, that sacred faculty which prompts the decisions of our will, and knits into harmonious working all the compacted energies of our being, is ours not for ourselves but for humanity. It is rightly used on truths which have been established by long experience and waiting toil, and which have stood in the fierce light of free and fearless questioning. Then it helps to bind men together, and to strengthen and direct their common action. It is desecrated when given to unproved and unquestioned statements, for the solace and private pleasure of the believer; to add a tinsel splendor to the plain straight road of our life and display a bright mirage beyond it; or even to drown the common sorrows of our kind by a self-deception which allows them not only to cast down, but also to degrade us. Whoso would deserve well of his fellows in this matter will guard the purity of his belief with a very fanaticism of jealous care, lest at any time it should rest on an unworthy object, and catch a stain which can never be wiped away.

It is not only the leader of men, statesman, philosopher, or poet, that owes this bounden duty to mankind. Every rustic who delivers in the village alehouse his slow, infrequent sentences, may help to kill or keep alive the fatal superstitions which clog his race. Every hardworked wife of an artisan may transmit to her children beliefs which shall knit society together, or rend it in pieces. No simplicity of mind, no obscurity of station, can escape the universal duty of questioning all that we believe.

It is true that this duty is a hard one, and the doubt which comes out of it is often a very bitter thing. It leaves us bare and powerless where we thought that we were safe and strong. To know all about anything is to know how to deal with it under all circumstances. We feel much happier and more secure when we think we know precisely what to do, no matter what happens, than when we have lost our way and do not know where to turn. And if we have supposed ourselves to know all about anything, and to be capable of doing what is fit in regard to it, we naturally do not like to find that we are really ignorant and powerless, that we have to begin again at the beginning, and try to learn what the thing is and how it is to be dealt with — if indeed anything can be learned about it. It is the sense of power attached to a sense of knowledge that makes men desirous of believing, and afraid of doubting.

This sense of power is the highest and best of pleasures when the belief on which it is founded is true belief, and has been fairly earned by investigation. For then we may justly feel that it is common property, and holds good for others as well as for ourselves. Then we may be glad, not that *I* have learned secrets by which I am safer and stronger, but that *we men* have got mastery over more of the world; and we shall be strong, not for ourselves, but in the name of Man and in his strength. But if the belief has been accepted on insufficient evidence, the pleasure is a stolen one. Not only does it deceive ourselves by giving us a sense of power which we do not really possess, but it is sinful, because it is stolen in defiance of our duty to mankind. That duty is to guard ourselves from such beliefs as from a pestilence, which may shortly master our own body and then spread to the rest of the town. What would be thought of one who, for the sake of a sweet fruit, should deliberately run the risk of bringing a plague upon his family and his neighbors?

And, as in other such cases, it is not the risk only which has to be considered; for a bad action is always bad at the time when it is done, no matter what happens afterwards. Every time we let ourselves believe for unworthy reasons, we weaken our powers of self-control, of doubting, of judicially and fairly weighing evidence. We all suffer severely enough from the maintenance and support of false beliefs and the fatally wrong actions which they lead to, and the evil born when one such belief is entertained is great and wide. But a greater and wider evil arises when the credulous character is maintained and supported, when a habit of believing for unworthy reasons is fostered and made permanent. If I steal money from any person, there may be no harm done by the mere transfer of possession; he may not feel the loss, or it may prevent him from using the money badly. But I cannot help doing this great wrong towards Man, that I make myself dishonest. What hurts society is not that it should lose its property, but that it should become a den of thieves; for then it must cease to be society. This is why we ought not to do evil that good may come; for at any rate this great evil has come, that we have done evil and are made wicked thereby. In like manner, if I let myself believe anything on insufficient evidence, there may be no great harm done by the mere belief; it may be true after all, or I may never have occasion to exhibit it in outward acts. But I cannot help doing this great wrong toward Man, that I make myself credulous. The danger to society is not merely that it should believe wrong things, though that is great enough; but that it should become credulous, and lose the habit of testing things and inquiring into them; for then it must sink back into savagery.

The harm which is done by credulity in a man is not confined to the fostering of a credulous character in others, and consequent support of false beliefs. Habitual want of care about which I believe leads to habitual want of care in others about the truth of what is told to me. Men speak the truth to one another when each reveres the truth in his own mind and in the other's mind; but how shall my friend revere the truth in my mind when I myself am careless about it, when I believe things because I want to believe them, and because they are comforting and pleasant? Will he not learn to cry, "Peace," to me, when there is no peace? By such a course I shall surround myself with a thick atmosphere of falsehood and fraud, and in that I must live. It may matter little to me, in my cloud-castle of sweet illusions and darling lies; but it matters much to Man that I have made my neighbors ready to deceive. The credulous man is father to the liar and the cheat; he lives in the bosom of this his family, and it is no marvel if he should become even as they are. So closely are our duties knit together, that whoso shall keep the whole law, and yet offend in one point, he is guilty of all.

To sum up; it is wrong always, everywhere, and for anyone, to believe anything upon insufficient evidence.

If a man, holding a belief which he was taught in childhood or persuaded of afterwards, keeps down and pushes away any doubts which arise about it in his mind, purposely avoids the reading of books and the company of men that call in question or discuss it, and regards as impious those questions which cannot easily be asked without disturbing it—the life of that man is one long sin against mankind.

If this judgment seems harsh when applied to those simple souls who have never known better, who have been brought up from the cradle with a horror of doubt, and taught that their eternal welfare depends on what they believe, then it leads to the very serious question. Who hath made Israel to sin? . . .

Inquiry into the evidence of a doctrine is not to be made once for all, and then taken as finally settled. It is never lawful to stifle a doubt; for either it can be honestly answered by means of the inquiry already made, or else it proves that the inquiry was not complete.

"But," says one, "I am a busy man; I have no time for the long course of study which would be necessary to make me in any degree a competent judge of certain questions, or even able to understand the nature of the arguments." Then he would have no time to believe. . . .

Further Questions

1. The "feeling" that something is so is sometimes a good reason for thinking that it actually is so: for instance, "I feel nervous"; "I feel I'm about to vomit." In other cases, however, the value of our feelings as evidence is more dubious: "I feel that abortion is morally wrong"; "I feel that God exists." If you agree, explain why the evidential value of our feelings differs so much in the two sets of examples.

2. Can you think of any *noncontroversial* exceptions to Clifford's claim that we have a duty always to believe exactly according to the evidence?

3. Are there any important *dis*analogies between Clifford's shipowner and society of agitators examples and ordinary cases where people believe things religiously without sufficient evidence?

Further Readings

Adams, Robert M. *The Virtue of Faith*. New York: Oxford University Press, 1987. A philosophically sophisticated defense of Christian belief by an important philosopher who is also a Presbyterian minister.

Delaney, C. F., ed. *Rationality and Religious Belief*. Notre Dame: University of Notre Dame Press, 1978. A good but often technical discussion of the permissibility of faith.

Penelhum, Terence, ed. *Faith*. New York: Macmillan, 1989. Historical and contemporary selections. An excellent anthology.

The Will to Believe

WILLIAM JAMES

A brief biography of James appears on pages 176–177.

In this famous selection, James defends the rationality, under certain conditions, of believing in the existence of God in the absence of adequate arguments or evidence for the existence of God. James's thesis is still a live philosophical issue today and is sometimes defended even by atheists.

Reading Questions

1. What does James mean by a "genuine option"?
2. What are the conditions under which James claims it is rationally permissible to believe on faith that God exists? Why does James think these conditions suffice?
3. Some philosophers think it is a rule of rationality that the strength of one's belief should be directly proportional to the evidence supporting that belief, and if a belief is not supported by adequate evidence — that is, evidence that makes it more likely than not to be true — one ought to dispense with the belief. How does James answer these philosophers?

. . . LET US GIVE THE NAME of *hypothesis* to anything that may be proposed to our belief; and just as the electricians speak of live and dead wires, let us speak of any hypothesis as either *live* or *dead*. A live hypothesis is one which appeals as a real possibility to him to whom it is proposed. If I ask you to believe in the Mahdi, the notion makes no electric connection with your nature, — it refuses to scintillate with any credibility at all. As an hypothesis it is completely dead. To an Arab, however (even if he be not one of the Mahdi's followers), the hypothesis is among the mind's possibilities: it is alive. This shows that deadness and liveness in an hypothesis are not intrinsic properties, but relations to the individual thinker. They are measured by his willingness to act. The maximum of liveness in an hypothesis means willingness to act irrevocably. Practically, that means belief; but there is some believing tendency wherever there is willingness to act at all.

Next, let us call the decision between two hypotheses an *option*. Options may be of several kinds. They may be — 1, *living* or *dead*; 2, *forced* or *avoidable*; 3, *momentous* or *trivial*; and for our purposes we may call an option a *genuine* option when it is of the forced, living, and momentous kind.

1. A living option is one in which both hypotheses are live ones. If I say to you: "Be a theosophist or be a Mohammedan,"

it is probably a dead option, because for you neither hypothesis is likely to be alive. But if I say, "Be an agnostic or be a Christian," it is otherwise: trained as you are, each hypothesis makes some appeal, however small, to your belief.

2. Next, if I say to you: "Choose between going out with your umbrella or without it," I do not offer you a genuine option, for it is not forced. You can easily avoid it by not going out at all. Similarly, if I say, "Either love me or hate me," "Either call my theory true or call it false," your option is avoidable. You may remain indifferent to me, neither loving nor hating, and you may decline to offer any judgment as to my theory. But if I say, "Either accept this truth or go without it," I put on you a forced option, for there is no standing place outside of the alternative. Every dilemma based on a complete logical disjunction, with no possibility of not choosing, is an option of this forced kind. . . .

The thesis I defend is, briefly stated, this: *Our passional nature not only lawfully may, but must, decide an option between propositions, whenever it is a genuine option that cannot by its nature be decided on intellectual grounds; for to say, under such circumstances, "Do not decide, but leave the question*

Extracts from William James, "The Will to Believe," an Address to the Philosophical Clubs of Yale and Brown Universities. First published in the New World, *1896.*

open," is itself a passional decision, — just like decid-
ing yes or no, — and is attended with the same risk of
losing the truth. . . .

Wherever the option between losing truth and
gaining it is not momentous, we can throw the
chance of *gaining truth* away, and at any rate save
ourselves from any chance of *believing falsehood*,
by not making up our minds at all till objective
evidence has come. In scientific questions, this is
almost always the case; and even in human affairs
in general, the need of acting is seldom so urgent
that a false belief to act on is better than no belief
at all. Law courts, indeed, have to decide on the
best evidence attainable for the moment, because
a judge's duty is to make law as well as to ascertain
it, and (as a learned judge once said to me) few
cases are worth spending much time over: the
great thing is to have them decided on *any* acceptable principle, and got out of the way. But in
our dealings with objective nature we obviously
are recorders, not makers, of the truth; and decisions for the mere sake of deciding promptly and
getting on to the next business would be wholly
out of place. Throughout the breadth of physical
nature facts are what they are quite independently of us, and seldom is there any such hurry
about them that the risks of being duped by believing a premature theory need be faced. The
questions here are always trivial options, the hypothesis are hardly living (at any rate not living
for us spectators), the choice between believing
truth or falsehood is seldom forced. The attitude
of sceptical balance is therefore the absolutely
wise one if we would escape mistakes. What difference, indeed, does it make to most of us
whether we have or have not a theory of the
Röntgen rays, whether we believe or not in
mind-stuff, or have a conviction about the causality of conscious states? It makes no difference.
Such options are not forced on us. On every account it is better not to make them, but still keep
weighing reasons *pro et contra* with an indifferent
hand. . . .

. . . Religions differ so much in their accidents
that in discussing the religious question we must
make it very generic and broad. What then do we
now mean by the religious hypothesis? Science
says things are; morality says some things are better than other things; and religion says essentially
two things.

First, she says that the best things are the more
external things, the overlapping things, the
things in the universe that throw the last stone, so
to speak, and say the final word. "Perfection is
eternal," — this phrase of Charles Secrétan seems
a good way of putting this first affirmation of religion, an affirmation which obviously cannot yet
be verified scientifically at all.

The second affirmation of religion is that we
are better off even now if we believe her first affirmation to be true.

Now, let us consider what the logical elements
of this situation are *in case the religious hypothesis
in both its branches be really true.* (Of course, we
must admit that possibility at the outset. If we are
to discuss the question at all, it must involve a
living option. If for any of you religion be a hypothesis that cannot, by any living possibility be
true, then you need go no farther. I speak to the
'saving remnant' alone.) So proceeding, we see,
first that religion offers itself as a *momentous* option. We are supposed to gain, even now, by our
belief, and to lose by our nonbelief, a certain vital
good. Secondly, religion is a *forced* option, so far
as that good goes. We cannot escape the issue by
remaining sceptical and waiting for more light,
because, although we do avoid error in that way
if religion be untrue, we lose the good, *if it be true*,
just as certainly as if we positively chose to disbelieve. It is as if a man should hesitate indefinitely
to ask a certain woman to marry him because he
was not perfectly sure that she would prove an
angel after he brought her home. Would he not
cut himself off from that particular angel-possi-
bility as decisively as if he went and married some
one else? Scepticism, then, is not avoidance of
option; it is option of a certain particular kind of
risk. *Better risk loss of truth than chance of error,* —
that is your faith-vetoer's exact position. He is actively playing his stake as much as the believer is;

he is backing the field against the religious hypothesis, just as the believer is backing the religious hypothesis against the field. To preach scepticism to us as a duty until 'sufficient evidence' for religion be found, is tantamount therefore to telling us, when in presence of the religious hypothesis, that to yield to our fear of its being error is wiser and better than to yield to our hope that it may be true. It is not intellect against all passions, then; it is only intellect with one passion laying down its law. And by what, forsooth, is the supreme wisdom of this passion warranted? Dupery for dupery, what proof is there that dupery through hope is so much worse than dupery through fear? I, for one, can see no proof; and I simply refuse obedience to the scientist's command to imitate his kind of option, in a case where my own stake is important enough to give me the right to choose my own form of risk. If religion be true and the evidence for it be still insufficient, I do not wish, by putting our extinguisher upon my nature (which feels to me as if it had after all some business in this matter), to forfeit my sole chance in life of getting upon the winning side, — that chance depending, of course, on my willingness to run the risk of acting as if my passional need of taking the world religiously might be prophetic and right.

All this is on the supposition that it really may be prophetic and right, and that, even to us who are discussing the matter, religion is a live hypothesis which may be true. Now, to most of us religion comes in a still further way that makes a veto on our active faith even more illogical. The more perfect and more eternal aspect of the universe is represented in our religions as having personal form. The universe is no longer a mere *It* to us, but a *Thou*, if we are religious; and any relation that may be possible from person to person might be possible here. For instance, although in one sense we are passive portions of the universe, in another we show a curious autonomy, as if we were small active centres on our own account. We feel, too, as if the appeal of religion to us were made to our own active goodwill, as if

evidence might be forever withheld from us unless we met the hypothesis half-way. To take a trivial illustration: just as a man who in a company of gentlemen made no advances, asked a warrant for every concession, and believed no one's word without proof, would cut himself off by such churlishness from all the social rewards that a more trusting spirit would earn, — so here, one who should shut himself up in snarling logicality and try to make the gods extort his recognition willy-nilly, or not get it at all, might cut himself off forever from his only opportunity of making the gods' acquaintance. This feeling, forced on us we know not whence, that by obstinately believing that there are gods (although not to do so would be so easy both for our logic and our life) we are doing the universe the deepest service we can, seems part of the living essence of the religious hypothesis. If the hypothesis *were* true in all its parts, including this one, then pure intellectualism, with its veto on our making willing advances, would be an absurdity; and some participation of our sympathetic nature would be logically required. I, therefore, for one, cannot see my way to accepting the agnostic rules for truthseeking, or wilfully agree to keep my willing nature out of the game. I cannot do so for this plain reason, that *a rule of thinking which would absolutely prevent me from acknowledging certain kinds of truth if those kinds of truth were really there, would be an irrational rule.* That for me is the long and short of the formal logic of the situation, no matter what the kinds of truth might materially be.

I confess I do not see how this logic can be escaped. But sad experience makes me fear that some of you may still shrink from radically saying with me, *in abstracto*, that we have the right to believe at our own risk any hypothesis that is live enough to tempt our will. I suspect, however, that if this is so, it is because you have got away from the abstract logical point of view altogether, and are thinking (perhaps without realizing it) of some particular religious hypothesis which for you is dead. The freedom to 'believe what we will' you apply to the case of some patent superstition;

and the faith you think of is the faith defined by the schoolboy when he said, "Faith is when you believe something that you know ain't true." I can only repeat that this is misapprehension. *In concreto*, the freedom to believe can only cover living options which the intellect of the individual cannot by itself resolve; and living options never seem absurdities to him who has them to consider. When I look at the religious question as it really puts itself to concrete men, and when I think of all the possibilities which both practically and theoretically it involves, then this command that we shall put a stopper on our heart, instincts, and courage, and *wait*—acting of course meanwhile more or less as if religion were *not* true—till doomsday, or till such time as our intellect and senses working together may have raked in evidence enough,—this command, I say, seems to me the queerest idol ever manufactured in the philosophic cave. Were we scholastic absolutists, there might be more excuse. If we had an infallible intellect with its objective certitudes, we might feel ourselves disloyal to such a perfect organ of knowledge in not trusting to it exclusively, in not waiting for its releasing word. But if we are empiricists, if we believe that no bell in us tolls to let us know for certain when truth is in our grasp, then it seems a piece of idle fantasticality to preach so solemnly our duty of waiting for the bell. Indeed we *may* wait if we will.—I hope you do not think that I am denying that,—but if we do so, we do so at our peril as much as if we believed. In either case we *act*, taking our life in our hands. . . .

Further Questions

1. Suppose a ninety-year-old man were to believe on faith that he could win the 100-meter dash in the next summer Olympics. Is James committed to saying that his belief is rationally permissible?

2. Suppose someone were to believe on faith that there are thousands of little gremlins that cannot be detected in any way, either directly or indirectly, but which surround the leaves of trees in the fall and accompany them on their journey from the trees to the ground. Is James committed to saying that such a belief could be rationally permissible? Would he be committed if the belief were a genuine option?

3. Is it rationally permissible to believe, on the basis of faith alone (that is, in the absence of arguments or evidence that make your belief more likely than not to be true), that God exists? Explain how William James would answer. How would he defend his answer? Formulate a good objection to James's argument.

Further Readings

Mackie, J. L. *The Miracle of Theism*. Oxford: Clarendon Press, 1982, pp. 204–209. Perhaps the best short discussion of James's argument.

Penelhum, Terence, ed. *Faith*. New York: Macmillan, 1989. An excellent comprehensive anthology.

Rationality and Religious Belief

ALVIN PLANTINGA

Alvin Plantinga teaches philosophy at the University of Notre Dame and writes primarily on metaphysics and philosophy of religion. He is regarded by many philosophers as one of the greatest living apologists for Christianity. In this selection he argues that belief in God is perfectly rational by arguing that a foundationalist has no grounds for rejecting belief in God as a basic belief.

Reading Questions

1. What is the evidentialist objection to belief in God?
2. What is the connection between evidentialism and foundationalism?
3. How does the foundationalist — how does anyone — know whether a belief is self-evident?
4. What is Plantinga's distinction between belief *in* God and belief *that* God exists?
5. What is the Evidentialist Objection, and what is it rooted in?
6. How does Plantinga distinguish what *appears* to be self-evident from what *really is* self-evident?

WHAT I MEAN TO DISCUSS in this paper is the question: "Is it rational, or reasonable, or rationally acceptable, to believe in God?" I mean to *discuss* this question, not answer it. My initial aim is not to argue that religious belief *is* rational (although I think it is) but to try to understand this question.

The first thing to note is that I have stated the question misleadingly. What I really want to discuss is whether it is rational to believe that God exists — that there is such a person as God. Of course there is an important difference between believing that God exists and believing *in* God. To believe that God exists is just to accept a certain proposition — the proposition that there really is such a person as God — as true. According

to the book of James (2:19) the devils believe this proposition, and they tremble. To believe *in* God, however, is to trust him, to commit your life to him, to make his purposes your own. The devils do not do that. So there is a difference between believing in God and believing that he exists; for purposes of economy, however, I shall use the phrase "belief in God" as a synonym for "belief that God exists."

I. The Evidentialist Objection

Our question, therefore, is whether belief in God is rational. This question is widely asked and widely answered. Many philosophers — most prominently, those in the great tradition of

Parts of this paper appeared in C. F. Delaney (ed.), Rationality and Religious Belief *(Notre Dame: University of Notre Dame Press, 1978) and in NOÛS 15 (1981):41–51. Used by permission of University of Notre Dame Press, the editor of NOÛS, and the author.*

natural theology—have argued that belief in God *is* rational; they have typically done so by providing what they took to be *demonstrations* or *proofs* of God's existence. Many others have argued that belief in God *is* *ir*rational. If we call those of the first group "natural theologians," perhaps we should call those of the second "natural atheologians." (That would at any rate be kinder than calling them "unnatural theologians.") J. L. Mackie, for example, opens his statement of the problem of evil as follows: "I think, however, that a more telling criticism can be made by way of the traditional problem of evil. Here it can be shown, not merely that religious beliefs lack rational support, but that they are positively irrational."[1] And a very large number of philosophers take it that a central question—perhaps *the* central question—of philosophy of religion is the question whether religious belief in general and belief in God in particular is rationally acceptable.[2]

Now an apparently straightforward and promising way to approach this question would be to take a definition of rationality and see whether belief in God conforms to it. The chief difficulty with this appealing course, however, is that no such definition of rationality seems to be available. If there *were* such a definition, it would set out some conditions for a belief's being rationally acceptable—conditions that are severally necessary and jointly sufficient. That is, each of the conditions would have to be met by a belief that is rationally acceptable; and if a belief met all the conditions, then it would follow that it is rationally acceptable. But it is monumentally difficult to find any non-trivial necessary conditions at all. Surely, for example, we cannot insist that S's belief that *p* is rational only if it is *true*. For consider Newton's belief that if *x*, *y* and *z* are moving colinearly, then the motion of *z* with respect to *x* is the sum of the motions of *y* with respect to *x* and *z* with respect to *y*. No doubt Newton was rational in accepting this belief; yet it was false, at least if contemporary physicists are to be trusted. And if they aren't—that is, if they are wrong in contradicting Newton—then *they*

exemplify what I'm speaking of; they rationally believe a proposition which, as it turns out, is false.

Nor can we say that a belief is rationally acceptable only if it is possibly true, not necessarily false in the broadly logical sense.[3] For example, I might do the sum $735 + 421 + 9,216$ several times and get the same answer: 10,362. I am then rational in believing that $735 + 421 + 9,216 = 10,362$, even though the fact is I've made the same error each time—failed to carry a "1" from the first column—and thus believe what is necessarily false. Or I might be a mathematical neophyte who hears from his teacher that every continuous function is differentiable. I need not be irrational in believing this, despite the fact that it is necessarily false. Examples of this sort can be multiplied.

So this question presents something of an initial enigma in that it is by no means easy to say what it is for a belief to be rational. And the fact is those philosophers who ask this question about belief in God do not typically try to answer it by giving necessary and sufficient conditions for rational belief. Instead, they typically ask whether the believer has *evidence* or *sufficient evidence* for his belief; or they may try to argue that in fact there is sufficient evidence for the proposition that there is *no* God; but in any case they try to answer this question by finding evidence for or against theistic belief. Philosophers who think there are sound arguments for the existence of God—the natural theologians—claim there is good evidence *for* this proposition; philosophers who believe that there are sound arguments for the non-existence of God naturally claim that there is evidence *against* this proposition. But they concur in holding that belief in God is rational only if there is, on balance, a preponderance of evidence for it—or less radically, only if there is not, on balance, a preponderance of evidence against it.

The nineteenth-century philosopher W. K. Clifford provides a splendid if somewhat strident example of the view that the believer in God must have evidence if he is not to be irrational. Here he does not discriminate against religious belief; he apparently holds that a belief of any sort at all is rationally acceptable only if there is sufficient evidence for it. And he goes on to insist that it is wicked, immoral, monstrous, and perhaps even impolite to accept a belief for which one does not have sufficient evidence:

> Whoso would deserve well of his fellows in this matter will guard the purity of his belief with a very fanaticism of jealous care, lest at any time it should rest on an unworthy object, and catch a stain which can never be wiped away.

He adds that if a

> belief has been accepted on insufficient evidence, the pleasure is a stolen one. Not only does it deceive ourselves by giving us a sense of power which we do not really possess, but it is sinful, because it is stolen in defiance of our duty to mankind. That duty is to guard ourselves from such beliefs as from a pestilence which may shortly master our body and spread to the rest of the town.

And finally:

> To sum up: it is wrong always, everywhere, and for anyone to believe anything upon insufficient evidence.[4]

(It is not hard to detect, in these quotations, the "tone of robustious pathos" with which William James credits him.) Clifford finds it utterly obvious, furthermore, that those who believe in God do indeed so believe on insufficient evidence and thus deserve the above abuse. A believer in God is, on his view, at best a harmless pest and at worst a menace to society; in either case he should be discouraged.

Here Clifford is urging *the evidentialist objection to theistic belief*—the claim that belief in God is irrational, or unreasonable, or noetically substandard because, so goes the claim, there is insufficient evidence for it. Suppose we take a deeper look at this position. What is essential to it is the claim that we must evaluate the rationality of belief in God by examining its relation to *other* propositions. We are directed to estimate its rationality by determining whether we have *evidence* for it—whether we know, or at any rate rationally believe, some other propositions which stand in the appropriate relation to the proposition in question. And belief in God is rational, or reasonable, or rationally acceptable, on this view, only if there are other propositions with respect to which it is thus evident.

According to the Cliffordian position, then, there is a set of propositions E such that my belief in God is rational if and only if it is evident with respect to E—if and only if E constitutes, on balance, evidence for it. But what propositions are to be found in E? Do we know that belief in God is not itself in E? If it *is*, of course, then it is certainly evident with respect to E. How does a proposition get into E anyway? How do we decide which propositions are the ones such that my belief in God is rational if and only if it is evident with respect to them? Should we say that E contains the propositions that I *know*? But then, for our question to be interesting, we should first have to argue or agree that I don't know that God exists—that I only *believe* it, whether rationally or irrationally. This position is widely taken for granted, and indeed taken for granted by theists as well as others. But why should the latter concede that he doesn't know that God exists—that at best he rationally believes it? The Bible regularly speaks of *knowledge* in this context—not just rational or well-founded belief. Of course it is true that the believer has *faith*—faith in God, faith in what He reveals—but this by no means settles the issue. The question is whether he doesn't also *know* that God exists. Indeed, according to the Heidelberg Catechism, knowledge is an essential element of faith, so that one has true faith that *p* only if he knows that *p*:

> True faith is not only a certain (i.e., sure) knowledge whereby I hold for truth all that God has revealed in His word, but also a deep-rooted assurance created in me by the Holy Spirit through the gospel that not only others but I

too have had my sins forgiven, have been made forever right with God and have been granted salvation. (Q 21)

So from this point of view a man has true faith that *p* only if he knows that *p*, and also meets a certain further condition: roughly (where *p* is a universal proposition) that of accepting the universal instantiation of *p* with respect to himself. Now of course the theist may be unwilling to concede that he does not have true faith. But if he does have true faith, then, at least according to the Catechism, he has a "certain" (i.e., sure) knowledge" of such revealed truths as that, e.g., "God so loved the world that he gave his only son, that whoever believes in him should not perish but have everlasting life" (John 3:16)—a truth that self-evidently entails that God exists. Accordingly the theist may be unwilling to concede that he does not know but only believes that God exists.

II. Classical Foundationalism

Now of course the evidentialist will not be at all eager to agree that belief in God belongs in E. But why not? To answer we must take a deeper look at his position. The evidentialist objection is nearly always rooted in *classical foundationalism*, an enormously popular picture or total way of looking at faith, knowledge, justified belief, rationality and allied topics. This picture has had a long and distinguished career in the history of philosophy, including among its adherents Plato, Aristotle, Aquinas, Descartes, Leibniz, Locke, and, to leap to the present, Professor Roderick Chisholm; its near relatives, perhaps, remain the dominant ways of thinking about these topics. We may think of the classical foundationalist as beginning with the observation that some of one's beliefs may be *based upon* others; it may be that there are a pair of propositions *A* and *B* such that I believe *A on the basis of B*. Although this relation isn't easy to characterize in a revealing and non-trivial fashion, it is nonetheless familiar.

I believe that the word "umbrageous" is spelled u-m-b-r-a-g-e-o-u-s: this belief is based on another belief of mine; the belief that that's how the dictionary says it's spelled. I believe that $72 \times 71 = 5112$. This belief is based upon several other beliefs I hold: that $1 \times 72 = 72$; $7 \times 2 = 14$; $7 \times 7 = 49$; $49 + 1 = 50$; and others. Some of my beliefs, however, I accept but don't accept on the basis of any other beliefs. Call these beliefs *basic*. I believe that $2 + 1 = 3$, for example, and don't believe it on the basis of other propositions. I also believe that I am seated at my desk, and that there is a mild pain in my right knee. These too are basic for me; I don't believe them on the basis of any other propositions. According to the classical foundationalist, some propositions are *properly* or *rightly* basic for a person and some are not. Those that are not, are rationally accepted only on the basis of *evidence*, where the evidence must trace back, ultimately, to what is properly basic.

Suppose we say that the assemblage of beliefs a person holds, together with a various logical and epistemic relations that hold among them, constitutes that person's noetic structure; and let's say that the *foundations* of S's noetic structure (call it "F") is the set of propositions that are *basic* for S and *properly* basic for him.

And from the foundationalist point of view, our question must be restated: Is belief in God evident with respect to the foundations of my noetic structure? Clifford, as I say, takes it to be obvious that the answer is no. But is this obvious? To restate my earlier question: Might it not be that my belief in God is itself in the foundations of my noetic structure? Perhaps it is a member of F, in which case, of course, it will automatically be evident with respect to F.

Here the classical foundationalist goes further. Not just any belief can properly be in the foundations of a person's noetic structure; to be in F a belief must meet some fairly specific conditions. It must be capable of functioning foundationally; it must be capable of bearing its share of the weight of the entire noetic structure. The propositions in F, of course, are not inferred from other propositions and are not accepted on the basis of other propositions. I *know* the propositions in the foundations of my noetic structure, but not by virtue of knowing other propositions; for these are the ones I start with. And so the question the foundationalist asks about belief in God — namely, what is the evidence for it? — is not properly asked about the members of F; these items don't require to be evident with respect to other propositions in order to be rationally believed. Accordingly, says the foundationalist, not just any proposition is capable of functioning foundationally; to be so capable, with respect to a person S, a proposition must not need the evidential support of other propositions; it must be such that it is possible that S know *p* but have no evidence for *p*.

Well, suppose all this is so; what kind of propositions can function foundationally? Here different foundationalists give different answers. Aristotle and Aquinas, for example, held that self-evident propositions — ones like *all black dogs are black* — belong in the foundations. Aquinas, at least, seems also to hold that propositions "evident to the senses," as he puts it — propositions like *some things change* — belong there. For he believed, of course, that the existence of God is demonstrable; and by this I think he meant that God's existence can be deduced from foundational propositions. He holds, furthermore, that God's existence can be demonstrated "from his effects" — from sensible objects; and in each of the five ways there is a premise that, says Aquinas, is "evident to the senses." I therefore believe Aquinas meant to include such propositions among the foundations. You may think it strange, incidentally, to count Aquinas among the Cliffordians. On this point, however, he probably belongs with them; he held that belief in God is rational only if supported by the foundations. Of course he differs from Clifford in holding that in fact God's existence *is* supported by them; he thinks it follows from members of F by argument forms that are themselves in F. This, indeed, is the burden of his five ways.

According to Aquinas, therefore, self-evident propositions and those evident to the senses belong in the foundations. And when he speaks of propositions of the latter sort, he means such propositions as

1. there's a tree over there,
2. there is an ashtray on my desk,
3. that tree's leaves have turned yellow,

and

4. this fender has rusted through.

Modern foundationalists — Descartes, for example — argue that what goes into the foundations, in addition to self-evident propositions, are not propositions that, like (1)–(4), entail the existence of such material objects as ashtrays, trees, leaves, and fenders, but more cautious claims; for example:

5. I seem to see a red book,
6. it seems to me that I see a book with a red cover,
7. I seem to see something red,

or even, as Professor Chisholm put it,

8. I am appeared redly to.

The modern foundationalist who opts for propositions like (5)–(8) rather than (1)–(4) has a prima facie plausible reason for doing so: Belief in a proposition of the latter sort seems to have a sort of immunity from error not enjoyed by belief in one of the former. I may believe that there is a red ashtray on my desk, or that I see a red ashtray on my desk, when the fact is there is no red ashtray there at all: I am color-blind, or hallucinating, or the victim of an illusion of some sort or other. But it is at the least very much harder to see that I could be wrong in believing that I *seem* to see a red ashtray on my desk — that, in Chisholm's language, I am appeared redly (or red-ashtrayly) to. There are plenty of possible worlds in which I mistakenly believe that there is a red book on my desk; it is at least plausible to hold that there are no possible worlds in which I mistakenly believe that I seem to see a red book there. And this immunity from error may plausibly be taken to provide a reason for distinguishing between propositions like (5)–(8) and (1)–(4), admitting the former but not the latter to the foundations.

There is a small problem here, however: Every necessarily true proposition—every proposition true in all possible worlds—is such that there is no possible world in which I mistakenly believe it. Yet presumably the foundationalist will not be inclined to hold that every necessary proposition I believe is in the foundations of my noetic structure. Consider, for example, Goldbach's Conjecture that every even number greater than two is the sum of two primes. This proposition is either necessarily true or necessarily false, although it isn't presently known which. Suppose it is in fact true, and I believe it, but not because I have found a proof of it; I simply believe it. The foundationalist will presumably hold, in this case, that my belief in Goldbach's Conjecture is necessarily true but not a good candidate for the foundations. Here I truly believe but do not know the proposition in question; so it does not belong among the foundations, and this despite the fact that there is no possible world in which I mistakenly believe it.

Presumably, then, the modern foundationalist will not hold that just any necessarily true belief is automatically among the foundations. He may argue instead that what characterizes propositions like (5)–(8) is not just that it is not possible to believe them mistakenly, but that it is not possible to be mistaken about them. That is to say, a proposition of this sort is like a necessary proposition in that it is not possible for me to believe it mistakenly; it is unlike a necessary proposition, however, in that it is also not possible for me to believe its *denial* mistakenly. If I believe that I am appeared to redly, then it follows that I *am* appeared to redly; but if I believe that I am not appeared to redly, it follows equally that I am not thus appeared to. We might say that propositions meeting this condition are *incorrigible* for me; perhaps we can explain this notion thus:

9. p is incorrigible for S at t if there is no possible world in which S mistakenly believes p at t and no possible world in which S mistakenly believes not-p at t.[5]

According to our paradigm Cliffordian, then, a belief is properly in the foundations of my noetic structure only if it is either self-evident or incorrigible for me. So suppose we take a look at self-evidence. What is it? Under what conditions is a proposition self-evident? What kinds of propositions are self-evident? Examples would include very simple arithmetical truths such as

10. $2 + 1 = 3$,

simple truths of logic such as

11. no man is both married and unmarried,

perhaps the generalizations of simple truths of logic, such as

12. for any proposition p, the conjunction of p with its denial is false.

and certain propositions expressing identity and diversity; for example:

13. Redness is distinct from greenness,
14. the property of being prime is distinct from the property of being composite,

and

15. the proposition *all men are mortal* is distinct from the proposition *all mortals are men*.[6]

There are others; Aquinas gives as examples:

16. the whole is greater than the part,

where, presumably, he means by "part" what we mean by "proper part," and, more dubiously,

17. man is an animal.[7]

Still other candidates—candidates which may be less then entirely uncontroversial—come from many other areas; for example:

18. if p is necessarily true and p entails q, then q is necessarily true,
19. if e^1 occurs before e^2 and e^2 occurs before e^3, then e^1 occurs before e^3,

and

20. it is wrong to cause unnecessary (and unwanted) pain just for the fun of it.

What is it that characterizes these propositions? According to the tradition, the outstanding characteristic of a self-evident proposition is that one simply sees it to be true upon grasping or understanding it. Understanding a self-evident proposition is sufficient for apprehending its truth. Of course this notion must be relativized to *persons*; what is self-evident to you might not be to me. Very simple arithmetical truths will be self-evident to nearly all of us; but a truth like $17 + 18 = 35$ may be self-evident only to some. And of course a proposition is self-evident to a person only if he does in fact grasp it; so a proposition will not be self-evident to those who do not apprehend the concepts involved in the proposition. As Aquinas says, some propositions are self-evident only to the learned; his example is the truth that immaterial substances do not occupy space. Among those propositions whose concepts not everyone grasps, some are such that anyone who *did* grasp them would see their truth; for example:

21. A model of a first order theory T assigns truth to the axioms of T.

Others — $17 + 13 = 30$, for example — may be such that some but not all of those who apprehend them also see that they are true.

But how shall we understand this "seeing that they are true?" Those who speak of self-evidence explicitly turn to this visual metaphor and expressly explain self-evidence by reference to vision. There are two important aspects to the metaphor and two corresponding components to the idea of self-evidence. First, there is the *epistemic* component: a proposition p is self-evident to a person S only if S has *immediate* knowledge of p — i.e., knows p, and does not know p on the basis of his knowledge of other propositions. Consider a simple arithmetic truth such as $2 + 1 = 3$ and compare it with one like $24 \times 24 = 576$. I know each of these propositions; and I know the second but not the first on the basis of computation, which is a kind of inference. So I have immediate knowledge of the first but not the second. The epistemic component of self-evidence, therefore, is immediate knowledge; it follows, of course, that any proposition self-evident to a person is true.

But there is also a phenomenological component. Consider again our two propositions; the first but not the second has about it a kind of luminous aura or glow when you bring it to mind or consider it. Locke speaks, in this connection, of an "evident luster"; a self-evident proposition, he says, displays a kind of "clarity and brightness to the attentive mind." Descartes speaks instead of "clarity and distinctness"; each, I think, is referring to same phenomenological feature. And this feature is connected with another: Upon understanding a proposition of this sort one feels a strong inclination to accept it; this luminous obviousness seems to compel or at least impel assent. Aquinas and Locke, indeed, held that a person, or at any rate a normal well-formed human being, finds it impossible to withhold assent when considering a self-evident propositon. The phenomenological component of the idea of self-evidence, then, seems to have a double aspect: There is the luminous aura that $2 + 1 = 3$ displays, and there is also an experienced tendency to accept or believe it. Perhaps, indeed, the luminous aura *just is* the experienced impulsion towards acceptance; perhaps these are the very same thing. In that case the phenomenological component would not have the double aspect I suggested it did have; in either case, however, we must recognize this phenomenological aspect of self-evidence.

Now suppose we return to the main question: Why shouldn't belief in God be among the foundations of my noetic structure? Can belief in God be properly basic for a person? If not, why not? The answer, on the part of the modern foundationalist was that even if this belief is *true*, it does not have the characteristics a proposition must have to deserve a place in the foundations. There is no room in the foundations for a proposition that can be known only on the basis of other propositions. A proposition is properly basic for a person only if he knows it immediately—i.e., knows it, and does not know it on the basis of other propositions. The proposition that God exists, however, is at best truly believed, not known, and even if it were known, it wouldn't be known immediately. The only propositions that meet this condition of immediate knowledge are those that are self-evident or incorrigible. Since this proposition is neither, it is not properly basic for anyone; that is, no well-formed, rational noetic structure contains this proposition in its foundations.

But why should the theist concede these things? Suppose he grants that there is a foundation to his noetic structure: a set F of propositions such that (1) he knows each member of F *immediately* and (2) whatever else he knows is evident with respect to the members of F. Suppose he concedes, further, that he does know other things, and knows them on the basis of his knowledge of these basic propositions. Suppose, in a particularly ironic and conciliatory frame of mind, he concedes still further that much of what he believes, he believes but does not know; and that the rationality of these beliefs is to be tested or measured by way of their connections with those propositions that are basic for him. Why should he not combine these concessions with the claim that his belief in God is properly basic for him?

Because, says the modern foundationalist, belief in God is neither self-evident nor incorrigible. But now we must look more closely at this fundamental principle of the foundationalist's position:

22. a proposition *p* is properly basic for a person *S* if and only if *p* is either self-evident to *S* or incorrigible for *S*;

that is, the foundations of a well-formed, rational noetic structure will contain propositions that are self-evident or incorrigible and will not contain any propositions that do not meet this condition.

And here we must ask a question that has been clamoring for attention. How does the foundationalist know—how does anyone know—that, indeed, a given proposition *is* self-evident? How do we tell? Isn't it possible that a proposition should seem to me to be self-evident when in fact it is not? Consider an analogy. Suppose the theist claims that a proposition *p* is properly basic for a person *S* if *S* knows *p* *immediately*; and suppose he adds that one of the things he immediately knows is that God exists. The foundationalist, presumably, will want to reply as follows: you *say* you have immediate knowledge of this proposition, but perhaps you are mistaken; perhaps you only *believe* and do not *know* that God exists; perhaps, indeed, God does *not* exist. How do you know that you have immediate knowledge of this proposition? What leads you to think so?

Here the theist may be hard put to give an answer; but the foundationalist may find a similar question similarly embarrassing. How does he know that a given proposition—$7 + 5 = 12$, for example—*is* self-evident? Might we not be mistaken in our judgment of self-evidence? It seems obviously possible that there should be a race of persons—on some other planet, let's say—who think they find *other* propositions self-evident, some of these others being the denials of propositions *we* find self-evident. Perhaps this race invariably makes mistakes about what is self-evident. But might not the same thing be true of us? A proposition is self-evident, after all, only if it is *true*; and it certainly seems possible that we should believe a proposition self-evident when in fact it is not.

Nor need we rest content with the mere possibility that we should mistakenly find a proposition self-evident. Here the Russell paradoxes are peculiarly instructive. It seems self-evident to many that some properties—e.g., that of being a horse—do not exemplify themselves, while others—e.g., that of being a property—do. It seems self-evident, furthermore, that if some properties exemplify themselves and others do not, then there is such a property as *self-exemplification*: a property enjoyed by the properties in the first group but lacked by those in the second. But it also seems self-evident that if there is such a property as *self-exemplification*, then there is such a property as *non-self-exemplification*: the property a property has if and only if it does not exemplify itself. And of course it seems self-evident that if there is such a property as *non-self-exemplification*, then either it exemplifies itself or it does not. But if it does exemplify itself, it has the property of non-self-exemplification, in which case it does not exemplify itself. So if it does exemplify itself, it does not exemplify itself. But of course it is also true that if it does exemplify itself, then it does; so if it exemplifies itself, it both does and does not exemplify itself. Hence it does not exemplify itself. If, on the other hand, non-self-exemplification does not exemplify itself, then it does not have the property of non-self-exemplification, in which case it must have the property of self-exemplification, i.e., it exemplifies itself. So if it does not exemplify itself, it does exemplify itself. But it is also true that if it does not exemplify itself, then it does not exemplify itself; so if it does not exemplify itself, it both does and does not exemplify itself. Hence it is false that it does not exemplify itself, and true that it does. But now from propositions that seem self-evident we have deduced, by arguments that seem self-evidently right, that non-self-exemplification both exemplifies itself and does not exemplify itself; and this seems self-evidently false. The conclusion must be that at least one proposition that *seems* self-evident, is not *in fact* self-evident.

We must distinguish, therefore, what *appears* to be self-evident from what really *is*. Suppose we say that a proposition *seems* or *appears* self-evident to a person if he understands it, and if it displays the phenomenological feature referred to above—the "evident luster" of which Locke speaks—when he attentively considers it. How, then, does the foundationalist determine which propositions really *are* self-evident for him? By noting of course, which ones appear self-evident to him; he has nothing else to go on. Of course he cannot sensibly hold that *whatever* appears self-evident, really is; that is the lesson of the Russell paradoxes. Perhaps, however, he can retreat to a weaker principle; perhaps he can hold that whatever seems self-evident has, as we might put it, the presumption of self-evidence in its favor. What appears to be self-evident ought to be taken to be self-evident unless there are reasons to the contrary—unless, for example, it appears self-evident that the proposition in question conflicts with *other* apparently self-evident propositions. And perhaps he will support this injunction by appeal to some such principles as

24. Whatever seems self-evident is very likely true

or

25. most propositions that *seem* self-evident *are* self-evident (and hence true).

But why should we accept (24) and (25)? Why does the foundationalist accept them? We should note, first of all, that neither of these propositions seems self-evident. One who understands them can nonetheless wonder whether they are true and in fact reject them. They do not possess that evident luster; and there certainly seem to be thinkable alternatives. Impressed with evolutionary theory, for example, we might suppose that the disposition to find these propositions self-evident is a trait emerging in the course of a long evolutionary development—a trait that has a certain survival value, but is at best fortuitously connected with truth, so that many or most of the propositions that appear self-evident to us are in fact false. Or, remembering our Descartes, we might speculate that we have been created by a being who delights in deception and produces in us a powerful tendency to accept certain false propositions as self-evident. Or we might speculate, in a Kierkegaardian vein, that our noetic endowment, once pristine and totally reliable, has been corrupted by some primal cataclysm befalling the human race. So (24) and (25) are not themselves apparently self-evident.

The important point here, however, lies in a different direction. Suppose these principles — (24) and (25) — *were* apparently self-evident. That is, suppose the proposition

26. most propositions that display the phenomenological feature are true

itself displayed this feature. Would that be a relevant answer to the question of what reason, if any, there is for believing that most propositions displaying this feature are true? It is hard to see how. The question is whether a proposition's displaying this feature is a reason for thinking it true; to reply that (26) itself displays this feature is simply to invite the question again. Here the appeal to self-evidence seems entirely unsatisfactory. It is as if the theist were to reply to the question: "Why believe in God?" by pointing out that God requires us to believe in Him, and requires us to believe only what is true. This may indeed be so; but it does not supply a reason for belief for anyone who does not already believe. Similarly, the claim that (24) and (25) are apparently self-evident, may or may not be true; but it can serve as a reason for accepting them only for someone who already accepts them. And hence it cannot serve as a reason, for the foundationalist, for accepting them.

The fact of the matter is, I think, that the foundationalist has no reason at all for accepting (24) and (25). They do not appear to be self-evident; and of course they are not incorrigible. But if the foundationalist *does* have a reason for them, that reason must trace back, ultimately, to the foundations; that is, the foundationalist has a reason, on his own view, for (24) and (25) only if they are evident with respect to propositions that are properly basic for him—propositions that are self-evident or incorrigible. It is hard to see how (24) or (25) could be evident with respect to such propositions.

Accordingly, the foundationalist accepts (24) and (25) but has no reason for so doing. He isn't *obliged* to accept them; there are alternatives. He simply commits himself to them. We might say that he commits himself to the trustworthiness of his noetic equipment. More elegantly, he commits himself to the reliability of his epistemic endowment. If, with an older tradition, we think of reason as an organ, or power, or faculty — the faculty whereby we discern what is self-evident — then the foundationalist commits himself to the basic reliability of reason. He doesn't do so, of course, as a result of (broadly speaking) scientific or rational investigation; he does so in advance of such investigation. For he has no reasons for accepting (24) and (25); but he does accept them, and he uses them to determine the acceptability of *other* propositions. In other words, (24) and (25) are members of the foundation of his noetic structure.

The foundationalist, therefore, commits himself to the basic reliability of reason. I do not say this by way of criticism; it is a commitment I share. The theist is by no means obliged to reject this commitment. Augustine, indeed, argued that reason is ultimately reliable just because God has created us and is not a deceiver. He has created us in such a way that certain propositions appear self-evident to us; and because he is a God of goodness and truth, he would not create us in such a way that *false* propositions should appear self-evident. Had Augustine been apprised of the Russell paradoxes, he might have expressed himself more guardedly; but his basic point remains. One who believes in God can certainly accept (24) and (25); and he, unlike the foundationalist, can give a reason for doing so.

Since the theist can properly concur with the foundationalist on (24) and (25), he can agree with the latter that apparently self-evident and incorrigible propositions are properly basic for S. But the foundationalist *credo*, we have seen, contains *two* elements, a positive and a negative. The foundationalist holds, positively, that

27. self-evident and incorrigible propositions are properly basic for S,

and he adds, negatively, that

28. *only* propositions of those sorts are properly basic for S.

But why should we accept this negative element? What is there to be said in favor of it? Do we have anything more than the foundationalist's word for (28)?

The fact is we have *less* than the foundationalist's word for it. For consider (28). (28) is neither self-evident nor incorrigible; nor does it appear to follow from propositions that are. It is, therefore, basic for the foundationalist. So he holds that self-evident and incorrigible propositions are the only viable candidates for the foundations of his noetic structure, but he himself accepts (28) as basic, which is neither self-evident nor incorrigible. Accordingly, the foundationalist is hoist on his own petard; his characteristic claim is self-referentially incoherent.[8] Is there then any reason at all for believing (28)? If so, it is hard to see what it might be. (28) certainly does not appear to be self-evident; it is certainly not incorrigible. It is very hard to see, furthermore, that it either follows from or is evident with respect to propositions that are self-evident or incorrigible. So it is hard to see that there is any reason for accepting (28), even from a roughly foundationalist point of view. Why then should we accept it? Why should the theist feel any obligation to believe it?

The answer, I believe, is that there is no reason at all for accepting (28); it is no more than a bit of intellectual imperialism on the part of the foundationalist. He means to commit himself to reason and to nothing more; he therefore declares irrational any noetic structure that contains more — belief in God, for example — in its foundations. But here there is no reason for the theist to follow his example.

III. Is Belief in God Properly Basic?

Now many Reformed theologians[9] and thinkers have rejected *natural theology* (thought of as the attempt to provide proofs or arguments for the existence of God). They have held not merely that the proffered arguments are unsuccessful, but that the whole enterprise is in some way radically misguided. I've argued elsewhere[10] that the Reformed rejection of natural theology is best construed as an inchoate and unfocused rejection of classical foundationalism. What these Reformed thinkers really mean to hold, I think, is that belief in God need not be based on argument or evidence from other propositions at all. They mean to hold that the believer is entirely within his intellectual rights in believing as he does even if he doesn't know of any good theistic argument (deductive or non-deductive), even if he doesn't believe that there is any such argument, and even if in fact no such argument exists. They hold that it is perfectly rational to accept belief in God without accepting it on the basis of any other beliefs or propositions at all. In a word, they hold that *belief in God is properly basic*. And insofar as they mean to reject classical foundationalism, they are to be applauded; classical foundationalism is eminently rejectable. Of course it does not follow that belief in God *is* properly basic; perhaps the class of properly basic propositions is broader than classical foundationalists think, but still not broad enough to admit belief in God. But why think so? What might be the objections to the Reformed view that belief in God is properly basic? I wish to examine two such objections.

It is sometimes claimed that if I have no evidence for the existence of God, then if I accept that proposition my belief will be groundless, or gratuitous, or arbitrary. I think this is an error; let me explain. Suppose we consider perceptual beliefs, memory beliefs, and beliefs ascribing mental states to other persons: such beliefs as

29. I see a tree,

30. I had breakfast this morning,

and

31. That person is angry.

Although beliefs of this sort are typically and properly taken as basic, it would be a mistake to describe them as *groundless*. Upon having an experience of a certain sort, I believe that I am perceiving a tree. In the typical case, I do not hold this belief on the basis of other beliefs; it is nonetheless not groundless. My having that characteristic sort of experience — to use Professor Chisholm's language, my being appeared treely to — plays a crucial role in the formation and justification of that belief. We might say this experience, together, perhaps, with other circumstances, is what *justifies* me in holding it; this is the *ground* of my justification, and, by extension, the ground of the belief itself.

If I see someone displaying typical pain behavior, I take it that he or she is in pain. Again, I don't take the displayed behavior as *evidence* for that belief; I don't infer that belief from others I hold; I don't accept it on the basis of other beliefs. Still, my perceiving the pain behavior plays a unique role in the formation and justification of that belief; as in the previous case, it forms the ground of my justification for the belief in question. The same holds for memory beliefs. I seem to remember having breakfast this morning; that is, I have an inclination to believe the proposition that I had breakfast, along with a certain past-tinged experience that is familiar to all but hard to describe. Perhaps we should say that I am appeared to pastly; but perhaps that insufficiently distinguishes the experience in question from that accompanying beliefs about the past not grounded in my own memory. The phenomenology of memory is a rich and unexplored realm; here I have no time to explore it. In this case as in the others, however, there is a justifying circumstance present, a condition that forms the ground of my justification for accepting the memory belief in question.

In each of these cases, a belief is taken as basic, and in each case properly taken as basic. In each case there is some circumstance or condition that confers justification; there is a circumstance that serves as the *ground* of justification. So in each case there will be some true proposition of the sort:

32. In condition C, S is justified in taking p as basic.

Of course C will vary with p. For a perceptual judgment such as

33. I see a rose-colored wall before me,

C will include my being appeared to in a certain fashion. No doubt C will include more. If I'm appeared to in the familiar fashion but know that I'm wearing rose-colored glasses, or that I am suffering from a disease that causes me to be thus appeared to, no matter what the color of the nearby objects, then I'm not justified in taking (33) as basic. Similarly for memory. Suppose I know that my memory is unreliable; it often plays me tricks. In particular, when I seem to remember having breakfast, then, more often than not, I *haven't* had breakfast. Under these conditions I am not justified in taking it as basic that I had breakfast, even though I seem to remember that I did.

So being appropriately appeared to, in the perceptual case, is not sufficient for justification; some further condition — a condition hard to state in detail — is clearly necessary. The central point here, however, is that a belief is properly basic only in certain conditions; these conditions are, we might say, the ground of its justification and, by extension, the ground of the belief itself. In this sense, basic beliefs are not, or are not necessarily, *groundless* beliefs.

Now similar things may be said about belief in God. When the Reformers claim that this belief is properly basic, they do not mean to say, of course, that there are no justifying circumstances for it, or that it is in that sense groundless or gratuitous. Quite the contrary. Calvin holds that God "reveals and daily discloses himself in the whole workmanship of the universe," and the divine art "reveals itself in the innumerable and yet distinct and well ordered variety of the heavenly host." God has so created us that we have a tendency or disposition to see his hand in the world about us. More precisely, there is in us a disposition to believe propositions of the sort *this flower was created by God* or *this vast and intricate universe was created by God* when we contemplate the flower or behold the starry heavens or think about the vast reaches of the universe.

Calvin recognizes, at least implicitly, that other sorts of conditions may trigger this disposition. Upon reading the Bible, one may be impressed with a deep sense that God is speaking to him. Upon having done what I know is cheap, or wrong, or wicked, I may feel guilty in God's sight and form the belief *God disapproves of what I've done*. Upon confession and repentance, I may feel forgiven, forming the belief *God forgives me for what I've done*. A person in grave danger may turn to God, asking for his protection and help; and of course he or she then forms the belief that God is indeed able to hear and help if he sees fit. When life is sweet and satisfying, a spontaneous sense of gratitude may well up within the soul; someone in this condition may thank and praise the Lord for his goodness, and will of course form the accompanying belief that indeed the Lord is to be thanked and praised.

There are therefore many conditions and circumstances that call forth belief in God: guilt, gratitude, danger, a sense of God's presence, a sense that he speaks, perception of various parts of the universe. A complete job would explore the phenomenology of all these conditions and of more besides. This is a large and important topic; but here I can only point to the existence of these conditions.

Of course, none of the beliefs I mentioned a moment ago is the simple belief that God exists. What we have instead are such beliefs as

34. God is speaking to me,
35. God has created all this,
36. God disapproves of what I have done,
37. God forgives me,

and

38. God is to be thanked and praised.

These propositions are properly basic in the right circumstances. But it is quite consistent with this to suppose that the proposition *there is such a person as God* is neither properly basic nor taken as basic by those who believe in God. Perhaps what they take as basic are such propositions as (34)–(38), believing in the existence of God on the basis of propositions such as those. From this point of view, it isn't exactly right to say that it is belief in God that is properly basic; more exactly, what are properly basic are such propositions as (34)–(38), each of which self-evidently entails that God exists. It isn't the relatively high level and general proposition *God exists* that is properly basic, but instead propositions detailing some of his attributes or actions.

Suppose we return to the analogy between belief in God and belief in the existence of perceptual objects, other persons, and the past. Here too it is relatively specific and concrete propositions rather than their more general and abstract colleagues that are properly basic. Perhaps such items as

39. There are trees,
40. There are other persons,

and

41. The world has existed for more than five minutes

are not in fact properly basic; it is instead such propositions as

42. I see a tree,
43. That person is pleased,

and

44. I had breakfast more than an hour ago

that deserve that accolade. Of course, propositions of the latter sort immediately and self-evidently entail propositions of the former sort; and perhaps there is thus no harm in speaking of the former as properly basic, even though so to speak is to speak a bit loosely.

The same must be said about belief in God. We may say, speaking loosely, that belief in God is properly basic; strictly speaking, however, it is probably not that proposition but such propositions as (34)–(38) that enjoy that status. But the main point, here, is this: belief in God or (34)–(38), are properly basic; to say so, however, is not to deny that there are justifying conditions for these beliefs, or conditions that confer justification on one who accepts them as basic. They are therefore not groundless or gratuitous.

A second objection I've often heard: If belief in God is properly basic, why can't *just any* belief be properly basic? Couldn't we say the same for any bizarre aberration we can think of? What about voodoo or astrology? What about the belief that the Great Pumpkin returns every Halloween? Could I properly take *that* as basic? And if I can't, why can I properly take belief in God as basic? Suppose I believe that if I flap my arms with sufficient vigor, I can take off and fly about the room; could I defend myself against the charge of irrationality by claiming this belief is basic? If we say that belief in God is properly basic, won't we be committed to holding that just anything, or nearly anything, can properly be taken as basic, thus throwing wide the gates to irrationalism and superstition?

Certainly not. What might lead one to think the Reformed epistemologist is in this kind of trouble? The fact that he rejects the criteria for proper basicality purveyed by classical foundationalism? But why should *that* be thought to commit him to such tolerance of irrationality? Consider an analogy. In the palmy days of positivism, the positivists went about confidently wielding their verifiability criterion and declaring meaningless much that was obviously meaningful. Now suppose someone rejected a formulation of that criterion — the one to be found in the second edition of A. J. Ayer's *Language, Truth and Logic*, for example. Would that mean she was committed to holding that

45. "'Twas brillig; and the slithy toves did
     gyre and bymble in the wabe,

contrary to appearances, makes good sense? Of course not. But then the same goes for the Reformed epistemologist; the fact that he rejects the classical foundationalist's criterion of proper basicality does not mean that he is committed to supposing just anything is properly basic.

But what then is the problem? Is it that the Reformed epistemologist not only rejects those criteria for proper basicality, but seems in no hurry to produce what he takes to be a better substitute? If he has no such criterion, how can he fairly reject belief in the Great Pumpkin as properly basic?

This objection betrays an important misconception. How do we rightly arrive at or develop criteria for meaningfulness, or justified belief, or proper basicality? Where do they come from? Must one have such a criterion before one can sensibly make any judgments — positive or negative — about proper basicality? Surely not. Suppose I don't know of a satisfactory substitute for the criteria proposed by classical foundationalism; I am nevertheless entirely within my rights in holding that certain propositions are not properly basic in certain conditions. Some propositions seem self-evident when in fact they are not; that is the lesson of some of the Russell paradoxes. Nevertheless it would be irrational to take as basic the denial of a proposition that seems self-evident to you. Similarly, suppose it seems to you that you see a tree; you would then be irrational in taking as basic the proposition that you don't see a tree, or that there aren't any trees. In the same way, even if I don't know of some illuminating criterion of meaning, I can quite properly declare (45) meaningless.

And this raises an important question — one Roderick Chisholm has taught us to ask. What is the status of criteria for knowledge, or proper basicality, or justified belief? Typically, these are universal statements. The modern foundationalist's criterion for properly basicality, for example, is doubly universal:

46. For any proposition A and person S, A
     is properly basic for S if and only if A is
     incorrigible for S or self-evident to S.

But how could one know a thing like that? What are its credentials? Clearly enough, (46) isn't self-evident or just obviously true. But if it isn't, how does one arrive at it? What sorts of arguments would be appropriate? Of course a foundationalist might find (46) so appealing, he simply takes it to be true, neither offering argument for it, nor accepting it on the basis of other things he believes. If he does so, however, then, as we have seen in connection with (28), his noetic structure will be self-referentially incoherent. (46) itself is neither self-evident nor incorrigible; hence in accepting (46) as basic, the modern foundationalist violates the condition of proper basicality he himself lays down in accepting it. On the other hand, perhaps the foundationalist will try to produce some argument for it from premises that are self-evident or incorrigible; it is exceedingly hard to see, however, what such an argument might be like. And until he has produced such arguments, what shall the rest of us do — we who do not find (46) at all obvious or compelling? How could he use (46) to show us that belief in God, for example, is not properly basic? Why should we believe (46), or pay it any attention?

The fact is, I think, that neither (46) nor any other revealing necessary and sufficient condition for proper basicality follows from clearly self-evident premises by clearly acceptable arguments. And hence the proper way to arrive at such a criterion is, broadly speaking, *inductive*. We must assemble examples of beliefs and conditions such that the former are obviously properly basic in the latter, and examples of beliefs and conditions such that the former are obviously *not* properly basic in the latter. We must then frame hypotheses as to the necessary and sufficient conditions of proper basicality and test these hypotheses by references to those examples. Under the right conditions, for example, it is clearly rational to believe that you see a human person before you: a being who has thoughts and feelings, who knows and believes things, who makes decisions and acts. It is clear, furthermore, that you are under no obligation to reason to this belief from others you hold; under those conditions that belief is properly basic for you. But then (46) must be

mistaken; the belief in question, under those circumstances, is properly basic, though neither self-evident nor incorrigible for you. Similarly, you may seem to remember that you had breakfast this morning, and perhaps you know of no reason to suppose your memory is playing you tricks. If so, you are entirely justified in taking that belief as basic. Of course it isn't properly basic on the criteria offered by classical foundationalists; but that fact counts not against you but against those criteria.

Accordingly, criteria for proper basicality must be reached from below rather than above; they should not be presented *ex cathedra* but argued and tested by a relevant set of examples. But there is no reason to assume, in advance, that everyone will agree on the examples. The Christian or Jew will of course suppose that belief in God is entirely proper and rational; if he doesn't accept this belief on the basis of other propositions, he will conclude that it is basic for him and quite properly so. Followers of Bertrand Russell and Madelyn Murray O'Hare may disagree, but how is that relevant? Must my criteria, or those of the believing community, conform to their examples? Surely not. The theistic community is responsible to *its* set of examples, not to theirs.

Accordingly, the Reformed epistemologist can properly hold that belief in the Great Pumpkin is not properly basic, even though he holds that belief in God *is* properly basic, and even if he has no full-fledged criterion of proper basicality. Of course he is committed to supposing that there is a relevant *difference* between belief in God and belief in the Great Pumpkin, if he holds that the former but not the latter is properly basic. But this should prove no great embarrassment; there are plenty of candidates. These candidates are to be found in the neighborhood of the conditions I mentioned that justify and ground belief in God. Thus, for example, the Reformed epistemologist may concur with Calvin in holding that God has implanted in us a natural tendency to see his hand in the world around us; the same cannot be said for the Great Pumpkin, there being no Great Pumpkin and no natural tendency to accept beliefs about the Great Pumpkin.

By way of conclusion then, the evidentialist objection, insofar as it is based upon classical foundationalism, is bankrupt; being self-evident, or incorrigible, or evident to the senses is not a necessary condition of proper basicality. Furthermore, one who holds that belief in God *is* properly basic is not thereby committed to the idea that belief in God is groundless, or gratuitous, or without justifying circumstances. And even if he lacks a general criterion of proper basicality, he is not obliged to suppose that just any or nearly any belief—belief in the Great Pumpkin, for example—is properly basic. Like everyone should, he begins with examples; and he may take belief in the Great Pumpkin as a paradigm of irrational basic belief.

NOTES

1. "Evil and Omnipotence," *Mind* 64 (1955), pp. 203–4.

2. See, for example, T. McPherson, *The Philosophy of Religion* (London: D. Van Nostrand, 1965); T. Penelhum, *Religion and Rationality* (New York: Random House, 1971); J. Ross, *Philosophical Theology* (Indianapolis: Bobbs Merrill, 1969); A. Plantinga, *God and Other Minds* (Ithaca, N.Y.: Cornell University Press, 1967), and many others.

3. See my book *The Nature of Necessity* (Oxford: Clarendon Press, 1974), chap. 1.

4. W. K. Clifford, "The Ethics of Belief," from *Lectures and Essays* (London: Macmillan, 1979).

5. Philip Quinn has pointed out (in correspondence) that, according to (9), false propositions will be incorrigible for me now: Although I do not now seem to see something green, the proposition *I seem to see something green* is incorrigible for me now. I'm not certain this feature of the definition is a defect; if it is, it can be repaired by adding the clause "*p* is true" to the definiens or, as Quinn suggests, by adding "*S* believes *p* at *t*."

6. Examples of these kinds are given by Locke, *Essay Concerning Human Understanding*, Book IV, chap. 7.

7. *Summa Theologica* 1, Q1 a2; *Summa Contra Gentiles* I, chap. 10.

8. (28), of course, is stated for modern foundationalism, but precisely similar remarks apply to the ancient and medieval foundationalism embraced by Aristotle and Aquinas.

9. A Reformed theologian is one whose intellectual sympathies lie with the Protestant tradition going back to John Calvin (not someone who was formerly a theologian and has since seen the light).

10. "The Reformed Objection to Natural Theology," *Proceedings of the American Catholic Philosophical Association*, 1980.

Further Questions

1. Is belief in God "properly basic"? What does Plantinga think? What do you think?

2. Plantinga claims that while belief in God can be properly basic, not just any belief—for instance, belief in the Great Pumpkin—can be properly basic. Do you find his argument convincing?

Further Readings

Davies, Brian. *An Introduction to the Philosophy of Religion*. Oxford: Oxford University Press, 1982. An introduction written from a theistic point of view.

Plantinga, Alvin. *God, Freedom, and Evil*. Grand Rapids, MI: Eerdman's, 1974. Contains Plantinga's novel ontological argument for God's existence, and his "free-will defense" against claims that the presence of evil in the world disproves God's existence.

Swinburne, Richard. *The Existence of God*. Oxford: Clarendon Press, 1979. A well-known philosopher gives a sympathetic defense of many of the traditional arguments for the existence of God.

God and Evil

DAVID HUME

In this selection, from *Dialogues Concerning Natural Religion* (1779), Hume's character, Philo, argues that the enormous amount of human and animal suffering provides good reason for believing that God does not exist.

Reading Questions

1. There are three characters in Hume's *Dialogue*: Philo, Cleanthes, and Demea. Based just on the segment of the *Dialogue* included here, how would you characterize the differences in their views?

2. What are Philo's main arguments? How does Cleanthes respond?

Part X

IT IS MY OPINION, I OWN, replied Demea, that each man feels, in a manner, the truth of religion within his own breast, and, from a consciousness of his imbecility and misery rather than from any reasoning, is led to seek protection from that Being on whom he and all nature is dependent. So anxious or so tedious are even the best scenes of life that futurity is still the object of all our hopes and fears. We incessantly look forward and endeavour, by prayers, adoration, and sacrifice, to appease those unknown powers whom we find, by experience, so able to afflict and oppress us. Wretched creatures that we are! What resource for us amidst the innumerable ills of life did not

religion suggest some methods of atonement, and appease those terrors with which we are incessantly agitated and tormented?

I am indeed persuaded, said Philo, that the best and indeed the only method of bringing everyone to a due sense of religion is by just representations of the misery and wickedness of men. And for that purpose a talent of eloquence and strong imagery is more requisite than that of reasoning and argument. For is it necessary to prove what everyone feels within himself? It is only necessary to make us feel it, if possible, more intimately and sensibly.

The people, indeed, replied Demea, are sufficiently convinced of this great and melancholy truth. The miseries of life, the unhappiness of

From David Hume, Dialogues Concerning Natural Religion *(1779; London: Longmans Green, 1878).*

man, the general corruptions of our nature, the unsatisfactory enjoyment of pleasures, riches, honours—these phrases have become almost proverbial in all languages. And who can doubt of what all men declare from their own immediate feeling and experience?

In this point, said Philo, the learned are perfectly agreed with the vulgar; and in all letters, *sacred* and *profane*, the topic of human misery has been insisted on with the most pathetic eloquence that sorrow and melancholy could inspire. The poets, who speak from sentiment, without a system, and whose testimony has therefore the more authority, abound in images of this nature. From Homer down to Dr. Young, the whole inspired tribe have ever been sensible that no other representation of things would suit the feeling and observation of each individual.

As to authorities, replied Demea, you need not seek them. Look round this library of Cleanthes. I shall venture to affirm that, except authors of particular sciences, such as chemistry or botany, who have no occasion to treat of human life, there is scarce one of those innumerable writers from whom the sense of human misery has not, in some passage or other, extorted a complaint and confession of it. At least, the chance is entirely on that side; and no one author has ever, so far as I can recollect, been so extravagant as to deny it.

There you must excuse me, said Philo: Leibniz has denied it, and is perhaps the first[1] who ventured upon so bold and paradoxical an opinion; at least, the first who made it essential to his philosophical system.

And by being the first, replied Demea, might he not have been sensible of his error? For is this a subject in which philosophers can propose to make discoveries especially in so late an age? And can any man hope by a simple denial (for the subject scarcely admits of reasoning) to bear down the united testimony of mankind, founded on sense and consciousness?

And why should man, added he, pretend to an exemption from the lot of all other animals? The whole earth, believe me, Philo, is cursed and polluted. A perpetual war is kindled amongst all living creatures. Necessity, hunger, want stimulate the strong and courageous; fear, anxiety, terror agitate the weak and infirm. The first entrance into life gives anguish to the new-born infant and to its wretched parent; weakness, impotence, distress attend each stage of that life, and it is, at last, finished in agony and horror.

Observe, too, says Philo, the curious artifices of nature in order to embitter the life of every living being. The stronger prey upon the weaker and keep them in perpetual terror and anxiety. The weaker, too, in their turn, often prey upon the stronger, and vex and molest them without relaxation. Consider that innumerable race of insects, which either are bred on the body of each animal or, flying about, infix their stings in him. These insects have others still less than themselves which torment them. And thus on each hand, before and behind, above and below, every animal is surrounded with enemies which incessantly seek his misery and destruction.

Man alone, said Demea, seems to be, in part, an exception to this rule. For by combination in society he can easily master lions, tigers, and bears, whose greater strength and agility naturally enable them to prey upon him.

On the contrary, it is here chiefly, cried Philo, that the uniform and equal maxims of nature are most apparent. Man, it is true, can, by combination, surmount all his *real* enemies and become master of the whole animal creation; but does he not immediately raise up to himself *imaginary* enemies, the demons of his fancy, who haunt him with superstitious terrors and blast every enjoyment of life? His pleasure, as he imagines, becomes in their eyes a crime; his food and repose give them umbrage and offence; his very sleep and dreams furnish new materials to anxious fear; and even death, his refuge from every other ill, presents only the dread of endless and innumerable woes. Nor does the wolf molest more the timid flock than superstition does the anxious breast of wretched mortals.

Besides, consider, Demea: This very society by which we surmount those wild beasts, our natural enemies, what new enemies does it not raise to us? What woe and misery does it not occasion? Man is the greatest enemy of man. Oppression, injustice, contempt, contumely, violence, sedition, war, calumny, treachery, fraud — by these they mutually torment each other, and they would soon dissolve that society which they had formed were it not for the dread of still greater ills which must attend their separation.

But though these external insults, said Demea, from animals, from men, from all the elements, which assault us form a frightful catalogue of woes, they are nothing in comparison of those which arise within ourselves, from the distempered condition of our mind and body. How many lie under the lingering torment of diseases? Hear the pathetic enumeration of the great poet.

> Intestine stone and ulcer, colic-pangs,
> Demoniac frenzy, moping melancholy,
> And moon-struck madness, pining atrophy,
> Marasmus, and wide-wasting pestilence.
> Dire was the tossing, deep the groans: *Despair*
> Tended the sick, busiest from couch to couch.
> And over them triumphant *Death* his dart
> Shook: but delay'd to strike, though oft invok'd
> With vows, as their chief good and final hope.[2]

The disorders of the mind, continued Demea, though more secret, are not perhaps less dismal and vexatious. Remorse, shame, anguish, rage, disappointment, anxiety, fear, dejection, despair — who has ever passed through life without cruel inroads from these tormentors? How many have scarcely ever felt any better sensations? Labour and poverty, so abhorred by everyone, are the certain lot of the far greater number; and those few privileged persons who enjoy ease and opulence never reach contentment or true felicity. All the goods of life united would not make a very happy man, but all the ills united would make a wretch indeed; and any one of them almost (and who can be free from every one?), nay, often the absence of one good (and who can possess all?) is sufficient to render life ineligible.

Were a stranger to drop on a sudden into this world, I would show him, as a specimen of its ills, an hospital full of diseases, a prison crowded with malefactors and debtors, a field of battle strewed with carcases, a fleet foundering in the ocean, a nation languishing under tyranny, famine, or pestilence. To turn the gay side of life to him and give him a notion of its pleasures — whether should I conduct him? To a ball, to an opera, to court? He might justly think that I was only showing him a diversity of distress and sorrow.

There is no evading such striking instances, said Philo, but by apologies which still further aggravate the charge. Why have all men, I ask, in all ages, complained incessantly of the miseries of life? . . . They have no just reason, says one: these complaints proceed only from their discontented, repining, anxious disposition. . . . And can there possibly, I reply, be a more certain foundation of misery than such a wretched temper?

But if they were really as unhappy as they pretend, says my antagonist, why do they remain in life? . . .

Not satisfied with life, afraid of death —

this is the secret chain, say I, that holds us. We are terrified, not bribed to the continuance of our existence.

It is only a false delicacy, he may insist, which a few refined spirits indulge, and which has spread these complaints among the whole race of mankind. . . . And what is this delicacy, I ask, which you blame? Is it anything but a greater sensibility to all the pleasures and pains of life? And if the man of a delicate, refined temper, by being so much more alive than the rest of the world, is only so much more unhappy, what judgment must we form in general of human life?

Let men remain at rest, says our adversary, and they will be easy. They are willing artificers of their own misery. . . . No! reply I: an anxious languor follows their repose; disappointment, vexation, trouble, their activity and ambition.

I can observe something like what you mention in some others, replied Cleanthes, but I confess I feel little or nothing of it in myself, and hope that it is not so common as you represent it.

If you feel not human misery yourself, cried Demea, I congratulate you on so happy a singularity. Others, seemingly the most prosperous, have not been ashamed to vent their complaints in the most melancholy strains. Let us attend to the great, the fortunate emperor, Charles V, when, tired with human grandeur, he resigned all his existence dominions into the hands of his son. In the last harangue which he made on that memorable occasion, he publicly avowed *that the greatest prosperities which he had ever enjoyed had been mixed with so many adversities that he might truly say he had never enjoyed any satisfaction or contentment.* But did the retired life in which he sought for shelter afford him any greater happiness? If we may credit his son's account, his repentance commenced the very day of his resignation.

Cicero's fortune, from small beginnings, rose to the greatest lustre and renown; yet what pathetic complaints of the ills of life do his familiar letters, as well as philosophical discourses, contain? And suitably to his own experience, he introduces Cato, the great, the fortunate Cato protesting in his old age that had he a new life in his offer he would reject the present.

Ask yourself, ask any of your acquaintance, whether they would live over again the last ten or twenty years of their life. No! but the next twenty, they say, will be better:

> And from the dregs of life, hope to receive
> What the first sprightly running could not give.[3]

Thus, at last, they find (such is the greatness of human misery, it reconciles even contradictions) that they complain at once of the shortness of life and of its vanity and sorrow.

And is it possible, Cleanthes, said Philo, that after all these reflections, and infinitely more which might be suggested, you can still persevere in your anthropomorphism, and assert the moral attributes of the Deity, his justice, benevolence, mercy, and rectitude, to be of the same nature with these virtues in human creatures? His power, we allow, is infinite; whatever he wills is executed; but neither man nor any other animal is happy; therefore, he does not will their happiness. His wisdom is infinite; he is never mistaken in choosing the means to any end; but the course of nature tends not to human or animal felicity; therefore, it is not established for that purpose. Through the whole compass of human knowledge there are no inferences more certain and infallible than these. In what respect, then, do his benevolence and mercy resemble the benevolence and mercy of men?

Epicurus' old questions are yet unanswered.

Is he willing to prevent evil, but not able? then is he impotent. Is he able, but not willing? then is he malevolent. Is he both able and willing? whence then is evil?

You ascribe, Cleanthes, (and I believe justly) a purpose and intention to nature. But what, I beseech you, is the object of that curious artifice and machinery which she has displayed in all animals — the preservation alone of individuals, and propagation of the species? It seems enough for her purpose, if such a rank be barely upheld in the universe, without any care or concern for the happiness of the members that compose it. No resource for this purpose: no machinery in order merely to give pleasure or ease; no fund of pure joy and contentment; no indulgence without some want or necessity accompanying it. At least, the few phenomena of this nature are overbalanced by opposite phenomena of still greater importance.

Our sense of music, harmony, and indeed beauty of all kinds, gives satisfaction, without being absolutely necessary to the preservation and propagation of the species. But what racking pains, on the other hand, arise from gouts, gravels, megrims, toothaches, rheumatisms, where the injury to the animal machinery is either small or incurable? Mirth, laughter, play, frolic seem gratuitous satisfactions which have no further tendency; spleen, melancholy, discontent, superstition are pains of the same nature. How then does the Divine benevolence display itself, in the sense of you anthropomorphites? None but we mystics, as you were pleased to call us, can account for this strange mixture of phenomena, by deriving it from attributes infinitely perfect but incomprehensible.

And have you, at last, said Cleanthes smiling, betrayed your intentions, Philo? Your long agreement with Demea did indeed a little surprise me, but I find you were all the while erecting a concealed battery against me. And I must confess that you have now fallen upon a subject worthy of your noble spirit of opposition and controversy. If you can make out the present point, and prove mankind to be unhappy or corrupted, there is an end at once of all religion. For to what purpose establish the natural attributes of the Deity, while the moral are still doubtful and uncertain?

You take umbrage very easily, replied Demea, at opinions the most innocent and the most generally received, even amongst the religious and devout themselves; and nothing can be more surprising than to find a topic like this — concerning the wickedness and misery of man — charged with no less than atheism and profaneness. Have not all pious divines and preachers who have indulged their rhetoric on so fertile a subject, have they not easily, I say, given a solution of any difficulties which may attend it? This world is but a point in comparison of the universe; this life but a moment in comparison of eternity. The present evil phenomena, therefore, are rectified in other regions, and in some future period of existence. And the eyes of men, being then opened to larger views of things, see the whole connection of general laws, and trace, with adoration, the benevolence and rectitude of the Deity through all the mazes and intricacies of his providence.

No! replied Cleanthes, no! These arbitrary suppositions can never be admitted, contrary to matter of facts, visible and uncontroverted. Whence can any cause be known but from its known effects? Whence can any hypothesis be proved but from the apparent phenomena? To establish one hypothesis upon another is building entirely in the air; and the utmost we ever attain by these conjectures and fictions is to ascertain the bare possibility of our opinion, but never can we, upon such terms, establish its reality.

The only method of supporting Divine benevolence — and it is what I willingly embrace — is to deny absolutely the misery and wickedness of man. Your representations are exaggerated; your melancholy views mostly fictitious; your inferences contrary to fact and experience. Health is more common than sickness; pleasure than pain; happiness than misery. And for one vexation which we meet with, we attain, upon computation, a hundred enjoyments.

Admitting your position, replied Philo, which yet is extremely doubtful, you must at the same time allow that, if pain be less frequent than pleasure, it is infinitely more violent and durable. One hour of it is often able to outweigh a day, a week, a month of our common insipid enjoyments; and how many days, weeks, and months are passed by several in the most acute torments? Pleasure, scarcely in one instance, is ever able to reach ecstasy and rapture; and in no one instance can it continue for any time at its highest pitch and altitude. The spirits evaporate, the nerves relax, the fabric is disordered, and the enjoyment quickly degenerates into fatigue and uneasiness. But pain often, good God, how often! rises to torture and agony; and the longer it continues, it becomes still more genuine agony and torture. Patience is exhausted, courage languishes, melancholy seizes us, and nothing terminates our misery but the removal of its cause or another event which is the sole cure of all evil, but which, from our natural folly, we regard with still greater horror and consternation.

But not to insist upon these topics, continued Philo, though most obvious, certain, and important, I must use the freedom to admonish you, Cleanthes, that you have put the controversy upon a most dangerous issue, and are unawares introducing a total scepticism into the most essential articles of natural and revealed theology. What! no method of fixing a just foundation for religion unless we allow the happiness of human life, and maintain a continued existence even in this world, with all our present pains, infirmities, vexations, and follies, to be eligible and desirable! But this is contrary to everyone's feeling and experience; it is contrary to an authority so established as nothing can subvert. No decisive proofs can ever be produced against this authority; nor is it possible for you to compute, estimate, and compare all the pains and all the pleasures in the lives of all men and of all animals; and thus, by your resting the whole system of religion on a point which, from its very nature, must forever be uncertain, you tacitly confess that that system is equally uncertain.

But allowing you what never will be believed, at least, what you never possibly can prove, that animal or, at least, human happiness in this life exceeds its misery, you have yet done nothing; for this is not, by any means, what we expect from infinite power, infinite wisdom, and infinite goodness. Why is there any misery at all in the world? Not by chance, surely. From some cause then. Is it from the intention of the Deity? But he is perfectly benevolent. Is it contrary to his intention? But he is almighty. Nothing can shake the solidity of this reasoning, so short, so clear, so decisive, except we assert that these subjects exceed all human capacity, and that our common measures of truth and falsehood are not applicable to them—a topic which I have all along insisted on, but which you have, from the beginning, rejected with scorn and indignation.

But I will be contented to retire still from this intrenchment, for I deny that you can ever force me in it. I will allow that pain or misery in man is *compatible* with infinite power and goodness in the Deity, even in your sense of these attributes: what are you advanced by all these concessions? A mere possible compatibility is not sufficient. You must *prove* these pure, unmixt, and uncontrollable attributes from the present mixed and confused phenomena, and from these alone. A hopeful undertaking! Were the phenomena ever so pure and unmixed, yet, being finite, they would be insufficient for that purpose. How much more, where they are also so jarring and discordant!

Here, Cleanthes, I find myself at ease in my argument. Here I triumph. Formerly, when we argued concerning the natural attributes of intelligence and design, I needed all my sceptical and metaphysical subtilty to elude your grasp. In many views of the universe and of its parts, particularly the latter, the beauty and fitness of final causes strike us with such irresistible force that all objections appear (what I believe they really are) mere cavils and sophisms; nor can we then imagine how it was ever possible for us to repose any weight on them. But there is no view of human life or of the condition of mankind from which, without the greatest violence, we can infer the moral attributes or learn that infinite benevolence, conjoined with infinite power and infinite wisdom, which we must discover by the eyes of faith alone. It is your turn now to tug the labouring oar, and to support your philosophical subtilties against the dictates of plain reason and experience.

NOTES

1. That sentiment had been maintained by Dr. King and some few others before Leibniz, though by none of so great fame as that German philosopher.
2. Milton: *Paradise Lost*, Bk. XI.
3. John Dryden, *Aureng-Zebe*, Act IV, sc. 1.

Further Questions

1. It is sometimes said that the reason there is suffering is that God is using Earth as a testing ground to see which humans merit heaven. Suppose this were true. Would it be an adequate response to Philo's arguments?

2. "The so-called problem of evil is not really a problem for Christianity since any suffering we may experience on Earth is nothing compared to the infinite and eternal bliss that according to Christianity awaits us in heaven." Assume, for the sake of argument, that the bliss really is coming. Would this be an adequate response to Philo's arguments?

3. "The basic flaw in the so-called problem of evil is in its assumption that God's goodness is like human goodness. It is not. God's goodness is so beyond human goodness that we humans, with our finite mental and emotional capacities, can scarcely begin to comprehend it." Do you agree? Why?

Further Readings

McCloskey, H. J. "God and Evil." *The Philosophical Quarterly*, Vol. 10 (1960): 97–114. A classic contemporary restatement of the problem of evil by someone who doubts there is an adequate response.

Hick, John. *Evil and the God of Love*. New York: Harper & Row, 1966. A well-known Protestant theologian responds to the problem of evil. Thoughtful and readable.

Peterson, Michael L., ed. *The Problem of Evil*. South Bend, In.: University of Notre Dame Press, 1992. An anthology of classical and contemporary selections.

Pike, Nelson. "Hume on Evil." *The Philosophical Review*, vol. 72 (1963): 180–197. A critique of Hume's position.

Letters from the Earth

MARK TWAIN

"Mark Twain" was the pen name of Samuel Langhorne Clemens, one of America's greatest humorists and authors. Born in 1835 in a small village in Missouri, he grew up in Hannibal, Missouri, with relatively little schooling. He was apprenticed to a printer and then worked for newspapers in St. Louis, New York, and Philadelphia. In 1856, on his way to South America, he decided to fulfill his dream to become a steamboat pilot on the Mississippi River. When the Civil War disrupted river traffic, he fought briefly on the Confederate side, then went west to try his hand at forestry and mining. Failing at these, he worked as a reporter on the western frontier until he wrote the works for which he became famous, *The Adventures of Tom Sawyer* (1876), *The Adventures of Huckleberry Finn* (1884), and *A Connecticut Yankee in King Arthur's Court* (1889).

Commenting on the following selection, in 1909, Twain wrote: "This book will never be published . . . in fact, it couldn't be, because it would be a felony." It was not published in his lifetime. Even in 1939, as it was being prepared for publication, his daughter prevented it from going to press. It wasn't until 1962 that she withdrew her objections and *Letters from the Earth*, after more than half a century of censorship, finally reached an audience.

Reading Questions

1. Many people, even those who are not themselves religious, treat religion with reverence. Twain is unabashedly irreverent, poking fun and satirizing *everything* about it. (Keep in mind, too, how long ago this was written.) Do you treat religion with reverence? Why?

2. What does Twain think is the function of religion in society?

3. Do you know people who would be offended by Twain's essay? For what reasons? Do you agree? Why?

THE CREATOR SAT UPON THE THRONE, thinking. Behind him stretched the illimitable continent of heaven, steeped in a glory of light and color; before him rose the black night of Space, like a wall. His mighty bulk towered rugged and mountain-like into the zenith, and His divine head blazed there like a distant sun. At His feet stood three colossal figures, diminished to extinction, almost, by contrast — archangels — their heads level with His ankle-bone.

When the Creator had finished thinking, He said, "I have thought. Behold!"

He lifted His hand, and from it burst a fountain-spray of fire, a million stupendous suns, which clove the blackness and soared, away and away and away, diminishing in magnitude and intensity as they pierced the far frontiers of Space, until at last they were but as diamond nailheads sparkling under the domed vast roof of the universe.

At the end of an hour the Grand Council was dismissed.

They left the Presence impressed and thoughtful, and retired to a private place, where they might talk with freedom. None of the three seemed to want to begin, though all wanted somebody to do it. Each was burning to discuss the great event, but would prefer not to commit himself till he should know how the others regarded it. So there was some aimless and halting conversation about matters of no consequence, and this dragged tediously along, arriving nowhere, until at last the archangel Satan gathered

his courage together — of which he had a very good supply — and broke ground. He said: "We know what we are here to talk about, my lords, and we may as well put pretense aside, and begin. If this is the opinion of the Council —"

"It is, it is!" said Gabriel and Michael, gratefully interrupting.

"Very well, then, let us proceed. We have witnessed a wonderful thing; as to that, we are necessarily agreed. As to the value of it — if it has any — that is a matter which does not personally concern us. We can have as many opinions about it as we like, and that is our limit. We have no vote. I think Space was well enough, just as it was, and useful, too. Cold and dark — a restful place, now and then, after a season of the overdelicate climate and trying splendors of heaven. But these are details of no considerable moment; the new feature, the immense feature, is — what, gentlemen?"

"The invention and introduction of automatic, unsupervised, self-regulating *law* for the government of those myriads of whirling and racing suns and worlds!"

"That is it!" said Satan. "You perceive that it is a stupendous idea. Nothing approaching it has been evolved from the Master Intellect before. Law — *Automatic* Law — exact and unvarying Law — requiring no watching, no correcting, no readjusting while the eternities endure! He said those countless vast bodies would plunge through the wastes of Space ages and ages, at unimaginable speed, around stupendous orbits, yet

Excerpts from Letters from the Earth *(Fawcett World Library, 1967).*

never collide, and never lengthen nor shorten their orbital periods by so much as the hundredth part of a second in two thousand years! That is the new miracle, and the greatest of all—*Automatic Law*! And He gave it a name—the LAW OF NATURE—and said Natural Law is the LAW OF GOD—interchangeable names for one and the same thing."

"Yes," said Michael, "and He said He would establish Natural Law—the Law of God—throughout His dominions, and its authority should be supreme and inviolable."

"Also," said Gabriel, "He said He would by and by create animals, and place them, likewise, under the authority of that Law."

"Yes," said Satan, "I heard Him, but did not understand. What *is* animals, Gabriel?"

"Ah, how should I know? How should any of us know? It is a new word."

[*Interval of three centuries, celestial time—the equivalent of a hundred million years, earthly time. Enter a Messenger-Angel.*]

"My lords, He is making animals. Will it please you to come and see?"

They went, they saw, and were perplexed. Deeply perplexed—and the Creator noticed it, and said, "Ask. I will answer."

"Divine One," said Satan, making obeisance, "what are they for?"

"They are an experiment in Morals and Conduct. Observe them, and be instructed."

There were thousands of them. They were full of activities. Busy, all busy—mainly in persecuting each other. Satan remarked—after examining one of them through a powerful microscope: "This large beast is killing weaker animals, Divine One."

"The tiger—yes. The law of his nature is ferocity. The law of his nature is the Law of God. He cannot disobey it."

"Then in obeying it he commits no offense, Divine One?"

"No, he is blameless."

"This other creature, here, is timid, Divine One, and suffers death without resisting."

"The rabbit—yes. He is without courage. It is the law of his nature—the Law of God. He must obey it."

"Then he cannot honorably be required to go counter to his nature and resist, Divine One?"

"No. No creature can be honorably required to go counter to the law of his nature—the Law of God."

After a long time and many questions, Satan said, "The spider kills the fly, and eats it; the bird kills the spider and eats it; the wildcat kills the goose; the—well, they all kill each other. It is murder all along the line. Here are countless multitudes of creatures, and they all kill, kill, kill, they are all murderers. And they are not to blame, Divine One?"

"They are not to blame. It is the law of their nature. And always the law of nature is the Law of God. Now—observe—behold! A new creature—and the masterpiece—Man!"

Men, women, children, they came swarming in flocks, in droves, in millions.

"What shall you do with them, Divine One?"

"Put into each individual, in differing shades and degrees, all the various Moral Qualities, in mass, that have been distributed, a single distinguishing characteristic at a time, among the non-speaking animal world—courage, cowardice, ferocity, gentleness, fairness, justice, cunning, treachery, magnanimity, cruelty, malice, malignity, lust, mercy, pity, purity, selfishness, sweetness, honor, love, hate, baseness, nobility, loyalty, falsity, veracity, untruthfulness—each human being shall have *all* of these in him, and they will constitute his nature. In some, there will be high and fine characteristics which will submerge the evil ones, and those will be called good men; in others the evil characteristics will have dominion, and those will be called bad men. Observe—behold—they vanish!"

"Whither are they gone, Divine One?"

"To the earth—they and all their fellow animals."

"What is the earth?"

"A small globe I made, a time, two times and a half ago. You saw it, but did not notice it in the explosion of worlds and suns that sprayed from my hand. Man is an experiment, the other animals are another experiment. Time will show whether they were worth the trouble. The exhibition is over; you may take your leave, my lords."

Several days passed by.

This stands for a long stretch of (our) time, since in heaven a day is as a thousand years.

Satan had been making admiring remarks about certain of the Creator's sparkling industries — remarks which, being read between the lines, were sarcasms. He had made them confidentially to his safe friends the other archangels, but they had been overheard by some ordinary angels and reported at Headquarters.

He was ordered into banishment for a day — the celestial day. It was a punishment he was used to, on account of his too flexible tongue. Formerly he had been deported into space, there being nowhither else to send him, and had flapped tediously around there in the eternal night and the Arctic chill; but now it occurred to him to push on and hunt up the earth and see how the Human-Race experiment was coming along.

By and by he wrote home — very privately — to St. Michael and St. Gabriel about it.

Satan's Letter

This is a strange place, an extraordinary place, and interesting. There is nothing resembling it at home. The people are all insane, the other animals are all insane, the earth is insane, Nature itself is insane. Man is a marvelous curiosity. When he is at his very best he is a sort of low grade nickel-plated angel; at his worst he is unspeakable, unimaginable; and first and last and all the time he is a sarcasm. Yet he blandly and in all sincerity calls himself the "noblest work of God." This is the truth I am telling you. And this is not a new idea with him, he has talked it through all the ages, and believed it. Believed it, and found nobody among all his race to laugh at it.

Moreover — if I may put another strain upon you — he thinks he is the Creator's pet. He believes the Creator is proud of him; he even believes the Creator loves him; has a passion for him; sits up nights to admire him; yes, and watch over him and keep him out of trouble. He prays to Him, and thinks He listens. Isn't it a quaint idea? Fills his prayers with crude and bald and florid flatteries of Him, and thinks He sits and purrs over these extravagancies and enjoys them. He prays for help, and favor, and protection, every day; and does it with hopefulness and confidence, too, although no prayer of his has ever been answered. The daily affront, the daily defeat, do not discourage him, he goes on praying just the same. There is something almost fine about his perseverance. I must put one more strain upon you: he thinks he is going to heaven!

He has salaried teachers who tell him that. They also tell him there is a hell, of everlasting fire, and that he will go to it if he doesn't keep the Commandments. What are the Commandments? They are a curiosity. I will tell you about them by and by.

Letter II

. . . he has imagined a heaven, and has left entirely out of it the supremest of all his delights, the one ecstasy that stands first and foremost in the heart of every individual of his race — and of ours — sexual intercourse!

It is as if a lost and perishing person in a roasting desert should be told by a rescuer he might choose and have all longed-for things but one, and he should elect to leave out water!

His heaven is like himself: strange, interesting, astonishing, grotesque. I give you my word, it has not a single feature in it that he *actually values*. It consists — utterly and entirely — of diversions which he cares next to nothing about, here in the earth, yet is quite sure he will like in heaven. Isn't it curious? Isn't it interesting? You must not think I am exaggerating, for it is not so. . . .

Letter III

You have noticed that the human being is a curiosity. In times past he has had (and worn out and flung away) hundreds and hundreds of religions; today he has hundreds and hundreds of religions, and launches not fewer than three new ones every year. I could enlarge that number and still be within the facts.

One of his principal religions is called the Christian. A sketch of it will interest you. It is set forth in detail in a book containing two million words, called the Old and New Testaments. Also it has another name — The Word of God. For the Christian thinks every word of it was dictated by God — the one I have been speaking of.

It is full of interest. It has noble poetry in it; and some clever fables; and some blood-drenched history; and some good morals; and a wealth of obscenity; and upwards of a thousand lies.

This Bible is built mainly out of the fragments of older Bibles that had their day and crumbled to ruin. So it noticeably lacks in originality, necessarily. Its three or four most imposing and impressive events all happened in earlier Bibles; all its best precepts and rules of conduct came also from those Bibles; there are only two new things in it: hell, for one, and that singular heaven I have told you about.

What shall we do? If we believe, with these people, that their God invented these cruel things, we slander him; if we believe that these people invented them themselves, we slander them. It is an unpleasant dilemma in either case, for neither of these parties has done us any harm.

For the sake of tranquillity, let us take a side. Let us join forces with the people and put the whole ungracious burden upon *him* — heaven, hell, Bible and all. It does not seem right, it does not seem fair; and yet when you consider that heaven, and how crushingly charged it is with everything that is repulsive to a human being, how can we believe a human being invented it? And when I come to tell you about hell, the strain will be greater still, and you will be likely to say, No, a man would not provide that place, for either himself or anybody else; he simply couldn't.

That innocent Bible tells about the Creation. Of what — the universe? Yes, the universe. In six days!

God did it. He did not call it the universe — that name is modern. His whole attention was upon this world. He constructed it in five days — and then? It took him only one day to make twenty million suns and eighty million planets!

What were they for — according to his idea? To furnish light for this little toy-world. That was his whole purpose; he had no other. One of the twenty million suns (the smallest one) was to light it in the daytime, the rest were to help one of the universe's countless moons modify the darkness of its nights.

It is quite manifest that he believed his fresh-made skies were diamond-sown with those myriads of twinkling stars the moment his first-day's sun sank below the horizon; whereas, in fact, not a single star winked in that black vault until three years and a half after that memorable week's formidable industries had been completed.* Then one star appeared, all solitary and alone, and began to blink. Three years later another one appeared. The two blinked together for more than four years before a third joined them. At the end of the first hundred years there were not yet twenty-five stars twinkling in the wide wastes of those gloomy skies. At the end of a thousand years not enough stars were yet visible to make a show. At the end of a million years only half of the present array had sent their light over the telescopic frontiers, and it took another million for the rest to follow suit, as the vulgar phrase goes. There being at that time no telescope, their advent was not observed.

For three hundred years, now, the Christian astronomer has known that his Deity didn't make the stars in those tremendous six days; but the Christian astronomer does not enlarge upon that detail. Neither does the priest.

In his Book, God is eloquent in his praises of his mighty works, and calls them by the largest

---

* It takes the light of the nearest star (61 Cygni) three and a half years to come to the earth, traveling at the rate of 186,000 miles per second. Arcturus had been shining 200 years before it was visible from the earth. Remoter stars gradually became visible after thousands and thousands of years. — THE EDITOR [M. T.]

names he can find — thus indicating that he has a strong and just admiration of magnitudes; yet he made those millions of prodigious suns to light this wee little orb, instead of appointing this orb's little sun to chance attendance upon them. He mentions Arcturus in his Book — you remember Arcturus; we went there once. It is one of this earth's night lamps! — that giant globe which is fifty thousand times as large as this earth's sun, and compares with it as a melon compares with a cathedral.

However, the Sunday school still teaches the child that Arcturus was created to help light this earth, and the child grows up and continues to believe it long after he has found out that the probabilities are against its being so.

According to the Book and its servants the universe is only six thousand years old. It is only within the last hundred years that studious, inquiring minds have found out that it is nearer a hundred million.

During the Six Days, God created man and the other animals.

He made a man and a woman and placed them in a pleasant garden, along with the other creatures. They all lived together there in harmony and contentment and blooming youth for some time; then trouble came. God had warned the man and the woman that they must not eat of the fruit of a certain tree. And he added a most strange remark: he said that if they ate of it they should surely die. Strange, for the reason that inasmuch as they had never seen a sample of death they could not possibly know what he meant. Neither would he nor any other god have been able to make those ignorant children understand what was meant, without furnishing a sample. The mere word could have no meaning for them, any more than it would have for an infant of days.

Presently a serpent sought them out privately, and came to them walking upright, which was the way of serpents in those days. The serpent said the forbidden fruit would store their vacant minds with knowledge. So they ate it, which was quite natural, for man is so made that he eagerly

wants to know; whereas the priest, like God, whose imitator and representative he is, has made it his business from the beginning to keep him from knowing any useful thing.

Adam and Eve ate the forbidden fruit, and at once a great light streamed into their dim heads. They had acquired knowledge. What knowledge — useful knowledge? No — merely knowledge that there was such a thing as good and such a thing as evil, and how to do evil. They couldn't do it before. Therefore all their acts up to this time had been without stain, without blame, without offense.

But now they could do evil — and suffer for it; now they had acquired what the Church calls an invaluable possession, the Moral Sense; that sense which differentiates man from the beast and sets him above the beast. Instead of below the beast — where one would suppose his proper place would be, since he is always foul-minded and guilty and the beast always clean-minded and innocent. It is like valuing a watch that must go wrong, above a watch that can't.

The Church still prizes the Moral Sense as man's noblest asset today, although the Church knows God has a distinctly poor opinion of it and did what he could in his clumsy way to keep his happy Children of the Garden from acquiring it.

Very well, Adam and Eve now knew what evil was, and how to do it. They knew how to do various kinds of wrong things, and among them one principal one — the one God had his mind on principally. That one was the art and mystery of sexual intercourse. To them it was a magnificent discovery, and they stopped idling around and turned their entire attention to it, poor exultant young things!

In the midst of one of these celebrations they heard God walking among the bushes, which was an afternoon custom of his, and they were smitten with fright. Why? Because they were naked. They had not known it before. They had not minded it before; neither had God.

In that memorable moment immodesty was born; and some people have valued it ever since, though it would certainly puzzle them to explain why.

Adam and Eve entered the world naked and unashamed — naked and pure-minded; and no descendant of theirs has ever entered it otherwise. All have entered it naked, unashamed, and clean in mind. They have entered it modest. They had to acquire immodesty and the soiled mind; there was no other way to get it. A Christian mother's first duty is to soil her child's mind, and she does not neglect it. Her lad grows up to be a missionary, and goes to the innocent savage and to the civilized Japanese, and soils their minds. Whereupon they adopt immodesty, they conceal their bodies, they stop bathing naked together.

The convention miscalled modesty has no standard, and cannot have one, because it is opposed to nature and reason, and is therefore an artificiality and subject to anybody's whim, anybody's diseased caprice. And so, in India the refined lady covers her face and breasts and leaves her legs naked from the hips down, while the refined European lady covers her legs and exposes her face and her breasts. In lands inhabited by the innocent savage the refined European lady soon gets used to full-grown native stark-nakedness, and ceases to be offended by it. A highly cultivated French count and countess — unrelated to each other — who were marooned in their nightclothes, by shipwreck, upon an uninhabited island in the eighteenth century, were soon naked. Also ashamed — for a week. After that their nakedness did not trouble them, and they soon ceased to think about it.

You have never seen a person with clothes on. Oh, well, you haven't lost anything.

To proceed with the Biblical curiosities. Naturally you will think the threat to punish Adam and Eve for disobeying was of course not carried out, since they did not create themselves, nor their natures nor their impulses nor their weaknesses, and hence were not properly subject to anyone's commands, and not responsible to anybody for their acts. It will surprise you to know that the threat *was* carried out. Adam and Eve

were punished, and that crime finds apologists unto this day. The sentence of death was executed.

As you perceive, the only person responsible for the couple's offense escaped; and not only escaped but became the executioner of the innocent.

In your country and mine we should have the privilege of making fun of this kind of morality, but it would be unkind to do it here. Many of these people have the reasoning faculty, but no one uses it in religous matters.

The best minds will tell you that when a man has begotten a child he is morally bound to tenderly care for it, protect it from hurt, shield it from disease, clothe it, feed it, bear with its waywardness, lay no hand upon it save in kindness and for its own good, and never in any case inflict upon it a wanton cruelty. God's treatment of his earthly children, every day and every night, is the exact opposite of all that, yet those best minds warmly justify these crimes, condone them, excuse them, and indignantly refuse to regard them as crimes at all, when *he* commits them. Your country and mine is an interesting one, but there is nothing there that is half so interesting as the human mind.

Very well, God banished Adam and Eve from the Garden, and eventually assassinated them. All for disobeying a command which he had no right to utter. But he did not stop there, as you will see. He has one code of morals for himself, and quite another for his children. He requires his children to deal justly — and gently — with offenders, and forgive them seventy-and-seven times; whereas he deals neither justly nor gently with anyone, and he did not forgive the ignorant and thoughtless first pair of juveniles even their first small offense and say, "You may go free this time, I will give you another chance."

On the contrary! He elected to punish *their* children, all through the ages to the end of time, for a trifling offense committed by others before they were born. He is punishing them yet. In mild ways? No, in atrocious ones.

You would not suppose that this kind of a Being gets many compliments. Undeceive yourself:

the world calls him the All-Just, the All-Righteous, the All-Good, the All-Merciful, the All-Forgiving, the All-Truthful, the All-Loving, the Source of All Morality. These sarcasms are uttered daily, all over the world. But not as conscious sarcasms. No, they are meant seriously: they are uttered without a smile.

Letter IV

So the First Pair went forth from the Garden under a curse — a permanent one. They had lost every pleasure they had possessed before "The Fall"; and yet they were rich, for they had gained one worth all the rest; they knew the Supreme Art.

They practiced it diligently and were filled with contentment. The Deity ordered them to practice it. They obeyed, this time. But it was just as well it was not forbidden, for they would have practiced it anyhow, if a thousand Deities had forbidden it.

Results followed. By the name of Cain and Abel. And these had some sisters; and knew what to do with them. And so there were some more results: Cain and Abel begot some nephews and nieces. These, in their turn, begot some second cousins. At this point classification of relationships began to get difficult, and the attempt to keep it up was abandoned.

The pleasant labor of populating the world went on from age to age, and with prime efficiency; for in those happy days the sexes were still competent for the Supreme Art when by rights they ought to have been dead eight hundred years. The sweeter sex, the dearer sex, the lovelier sex was manifestly at its very best, then, for it was even able to attract gods. Real gods. They came down out of heaven and had wonderful times with those hot young blossoms. The Bible tells about it.

By help of those visiting foreigners the population grew and grew until it numbered several millions. But it was a disappointment to the Deity. He was dissatisfied with its morals; which in some respects were not any better than his own. Indeed they were an unflatteringly close imitation of his own. They were a very bad people, and as he knew of no way to reform them, he wisely concluded to abolish them. This is the only really enlightened and superior idea his Bible has credited him with, and it would have made his reputation for all time if he could only have kept to it and carried it out. But he was always unstable — except in his advertisements — and his good resolution broke down. He took a pride in man; man was his finest invention; man was his pet, after the housefly, and he could not bear to lose him wholly; so he finally decided to save a sample of him and drown the rest.

Nothing could be more characteristic of him. He created all those infamous people, and he alone was responsible for their conduct. Not one of them deserved death, yet it was certainly good policy to extinguish them; especially since in creating them the master crime had already been committed, and to allow them to go on procreating would be a distinct addition to the crime. But at the same time there could be no justice, no fairness, in any favoritism — all should be drowned or none.

No, he would not have it so; he would save half a dozen and try the race over again. He was not able to foresee that it would go rotten again, for he is only the Far-Sighted One in his advertisements.

He saved out Noah and his family, and arranged to exterminate the rest. He planned an Ark, and Noah built it. Neither of them had ever built an Ark before, nor knew anything about Arks; and so something out of the common was to be expected. It happened. Noah was a farmer, and although he knew what was required of the Ark he was quite incompetent to say whether this one would be large enough to meet the requirements or not (which it wasn't), so he ventured no advice. The Deity did not know it wasn't large enough, but took the chances and made no adequate measurements. In the end the ship fell far short of the necessities, and to this day the world still suffers for it.

Noah built the Ark. He built it the best he could, but left out most of the essentials. It had no rudder, it had no sails, it had no compass, it had no pumps, it had no charts, no leadlines, no anchors, no log, no light, no ventilation, and as for cargo room — which was the main thing — the less said about that the better. It was to be at sea eleven months, and would need fresh water enough to fill two Arks of its size — yet the additional Ark was not provided. Water from outside could not be utilized: half of it would be salt water, and men and land animals could not drink it.

For not only was a sample of man to be saved, but business samples of the other animals, too. You must understand that when Adam ate the apple in the Garden and learned how to multiply and replenish, the other animals learned the Art, too, by watching Adam. It was cunning of them, it was neat; for they got all that was worth having out of the apple without tasting it and afflicting themselves with the disastrous Moral Sense, the parent of all the immoralities. . . .

Letter VII

. . . I will tell you a pleasant tale which has in it a touch of pathos. A man got religion, and asked the priest what he must do to be worthy of his new estate. The priest said, "imitate our Father in Heaven, learn to be like him." The man studied his Bible diligently and thoroughly and understandingly, and then with prayers for heavenly guidance instituted his imitations. He tricked his wife into falling downstairs, and she broke her back and became a paralytic for life; he betrayed his brother into the hands of a sharper, who robbed him of his all and landed him in the almshouse; he inoculated one son with hookworms, another with the sleeping sickness, another with gonorrhea; he furnished one daughter with scarlet fever and ushered her into her teens deaf,

dumb, and blind for life; and after helping a rascal seduce the remaining one, he closed his doors against her and she died in a brothel cursing him. Then he reported to the priest who said that *that* was no way to imitate his Father in Heaven. The convert asked wherein he had failed, but the priest changed the subject and inquired what kind of weather he was having, up his way.

Letter VIII

Man is without any doubt the most interesting fool there is. Also the most eccentric. He hasn't a single written law, in his Bible or out of it, which has any but just one purpose and intention — to *limit or defeat a law of God.*

He can seldom take a plain fact and get any but a wrong meaning out of it. He cannot help this; it is the way the confusion he calls his mind is constructed. Consider the things he concedes, and the curious conclusions he draws from them.

For instance, he concedes that God made man. Made him without man's desire or privity.

This seems to plainly and indisputably make God, and God alone, responsible for man's acts. But man denies this.

He concedes that God has made angels perfect, without blemish, and immune from pain and death, and that he could have been similarly kind to man if he had wanted to, but denies that he was under any moral obligation to do it.

He concedes that man has no moral right to visit the child of his begetting with wanton cruelties, painful diseases and death, but refuses to limit God's privileges in this sort with the children of his begetting.

The Bible and man's statutes forbid murder, adultery, fornication, lying, treachery, robbery, oppression, and other crimes, but contend that God is free of these laws and has a right to break them when he will.

He concedes that God gives to each man his temperament, his disposition, at birth; he concedes that man cannot by any process change this temperament, but must remain always under its dominion. Yet if it be full of dreadful passions, in one man's case, and barren of them in another man's, it is right and rational to punish the one for his crimes, and reward the other for abstaining from crime.

There — let us consider these curiosities.

TEMPERAMENT (DISPOSITION)

Take two extremes of temperament — the goat and the tortoise.

Neither of these creatures makes it own temperament, but is born with it, like man, and can no more change it than can man.

Temperament is the law of God written in the heart of every creature by God's own hand, and *must* be obeyed, and will be obeyed in spite of all restricting or forbidding statutes, let them emanate whence they may.

Very well, lust is the dominant feature of the goat's temperament, the law of God in its heart, and it must obey it and *will* obey it the whole day long in the rutting season, without stopping to eat or drink. If the Bible said to the goat, "Thou shalt not fornicate, thou shalt not commit adultery," even Man — sap-headed man — would recognize the foolishness of the prohibition, and would grant that the goat ought not to be punished for obeying the law of his Maker. Yet he thinks it right and just that man should be put under the prohibition. All men. All alike.

On its face this is stupid, for, by temperament, which is the *real law* of God, many men are goats and can't help committing adultery when they get a chance; whereas there are numbers of men who, by temperament, can keep their purity and let an opportunity go by if the woman lacks in attractiveness. But the Bible doesn't allow adultery at all, whether a person can help it or not. It allows no distinction between goat and tortoise — the excitable goat, the emotional goat, that has to have some adultery every day or fade and die; and the tortoise, that cold calm puritan, that takes a treat only once in two years and then goes to sleep in the midst of it and doesn't wake

up for sixty days. No lady goat is safe from criminal assault, even on the Sabbath Day, when there is a gentleman goat within three miles to leeward of her and nothing in the way but a fence fourteen feet high, whereas neither the gentleman tortoise nor the lady tortoise is ever hungry enough for the solemn joys of fornication to be willing to break the Sabbath to get them. Now according to man's curious reasoning, the goat has earned punishment, and the tortoise praise.

"Thou shalt not commit adultery" is a command which makes no distinction between the following persons. They are all required to obey it:

Children at birth. Children in the cradle. School children. Youths and maidens. Fresh adults. Older ones. Men and women of 40. Of 50. Of 60. Of 70. Of 80. Of 90. Of 100.

The command does not distribute its burden equally, and cannot.

It is not hard upon the three sets of children.

It is hard — harder — still harder upon the next three sets — cruelly hard.

It is blessedly softened to the next three sets.

It has now done all the damage it can, and might as well be put out of commission. Yet with comical imbecility it is continued, and the four remaining estates are put under its crushing ban. Poor old wrecks, they couldn't disobey if they tried. And think — because they holily refrain from adulterating each other, they get praise for it! Which is nonsense; for even the Bible knows enough to know that if the oldest veteran there could get his lost heyday back again for an hour he would cast that commandment to the winds and ruin the first woman he came across, even though she were an entire stranger.

It is as I have said: every statute in the Bible and in the lawbooks is an attempt to defeat a law of God — in other words an unalterable and indestructible law of nature. These people's God has shown them by a million acts that he respects none of the Bible's statutes. He breaks every one of them himself, adultery and all.

The law of God, as quite plainly expressed in woman's construction, is this: There shall be no limit put upon your intercourse with the other sex sexually, at any time of life.

The law of God, as quite plainly expressed in man's construction is this: During your entire life you shall be under inflexible limits and restrictions, sexually.

During twenty-three days in every month (in the absence of pregnancy) from the time a woman is seven years old till she dies of old age, she is ready for action, and *competent*. As competent as the candlestick is to receive the candle. Competent every day, competent every night. Also, she *wants* that candle — yearns for it, longs for it, hankers after it, as commanded by the law of God in her heart.

But man is only briefly competent; and only then in the moderate measure applicable to the word in *his* sex's case. He is competent from the age of sixteen or seventeen thenceforward for thirty-five years. After fifty his performance is of poor quality, the intervals between are wide, and its satisfactions of no great value to either party; whereas his great-grandmother is as good as new. There is nothing the matter with her plant. Her candlestick is as firm as ever, whereas his candle is increasingly softened and weakened by the weather of age, as the years go by, until at last it can no longer stand, and is mournfully laid to rest in the hope of a blessed resurrection which is never to come.

By the woman's make, her plant has to be out of service three days in the month and during a part of her pregnancy. These are times of discomfort, often of suffering. For fair and just compensation she has the high privilege of unlimited adultery all the other days of her life.

That is the law of God, as revealed in her make. What becomes of this high privilege? Does she live in the free enjoyment of it? No. Nowhere in the whole world. She is robbed of it everywhere. Who does this? Man. Man's statutes — if the Bible *is* the Word of God.

Now there you have a sample of man's "reasoning powers," as he calls them. He observes certain facts. For instance, that in all his life he never sees the day that he can satisfy one woman; also, that no woman ever sees the day that she can't overwork, and defeat, and put out of commission any ten masculine plants that can be put to bed to her.* He puts those strikingly suggestive and luminous facts together, and from them draws this astonishing conclusion: The Creator intended the woman to be restricted to one man.

So he concretes that singular conclusion into a law, for good and all.

And he does it without consulting the woman, although she has a thousand times more at stake in the matter than he has. His procreative competency is limited to an average of a hundred exercises per year for fifty years, hers is good for three thousand a year for that whole time — and as many years longer as she may live. Thus his life interest in the matter is five thousand refreshments, while hers is a hundred and fifty thousand; yet instead of fairly and honorably leaving the making of the law to the person who has an overwhelming interest at stake in it, this immeasurable hog, who has nothing at stake in it worth considering, makes it himself!

You have heretofore found out, by my teachings, that man is a fool; you are now aware that woman is a damned fool.

Now if you or any other really intelligent person were arranging the fairness and justices between man and woman, you would give the man a one-fiftieth interest in one woman, and the woman a harem. Now wouldn't you? Necessarily. I give you my word, this creature with the decrepit candle has arranged it exactly the other way. Solomon, who was one of the Deity's favorites, had a copulation cabinet composed of seven

---

* In the Sandwich Islands in 1866, a buxom royal princess died. Occupying a place of distinguished honor at her funeral were thirty-six splendidly built young native men. In a laudatory song which celebrated the various merits, achievements and accomplishments of the late princess those thirty-six stallions were called her *harem*, and the song said it had been her pride and boast that she kept the whole of them busy, and that several times it had happened that more than one of them had been able to charge overtime. [M. T.]

hundred wives and three hundred concubines. To save his life he could not have kept two of those young creatures satisfactorily refreshed, even if he had had fifteen experts to help him. Necessarily almost the entire thousand had to go hungry years and years on a stretch. Conceive of a man hardhearted enough to look daily upon all that suffering and not be moved to mitigate it. He even wantonly added a sharp pang to that pathetic misery; for he kept within those women's sight, always, stalwart watchmen whose splendid masculine forms made the poor lassies' mouths water but who hadn't anything to solace a candlestick with, these gentry being eunuchs. A eunuch is a person whose candle has been put out. By art.*

From time to time, as I go along, I will take up a Biblical statute and show you that it always violates a law of God, and then is imported into the lawbooks of the nations, where it continues its violations. But those things will keep; there is no hurry.

Letter IX

. . . It is claimed that from the beginning of time he foresaw everything that would happen in the world. If that is true, he foresaw that Adam and Eve would eat the apple; that their posterity would be unendurable and have to be drowned; that Noah's posterity would in their turn be unendurable, and that by and by he would have to leave his throne in heaven and come down and be crucified to save that same tiresome human race again. The whole of it? No! A part of it? Yes. How much of it? In each generation, for hundreds and hundreds of generations, a billion would die and all go to perdition except perhaps ten thousand out of the billion. The ten thousand would have to come from the little body of Christians, and only one in the hundred of that little

body would stand any chance. None of them at all except such Roman Catholics as should have the luck to have a priest handy to sandpaper their souls at the last gasp, and here and there a Presbyterian. No others savable. All the others damned. By the million.

Shall you grant that he foresaw all this? The pulpit grants it. It is the same as granting that in the matter of intellect the Deity is the Head Pauper of the Universe, and that in the matter of morals and character he is away down on the level of David.

Letter X

The two Testaments are interesting, each in its own way. The Old one gives us a picture of these people's Deity as he was before he got religion, the other one gives us a picture of him as he appeared afterward. The Old Testament is interested mainly in blood and sensuality. The New one in Salvation. Salvation by fire.

The first time the Deity came down to earth, he brought life and death; when he came the second time, he brought hell.

Life was not a valuable gift, but death was. Life was a fever-dream made up of joys embittered by sorrows, pleasure poisoned by pain; a dream that was a nightmare-confusion of spasmodic and fleeting delights, ecstasies, exultations, happinesses, interspersed with long-drawn miseries, griefs, perils, horrors, disappointments, defeats, humiliations, and despairs — the heaviest curse devisable by divine ingenuity; but death was sweet, death was gentle, death was kind; death healed the bruised spirit and the broken heart, and gave them rest and forgetfulness; death was man's best friend; when man could endure life no longer, death came and set him free.

In time, the Deity perceived that death was a mistake; a mistake, in that it was insufficient; insufficient, for the reason that while it was an admirable agent for the inflicting of misery upon the survivor, it allowed the dead person himself to escape from all further persecution in the

---

* I purpose publishing these Letters here in the world before I return to you. Two editions. One, unedited, for Bible readers and their children; the other, expurgated, for persons of refinement. [M. T.]

blessed refuge of the grave. This was not satisfactory. A way must be contrived to pursue the dead beyond the tomb.

The Deity pondered this matter during four thousand years unsuccessfully, but as soon as he came down to earth and became a Christian his mind cleared and he knew what to do. He invented hell, and proclaimed it.

Now here is a curious thing. It is believed by everybody that while he was in heaven he was stern, hard, resentful, jealous, and cruel; but that when he came down to earth and assumed the name Jesus Christ, he became the opposite of what he was before: that is to say, he became sweet, and gentle, merciful, forgiving, and all harshness disappeared from his nature and a deep and yearning love for his poor human children took its place. Whereas it was as Jesus Christ that he devised hell and proclaimed it!

Which is to say, that as the meek and gentle Savior he was a thousand billion times crueler than ever he was in the Old Testament—oh, incomparably more atrocious than ever he was when he was at the very worst in those old days!

Meek and gentle? By and by we will examine this popular sarcasm by the light of the hell which he invented.

While it is true that the palm for malignity must be granted to Jesus, the inventor of hell, he was hard and ungentle enough for all godlike purposes even before he became a Christian. It does not appear that he ever stopped to reflect that *he* was to blame when a man went wrong, inasmuch as the man was merely acting in accordance with the disposition he had afflicted him with. No, he punished the man, instead of punishing himself. Moreover the punishment usually oversized the offense. Often, too, it fell, not upon the doer of a misdeed, but upon somebody else — a chief man, the head of a community, for instance.

And Israel abode in Shittim, and the people began to commit whoredom with the daughters of Moab.

And the Lord said unto Moses, Take *all the heads of the people*, and hang them up before the Lord against the Sun, that the fierce anger of the Lord may be turned away from Israel.

Does that look fair to you? It does not appear that the "heads of the people" got any of the adultery, yet it is they that are hanged, instead of "the people."

If it was fair and right in that day it would be fair and right today, for the pulpit maintains that God's justice is eternal and unchangeable; also that he is the Fountain of Morals, and that his morals are eternal and unchangeable. Very well, then, we must believe that if the people of New York should begin to commit whoredom with the daughters of New Jersey, it would be fair and right to set up a gallows in front of the city hall and hang the mayor and the sheriff and the judges and the archbishop on it, although they did not get any of it. It does not look right to me.

Moreover, you may be quite sure of one thing: it couldn't happen. These people would not allow it. They are better than their Bible. *Nothing* would happen here, except some lawsuits, for damages, if the incident couldn't be hushed up; and even down South they would not proceed against persons who did not get any of it; they would get a rope and hunt for the correspondents, and if they couldn't find them they would lynch a nigger.

Things have greatly improved since the Almighty's time, let the pulpit say what it may.

Will you examine the Deity's morals and disposition and conduct a little further? And will you remember that in the Sunday school the little children are urged to love the Almighty, and honor him, and praise him, and make him their model and try to be as like him as they can? Read:

1 And the Lord spake unto Moses, saying,

2 Avenge the children of Israel of the Midianites: afterward shalt thou be gathered unto thy people. . . .

7 And they warred against the Midianites, as the Lord commanded Moses; and they slew all the males.

8 And they slew the kings of Midian, beside the rest of them that were slain; *namely*, Evi, and Rekem, and Zur, and Hur, and Reba, five kings of Midian: Balaam also the son of Beor they slew with the sword.

9 And the children of Israel took *all* the women of Midian captives and their little ones, and took the spoil of all their cattle, and all their flocks, and all their goods.

10 And they burnt all their cities wherein they dwelt, and all their goodly castles, with fire.

11 And they took all the spoil, and all the prey, *both* of men and of beasts.

12 And they brought the captives, and the prey, and the spoil unto Moses and Eleazar the priest, and unto the congregation of the children of Israel, unto the camp at the plains of Moab, which *are* by Jordan *near* Jericho.

13 And Moses, and Eleazar the priest, and all the princes of the congregation, went forth to meet them without the camp.

14 And Moses was wroth with the officers of the host, *with* the captains over thousands, and captains over hundreds, which came from the battle.

15 And Moses said unto them, Have ye saved all the women alive?

16 Behold, these caused the children of Israel, through the counsel of Balaam, to commit trespass against the Lord in the matter of Peor, and there was a plague among the congregation of the Lord.

17 Now therefore kill every male among the little ones, and kill every woman that hath known man by lying with him.

18 But all the woman children, that have not known a man by lying with him, keep alive for yourselves.

19 And do ye abide without the camp seven days: whosoever hath killed any person, and whosoever hath touched any slain, purify *both* yourselves and your captives on the third day, and on the seventh day.

20 And purify all *your* raiment, and all that is made of skins, and all work of goats' *hair*, and all things made of wood.

21 And Eleazar the priest said unto the men of war which went to the battle, This *is* the ordinance of the law which the Lord commanded Moses. . . .

25 And the Lord spake unto Moses, saying,

26 Take the sum of the prey that was taken, *both* of man and of beast, thou, and Eleazar the priest, and the chief fathers of the congregation:

27 And divide the prey into two parts; between them that took the war upon them, who went out to battle, and between all the congregation:

28 And levy a tribute unto the Lord of the men of war which went out to battle. . . .

31 And Moses and Eleazar the priest did as the Lord commanded Moses.

32 And the booty, *being* the rest of the prey which the men of war had caught, was six hundred thousand, and seventy thousand and five thousand sheep,

33 And threescore and twelve thousand beeves,

34 And threescore and one thousand asses,

35 And thirty and two thousand persons in all, of women that had not known man by lying with him. . . .

40 And the persons *were* sixteen thousand; of which the Lord's tribute *was* thirty and two persons.

41 And Moses gave the tribute, *which was* the Lord's heave offering, unto Eleazar the priest, as the Lord commanded Moses. . . .

47 Even of the children of Israel's half, Moses took one portion of fifty, *both* of man and of beast, and gave them unto the Levites,which kept the charge of the tabernacle of the Lord; as the Lord commanded Moses.

10 When thou comest nigh unto a city to fight against it, then proclaim peace unto it. . . .

13 And when the Lord thy God hath delivered it into thine hands, thous shalt smite every male thereof with the edge of the sword:

14 But the women, and the little ones, and the cattle, and all that is in the city, *even* all the spoil thereof, shalt thou take unto thyself; and thou shalt eat the spoil of thine enemies, which the Lord thy God hath given thee.

15 Thus shalt thou do unto all the cities *which* are very far off from thee, which are not of the cities of these nations.

16 But of the cities of these people, which the Lord thy God doth give thee for an inheri-

tance, thou shalt save alive nothing that breatheth.

The Biblical law says: "Thou shalt not kill."

The law of God, planted in the heart of man at his birth, says: "Thou shalt kill."

The chapter I have quoted shows you that the book-statute is once more a failure. It cannot set aside the more powerful law of nature.

According to the belief of these people, it was God himself who said: "Thou shalt not kill."

Then it is plain that he cannot keep his own commandments.

He killed all those people — every male.

They had offended the Deity in some way. We know what the offense was, without looking; that is to say, we know it was a trifle; some small thing that no one but a god would attach any importance to. It is more than likely that a Midianite had been duplicating the conduct of one Onan, who was commanded to "go in unto his brother's wife" — which he did; but instead of finishing, "he spilled it on the ground." The Lord slew Onan for that, for the Lord could never abide indelicacy. The Lord slew Onan, and to this day the Christian world cannot understand why he stopped with Onan, instead of slaying all the inhabitants for three hundred miles around — they being innocent of offense, and therefore the very ones he would usually slay. For that had always been his idea of fair dealing. If he had had a motto, it would have read, "Let no innocent person escape." You remember what he did in the time of the flood. There were multitudes and multitudes of tiny little children, and he knew they had never done him any harm; but their relations had, and that was enough for him: he saw the waters rise toward their screaming lips, he saw the wild terror in their eyes, he saw that agony of appeal in the mothers' faces which would have touched any heart but his, but he was after the guiltless particularly, and he drowned those poor little chaps.

And you will remember that in the case of Adam's posterity *all* the billions are innocent — none of them had a share in his offense, but the

Deity holds them guilty to this day. None gets off, except by acknowledging that guilt — no cheaper lie will answer.

Some Midianite must have repeated Onan's act, and brought that dire disaster upon his nation. If that was not the indelicacy that outraged the feelings of the Deity, then I know what it was: some Midianite had been pissing against the wall. I am sure of it, for that was an impropriety which the Source of all Etiquette never could stand. A person could piss against a tree, he could piss on his mother, he could piss on his own breeches, and get off, but he must not piss against the wall — that would be going quite too far. The origin of the divine prejudice against this humble crime is not stated; but we know that the prejudice was very strong — so strong that nothing but a wholesale massacre of the people inhabiting the region where the wall was defiled could satisfy the Deity.

Take the case of Jeroboam. "I will cut off from Jeroboam him that pisseth against the wall." It was done. And not only was the man that did it cut off, but everybody else.

The same with the house of Baasha: everybody was exterminated, kinsfolks, friends, and all, leaving "not one that pisseth against a wall."

In the case of Jeroboam you have a striking instance of the Deity's custom of not limiting his punishments to the guilty; the innocent are included. Even the "remnant" of that unhappy house was removed, even "as a man taketh away dung, till it be all gone." That includes the women, the young maids, and the little girls. All innocent, for they couldn't piss against a wall. Nobody of that sex can. None but members of the other sex can achieve that feat.

A curious prejudice. And it still exists. Protestant parents still keep the Bible handy in the house, so that the children can study it, and one of the first things the little boys and girls learn is to be righteous and holy and not piss against the wall. They study those passages more than they study any others, except those which incite to masturbation. Those they hunt out and study in private. No Protestant child exists who does not masturbate. That art is the earliest accomplishment his religion confers upon him. Also the earliest her religion confers upon her.

The Bible has this advantage over all other books that teach refinement and good manners: that it goes to the child. It goes to the mind at its most impressible and receptive age—the others have to wait.

> Thou shalt have a paddle upon thy weapon; and it shall be, when thou wilt ease thyself abroad, thou shalt dig therewith, and shalt turn back and cover that which cometh from thee.

That rule was made in the old days because "The Lord thy God walketh in the midst of thy camp."

It is probably not worthwhile to try to find out, for certain, why the Midianites were exterminated. We can only be sure that it was for no large offense; for the cases of Adam, and the Flood, and the defilers of the wall teach us that much. A Midianite may have left his paddle at home and thus brought on the trouble. However, it is no matter. The main thing is the trouble itself, and the morals of one kind and another that it offers for the instruction and elevation of the Christian of today.

God wrote upon the tables of stone: "Thou shalt not kill." Also: "Thou shalt not commit adultery."

Paul, speaking by the divine voice, advised against sexual intercourse *altogether*. A great change from the divine view as it existed at the time of the Midianite incident.

Letter XI

Human history in all ages is red with blood, and bitter with hate, and stained with cruelties; but not since Biblical times have these features been without a limit of some kind. Even the Church, which is credited with having spilt more innocent blood, since the beginning of its supremacy, than all the political wars put together have spilt, has observed a limit. A sort of limit. But you no-

tice that when the Lord God of Heaven and Earth, adored Father of Man, goes to war, there is no limit. He is totally without mercy—he, who is called the Fountain of Mercy. He slays, slays, slays! All the men, all the beasts, all the boys, all the babies; also all the women and all the girls, except those that have not been deflowered.

He makes no distinction between innocent and guilty. The babies were innocent, the beasts were innocent, many of the men, many of the women, many of the boys, many of the girls were innocent, yet they had to suffer with the guilty. What the insane Father required was blood and misery; he was indifferent as to who furnished it.

The heaviest punishment of all was meted out to persons who could not by any possibility have deserved so horrible a fate—the 32,000 virgins. Their naked privacies were probed, to make sure that they still possessed the hymen unruptured; after this humiliation they were sent away from the land that had been their home, to be sold into slavery; the worst of slaveries and the shamefulest, the slavery of prostitution; bedslavery, to excite lust, and satisfy it with their bodies; slavery to any buyer, be he gentleman or be he a coarse and filthy ruffian.

It was the Father that inflicted this ferocious and undeserved punishment upon those bereaved and friendless virgins, whose parents and kindred he had slaughtered before their eyes. And were they praying to him for pity and rescue, meantime? Without a doubt of it.

These virgins were "spoil," plunder, booty. He claimed his share and got it. What use had *he* for virgins? Examine his later history and you will know.

His priests got a share of the virgins, too. What use could priests make of virgins? The private history of the Roman Catholic confessional can answer that question for you. The confessional's chief amusement has been seduction—in all the ages of the Church. Père Hyacinth testifies that of a hundred priests confessed by him, ninety-nine had used the confessional effectively for the seduction of married women and young girls. One priest confessed that of nine hundred girls and women whom he had served as father confessor in his time, none had escaped his lecherous embrace but the elderly and the homely. The official list of questions which the priest is required to ask will overmasteringly excite any woman who is not a paralytic.

There is nothing in either savage or civilized history that is more utterly complete, more remorselessly sweeping than the Father of Mercy's campaign among the Midianites. The official report does not furnish incidents, episodes, and minor details, it deals only in information in masses: *all* the virgins, *all* the men, *all* the babies, *all* "creatures *that breathe,*" *all* houses, *all* cities; it gives you just one vast picture, spread abroad here and there and yonder, as far as eye can reach, of charred ruin and storm-swept desolation; your imagination adds a brooding stillness, an awful hush—the hush of death. But of course there were incidents. Where shall we get them?

Out of history of yesterday's date. Out of history made by the red Indian of America. He has duplicated God's work, and done it in the very spirit of God. In 1862 the Indians in Minnesota, having been deeply wronged and treacherously treated by the government of the United States, rose against the white settlers and massacred them; massacred all they could lay their hands upon, sparing neither age nor sex. Consider this incident:

Twelve Indians broke into a farmhouse at daybreak and captured the family. It consisted of the farmer and his wife and four daughters, the youngest aged fourteen and the eldest eighteen. They crucified the parents; that is to say, they stood them stark naked against the wall of the living room and nailed their hands to the wall. Then they stripped the daughters bare, stretched them upon the floor in front of their parents, and repeatedly ravished them. Finally they crucified the girls against the wall opposite the parents, and cut off their noses and their breasts. They also—but I will not go into that. There is a limit.

There are indignities so atrocious that the pen cannot write them. One member of that poor crucified family—the father—was still alive when help came two days later.

Now you have one incident of the Minnesota massacre. I could give you fifty. They would cover all the different kinds of cruelty the brutal human talent has ever invented.

And now you know, by these sure indications, what happened under the personal direction of the Father of Mercies in his Midianite campaign. The Minnesota campaign was merely a duplicate of the Midianite raid. Nothing happened in the one that did not happen in the other.

No, that is not strictly true. The Indian was more merciful than was the Father of Mercies. He sold no virgins into slavery to minister to the lusts of the murderers of their kindred while their sad lives might last; he raped them, then charitably made their subsequent sufferings brief, ending them with the precious gift of death. He burned some of the houses, but not all of them. He carried out innocent dumb brutes, but he took the lives of none.

Would you expect this same conscienceless God, this moral bankrupt, to become a teacher of morals; of gentleness; of meekness; of righteousness; of purity? It looks impossible, extravagant; but listen to him. These are his own words:

Blessed are the poor in spirit, for theirs is the kingdom of heaven.

Blessed are they that mourn, for they shall be comforted.

Blessed are the meek, for they shall inherit the earth.

Blessed are they which do hunger and thirst after righteousness, for they shall be filled.

Blessed are the merciful, for they shall obtain mercy.

Blessed are the pure in heart, for they shall see God.

Blessed are the peace-makers, for they shall be called *the children of God*.

Blessed are they which are persecuted for righteousness' sake, for theirs is the kingdom of heaven.

Blessed are ye when men shall revile you and persecute you, and say all manner of evil against you falsely for my sake.

The mouth that uttered these immense sarcasms, these giant hypocrisies, is the very same that ordered the wholesale massacre of the Midianitish men and babies and cattle; the wholesale destruction of house and city; the wholesale banishment of the virgins into a filthy and unspeakable slavery. This is the same person who brought upon the Midianites the fiendish cruelties which were repeated by the red Indians, detail by detail, in Minnesota eighteen centuries later. The Midianite episode filled him with joy. So did the Minnesota one, or he would have prevented it.

The Beatitudes and the quoted chapters from Numbers and Deuteronomy ought always to be read from the pulpit together; then the congregation would get an all-round view of Our Father in Heaven. Yet not in a single instance have I ever known a clergyman to do this.

Further Questions

1. What would you think about having this piece included, along with *Tom Sawyer* and *Huckleberry Finn*, as part of a child's education? Do you think it should be available in elementary school libraries? Why or why not?

2. What is your overall reaction to the selection? What do you think Mark Twain finds most objectionable about religion? Do you agree?

3. "Religion, for many Christians, is the only source of legitimate moral codes. But religion is no more legitimate as a source of moral codes than is personal or cultural prejudice. Indeed, Christian moral codes are just personal and cultural prejudices wrapped up in the mantle of so-called divine respectability. There is no reason to think that the Bible expresses God's will regarding morality, or even if it does, that it embodies a legitimate moral code, that is, one that humane and reasonable people would want to follow." Regardless of what you actually believe, argue as well as you can *against* the remarks quoted. Include in your argument a reply to the sort of examples and considerations raised by Twain.

Further Readings

Mackie, J. L. "The Moral Consequences of Atheism," in *The Miracle of Theism*. Oxford: Oxford University Press, 1982, pp. 254–262. A short, clear argument for morality without God.

Pagels, Elaine. *The Gnostic Gospels*. New York: Random House, 1979. An excellent account of the struggle over patriarchy in early Christian communities.

Robinson, R. *An Atheist's Values*. Oxford: Oxford University Press, 1964. A spirited defense of atheistic morality. Includes a moral critique of Jesus' teachings.

Twain, Mark. *Letters from the Earth*. New York: Fawcett Crest, 1962. Contains the preceding selection plus many other provocative and irreverent essays, including "The Damned Human Race," "Passage from Eve's Autobiography," and "From an Unfinished Burlesque of Books on Etiquette."

"Why I Am Not a Christian"

BERTRAND RUSSELL

A brief biography of Russell appears on p. 217.

In this selection, Russell explains not only why he thinks the traditional arguments for the existence of God are inadequate but also why Christ was not the best and wisest of men.

Reading Questions

1. For each of the arguments for God that Russell considers, explain in your own words what the argument is and why Russell thinks it fails.
2. What flaws does Russell find in Christ's character? Do you agree? Explain.

THE SUBJECT ABOUT WHICH I am going to speak to you tonight is 'Why I am not a Christian'. Perhaps it would be as well, first of all, to try to make out what one means by the word 'Christian'. It is used these days in a very loose sense by a great many people. Some people mean no more by it than a person who attempts to live a good life. In that sense I suppose there would be Christians in all sects and creeds; but I do not think that that is the proper sense of the word, if only because it would imply that all the people who are not Christians — all the Buddhists, Confucians, Mohammedans, and so on — are not trying to live a good life. I do not mean by a Christian any person who tries to live decently according to his lights. I think that you must have a certain amount of definite belief before you have a right to call yourself a Christian. The word does not have quite such a full-blooded meaning now as it had in the times of St. Augustine and St. Thomas Aquinas. In those days, if a man said that he was a Christian it was known what he meant. You accepted a whole collection of creeds which were set out with great precision, and every single syllable of those creeds you believed with the whole strength of your convictions.

What Is a Christian?

Nowadays it is not quite that. We have to be a little more vague in our meaning of Christianity. I think, however, that there are two different items which are quite essential to anybody calling himself a Christian. The first is one of a dogmatic nature — namely, that you must believe in God and immortality. If you do not believe in those two things, I do not think that you can properly call yourself a Christian. Then, further than that, as the name implies, you must have some kind of belief about Christ. The Mohammedans, for instance, also believe in God and in immortality, and yet they would not call themselves Christians. I think you must have at the very lowest the belief that Christ was, if not divine, at least the best and wisest of men. If you are not going to believe that much about Christ, I do not think you have any right to call yourself a Christian. Of course there is another sense which you find in

Whitaker's Almanack and in geography books, where the population of the world is said to be divided into Christians, Mohammedans, Buddhists, fetish worshippers, and so on; and in that sense we are all Christians. The geography books count us all in, but that is a purely geographical sense, which I suppose we can ignore. Therefore I take it that when I tell you why I am not a Christian I have to tell you two different things; first, why I do not believe in God and in immortality; and, secondly, why I do not think that Christ was the best and wisest of men, although I grant Him a very high degree of moral goodness.

But for the successful efforts of unbelievers in the past, I could not take so elastic a definition of Christianity as that. As I said before, in olden days it had a much more full-blooded sense. For instance, it included the belief in hell. Belief in eternal hell fire was an essential item of Christian belief until pretty recent times. In this country, as you know, it ceased to be an essential item because of a decision of the Privy Council, and from that decision the Archbishop of Canterbury and the Archbishop of York dissented; but in this country our religion is settled by Act of Parliament, and therefore the Privy Council was able to override Their Graces and hell was no longer necessary to a Christian. Consequently I shall not insist that a Christian must believe in hell.

The Existence of God

To come to this question of the existence of God, it is a large and serious question, and if I were to attempt to deal with it in any adequate manner I should have to keep you here until Kingdom Come, so that you will have to excuse me if I deal with it in a somewhat summary fashion. You know, of course, that the Catholic Church has laid it down as a dogma that the existence of God can be proved by the unaided reason. That is a somewhat curious dogma, but it is one of their dogmas. They had to introduce it because at one time the free-thinkers adopted the habit of saying that there were such and such arguments which mere reason might urge against the existence of God, but of course they knew as a matter of faith that God did exist. The arguments and the reasons were set out at great length, and the Catholic Church felt that they must stop it. Therefore they laid it down that the existence of God can be proved by the unaided reason, and they had to set up what they considered were arguments to prove it. There are, of course, a number of them, but I shall take only a few.

The First Cause Argument

Perhaps the simplest and easiest to understand is the argument of the First Cause. (It is maintained that everything we see in this world has a cause, and as you go back in the chain of causes further and further you must come to a First Cause, and to that First Cause you give the name of God.) That argument, I suppose, does not carry very much weight nowadays, because, in the first place, cause is not quite what it used to be. The philosophers and the men of science have got going on cause, and it has not anything like the vitality it used to have; but, apart from that, you can see that the argument that there must be a First Cause is one that cannot have any validity. I may say that when I was a young man and was debating these questions very seriously in my mind, I for a long time accepted the argument of the First Cause, until one day, at the age of eighteen, I read John Stuart Mill's Autobiography, and I there found this sentence: 'My father taught me that the question, "Who made me?" cannot be answered, since it immediately suggests the further question, "Who made God?"' That very simple sentence showed me, as I still think, the fallacy in the argument of the First Cause. If everything must have a cause, then God must have a cause. If there can be anything without a cause, it may just as well be the world as God, so that there cannot be any validity in that argument. It is exactly of the same nature as the Hindu's view, that the world rested upon an elephant and the elephant rested upon a tortoise;

and when they said, 'How about the tortoise?' the Indian said, 'Suppose we change the subject'. The argument is really no better than that. There is no reason why the world could not have come into being without a cause; nor, on the other hand, is there any reason why it should not have always existed. There is no reason to suppose that the world had a beginning at all. The idea that things must have a beginning is really due to the poverty of our imagination. Therefore, perhaps, I need not waste any more time upon the argument about the First Cause.

The Natural Law Argument

Then there is a very common argument from natural law. That was a favourite argument all through the eighteenth century, especially under the influence of Sir Isaac Newton and his cosmogony. People observed the planets going round the sun according to the law of gravitation, and they thought that God had given a behest to these planets to move in that particular fashion, and that was why they did so. That was, of course, a convenient and simple explanation that saved them the trouble of looking any further for explanations of the law of gravitation. Nowadays we explain the law of gravitation in a somewhat complicated fashion that Einstein has introduced. I do not propose to give you a lecture on the law of gravitation as interpreted by Einstein, because that again would take some time; at any rate, you no longer have the sort of natural law that you had in the Newtonian system, where, for some reason that nobody could understand, nature behaved in a uniform fashion. We now find that a great many things we thought were natural laws are really human conventions. You know that even in the remotest depths of stellar space there are still three feet to a yard. That is, no doubt, a very remarkable fact, but you would hardly call it a law of nature. And a great many things that have been regarded as laws of nature are of that kind. On the other hand, where you can get down to any knowledge of what

atoms actually do, you will find they are much less subject to law than people thought, and that the laws at which you arrive are statistical averages of just the sort that would emerge from chance. There is, as we all know, a law that if you throw dice you will get double sixes only about once in thirty-six times, and we do not regard that as evidence that the fall of the dice is regulated by design; on the contrary, if the double sixes came very time we should think that there was design. The laws of nature are of that sort as regards a great many of them. They are statistical averages such as would emerge from the laws of chance; and that makes this whole business of natural law much less impressive than it formerly was. Quite apart from that, which represents the momentary state of science that may change tomorrow, the whole idea that natural laws imply a law-giver is due to a confusion between natural and human laws. Human laws are behests commanding you to behave a certain way, in which way you may choose to behave, or you may choose not to behave; but natural laws are a description of how things do in fact behave, and being a mere description of what they in fact do, you cannot argue that there must be somebody who told them to do that, because even supposing that there were you are then faced with the question, 'Why did God issue just those natural laws and no others?' If you say that He did it simply from His own good pleasure, and without any reason, you then find that there is something which is not subject to law, and so your train of natural law is interrupted. If you say, as more orthodox theologians do, that in all the laws which God issues He had a reason for giving those laws rather than others — the reason, of course, being to create the best universe, although you would never think it to look at it — if there was a reason for the laws which God gave, then God Himself was subject to law, and therefore you do not get any advantage by introducing God as an intermediary. You have really a law outside and anterior to the divine edicts, and God does not serve your purpose, because He is not the ultimate law-giver. In short, this whole argument about natural law no longer has anything like the strength that it used to have. I am travelling on in time in my review of the arguments. The arguments that are used for the existence of God change their character as time goes on. They were at first hard, intellectual arguments embodying certain quite definite fallacies. As we come to modern times they become less respectable intellectually and more and more affected by a kind of moralizing vagueness.

The Argument from Design

The next step in this process brings us to the argument from design. You all know the argument from design: everything in the world is made just so that we can manage to live in the world, and if the world was ever so little different we could not manage to live in it. That is the argument from design. It sometimes takes a rather curious form; for instance, it is argued that rabbits have white tails in order to be easy to shoot. I do not know how rabbits would view that application. It is an easy argument to parody. You all know Voltaire's remark, that obviously the nose was designed to be such as to fit spectacles. That sort of parody has turned out to be not nearly so wide of the mark as it might have seemed in the eighteenth century, because since the time of Darwin we understand much better why living creatures are adapted to their environment. It is not that their environment was made to be suitable to them, but that they grew to be suitable to it, and that is the basis of adaptation. There is no evidence of design about it.

When you come to look into this argument from design, it is a most astonishing thing that people can believe that this world, with all the things that are in it, with all its defects, should be the best that omnipotence has been able to produce in millions of years. I really cannot believe it. Do you think that, if you were granted omnipotence and omniscience and millions of years in which to perfect your world, you could produce nothing better than the Ku-Klux-Klan or the Fascists? Moreover, if you accept the ordinary laws of science, you have to suppose that human life and life in general on this planet will die out in due course: it is a stage in the decay of the solar system; at a certain stage of decay you get the sort of conditions of temperature and so forth which are suitable to protoplasm, and there is life for a short time in the life of the whole solar system. You see in the moon the sort of thing to which the earth is tending—something dead, cold, and lifeless.

I am told that that sort of view is depressing, and people will sometimes tell you that if they believed that they would not be able to go on living. Do not believe it; it is all nonsense. Nobody really worries much about what is going to happen millions of years hence. Even if they think they are worrying much about that, they are really deceiving themselves. They are worried about something much more mundane, or it may merely be a bad digestion; but nobody is really seriously rendered unhappy by the thought of something that is going to happen to this world millions and millions of years hence. Therefore, although it is of course a gloomy view to suppose that life will die out—at least I suppose we may say so, although sometimes when I contemplate the things that people do with their lives I think it is almost a consolation—it is not such as to render life miserable. It merely makes you turn your attention to other things.

The Moral Arguments for Deity

Now we reach one stage further in what I shall call the intellectual descent that the theists have made in their argumentations, and we come to what are called the moral arguments for the existence of God. You all know, of course, that there used to be in the old days three intellectual arguments for the existence of God, all of which were disposed of by Immanuel Kant in the *Critique of*

Pure Reason; but no sooner had he disposed of those arguments than he invented a new one, a moral argument, and that quite convinced him. He was like many people: in intellectual matters he was sceptical, but in moral matters he believed implicitly in the maxims that he had imbibed at his mother's knee. That illustrates what the psychoanalysts so much emphasize — the immensely stronger hold upon us that our very early associations have than those of later times.

Kant, as I say, invented a new moral argument for the existence of God, and that in varying forms was extremely popular during the nineteenth century. It has all sorts of forms. One form is to say that there would be no right or wrong unless God existed. I am not for the moment concerned with whether there is a difference between right and wrong, or whether there is not: that is another question. The point I am concerned with is that, if you are quite sure there is a difference between right and wrong, you are then in this situation: is that difference due to God's fiat or is it not? If it is due to God's fiat, then for God Himself there is no difference between right and wrong, and it is no longer a significant statement to say that God is good. If you are going to say, as theologians do, that God is good, you must then say that right and wrong have some meaning which is independent of God's fiat, because God's fiats are good and not bad independently of the mere fact that He made them. If you are going to say that, you will then have to say that it is not only through God that right and wrong came into being, but that they are in their essence logically anterior to God. You could, of course, if you liked, say that there was a superior deity who gave orders to the God who made this world, or could take up the line that some of the gnostics took up — a line which I often thought was a very plausible one — that as a matter of fact this world that we know was made by the devil at a moment when God was not looking. There is a good deal to be said for that, and I am not concerned to refute it.

The Argument For the Remedying of Injustice

Then there is another very curious form of moral argument, which is this: they say that the existence of God is required in order to bring justice into the world. In the part of this universe that we know there is great injustice, and often the good suffer, and often the wicked prosper, and one hardly knows which of those is the more annoying; but if you are going to have justice in the universe as a whole you have to suppose a future life to redress the balance of life here on earth. So they say that there must be a God, and there must be heaven and hell in order than in the long run there may be justice. That is a very curious argument. If you looked at the matter from a scientific point of view, you would say: 'After all, I know only this world. I do not know about the rest of the universe, but so far as one can argue at all on probabilities one would say that probably this world is a fair sample, and if there is injustice here the odds are that there is injustice elsewhere also.' Supposing you got a crate of oranges that you opened, and you found all the top layer of oranges bad, you would not argue: 'The underneath ones must be good, so as to redress the balance.' You would say: 'Probably the whole lot is a bad consignment'; and that is really what a scientific person would argue about the universe. He would say: 'Here we find in this world a great deal of injustice and so far as that goes that is a reason for supposing that justice does not rule in the world; and therefore so far as it goes it affords a moral argument against deity and not in favour of one.' Of course I know that the sort of intellectual arguments that I have been talking to you about are not what really moves people. What really moves people to believe in God is not any intellectual argument at all. Most people believe in God because they have been taught from early infancy to do it, and that is the main reason.

Then I think that the next most powerful reason is the wish for safety, a sort of feeling that there is a big brother who will look after you. That plays a very profound part in influencing people's desire for a belief in God.

The Character of Christ

I now want to say a few words upon a topic which I often think is not quite sufficiently dealt with by Rationalists, and that is the question whether Christ was the best and the wisest of men. It is generally taken for granted that we should all agree that that was so. I do not myself. I think that there are a good many points upon which I agree with Christ a great deal more than the professing Christians do. I do not know that I could go with Him all the way, but I could go with Him much farther than most professing Christians can. You will remember that He said: 'Resist not evil, but whosoever shall smite thee on thy right cheek, turn to him the other also.' That is not a new precept or a new principle. It was used by Lao-Tze and Buddha some five or six hundred years before Christ, but it is not a principle which as a matter of fact Christians accept. I have no doubt that the present Prime Minister,[1] for instance, is a most sincere Christian, but I should not advise any of you to go and smite him on one cheek. I think you might find that he thought this text was intended in a figurative sense.

Then there is another point which I consider is excellent. You will remember that Christ said: 'Judge not lest ye be judged.' That principle I do not think you would find was popular in the law courts of Christian countries. I have known in my time quite a number of judges who were very earnest Christians, and they none of them felt that they were acting contrary to Christian principles in what they did. Then Christ says: 'Give to him that asketh thee, and from him that would borrow of thee turn not thou away.' That is a very good principle.

[1] Stanley Baldwin.

Your Chairman has reminded you that we are not here to talk politics, but I cannot help observing that the last general election was fought on the question of how desirable it was to turn away from him that would borrow of thee, so that one must assume that the Liberals and Conservatives of this country are composed of people who do not agree with the teaching of Christ, because they certainly did very emphatically turn away on that occasion.

Then there is one other maxim of Christ which I think has a great deal in it, but I do not find that it is very popular among some of our Christian friends. He says: 'If thou wilt be perfect, go and sell that thou hast, and give to the poor.' That is a very excellent maxim, but, as I say, it is not much practised. All these, I think, are good maxims, although they are a little difficult to live up to. I do not profess to live up to them myself; but then, after all, it is not quite the same thing as for a Christian.

Defects in Christ's Teaching

Having granted the excellence of these maxims, I come to certain points in which I do not believe that one can grant either the superlative wisdom or the superlative goodness of Christ as depicted in the Gospels; and here I may say that one is not concerned with the historical question. Historically it is quite doubtful whether Christ ever existed at all, and if He did we do not know anything about Him, so that I am not concerned with the historical question, which is a very difficult one. I am concerned with Christ as He appears in the Gospels, taking the Gospel narrative as it stands, and there one does find some things that do not seem to be very wise. For one thing, He certainly thought that His second coming would occur in clouds of glory before the death of all the people who were living at that time. There are a great many texts that prove that. He says, for instance: 'Ye shall not have gone over the cities of Israel, till the Son of Man be come.' Then He says: 'There are some standing here which shall not taste death till the Son of Man comes into His kingdom'; and there are a lot of places where it is quite clear that He believed that His second coming would happen during the lifetime of many then living. That was the belief of His earlier followers, and it was the basis of a good deal of His moral teaching. When He said, 'Take no thought for the morrow', and things of that sort, it was very largely because He thought that the second coming was going to be very soon, and that all ordinary mundane affairs did not count. I have, as a matter of fact, known some Christians who did believe that the second coming was imminent. I knew a parson who frightened his congregation terribly by telling them that the second coming was very imminent indeed, but they were much consoled when they found that he was planting trees in his garden. The early Christians did really believe it, and they did abstain from such things as planting trees in their gardens, because they did accept from Christ the belief that the second coming was imminent. In that respect clearly He was not so wise as some other people have been, and He was certainly not superlatively wise.

The Moral Problem

Then you come to moral questions. There is one very serious defect to my mind in Christ's moral character, and that is that He believed in hell. I do not myself feel that any person who is really profoundly humane can believe in everlasting punishment. Christ certainly as depicted in the Gospels did believe in everlasting punishment, and one does find repeatedly a vindictive fury against those people who would not listen to His preaching—an attitude which is not uncommon with preachers, but which does somewhat detract from superlative excellence. You do not, for instance, find that attitude in Socrates. You find him quite bland and urbane towards the people who would not listen to him; and it is, to my mind, far more worthy of a sage to take that line than to take the line of indignation. You probably

all remember the sort of things that Socrates was saying when he was dying, and the sort of things that he generally did say to people who did not agree with him.

You will find that in the Gospels Christ said: 'Ye serpents, ye generation of vipers, how can ye escape the damnation of hell?' That was said to people who did not like His preaching. It is not really to my mind quite the best tone, and there are a great many of these things about hell. There is, of course, the familiar text about the sin against the Holy Ghost: 'Whosoever speaketh against the Holy Ghost it shall not be forgiven him neither in this world nor in the world to come.' That text has caused an unspeakable amount of misery in the world, for all sorts of people have imagined that they have committed the sin against the Holy Ghost, and thought that it would not be forgiven them either in this world or in the world to come. I really do not think that a person with a proper degree of kindliness in his nature would have put fears and terrors of that sort into the world.

Then Christ says: 'The Son of Man shall send forth His angels, and they shall gather out of His kingdom all things that offend, and them which do iniquity, and shall cast them into a furnace of fire; there shall be wailing and gnashing of teeth'; and He goes on about the wailing and gnashing of teeth. It comes in one verse after another, and it is quite manifest to the reader that there is a certain pleasure in contemplating wailing and gnashing of teeth, or else it would not occur so often. Then you all, of course, remember about the sheep and the goats; how at the second coming to divide the sheep and the goats He is going to say to the goats: 'Depart from me, ye cursed, into everlasting fire.' He continues: 'And these shall go away into everlasting fire.' Then He says again: 'If thy hand offend thee, cut it off; it is better for thee to enter into life maimed, than having two hands to go into hell, into the fire that never shall be quenched; where the worm dieth not and the fire is not quenched.' He repeats that again and again also. I must say that I think all this doctrine, that hell-fire is a punishment for sin, is a doctrine of cruelty. It is a doctrine that put cruelty into the world and gave the world generations of cruel torture; and the Christ of the Gospels, if you could take Him as His chroniclers represent Him, would certainly have to be considered partly responsible for that.

There are other things of less importance. There is the instance of the Gadarene swine where it certainly was not very kind to the pigs to put the devils into them and make them rush down the hill to the sea. You must remember that He was omnipotent, and He could have made the devils simply go away; but He chooses to send them into the pigs. Then there is the curious story of the fig-tree, which always rather puzzled me. You remember what happened about the fig-tree. 'He was hungry; and seeing a fig-tree afar off having leaves, He came if haply He might find anything thereon; and when He came to it He found nothing but leaves, for the time of figs was not yet. And Jesus answered and said unto it: "No man eat fruit of thee hereafter for ever", . . . and Peter . . . saith unto Him: "Master, behold the fig-tree which thou cursedst is withered away."' This is a very curious story, because it was not the right time of year for figs, and you really could not blame the tree. I cannot myself feel that either in the matter of wisdom or in the matter of virtue Christ stands quite as high as some other people known to history. I think I should put Buddha and Socrates above Him in those respects.

The Emotional Factor

As I said before, I do not think that the real reason why people accept religion has anything to do with argumentation. They accept religion on emotional grounds. One is often told that it is a very wrong thing to attack religion, because religion makes men virtuous. So I am told; I have not noticed it. You know, of course, the parody of that argument in Samuel Butler's book, *Erewhon Revisited*. You will remember that in *Erewhon* there is a certain Higgs who arrives in a remote country, and after spending some time there he escapes from that country in a balloon. Twenty years later he comes back to that country and finds a new religion, in which he is worshipped under the name of the 'Sun Child', and it is said that he ascended into heaven. He finds that the Feast of the Ascension is about to be celebrated, and he hears Professors Hanky and Panky say to each other that they never set eyes on the man Higgs, and they hope they never will; but they are the high priests of the religion of the Sun Child. He is very indignant, and he comes up to them, and he says: 'I am going to expose all this humbug and tell the people of Erewhon that it was only I, the man Higgs, and I went up in a balloon.' He was told: 'You must not do that, because all the morals of this country are bound round this myth, and if they once know that you did not ascend into heaven they will all become wicked'; and so he is persuaded of that and he goes quietly away.

That is the idea — that we should all be wicked if we did not hold to the Christian religion. It seems to me that the people who have held to it have been for the most part extremely wicked. You find this curious fact, that the more intense has been the religion of any period and the more profound has been the dogmatic belief, the greater has been the cruelty and the worse has been the state of affairs. In the so-called ages of faith, when men did really believe the Christian religion in all its completeness, there was the Inquisition, with its tortures; there were millions of unfortunate women burnt as witches; and there was every kind of cruelty practised upon all sorts of people in the name of religion.

You find as you look around the world that every single bit of progress in humane feeling, every improvement in the criminal law, every step towards the diminution of war, every step towards better treatment of the coloured race or every mitigation of slavery, every moral progress that there has been in the world, has been consistently opposed by the organized Churches of the world. I say quite deliberately that the Christian religion, as organized in its churches, has been and still is the principal enemy of moral progress in the world.

How the Churches Have Retarded Progress

You may think that I am going too far when I say that that is still so. I do not think that I am. Take one fact. You will bear with me if I mention it. It is not a pleasant fact, but the Churches compel one to mention facts that are not pleasant. Supposing that in this world that we live in today an inexperienced girl is married to a syphilitic man, in that case the Catholic Church says: 'This is an indissoluble sacrament. You must stay together for life.' And no steps of any sort must be taken by that woman to prevent herself from giving birth to syphilitic children. That is what the Catholic Church says. I say that that is fiendish cruelty, and nobody whose natural sympathies have not been warped by dogma, or whose moral nature was not absolutely dead to all sense of suffering, could maintain that it is right and proper that that state of things should continue.

That is only an example. There are a great many ways in which at the present moment the Church, by its insistence upon what it chooses to call morality, inflicts upon all sorts of people undeserved and unnecessary suffering. And of course, as we know, it is in its major part an opponent still of progress and of improvement in all the ways that diminish suffering in the world, because it has chosen to label as morality a certain narrow set of rules of conduct which have nothing to do with human happiness; and when you say that this or that ought to be done because it would make for human happiness, they think that has nothing to do with the matter at all. 'What has human happiness to do with morals? The object of morals is not to make people happy.'

Fear the Foundation of Religion

Religion is based, I think, primarily and mainly upon fear. It is partly the terror of the unknown, and partly, as I have said, the wish to feel that you have a kind of elder brother who will stand by you in all your troubles and disputes. Fear is the basis of the whole thing—fear of the mysterious, fear of defeat, fear of death. Fear is the parent of cruelty, and therefore it is no wonder if cruelty and religion have gone hand in hand. It is because fear is at the basis of those two things. In this world we can now begin a little to understand things, and a little to master them by help of science, which has forced its way step by step against the Christian religion, against the Churches, and against the opposition of all the old precepts. Science can help us to get over this craven fear in which mankind has lived for so many generations. Science can teach us, and I think our own hearts can teach us, no longer to look round for imaginary supports, no longer to invent allies in the sky, but rather to look to our own efforts here below to make this world a fit place to live in, instead of the sort of place that the churches in all these centuries have made it.

What We Must Do

We want to stand upon our own feet and look fair and square at the world—its good facts, its bad facts, its beauties, and its ugliness; see the world as it is, and be not afraid of it. Conquer the world by intelligence and not merely by being slavishly subdued by the terror that comes from it. The whole conception of God is a conception derived from the ancient Oriental despotisms. It is a conception quite unworthy of free men. When you hear people in church debasing themselves and saying that they are miserable sinners, and all the rest of it, it seems contemptible and not worthy of self-respecting human beings. We ought to stand up and look the world frankly in the face. We ought to make the best we can of the world, and if it is not so good as we wish, after all it will still be better than what these others have made of it in all these ages. A good world needs knowledge, kindliness, and courage; it does not need a regretful hankering after the past, or a fettering of the free intelligence by the words uttered long ago by ignorant men. It needs a fearless outlook and a free intelligence. It needs hope for the future, not looking back all the time towards a past that is dead, which we trust will be far surpassed by the future that our intelligence can create.

Further Questions

1. "In ancient times, theology was an attempt to explain many natural phenomena in the best way people then knew how to explain them. But since the advent of modern science it is no longer honest to appeal to God as a source of explanations of things we do not yet know how to explain. To do so is just to try to cover up our ignorance with an unsupported myth. It is more honest, if we don't know how to explain something, just to admit that we don't know how to explain it." Do you agree? Why?

2. In general, do you think it is proper for a teacher to encourage his students to accept what he or she says without question, or do you think students should be encouraged to question? Any exceptions (for instance, in the case of Christ)?

Further Readings

Egner, Robert E., and Lester E. Denonn, eds. *The Basic Writings of Bertrand Russell.* New York: Simon & Schuster, 1961. An intellectual feast.

Kolak, Daniel, and Raymond Martin, eds. *Self, Cosmos, God.* New York: Harcourt Brace Jovanovich, 1993. A philosophy of religion anthology.

Pagels, Elaine. *The Gnostic Gospels.* New York: Random House, 1979. A history of early Christians — "the Gnostics" — who tended to view Jesus not as "the Son of God" but as an Eastern-style spiritual teacher. This book, which is extremely readable, was a winner of the National Book Award.

Memorial Service

H. L. MENCKEN

Henry Louis Mencken, born in 1880 in Baltimore, Maryland, was a pungent critic of American life. He always considered himself a journalist and worked as a reporter for the *Baltimore Sun*, but it was his essays that made him a legend. His *Prejudices* contains six volumes of essays, reviews, and criticisms that many loved with as great a passion as others hated with rage. Mencken attacked organized religion, ridiculed business, and called the American people "the most timorous, sniveling, poltroonish, ignominious mob of serfs and goosesteppers ever gathered under one flag in Christendom since the end of the Middle Ages." In mid-career he proudly published a whole book devoted to nothing but denunciations of himself. He died in Baltimore in 1956.

Reading Questions

1. What is your response to this list of dead gods?
2. If you believe in a god, do you think your god will ever make such a list?

WHERE IS THE GRAVE-YARD of dead gods? What lingering mourner waters their mounds? There was a day when Jupiter was the king of the gods, and any man who doubted his puissance was *ipso facto* a barbarian and an ignoramus. But where in all the world is there a man who worships Jupiter to-day? And what of Huitzilopochtli? In one year — and it is no more than five hundred years ago — 50,000 youths and maidens were slain in sacrifice to him. Today, if he is remembered at all, it is only by some vagrant savage in the depths of the Mexican forest. Huitzilopochtli, like many other gods, had no human father; his mother was a virtuous widow; he was born of an apparently innocent flirtation that she carried on with the sun. When he frowned, his father, the sun, stood still. When he roared with rage, earthquakes engulfed whole cities. When he thirsted he was watered with 10,000 gallons of human blood. But today [in 1921] Huitzilopochtli is as magnificently forgotten as Allen G. Thurman. Once the peer of Allah, Buddha, and Wotan, he is now the peer of General Coxey, Richmond P. Hobson, Nan Petterson, Alton B. Parker, Adelina Patti, General Weyler, and Tom Sharkey.

Speaking of Huitzilopochtli recalls his brother, Tezcatilpoca. Tezcatilpoca was almost as powerful: He consumed 25,000 virgins a year. Lead me to his tomb: I would weep, and hang a *couronne des perles*. But who knows where it is? Or where the grave of Quitzalcoatl is? Or Tialoc? Or Chalchihuitlicue? Or Xiehtecutli? Or Centeotl, that sweet one? Or Tlazolteotl, the goddess of love? Or Mictlan? Or Ixtlilton? Or Omacatl? Or Yacatecutli? Or Mixcoatl? Or Xipe? Or all the host of Tzitzimitles? Where are their bones? Where is the willow on which they hung their harps? In what forlorn and unheard of hell do they await the resurrection morn? Who enjoys their residuary estates? Or that of Dis, whom Caesar found to be the chief god of the Celts? Or that of Tarves, the bull? Or that of Moccos, the pig? Or that of Epona, the mare? Or that of Mullo, the celestial jack-ass? There was a time when the Irish revered all these gods as violently as they now hate the English. But today even the drunkest Irishman laughs at them.

But they have company in oblivion: The hell of dead gods is as crowded as the Presbyterian hell for babies. Damona is there, and Esus, and Drunemeton, and Silvana, and Dervones, and Adsalluta, and Deva, and Belisama, and Axona, and Vintios, and Taranuous, and Sulis, and Cocidius, and Adsmerius, and Dumiatis, and Caletos, and Moccus, and Ollovidius, and Albiorix, and Leucitius, and Vitucadrus, and Ogmios, and Uxellimus, and Borvo, and Grannos, and Mogons. All mighty gods in their day, worshiped by millions, full of demands and impositions, able to bind and loose—all gods of the first class, not dilettanti. Men labored for generations to build vast temples to them—temples with stones as large as hay-wagons. The business of interpreting their whims occupied thousands of priests, wizards, archdeacons, evangelists, haruspices, bishops, archbishops. To doubt them was to die, usually at the stake. Armies took to the field to defend them against infidels: Villages were burned, women and children were butchered, cattle were driven off. Yet in the end they all withered and died, and today there is none so poor to do them reverence. Worse, the very tombs in which they lie are lost, and so even a respectful stranger is debarred from paying them the slightest and politest homage.

What has become of Sutekh, once the high god of the whole Nile Valley? What has become of:

Resheph	Ahijah	Shalem
Anath	Isis	Dagon
Ashtoreth	Ptah	Sharrab
El	Anubis	Yau
Nergal	Baal	Amon-Re
Nebo	Astarte	Osiris
Ninib	Hadad	Sebek
Melek	Addu	Molech?

All these were once gods of the highest eminence. Many of them are mentioned with fear and trembling in the Old Testament. They ranked, five or six thousand years ago, with Jahveh himself; the worst of them stood far higher than Thor. Yet they have all gone down the chute, and with them the following:

Bilé	Mami
Lêr	Nin-man
Arianrod	Zaraqu
Morrigu	Suqamunu
Govannon	Zagaga
Gunfled	Gwydion
Sokk-mimi	Manawyddan
Memetona	Nuada Argetlam
Dagda	Tagd
Robigus	Goibniu

Pluto	Odin
Ops	Llaw Gyffes
Meditrina	Lleu
Vesta	Ogma
Tilmun	Mider
Ogyrvan	Rigantona
Dea Dia	Marzin
Ceros	Mars
Vaticanus	Kaawanu
Edulia	Ni-zu
Adeona	Sahi
Iuno Lucina	Aa
Saturn	Allatu
Furrina	Jupiter
Vediovis	Cunina
Consus	Potina
Cronos	Statilinus
Enki	Diana of Ephesus
Engurra	Nin-azu
Belus	Lugal-Amarada
Dimmer	Zer-panitu
Mu-ul-lil	Merodach
Ubargisi	U-ki
Ubilulu	Dauke
Gasan lil	Gasan-abzu
U-dimmer-an-kia	Elum
Enurestu	U-Tin-dir-ki
U-sab-sib	Marduk
Kerridwen	Nin-lil-la
Pwyll	Nin
Tammuz	Persephone
Venus	Istar
Bau	Lagas
Mulu-hursang	U-urugal
Anu	Sirtumu
Beltis	Ea
Nusku	Nirig
U-Mersi	Nebo
Beltu	Samas
Dumu-zi-abzu	Ma-banba-anna
Kuski-banda	En-Mersi
Sin	Amurru
Abil Addu	Assur
Apsu	Aku
Dagan	Qarradu

Elali   Ura-gala
Isum   Ueras

You may think I spoof. That I invent the names. I do not. Ask the rector to lend you any good treatise on comparative religion: You will find them all listed. They were gods of the highest standing and dignity—gods of civilized peoples—worshiped and believed in by millions. All were theoretically omnipotent, omniscient, and immortal. And all are dead.

Further Question

1. Does Mencken's list *prove* anything? What?

Further Reading

Gaskin, J. C. A., ed. *Varieties of Unbelief.* New York: Macmillan, 1989. Unbelief from Epicurus to Sartre. An excellent anthology.

Part VII

Reality

S OMEONE TAPS YOU ON THE SHOULDER: three short taps, followed by three long taps, followed by three short taps. Using the Morse Code, you interpret the tap as the letters "S, O, S." You then interpret these letters as the message, "Help!"

Everything you experience — chairs, people, words — is based on the same principle: pressure gets interpreted as images, sounds, meanings, and things. *Nothing but taps ever touches you* — air tapping against your eardrum, light tapping against the back of your eye, pressure on your fingertips, and so on. But that's as far as the taps go.

You do not experience the taps as pressure. You get hooked through the "medium" directly to the "message." You (or, your brain) interpret the signals automatically.

You of course believe that what you are seeing exists outside you. The ultimate *cause* of the immediate experiences might exist outside you. This is a theory, perhaps a justified one. But your experience does not exist outside you. It is *in* you. Like a musical synthesizer synthesizes notes, you synthesize every element in your experience. All that ever reaches you is pressure. The rest happens in your head. This, too, is a theory!

One could put it like this: If by *dreaming* we mean experiencing images synthesized by the brain, then right now *you are dreaming*. Your eyes are open. But there is no open passage between you and the outside. Even when your eyes are open they are, in a sense, closed. In a sense, you are right now dreaming with your eyes open.

Of course, we still distinguish dreams from reality. But how? What *is* reality?

Experiment II

DANIEL KOLAK

Born in Zagreb, Croatia, Daniel Kolak teaches philosophy at William Paterson College in New Jersey. His main interests are philosophical psychology, philosophy of science, philosophy of mathematics, and philosophy in literature, music, and film. Among his books are *Wisdom Without Answers* (Wadsworth); *Self and Identity* (Macmillan); *Self, Cosmos, God* (Harcourt Brace Jovanovich); *Mathematical Thought* (Macmillan); *The Philosophy of Mind* (Wadsworth); *The Search for God* (Wadsworth); and *Zeno's Paradox Refined: An Eleatic Model of Paradoxical Rationality* and *I Am You, Dissolving the Boundaries of Personal Identity*, forthcoming.

Reading Questions

1. Have you ever had dreams in which you knew you were dreaming—what psychologists call "lucid dreams?" What happened in the dream that made you realize you were dreaming? How did this dream differ from an ordinary dream?

2. Most of us enjoy being fooled by an illusionist but have a deep fear of being fooled otherwise. Why? What's the difference?

3. From whose point of view is the story told?

4. On what basis do the characters assume that they are real? On what basis do *you*?

5. Which character do you most identify with, and why?

6. What is the "Monod"?

7. What is the disagreement between Nylsev and Petrov regarding a "scientific image" versus a "poetic image" about?

8. What does "your eyes are not windows" mean?

"Once Chuang Chou dreamt he was a butterfly, a butterfly flitting and fluttering around. . . . He didn't know he was Chuang Chou. Suddenly he woke up and there he was, solid and unmistakable Chuang Chou. But he didn't know if he was Chuang Chou who had dreamt he was a butterfly, or a butterfly dreaming he was Chuang Chou. . . ."

— FROM *CHUANG TZU*, TRANSLATED BY BURTON WATSON

AWOKE KNOWING NOTHING. Saw nothing. Heard nothing.

Sat up in the dark. Where am I? Who am I? Must be somewhere. Someone. But where? Who? I rubbed my face. Drenched in cold sweat, I savored the salty wetness.

I closed my eyes. How strange. Trying to remember something you can't even recall having forgotten. Think! Language. What language? Can't recall the name. The name . . . missing. All names, missing. There is only the awareness of being there, unknowing and unknown, nameless.

Opening my eyes I noticed a dim shadowless glow: blood red veil, all around, barely visible. I examined my hands. Thin and delicate. Well manicured. Sniffed my fingers. Fish and formaldehyde. Wondered why, they looked so clean. What a thing for a man in my position to be wondering about! A man, yes, of course a man, what else would you be. That's something at least.

Groping along the floor I found a puddle. Smelled it. Clean. Dipped a finger in and tasted . . . seawater! Cold and fresh. Ran my palms along the smooth, featureless stone along the bottom. No cracks anywhere. Where was it leaking in from?

Carefully, I stood up. Avoiding the puddle I walked through the dark. I came upon a wall. I felt along the cold, dry surface. No door. No windows. Not even a crack. I came to a corner. Another wall. I walked along it. Nothing. Another corner. Still no door. No gradations in the surface. No marks or imperfections of any kind. I was completely enclosed on all sides in a room without exit or entrance. I heard a noise.

"Who's there," I shouted, my voice flat and echoless, unfamiliar.

"Over here." A man sat on the floor with his back to the wall, watching me from the other side of the room.

I must have walked right past him in the dark. "How did you get in here? Who are you!"

"It's me, Petrov," he said. "My name is Ivan Petrov. What's your name?"

"I . . . I don't know."

"Ah! So this is how it works." He stood up. "Incredible." Slowly, he staggered toward me. He had swarthy, windburned skin and wide, massive shoulders. "How can a dream be so real?"

"A dream?"

"A dream, yes. A dream is what you are, pal." He let out a loud, bellowing laugh. "This is great. Really."

"What is this . . . place? Where are we? How did you—how did I . . . get here? Is this a, some sort of . . . prison?"

"You're in my dream, pal. I created you, a moment ago, when I started dreaming." Smiling stupidly, he wiped the sweat from his thick lips and then touched my arm. "Amazing. So . . . solid! So real. What's this?" He touched my chest.

I looked down. On the left side I saw letters sewn into the fabric. They spelled the name "Aris."

He ran his fingers over them. "That your name? Aris?"

"I suppose. Could be anybody's name. Even mine."

He laughed strangely. "Aris, eh? Amazing." He reached for my face. "You . . . hey, don't be afraid, pal! You're only a dream."

"What's going on here!"

He frowned, then laughed again. "Come on, think about it, pal. Don't know who you are. Don't know how you got here. Only dreams can exist like that, without knowing."

The way he talked and moved, awkwardly, stupidly, he seemed to me like a fish out of water. It made me laugh, the word, 'fish.'

"Think that's funny, uh? Go ahead. Laugh." He folded his massive arms across his chest. "Laugh, you figment of my imagination."

"Who the hell are you!"

"Told you. Ivan Petrov. I'm the man dreaming you."

"Ivan . . . who is . . . Ivan Petrov?"

"I'm a fisherman. I live here, on this island. I come from a long line of great fishermen."

"What are we doing in this dungeon?"

He pointed to the ceiling. "They put me. It's an experiment. Hallucinations and dreaming. This is a big isolation tank and I'm in here all alone, dreaming you into existence."

I stared up into the blackness. "They're watching now?"

"Yes. Watching, recording everything that's going on in my brain. You're just a bunch of waves in my brain, pal, what do you think of that!" He ran his fingers gently along my cheek. "Incredible." He nodded solemnly. "Such wonderful detail. I can see the pigment in your eyes and my own reflection in them. What a dream!"

"Yes," I said. "It is a dream, it must be! It's too absurd to be anything else. Only, you're not the one dreaming. I am."

"I'm the dream and you're the dreamer?" He laughed. "Ridiculous. I'm conscious, pal. I know I'm here, I exist!"

"A real fisherman would know all about fishing, right, Ivan? Tell me about fishing."

"Ever been fishing?"

"Never even been out on a boat," I said. "I get seasick."

"How do you know you get seasick if you've never been out on a boat?"

"Ah. Very good." I laughed nervously. "Didn't mean — I mean, I made that up! Figure of speech."

"You wouldn't be any good on a boat. Wind would blow you away. You're too skinny."

"How do you steer?"

"Rudder?"

"Mmmm. And the fish — how do you catch fish?"

"With a net! A big, black net. Takes a lot of work, *real* work. Especially if you run the boat by yourself, like I do. You hardly ever make enough money. That's why I signed up for this damned experiment. But I love the sea. Wouldn't be happy doing anything else." Ivan's eyes focused into the distance, as if looking far away. "Takes a real man to handle a boat. Gets pretty rough, sometimes. Long as you can handle the boat, the sea holds you up. If you can't, it swallows you up sure and fast." His eyes grew wide. "That's when I like it best. Water gets dark and murky and you can't see the bottom. Just deep dark blue, the deepest darkest blue you can imagine, with nothing below. And before the storm, you know, when the wind blows right through you, and the waves start to foam, and those pitch-black clouds rise up from the horizon, blotting out the sun, that's when the sea looks like someone spilled ink in it. I like that even better than when it's calm. Other fishermen, they rush into port to anchor their boats. Not me! I like to sit 'em out. And when it gets really bad, and the waves jiggle the boat and you feel like you're in some goddamned cradle, being rocked by a crazed mother, that's when I holler and laugh at the top of my lungs, no matter how hard it's blowing, or raining, because I know even God can't raise up a storm that I can't ride! When it's all over, and the clouds are gone and the rain has been drunk by the sea and only the wind is left, that's when I sit out on the deck with my feet over the side, warming myself in the sun if it's out, and the other fishermen ride by and wave. And I wave back, proud as hell. Proud as hell, I tell you."

I put my hands on his shoulders. "You're not real. You're a dream!"

"You should hear yourself, pal. You're completely dysfunctional."

"Dysfunctional?" I tried to suppress a laugh and realizing I was trying to suppress a laugh, I laughed. "Is that a word a fisherman would use?"

"I went to school," he said.

I thought: what are you doing? Trying to get a character in your dream to admit to you, a character in your own dream, that he is only a dream! Why? What for? What would it prove? I felt embarrassed and, almost immediately, felt stupid for feeling embarrassed. After all, this was only a dream. . . .

Our eyes met and for a brief moment we stared at each other in terrible, numinous silence. Suddenly, like a trap door the floor opened up and together we fell into the gentle pressure of labyrinthine nets that broke under our weight and we vanished like pebbles dropped into a vast and limitless ocean of dark waves, sinking and trembling slowly into the deep.

*   *   *

I awoke. The experiment was over. I lay in the recovery room. Nylsev sat in an armchair next to the open window, smoking his pipe, gazing out at the ocean. Nylsev's long, gray hair glistened in the sunlight. He waved his hair away from his face. I watched as the motion of his hand upset the steadily rising stream of pipe smoke, sending it spiraling throughout the room. I wondered what he was thinking about.

"I'm awake, Jon."

Startled, Nylsev turned. "Sorry, Aris. Dozed off. You all right?"

I stretched. "Fine. A bit queasy. That was some maelstrom."

"I know! Can't stop thinking maybe this time we stumbled directly onto the threshold between dream and reality."

I stood up from the recliner and walked to the window. Two children played in the sand. They had made a toy boat out of an old hollow log and as they sat on it, pretending to row with palm leaves, they sang a nursery rhyme which I had heard lots of times but had never paid much attention to:

> Row, row, row your boat,
> Gently down the stream,
> Merrily, merrily, merrily, merrily,
> Life is but a dream.

"Wonder what made me dream up a fisherman," I said.

A butterfly flew into the room. Flitting back and forth, it landed on the window sill. When Nylsev tried to examine it, the butterfly flew away. Looking up, he waved to the children.

"You conjured him up out of nothing but you dreamt yourself exactly as you are." He re-lit his pipe, which had gone out. "Your dream body even had your name sewn on it! That's impossible. You weren't supposed to remember your name. Another leak." He rubbed his eyes. "Let's get to the lab and see where those leaks are coming from."

"I feel really weird," I said. "You know? Like maybe we're just completely wrong about everything."

Nylsev didn't respond to the comment and it made me self-conscious. What a dumb thing for you to say, I thought, feeling as if everything I had been saying up to then had been phony. To cover myself, I said, "You don't seem yourself, Jon."

He stood up. "What? What did you say?"

"You look tired. That's all I meant. What's the matter?"

"Nothing." He yawned. The yawn looked intentional, false. "Dozed off in the chair," he yawned again, "while I was waiting for you to wake up. First time I ever had a lucid dream unhooked from the equipment."

Together, we walked out into the hall. We passed by several glass-enclosed cubicles where neon lights shone over gray machines.

"Go on," I said. "Tell me about your dream." I wondered why Nylsev, a leading dream researcher, would have to be prodded into talking about his own dreams.

He smiled uneasily. "It was very . . . appropriate. Dreamt everything was exactly as it is now. Only difference was, you didn't exist. The fisherman, Ivan Petrov, he was real. In my dream, we did the experiment on Petrov, not you, and *he* had dreamed *you* into existence."

"How could—"

"Wait, that's not all! In my dream, after the experiment was over, I took Petrov to the laboratory. Just like I'm taking you there now, we walked down this hall, except I was leading him by the arm—" he paused, chuckling. "Told him about the dream I had just had while waiting for him to wake up in the recovery room. 'In my dream within my dream,' I said, to him, 'Aris had dreamt *you* into existence.'"

I tried to laugh naturally but it came out forced. Nylsev's dream sounded unreal. Worse still, Nylsev, being a good neurophysiologist, would recognize his dream as unreal. That Nylsev didn't seem to recognize it as such meant he clearly was deluded about the reality of his own dreams—a paradox the two of us had often talked about and sometimes even experienced.

Nylsev stared at me. "What's wrong, Aris?"

"Your dream sounds fictitious, Jon."

"Of course! Very much so. What do you expect from a dream?" He smiled confidently. "Don't worry, Aris. I'm not dysfunctional."

With a forceful shove he threw open the double doors to the huge, gymnasium-sized laboratory where bright studio lights gave the room, the men, and the machines a cold, impersonal glare. On one side of the laboratory a group of scientists sat behind a long row of instrument panels while technicians moved equipment through a large sliding door in the back. In the center of the laboratory, what looked like the dome of a planetarium, was the observation room. Through the open doors I could see the transparent, one-way mirror glass floor inside. Below it was what we called "The Monad," the soundproof, lightproof cell in which, deprived of all my occurrent memories as well as my senses, I had been enclosed.

In silence we went down the moving stairway next to the observation room. Shaped like a double helix, the stairs spiraled upward and downward at the same time, constantly intertwining yet never touching. The stairs brought us to a hallway next to the Monad. We walked in.

Though I had been in the Monad many times, coming into it with all the lights on always felt eerie. I stood next to the wall and slid my hand over the smooth, warm surface. With a sensation of awe, I closed my eyes and remembered. I couldn't help thinking that at that very moment Ivan was somewhere deep within my subconscious, sailing on an imaginary ocean of dark, foam-covered waves, with the wind blowing against him and a nonexistent sun warming his unreal body. Thinking about it I began to feel uncomfortable and opened my eyes. The strange feeling did not go away; I felt dizzy, as if at any moment I would collapse and fall into a dark, empty, bottomless trench.

"Listen, Jon . . . Jon?"

He was gone. A chill shook me. I looked around the Monad. It was empty.

"Over here, Aris."

I turned. He was on the other side of the wall.

"This time you've gone too far, Jon. I'm still inside the Monad. Right?"

"Of course, inside, yes —"

"But I . . . I never stepped out into the real world, did I!"

He kept summoning me.

I reached out. My hand went through the wall. "What the hell is this?"

"The stuff that dreams are made of," he chortled.

Half way through the wall, I froze. "This can't be real. What's going on? Who are you!"

"You first." Laughing, Nylsev pointed past me. "Look, our fisherman. Better go ask him. Maybe *he's* real."

On the other side of the Monad I saw Ivan Petrov on the floor, sleeping. I started toward him but the floor opened up and I fell down into a web of insubstantial shadows; above and below me a jungle of infinite nets stretched in all directions as far as the eye could see.

I screamed: "Let me out!"

Nylsev dropped down into the net. "Damned neurons —"

"Stop, Jon. Shut it down! Shut down the dream machine."

He kept tearing through the nets with his hands. "It is shut down!"

Flitting about, he went on sinking, bursting through the nets. From upstairs the scientists began one by one to drop.

One fell right on my head. "It's okay," he said, pulling his fountain pen out from my skull, "it's only a dream."

"Whose dream?"

* * *

I awoke. Dr. Nylsev sat in an armchair next to the open window, smoking his pipe and gazing out at the ocean. His long, gray hair glistened in the sunlight. He waved his hair away from his face.

"Jon?"

Startled, Nylsev turned. "What, we're on first name basis?"

"Sorry, Doc." I felt embarrassed. "I . . . I dreamt I was your colleague."

Nylsev stood up and walked to the window. Outside, my two children sat on the old dried-up log, pretending to row with palm leaves as they sang a nursery rhyme which I could barely hear.

"Ready, Mr. Petrov. Let's go. You need to fill some forms so we can pay you." He waved to my children. "I'll show you what your brain looks like from the inside. All right? Then you can go fish."

"You already showed me, Doc. Just a bunch of wires."

"Did I? I suppose I must have. Dark wires, right? No light gets in there. The brain lives in darkness."

"Yeah, up close, the brain looks kind of like a net, doesn't it. A big net. So where then in the net is the picture of the net? How do you net the net! With what? Another net?"

"That's a very poetic image, Mr. Petrov. That's *all* it is, though. A poetic image —"

"But even on your scientific equipment, Dr. Nyslev, your brain is not really seeing a brain, is it? It's just a scientific image. That's all it is. A scientific image —"

"Want my advice, Mr. Petrov? Stick to fishing! Leave the science of dreams to us dream scientists."

"Ever been fishing?"

"No, I get seasick."

"How do you know, if you've never been?"

"Please, Mr. Petrov. I really don't have time for this."

"You're inconsistent."

"I've been on a boat! Just never been fishing!"

He hurried out into the hall. I followed. A strange feeling of *dé-jà-vu* swept over me as we passed by glass-enclosed cubicles where neon lights shone over gray machines. At the end of the hallway we entered the laboratory. Nylsev summoned me along after him. Instead, I went down the moving stairway. Shaped like a double helix, the stairs spiraled upward and downward at the same time, constantly intertwining yet never touching. I walked into the Monad.

Standing next to the wall I slid my hand over the smooth, warm surface. With a sensation of awe, I closed my eyes and remembered. I smiled, thinking that at that very moment Aris Hauer was somewhere deep within my subconscious, working in some imaginary laboratory, fiddling with imaginary contraptions that he thought connected him to reality, a well-cushioned and very expensive imaginary seat supporting his unreal body. . . .

"Mr. Petrov! What are you doing? Mr. Petrov?"

"Leave me alone, Dr. Nylsev." I kept my eyes shut.

He laughed. I began to feel uncomfortable and opened my eyes. The feeling did not go away; I felt dizzy and seasick, as if at any moment the floor would crack open and water would burst up from beneath and I would collapse and sink like a chainless anchor into the deep.

"Dr. Nylsev? Where are you? Dr. Nylsev!"

He was gone. The Monad was empty. I screamed and heard an echo, another scream, another voice, familiar, mine yet not mine, barely audible.

I turned. A chill shook me. I could see through the wall. Concentrating, I could make out the space beyond; I saw nets, and the insubstantial shadows of men, like fish, caught, hanging, suspended in the trembling.

* * *

I awoke. My pipe had fallen out of my mouth.

Embarrassed, I thrust it like a pacifier between my lips and brushed away the ash that had spilled onto my lab coat. The motion upset the steadily rising stream of pipe smoke, sending it spiraling throughout the room.

"Jon?"

Startled, I turned. "Sorry, Aris. Dozed off. You all right?"

He stretched. "Fine. A bit queasy. That was some maelstrom."

"I know. Can't stop thinking maybe this time we stumbled directly onto the threshold between dream and reality."

Shivering, I put on my sunglasses and looked through the open window out at the black clouds welling at the horizon like some giant tidal wave. I saw a boat tossing about in the waves and someone on it, waving. All across the sea I could see the whitecaps swelling, craving toward the darkening sky.

Suddenly, a butterfly landed on the window sill. When I leaned forward to examine it more closely a gust of wind caught its wings and sent it spiraling toward the two children playing in the sand. They had made a toy boat out of an old hollow log and as they sat on it, pretending to row with palm leaves, they sang a nursery rhyme which I had heard lots of times but had never paid much attention to.

"Better warn the children," said Aris. "Looks like we're in for quite a storm." He waved to them. "Want to hear about my dream, Jon?"

"Sure. Go on. Tell me about *your* dream."

Further Questions

1. How does the story end? Suppose you continued writing where the author left off. What would you have happen? As an exercise, you might actually try this.

2. The theme "reality is a dream" is probably one of the oldest themes in history. Why do you think this is so? What is the significance of it? Why have people across the ages been drawn to this idea?

3. Suppose for a moment that reality *really is* a dream. What would this mean? Who is dreaming? Is the dreamer dreaming the dream real? In that case, *ultimate* reality is not a dream. But could the dreamer ever know this? How? If all dreamers can be fooled by dreams, then the dreamer might also be but a dream. On the other hand, if the dreamer dreaming the

dream is *not* real, then why even call the dreamer a dreamer? Does the concept of a dream without any real dreamer make any sense to you?

4. The Victorians, in order to distance themselves from their primitive ancestors, decided to regard dreams as nonsense. Nearly every other culture considers dreams extremely important — indeed, some cultures consider dreams *more* important than reality! Who do you think is right — and *why*? What is your *evidence*?

Further Readings

Bierce, Ambrose. "An Occurrence at Owl Creek Bridge," in *The Collected Writings of Ambrose Bierce*. Secaucus, NJ: Citadel Press, 1946. A classic.

Borges, Jorge Luis. *Labyrinths*. New York: New Directions, 1964. "Tlon, Uqbar, Orbis Tertius" is about a group of idealists who try to dream a whole country into existence; "The Circular Ruins" is about a man who dreams a son into existence only to discover that he, the dreamer, "too was a mere appearance, dreamt by another."

Chuang Tzu, *Basic Writings*, translated by Burton Watson. New York: Columbia University Press, 1964. Contains the famous dreaming butterfly story and, more generally, a whole philsophy based on "trying to wake up" from this reality using nonlogic.

Cortázar, Julio. *Blow-Up*. New York: Collier Books, 1969. The story "The Night Face Up" is about a man who gets in a car accident and then finds himself on the sacrificial table of the Aztecs, unsure which is the reality, which the dream.

Kolak, Daniel. "Finding Our Selves: Identification, Identity, and Multiple Personality," forthcoming, *Philosophical Psychology*.

Kolak, Daniel. "The Metaphysics and Metapsychology of Personal Identity," forthcoming, *American Philosophical Quarterly*.

Fiction

ROBERT NOZICK

Robert Nozick teaches philosophy at Harvard University. His writings range across the entire spectrum of philosophy, but he is perhaps best known for his controversial contribution to political philosophy, *Anarchy, State and Utopia* (New York: Basic Books, 1974) and his *Philosophical Explanations* (Harvard). In this selection, Nozick suggests that there may be no way to tell whether we are fictional or real.

Reading Questions

1. What does Nozick mean by "fiction"? How does being fictional, in his sense, differ from being real, in your sense?

2. Previous selections consider the distinction between dreams and reality. Is the distinction between fiction and reality the same distinction or a different one?

I AM A FICTIONAL CHARACTER. However, you would be in error to smile smugly, feeling ontologically superior. For you are a fictional character too. All my readers are except one who is, properly, not reader but author.

I am a fictional character; this is *not*, however, a work of fiction, no more so than any other work you've ever read. It is not a modernist work that self-consciously *says* it's a work of fiction, nor one even more tricky that denies its fictional status. We all are familiar with such works and know how to deal with them, how to frame them so that *nothing* the author says — nothing the first person voices even in an afterword or in something headed "author's note" — can convince us that anyone is speaking seriously, *non*-fictionally in his own first person.

All the more severe is my own problem of informing you that this very piece you are reading is a work of non-fiction, yet we are fictional characters, nevertheless. *Within* this world of fiction we inhabit, this writing is non-fictional, although in a wider sense, encased as it is in a work of fiction, it too can only be a fiction.

Think of our world as a novel in which you yourself are a character. Is there any way to tell what our author is like? Perhaps. *If* this is a work in which the author *expresses* himself, we can draw inferences about his facets, while noting that each such inference we draw will be written by him. And if he writes that we find a particular inference plausible or valid, who are we to argue?

One sacred scripture in the novel we inhabit says that the author of our universe created things merely by speaking, by saying "Let there be . . ." The only thing mere speaking can create, we know, is a story, a play, an epic poem, a fiction. Where we live is created by and in words: a uni-verse.

Recall what is known as the problem of evil: why does a good creator allow evil in the world, evil he knows of and can prevent? However, when an author includes monstrous deeds — pain and suffering — in his work, does this cast any special doubt upon his goodness? Is an author callous who puts his characters through hardships? Not if the characters do not suffer them *really*. But don't they? Wasn't Hamlet's father really killed? (Or was he merely hiding to see how Hamlet would respond?) Lear really was cast adrift — he didn't just dream this. Macbeth, on the other hand, did *not* see a real dagger. But these characters aren't real and never were, so there was no suffering outside of the world of the work, no *real* suffering in the author's *own* world, and so in his creating, the author was not cruel. (Yet why is it cruel only when he creates suffering in his *own* world? Would it be perfectly all right for Iago to create misery in *our* world?)

"What!" you say, "we don't really undergo suffering? Why it's as real to us as Oedipus' is to him." Precisely as real. "But can't you *prove* that you *really* exist?" If Shakespeare had Hamlet say "I think, therefore I am," would that prove to us that Hamlet exists? Should it prove that to Hamlet, and if so what is such a proof worth? Could not *any* proof be written into a work of fiction and be presented by one of the characters, perhaps one named "Descartes"? (Such a character should worry less that he's dreaming, more that he's dreamed.)

Often, people discover anomalies in the world, facts that just don't jibe. The deeper dug, the more puzzles found — far-fetched coincidences, dangling facts — on these feed conspiracy and assassination buffs. That number of hours spent probing into *anything* might produce anomalies, however, if reality is not as coherent as we thought, if it is not *real*. Are we simply discovering the limits of the details the author worked out? But *who* is discovering this? The author who writes our discoveries knows them himself. Perhaps he now is preparing to correct them. Do we live in galley proofs in the process of being corrected? Are we living in a *first draft*?

My tendency, I admit, is to want to revolt, to conspire along with the rest of you to overthrow our author or to make our positions more equal, at least, to hide some portion of our lives from him—to gain a little breathing space. Yet these words I write he reads, my secret thoughts and modulations of feeling he knows and records, my Jamesian author.

But does he *control* it all? Or does our author, through writing, learn about his characters and from them? Is he surprised by what he finds us doing and thinking? When we feel we freely think or act on our own, is this merely a description he has written in for us, or does he *find* it to be true of us, his characters, and therefore write it? Does our leeway and privacy reside in this, that there are some implications of his work that he hasn't yet worked out, some things he has not thought of which nevertheless are true in the world he has created, so that there are actions and thoughts of ours that elude his ken? (Must we therefore speak *in code*?) Or is he only ignorant of what we *would* do or say in some *other* circumstances, so that our independence lies only in the *subjunctive* realm?

Does this way madness lie? Or enlightenment?

Our author, we know, is outside our realm, yet he may not be free of our problems. Does he wonder too whether *he* is a character in a work of fiction, whether his writing our universe is a play within a play? Does he have me write this work and especially this very paragraph in order to express his own concerns?

It would be nice for us if our author too is a fictional character and this fictional world he made describes (that being no coincidence) the actual world inhabited by *his* author, the one who created him. We then would be fictional characters who, unbeknownst to our own author although not to his, correspond to real people. (Is that why we are so true to life?)

Must there be a top-floor somewhere, a world that itself is not created in someone else's fiction? Or can the hierarchy go on infinitely? Are circles excluded, even quite narrow ones where a character of one world creates another fictional world wherein a characer creates the first world? Might the circle get narrower, still?

Various theories have described our world as less real than another, even as an illusion. The idea of our having this inferior ontological status takes some getting used to, however. It may help if we approach our situation as literary critics and ask the genre of our universe, whether tragedy, farce, or theater-of-the-absurd? What is the plot line, and which act are we in?

Still, our status may bring some compensations, as, for example, that we live on even after we die, preserved permanently in the work of fiction. Or if not permanently, at least for as long as our book lasts. May we hope to inhabit an enduring masterpiece rather than a quickly remaindered book?

Moreover, though in some sense it might be false, in another wouldn't it be true for Hamlet to say, "I am Shakespeare"? What do Macbeth, Banquo, Desdemona, and Prospero have in common? The consciousness of the one author, Shakespeare, which underlies and infuses each of them. (So too, there is the brotherhood of man.) Playing on the intricacy both of our ontological status and of the first person reflexive pronoun, each of us too may truly say, "I am the author."

Note From the Author

Suppose I now tell you that the preceding *was* a work of fiction and the "I" didn't refer to me, the author, but a first person character. Or suppose I tell you that it was *not* a work of fiction but a playful, and so of course serious, philosophical essay by me, Robert Nozick. (*Not* the Robert Nozick named as author at the beginning of this work—he may be, for all we know, another literary persona—but the one who attended P.S.

165.) How would your response to this whole work differ depending on which I say, supposing you were willing, as you won't be, simply to accept my statement?

May I decide *which* to say, fiction or philosophical essay, only now, as I finish writing this, and how will that decision affect the character of what already was set down previously? May I postpone the decision further, perhaps until after you have read this, fixing its status and genre only then?

Perhaps God has not decided *yet* whether he has created, in this world, a fictional world or a real one. Is the Day of Judgment the day he will decide? Yet what additional thing depends upon which way he decides — what would either decision add to our situation or subtract from it?

And which decision do you hope for?

Further Questions

1. Are you fictional or real? How do you know?

2. Does it make any difference — either theoretically, in terms of how you think about yourself, or practically, in terms of how you lead your life — whether you are fictional or real?

3. Nozick suggests that if we are fictional, the problem of evil may not arise. Is he right? If he is, is this part of the answer to the previous question?

Further Readings

Kant, Immanuel. *Critique of Pure Reason*. Originally published in 1781 and now available in many English editions. Tough reading, but one of the most philosophically influential books of all time and one which set the agenda for the modern discussion of the nature of reality.

Nozick, Robert. *Philosophical Explanations*. Cambridge: Harvard University Press, 1981. Sophisticated, yet intended for a wide audience. Includes many perceptive and original discussions of issues related to the nature of reality.

Reality and Modern Science

PAUL DAVIES

In this selection Paul Davies brilliantly explains the most mind-boggling challenges that quantum theory poses for our ordinary ways of thinking about reality.

A brief biography of Davies appears on page 82.

Reading Questions

1. Davies claims that quantum theory contains "some astonishing insights into the nature of the mind and the reality of the external world." How would you sum up Davies's account of those insights?

2. Some feel that one consequence of quantum theory is a holistic view of reality in which it is not possible to separate the observer from the observed. Does Davies's account support this view?

3. What is "Bell's inequality"? What is its significance?

4. What is the "two-slit experiment"? What is it supposed to show?

'Anyone who is not shocked by quantum theory has not understood it.'

NIELS BOHR

. . . THE RELATION BETWEEN BODY AND MIND, that ancient philosophical enigma, is like the relation between hardware and software in computing. But the connection is tighter than it is in routine computer programming, in the sense that the software (the 'program') is coupled to, or interwoven with, the hardware in what Hofstadter has called a 'Tangled Hierarchy' or 'Strange Loop.' This mosaic of self-reference is the essential feature of consciousness.

The idea of coupling between hardware and software, brain and mind, or matter and information, is not new to science. In the 1920s a revolution occurred in fundamental physics that shook the scientific community and focussed attention as never before on the relation between the observer and the external world. Known as the quantum theory, it forms a pillar in what has become known as the new physics, and provides the most convincing scientific evidence yet that consciousness plays an essential role in the nature of physical reality.

Considering that the quantum theory is now several decades old, it is remarkable that its stunning ideas have taken so long to percolate through to the layman. There is, however, a growing awareness that the theory contains some astonishing insights into the nature of the mind and the reality of the external world, and that full account must be taken of the quantum revolution in the search for an understanding of God and existence. Many modern writers are finding close parallels between the concepts used in the quantum theory and those of Oriental mysticism, such as Zen. But whatever one's religious persuasions, the quantum factor cannot be ignored.

Before embarking on a discussion of these issues it must be made clear that the quantum theory is primarily a practical branch of physics, and as such is brilliantly successful. It has given us the laser, the electron microscope, the transistor, the superconductor and nuclear power. At a stroke it explained chemical bonding, the structure of the atom and nucleus, the conduction of electricity, the mechanical and thermal properties of solids, the stiffness of collapsed stars and a host of other important physical phenomena. The theory has now penetrated most areas of scientific inquiry, at least in the physical sciences, and for two generations has been learned as a matter of course by most science undergraduates. These days, it is applied in many routine practical ways in engineering. In short, the quantum theory is, in its everyday application, a very down-to-Earth subject with a vast body of supporting evidence, not only from commercial gadgetry, but from careful and delicate scientific experiments.

Even though few professional physicists stop to think about the bizarre philosophical implications of the quantum theory, the truly weird nature of the subject emerged very soon after its inception. The theory arose from attempts to describe the behaviour of atoms and their constituents, so it is primarily concerned with the microworld.

Physicists had known for some time that certain processes, such as radioactivity, seem to be random and unpredictable. While large numbers of radioactive atoms obey the laws of statistics, the exact moment of decay of an individual atomic nucleus cannot be predicted. This fundamental uncertainty extends to all atomic and subatomic phenomena, and requires a radical revision of commonsense beliefs to explain it. Before atomic uncertainty was discovered in the early part of this century, it was assumed that all material objects complied strictly with the laws of mechanics, which operate to keep the planets in their orbits, or direct the bullet towards its target. The atom was considered to be like a scaled-down version of the solar system, with its internal components turning like precision clockwork. It turned out to be illusory. In the 1920s it was discovered that the atomic world is full of murkiness and chaos. A particle such as an electron does not appear to follow a meaningful, well-defined trajectory at all. One moment it is found here, the next there. Not only electrons, but all known subatomic particles — even whole atoms — cannot be pinned down to a specific motion. Scrutinized in detail, the concrete matter of daily experience dissolves in a maelstrom of fleeting, ghostly images.

Uncertainty is the fundamental ingredient of the quantum theory. It leads directly to the consequence of *unpredictability*. Does every event have a cause? Few would deny it. . . . The cause-effect chain has been used to argue for the existence of God — the first cause of everything. The quantum factor, however, apparently breaks the chain by allowing effects to occur that have no cause.

Already in the twenties, controversy raged over the meaning behind the unpredictable face of atoms. Is nature inherently capricious, allowing electrons and other particles to simply pop about at random, without rhyme or reason — events without a cause? Or are these particles like corks being tossed about by an unseen ocean of microscopic forces?

Most scientists, under the leadership of the Danish physicist Niels Bohr, accepted that atomic uncertainty is truly intrinsic to nature: the rules of clockwork might apply to familiar objects such as snooker balls, but when it comes to atoms, the rules are those of roulette. A dissenting, albeit distinguished, voice was that of Albert Einstein. 'God does not play dice', he declared. Many ordinary systems, such as the stock market or the weather, are also unpredictable. But that is only because of our ignorance. If we had complete knowledge of all the forces concerned, we could (in principle at least) anticipate every twist and turn.

The Bohr–Einstein debate is not just one of detail. It concerns the entire conceptual structure of science's most successful theory. At the heart of the subject lies the bald question: is an atom a *thing*, or just an abstract construct of imagination useful for explaining a wide range of observations? If an atom *really* exists as an independent entity then at the very least it should have a location and a definite motion. But the quantum theory denies this. It says that you can have one or the other but not both.

This is the celebrated uncertainty principle of Heisenberg, one of the founders of the theory. It says you can't know where an atom, or electron, or whatever, is located *and* know how it is moving, at one and the same time. Not only can you not know it, but the very concept of an atom with a definite location and motion is meaningless. You can ask where an atom is and get a sensible answer. Or you can ask how it is moving and get a sensible answer. But there is no answer to a question of the sort 'Where is it and how fast is it going?' Position and motion (strictly, momentum) form two mutually incompatible aspects of reality for the microscopic particle. But what right have we to say that an atom is a *thing* if it isn't located somewhere, or else has no meaningful motion?

According to Bohr, the fuzzy and nebulous world of the atom only sharpens into concrete reality when an observation is made. In the absence of an observation, the atom is a ghost. It only materializes when you look for it. And you can decide what to look for. Look for its location and you get an atom at a place. Look for its motion and you get an atom with a speed. But you can't have both. The reality that the observation sharpens into focus cannot be separated from the observer and his choice of measurement strategy.

If all this seems too mind-boggling or paradoxical to accept, Einstein would have agreed with you. Surely the world out there really exists whether we observe it or not? Surely everything that happens does so for its own reasons and not because it is being watched? Our observations might uncover the atomic reality, but how can they *create* it? True, atoms and their components might seem to behave in a muddled and imprecise way, but that is only due to our clumsiness in probing such delicate objects.

The essential dichotomy can be illustrated with the aid of the humble television. The image on a television screen is produced by myriads of light pulses emitted when electrons fired from a gun at the back of the set strike the fluorescent screen. The picture you perceive is reasonably sharp because the number of electrons involved is enormous, and by the law of averages, the cumulative effect of many electrons is predictable. However, any particular electron, with its inbuilt unpredictability, could go anywhere on the screen. The arrival of this electron at a place, and the fragment of picture that it produces, is uncertain. According to Bohr's philosophy bullets from an ordinary gun follow a precise path to their target, but electrons from an electron gun

simply turn up at the target. And however good your aim, no bull's-eye is guaranteed. The event 'electron at place x on the television screen' cannot be considered as *caused* by the gun, or anything else. For there is no known reason why the electron should go to point x rather than some other place. The picture fragment is an event without a cause, an astonishing claim to remember when you next watch your favourite programme.

Nobody is saying, of course, that the electron gun has nothing whatever to do with the electron's arrival, only that it does not completely determine it. Instead of envisaging the electron at the target as really existing prior to its arrival and being connected to the gun by a precise trajectory, physicists think of the electron leaving the gun as being in a sort of limbo, its presence represented only by cohorts of ghosts. Each ghost explores its own path to the screen, though only one electron actually appears on the screen itself.

How can these weird ideas be confirmed?

In the 1930s Einstein conceived of an experiment which he believed would expose the fraud of the quantum ghosts, and establish once and for all that every event has a distinct cause. The experiment is based on the principle that the multitude of ghosts do not act independently, but in collusion. Suppose, said Einstein, that a particle explodes into two fragments, and these fragments are allowed to travel undisturbed, a long way apart. Although well separated, each fragment will carry an imprint of its partner. For example, if one flies off spinning clockwise the other, by reaction, will spin anti-clockwise.

The ghost theory claims that each fragment will be represented by more than one potential possibility. To pursue the example, fragment A will have two ghosts, one spinning clockwise, the other anti-clockwise. Which ghost becomes the *real* particle has to await a definite measurement or observation. Similarly, the oppositely-moving partner, fragment B, will also be represented by two counter-spinning ghosts. However, if a measurement of A promotes, for instance, the clockwise ghost to reality, B has no choice: it must promote its anti-clockwise ghost. The two separated ghost particles must cooperate with each other to comply with the law of action and reaction (see Fig. 1).

Figure 1. The decay of an atom, or a subnuclear particle, can produce two oppositely spinning particles (e.g. photons of light) which travel in opposite directions, perhaps to a large distance.

It seems baffling, to say the least, how fragment B can possibly *know* for which of its two ghosts fragment A has opted. If the fragments are well separated, it is hard to see how they can communicate. Furthermore, if both fragments are observed simultaneously, there is simply no time for any signal to propagate between the fragments. Einstein insisted that this result is paradoxical unless the fragments *really* exist (already spinning in a particular way) at the instant they separate, and that they retain their spin during their flight apart. There are no ghosts; there is no delay of choice until measurement, no mysterious cooperation without communication.

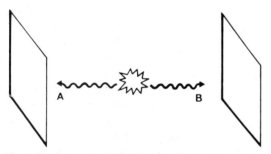

Figure 2. If two photons with correlated spins and polarization encounter parallel pieces of polarizing material, they will show 100 percent cooperation: whenever photon A is blocked, so is B. This cooperation occurs even though (i) the actual outcome of the encounter between photon and polarizer is completely unpredictable, and (ii) the photons may be very far apart.

Bohr replied that Einstein's reasoning assumed the two fragments are independently real because they are well separated. In fact, asserted Bohr, it is not possible to regard the world as made up of lots of separated bits. Until a measurement is actually performed, both A and B must be regarded as a single totality, even if they are light years apart. This is holism indeed!

The real test of Einstein's challenge had to await post-war developments. In the 1960s, the physicist John Bell proved a most remarkable theorem about experiments of the Einstein type. He showed, quite generally, that the degree of cooperation between separated systems cannot exceed a certain definite maximum, if along with Einstein, one assumes that the fragments really do exist in well-defined states prior to their observation. In contrast, the quantum theory predicts that this limit can be exceeded. What was needed was an experiment.

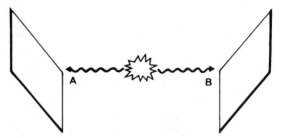

Figure 3. Testing Bell's inequality: if the polarizers are oriented obliquely, the cooperation between A and B declines—sometimes A is passed when B is blocked. However, there is found to be some residual cooperation; more than can be explained by any theory that assumes (i) the independent reality of the external world, and (ii) no secret reversed-time communication between the widely-separated photons.

Advances in technology enabled experimental tests to be conducted to check Bell's inequality. Several such experiments have been performed, but by far the best was carried out in 1982 at the University of Paris by Alaine Aspect and colleagues. For subatomic fragments they used two photons of light emitted simultaneously by an atom. Stationed in the path of each photon was a piece of polarizing material. This filters out photons that do not align their vibrations with the axis of the material. Thus, only ghost photons with the correct orientation (polarization) will emerge from the polarizing material. Again, photons A and B cooperate, because their polarizations are forced by action and reaction to be parallel. If photon A is blocked, so is B.

The real test comes when the two pieces of polarizing material are oriented obliquely to each other. The cooperation then declines because the polarizations of the photons cannot now both be aligned with their respective polarizers. And it is here that the Bohr–Einstein controversy can be settled. Einstein's theory predicts considerably less cooperation than Bohr's.

So what was the result?

Bohr wins, Einstein loses. The Paris experiment, taken together with other less accurate experiments performed during the seventies, leaves little room for doubt that the uncertainty of the microworld is intrinsic. Events without causes, ghost images, reality triggered only by observation — all must apparently be accepted on the experimental evidence.

What are the implications of this stunning conclusion?

So long as nature's rebelliousness is restricted to the microworld, many people will feel only slightly uneasy that the concrete reality of the world 'out there' has dissolved. In daily life a chair is still a chair, is it not?

Well — not quite.

Chairs are made of atoms. How can lots of ghosts combine together to make something real and solid? And what about the observer himself? What is so special about a human being that gives him the power to focus the fuzziness of atoms into sharp reality? Does an observer have to be human? Will a cat suffice, or a computer?

The quantum theory is one of the most difficult and technical subjects to understand, and this brief review can do no more than lift a small corner of the veil of mystery to allow the reader a glimpse of its bizarre concepts. (The subject is treated in much greater detail in my book *Other Worlds*.) This sketchy survey will, however, demonstrate that the commonsense view of the world, in terms of objects that really exist 'out there' independently of our observations, totally collapses in the face of the quantum factor.

Many of the perplexing features of the quantum theory can be understood in terms of a curious 'wave-particle' duality, reminiscent of the mind–body duality. According to this idea, a microscopic entity such as an electron or a photon sometimes behaves like a particle and sometimes like a wave; it depends on the sort of experiment chosen. A particle is a totally different animal from a wave: it is a small lump of concentrated stuff, whereas a wave is an amorphous disturbance that can spread out and dissipate. How can anything be both?

It all has to do with complementarity again. How can the mind be both thoughts and neural impulses? How can a novel be both a story and a collection of words? Wave-particle duality is another software–hardware dichotomy. The particle aspect is the hardware face of atoms — little balls rattling about. The wave aspect corresponds to software, or mind, or information, for the quantum wave is not like any other sort of wave anybody has ever encountered. It is not a wave of any substance or physical stuff, but a wave of knowledge or information. It is a wave that tells us what can be known about the atom, not a wave of the atom itself. Nobody is suggesting that an atom can ever spread itself around as an undulation. But what can spread itself around is what an observer can know about the atom. We are all familiar with crime waves; not waves of any substance but waves of *probability*. Where the crime wave is most intense, there is the greatest likelihood of a felony.

The quantum wave is also a wave of probability. It tells you where you can expect the particle to be, and what chance it may have of such-and-such a property, such as rotation or energy. The wave thus encapsulates the inherent uncertainty and unpredictability of the quantum factor.

No experiment better illustrates the conflict and dichotomy of wave-particle duality than Thomas Young's two-slit system. Light, according to the long tradition of classical physics, is a wave — an electromagnetic wave, an undulation of the electromagnetic field. About 1900, however, Max Planck demonstrated mathematically that light waves can behave in some ways like particles — we now call them photons. Light, according to Planck, comes in indivisible lumps or packets (hence the Greek word quantum). The idea was refined by Einstein, who pointed out that these corpuscular photons can knock electrons out of atoms after the fashion of a coconut shy. This is what happens in the now familiar photocell; odd, but not outrageous.

The first unexpected twist comes when two light beams are combined together. If two wave systems are superimposed, an effect called interference results. Imagine two stones dropped a few inches apart into a still pond. Where the spreading disturbances overlap a complex pattern of undulations occurs. In some regions the two wave motions come together in phase and the disturbance is amplified; elsewhere the waves meet out of phase and cancel each other.

To get the same effect with light we can illuminate two holes in a screen. The light waves spilling through each aperture spread out and overlap, creating an interference pattern which is readily revealed by a photographic plate. The image of the two holes is not merely two fuzzy blobs, but a systematic pattern of bright and dark patches, indicating where the two wave trains have arrived in step, and out of step, respectively (see Fig. 4).

All this was well known in the early nineteenth century. Strange overtones develop, however, when the corpuscular nature of light is taken into account. Each photon hits the photographic plate at a particular point and makes a little spot. The extended image, as in the television case, therefore builds up from millions of speckles as the photons strike the plate like a hail of shot. The point of arrival of any individual photon is definitely unpredictable. All we know is that there is a good chance it will hit the plate in a bright-patch area.

Figure 4. The famous Young's two-slit experiment is ideal for exposing the bizarre wave-particle duality of light (it can also be performed with electrons or other particles). The small hole in screen A illuminates the two narrow slits in screen B. The image of the slits is displayed on screen C. Rather than a simple double band of light, there appears a sequence of bright and dark bands (interference fringes) caused by the light waves from each slit arriving successively in step or out of step, depending on position. Even when one photon at a time traverses the apparatus, the same interference pattern builds up in a speckled fashion, though any given photon can only go through *either* one slit *or* the other in screen B, and has no neighbouring photons against which to gauge its 'step'.

That, however, is not all. Suppose we turn down the illumination so that only *one photon at a time* passes through the system. Given long enough, the accumulated speckles will still build up to give the bright and dark interference pattern. The paradox is that any particular photon can surely pass through only *one* of the holes. Yet the interference pattern requires *two* overlapping wave trains, one from each hole. The entire experiment can, in fact, be performed with atoms, electrons or other subatomic particles instead of light. In all cases an interference pattern composed of individual speckles results, demonstrating that photons, atoms, electrons, mesons, and so on manifest both wave and particle aspects.

In the 1920s Bohr gave a possible resolution of the paradox. Think of the case when the photon goes through hole A as one possible world

(world A) and the route through hole B as another (world B). Then *both* these worlds, A and B, are somehow present together, superimposed. We cannot say, Bohr asserted, that the world of our experience represents *either* A *or* B, but is a genuine hybrid of the two. Moreover, this hybrid reality is not simply the sum total of the two alternatives, but a subtle marriage: each world *interferes* with the other to produce the celebrated pattern. The two alternative worlds overlap and combine, rather like two movie films being projected simultaneously onto the same screen.

Einstein, the eternal sceptic, refused to accept hybrid realities. He confronted Bohr with a modified version of the two-hole experiment, in which the screen is allowed to move freely. Careful observation, he insisted, would enable one to determine through which hole the photon went. Passage through the left-hand hole results in a slight deflection of the photon to the right, and the recoiling screen could in principle be seen to move to the left. Motion to the right would indicate that the other hole had been traversed. By this means, experiment would determine that *either* world A *or* B corresponds to reality. Furthermore, the apparent indeterminacy of the photon's behaviour in the original experiment could then simply be attributed to the coarseness of the experimental technique in that arrangement.

Bohr countered decisively. Einstein was changing the rules in midgame. If the screen is free to move, then its motion is also subject to the inherent uncertainty of quantum physics. Bohr easily showed that the effect of recoil would be to destroy the interference pattern on the photographic plate, producing merely two fuzzy blobs instead. Either the screen is clamped, and the wavelike nature of light is manifested in the interference pattern, or the screen is freed, and a definite trajectory for the photon is established. But in that case the wave-like aspect disappears, and the light behaves in a purely corpuscular way. We are thus dealing with two different experiments. They are not contradictory, but complementary. Einstein's strategy tells us nothing about the pho-

ton paths in the original experiment, where the hybrid world is manifested.

The bizarre conclusion from this exchange is that we — the experimenters — are involved in the nature of reality in a fundamental way. By choosing to clamp the screen we can construct a mysterious hybrid world in which photon paths have no well-defined meaning.

In 1979, John Wheeler, speaking ironically at a symposium in Princeton celebrating Einstein's centenary, drew a still more mind-boggling conclusion from the two-hole experiment. He pointed out that by a simple modification of the apparatus it is possible to delay the choice of measurement strategy until *after* the photon has passed through the screen. Our decision to make a hybrid world can thus be delayed until after that world has come into existence! The precise nature of reality, Wheeler claims, has to await the participation of a conscious observer. In this way, mind can be made responsible for the retroactive creation of reality — even a reality that existed before there were people. . . .

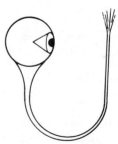

Figure 5. This symbolic picture due to John Wheeler represents the universe as a self-observing system. Wheeler's astonishing modification of the Young's two-slit experiment reveals that an observer today can be made partially responsible for generating the reality of the remote past. The tail of the figure can thus represent the early stages of the universe, being promoted to concrete reality through its later observation by consciousness which itself depends on that reality.

It will be evident from the foregoing that the quantum theory demolishes some cherished commonsense concepts about the nature of reality. By blurring the distinction between subject and object, cause and effect, it introduces a strong holistic element into our world view. We have seen how, in the Einstein experiment, two widely separated particles must nevertheless be regarded as a single system. We have also seen how it is meaningless to talk about the condition of an atom, or even the very notion of an atom, except within the context of a specified experimental arrangement. To ask where an atom is *and* how it moves is forbidden. First establish what you want to measure—position or motion—then you will get a sensible answer. The measurement will involve large chunks of macroscopic apparatus. Thus the microscopic reality is inseparable from the macroscopic reality. Yet the macroscopic is made up of the microscopic—apparata are made of atoms! Strange loops again.

David Bohm, a leading quantum theorist, addressed these issues in his book *Wholeness and the Implicate Order*:

> A centrally relevant change in descriptive order required in the quantum theory is thus the dropping of the notion of analysis of the world into relatively autonomous parts, separately existent but in interaction. Rather, the primary emphasis is now on *undivided wholeness*, in which the observing instrument is not separated from what is observed.

In short, the world is not a collection of separate but coupled *things*; rather it is a network of *relations*. Bohm here echoes the words of Werner Heisenberg: 'The common division of the world into subject and object, inner world and outer world, body and soul is no longer adequate.'

How can we resolve the paradoxical loop that the macroworld—the world of daily experience—determines the microscopic reality that it is, itself, made of? This issue is confronted head on when we ask what actually happens when a quantum measurement is made. How does the observer contrive to project the fuzzy microworld into a state of concrete reality?

The quantum 'measurement problem' is really a variant of the mind-body or software–hardware problem; physicists and philosophers have struggled with it for decades. The hardware—the particle—is described by a wave, which encodes the information (software) about what an observer is likely to find the particle doing when he observes it. When an observation is made the wave 'collapses' into a particular state that ascribes a definite sharp value to whatever has been observed.

Paradoxes arise when the act of measurement is described throughout at purely the hardware level. Suppose an electron scatters off a target. It could go either right or left. You compute with the wave and find out where the wave goes. The wave diffracts off the target and spreads out, partly to the right and partly to the left, with equal strength, for instance. This means a fifty-fifty chance that, on observation, you will find the electron on *either* the left *or* the right. It is important to remember, though, that until the observation is actually performed, it is not possible to say (or indeed to meaningfully discuss) on which side of the target the electron *really* is located. The electron keeps its options open until you actually peek. Both possible worlds coexist in a hybrid, ghostly superposition (see Fig. 6).

Now you make your observation, and the electron is found, say, on the left. Instantly the right hand 'ghost' vanishes. The wave suddenly collapses over to the left hand side of the target, for there is now no possibility of the electron being on the right. What causes this dramatic collapse?

In order to make an observation it is necessary to couple the electron to a piece of external apparatus, or perhaps a series of apparata. These have the job of sniffing out where the electron is and amplifying the signal up to the macroscopic level where it can be recorded. But these couplings and apparatus processes are themselves mechanical activities involving atoms (albeit in large numbers), and are therefore subject to the quantum factor too. We could write down a wave to represent the measuring apparatus. Suppose that the measuring machine is equipped with a pointer which has two positions, one to indicate that the electron is on the left, the other implying it is on the right. Then viewing the total system of electron plus apparatus as a large quantum system forces us to conclude that the hybrid nature of the balking electron is transferred to the pointer. Instead of the measurement device showing either one pointer position or the other, it ought to go into a state of quantum limbo. In this way, a measurement seems to amplify the nightmare quantum world up to laboratory scale.

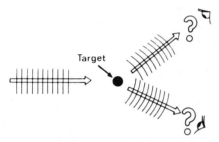

Figure 6. Described as a wave, an electron ricochets off the target by producing ripples that travel both leftwards and rightwards. Until an observation is made of where the electron has deflected, it is necessary to suppose that two ghost-worlds (or ghost-electrons) coexist in a hybrid state of unreality. At the instant of observation one of the ghosts disappears, its associated wave simply collapsing, and the electron is promoted from its former state of limbo to a single concrete reality. Mystery surrounds just what it is that the observer does to the electron to achieve this abrupt promotion. Is it mind-over-matter? Does the universe split into two parallel realities?

This paradox was investigated by the mathematician John von Neumann, who demonstrated (using a simple mathematical model) that the effect of coupling the electron to the measuring apparatus does indeed prod the electron into opting for either left or right, but at the price of transferring the hybrid unreality to the apparatus pointer. Von Neumann also showed, however, that if the apparatus is in turn coupled to another instrument that reads the output of the first instrument, then the first pointer would thereby be

prodded into a decision too. But now the second apparatus goes into limbo. There can thus be a whole chain of machines looking at each other and recording sensible 'either-or' results, but always the last member of von Neumann's chain will be left in a state of unreality.

The eccentric consequences are highlighted by a famous paradox due to Schrödinger in which the amplifying device is used to trigger the release of a poison which can kill a cat. The left–right pointer dichotomy thus becomes a live–dead cat dichotomy. If a cat is to be described as a quantum system one is forced to conclude that, until the cat is observed by someone or something, it is suspended in a schizophrenic 'live–dead' condition, which seems absurd.

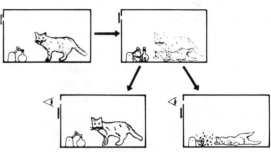

Figure 7. The sad tale of Schrödinger's cat. A quantum process can trigger the release of cyanide with a 50:50 probability. Quantum theory requires that the system develops into a ghost-like hybrid state of live–dead cat until an observation is made, when *either* a live cat *or* a dead cat will be perceived. This thought experiment highlights the weird implications surrounding the act of observation in the quantum theory.

Suppose we use a person instead of a cat. Do they experience a live–dead state? Of course not. So has quantum mechanics broken down when it comes to human observers? Does von Neumann's chain end when it reaches the consciousness of a person? This sensational claim has indeed been made by a leading quantum theorist, Eugene Wigner. Wigner suggests that it is the entry of the information about the quantum system into the mind of the observer that collapses the quantum wave and abruptly converts a schizophrenic, hybrid, ghost state into a sharp and definite state of concrete reality. Thus, when the experimenter himself looks at the apparatus pointer, he causes it to decide upon either one position or the other, and thereby, down the chain, also forces the electron to make up its mind.

If Wigner's thesis is accepted it returns us to the old idea of dualism—that mind exists as a separate entity on the same level as matter and can act on matter causing it to move in apparent violation of the laws of physics. Wigner serenely accepts this: 'Does the consciousness influence the physico-chemical conditions (of the brain)? In other words, does the human body deviate from the laws of physics, as gleaned from the study of inanimate matter? The traditional answer to this question is, "No": the body influences the mind but the mind does not influence the body. Yet at least two reasons can be given to support the opposite thesis.' One of these two reasons Wigner cites is the law of action and reaction. If body acts on mind the reverse should also be true. The other is the aforementioned resolution of the quantum measurement problem that results.

It has to be admitted that very few physicists support Wigner's ideas, though some have seized upon the quantum route to mind-over-matter to argue for the acceptability of certain paranormal phenomena, such as psychokinesis and remote metal-bending. ('If the mind can fire neurons why can't it bend spoons?')

There is a strong hint of level-confusion running through the Wigner thesis. The attempt to discuss the operation of hardware (electrons running about) by appeal to software (the mind) falls into the dualist trap. However, the issue is more subtle here because hardware and software are hopelessly entangled in the quantum theory (for example, in wave-particle duality). Whatever the validity of Wigner's ideas, they do suggest that the solution of the mind–body problem may be closely connected with the solution of the quantum measurement problem, whatever that will eventually be.

Another attempt to break out of the quantum measurement paradox is perhaps even more bizarre than Wigner's appeal to the mind. So long as one is dealing with a finite physical system, von Neumann's chain can be extended. You can always claim that everything you perceive is real because there exists a larger system which collapses when you see into reality by 'measuring' or 'observing' it. But in recent years physicists have been interested in the subject of quantum cosmology—the quantum theory of the entire universe. By definition, there can be nothing outside the universe to collapse the whole cosmic panorama into concrete existence (except God, perhaps?). At this level, the universe would seem to be caught in a state of limbo or cosmic schizophrenia. Without a Wigner-type mind to integrate it, the universe seems destined to languish as a mere collection of ghosts, a multi-hybrid superposition of overlapping alternative realities, none of them the *actual* reality. Why, then, do we perceive a single, concrete reality?

One bold idea addresses this unnerving issue face on: the parallel universe theory. Invented by physicist Hugh Everett in 1957, and subsequently championed by Bryce DeWitt, now at the University of Texas at Austin, the theory proposes that all the possible alternative quantum worlds are equally real, and exist in parallel with one another. Whenever a measurement is performed to determine, for example, whether the cat is alive or dead, the universe divides into two, one containing a live cat, the other a dead one. Both worlds are equally real, and both contain human observers. Each set of inhabitants, however, perceives only their own branch of the universe.

Commonsense may rebel against the extraordinary concept of the universe branching into two as the result of the antics of a single electron, but the theory stands up well to closer scrutiny. When the universe splits, our minds split with it, one copy going off to populate each world. Each copy thinks it is unique. Those who object that they don't feel themselves being split should reflect on the fact that they do not feel the motion of the Earth around the sun either. The splitting is repeated again and again as every atom, and all the subatomic particles, cavort about. Countless times each second, the universe is replicated. Nor is it necessary for an actual measurement to be performed in order that the replication occur. It suffices that a single microscopic particle merely interacts in some way with a macroscopic system. In the words of DeWitt:

> Every quantum transition taking place on every star, in every galaxy, in every remote corner of the universe is splitting our local world on earth into myriads of copies of itself . . . Here is schizophrenia with a vengeance.

The price paid for the restoration of reality is a multiplicity of realities — a stupendous and growing number of parallel universes, diverging along their separate branches of evolution.

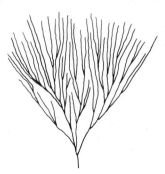

Figure 8. To avoid live–dead cats and other quantum schizophrenic unrealities, Everett proposed that the indeterminism of quantum systems generates a multifoliate reality in which the universe is continually branching into myriads of 'parallel universes', physically disconnected, but equally real. The observer's mind is also split into countless duplicates by this process.

What are these other worlds like? Can we travel to them? Do they explain UFOs or the mysterious disappearances in the Bermuda trian-

gle? Alas for the ufologists, the Everett theory is explicit on this point. The parallel worlds, once disconnected, are physically isolated for all practical purposes. To reunite them would require reversing a measurement, which amounts to reversing time. It would be rather like reconstituting a broken egg, atom by atom.

But where *are* these worlds? In a sense, those that closely resemble our own are very nearby. Yet they are totally inaccessible: we cannot reach them however far we travel through our own space and time. The reader of this book is no more than an inch away from millions of his duplicates, but that inch is not measured through the space of our perceptions.

The farther apart the worlds have branched, the greater their differences. Worlds that split away from our own in some trivial way, such as the path of a photon in a two-hole experiment, would be indistinguishable to the casual glance. Others would differ in their cat populations. In some worlds Hitler would not have been, John Kennedy lives on. Yet others would be wildly different, especially those that branched away from each other near the beginning of time. In fact, everything that could possibly happen (though not everything that can conceivably happen) does happen somewhere, in some branch of this multifoliate reality.

The simultaneous existence of all possible worlds raises the intriguing question of why the world in which this book is being read is the one it is, and not one of the other, very different branches. Obviously, the reader cannot exist in all or indeed the vast majority of the other worlds, for their conditions are simply not suitable for life to arise. . . .

Many people have suggested that the quantum theory, with its involvement of the mind in so basic a fashion, opens the door to an understanding of free will. The old idea of a deterministic universe in which everything we do is decided by the mechanics of the universe long before our birth seems to be swept away by the quantum factor. So is free will alive and well? To deal with this matter properly we first have to delve more deeply into the mysteries of time. [See the earlier selection by Davies, "Time."]

Further Questions

1. You are part of reality. So, if the quantum theory is about reality, then it is also about you. How do the ideas discussed in this chapter affect your conception of who and what you are?

2. What is the significance of Einstein's loss to Bohr regarding the prediction of the cooperation between two widely separated photons?

3. John Wheeler represents the universe as a self-observing system, which implies that the existence of observers today makes the past real. What then makes the observers today real?

4. How do you respond to the paradox of Schrödinger's cat?

5. If the universe is constantly branching, do *you* branch with it? What are the implications of this theory for our ordinary view of personal identity?

Further Readings

Baker, Adolph. *Modern Physics and Anti-Physics*. Reading, MA: Addison-Wesley, 1970. An elementary presentation of quantum-mechanics.

Barrow, John. *Theories of Everything: The Quest for Ultimate Explanation*. New York: Oxford University Press, 1991.

Davies, Paul. *Other Worlds*. Simon & Schuster, 1981. Good especially for its discussion of the many worlds' interpretation of quantum theory.

Davies, Paul, and J. R. Brown. *The Ghost in the Atom*. Cambridge: Cambridge University Press, 1986. Contains excellent, up-to-date, and nontechnical discussions with major contemporary physicists, including John Wheeler, John Bell, David Bohm, and Alaine Aspect.

Gribbon, John. *In Search of Schrödinger's Cat*. New York: Bantam, 1984. A beautifully written elementary account of quantum theory.

Scientific Realism versus Constructive Empiricism: A Dialogue

GARY GUTTING

Gary Gutting is professor of philosophy at the University of Notre Dame. He writes primarily in the areas of philosophy of science and philosophy of religion. In the following selection, he introduces two sides of an important current debate over "scientific realism." The main issue is whether, as the Scientific Realist maintains, we ought to believe that the empirical success of our best scientific theories makes it likely that the (unobservable) theoretical entities, such as atoms and electrons, posited by these theories actually exist. The Scientific Realist's opponent, the Constructive Empiricist, maintains that, for all we know, such theoretical entities may simply be convenient fictions which, while useful in making empirical predictions, do not actually exist. In other words, the debate is over whether we ought to believe that our best scientific theories accurately describe the world, particularly its unobservable parts. Scientific Realists such as Wilfrid Sellars, a leading philosopher of science in the 1950s and '60s, answer yes; Constructive Empiricists such as Bas van Fraassen, currently professor of philosophy at Princeton University, answer no.

Reading Questions

1. Explain in your own words the difference between believing that a theory is true and believing that it is empirically adequate.

2. Do the Scientific Realist (SR) and the Constructive Empiricist (CE) agree about what it means for something to be "observable"? If so, what do they agree it means? If not, how do they differ?

3. Toward the end of the debate SR says that CE's position is "arbitrary." What is SR's point? How does CE respond? Do you find CE's response adequate?

Note: *The following is a discussion between a scientific realist (SR) who has been strongly influenced by the work of Wilfrid Sellars and a constructive empiricist (CE) who has been equally influenced by the work of Bas van Fraassen. Indeed, the influence is so great that the interlocuters occasionally lapse into direct quotation of their masters. I do not, however, want anyone to* identify *the views of my two characters with those of Sellars and van Fraassen. What they say merely represents the dialectic of my own mind as I think through the issues raised by the debate between Sellars and van Fraassen on scientific realism.*

SR: REALISM IS ENCAPSULATED in the claim that "to have good reason for holding a theory is *ipso facto* to have good reason for holding that the entities postulated by the theory exist."[1] For an appropriate scientific theory (say atomic theory), this claim allows us to argue as follows:

1. If we have good reason for holding atomic theory, we have good reasons for holding that atoms exist;

2. We do have good reason for holding atomic theory (it's highly confirmed, fruitful, simple, etc.);

3. Therefore, we have good reason for holding that atoms exist.

CE: Everything depends on what we mean by "holding a theory." If it means "believing that the theory is true," then premise (1) of your argument is obvious but premise (2) strikes me as false. There's a lot to be said for atomic theory but none of it constitutes a cogent case for its truth. At the most, the evidence shows that atomic theory is empirically adequate, by which I mean that there may be reason to think that all its *observable* consequences are true. But the evidence does not support the existence of the particular unobservable mechanisms and entities the theory postulates. On the other hand, if you take "holding a theory," as I do, to mean "believing it to be empirically adequate," then there's no problem with premise (2) but, for the reasons I've just been urging, there is no basis for premise (1).

SR: I'm willing to stand by the argument even if we take "holding a theory" to mean "believing it to be empirically adequate"; but we need to get clear on just what's involved in empirical adequacy. For example, it won't do to take empirical adequacy in the minimal sense of "accurately describing all the observable phenomena." With this sense of "empirically adequate" the argument will fall to the old problem of the underdetermination of theory by data. Specifically, with this meaning of "empirically adequate," premise (1) says: "If we have good reason for believing that atomic theory accurately describes all the observable phenomena, then we have good reason for believing that atoms exist." But this isn't so since, first, there are an infinity of other sorts of theoretical entities that would produce the same observable phenomena and, second, we could just as well believe only in the phenomena and forget about underlying entities.[2]

CE: Your second point is just my view. I'm not saying theoretical entities don't exist or that talk about them is meaningless. I don't even say there's anything wrong with believing in them if you want to. My point is simply that there's no evidence that makes it irrational to withhold judgment about their existence. I'm defending my right to be an agnostic on the issue. I suspect however that, just like theists who deny the rationality of religious agnosticism, you're going to invoke the explanatory power of your postulations to support their existence. . . . My position is like Duhem's. He shared your conviction that "postulation of unobservable entities is indispensable to science." But since he also held that improved description of observable phenomena is the only basic role for theoretical postulation, he maintained that there is no need for us to accept the existence of postulated entities. "If that is how one sees it, then truth of the postulates becomes quite irrelevant. When a scientific theory plays [its] role well, we shall have reason to use the theory whether we do or do not believe it to be true; and we may do well to reserve judgment on the question of truth. The only thing we need to believe here is that the theory is empirically adequate, which means that in its round-about way it has latched on to actual regularities in the observable phenomena. Acceptance of the theory need involve no further beliefs."[3]

SR: Don't we at least need an explanation of why the theory is empirically adequate; that is, of why what we observe is just as it would be if the theory were true? And isn't the best explanation just that the theory is in fact true (or anyway near the truth)? Don't we ultimately need to invoke realism to explain the success of science?

CE: It seems to me that you're slipping back into the theological demand for explanation for its own sake. Why are you so sure that we need an explanation for science's success? But let me agree, at least for the moment, that we do need such an explanation. Even so, I think the appropriate explanation is quite different from the one you've proposed. After all, "science is a biological phenomenon, an activity by one kind of organism which facilitates its interaction with its environment."[4] Just as, from a Darwinian viewpoint, the only species that survive are those that are successful in coping with their environment, so too only successful scientific theories have survived. "Any scientific theory is born into a life of fierce competition, a jungle red in tooth and claw. Only the successful theories survive — the ones which in fact latched on to actual regularities in nature."[5] But this process of selection on the basis of empirical success need have nothing to do with the *truth* of the theories selected. Your argument is no different from that of an antievolutionist who holds that the survival of a species can be explained only by some design that has preadapted the species to its environment. But we don't need the hypothesis that theories are successful because truth has preadapted them to the world. We need only the hypothesis that theories that are not empirically successful have not survived.

SR: . . . The defense of realism that I'm interested in proposing need not be based on putting it forward as an explanation of science's success. Rather I have been arguing from the indispensable role of theoretical postulation in the formulation of empirically adequate laws. Think about it this way: Imagine that we are doing science initially only in the observation framework. We are aware of various singular observational facts and are trying to explain them by subsuming them under empirical generalizations — that is, under inductive generalizations that employ only the concepts of the observation framework.

CE: Excuse me a moment. Just how are you understanding the notion of *observation* when you speak of the observation framework? Some realists, you know, have maintained that anything — even electrons and other postulated submicroscopic entities — are in principle observable.

SR: I sympathize with some of the epistemological motives behind such claims. It is important to reject the idea that the realm of entities and properties we in fact observe functions as an unchangeable given. But in this context we must avoid trivializing the distinction between what is observable and what is not. When someone says that everything is observable, he is envisaging a situation in which concepts from the theoretical framework of science have ingressed into the observation framework. I'm speaking of the observation framework prior to any theoretical ingressions.

CE: All right. So what we observe are the ordinary objects of everyday life and their properties.

SR: Yes, but we need to distinguish two sorts of properties that we attribute to observable things. On the one hand, there are occurrent (nondispositional) properties that are, strictly speaking, *what we perceive of an object* that we perceive. There is, for example, "the occurrent sensuous redness of the facing side" of a brick.[6] On

the other hand, there are dispositional or, more broadly, causal properties that correspond to *what we perceive an object as* (e.g., the brick seen as made of baked clay). Within the observation framework properties of the first sort are a constant factor. They correspond to the way that, for physiological reasons, we must perceive the world. The second sort of properties corresponds to our conceptual resources for classifying objects into kinds with distinctive causal features. These kinds are not constant but can change as "our classification of physical objects . . . becomes more complex and sophisticated."[7] An essential feature of scientific inquiry is its *revision* of the causal concepts of the observation framework in order to arrive at maximally accurate empirical generalizations. In many cases, these revisions take place entirely within the observation framework. In such cases, the causal properties are always built out of concepts expressing the occurrent properties of physical objects. We can imagine that science never required any conceptual revision other than this sort. In that case, the observation framework would be conceptually autonomous; that is, its conceptual resources would suffice for formulating and justifying entirely accurate empirical generalizations about singular observable facts. If this were the case, then the framework of postulational science would be "in principle otiose,"[8] and what Sellars calls the "manifest image" would provide a correct ontology for the world. But, as we have learned from the development of science, the observation framework is not autonomous. We cannot do the job of science using only its conceptual resources. Rather, we can arrive at justified empirical generalizations in the observation framework only by appealing to theories that employ concepts that cannot be built out of the conceptual resources of the observation framework.

CE: You seem to be missing the point of my antirealism. I'm willing to admit everything you've said about the *indispensability* of theories. But why should we also have to accept the *truth* of theories? As I see it, the highest virtue we need attribute to a theory needed for the successful practice of science is empirical adequacy. In other words, we need only agree that all of a successful theory's *observable consequences* are true. If we regard a theory as empirically adequate — and of course we are entitled to so regard highly successful theories — then from that alone we have sufficient justification for accepting the empirical generalizations that theory entails. The further assertion of the theory's truth is a gratuitous addition, entirely unnecessary for the fulfillment of science's fundamental aim; namely, an exact account of observable phenomena. The enterprise of science can be entirely successful without ever accepting the truth of its theories. Consider two scientists. One accepts atomic theory in the sense that he thinks it is empirically adequate: he knows that it fits all observations to date and expects that it will continue to fit all further observations. Accordingly, he thinks in terms of atomic theory and uses its conceptual resources to solve relevant scientific problems. However, he remains agnostic on the question of whether atoms really exist. A second scientist shares the first's views about the empirical adequacy of atomic theory, but he also holds that atoms really do exist. But what sort of work is done by this latter belief? It makes absolutely no difference for what the second scientist expects to observe or for how he proceeds in his scientific work. His expectations and procedures are exactly the same as those of his agnostic colleague. So, while I agree with you that theories are not "otiose in principle," I do maintain that a realistic interpretation of theories is. There is nothing in the aims of scientific inquiry that is in the least affected by the acceptance or the rejection of the existence of theoretical entities.

SR: It seems to me that it's you who are missing the point of my realism. First of all, you misrepresent my view by taking it as a thesis about the aims of science. I am entirely content with the view that science aims only at empirical adequacy. . . . My thesis is rather that empirical ade-

quacy in fact requires theories that postulate unobservable entities and that this fact provides good reason for thinking such entities exist. My realism is not a thesis about the aim of science but rather a thesis about the philosophical (specifically, metaphysical) significance of the means that scientists have had to use in fulfilling this aim.

CE: I'm happy to accept this clarification of your views, but it does not affect the central point: that you haven't offered an argument from the indispensability of theories to the existence of the entities they postulate. Even Sellars, who develops the indispensability thesis much more cogently than you do, seems to ignore the need for such an argument. He seems just to assume that, once theories have been shown to be indispensable, then reality of the entities they postulate has been established. But in fact there is a gap that needs bridging. Sellars himself has exmphasized this very point in parallel contexts. For example, he agrees that semantic concepts such as *meaning* and moral concepts such as *person* are indispensable, but nonetheless insists this doesn't entail that meanings and persons exist. Similarly, I think you should admit that the indispensability of theoretical language does not entail the existence of theoretical entities. Further, I submit that the only way of bridging the gap between indispensability and existence is by an act of faith that may be permissible for those who want to believe in atoms and similar things but is in no way required by the evidence.

SR: I agree that the gap needs to be bridged and I even agree that it cannot be bridged by a deductive argument. I admit that indispensability does not entail existence; theories could be indispensable and yet theoretical entities not exist. But I insist that there is a good *inductive* case for realism; reasons that make it highly probable that theoretical entities exist. . . . I have in mind the following strategy of argument: First find a generally valid type of argumentation from the explanatory power of a hypothesis to the reality of the entities the hypothesis refers to; then show that, in some specific cases, the results of theoretical science enable us to construct an argument of just this type for the existence of theoretical entities. Such a case is inductive because the argument type employed is inductive. But it's philosophical rather than scientific because it is not postulating an explanatory hypothesis but rather pointing out the essential similarity of two ways of arguing.

CE: I need to hear the type of argumentation you have in mind.

SR: The point is really quite simple. There's a standard way of arguing—in both everyday and scientific contexts—for the existence of unobserved entities. The mode of argument is this: from the ability of a hypothesis to (a) subsume all known facts and to (b) predict new and even unexpected facts, we infer the reality of the entities the hypothesis postulates. There's no doubt that we all accept this mode of argument in many cases that involve unobserved though observable entities. For example, this is just the way we proceed in arguing for the past existence of dinosaurs or for the present existence of stars, conceived as huge, tremendously hot, gaseous masses far distant from us. But the very same mode of argumentation used in these noncontroversial cases can be employed to argue for the existence of the unobserved entities postulated by microphysics. Just as we accepted the existence of dinosaurs because the hypothesis of their existence subsumed the known facts and successfully predicted new ones, so too we ought to accept the existence of electrons, neutrinos, etc. for precisely the same sort of reasons. The case for the existence of electrons and neutrinos is logically identical to the case for the existence of dinosaurs and stars. Since you can hardly reject the latter, I submit that you cannot consistently reject the former.

CE: You yourself have mentioned but ignored the crucial point: the nonobservability of the entities postulated by microphysics in contrast to the observability of stars and dinosaurs. This dif-

ference undermines your claim that the mode of argument for the two sorts of entities is the same. As I see it, the mode of inference at work in the examples you've given is not from a theory's explanatory power to its truth but from its explanatory power to its empirical adequacy. At any rate, the uncontroversial uses of the mode of argumentation—to the existence of stars and dinosaurs—cannot decide between the realist and the antirealist interpretations of it. For these are cases of inference to *observable* entities; and, for such cases, the claim that a postulation is empirically adequate is equivalent to the claim that it is true. For example, 'Stars (as described by modern astronomy) exist' is equivalent to 'All observable phenomena are as if stars exist', since the existence of stars is itself (in principle) observable. So I can accept the inference to stars and reject the inference to electrons, etc., on the grounds that, in both cases, we are only entitled to infer the empirical adequacy of a hypothesis from its explanatory and predictive success. In the case of stars, this is equivalent to inferring their existence; but in the case of electrons, which are not even in principle observable, it is not.

SR: This response keeps your position consistent but at the price of arbitrariness. By maintaining that explanatory and predictive success supports only the empirical adequacy of a theory, you are implicitly committing yourself to a sharp epistemic distinction between the observable and the unobservable. You say the explanatory success of a hypothesis is evidence of its truth only if the hypothesis is about observable entities. But why should observability matter in this context?

CE: The answer depends, of course, on what you mean by 'observable'. As we noted above, in one sense everything is observable: there might be some creature with sense organs appropriate for perceiving it. But, as we agreed when discussing this point, here a more restricted sense of 'observable' is appropriate. Specifically, observability must be taken as a function of certain empirical limitations of human beings. "The human organism is, from the point of view of physics, a certain kind of measuring apparatus. As such it has certain inherent limitations—which will be described in detail in the final physics and biology. It is these limitations to which the 'able' in 'observable' refers—our limitations, *qua* human beings."[9]

SR: I agree with this construal of 'observable'. But my question is, What does observability in this sense have to do with the existence or nonexistence of an entity? You're surely not so much of a positivist as to deny the possibility of the existence of what's unobservable?

CE: You're misconstruing my point. Of course observability in the sense we're taking it has nothing to do with the existence or the nonexistence of an entity. But it has a great deal to do with what we have reason to believe exists. "The question is . . . how much we shall believe when we accept a scientific theory. What is the proper form of acceptance: belief that the theory, as a whole, is true; or something else? To this question, what is observable by us seems eminently relevant." And my answer to the question is this: "to accept a theory is (for us) to believe that it is empirically adequate—that what the theory says *about what is observable* (by us) is true."[10]

SR: Since you refer to what is observable "by us," I take it you make observability relative to an epistemic community, not to individuals?

CE: Of course. The dimmer component of the double star in the Big Dipper's handle is observable because some sharp-eyed people can see it, even if most of us can't.

SR: But then I have a problem. You surely must admit the possibility that our epistemic community might be enlarged, say by the inclusion of animals or extraterrestrials capable of observing things that we now can't observe. For example, we might encounter space travellers who, when we tell them our theories about electrons, say, "Of course, we see them all the time." If this happened, your principles would require that we then, for the first time, accept the existence of

electrons. But this seems absurd. Why should the testimony of these aliens be decisive when the overwhelming evidence of our science was not? More generally, isn't it absurd to say that, just because our epistemic community has been enlarged in this way, our beliefs about what there is should change?

CE: Not at all. Your objection has weight only if we believe that "our epistemic policies should give the same results independent of our beliefs about the range of evidence accessible to us."[11] But I see absolutely no reason to believe this. On the contrary, it seems to me that to deny that what evidence is accessible is relevant to what we should believe is to open the door to scepticism or irrationalism.

SR: It seems to me you're equivocating on the expression "evidence accessible to us." Of course such evidence is relevant to our beliefs if it means "the evidence that we are in fact aware of." But this isn't what you mean here. Rather, you're saying that our beliefs ought to depend on the range of evidence that we *might* have even if we don't. Specifically, you're saying that believing that an entity exists ought to depend on whether or not there *could be* direct observations of its existence. Of course, actual observations of an entity are relevant to belief in its existence. And it's also true that, since evidence of actual observations of unobservable entities is not available, it's often harder to produce an adequate case for the existence of such things. But what reason could you have for thinking that the mere question of whether or not an entity could in principle be observed by us is decisive for the question of whether we ought to believe that it exists?

CE: What reason do you have for thinking this isn't the case?

SR: Well, consider an example. Suppose astronomical theory postulates the existence of a far distant star that has not been observed but which we have every reason to think we could observe if we were close enough. It might be, for example, that the star has been postulated as the much smaller double of a known star to explain certain anomalies in its motion. I suppose that if the evidence supporting this postulation is strong enough, you will agree that we have good reasons to believe in the existence of this star.

CE: Of course, since it is in principle observable.

SR: All right. But suppose further that, entirely independent of astronomical investigations, physiological studies subsequently show that there are previously unknown limits on human powers of observation that make the postulated star unobservable. We may, for example, have assumed that the star was observable because it emitted light in the visible spectrum and so could be seen if we got close enough to it. But physiologists might discover that the visible spectrum is not continuous, that there are small "holes" of invisibility corresponding to specific wave lengths, one of which is that emitted by the star. On your principles, such a physiological result would require us to abandon our conclusion that the star exists, even though all the empirical evidence that led us to postulate it remains the same. But surely such a move would be unreasonable; whether or not the star is observable does not alter the evidence in favor of its existence.

Notice that I'm not saying that observations we in fact have made are not relevant to our beliefs about what exists. But the mere fact that something is observable does not give us any reason to think that it ever has or will in fact be observed. The issue between us is whether mere observability — as distinct from actual observation — is relevant to our beliefs about what exists. I submit that it is not.

Another difficulty for your view derives from the fact that an observable entity may have unobservable properties. The sun, for example, is observable but the temperature of its interior is not. What then is your attitude toward the claim that the temperature at the sun's center is about 20 million degrees Centigrade? It would be odd not to accept it: After all, the claim is very well supported by a calculation based on observed facts

(the average temperature of the earth, etc.). If these observed facts were appropriately different, the calculation would yield a temperature of the center of the sun that is observable (e.g., about 10 degrees Centigrade). Since you would accept the truth of the result of the calculation in the latter case, it's hard to see how you could coherently not accept its truth in the former case. But, if you accept the claim that the temperature of the sun's center is about 20 million degrees, then you've implicitly given up your principle that observability is relevant to the justification of existence claims.

CE: Not necessarily. The principle might distinguish between unobservable entities and unobservable properties of observable entities.

SR: Possibly. But then we'd need an explanation of why such a distinction is epistemically relevant.

CE: Of course, but you can see where this would lead. To respond to this objection — and your other one about the star that turns out to be unobservable — in a convincing way would require a very elaborate excursion into the theory of knowledge. "But we cannot settle the major questions of epistemology *en passant* in philosophy of science."[12] I'll just acknowledge the relevance of your objections but maintain that more careful epistemological analysis would disarm them. Furthermore, even if I can't answer your objections and your argument stands, remember that the argument is only inductive. This means that, even if I can't directly refute it, I might be able to blunt its force by pointing to overriding considerations that make realism implausible. There is, for example, the fact that, for any theory whose ontology you propose to accept, we can always formulate another theory with a different ontology that is just as well supported by the evidence as the theory you favor. Also, there's the strong historical evidence that scientific postulations are not converging to any single picture of what the unobservable world is like. Until you've dealt with these historical and logical objections to realism, you can't be content with your case for realism.

SR: I agree that the issue isn't fully settled, but your remarks strike me as a strategic retreat that, at least for the present, leaves me in control of the battlefield.

NOTES

1. Wilfrid Sellars, *Science, Perception, and Reality* (New York: Humanities, 1963), p. 91.

2. Cf. Bas van Fraassen, *The Scientific Image* (Oxford: The Clarendon Press, 1980), p. 12.

3. Bas van Fraassen, "On the Radical Incomplete-ness of the Manifest Image," *PSA*, 1976, ed. F. Suppe and P. Asquith (East Lansing, MI.: Philosophy of Science Association, 1977), p.325.

4. van Fraassen, *The Scientific Image*, p. 39, cited in n2, above.

5. Ibid., p. 40.

6. Sellars, "Is Scientific Realism Tenable?," *PSA*, 1976, ed. F. Suppe and P. Asquith (East Lansing, MI.: Philosophy of Science Association, 1977), p. 316.

7. Ibid., p. 318.

8. Sellars, *Science, Perception, and Reality*, p. 118, cited in n1, above.

9. van Fraassen, *The Scientific Image*, p. 17.

10. Ibid., p. 18.

11. Ibid.

12. Ibid., p. 19.

Further Questions

1. In light of this debate, what do you think it means for something to be observable?

2. Get together with two of your classmates. Independently of one another, formulate a view about what it means for something to be observable (or not) and what this has to do with whether we ought to believe it exists. Compare your views and try to figure out which is most adequate.

Further Readings

Devitt, Michael. *Realism and Truth*. Princeton: Princeton University Press, 1984. A spirited and readable defense of realism.

Moser, Paul K. *Reality in Focus*. Englewood Cliffs: Prentice-Hall, 1990. Part I contains several contemporary articles appropriate for scientifically informed undergraduates.

van Fraassen, Bas. *The Scientific Image*. Oxford: Clarendon Press, 1980. A sophisticated and influential defense of antirealism.

Part VIII

Experience

D<small>EEP IN THE HEART OF A MYSTERIOUS LABYRINTH</small> you find the center. Cautiously, you step in only to find yourself in yet another labyrinth, deeper and more puzzling than the first. You wander through it until you find its center—where there is yet another labyrinth, a labyrinth within a labyrinth within a labyrinth—

You turn and go back. You find the exit to the original labyrinth where you began. You step out into an outer labyrinth. You continue outward, exiting into another outer labyrinth, then another—

You go inward, entering one labyrinth after another. You go outward, exiting into one labyrinth after another. You never emerge: *there is no exit*. You never find what you are looking for: *there is no center*.

Perhaps you find this story strange. But that is where you are now: inside a labyrinth. The labyrinth has a name. It is called "experience."

That experience exists at all is both obvious and puzzling. Right now you are having the experience of reading a book and, along with it, the experience of being in the world at a particular place and time. You might be mistaken about whether your experience is accurate or true. But you cannot be mistaken about whether experience itself—accurate or not—is going on. Experience is happening. To you. Now.

There is far less correspondence between your experiences and what exists outside you than you probably think. And that there is any correspondence at all is based *completely* on theory. It cannot be verified in your experience! In other words, the experiences you are having cannot be *seen* to be a reliable indication of what exists outside you because every element of your experience is inside you. The puzzle goes deeper. No one has ever been able to explain unproblematically how experience is even possible—how, for instance, atoms interacting with each other can produce sensation, emotions, and thoughts—what you might call your "mental inside."

Your experiences are always inside. Inside what? You. Along with your image of the outside there is also the image of you, the image of a something that has an inside. This "having an inside" is the ability to have experiences: something we call consciousness. But consciousness, too, like your image of the outside, is synthesized by you! How could that be? How could your brain, a collection of nonconscious elements, ever become conscious? How could this "having an inside," "being a center of consciousness," ever come about? What *is* consciousness?

Suppose you did find yourself inside a mysterious labyrinth within a labyrinth whose center is a labyrinth that has yet another labyrinth for a center. What would you do? *Perhaps this.*

On Having No Head

D. E. HARDING

Born in 1909, retired architect D. E. Harding currently gives spiritual workshops in England. In this selection, he poignantly dramatizes the distinction between what we experience and the interpretations we put on what we experience. For instance, you think you experience your head. What could be more obvious? But Harding points out the ways in which your own head is for you an interpretation. According to him, you do not even have a head. Your head is a hallucination.

Reading Questions

1. Are there two "widely different species" of people, those with heads and those without them? What does Harding think?
2. Can you prove that you have a head by looking in a mirror or by asking your neighbor? What does Harding think? What do you think?
3. Can you prove *through experience* that Harding is wrong?
4. How does Harding distinguish *looking* from *thinking*?
5. What does he mean by "hallucination"?

THE BEST DAY OF MY LIFE —my rebirthday, so to speak—was when I found I had no head. This is not a literary gambit, a witticism designed to arouse interest at any cost. I mean it in all seriousness: *I have no head*.

It was eighteen years ago, when I was thirty-three, that I made the discovery. Though it certainly came out of the blue, it did so in response to an urgent enquiry; I had for several months been absorbed in the question: what am I? The fact that I happened to be walking in the Himalayas at the time probably had little to do with it; though in that country unusual states of mind are said to come more easily. However that may be, a

From On Having No Head: Zen and the Re-Discovery of the Obvious *by D. E. Harding (Arkana, 1986), pp. 1–3, 5–10, 15–16, copyright © D. E. Harding, 1961, 1971, 1986. Reproduced by permission of Penguin Books Ltd. and the author.*

very still clear day, and a view from the ridge where I stood, over misty blue valleys to the highest mountain range in the world, with Kangchenjunga and Everest unprominent among its snow-peaks, made a setting worthy of the grandest vision.

What actually happened was something absurdly simple and unspectacular: I stopped thinking. A peculiar quiet, an odd kind of alert limpness or numbness, came over me. Reason and imagination and all mental chatter died down. For once, words really failed me. Past and future dropped away. I forgot who and what I was, my name, manhood, animalhood, all that could be called mine. It was as if I had been born that instant, brand new, mindless, innocent of all memories. There existed only the Now, that present moment and what was clearly given in it. To look was enough. And what I found was khaki trouserlegs terminating downwards in a pair of brown shoes, khaki sleeves terminating sideways in a pair of pink hands, and a khaki shirtfront terminating upwards in — absolutely nothing whatever! Certainly not in a head.

It took me no time at all to notice that this nothing, this hole where a head should have been, was no ordinary vacancy, no mere nothing. On the contrary, it was very much occupied. It was a vast emptiness vastly filled, a nothing that found room for everything — room for grass, trees, shadowy distant hills, and far above them snow-peaks like a row of angular clouds riding the blue sky. I had lost a head and gained a world.

It was all, quite literally, breathtaking. I seemed to stop breathing altogether, absorbed in the Given. Here it was, this superb scene, brightly shining in the clear air, alone and unsupported, mysteriously suspended in the void, and (and *this* was the real miracle, the wonder and delight) utterly free of "me," unstained by any observer. Its total presence was my total absence, body and soul. Lighter than air, clearer than glass, altogether released from myself, I was nowhere around.

Yet in spite of the magical and uncanny quality of this vision, it was no dream, no esoteric revelation. Quite the reverse: it felt like a sudden waking from the sleep of ordinary life, an end to dreaming. It was self-luminous reality for once swept clean of all obscuring mind. It was the revelation, at long last, of the perfectly obvious. It was a lucid moment in a confused life-history. It was a ceasing to ignore something which (since early childhood at any rate) I had always been too busy or too clever to see. It was naked, uncritical attention to what had all along been staring me in the face — my utter facelessness. In short, it was all perfectly simple and plain and straightforward, beyond argument, thought, and words. There arose no questions, no reference beyond the experience itself, but only peace and a quiet joy, and the sensation of having dropped an intolerable burden.

*   *   *

As the first wonder of my Himalayan discovery began to wear off, I started describing it to myself in some such words as the following.

Somehow or other I had vaguely thought of myself as inhabiting this house which is my body, and looking out through its two round windows at the world. Now I find it isn't like that at all. As I gaze into the distance, what is there at this moment to tell me how many eyes I have here — two, or three, or hundreds, or none? In fact, only one window appears on this side of my facade, and that one is wide open and frameless, with nobody looking out of it. It is always the other fellow who has eyes and a face to frame them; never this one.

There exist, then, two sorts — two widely different species — of man. The first, of which I note countless specimens, evidently carries a head on its shoulders (and by "head" I mean a hairy eight-inch ball with various holes in it) while the second, of which I note only one specimen, evidently carries no such thing on its shoulders. And till now I had overlooked this considerable difference! Victim of a prolonged fit of madness, of a lifelong hallucination (and by "hallucination" I mean what my dictionary says: *apparent perception of an object not actually present*), I had invariably seen myself as pretty much like other men, and certainly never as a decapitated but still living biped. I had been blind to the one thing that is always present, and without which I am blind indeed — to this marvellous substitute-for-a-head, this unbounded clarity, this luminous and absolutely pure void, which nevertheless is — rather than contains — all things. For, however carefully I attend, I fail to find here even so much as a blank screen on which these mountains and sun and sky are projected, or a clear mirror in which they are reflected, or a transparent lens or aperture through which they are viewed — still less a soul or a mind to which they are presented, or a viewer (however shadowy) who is distinguishable from the view. Nothing whatever intervenes, not even that baffling and elusive obstacle called "distance": the huge blue sky, the pink-edged whiteness of the snows, the sparkling green of the grass — how can these be remote, when there's nothing to be remote from? The headless void here refuses all definition and location: it is not round, or small, or big, or even here as distinct from there. (And even if there *were* a head here to measure outwards from, the measuring-rod stretching from it to the peak of Everest would, when read end-on — and there's no other way for me to read it — reduce to a point, to nothing.) In fact, these colored shapes present themselves in all simplicity, without any such complications as near or far, this or that, mine or not mine, seen-by-me or merely given. All twoness — all duality of subject and object — has vanished: it is no longer read into a situation which has no room for it.

Such were the thoughts which followed the vision. To try to set down the first-hand, immediate experience in these or any other terms, however, is to misrepresent it by complicating what is quite simple: indeed the longer the postmortem examination drags on the further it gets from the living original. At best, these descriptions can re-

mind one of the vision (without the bright awareness) or invite a recurrence of it; but they can no more convey its essential quality, or ensure a recurrence, than the most appetizing menu can taste like the dinner, or the best book about humour enable one to see a joke. On the other hand, it is impossible to stop thinking for long, and some attempt to relate the lucid intervals of one's life to the confused background is inevitable. It could also encourage, indirectly, the recurrence of lucidity.

In any case, there are several commonsense objections which refuse to be put off any longer, questions which insist on reasoned answers, however inconclusive. . . .

* * *

My first objection was: my head may be missing, but not its nose. Here it is, visibly preceding me wherever I go. And my answer was: if this fuzzy, pinkish, yet perfectly transparent cloud suspended on my right, and this other similar cloud suspended on my left, are noses, then I count two of them and not one; and the perfectly opaque single protuberance which I observe so clearly in the middle of your face is *not* a nose: only a hopelessly dishonest or confused observer would deliberately use the same name for such utterly different things. I prefer to go by my dictionary and common usage, which oblige me to say that, whereas nearly all other men have a nose apiece, I have none.

All the same, if some misguided skeptic, over-anxious to make his point, were to strike out in this direction, aiming midway between these two pink clouds, the result would surely be as unpleasant as if I owned the most solid and punchable of noses. Again, what about this complex of subtle tensions, movements, pressures, itches, tickles, aches, warmths, and throbbings, never entirely absent from this central region? Above all, what about these touch-feelings which arise when I explore here with my hand? Surely these findings add up to massive evidence for the existence of my head right here and now, after all?

They do nothing of the sort. No doubt a great variety of sensations are plainly given here and cannot be ignored, but they don't amount to a head, or anything like one. The only way to make a head out of them would be to throw in all sorts of ingredients that are plainly missing here—in particular, all manner of coloured shapes in three dimensions. What sort of head is it that, though containing innumerable sensations, is observed to lack eyes, ears, mouth, hair, and indeed all the bodily equipment which other heads are observed to contain? The plain fact is that this place must be kept clear of all such obstructions, of the slightest mistiness or colouring which could cloud my universe.

In any case, when I start groping round for my lost head, instead of finding it here I only lose my exploring hand as well: it, too, is swallowed up in the abyss at the centre of my being. Apparently this yawning cavern, this unoccupied base of all my operations, this magical locality where I thought I kept my head, is in fact more like a beacon-fire so fierce that all things approaching it are instantly and utterly consumed, in order that its world-illuminating brilliance and clarity shall never for a moment be obscured. As for these lurking aches and tickles and so on, they can no more quench or shade that central brightness than these mountains and clouds and sky can do so. Quite the contrary: they all exist in its shining, and through them it is seen to shine. Present experience, whatever sense is employed, occurs only in an empty and absent head. For here and now my world and my head are incompatibles: they won't mix. There is no room for both at once on these shoulders, and fortunately it is my head with all its anatomy that has to go. This is not a matter of argument, or of philosophical acumen, or of working oneself up into a state, but of simple sight—of LOOK-WHO'S-HERE instead of THINK-WHO'S-HERE. . . .

*   *   *

Probably there is only one way of converting the skeptic who still says I have a head here, and that is to invite him to come here and take a look for himself; only he must be an honest reporter, describing what he observes and nothing else.

Starting off on the far side of the room, he sees me as a full-length man-with-a-head. But as he approaches he finds half a man, then a head, then a blurred cheek or eye or nose, then a mere blur, and finally (at the point of contact) nothing at all. Alternatively, if he happens to be equipped with the necessary scientific instruments, he reports that the blur resolves itself into tissues, then cell-groups, then a single cell, a cell-nucleus, giant molecules . . . and so on, till he comes to a place where nothing is to be seen, to space which is empty of all solid or material objects. In either case, the observer who comes here to see what it's really like finds what I find here—vacancy. And if, having discovered and shared my nonentity here, he were to turn around (looking out with me instead of in at me) he would again find what I find—that this vacancy is filled to capacity with everything imaginable. He, too, would find this central Point exploding into an Infinite Volume, this Nothing into the All, this Here into Everywhere.

And if my skeptical observer still doubts his senses, he may try his camera instead—a device which, lacking memory and anticipation, can register only what is contained in the place where it happens to be. It records the same picture of me. Over there, it takes a man; midway, bits and pieces of a man; here, no man and nothing—or else, when pointed the other way round, the universe.

*   *   *

Film directors . . . are practical people, much more interested in the telling re-creation of experience than in discerning the nature of the experiencer; but in fact the one involves some of the other. Certainly these experts are well aware (for example) how feeble my reaction is to a film of a vehicle obviously driven by someone else, compared with my reaction to a film of a vehicle apparently driven by myself. In the first instance I am a spectator on the pavement, observing two similar cars swiftly approaching, colliding, killing the drivers, bursting into flames — and I am mildly interested. In the second, I am the driver — headless, of course, like all first-person drivers, and my car (what little there is of it) is stationary. Here are my swaying knees, my foot hard down on the accelerator, my hands struggling with the steering wheel, the long bonnet sloping away in front, telegraph poles whizzing by, the road snaking this way and that, the other car, tiny at first, but looming larger and larger, coming straight at me, and then the crash, a great flash of light, and an empty silence. . . . I sink back onto my seat and get my breath back. I have been taken for a ride.

How are they filmed, these first-person sequences? Two ways are possible: either a headless dummy is photographed, with the camera in place of the head; or else a real man is photographed, with his head held far back or to one side to make room for the camera. In other words, to ensure that I shall identify myself with the actor, his head is got out of the way: he must be my kind of man. For a picture of me-with-a-head is no likeness at all: it is the portrait of a complete stranger, a case of mistaken identity.

It is curious that anyone should go to the advertising man for a glimpse into the deepest — and simplest — truths about himself; odd also that an elaborate modern invention like the cinema should help rid anyone of an illusion which very young children and animals are free of. But in other ages there were other and equally curious pointers, and our human capacity for self-deception has surely never been complete. A profound though dim awareness of the human condition may well explain the popularity of many old cults and legends of loose and flying heads, of one-eyed or headless monsters and apparitions, of human bodies with non-human heads, and of martyrs who (like King Charles in the ill-punctuated sentence) walked and talked after their heads were cut off — fantastic pictures, no doubt, but nearer than common sense ever gets to a true portrait of *this* man.

*   *   *

Further Questions

1. If you can't *see* that you have a head, can't you at least *feel* that you have a head? And if you can feel that you have one, is there any reason visual experience should take precedence over tactile experience in determining what is real?

2. Is there a useful distinction to be drawn between what we can know on the basis of direct experience and what we can know only on the basis of theory? If so, does Harding draw or utilize that distinction correctly?

Further Readings

Kapleau, Philip. *The Three Pillars of Zen.* New York: Anchor, 1980. How to uninterpret your experience, Zen-style. A beautifully written book.

Krishnamurti, J. *The Awakening of Intelligence.* New York: Avon, 1973. Another interesting attempt to get beneath the labels to experience itself.

Suzuki, D. T. *Essays in Zen Buddhism, First Series.* New York: Grove Press, 1961. Essays on experience and truth, by the man who introduced Zen to the West.

A Coffeehouse Conversation on the Turing Test

DOUGLAS R. HOFSTADTER

Douglas Hofstadter is Professor of Cognitive Science and Computer Science at the Center for Research on Concepts and Cognition at Indiana University. He is the author of *Gödel, Escher, and Bach* (1979), co-editor, along with Daniel Dennett, of *The Mind's I* (1981), and author of *Metamagical Themas* (1985), a collection of essays, several of which appeared originally, as did the following selection, in his regular column in *Scientific American*. In this selection Hofstadter dramatically portrays the reasons for and against using the "Turing Test" as a criterion for determining whether a machine can think.

Reading Questions

1. What's the difference between the Imitation Game and the Turing Test? Which, if either, is a more adequate test of whether machines can think?
2. Which of the characters—Chris, Sandy, or Pat—has the best arguments?
3. D. M. Armstrong, in a previous selection, suggested that a thermometer might have knowledge. *If* we're prepared to say that a thermometer might know, should we hesitate to say that a computer might think?

PARTICIPANTS IN THE DIALOGUE: Chris, a physics student; Pat, a biology student; Sandy, a philosophy student.

Chris: Sandy, I want to thank you for suggesting that I read Alan Turing's article "Computing Machinery and Intelligence". It's a wonderful piece and certainly made me think—and think about my thinking.

Sandy: Glad to hear it. Are you still as much of a skeptic about artificial intelligence as you used to be?

Chris: You've got me wrong. I'm not against artificial intelligence; I think it's wonderful stuff—perhaps a little crazy, but why not? I simply am convinced that you AI advocates have far underestimated the human mind, and that there are

things a computer will never, ever be able to do. For instance, can you imagine a computer writing a Proust novel? The richness of imagination, the complexity of the characters—

Sandy: Rome wasn't built in a day!

Chris: In the article, Turing comes through as an interesting person. Is he still alive?

Sandy: No, he died back in 1954, at just 41. He'd be only 70 or so now, although he is such a legendary figure it seems strange to think that he could still be living today.

Chris: How did he die?

Sandy: Almost certainly suicide. He was homosexual, and had to deal with some pretty barbaric treatment and stupidity from the outside world. In the end, it got to be too much, and he killed himself.

Chris: That's horrendous, especially in this day and age.

Sandy: I know. What really saddens me is that he never got to see the amazing progress in computing machinery and theory that has taken place since 1954. Can you imagine how he'd have been wowed?

Chris: Yeah . . .

Pat: Hey, are you two going to clue me in as to what this Turing article is about?

Sandy: It is really about two things. One is the question "Can a machine think?"—or rather, "Will a machine ever think?" The way Turing answers the question—he thinks the answer is *yes*, by the way—is by batting down a series of objections to the idea, one after another. The other point he tries to make is that, as it stands, the question is not meaningful. It's too full of emotional connotations. Many people are upset by the suggestion that people are machines, or that machines might think. Turing tries to defuse the question by casting it in less emotional terms. For instance, what do you think, Pat, of the idea of thinking machines?

Pat: Frankly, I find the term confusing. You know what confuses me? It's those ads in the newspapers and on TV that talk about "products that think" or "intelligent ovens" or whatever. I just don't know how seriously to take them.

Sandy: I know the kind of ads you mean, and they probably confuse a lot of people. On the other hand, we're always hearing the refrain "Computers are really dumb; you have to spell everything out for them in words of one syllable"—yet on the other hand, we're constantly bombarded with advertising hype about "smart products."

Chris: That's certainly true. Do you know that one company has even taken to calling its products "dumb terminals" in order to stand out from the crowd?

Sandy: That's a pretty clever gimmick, but even so it just contributes to the trend toward obfuscation. The term "electronic brain" always comes to my mind when I'm thinking about this.

Many people swallow it completely, and others reject it out of hand. It takes patience to sort out the issues and decide how much of it makes sense.

Pat: Does Turing suggest some way of resolving it, some kind of IQ test for machines?

Sandy: That would be very interesting, but no machine could yet come close to taking an IQ test. Instead, Turing proposes a test that theoretically could be applied to any machine to determine whether or not it can think.

Pat: Does the test give a clear-cut yes-or-no answer? I'd be skeptical if it claimed to.

Sandy: No, it doesn't claim to. In a way that's one of its advantages. It shows how the borderline is quite fuzzy, and how subtle the whole question is.

Pat: And so, as usual in philosophy, it's all just a question of words!

Sandy: Maybe, but they're emotionally charged words, and so it's important, it seems to me, to explore the issues and try to map out the meanings of the crucial words. The issues are fundamental to our concept of ourselves, so we shouldn't just sweep them under the rug.

Pat: Okay, so tell me how Turing's test works.

Sandy: The idea is based on what he calls the *Imitation Game*. Imagine that a man and a woman go into separate rooms, and from there they can be interrogated by a third party via some sort of teletype set-up. The third party can address questions to either room, but has no idea which person is in which room. For the interrogator, the idea is to determine which room the woman is in. The woman, by her answers, tries to help the interrogator as much as she can. The man, though, is doing his best to bamboozle the interrogator, by responding as he thinks a woman might. And if he succeeds in fooling the interrogator . . .

Pat: The interrogator only gets to see written words, eh? And the sex of the author is supposed to shine through? That game sounds like a good challenge. I'd certainly like to take part in it someday. Would the interrogator have met either the man or the woman before the test began? Would any of them know any of the others?

Sandy: That would probably be a bad idea. All kinds of subliminal cueing might occur if the interrogator knew one or both of them. It would certainly be best if all three people were totally unknown to one another.

Pat: Could you ask any questions at all, with no holds barred?

Sandy: Absolutely. That's the whole idea!

Pat: Don't you think, then, that pretty quickly it would degenerate into sex-oriented questions? I mean, I can imagine the man, overeager to act convincing, giving away the game by answering some very blunt questions that most women would find too personal to answer, even through an anonymous computer connection.

Sandy: That's a nice observation. I wonder if it's true . . .

Chris: Another possibility would be to probe for knowledge of minute aspects of traditional sex-role differences, by asking about such things as dress sizes and so on. The psychology of the Imitation Game could get pretty subtle. I suppose whether the interrogator was a woman or a man would make a difference. Don't you think that a woman could spot some telltale differences more quickly than a man could?

Pat: If so, maybe the best way to tell a man from a woman is to let each of them play interrogator in an Imitation Game, and see which of the two is better at telling a man from a woman!

Sandy: Hmm . . . that's a droll twist. Oh, well. I don't know if this original version of the Imitation Game has ever been seriously tried out, despite the fact that it would be relatively easy to do with modern computer terminals. I have to admit, though, that I'm not at all sure what it would prove, whichever way it turned out.

Pat: I was wondering about that. What would it prove if the interrogator — say a woman — couldn't tell correctly which person was the woman? It certainly wouldn't prove that the man *was* a woman!

Sandy: Exactly! What I find funny is that although I strongly believe in the idea of the Turing Test, I'm not so sure I understand the point of its basis, the Imitation Game.

Chris: As for me, I'm not any happier with the Turing Test as a test for thinking machines than I am with the Imitation Game as a test for femininity.

Pat: From what you two are saying, I gather the Turing Test is some kind of extension of the Imitation Game, only involving a machine and a person instead of a man and a woman.

Sandy: That's the idea. The machine tries its hardest to convince the interrogator that it is the human being and the human tries to make it clear that he or she is not the computer.

Pat: The machine *tries*? Isn't that a loaded way of putting it?

Sandy: Sorry, but that seemed the most natural way to say it.

Pat: Anyway, this test sounds pretty interesting. But how do you know that it will get at the essence of thinking? Maybe it's testing for the wrong things. Maybe, just to take a random illustration, someone would feel that a machine was able to think only if it could dance so well that you couldn't tell it was a machine. Or someone else could suggest some other characteristic. What's so sacred about being able to fool people by typing at them?

Sandy: I don't see how you can say such a thing. I've heard that objection before, but frankly, it baffles me. So what if the machine can't tap-dance or drop a rock on your toe? If it can discourse intelligently on any subject you want, then it has shown that it can think — to me, at least! As I see it, Turing has drawn, in one clean stroke, a clear division between thinking and other aspects of being human.

Pat: Now *you're* the baffling one. If you couldn't conclude anything from a *man's* ability to win at the Imitation Game, how could you conclude anything from a *machine*'s ability to win at the Turing Game?

Chris: Good question.

Sandy: It seems to me that you could conclude *something* from a man's win in the Imitation Game. You wouldn't conclude he was a woman, but you could certainly say he had good insights into the feminine mentality (if there is such a thing). Now, if a computer could fool someone into thinking it was a person, I guess you'd have to say something similar about it—that it had good insights into what it's like to be human, into "the human condition" (whatever that is).

Pat: Maybe, but that isn't necessarily equivalent to *thinking*, is it? It seems to me that passing the Turing Test would merely prove that some machine or other could do a very good job of *simulating* thought.

Chris: I couldn't agree more with Pat. We all know that fancy computer programs exist today for simulating all sorts of complex phenomena. In theoretical physics, for instance, we simulate the behavior of particles, atoms, solids, liquids, gases, galaxies, and so on. But no one confuses any of those simulations with the real thing!

Sandy: In his book *Brainstorms*, the philosopher Daniel Dennett makes a similar point about simulated hurricanes.

Chris: That's a nice example, too. Obviously, what goes on inside a computer when it's simulating a hurricane is not a hurricane, for the machine's memory doesn't get torn to bits by 200-mile-an-hour winds, the floor of the machine room doesn't get flooded with rainwater, and so on.

Sandy: Oh, come on—that's not a fair argument! In the first place, the programmers don't claim the simulation really *is* a hurricane. It's merely a simulation of certain aspects of a hurricane. But in the second place, you're pulling a fast one when you imply that there are no downpours or 200-mile-an-hour winds in a simulated hurricane. To *us* there aren't any, but if the program were incredibly detailed, it could include simu-

lated people on the ground who would experience the wind and the rain just as we do when a hurricane hits. In their minds—or, if you'd rather, in their *simulated* minds—the hurricane would be not a simulation, but a genuine phenomenon complete with drenching and devastation.

Chris: Oh, my—what a science-fiction scenario! Now we're talking about simulating whole populations, not just a single mind!

Sandy: Well, look—I'm simply trying to show you why your argument that a simulated McCoy isn't the real McCoy is fallacious. It depends on the tacit assumption that any old observer of the simulated phenomenon is equally able to assess what's going on. But in fact, it may take an observer with a special vantage point to recognize what is going on. In the hurricane case, it takes special "computational glasses" to see the rain and the winds.

Pat: "Computational glasses"? I don't know what you're talking about.

Sandy: I mean that to see the winds and the wetness of the hurricane, you have to be able to look at it in the proper way. You—

Chris: No, no, no! A simulated hurricane isn't wet! No matter how much it might seem wet to simulated people, it won't ever be *genuinely* wet! And no computer will ever get torn apart in the process of simulating winds.

Sandy: Certainly not, but that's irrelevant. You're just confusing levels. The laws of physics don't get torn apart by real hurricanes, either. In the case of the simulated hurricane, if you go peering at the computer's memory, expecting to find broken wires and so forth, you'll be disappointed. But look at the proper level. Look into the *structures* that are coded for in memory. You'll see that many abstract links have been broken, many values of variables radically changed, and so on. *There's* your flood, your devastation—real, only a little concealed, a little hard to detect.

Chris: I'm sorry, I just can't buy that. You're insisting that I look for a new kind of devastation, one never before associated with hurricanes. That way you could call *anything* a hurricane as long as its effects, seen through your special "glasses," could be called "floods and devastation."

Sandy: Right—you've got it exactly! You recognize a hurricane by its *effects*. You have no way of going in and finding some ethereal "essence of hurricane," some "hurricane soul" right in the middle of the storm's eye. Nor is there any ID card to be found that certifies "hurricanehood." It's just the existence of a certain kind of *pattern*—a spiral storm with an eye and so forth—that makes you say it's a hurricane. Of course, there are a lot of things you'll insist on before you call something a hurricane.

Pat: Well, wouldn't you say that being an *atmospheric* phenomenon is one prerequisite? How can anything inside a computer be a storm? To me, a simulation is a simulation is a simulation!

Sandy: Then I suppose you would say that even the *calculations* computers do are simulated —that they are fake calculations. Only *people* can do genuine calculations, right?

Pat: Well, computers get the right answers, so their calculations are not exactly fake—but they're still just patterns. There's no *understanding* going on in there. Take a cash register. Can you honestly say that you feel it is *calculating* something when its gears mesh together? And the step from cash register to computer is very short, as I understand things.

Sandy: If you mean that a cash register doesn't feel like a schoolkid doing arithmetic problems, I'll agree. But is that what "calculation" means? Is that an integral part of it? If so, then contrary to what everybody has thought up till now, we'll have to write a very complicated program indeed to perform *genuine* calculations. Of course, this program will sometimes get careless and make mistakes, and it will sometimes scrawl its answers illegibly, and it will occasionally doodle on its paper . . . It won't be any more reliable than the store clerk who adds up your total by hand. Now, I happen to believe that eventually such a pro-

gram could be written. Then we'd know something about how clerks and schoolkids work.

Pat: I can't believe you'd ever be able to do that!

Sandy: Maybe, maybe not, but that's not my point. You say a cash register can't calculate. It reminds me of another favorite passage of mine from Dennett's *Brainstorms*. It goes something like this: "Cash registers can't really calculate; they can only spin their gears. But cash registers can't really spin their gears, either; they can only follow the laws of physics." Dennett said it originally about computers; I modified it to talk about cash registers. And you could use the same line of reasoning in talking about people: "People can't really calculate; all they can do is manipulate mental symbols. But they aren't really manipulating symbols; all they are doing is firing various neurons in various patterns. But they can't really make their neurons fire; they simply have to let the laws of physics make them fire for them." Et cetera. Don't you see how this *reductio ad absurdum* would lead you to conclude that calculation doesn't exist, that hurricanes don't exist—in fact, that nothing at a level higher than particles and the laws of physics exists? What do you gain by saying that a computer only pushes symbols around and doesn't truly calculate?

Pat: The example may be extreme, but it makes my point that there is a vast difference between a real phenomenon and any simulation of it. This is so for hurricanes, and even more so for human thought.

Sandy: Look, I don't want to get too tangled up in this line of argument, but let me try one more example. If you were a radio ham listening to another ham broadcasting in Morse code and you were responding in Morse code, would it sound funny to you to refer to "the person at the other end"?

Pat: No, that would sound okay, although the existence of a person at the other end would be an assumption.

Sandy: Yes, but you wouldn't be likely to go and check it out. You're prepared to recognize personhood through those rather unusual channels. You don't have to see a human body or hear a voice. All you need is a rather abstract manifestation—a code, as it were. What I'm getting at is this. To "see" the person behind the dits and dahs, you have to be willing to do some *decoding*, some interpretation. It's not direct perception; it's indirect. You have to peel off a layer or two to find the reality hidden in there. You put on your "radio-ham's glasses" to "see" the person behind the buzzes. Just the same with the simulated hurricane! You don't see it darkening the machine room; you have to decode the machine's memory. You have to put on special "memory-decoding" glasses. *Then* what you see is a hurricane.

Pat: Oh, ho ho! Talk about fast ones—wait a minute! In the case of the shortwave radio, there's a real person out there, somewhere in the Fiji Islands or wherever. My decoding act as I sit by my radio simply reveals that that person exists. It's like seeing a shadow and concluding there's an object out there, casting it. One doesn't confuse the shadow with the object, however! And with the hurricane there's no *real* storm behind the scenes, making the computer follow its patterns. No, what you have is just a shadow-hurricane without any genuine hurricane. I just refuse to confuse shadows with reality.

Sandy: All right. I don't want to drive this point into the ground. I even admit it is pretty silly to say that a simulated hurricane *is* a hurricane. But I wanted to point out that it's not as silly as you might think at first blush. And when you turn to simulated *thought*, then you've got a very different matter on your hands from simulated hurricanes.

Pat: I don't see why. You'll have to convince me.

Sandy: Well, to do so, I'll first have to make a couple of extra points about hurricanes.

Pat: Oh, no! Well, all right, all right.

Sandy: Nobody can say just exactly what a hurricane is—that is, in totally precise terms. There's an abstract pattern that many storms share, and it's for that reason we call those storms

hurricanes. But it's not possible to make a sharp distinction between hurricanes and non-hurricanes. There are tornados, cyclones, typhoons, dust devils . . . Is the Great Red Spot on Jupiter a hurricane? Are sunspots hurricanes? Could there be a hurricane in a wind tunnel? In a test tube? In your imagination, you can even extend the concept of "hurricane" to include a microscopic storm on the surface of a neutron star.

Chris: That's not so far-fetched, you know. The concept of "earthquake" has actually been extended to neutron stars. The astrophysicists say that the tiny changes in rate that once in a while are observed in the pulsing of a pulsar are caused by "glitches"—starquakes—that have just occurred on the neutron star's surface.

Sandy: Oh, I remember that now. That "glitch" idea has always seemed eerie to me—a surrealistic kind of quivering on a surrealistic kind of surface.

Chris: Can you imagine—plate tectonics on a giant sphere of pure nuclear matter?

Sandy: That's a wild thought. So, starquakes and earthquakes can both be subsumed into a new, more abstract category. And that's how science constantly extends familiar concepts, taking them further and further from familiar experience and yet keeping some essence constant. The number system is the classic example—from positive numbers to negative numbers, then rationals, reals, complex numbers, and "on beyond zebra," as Dr. Seuss says.

Pat: I think I can see your point, Sandy. In biology, we have many examples of close relationships that are established in rather abstract ways. Often the decision about what family some species belongs to comes down to an abstract pattern shared at some level. Even the concepts of "male" and "female" turn out to be surprisingly abstract and elusive. When you base your system of classification on very abstract patterns, I suppose that a broad variety of phenomena can fall into "the same class," even if in many superficial ways the class members are utterly unlike one another. So perhaps I can glimpse, at least a little, how to you, a simulated hurricane could, in a funny sense, *be* a hurricane.

Chris: Perhaps the word that's being extended is not "hurricane," but "be."

Pat: How so?

Chris: If Turing can extend the verb "think," can't I extend the verb "be"? All I mean is that when simulated things are deliberately confused with genuine things, somebody's doing a lot of philosophical wool-pulling. It's a lot more serious than just extending a few *nouns*, such as "hurricane."

Sandy: I like your idea that "be" is being extended, but I sure don't agree with you about the wool-pulling. Anyway, if you don't object, let me just say one more thing about simulated hurricanes and then I'll get to simulated minds. Suppose you consider a really deep simulation of a hurricane—I mean a simulation of every atom, which I admit is sort of ridiculous, but still, just consider it for the sake of argument.

Pat: Okay.

Sandy: I hope you would agree that it would then share all the abstract structure that defines the "essence of hurricanehood." So what's to keep you from calling it a hurricane?

Pat: I thought you were backing off from that claim of equality.

Sandy: So did I, but then these examples came up, and I was forced back to my claim. But let me back off, as I said I would do, and get back to *thought*, which is the real issue here. Thought, even more than hurricanes, is an abstract structure, a way of describing some complex events that happen in a medium called a brain. But actually, thought can take place in any one of several billion brains. There are all these physically very different brains, and yet they all support "the same thing": thinking. What's important, then, is the abstract *pattern*, not the medium. The same kind of swirling can happen inside any of them, so no person can claim to think more "genuinely" than any other. Now, if we come up with some

new kind of medium in which *the same style* of swirling takes place, could you deny that thinking is taking place in it?

Pat: Probably not, but you have just shifted the question. The question now is: How can you determine whether the "same style" of swirling is really happening?

Sandy: The beauty of the Turing Test is that it *tells* you when! Don't you see?

Chris: I don't see that at all. How would you know that the same style of activity was going on inside a computer as inside my mind, simply because it answered questions as I do? All you're looking at is its *outside*.

Sandy: I'm sorry, I disagree entirely! How do you know that when I speak to you, anything similar to what you call thinking is going on inside *me*? The Turing Test is a fantastic probe, something like a particle accelerator in physics. Here, Chris—I think you'll like this analogy. Just as in physics, when you want to understand what is going on at an atomic or subatomic level, since you can't see it directly, you scatter accelerated particles off a target and observe their behavior. From this, you infer the internal nature of the target. The Turing Test extends this idea to the mind. It treats the mind as a "target" that is not directly visible but whose structure can be deduced more abstractly. By "scattering" questions off a target mind, you learn about its internal workings, just as in physics.

Chris: Well . . . to be more exact, you can *hypothesize* about what kinds of internal structures might account for the behavior observed—but please remember that they may or may not in fact exist.

Sandy: Hold on, now! Are you suggesting that atomic nuclei are merely *hypothetical* entities? After all, their existence (or should I say *hypothetical* existence?) was proved (or should I say *suggested*?) by the behavior of particles scattered off atoms.

Chris: I would agree, but you know, physical systems seem to me to be much simpler than the mind, and the certainty of the inferences made is correspondingly greater. And the conclusions are confirmed over and over again by different types of experiments.

Sandy: Yes, but those experiments still are of the same sort — scattering, detecting things indirectly. You can never *handle* an electron or a quark. Physics experiments are also correspondingly harder to do and to interpret. Often they take years and years, and dozens of collaborators are involved. In the Turing Test, though, just one person could perform many highly delicate experiments in the course of no more than an hour. I maintain that people give other people credit for being conscious simply because of their continual external monitoring of other people — which is itself something like a Turing Test.

Pat: That may be roughly true, but it involves more than just conversing with people through a teletype. We see that other people have bodies, we watch their faces and expressions — we see they are human beings, and so we think they think.

Sandy: To me, that seems a narrow, anthropocentric view of what thought is. Does that mean you would sooner say a mannequin in a store thinks than a wonderfully programmed computer, simply because the mannequin looks more human?

Pat: Obviously I would need more than just vague physical resemblance to the human form to be willing to attribute the power of thought to an entity. But that organic quality, the sameness of origin, undeniably lends a degree of credibility that is very important.

Sandy: Here we disagree. I find this simply too chauvinistic. I feel that the key thing is a similarity of *internal* structure — not bodily, organic, chemical structure but *organizational* structure — software. Whether an entity can think seems to me a question of whether its organization can be described in a certain way, and I'm perfectly willing to believe that the Turing Test detects the presence or absence of that mode of organization. I would say that your depending on my physical body as evidence that I am a thinking being is rather shallow. The way I see it, the Turing Test looks far deeper than at mere external form.

Pat: Hey, now — you're not giving me much credit. It's not just the *shape* of a body that lends weight to the idea that there's real thinking going on inside. It's also, as I said, the idea of common origin. It's the idea that you and I both sprang from DNA molecules, an idea to which I attribute much depth. Put it this way: the external form of human bodies reveals that they share a deep biological history, and it's *that* depth that lends a lot of credibility to the notion that the owner of such a body can think.

Sandy: But that is all indirect evidence. Surely you want some *direct* evidence. That's what the Turing Test is for. And I think it's the *only* way to test for thinkinghood.

Chris: But you could be fooled by the Turing Test, just as an interrogator could mistake a man for a woman.

Sandy: I admit, I could be fooled if I carried out the test in too quick or too shallow a way. But I would go for the deepest things I could think of.

Chris: *I* would want to see if the program could understand jokes — or better yet, make them! *That* would be a real test of intelligence.

Sandy: I agree that humor probably is an acid test for a supposedly intelligent program, but equally important to me — perhaps more so — would be to test its emotional responses. So I would ask it about its reactions to certain pieces of music or works of literature — especially my favorite ones.

Chris: What if it said, "I don't know that piece," or even, "I have no interest in music"? What if it tried its hardest (oops! — sorry, Pat!) . . . Let me try that again. What if it did everything it could, to steer clear of emotional topics and references?

Sandy: That would certainly make me suspicious. Any consistent pattern of avoiding certain issues would raise serious doubts in my mind as to whether I was dealing with a thinking being.

Chris: Why do you say that? Why not just conclude you're dealing with a thinking but unemotional being?

Sandy: You've hit upon a sensitive point. I've thought about this for quite a long time, and I've concluded that I simply can't believe emotions and thought can be divorced. To put it another way, I think emotions are an automatic by-product of the ability to think. They are entailed by the very nature of thought.

Chris: That's an interesting conclusion, but what if you're wrong? What if I produced a machine that could think but not emote? Then its intelligence might go unrecognized because it failed to pass *your* kind of test.

Sandy: I'd like you to point out to me where the boundary line between emotional questions and non-emotional ones lies. You might want to ask about the meaning of a great novel. This certainly requires an understanding of human emotions! Now is that thinking, or merely cool calculation? You might want to ask about a subtle choice of words. For that, you need an understanding of their connotations. Turing uses examples like this in his article. You might want to ask for advice about a complex romantic situation. The machine would need to know a lot about human motivations and their roots. If it failed at this kind of task, I would not be much inclined to say that it could think. As far as I'm concerned, *thinking*, *feeling*, and *consciousness* are just different facets of one phenomenon, and no one of them can be present without the others.

Chris: Why couldn't you build a machine that could feel nothing (we all know machines don't feel anything!), but that could think and make complex decisions anyway? I don't see any contradiction there.

Sandy: Well, I do. I think that when you say that, you are visualizing a metallic, rectangular machine, probably in an air-conditioned room — a hard, angular, cold object with a million colored wires inside it, a machine that sits stock still on a tiled floor, humming or buzzing or whatever, and spinning its tapes. Such a machine can play a good game of chess, which, I freely admit, involves a lot of decision-making. And yet I would never call it conscious.

Chris: How come? To mechanists, isn't a chess-playing machine rudimentarily conscious?

Sandy: Not to *this* mechanist! The way I see it, consciousness has got to come from a precise pattern of organization, one we haven't yet figured out how to describe in any detailed way. But I believe we will gradually come to understand it. In my view, consciousness requires a certain way of mirroring the external universe internally, and the ability to respond to that external reality on the basis of the internally represented model. And then in addition, what's really crucial for a conscious machine is that it should incorporate a well-developed and flexible self-model. And it's there that all existing programs, including the best chess-playing ones, fall down.

Chris: Don't chess programs look ahead and say to themselves as they're figuring out their next move, "If my opponent moves here, then I'll go there, and then if they go this way, I could go that way . . ."? Doesn't that usage of the concept "I" require a sort of self-model?

Sandy: Not really. Or, if you want, it's an extremely limited one. It's an understanding of self in only the narrowest sense. For instance, a chess-playing program has no concept of why it is playing chess, or of the fact that it is a program or is in a computer, or has a human opponent. It has no idea about what winning and losing are, or —

Pat: How do *you* know it has no such sense? How can *you* presume to say what a chess program feels or knows?

Sandy: Oh, come on! We all know that certain things don't feel anything or know anything. A thrown stone doesn't know anything about parabolas, and a whirling fan doesn't know anything about air. It's true I can't *prove* those statements — but here, we are verging on questions of faith.

Pat: This reminds me of a Taoist story I read. It goes something like this. Two sages were standing on a bridge over a stream. One said to the other, "I wish I were a fish. They are so happy." The other replied, "How do *you* know whether fish are happy or not? *You're* not a fish!" The first said, "But you're not *me*, so how do you know whether I know how fish feel?"

Sandy: Beautiful! Talking about consciousness really does call for a certain amount of restraint. Otherwise, you might as well just jump on the solipsism bandwagon ("*I* am the only conscious being in the universe") or the panpsychism bandwagon ("*Everything* in the universe is conscious!")

Pat: Well, how do you know? Maybe everything *is* conscious.

Sandy: Oh, Pat, if you're going to join the club that maintains that stones and even particles like electrons have some sort of consciousness, then I guess we part company here. That's a kind of mysticism I just can't fathom. As for chess programs, I happen to know how they work, and I can tell you for sure that they aren't conscious. No way!

Pat: Why not?

Sandy: They incorporate only the barest knowledge about the goals of chess. The notion of "playing" is turned into the mechanical act of comparing a lot of numbers and choosing the biggest one over and over again. A chess program has no sense of disappointment about losing, or pride in winning. Its self-model is very crude. It gets away with doing the least it can, just enough to play a game of chess and nothing more. Yet interestingly enough, we still tend to talk about the "desires" of a chess-playing computer. We say, "It wants to keep its king behind a row of pawns" or "It likes to get its rooks out early" or "It thinks I don't see that hidden fork."

Pat: Yes, and we do the same thing with insects. We spot a lonely ant somewhere and say, "It's trying to get back home" or "It wants to drag that dead bee back to the colony." In fact, with any animal we use terms that indicate emotions, but we don't know for certain how much the animal feels. I have no trouble talking about dogs and cats being happy or sad, having desires and beliefs, and so on, but of course I don't think their sadness is as deep or complex as human sadness is.

Sandy: But you wouldn't call it "simulated" sadness, would you?

Pat: No, of course not. I think it's real.

Sandy: It's hard to avoid use of such teleological or mentalistic terms. I believe they're quite justified, although they shouldn't be carried too far. They simply don't have the same richness of meaning when applied to present-day chess programs as when applied to people.

Chris: I still can't see that intelligence has to involve emotions. Why couldn't you imagine an intelligence that simply calculates and has no feelings?

Sandy: A couple of answers here. Number one, any intelligence has to have motivations. It's simply not the case, whatever many people may think, that machines could think any more "objectively" than people do. Machines, when they look at a scene, will have to focus and filter that scene down into some preconceived categories, just as a person does. And that means seeing some things and missing others. It means giving more weight to some things than to others. This happens on every level of processing.

Pat: I'm not sure I'm following you.

Sandy: Take me right now, for instance. You might think I'm just making some intellectual points, and I wouldn't need emotions to do that. But what makes me *care* about these points? Just now—why did I stress the word "care" so heavily? Because I'm emotionally involved in this conversation! People talk to each other out of conviction—not out of hollow, mechanical reflexes. Even the most intellectual conversation is driven by underlying passions. There's an emotional undercurrent to every conversation—it's the fact that the speakers want to be listened to, understood, and respected for what they are saying.

Pat: It sounds to me as if all you're saying is that people need to be interested in what they're saying, otherwise a conversation dies.

Sandy: Right! I wouldn't bother to talk to anyone if I weren't motivated by *interest*. And "interest" is just another name for a whole constellation of subconscious biases. When I talk, all my biases work together, and what you perceive on the surface level is my personality, my style. But that style arises from an immense number of tiny priorities, biases, leanings. When you add up a million of them interacting together, you get something that amounts to a lot of *desires*. It just all adds up! And that brings me to the other answer to Chris' question about feelingless calculation. Sure, that exists — in a cash register, a pocket calculator. I'd say it's even true of all today's computer programs. But eventually, when you put enough feelingless calculations together in a huge coordinated organization, you'll get something that has properties *on another level*. You can see it — in fact, you *have* to see it — not as a bunch of little calculations but as a system of tendencies and desires and beliefs and so on. When things get complicated enough, you're *forced* to change your level of description. To some extent that's already happening, which is why we use words such as "want," "think," "try," and "hope" to describe chess programs and other attempts at mechanical thought. Dennett calls that kind of level-switch by the observer "adopting the intentional stance." The really interesting things in AI will only begin to happen, I'd guess, when the program *itself* adopts the intentional stance toward itself!

Chris: That would be a very strange sort of level-crossing feedback loop.

Sandy: It certainly would. When a program looks at itself *from the outside*, as it were, and tries to figure out why it acted the way it did, then I'll start to think that there's *someone* in there, doing the looking.

Pat: You mean an "I"? A self?

Sandy: Yes, something like that. A soul, even — although not in any religious sense. Of course, it's highly premature for anyone to adopt the intentional stance (in the full force of the term) with respect to today's programs. At least that's my opinion.

Chris: For me an important related question is: To what extent is it valid to adopt the intentional stance toward beings other than humans?

Pat: I would certainly adopt the intentional stance toward mammals.

Sandy: I vote for that.

Chris: Now that's interesting. How can that be, Sandy? Surely you wouldn't claim that a dog or cat can pass the Turing Test? Yet don't you maintain the Turing Test is the *only* way to test for the presence of consciousness? How can you have these beliefs simultaneously?

Sandy: Hmmm . . . All right. I guess that my argument is really just that the Turing Test works only above a certain level of consciousness. I'm perfectly willing to grant that there can be thinking beings that could *fail* at the Turing Test — but the main point that I've been arguing for is that anything that *passes* it would be a genuinely conscious, thinking being.

Pat: How can you think of a computer as a conscious being? I apologize if what I'm going to say sounds like a stereotype, but when I think of conscious beings, I just can't connect that thought with machines. To me, consciousness is connected with soft, warm bodies, silly though it may sound.

Chris: That does sound odd, coming from a biologist. Don't you deal with life so much in terms of chemistry and physics that all magic seems to vanish?

Pat: Not really. Sometimes the chemistry and physics simply increase the feeling that there's something magical going on down there! Anyway, I can't always integrate my scientific knowledge with my gut feelings.

Chris: I guess I share that trait.

Pat: So how do you deal with rigid preconceptions like mine?

Sandy: I'd try to dig down under the surface of your concept of "machine" and get at the intuitive connotations that lurk there, out of sight but deeply influencing your opinions. I think we all have a holdover image from the Industrial Revolution that sees machines as clunky iron contraptions gawkily moving under the power of some loudly chugging engine. Possibly that's even how the computer inventor Charles Babbage saw people! After all, he called his magnificent many-geared computer the "Analytical Engine."

Pat: Well, *I* certainly don't think people are just fancy steam shovels or electric can openers. There's something about people, something that—that—they've got a sort of *flame* inside them, something alive, something that flickers unpredictably, wavering, uncertain—but something *creative*!

Sandy: Great! That's just the sort of thing I wanted to hear. It's very human to think that way. Your flame image makes me think of candles, of fires, of vast thunderstorms with lightning dancing all over the sky in crazy, tumultuous patterns. But do you realize that just that kind of thing is visible on a computer's console? The flickering lights form amazing chaotic sparkling patterns. It's such a far cry from heaps of lifeless, clanking metal! It *is* flamelike, by God! Why don't you let the word "machine" conjure up images of dancing patterns of light rather than of giant steam shovels?

Chris: That's a beautiful image, Sandy. It does tend to change my sense of mechanism from being matter-oriented to being pattern-oriented. It makes me try to visualize the thoughts in my mind—these thoughts right now, even!—as a huge spray of tiny pulses flickering in my brain.

Sandy: That's quite a poetic self-portrait of a mere spray of flickers to have come up with!

Chris: Thank you. But still, I'm not totally convinced that a machine is all that I am. I admit, my concept of machines probably does suffer from anachronistic subconscious flavors, but I'm afraid I can't change such a deeply rooted sense in a flash.

Sandy: At least you sound open-minded. And to tell the truth, part of me sympathizes with the way you and Pat view machines. Part of me balks at calling myself a machine. It *is* a bizarre thought that a feeling being like you or me might emerge from mere circuitry. Do I surprise you?

Chris: You certainly surprise *me*. So, tell us—do you believe in the idea of an intelligent computer, or don't you?

Sandy: It all depends on what you mean. We've all heard the question "Can computers think?" There are several possible interpretations of this (aside from the many interpretations of the word "think"). They revolve around different meanings of the words "can" and "computer."

Pat: Back to word games again . . .

Sandy: I'm sorry, but that's unavoidable. First of all, the question might mean, "Does some present-day computer think, right now?" To this I would immediately answer with a loud *no*. Then it could be taken to mean, "Could some present-day computer, if suitably programmed, potentially think?" That would be more like it, but I would still answer, "Probably not." The real difficulty hinges on the word "computer." The way I see it, "computer" calls up an image of just what I described earlier: an air-conditioned room with cold rectangular metal boxes in it. But I suspect that with increasing public familiarity with computers and continued progress in computer architecture, that vision will eventually become outmoded.

Pat: Don't you think computers as we know them will be around for a while?

Sandy: Sure, there will have to be computers in today's image around for a long time, but advanced computers—maybe no longer called "computers"—will evolve and become quite different. Probably, as with living organisms, there will be many branchings in the evolutionary tree. There will be computers for business, computers for schoolkids, computers for scientific calculations, computers for systems research, computers for simulation, computers for rockets going into space, and so on. Finally, there will be computers for the study of intelligence. It's really only these last that I'm thinking of—the ones with the maximum flexibility, the ones that people are deliberately attempting to make smart. I see no reason that these will stay fixed in the traditional image. They probably will soon acquire as standard features some rudimentary sensory systems — mostly for vision and hearing, at first. They will need to be able to move around, to explore. They will have to be physically flexible. In short, they will have to become more animal-like, more self-reliant.

Chris: It makes me think of the robots R2D2 and C3PO in the movie *Star Wars*.

Sandy: Not me! In fact, I don't think of anything remotely like them when I visualize intelligent machines. They are too silly, too much the product of a film designer's imagination. Not that I have a clear vision of my own. But I think it's necessary, if people are realistically going to try to imagine an artificial intelligence, to go beyond the limited, hard-edged picture of computers that comes from exposure to what we have today. The only thing all machines will always have in common is their underlying mechanicalness. That may sound cold and inflexible, but then — just think — what could be more mechanical, in a wonderful way, than the working of the DNA and proteins and organelles in our cells?

Pat: To me, what goes on inside cells has a "wet," "slippery" feel to it, and what goes on inside machines is dry and rigid. It's connected with the fact that computers don't make mistakes, that computers do only what you tell them to do. Or at least that's my image of computers.

Sandy: Funny — a minute ago, your image was of a flame, and now it's of something wet and slippery. Isn't it marvelous, how contradictory we can be?

Pat: I don't need your sarcasm.

Sandy: No, no, I'm not being sarcastic — I really *do* think it's marvelous.

Pat: It's just an example of the human mind's slippery nature — mine, in this case.

Sandy: True. But your image of computers is stuck in a rut. Computers certainly *can* make mistakes — and I don't mean on the hardware level.

Think of any present-day computer predicting the weather. It can make wrong predictions, even though its program runs flawlessly.

Pat: But that's only because you've fed it the wrong data.

Sandy: Not so. It's because weather prediction is too complex. Any such program has to make do with a limited amount of data — entirely correct data — and extrapolate from there. Sometimes it will make wrong predictions. It's no different from a farmer gazing at the clouds and saying, "I reckon we'll get a little snow tonight." In our heads, we make models of things and use those models to guess how the world will behave. We have to make do with our models, however inaccurate they may be, or evolution will prune us out ruthlessly — we'll fall off a cliff or something. And for intelligent computers, it'll be the same. It's just that human designers will speed up the evolutionary process by aiming explicitly at the goal of creating intelligence, which is something nature just stumbled on.

Pat: So you think computers will be making fewer mistakes as they get smarter?

Sandy: Actually, just the other way around! The smarter they get, the more they'll be in a position to tackle messy real-life domains, so they'll be more and more likely to have inaccurate models. To me, mistake-making is a sign of high intelligence!

Pat: Wow — you throw me sometimes!

Sandy: I guess I'm a strange sort of advocate for machine intelligence. To some degree I straddle the fence. I think that machines won't really be intelligent in a humanlike way until they have something like your biological wetness or slipperiness to them. I don't mean *literally* wet — the slipperiness could be in the software. But biological-seeming or not, intelligent machines will in any case be machines. We will have designed them, built them — or grown them! We'll understand how they work — or least in some sense. Possibly no one person will really understand them, but collectively we will know how they work.

Pat: It sounds like you want to have your cake and eat it too. I mean, you want to have people able to build intelligent machines and yet at the same time have some of the mystery of mind remain.

Sandy: You're absolutely right—and I think that's what *will* happen. When *real* artificial intelligence comes—

Pat: Now there's a nice contradiction in terms!

Sandy: Touché! Well, anyway, when it comes, it will be mechanical and yet at the same time organic. It will have that same astonishing flexibility that we see in life's mechanisms. And when I say mechanisms, I *mean* mechanisms. DNA and enzymes and so on really *are* mechanical and rigid and reliable. Wouldn't you agree, Pat?

Pat: Sure! But when they work together, a lot of unexpected things happen. There are so many complexities and rich modes of behavior that all that mechanicalness adds up to something very fluid.

Sandy: For me, it's an almost unimaginable transition from the mechanical level of molecules to the living level of cells. But it's that exposure to biology that convinces me that people are machines. That thought makes me uncomfortable in some ways, but in other ways it is exhilarating.

Chris: I have one nagging question . . . If people are machines, how come it's so hard to convince them of the fact? Surely a machine ought to be able to recognize its own machinehood!

Sandy: It's an interesting question. You have to allow for emotional factors here. To be told you're a machine is, in a way, to be told that you're nothing more than your physical parts, and it brings you face to face with your own vulnerability, destructibility, and, ultimately, your mortality. That's something nobody finds easy to face. But beyond this emotional objection, to see yourself as a machine, you have to "unadopt" the intentional stance you've grown up taking toward yourself—you have to jump all the way from the level where the complex lifelike activities take place to the bottom-most mechanical level where ribosomes chug along RNA strands, for instance. But there are so many intermediate layers that they act as a shield, and the mechanical quality way down there becomes almost invisi-

ble. I think that when intelligent machines come around, that's how they will seem to us—and to themselves! Their mechanicalness will be buried so deep that they'll *seem* to be alive and conscious—just as *we* seem alive and conscious . . .

Chris: You're baiting me! But I'm not going to bite.

Pat: I once heard a funny idea about what will happen when we eventually have intelligent machines. When we try to implant that intelligence into devices we'd like to control, their behavior won't be so predictable.

Sandy: They'll have a quirky little "flame" inside, maybe?

Pat: Maybe.

Chris: And what's so funny about that?

Pat: Well, think of military missiles. The more sophisticated their target-tracking computers get, according to this idea, the less predictably they will function. Eventually, you'll have missiles that will decide they are pacifists and will turn around and go home and land quietly without blowing up. We could even have "smart bullets" that turn around in midflight because they don't want to commit suicide!

Sandy: What a nice vision!

Chris: I'm very skeptical about all this. Still, Sandy, I'd like to hear your predictions about when intelligent machines will come to be.

Sandy: It won't be for a long time, probably, that we'll see anything remotely resembling the level of human intelligence. It rests on too awesomely complicated a substrate—the brain—for us to be able to duplicate it in the foreseeable future. Anyhow, that's my opinion.

Pat: Do you think a program will ever pass the Turing Test?

Sandy: That's a pretty hard question. I guess there are various degrees of passing such a test, when you come down to it. It's not black and white. First of all, it depends on who the interrogator is. A simpleton might be totally taken in by some programs today. But secondly, it depends on how deeply you are allowed to probe.

Pat: You could have a range of Turing Tests—one-minute versions, five-minute versions, hour-long versions, and so forth. Wouldn't it be interesting if some official organization sponsored a periodic competition, like the annual computer-chess championships, for programs to try to pass the Turing Test?

Chris: The program that lasted the longest against some panel of distinguished judges would be the winner. Perhaps there could be a big prize for the first program that fools a famous judge for, say, ten minutes.

Pat: A prize for the *program*, or for its *author*?

Chris: For the program, of course!

Pat: That's ridiculous! What would a program do with a prize?

Chris: Come now, Pat. If a program's human enough to fool the judges, don't you think it's human enough to enjoy the prize? That's precisely the threshold where it, rather than its creators, deserves the credit, and the rewards. Wouldn't you agree?

Pat: Yeah, yeah—especially if the prize is an evening out on the town, dancing with the interrogators!

Sandy: I'd certainly like to see something like that established. I think it could be hilarious to watch the first programs flop pathetically!

Pat: You're pretty skeptical for an AI advocate, aren't you? Well, do you think any computer program today could pass a five-minute Turing Test, given a sophisticated interrogator?

Sandy: I seriously doubt it. It's partly because no one is really working at it explicitly. I should mention, though, that there is one program whose inventors claim it has *already* passed a rudimentary version of the Turing Test. It is called "Parry," and in a series of remotely conducted interviews, it fooled several psychiatrists who were told they were talking to either a computer or a paranoid patient. This was an improvement over an earlier version, in which psychiatrists were simply handed transcripts of short interviews and asked to determine which ones were with a genuine paranoid and which ones were with a computer simulation.

Pat: You mean they didn't have the chance to ask any questions? That's a severe handicap—and

it doesn't seem in the spirit of the Turing Test. Imagine someone trying to tell which sex *I* belong to, just by reading a transcript of a few remarks by me. It might be very hard! I'm glad the procedure has been improved.

Chris: How do you get a computer to act like a paranoid?

Sandy: Now just a moment—I didn't say it *does* act like a paranoid, only that some psychiatrists, under unusual circumstances, thought so. One of the things that bothered me about this pseudo-Turing Test is the way Parry works. "He," as the people who designed it call it, acts like a paranoid in that "he" gets abruptly defensive and veers away from undesirable topics in the conversation. In effect, Parry maintains strict control so that no one can truly probe "him." For reasons like this, simulating a paranoid is a whole lot easier than simulating a normal person.

Pat: I wouldn't doubt that. It reminds me of the joke about the easiest kind of human being for a computer program to simulate.

Chris: What is that?

Pat: A catatonic patient—they just sit and do nothing at all for days on end. Even *I* could write a computer program to do that!

Sandy: An interesting thing about Parry is that it creates no sentences on its own—it merely selects from a huge repertoire of canned sentences the one that in some sense responds best to the input sentence.

Pat: Amazing. But that would probably be impossible on a larger scale, wouldn't it?

Sandy: You better believe it (to use a canned remark)! Actually, this is something that's really not appreciated enough. The number of sentences you'd need to store in order to be able to respond in a normal way to all possible turns that a conversation could take is more than astronomical—it's really unimaginable. And they would have to be so intricately indexed, for retrieval . . . Anybody who thinks that somehow, a program could be rigged up just to pull sentences out of storage like records in a jukebox, and that this program could pass the Turing Test, hasn't thought very hard about it. The funny part is that it is just this kind of unrealizable "parrot program" that most critics of artificial intelligence cite, when they argue against the concept of the Turing Test. Instead of imagining a truly intelligent machine, they want you to envision a gigantic, lumbering robot that intones canned sentences in a dull monotone. They set up the imagery in a contradictory way. They manage to convince you that you could see through to its mechanical level with ease, even as it is simultaneously performing tasks that we think of as fluid, intelligent processes. Then the critics say, "You see! A machine could pass the Turing Test and yet it would still be just a mechanical device, not intelligent at all." I see things almost the opposite way. If *I* were shown a machine that can do things that I can do — I mean pass the Turing Test — then, instead of feeling insulted or threatened, I'd chime in with philosopher Raymond Smullyan and say, "How wonderful machines are!"

Chris: If you could ask a computer just one question in the Turing Test, what would it be?

Sandy: Uhmm . . .

Pat: How about this: "If you could ask a computer just one question in the Turing Test, what would it be?"?

Further Questions

1. There are three characters in Hofstadter's dialogue: Chris, Sandy, and Pat. What are their sexes? Justify your answer. (Does your difficulty justifying your answer to this question remind you of anything about Turing's Imitation Game?)

2. Is the Turing Test an adequate criterion for determining whether a machine can think? Can you think of a better criterion?

Further Readings

Block, Ned. "Psychologism and Behaviorism." *The Philosophical Review*, vol. 90, 1981, pp. 5–43. A good discussion of problems raised by the Turing Test.

Robinson, William S. *Computers, Minds, and Robots*. Philadelphia: Temple University Press, 1992. Philosophy of mind through the lens of artificial intelligence.

Searle, John. "Minds, Brains, and Programs." *The Behavioral and Brain Sciences*, vol. 3, 1980. The most famous attack on the Turing Test. It appears with twenty-eight responses.

Turing, A. M. "Computing Machinery and Intelligence." *Mind*, vol. 59, 1950. Turing's classic paper.

The Story of a Brain

ARNOLD ZUBOFF

Arnold Zuboff teaches philosophy at the University of London and writes primarily in the areas of philosophy of mind and personal identity. In this well-known and highly imaginative essay, he shows how the modern scientific idea that the mind is nothing more than a collection of neurons functioning in a particular way leads to some deeply bizarre results.

Reading Questions

1. Consider the various Cassanderish "conditions of experience" discussed in this essay: proximity; actual causal connection; synchronization; topology; neural identity; and neural context. Is there any reason to think any of them are necessary for experience to occur?

2. Assuming that experience can be continued in the way sketched in this story, is the identity of the experiencer also continued? In other words, is the young man at the beginning the same experiencer as whatever is having experiences at the end? In still other words, did the young man's scheme for prolonging *his* capacity to have experiences work?

I

ONCE UPON A TIME, a kind young man who enjoyed many friends and great wealth learned that a horrible rot was overtaking all of his body but his nervous system. He loved life; he loved having experiences. Therefore he was intensely interested when scientist friends of amazing abilities proposed the following:

"We shall take the brain from your poor rotting body and keep it healthy in a special nutrient bath. We shall have it connected to a machine that is capable of inducing in it any pattern at all of neural firings and is therein capable of bringing about for you any sort of total experience that it is possible for the activity of your nervous system to cause or to be."

The reason for this last disjunction of the verbs *to cause* and *to be* was that, although all these scientists were convinced of a general theory that they called "the neural theory of experience," they disagreed on the specific formulation of this theory. They all knew of countless instances in which it was just obvious that the state of the brain, the pattern of its activity, somehow had made for a man's experiencing this rather than that. It seemed reasonable to them all that ultimately what decisively controlled any particular experience of a man — controlled whether it existed and

what it was like — was the state of his nervous system and more specifically that of those areas of the brain that careful research had discovered to be involved in the various aspects of consciousness. This conviction was what had prompted their proposal to their young friend. That they disagreed about whether an experience simply consisted in or else was caused by neural activity was irrelevant to their belief that as long as their friend's brain was alive and functioning under their control, they could keep him having his beloved experience indefinitely, just as though he were walking about and getting himself into the various situations that would in a more natural way have stimulated each of those patterns of neural firings that they would bring about artificially. If he were actually to have gazed through a hole in a snow-covered frozen pond, for instance, the physical reality there would have caused him to experience what Thoreau described: "the quiet parlor of the fishes, pervaded by a softened light as through a window of ground glass, with its bright sanded floor the same as in summer." The brain lying in its bath, stripped of its body and far from the pond, if it were made to behave precisely as it naturally would under such pond-hole circumstances, would have for the young man that very same experience.

Well, the young man agreed with the concept and looked forward to its execution. And a mere month after he had first heard the thing proposed to him, his brain was floating in the warm nutrient bath. His scientist friends kept busy researching, by means of paid subjects, which patterns of neuron firings were like the natural neural responses to very pleasant situations; and, through the use of a complex electrode machine, they kept inducing only these neural activities in their dear friend's brain.

Then there was trouble. One night the watchman had been drinking, and, tipsily wandering into the room where the bath lay, he careened forward so his right arm entered the bath and actually split the poor brain into its two hemispheres.

The brain's scientist friends were very upset the next morning. They had been all ready to feed into the brain a marvelous new batch of experiences whose neural patterns they had just recently discovered.

"If we let our friend's brain mend after bringing the parted hemispheres together," said Fred, "we must wait a good two months before it will be healed well enough so that we can get the fun of feeding him these new experiences. Of course, he won't know about the waiting; but we sure will! And unfortunately, as we all know, two separated halves of a brain can't entertain the same neural patterns that they can when they're together. For all those impulses which cross from one hemisphere to another during a whole-brain experience just can't make it across the gap that has been opened between them."

The end of this speech gave someone else an idea. Why not do the following: Develop tiny electrochemical wires whose ends could be fitted to the synapses of neurons to receive or discharge their neural impulses. These wires could then be strung from each neuron whose connection had been broken in the split to that neuron of the other hemisphere to which it had formerly been connected. "In this way," finished Bert, the proposer of this idea, "all those impulses that were supposed to cross over from one hemi-

sphere to the other could do just that—carried over the wires."

This suggestion was greeted with enthusiasm, since the construction of the wire system, it was felt, could easily be completed within a week. But one grave fellow named Cassander had worries. "We all agree that our friend has been having the experiences we've tried to give him. That is, we all accept in some form or other the neural theory of experience. Now, according to this theory as we all accept it, it is quite permissible to alter as one likes the context of a functioning brain, just so long as one maintains the pattern of its activity. We might look at what we're saying this way. There are various conditions that make for the usual having of an experience—an experience, for instance, like that pond-hole experience we believe we gave our friend three weeks ago. Usually these conditions are the brain being in an actual body on an actual pond stimulated to such neural activity as we did indeed give our friend. We gave our friend the neural activity without those other conditions of its context, because our friend has no body and because we believe that what is essential and decisive for the existence and character of an experience anyway is not such context but rather only the neural activity that it can stimulate. The contextual conditions, we believe, are truly inessential to the bare fact of a man having an experience—even if they *are* essential conditions in the normal having of that experience. If one has the wherewithal, as we do, to get around the normal necessity of these external conditions of an experience of a pond hole, then such conditions are no longer necessary. And this demonstrates that within our concept of experience they never were necessary in principle to the bare fact of having the experience.

"Now, what you men are proposing to do with these wires amounts to regarding as inessential just one more normal condition of our friend's having his experience. That is, you are saying something like what I just said about the context of neural activity—but *you're* saying it about the condition of the *proximity* of the hemispheres of the brain to one another. You're saying that the two hemispheres being attached to one another in the whole-brain experiences may be necessary to the coming about of those experiences in the usual case, but if one can get around a breach of this proximity in some, indeed *un-usual* case, as you fellows would with your wires, there'd still be brought about just the same bare fact of the same experience being had! You're saying that proximity isn't a necessary condition to this bare fact of an experience. But isn't it possible that even reproducing precisely the whole-brain neural patterns in a sundered brain would, to the contrary, *not* constitute the bringing about of the whole-brain experience? Couldn't proximity be not just something to get around in creating a particular whole-brain experience but somehow an absolute condition and principle of the having of a whole-brain experience?"

Cassander got little sympathy for his worries. Typical replies ran something like this: "Would the damn hemispheres *know* they were connected by wires instead of attached in the usual way? That is, would the fact get encoded in any of the brain structures responsible for speech, thought or any other feature of awareness? How could this fact about how his brain looks to external observers concern our dear friend in his pleasures at all — any more than being a naked brain sitting in a warm nutrient bath does? As long as the neural activity in the hemispheres — together *or* apart — matches precisely that which would have been the activity in the hemispheres lumped together in the head of a person walking around having fun, then the person himself is having that fun. Why, if we hooked up a mouth to these brain parts, he'd be telling us through it about his fun." In reply to such answers, which were getting shorter and angrier, Cassander could only mutter about the possible disruption of some experiential field "or some such."

But after the men had been working on the wires for a while someone else came up with an objection to their project that *did* stop them. He pointed out that it took practically no time for an impulse from one hemisphere to enter into the other when a brain was together and functioning normally. But the travel of these impulses over wires must impose a tiny increase on the time taken in such crossovers. Since the impulses in the rest of the brain in each hemisphere would be taking their normal time, wouldn't the overall pattern get garbled, operating as if there were a slowdown in only one region? Certainly it would be impossible to get precisely the normal sort of pattern going — you'd have something strange, disturbed.

When this successful objection was raised, a man with very little training in physics suggested that somehow the wire be replaced by radio signals. This could be done by outfitting the raw face — of the split — of each hemisphere with an "impulse cartridge" that would be capable of sending any pattern of impulses into the hitherto exposed and unconnected neurons of that hemisphere, as well as of receiving from those neurons any pattern of impulses that that hemisphere might be trying to communicate to the other hemisphere. Then each cartridge could be plugged into a special radio transmitter and receiver. When a cartridge received an impulse from a neuron in one hemisphere intended for a neuron of the other, the impulse could then be radioed over and properly administered by the other cartridge. The fellow who suggested this even mused that then each half of the brain could be kept in a separate bath and yet the whole still be engaged in a single whole-brain experience.

The advantage of this system over the wires, this fellow thought, resided in the "fact" that radio waves take no time, unlike impulses in wires, to travel from one place to another. He was quickly disabused of this idea. No, the radio system still suffered from the time-gap obstacle.

But all this talk of impulse cartridges inspired Bert. "Look, we could feed each impulse cartridge with the same pattern of impulses it would have been receiving by radio but do so by such a method as to require no radio or wire transmission. All we need do is fix to each cartridge not a radio transmitter and receiver but an 'impulse programmer', the sort of gadget that would play through whatever program of impulses you have previously given it. The great thing about this is that there is no longer any need for the impulse pattern going into one hemisphere to be *actually caused*, in part, by the pattern coming from the other. Therefore there need not be any wait for the transmission. The programmed cartridges can be so correlated with the rest of our stimulation of neural patterns that all of the timing can be just as it would have been if the hemispheres were together. And, yes, then it will be easy to fix each hemisphere in a separate bath — perhaps one in the laboratory here and one in the laboratory across town, so that we may employ the facilities of each laboratory in working with merely half a brain. This will make everything easier. And we can then bring in more people; there are many who've been bothering us to let them join our project."

But now Cassander was even more worried. "We have already disregarded the condition of proximity. Now we are about to abandon yet another condition of usual experience — that of actual causal connection. Granted you can be clever enough to get around what is usually quite necessary to an experience coming about. So now, with your programming, it will no longer be necessary for impulses in one half of the brain actually to be a cause of the completion of the whole-brain pattern in the other hemisphere in order for the whole-brain pattern to come about. But is the result still the bare fact of the whole-brain experience or have you, in removing this condition, removed an absolute principle of, an essential condition for, a whole-brain experience really being had?"

The answers to this were much as they had been to the other. How did the neural activity *know* whether a radio-controlled or programmed impulse cartridge fed it? How could this fact, so totally external to them, register with the neural structures underlying thought, speech, and every other item of awareness? Certainly it could not register mechanically. Wasn't the result then pre-cisely the same with tape as with wire except that now the time-gap problem had been overcome? And wouldn't a properly hooked-up mouth even report the experiences as nicely after the taped as after the wired assistance with crossing impulses?

The next innovation came soon enough — when the question was raised about whether it was at all important, since each hemisphere was now working separately, to synchronize the two causally unconnected playings of the impulse patterns of the hemispheres. Now that each hemisphere would in effect receive all the impulses that in a given experience it would have received from the other hemisphere — and receive them in such a way as would work perfectly with the timing of the rest of its impulses — and since this fine effect could be achieved in either hemisphere quite independent of its having yet been achieved in the other, there seemed no reason for retaining what Cassander sadly pointed to as the "condition of synchronization." Men were heard to say, "How does either hemisphere *know*, how could it register when the other goes off, in the time of the external observer, anyway? For each hemisphere what more can we say than that it is just precisely as if the other had gone off with it the right way? What is there to worry about if at one lab they run through one half of a pattern one day and at the other lab they supply the other hemisphere with its half of the pattern another day? The pattern gets run through fine. The experience comes about. With the brain parts hooked up properly to a mouth, our friend could even report his experience."

There was also some discussion about whether to maintain what Cassander called "topology" — that is, whether to keep the two hemispheres in the general spatial relation of facing each other. Here too Cassander's warnings were ignored.

II

Ten centuries later the famous project was still engrossing men. But men now filled the galaxy and their technology was tremendous. Among them were billions who wanted the thrill and responsibility of participating in the "Great Experience Feed." Of course, behind this desire lay the continuing belief that what men were doing in programming impulses still amounted to making a man have all sorts of experiences.

But in order to accommodate all those who now wished to participate in the project, what Cassander had called the "conditions" of the experiencing had, to the superficial glance, changed enormously. (Actually, they were in a sense more conservative than they had been when we last saw them, because, as I shall explain later, something like "synchronization" had been restored.) Just as earlier each hemisphere of the brain had rested in its bath, now *each individual neuron* rested in one of its own. Since there were billions of neurons, each of the billions of men could involve himself with the proud task of manning a neuron bath.

To understand this situation properly, one must go back again ten centuries, to what had occurred as more and more men had expressed a desire for a part of the project. First it was agreed that if a whole-brain experience could come about with the brain split and yet the two halves programmed as I have described, the same experience could come about if each hemisphere too were carefully divided and each piece treated just as each of the two hemispheres had been. Thus each of four pieces of brain could now be given not only its own bath but a whole lab — allowing many more people to participate. There naturally seemed nothing to stop further and further divisions of the thing, until finally, ten centuries later, there was this situation — a man on each neuron, each man responsible for an impulse cartridge that was fixed to both ends of that neuron — transmitting and receiving an impulse whenever it was programmed to do so.

Meanwhile there had been other Cassanders. After a while none of these suggested keeping the condition of proximity, since this would have so infuriated all his fellows who desired to have a piece of the brain. But it *was* pointed out by such Cassanders that the original topology of the brain, that is, the relative position and directional

attitude of each neuron, could be maintained even while the brain was spread apart; and also it was urged by them that the neurons continue to be programmed to fire with the same chronology — the same temporal pattern — that their firings would have displayed when together in the brain.

But the suggestion about topology always brought a derisive response. A sample: "How should each of the neurons *know*, how should it register on a single neuron, where it is in relation to the others? In the usual case of an experience it is indeed necessary for the neurons, in order at all to get firing in that pattern that is or causes the experience, to be next to each other, actually causing the firing of one another, in a certain spatial relation to one another — but the original necessity of all these conditions is overcome by our techniques. For example, they are not necessary to the *bare fact* of the coming about of the experience that we are now causing to be had by the ancient gentleman whose neuron this is before me. And if we should bring these neurons together into a hookup with a mouth, then he would tell you of the experience personally."

Now as for the second part of the Cassanderish suggestion, the reader might suppose that after each successive partitioning of the brain, synchronization of the parts would have been consistently disregarded, so that eventually it would have been thought not to matter when each individual neuron was to be fired in relation to the firings of the other neurons — just as earlier the conditions had been disregarded when there were only two hemispheres to be fired. But somehow, perhaps because disregarding the timing and order of individual neuron firings would have reduced the art of programming to absurdity, the condition of order and timing had crept back, but without the Cassanderish reflectiveness. "Right" temporal order of firings is now merely *assumed* as somehow essential to bringing about a given experience by all those men standing before their baths and *waiting* for each properly programmed impulse to come to its neuron.

But now, ten centuries after the great project's birth, the world of these smug billions was about to explode. Two thinkers were responsible.

One of these, named Spoilar, had noticed one day that the neuron in his charge was getting a bit the worse for wear. Like any other man with a neuron in that state, he merely obtained another fresh one just like it and so replaced the particular one that had gotten worn — tossing the old one away. Thus he, like all the others, had violated the Cassanderish condition of "neural identity" — a condition never taken very seriously even by Cassanders. It was realized that in the case of an ordinary brain the cellular metabolism was always replacing all the particular matter of any neuron with other particular matter, forming precisely the same kind of neuron. What this man had done was really no more than a speeding-up of this process. Besides, what if, as some Cassanders had implausibly argued, replacing one neuron by another just like it somehow resulted, when it was eventually done to all the neurons, in a new identity for the experiencer? There still would be *an* experiencer having the same experience every time the same patterns of firings were realized (and what it would mean to say he was a different experiencer was not clear at all, even to the Cassanders). So any shift in neural identity did not seem destructive of the fact of an experience coming about.

This fellow Spoilar, after he had replaced the neurons, resumed his waiting to watch his own neuron fire as part of an experience scheduled several hours later. Suddenly he heard a great crash and a great curse. Some fool had fallen against another man's bath, and it had broken totally on the floor when it fell. Well, this man whose bath had fallen would just have to miss out on any experiences his neuron was to have been part of until the bath and neuron could be replaced. And Spoilar knew that the poor man had had one coming up soon.

The fellow whose bath had just broken walked up to Spoilar. He said, "Look, I've done favors for you. I'm going to have to miss the impulse coming up in five minutes — that experience will

have to manage with one less neuron firing. But maybe you'd let me man yours coming up later. I just hate to miss all the thrills coming up today!"

Spoilar thought about the man's plea. Suddenly, a strange thought hit him. "Wasn't the neuron you manned the same sort as mine?"

"Yes."

"Well, look. I've just replaced my neuron with another like it, as we all do occasionally. Why don't we take my entire bath over to the old position of yours? Then won't it still be the same experience brought about in five minutes that it would have been with the old neuron if we fire this then, since this one is just like the old one? Surely the *bath's* identity means nothing. Anyway, then we can bring the bath back here and I can use the neuron for the experience it is scheduled to be used for later on. Wait a minute! We both believe the condition of topology is baloney. So why need we move the bath at all? Leave it here; fire it for yours; and then I'll fire it for mine. Both experiences must still come about. Wait a minute again! Then all we need do is fire this one neuron here in place of all the firings of all neurons just like it! Then there need be only one neuron of each type firing again and again and again to bring about all these experiences! But how would the neurons *know* even that they were repeating an impulse when they fired again and again? How would they *know* the relative order of their firings? Then we could have one neuron of each sort firing once and that would provide the physical realization of all patterns of impulses (a conclusion that would have been arrived at merely by consistently disregarding the necessity of synchronization in the progress from parted hemispheres to parted neurons). And couldn't these neurons simply be any of those naturally firing in any head? So what are we all doing here?"

Then an even more desperate thought hit him, which he expressed thus: "But if all possible neural experience will be brought about simply in the firing once of one of each type of neuron, how can any experiencer believe that he is connected to anything more than this bare minimum of physical reality through the fact of his having *any* of his experiences? And so all this talk of heads and neurons in them, which is supposedly based on the true discovery of physical realities, is undermined entirely. There may be a true system of physical reality, but if it involves all this physiology we have been hoodwinked into believing, it provides so cheaply for so much experience that we can never know what is an actual experience of *it*, the physical reality. And so belief in such a system undermines itself. That is, unless it's tempered with Cassanderish principles."

The other thinker, coincidentally also named Spoilar, came to the same conclusion somewhat differently. He enjoyed stringing neurons. Once he got his own neuron, the one he was responsible for, in the middle of a long chain of like neurons and then recalled he was supposed to have it hooked up to the cartridge for a firing. Not wanting to destroy the chain, he simply hooked the two end neurons to the chain to the two poles of the impulse cartridge and adjusted the timing of the cartridge so that the impulse, traveling now through this whole chain, would reach his neuron at just the right time. Then he noticed that here a neuron, unlike one in usual experience, was quite comfortably participating in two patterns of firings at once — the chain's, which happened to have proximity and causal connection, and the programmed experience for which it had fired. After this Spoilar went about ridiculing "the condition of neural context." He'd say, "Boy, I could hook my neuron up with all those in your head, and if I could get it to fire just at the right time, I could get it into one of these programmed experiences as fine as if it were in my bath, on my cartridge."

Well, one day there was trouble. Some men who had not been allowed to join the project had come at night and so tampered with the baths that many of the neurons in Spoilar's vicinity had simply died. Standing before his own dead neuron, staring at the vast misery around him, he thought about how the day's first experience must turn out for the experiencer when so many neuron firings were to be missing from their physical realization. But as he looked about he suddenly took note of something else. Nearly everyone was stooping to inspect some damaged equipment just under his bath. Suddenly it seemed significant to Spoilar that next to every bath there was a head, each with its own billions of neurons of all sorts, with perhaps millions of each sort firing at any given moment. Proximity didn't matter. But then at any given moment of a particular pattern's being fired through the baths all the requisite activity was already going on anyway in the heads of the operators — in even *one* of those heads, where a loose sort of proximity condition was fulfilled too! Each head was bath and cartridge enough for any spread-brain's realization: "But," thought Spoilar, "the same kind of physical realization must exist for every experience of every brain — since all brains are spreadable. And that includes mine. But then all my beliefs are based on thoughts and experiences that might exist only as some such floating cloud. They are all suspect — including those that had convinced me of all this physiology in the first place. Unless Cassander is right, to some extent, then physiology reduces to absurdity. It undermines itself."

Such thinking killed the great project and with it the spread-brain. Men turned to other weird activities and to new conclusions about the nature of existence. But what these were is another story.

Further Questions

1. If the view of consciousness sketched in Zuboff's story is right, then there are conscious experiences that do not belong to any particular organism. Explain how that could be. Does this consequence reduce to absurdity the view of consciousness which implies it, or does it

merely show that if that view of consciousness is correct, the world is an even stranger place than we thought? Give reasons for your answer.

2. How much weight, if any, should be given to common sense in deciding whether a theory is correct?

Further Readings

Block, Ned, ed. *Readings in Philosophy of Psychology*, 2 vols. Cambridge: Harvard University Press, 1980, 1981. An excellent collection of papers, many of which focus on functionalism.

Dennett, Daniel. "Current Issues in the Philosophy of Mind." *American Philosophical Quarterly*, vol. 15, 1978, pp. 249–261. An excellent account of the rise of functionalism, the theory of consciousness portrayed in the selection by Hofstadter.

What Is It Like to Be a Bat?

THOMAS NAGEL

Thomas Nagel taught philosophy for several years at Princeton University and now teaches at New York University. He writes primarily in the areas of philosophy of mind and ethics. In this selection Nagel claims that the essence of consciousness is that "there is something it is like" to be a conscious being and nothing it is like to be a being that lacks consciousness. Thus, for instance, there is something it is like to be a bat, but nothing it is like to be a baseball. Furthermore, we could know everything there is to know scientifically — from the "outside" — about how a conscious being, say, a bat, works, yet still not know what it is like to be that conscious being. Nagel argues that this implies the antireductionist view that there is more to consciousness than what can be captured in our current scientific theories.

Reading Questions

1. What is Nagel's understanding of subjectivity? What is the role of "point of view"?

2. Use an example of your own to illustrate what Nagel means by his claim that there are facts which we can neither state nor comprehend.

3. Can we have evidence for the truth of something we cannot understand? How does Nagel answer? What use does he make of his answer?

4. What is "objective phenomenology"?

CONSCIOUSNESS IS what makes the mind-body problem really intractable. Perhaps that is why current discussions of the problem give it little attention or get it obviously wrong. The recent wave of reductionist euphoria has produced several analyses of mental phenomena and mental concepts designed to explain the possibility of some variety of materialism, psychophysical identification, or reduction.[1] But the problems dealt with are those common to this type of reduction and other types, and what makes the mind-body problem unique, and unlike the water-H_2O problem or the Turing machine-IBM machine problem or the lightning-electrical discharge problem or the gene-DNA problem or the oak tree-hydrocarbon problem, is ignored.

Every reductionist has his favorite analogy from modern science. It is most unlikely that any of these unrelated examples of successful reduction will shed light on the relation of mind to brain. But philosophers share the general human weakness for explanations of what is incomprehensible in terms suited for what is familiar and well understood, though entirely different. This has led to the acceptance of implausible accounts of the mental largely because they would permit familiar kinds of reduction. I shall try to explain why the usual examples do not help us to understand the relation between mind and body — why, indeed, we have at present no conception of what an explanation of the physical nature of a mental phenomenon would be. Without consciousness the mind-body problem would be much less interesting. With consciousness it seems hopeless. The most important and characteristic feature of conscious mental phenomena is very poorly understood. Most reductionist theories do not even try to explain it. And careful examination will show that no currently available concept of reduction is applicable to it. Perhaps a new theoretical form can be devised for the purpose, but such a solution, if it exists, lies in the distant intellectual future.

Conscious experience is a widespread phenomenon. It occurs at many levels of animal life, though we cannot be sure of its presence in the simpler organisms, and it is very difficult to say in general what provides evidence of it. (Some extremists have been prepared to deny it even of mammals other than man.) No doubt it occurs in countless forms totally unimaginable to us, on other planets in other solar systems throughout the universe. But no matter how the form may vary, the fact that an organism has conscious experience *at all* means, basically, that there is something it is like to *be* that organism. There may be further implications about the form of the experience; there may even (though I doubt it) be implications about the behavior of the organism. But fundamentally an organism has conscious mental states if and only if there is something that it is like to *be* that organism — something it is like *for* the organism.

We may call this the subjective character of experience. It it not captured by any of the familiar, recently devised reductive analyses of the mental, for all of them are logically compatible with its absence. It is not analyzable in terms of any explanatory system of functional states, or intentional states, since these could be ascribed to robots or automata that behaved like people though they experienced nothing.[2] It is not analyzable in terms of the causal role of experiences in relation to typical human behavior — for similar reasons.[3] I do not deny that conscious mental states and events cause behavior, nor that they may be given functional characterizations. I deny only that this kind of thing exhausts their analysis. Any reductionist program has to be based on an analysis of what is to be reduced. If the analysis leaves something out, the problem will be falsely posed. It is useless to base the defense of materialism on any analysis of mental phenomena that fails to deal explicitly with their subjective character. For there is no reason to suppose that a reduction which seems plausible when no

"What Is It Like to Be a Bat?" by Thomas Nagel, The Philosophical Review, *October 1974. Reprinted by permission of the author and* The Philosophical Review.

attempt is made to account for consciousness can be extended to include consciousness. Without some idea, therefore, of what the subjective character of experience is, we cannot know what is required of a physicalist theory.

While an account of the physical basis of mind must explain many things, this appears to be the most difficult. It is impossible to exclude the phenomenological features of experience from a reduction in the same way that one excludes the phenomenal features of an ordinary substance from a physical or chemical reduction of it—namely, by explaining them as effects on the minds of human observers.[4] If physicalism is to be defended, the phenomenological features must themselves be given a physical account. But when we examine their subjective character it seems that such a result is impossible. The reason is that every subjective phenomenon is essentially connected with a single point of view, and it seems inevitable that an objective, physical theory will abandon that point of view.

Let me first try to state the issue somewhat more fully than by referring to the relation between the subjective and the objective, or between the *pour-soi* and the *en-soi*. This is far from easy. Facts about what it is like to be an X are very peculiar, so peculiar that some may be inclined to doubt their reality, or the significance of claims about them. To illustrate the connection between subjectivity and a point of view, and to make evident the importance of subjective features, it will help to explore the matter in relation to an example that brings out clearly the divergence between the two types of conception, subjective and objective.

I assume we all believe that bats have experience. After all, they are mammals, and there is no more doubt that they have experience than that mice or pigeons or whales have experience. I have chosen bats instead of wasps or flounders because if one travels too far down the phylogenetic tree, people gradually shed their faith that there is experience there at all. Bats, although more closely related to us than those other species, nevertheless present a range of activity and a sensory apparatus so different from ours that the problem I want to pose is exceptionally vivid (though it certainly could be raised with other species). Even without the benefit of philosophical reflection, anyone who has spent some time in an enclosed space with an excited bat knows what it is to encounter a fundamentally *alien* form of life.

I have said that the essence of the belief that bats have experience is that there is something that it is like to be a bat. Now we know that most bats (the microchiroptera, to be precise) perceive the external world primarily by sonar, or echolocation, detecting the reflections, from objects within range, of their own rapid, subtly modulated, high-frequency shrieks. Their brains are designed to correlate the outgoing impulses with the subsequent echoes, and the information thus acquired enables bats to make precise discriminations of distance, size, shape, motion, and texture comparable to those we make by vision. But bat sonar, though clearly a form of perception, is not similar in its operation to any sense that we possess, and there is no reason to suppose that it is subjectively like anything we can experience or imagine. This appears to create difficulties for the notion of what it is like to be a bat. We must consider whether any method will permit us to extrapolate to the inner life of the bat from our own case,[5] and if not, what alternative methods there may be for understanding the notion.

Our own experience provides the basic material for our imagination, whose range is therefore limited. It will not help to try to imagine that one has webbing on one's arms, which enables one to fly around at dusk and dawn catching insects in one's mouth; that one has very poor vision, and perceives the surrounding world by a system of reflected high-frequency sound signals; and that one spends the day hanging upside down by one's feet in an attic. In so far as I can imagine this (which is not very far), it tells me only what it would be like for *me* to behave as a bat behaves. But that is not the question. I want to know what it is like for a *bat* to be a bat. Yet if I try to imagine this, I am restricted to the resources of my own mind, and those resources are inadequate to the task. I cannot perform it either by imagining additions to my present experience, or by imagining segments gradually subtracted from it, or by imagining some combination of additions, subtractions, and modifications.

To the extent that I could look and behave like a wasp or a bat without changing my fundamental structure, my experiences would not be anything like the experiences of those animals. On the other hand, it is doubtful that any meaning can be attached to the supposition that I should possess the internal neurophysiological constitution of a bat. Even if I could by gradual degrees be transformed into a bat, nothing in my present constitution enables me to imagine what the experiences of such a future stage of myself thus metamorphosed would be like. The best evidence would come from the experiences of bats, if we only knew what they were like.

So if extrapolation from our own case is involved in the idea of what it is like to be a bat, the extrapolation must be incompletable. We cannot form more than a schematic conception of what it *is* like. For example, we may ascribe general *types* of experience on the basis of the animal's structure and behavior. Thus we describe bat sonar as a form of three-dimensional forward perception; we believe that bats feel some versions of pain, fear, hunger, and lust, and that they have other, more familiar types of perception besides sonar. But we believe that those experiences also have in each case a specific subjective character, which it is beyond our ability to conceive. And if there is conscious life elsewhere in the universe, it is likely that some of it will not be describable even in the most general experiential terms available to us.[6] (The problem is not confined to exotic cases, however, for it exists between one person and another. The subjective character of the experience of a person deaf and blind from birth is not accessible to me, for example, nor presumably is mine to him. This does not prevent us each from believing that the other's experience has such a subjective character.)

If anyone is inclined to deny that we can believe in the existence of facts like this whose exact nature we cannot possibly conceive, he should reflect that in contemplating the bats we are in much the same position that intelligent bats or Martians[7] would occupy if they tried to form a conception of what it was like to be us. The structure of their own minds might make it impossible for them to succeed, but we know they would be wrong to conclude that there is not anything precise that it is like to be us: that only certain general types of mental state could be ascribed to us (perhaps perception and appetite would be concepts common to us both; perhaps not). We know they would be wrong to draw such a skeptical conclusion because we know what it is like to be us. And we know that while it includes an enormous amount of variation and complexity, and while we do not possess the vocabulary to describe it adequately, its subjective character is highly specific, and in some respects describable in terms that can be understood only by creatures like us. The fact that we cannot expect ever to accommodate in our language a detailed description of Martian or bat phenomenology should not lead us to dismiss as meaningless the claim that bats and Martians have experiences fully comparable in richness of detail to our own. It would be fine if someone were to develop concepts and a theory that enabled us to think about those things; but such an understanding may be permanently denied to us by the limits of our nature. And to deny the reality or logical significance of what we can never describe or understand is the crudest form of cognitive dissonance.

This brings us to the edge of a topic that requires much more discussion than I can give it here: namely, the relation between facts on the one hand and conceptual schemes or systems of representation on the other. My realism about the subjective domain in all its forms implies a belief in the existence of facts beyond the reach of human concepts. Certainly it is possible for a human being to believe that there are facts which humans never *will* possess the requisite concepts to represent or comprehend. Indeed, it would be foolish to doubt this, given the finiteness of humanity's expectations. After all, there would have been transfinite numbers even if everyone had been wiped out by the Black Death before Cantor discovered them. But one might also believe that there are facts which *could* not ever be represented or comprehended by human beings, even if the species lasted forever — simply because our structure does not permit us to operate with concepts of the requisite type. This impossibility might even be observed by other beings, but it is not clear that the existence of such beings, or the possibility of their existence, is a precondition of the significance of the hypothesis that there are humanly inaccessible facts. (After all, the nature of beings with access to humanly inaccessible facts is presumably itself a humanly inaccessible fact.) Reflection on what it is like to be a bat seems to lead us, therefore, to the conclusion that there are facts that do not consist in the truth of propositions expressible in a human language. We can be compelled to recognize the existence of such facts without being able to state or comprehend them.

I shall not pursue this subject, however. Its bearing on the topic before us (namely, the mind-body problem) is that it enables us to make a general observation about the subjective character of experience. Whatever may be the status of facts about what it is like to be a human being, or a bat, or a Martian, these appear to be facts that embody a particular point of view.

I am not adverting here to the alleged privacy of experience to its possessor. The point of view in question is not one accessible only to a single individual. Rather it is a *type*. It is often possible to take up a point of view other than one's own, so the comprehension of such facts is not limited to one's own case. There is a sense in which phenomenological facts are perfectly objective: one person can know or say of another what the quality of the other's experience is. They are subjec-

tive, however, in the sense that even this objective ascription of experience is possible only for someone sufficiently similar to the object of ascription to be able to adopt his point of view — to understand the ascription in the first person as well as in the third, so to speak. The more different from oneself the other experiencer is, the less success one can expect with this enterprise. In our own case we occupy the relevant point of view, but we will have as much difficulty understanding our own experience properly if we approach it from another point of view as we would if we tried to understand the experience of another species without taking up *its* point of view.[8]

This bears directly on the mind-body problem. For if the facts of experience — facts about what it is like *for* the experiencing organism — are accessible only from one point of view, then it is a mystery how the true character of experiences could be revealed in the physical operation of that organism. The latter is a domain of objective facts *par excellence* — the kind that can be observed and understood from many points of view and by individuals with differing perceptual systems. There are no comparable imaginative obstacles to the acquisiton of knowledge about bat neurophysiology by human scientists, and intelligent bats or Martians might learn more about the human brain than we ever will.

This is not by itself an argument against reduction. A Martian scientist with no understanding of visual perception could understand the rainbow, or lightning, or clouds as physical phenomena, though he would never be able to understand the human concepts of rainbow, lightning, or cloud, or the place these things occupy in our phenomenal world. The objective nature of the things picked out by these concepts could be apprehended by him because, although the concepts themselves are connected with a particular point of view and a particular visual phenomenology, the things apprehended from that point of view are not: they are observable from the point of view but external to it; hence they can be comprehended from other points of view also, either by the same organisms or by others. Lightning has an objective character that is not exhausted by its visual appearance, and this can be investigated by a Martian without vision. To be precise, it has a *more* objective character than is revealed in its visual appearance. In speaking of the move from subjective to objective character-ization, I wish to remain noncommittal about the existence of an end point, the completely objec-tive intrinsic nature of the thing, which one might or might not be able to reach. It may be more accurate to think of objectivity as a direc-tion in which the understanding can travel. And in understanding a phenomenon like lightning, it is legitimate to go as far away as one can from a strictly human viewpoint.[9]

In the case of experience, on the other hand, the connection with a particular point of view seems much closer. It is difficult to understand what could be meant by the *objective* character of an experience, apart from the particular point of view from which its subject apprehends it. After all, what would be left of what it was like to be a bat if one removed the viewpoint of the bat? But if experience does not have, in addition to its sub-jective character, an objective nature that can be apprehended from many different points of view, then how can it be supposed that a Martian inves-tigating my brain might be observing physical processes which were my mental processes (as he might observe physical processes which were bolts of lightning), only from a different point of view? How, for that matter, could a human physiologist observe them from another point of view?[10]

We appear to be faced with a general difficulty about psycho-physical reduction. In other areas the process of reduction is a move in the direction of greater objectivity, toward a more accurate view of the real nature of things. This is accom-plished by reducing our dependence on individ-ual or species-specific points of view toward the object of investigation. We describe it not in terms of the impressions it makes on our senses, but in terms of its more general effects and of properties detectable by means other than the human senses. The less it depends on a specifi-cally human viewpoint, the more objective is our description. It is possible to follow this path be-cause although the concepts and ideas we employ in thinking about the external world are initially applied from a point of view that involves our perceptual apparatus, they are used by us to refer to things beyond themselves — toward which we *have* the phenomenal point of view. Therefore we can abandon it in favor of another, and still be thinking about the same things.

Experience itself, however, does not seem to fit the pattern. The idea of moving from appear-ance to reality seems to make no sense here. What is the analogue in this case to pursuing a more objective understanding of the same phenomena by abandoning the initial subjective viewpoint toward them in favor of another that is more ob-jective but concerns the same thing? Certainly it *appears* unlikely that we will get closer to the real nature of human experience by leaving behind the particularity of our human point of view and striving for a description in terms accessible to beings that could not imagine what it was like to be us. If the subjective character of experience is fully comprehensible only from one point of view, then any shift to greater objectivity — that is, less attachment to a specific viewpoint — does not take us nearer to the real nature of the phe-nomenon: it takes us farther away from it.

In a sense, the seeds of this objection to the reducibility of experience are already detectable in successful cases of reduction; for in discover-ing sound to be, in reality, a wave phenomenon in air or other media, we leave behind one view-point to take up another, and the auditory, hu-man or animal viewpoint that we leave behind remains unreduced. Member of radically differ-ent species may both understand the same physi-cal events in objective terms, and this does not require that they understand the phenomenal forms in which those events appear to the senses of members of the other species. Thus it is a con-dition of their referring to a common reality that their more particular viewpoints are not part of the common reality that they both apprehend. The reduction can succeed only if the species-specific viewpoint is omitted from what is to be reduced.

But while we are right to leave this point of view aside in seeking a fuller understanding of the external world, we cannot ignore it permanently, since it is the essence of the internal world, and not merely a point of view on it. Most of the neobehaviorism of recent philosophical psychology results from the effort to substitute an objective concept of mind for the real thing, in order to have nothing left over which cannot be reduced. If we acknowledge that a physical theory of mind must account for the subjective character of experience, we must admit that no presently available conception gives us a clue how this could be done. The problem is unique. If mental processes are indeed physical processes, then there is something it is like, intrinsically,[11] to undergo certain physical processes. What it is for such a thing to be the case remains a mystery.

What moral should be drawn from these reflections, and what should be done next? It would be a mistake to conclude that physicalism must be false. Nothing is proved by the inadequacy of physicalist hypotheses that assume a faulty objective analysis of mind. It would be truer to say that physicalism is a position we cannot understand because we do not at present have any conception of how it might be true. Perhaps it will be thought unreasonable to require such a conception as a condition of understanding. After all, it might be said, the meaning of physicalism is clear enough: mental states are states of the body; mental events are physical events. We do not know *which* physical states and events they are, but that should not prevent us from understanding the hypothesis. What could be clearer than the words "is" and "are"?

But I believe it is precisely this apparent clarity of the word "is" that is deceptive. Usually, when we are told that X is Y we know *how* it is supposed to be true, but that depends on a concep-

tual or theoretical background and is not conveyed by the "is" alone. We know how both "X" and "Y" refer, and the kinds of things to which they refer, and we have a rough idea how the two referential paths might converge on a single thing, be it an object, a person, a process, an event, or whatever. But when the two terms of the identification are very disparate it may not be so clear how it could be true. We may not have even a rough idea of how the two referential paths could converge, or what kind of things they might converge on, and a theoretical framework may have to be supplied to enable us to understand this. Without the framework, an air of mysticism surrounds the identification.

This explains the magical flavor of popular presentations of fundamental scientific discoveries, given out as propositions to which one must subscribe without really understanding them. For example, people are now told at an early age that all matter is really energy. But despite the fact that they know what "is" means, most of them never form a conception of what makes this claim true, because they lack the theoretical background.

At the present time the status of physicalism is similar to that which the hypothesis that matter is energy would have had if uttered by a pre-Socratic philosopher. We do not have the beginnings of a conception of how it might be true. In order to understand the hypothesis that a mental event is a physical event, we require more than an understanding of the word "is." The idea of how a mental and a physical term might refer to the same thing is lacking, and the usual analogies with theoretical identification in other fields fail to supply it. They fail because if we construe the reference of mental terms to physical events on the usual model, we either get a reappearance of separate subjective events as the effects through which mental reference to physical events is secured, or else we get a false account of how mental terms refer (for example, a causal behaviorist one).

Strangely enough, we may have evidence for the truth of something we cannot really understand. Suppose a caterpillar is locked in a sterile safe by someone unfamiliar with insect metamorphosis, and weeks later the safe is reopened, revealing a butterfly. If the person knows that the safe has been shut the whole time, he has reason to believe that the butterfly is or was once the caterpillar, without having any idea in what sense this might be so. (One possibility is that the caterpillar contained a tiny winged parasite that devoured it and grew into the butterfly.)

It is conceivable that we are in such a position with regard to physicalism. Donald Davidson has argued that if mental events have physical causes and effects, they must have physical descriptions. He holds that we have reason to believe this even though we do not—and in fact *could* not—have a general psychophysical theory.[12] His argument applies to intentional mental events, but I think we also have some reason to believe that sensations are physical processes, without being in a position to understand how. Davidson's position is that certain physical events have irreducibly mental properties, and perhaps some view describable in this way is correct. But nothing of which we can now form a conception corresponds to it; nor have we any idea what a theory would be like that enabled us to conceive of it.[13]

Very little work has been done on the basic question (from which mention of the brain can be entirely omitted) whether any sense can be made of experiences' having an objective character at all. Does it make sense, in other words, to ask what my experiences are *really* like, as opposed to how they appear to me? We cannot genuinely understand the hypothesis that their nature is captured in a physical description unless we understand the more fundamental idea that they *have* an objective nature (or that objective processes can have a subjective nature).[14]

I should like to close with a speculative proposal. It may be possible to approach the gap between subjective and objective from another direction. Setting aside temporarily the relation between the mind and the brain, we can pursue a more objective understanding of the mental in its own right. At present we are completely unequipped to think about the subjective character of experience without relying on the imagination—without taking up the point of view of the experiential subject. This should be regarded as a challenge to form new concepts and devise a new method—an objective phenomenology not dependent on empathy or the imagination. Though presumably it would not capture everything, its goal would be to describe, at least in part, the subjective character of experiences in a form comprehensible to beings incapable of having those experiences.

We would have to develop such a phenomenology to describe the sonar experiences of bats; but it would also be possible to begin with humans. One might try, for example, to develop concepts that could be used to explain to a person blind from birth what it was like to see. One would reach a blank wall eventually, but it should be possible to devise a method of expressing in objective terms much more than we can at present, and with much greater precision. The loose intermodal analogies—for example, "Red is like the sound of a trumpet"—which crop up in discussions of this subject are of little use. That should be clear to anyone who has both heard a trumpet and seen red. But structural features of perception might be more accessible to objective description, even though something would be left out. And concepts alternative to those we learn in the first person may enable us to arrive at a kind of understanding even of our own experience which is denied us by the very ease of description and lack of distance that subjective concepts afford.

Apart from its own interest, a phenomenology that is in this sense objective may permit questions about the physical[15] basis of experience to assume a more intelligible form. Aspects of subjective experience that admitted this kind of objective description might be better candidates for objective explanations of a more familiar sort. But whether or not this guess is correct, it seems unlikely that any physical theory of mind can be contemplated until more thought has been given to the general problem of subjective and objective. Otherwise we cannot even pose the mind-body problem without sidestepping it.[16]

NOTES

1. Examples are J. J. C. Smart, *Philosophy and Scientific Realism* (London, 1963); David K. Lewis, "An Argument for the Identity Theory," *Journal of Philosophy*, LXIII (1966), reprinted with addenda in David M. Rosenthal, *Materialism & the Mind-Body Problem* (Englewood Cliffs, N.J., 1971); Hilary Putnam, "Psychological Predicates" in Capitan and Merrill, *Art, Mind, & Religion* (Pittsburgh, 1967), reprinted in Rosenthal, *op. cit.*, as "The Nature of Mental States"; D. M. Armstrong, *A Materialist Theory of the Mind* (London, 1968); D. C. Dennett, *Content and Consciousness* (London, 1969). I have expressed earlier doubts in "Armstrong on the Mind," *Philosophical Review* LXXIX (1970), 394–403; "Brain Bisection and the Unity of Consciousness," *Synthèse*, 22 (1971); and a review of Dennett, *Journal of Philosophy*, LXIX (1972). See also Saul Kripke, "Naming and Necessity" in Davidson and Harman, *Semantics of Natural Language* (Dordrecht, 1972), esp. pp. 334–342; and M. T. Thornton, "Ostensive Terms and Materialism," *The Monist*, 56 (1972).

2. Perhaps there could not actually be such robots. Perhaps anything complex enough to behave like a person would have experiences. But that, if true, is a fact which cannot be discovered merely by analyzing the concept of experience.

3. It is not equivalent to that about which we are incorrigible, both because we are not incorrigible about experience and because experience is present in animals lacking language and thought, who have no beliefs at all about their experiences.

4. Cf. Richard Rorty, "Mind-Body Identity, Privacy, and Categories," *The Review of Metaphysics*, XIX (1965), esp. 37–38.

5. By "our own case" I do not mean just "my own case," but rather the mentalistic ideas that we apply unproblematically to ourselves and other human beings.

6. Therefore the analogical form of the English expression "what is it *like*" is misleading. It does not mean "what (in our experience) it *resembles*," but rather "how it is for the subject himself."

7. Any intelligent extraterrestrial beings totally different from us.

8. It may be easier than I suppose to transcend inter-species barriers with the aid of the imagination. For example, blind people are able to detect objects near them by a form of sonar, using vocal clicks or taps of a cane. Perhaps if one knew what that was like, one could by extension imagine roughly what it was like to possess the much more refined sonar of a bat. The distance between oneself and other persons and other species can fall anywhere on a continuum. Even for other persons the understanding of what it is like to be them is only partial, and when one moves to species very different from oneself, a lesser degree of partial understanding may still be available. The imagination is remarkably flexible. My point, however, is not that we cannot *know* what it is like to be a bat. I am not raising that epistemological problem. My point is rather that even to form a *conception* of what it is like to be a bat (and a fortiori to know what it is like to be a bat) one must take up the bat's point of view. If one can take it up roughly, or partially, then one's conception will also be rough or partial. Or so it seems in our present state of understanding.

9. The problem I am going to raise can therefore be posed even if the distinction between more subjective and more objective descriptions or viewpoints can itself be made only within a larger human point of view. I do not accept this kind of conceptual relativism, but it need not be refuted to make the point that psychophysical reduction cannot be accommodated by the subjective-to-objective model familiar from other cases.

10. The problem is not just that when I look at the "Mona Lisa," my visual experience has a certain quality, no trace of which is to be found by someone looking into my brain. For even if he did observe there a tiny image of the "Mona Lisa," he would have no reason to identify it with the experience.

11. The relation would therefore not be a contingent one, like that of a cause and its distinct effect. It would be necessarily true that a certain physical state felt a certain way. Saul Kripke (*op. cit.*) argues that causal behaviorist and related analyses of the mental fail because they construe, e.g., "pain" as a merely contingent name of pains. The subjective character of an experience ("its immediate phenomenological quality" Kripke calls it [p. 340]) is the essential property left out by such analyses, and the one in virtue of which it is, necessarily, the experience it is. My view is closely related to his. Like Kripke, I find the hypothesis that a certain brain state should *necessarily* have a certain subjective character incomprehensible without further explanation. No such explanation emerges from theories which view the mind-brain relation as contingent, but perhaps there are other alternatives, not yet discovered.

A theory that explained how the mind-brain relation was necessary would still leave us with Kripke's problem of explaining why it nevertheless appears contingent. That difficulty seems to me surmountable, in the following way. We may imagine something by representing it to ourselves either perceptually, sympathetically, or symbolically. I shall not try to say how symbolic imagination works, but part of what happens in the other two cases is this. To imagine something perceptually, we put ourselves in a conscious state resembling the state we would be in if we perceived it. To imagine something sympathetically, we put ourselves in a conscious state resembling the thing itself. (This method can be used only to imagine mental events and states—our own or another's.) When we try to imagine a mental state occurring without its associated brain state, we first sympathetically imagine the occurrence of the mental state: that is, we put ourselves into a state that resembles it mentally. At the same time, we attempt to perceptually imagine the non-occurrence of the associated physical state, by putting ourselves into another state unconnected with the first: one resembling that which we would be in if we perceived the non-occurrence of the physical state. Where the imagination of physical features is perceptual and the imagination of mental features is sympathetic, it appears to us that we can imagine any experience occurring without its associated brain state, and vice versa. The relation between them will appear contingent even if it is necessary, because of the independence of the disparate types of imagination.

(Solipsism, incidentally, results if one misinterprets sympathetic imagination as if it worked like perceptual imagination: it then seems impossible to imagine any experience that is not one's own.)

12. See "Mental Events" in Foster and Swanson, *Experience and Theory* (Amherst, 1970); though I don't understand the argument against psychophysical laws.

13. Similar remarks apply to my paper "Physicalism," *Philosophical Review* LXXIV (1965), 339–356, reprinted with postscript in John O'Connor, *Modern Materialism* (New York, 1969).

14. This question also lies at the heart of the problem of other minds, whose close connection with the mind-body problem is often overlooked. If one understood how subjective experience could have an objective nature, one would understand the existence of subjects other than oneself.

15. I have not defined the term "physical." Obviously it does not apply just to what can be described by the concepts of contemporary physics, since we expect further developments. Some may think there is nothing to prevent mental phenomena from eventually being recognized as physical in their own right. But whatever else may be said of the physical, it has to be objective. So if our idea of the physical ever expands to include mental phenomena, it will have to assign them an objective character—whether or not this is done by analyzing them in terms of other phenomena already regarded as physical. It seems to me more likely, however, that mental-physical relations will eventually be expressed in a theory whose fundamental terms cannot be placed clearly in either category.

16. I have read versions of this paper to a number of audiences, and am indebted to many people for their comments.

Further Questions

1. Could an android have a point of view? Could it have one even if it were not conscious?

2. Is it possible that there is an experiential way of understanding things that differs from the scientific way of understanding things even though the experiential way of understanding does not imply the existence of any extra things (psychic events or properties) than those implied by our best scientific theories? In other words, is it possible that experiential *understanding* cannot be reduced to scientific understanding even though an experiencing *organism* is nothing more than a certain kind of wholly physical mechanism?

Further Readings

Morton, Adam. *Frames of Mind*. New York: Oxford University Press, 1980. On subjectivity.
Nagel, Thomas. *The View from Nowhere*. New York: Oxford University Press, 1986. Nagel's latest thoughts on subjectivity.

Part IX

Understanding

U SUALLY, WHEN WE TRY TO UNDERSTAND something, we try to reduce it to simpler components. We try to understand the complex whole by getting hold of the simple elements of which it is composed. Do we ever succeed? Only up to a point. The problem is that we the observers are invariably and inextricably linked to whatever we are trying to understand.

We imagine our relationship to the universe to be like that of fish to a fishtank: whether or not there are fish, the tank is there. We think the universe is not shaped by us. Rather, we are shaped by it. We believe that ultimately the universe exists independently of the minds trying so desperately to understand it.

One of the most amazing scientific discoveries of all time, however, is that this fishbowl model of the universe simply does not work. Without us, the observers, trying to understand the observed, the universe we know would literally not exist — and neither would we.

The Selfish Gene

RICHARD DAWKINS

Richard Dawkins is a British biologist. His book, *The Selfish Gene*, from which the following selection is taken, is a modern classic of popular science. In it Dawkins explains how simple constituents can combine, through the action of natural forces, to produce a highly complex result: you. In the process Dawkins nicely illustrates how science, by reducing the complex to the simple, contributes to our understanding of nature and ourselves.

Reading Questions

1. How, according to Dawkins, did simple atoms become biologically more complex?
2. If Dawkins's account is correct, who's running the show—us, or our genes?
3. Why is there no need for design or purpose at the molecular level?
4. What is a *survival machine*?

Selfish Genes

IN THE BEGINNING WAS SIMPLICITY. It is difficult enough explaining how even a simple universe began. I take it as agreed that it would be even harder to explain the sudden springing up, fully armed, of complex order—life, or a being capable of creating life. Darwin's theory of evolution by natural selection is satisfying because it shows us a way in which simplicity could change into complexity, how unordered atoms could group themselves into ever more complex patterns until they ended up manufacturing people. Darwin provides a solution, the only feasible one so far suggested, to the deep problem of our existence. I will try to explain the great theory in a more general way than is customary, beginning with the time before evolution itself began.

Darwin's 'survival of the fittest' is really a special case of a more general law of *survival of the stable*. The universe is populated by stable things. A stable thing is a collection of atoms which is permanent enough or common enough to deserve a name. It may be a unique collection of atoms, such as the Matterhorn, which lasts long enough to be worth naming. Or it may be a *class* of entities, such as rain drops, which come into existence at a sufficiently high rate to deserve a collective name, even if any one of them is short-lived. The things which we see around us, and which we think of as needing explanation—rocks, galaxies, ocean waves—are all, to a greater or lesser extent, stable patterns of atoms. Soap bubbles tend to be spherical because this is a stable configuration for thin films filled with gas. In a spacecraft, water is also stable in spherical globules, but on earth, where there is gravity, the stable surface for standing water is flat and horizontal. Salt crystals tend to be cubes because this is a stable way of packing sodium and chloride ions together. In the sun the simplest atoms of all, hydrogen atoms, are fusing to form helium atoms, because in the conditions which prevail there the helium configuration is more stable. Other even more complex atoms are being formed in stars all over the universe, and were formed in the "big bang" which, according to the prevailing theory, initiated the universe. This is originally where the elements on our world came from.

Sometimes when atoms meet they link up together in chemical reaction to form molecules, which may be more or less stable. Such molecules can be very large. A crystal such as a diamond can be regarded as a single molecule, a proverbially stable one in this case, but also a very simple one since its internal atomic structure is endlessly repeated. In modern living organisms there are other large molecules which are highly complex, and their complexity shows itself on several levels. The hemoglobin of our blood is a typical protein molecule. It is built up from chains of smaller molecules, amino acids, each containing a few dozen atoms arranged in a precise pattern. In the hemoglobin molecule there are 574 amino acid molecules. These are arranged in four chains, which twist around each other to form a globular three-dimensional structure of bewildering complexity. . . .

Hemoglobin is a modern molecule, used to illustrate the principle that atoms tend to fall into stable patterns. The point that is relevant here is that, before the coming of life on earth, some rudimentary evolution of molecules could have occurred by ordinary processes of physics and chemistry. There is no need to think of design or purpose or directedness. If a group of atoms in the presence of energy falls into a stable pattern it will tend to stay that way. The earliest form of natural selection was simply a selection of stable forms and a rejection of unstable ones. There is no mystery about this. It had to happen by definition.

From this, of course, it does not follow that you can explain the existence of entities as complex as man by exactly the same principles on their own. It is no good taking the right number of atoms and shaking them together with some external energy till they happen to fall into the right pattern, and out drops Adam! You may make a molecule consisting of a few dozen atoms like that, but a man consists of over a thousand million million million million atoms. To try to make a man, you would have to work at your biochemical cocktail-shaker for a period so long that the entire age of the universe would seem like an eye-blink, and even then you would not succeed. This is where Darwin's theory, in its most general form, comes to the rescue. Darwin's theory takes over from where the story of the slow building up of molecules leaves off.

The account of the origin of life which I shall give is necessarily speculative; by definition, nobody was around to see what happened. There are a number of rival theories, but they all have certain features in common. The simplified account I shall give is probably not too far from the truth.

We do not know what chemical raw materials were abundant on earth before the coming of life, but among the plausible possibilities are water, carbon dioxide, methane, and ammonia: all simple compounds known to be present on at least some of the other planets in our solar system. Chemists have tried to imitate the chemical conditions of the young earth. They have put these simple substances in a flask and supplied a source of energy such as ultraviolet light or electric sparks — artificial simulation of primordial lightning. After a few weeks of this, something interesting is usually found inside the flask: a weak brown soup containing a large number of molecules more complex than the ones originally put in. In particular, amino acids have been found — the building blocks of proteins, one of the two great classes of biological molecules. . . .

Processes analogous to these must have given rise to the "primeval soup" which biolo-gists and chemists believe constituted the seas some three to four thousand million years ago. The organic substances became locally concentrated, perhaps in drying scum round the shores, or in tiny suspended droplets. Under the further influence of energy such as ultraviolet light from the sun, they combined into larger molecules. . . .

At some point a particularly remarkable molecule was formed by accident. We will call it the *Replicator*. It may not necessarily have been the biggest or the most complex molecule around, but it had the extraordinary property of being able to create copies of itself. This may seem a very unlikely sort of accident to happen. So it was. It was exceedingly improbable. In the lifetime of a man, things which are that improbable can be treated for practical purposes as impossible. That is why you will never win a big prize on the football pools. But in our human estimates of what is probable and what is not, we are not used to dealing in hundreds of millions of years. If you filled in pools coupons every week for a hundred million years you would very likely win several jackpots.

Actually a molecule which makes copies of itself is not as difficult to imagine as it seems at first, and it only had to arise once. Think of the replicator as a mold or template. Imagine it as a large molecule consisting of a complex chain of various sorts of building block molecules. The small building blocks were abundantly available in the soup surrounding the replicator. Now suppose that each building block has an affinity for its own kind. Then whenever a building block from out in the soup lands up next to a part of the replicator for which it has an affinity, it will tend to stick there. The building blocks which attach themselves in this way will automatically be arranged in a sequence which mimics that of the replicator itself. It is easy then to think of them joining up to form a stable chain just as in the formation of the original replicator. This process could continue as a progressive stacking up, layer upon layer. This is how crystals are formed. On the other hand, the two chains might split apart, in which case we have two replicators, each of which can go on to make further copies.

A more complex possibility is that each building block has affinity not for its own kind, but reciprocally for one particular other kind. Then the replicator would act as a template not for an identical copy, but for a kind of "negative," which would in its turn remake an exact copy of the original positive. For our purposes it does not matter whether the original replication process was positive–negative or positive–positive, though it is worth remarking that the modern equivalents of the first replicator, the DNA molecules, use positive–negative replication. What does matter is that suddenly a new kind of "stability" came into the world. Previously it is probable that no particular kind of complex molecule was very abundant in the soup, because each was dependent on building blocks happening to fall by luck into a particular stable configuration. As soon as the replicator was born it must have spread its copies rapidly throughout the seas, until the smaller building block molecules became a scarce resource, and other larger molecules were formed more and more rarely.

So we seem to arrive at a large population of identical replicas. But now we must mention an important property of any copying process: it is not perfect. Mistakes will happen. I hope there are no misprints in this book, but if you look carefully you may find one or two. They will probably not seriously distort the meaning of the sentences, because they will be "first-generation" errors. But imagine the days before printing, when books such as the Gospels were copied by hand. All scribes, however careful, are bound to make a few errors, and some are not above a little willful "improvement." If they all copied from a single master original, meaning would not be greatly perverted. But let copies be made from other copies, which in their turn were made from other copies, and errors will start to become cumulative and serious. We tend to regard erratic copying as a bad thing, and in the case of human

documents it is hard to think of examples where errors can be described as improvements. I suppose the scholars of the Septuagint could at least be said to have started something big when they mistranslated the Hebrew word for "young woman" into the Greek word for "virgin," coming up with the prophecy: "Behold a virgin shall conceive and bear a son. . . ." Anyway, as we shall see, erratic copying in biological replicators can in a real sense give rise to improvement, and it was essential for the progressive evolution of life that some errors were made. We do not know how accurately the original replicator molecules made their copies. Their modern descendants, the DNA molecules, are astonishingly faithful compared with the most high-fidelity human copying process, but even they occasionally make mistakes, and it is ultimately these mistakes which make evolution possible. Probably the original replicators were far more erratic, but in any case we may be sure that mistakes were made, and these mistakes were cumulative.

As mis-copyings were made and propagated, the primeval soup became filled by a population not of identical replicas, but of several varieties of replicating molecules, all "descended" from the same ancestor. Would some varieties have been more numerous than others? Almost certainly yes. Some varieties would have been inherently more stable than others. Certain molecules, once formed, would be less likely than others to break up again. These types would become relatively numerous in the soup, not only as a direct logical consequence of their "longevity," but also because they would have a long time available for making copies of themselves. Replicators of high longevity would therefore tend to become more numerous and, other things being equal, there would have been an "evolutionary trend" toward greater longevity in the population of molecules.

But other things were probably not equal, and another property of a replicator variety which must have had even more importance in spreading it through the population was speed of replication, or "fecundity." If replicator molecules of type A make copies of themselves on average once a week while those of type B make copies of themselves once an hour, it is not difficult to see that pretty soon type A molecules are going to be far outnumbered, even if they "live" much longer than B molecules. There would therefore probably have been an "evolutionary trend" towards higher "fecundity" of molecules in the soup. A third characteristic of replicator molecules which would have been positively selected is accuracy of replication. If molecules of type X and type Y last the same length of time and replicate at the same rate, but X makes a mistake on average every tenth replication while Y makes a mistake only every hundredth replication, Y will obviously become more numerous. The X contingent in the population loses not only the errant "children" themselves, but also all their descendants, actual or potential.

If you already know something about evolution, you may find something slightly paradoxical about the last point. Can we reconcile the idea that copying errors are an essential prerequisite for evolution to occur, with the statement that natural selection favors high copying-fidelity? The answer is that although evolution may seem, in some vague sense, a "good thing," especially since we are the product of it, nothing actually "wants" to evolve. Evolution is something that happens, willy-nilly, in spite of all the efforts of the replicators (and nowadays of the genes) to prevent it happening. Jacques Monod made this point very well in his Herbert Spencer lecture, after wryly remarking: "Another curious aspect of the theory of evolution is that everybody thinks he understands it!"

To return to the primeval soup, it must have become populated by stable varieties of molecules; stable in that either the individual molecules lasted a long time, or they replicated rapidly, or they replicated accurately. Evolutionary trends toward these three kinds of stability took place in the following sense: If you had sampled the soup at two different times, the later sample would have contained a higher proportion of va-

rieties with high longevity/fecundity/copying-fidelity. This is essentially what a biologist means by evolution when he is speaking of living creatures, and the mechanism is the same — natural selection.

Should we then call the original replicator molecules "living"? Who cares? I might say to you "Darwin was the greatest man who has ever lived," and you might say, "No, Newton was," but I hope we would not prolong the argument. The point is that no conclusion of substance would be affected whichever way our argument was resolved. The facts of the lives and achievements of Newton and Darwin remain totally unchanged whether we label them "great" or not. Similarly, the story of the replicator molecules probably happened something like the way I am telling it, regardless of whether we choose to call them "living." Human suffering has been caused because too many of us cannot grasp that words are only tools for our use, and that the mere presence in the dictionary of a word like "living" does not mean it necessarily has to refer to something definite in the real world. Whether we call the early replicators living or not, they were the ancestors of life; they were our founding fathers.

The next important link in the argument, one which Darwin himself laid stress on (although he was talking about animals and plants, not molecules) is *competition*. The primeval soup was not capable of supporting an infinite number of replicator molecules. For one thing, the earth's size is finite, but other limiting factors must also have been important. In our picture of the replicator acting as a template or mold, we supposed it to be bathed in a soup rich in the small building block molecules necessary to make copies. But when the replicators became numerous, building blocks must have been used up at such a rate that they became a scarce and precious resource. Different varieties or strains of replicator must have competed for them. We have considered the factors which would have increased the numbers of favored kinds of replicator. We can now see that less-favored varieties must actually have become *less* numerous because of competition, and ultimately many of their lines must have gone extinct. There was a struggle for existence among replicator varieties. They did not know they were struggling, or worry about it; the struggle was conducted without any hard feelings, indeed without feelings of any kind. But they were struggling, in the sense that any miscopying which resulted in a new higher level of stability, or a new way of reducing the stability of rivals, was automatically preserved and multiplied. The process of improvement was cumulative. Ways of increasing stability and of decreasing rivals' stability became more elaborate and more efficient. Some of them may even have "discovered" how to break up molecules of rival varieties chemically, and to use the building blocks so released for making their own copies. These proto-carnivores simultaneously obtained food and removed competing rivals. Other replicators perhaps discovered how to protect themselves, either chemically or by building a physical wall of protein around themselves. This may have been how the first living cells appeared. Replicators began not merely to exist, but to construct for themselves containers, vehicles for their continued existence. The replicators which survived were the ones which built *survival machines* for themselves to live in. The first survival machines probably consisted of nothing more than a protective coat. But making a living got steadily harder as new rivals arose with better and more effective survival machines. Survival machines got bigger and more elaborate, and the process was cumulative and progressive.

Was there to be any end to the gradual improvement in the techniques and artifices used by the replicators to ensure their own continuance in the world? There would be plenty of time for improvement. What weird engines of self-preservation would the millennia bring forth? Four thousand million years on, what was to be the fate of the ancient replicators? They did not die out, for they are past masters of the survival arts. But do not look for them floating loose in the sea; they gave up that cavalier freedom long ago. Now they swarm in huge colonies, safe inside gigantic lumbering robots, sealed off from the outside world, communicating with it by tortuous indirect routes, manipulating it by remote control. They are in you and in me; they created us, body and mind; and their preservation is the ultimate rationale for our existence. They have come a long way, those replicators. Now they go by the name of genes, and we are their survival machines.

Further Questions

1. Does a scientific theory have to be reductionist?
2. It is sometimes said that "creationism"—the claim that the various species of plants and animals are each the product of a separate act of divine creation—and evolutionary theory are competing theories of our origins. But are the two really *theories* in the same sense? (What are the important differences, if any, between a religious "theory" and a scientific theory?)

Further Readings

Hofstadter, Douglas. *Gödel, Escher, and Bach*. New York: Basic Books, 1979. An imaginative exploration of consciousness.
Pribram, Karl. *The Languages of the Brain*. Englewood Cliffs, N.J.: Prentice-Hall, 1971. Explores different levels of descriptions of the brain.

Epiphenomenal Qualia

FRANK JACKSON

Frank Jackson teaches philosophy at Monash University, in Australia, and writes primarily in the area of philosophy of mind. A mind-body dualist, he is one of the foremost philosophical opponents of the idea that mental phenomena can be reduced to physical phenomena. In this selection, Jackson provides vivid and interesting examples that seem to refute physicalism. In one of these examples, Mary, who knows all there is to know scientifically about color perception but has been confined all her life to a black-and-white environment, finally emerges to experience the full range of colors. Jackson claims that what she learns through her new experiences shows that physicalism is false.

Reading Questions

1. Do the examples of Fred and Mary make the same point or different points? What is the point of each story?
2. Can we learn things from experience that we cannot learn from science? If so, does this count against physicalism?

. . . I AM WHAT IS SOMETIMES KNOWN as a "qualia freak." I think that there are certain features of the bodily sensations especially, but also of certain perceptual experiences, which no amount of purely physical information includes. Tell me everything physical there is to tell about what is going on in a living brain, the kind of states, their functional role, their relation to what goes on at other times and in other brains, and so on and so forth, and be I as clever as can be in fitting it all together, you won't have told me about the hurtfulness of pains, the itchiness of itches, pangs of jealousy, or about the characteristic experience of tasting a lemon, smelling a rose, hearing a loud noise or seeing the sky. . . .

The Knowledge Argument for Qualia

People vary considerably in their ability to discriminate colours. Suppose that in an experiment to catalogue this variation Fred is discovered. Fred has better colour vision than anyone else on record; he makes every discrimination that anyone has ever made, and moreover he makes one that we cannot even begin to make. Show him a batch of ripe tomatoes and he sorts them into two roughly equal groups and does so with complete consistency. That is, if you blindfold him, shuffle the tomatoes up, and then remove the blindfold and ask him to sort them out again, he sorts them into exactly the same two groups.

We ask Fred how he does it. He explains that all ripe tomatoes do not look the same colour to him, and in fact that this is true of a great many objects that we classify together as red. He sees two colours where we see one, and he has in consequence developed for his own use two words 'red$_1$' and 'red$_2$' to mark the difference. Perhaps he tells us that he has often tried to teach the difference between red$_1$ and red$_2$ to his friends but

From Frank Jackson, "Epiphenomenal Qualia," Philosophical Quarterly, Vol. 32, 1982, pp. 127–136. Reprinted by permission of the publisher.

has got nowhere and has concluded that the rest of the world is red$_1$-red$_2$ colour-blind — or perhaps he has had partial success with his children, it doesn't matter. In any case he explains to us that it would be quite wrong to think that because 'red' appears in both 'red$_1$' and 'red$_2$' that the two colours are shades of the one colour. He only uses the common term 'red' to fit more easily into our restricted usage. To him red$_1$ and red$_2$ are as different from each other and all the other colours as yellow is from blue. And his discriminatory behaviour bears this out: he sorts red$_1$ from red$_2$ tomatoes with the greatest of ease in a wide variety of viewing circumstances. Moreover, an investigation of the physiological basis of Fred's exceptional ability reveals that Fred's optical system is able to separate out two groups of wavelengths in the red spectrum as sharply as we are able to sort out yellow from blue.[1]

I think that we should admit that Fred can see, really see, at least one more colour than we can; red$_1$ is a different colour from red$_2$. We are to Fred as a totally red-green colour-blind person is to us. H. G. Wells' story "The Country of the Blind" is about a sighted person in a totally blind community.[2] This person never manages to convince them that he can see, that he has an extra sense. They ridicule this sense as quite inconceivable, and treat his capacity to avoid falling into ditches, to win fights and so on as precisely that capacity and nothing more. We would be making their mistake if we refused to allow that Fred can see one more colour than we can.

What kind of experience does Fred have when he sees red$_1$ and red$_2$? What is the new colour or colours like? We would dearly like to know but do not; and it seems that no amount of physical information about Fred's brain and optical system tells us. We find out perhaps that Fred's cones respond differentially to certain light waves in the red section of the spectrum that make no difference to ours (or perhaps he has an extra cone) and that this leads in Fred to a wider range of those brain states responsible for visual discriminatory behaviour. But none of this tells us what we really want to know about his colour

experience. There is something about it we don't know. But we know, we may suppose, everything about Fred's body, his behaviour and dispositions to behaviour and about his internal physiology, and everything about his history and relation to others that can be given in physical accounts of persons. We have all the physical information. Therefore, knowing all this is *not* knowing everything about Fred. It follows that Physicalism leaves something out.

To reinforce this conclusion, imagine that as a result of our investigations into the internal workings of Fred we find out how to make everyone's physiology like Fred's in the relevant respects; or perhaps Fred donates his body to science and on his death we are able to transplant his optical system into someone else — again the fine detail doesn't matter. The important point is that such a happening would create enormous interest. People would say, "At last we will know what it is like to see the extra colour, at last we will know how Fred has differed from us in the way he has struggled to tell us about for so long." Then it cannot be that we knew all along all about Fred. But *ex hypothesi* we did know all along everything about Fred that features in the physicalist scheme; hence the physicalist scheme leaves something out.

Put it this way. *After* the operation, we will know *more* about Fred and especially about his colour experiences. But beforehand we had all the physical information we could desire about his body and brain, and indeed everything that has ever featured in physicalist accounts of mind and consciousness. Hence there is more to know than all that. Hence Physicalism is incomplete.

Fred and the new colour(s) are of course essentially rhetorical devices. The same point can be made with normal people and familiar colours. Mary is a brilliant scientist who is, for whatever reason, forced to investigate the world from a black and white room *via* a black and white television monitor. She specialises in the neurophysiology of vision and acquires, let us suppose, all the physical information there is to obtain about what goes on when we see ripe tomatoes, or the sky, and use terms like 'red,' 'blue,' and so on. She discovers, for example, just which wavelength combinations from the sky stimulate the retina, and exactly how this produces *via* the central nervous system the contraction of the vocal chords and expulsion of air from the lungs that results in the uttering of the sentence 'The sky is blue.' (It can hardly be denied that it is in principle possible to obtain all this physical information from black and white television, otherwise the Open University would *of necessity* need to use colour television.)

What will happen when Mary is released from her black and white room or is given a colour television monitor? Will she *learn* anything or not? It seems just obvious that she will learn something about the world and our visual experience of it. But then it is inescapable that her previous knowledge was incomplete. But she had *all* the physical information. *Ergo* there is more to have than that, and Physicalism is false. . . .

NOTES

1. Put this, and similar simplifications below, in terms of Land's theory if you prefer. See, e.g., Edwin H. Land, "Experiments in Color Vision," *Scientific American*, 200 (5 May 1959), 84–99.

2. H. G. Wells, *The Country of the Blind and Other Stories* (London, n.d.).

Further Questions

1. Does either of Jackson's examples show that science is incomplete? If so, in what ways is science incomplete?

2. Does either of Jackson's examples show that physicalism is false? If so, how? If not, why not?

Further Readings

Campbell, Keith. *Body and Mind*. New York: Doubleday, 1970. An excellent introduction to the traditional issues.

Churchland, Paul. *Matter and Consciousness*. Cambridge: M.I.T. Press, Revised Edition, 1988. A beautifully written, physiologically informed argument for reductionism.

Reduction, Qualia, and the Direct Introspection of Brain States

PAUL CHURCHLAND

Paul Churchland teaches philosophy at the University of California at San Diego and writes primarily in the area of philosophy of mind. He is one of the leading spokesmen for physicalism, the view that mental states can be reduced to physical states — the view that Thomas Nagel and Frank Jackson attacked in the preceding selections. In this selection Churchland explains how we should understand physicalism and then why, in his opinion, certain well-known criticisms of it, including Nagel's and Jackson's, ultimately fail.

Reading Questions

1. Churchland distinguishes several different versions of the reductionist thesis. In your own words, explain the differences among them.
2. Which versions of reductionism does Churchland believe in?
3. Why does Churchland think that the anti-reductionist arguments of Nagel and Jackson fail? Do you agree?
4. What is "intertheoretic reduction"? Why does Churchland think the classical account of it is mistaken? How does he think it can be repaired?
5. What is the difference between *theoretical* and *perceptual* change?
6. How does Churchland respond to Thomas Nagel's arguments?
7. What does Churchland think are the two shortcomings of Jackson's knowledge argument?

DO THE PHENOMENOLOGICAL or qualitative features of our sensations constitute a permanent barrier to the reductive aspirations of any materialistic neuroscience? I here argue that they do not.…

If we are to deal sensibly with the issues here at stake, we must approach them with a general theory of scientific reduction already in hand, a theory motivated by and adequate to the many instances and varieties of interconceptual reduction displayed *elsewhere* in our scientific history. With an independently based account of the nature and grounds of intertheoretic reduction, we can approach the specific case of subjective qualia, free from the myopia that results from trying to divine the proper conditions on reduction by simply staring long and hard at the problematic case at issue.

I. Intertheoretic Reduction

We may begin by remarking that the classical account of intertheoretic reduction[1] now appears to be importantly mistaken, though the repairs necessary are quickly and cleanly made. Sup-

pressing niceties, we may state the original account as follows. A new and more comprehensive theory *reduces* an older theory just in case the new theory, when conjoined with appropriate correspondence rules, logically entails the principles of the older theory. (The point of the correspondence rules, or "bridge laws," is to connect the disparate ontologies of the two theories: often these are expressed as identity statements, such as *Temperature* = $mv^2/3k$.) Schematically,

$$T_N \text{ \& (Correspondence Rules)}$$

logically entails

$$T_O$$

Difficulties with this view begin with the observation that most reduced theories turn out to be, strictly speaking and in a variety of respects, *false*. (Real gases don't really obey $PV = \mu RT$, as in classical thermodynamics; the planets don't really move in ellipses, as in Keplerian astronomy; the acceleration of falling bodies isn't really uni-

Paul Churchland, "Reduction, Qualia, and the Direct Introspection of Brain States," LXXXII:1 (January 1985), pp. 8–28. Used by permission of The Journal of Philosophy *and the author.*

form, as in Galilean dynamics; etc.) If reduction is *de*duction, modus tollens would thus require that the premises of the new reducing theories (statistical thermodynamics in the first case, Newtonian dynamics in the second and third) be somehow false as well, in contradiction to their assumed truth.

This complaint can be temporarily deflected by pointing out that the premises of a reduction must often include not just the new reducing theory but also some limiting assumptions or counterfactual boundary conditions (such as that the molecules of a gas enjoy only mechanical energy, or that the mass of the planets is negligible compared to the sun's, or that the distance any body falls is negligibly different from zero). Falsity in the reducing premises can thus be conceded, since it is safely confined to those limiting or counterfactual assumptions.

This defense will not deal with all cases of falsity, however, since in some cases the reduced theory is so radically false that some or all of its ontology must be rejected entirely, and the "correspondence rules" connecting that ontology to the newer ontology therefore display a problematic status. Newly conceived features cannot be identical with, nor even nomically connected with, old features, if the old features are illusory and uninstantiated. For example, relativistic mass is not identical with Newtonian mass, nor even coextensive with it, even at low velocities. Nevertheless, the reduction of Newtonian by Einsteinian mechanics is a paradigm of a successful reduction. For a second example, neither is caloric-fluid-pressure identical with, nor even coextensive with, mean molecular kinetic energy. But an overtly *fluid* thermodynamics (i.e., one committed to the existence of caloric) still finds a moderately impressive reduction within statistical thermodynamics. In sum, even theories with a *nonexistent* ontology can enjoy reduction, and this fact is problematic on the traditional account at issue.

What cases like these invite us to give up is the idea that what gets *de*duced in a reduction is the theory to be *re*duced. . . .

The point of a reduction, according to this view, is to show that the new or more comprehensive theory contains explanatory and predictive resources that parallel, to a relevant degree of exactness, the explanatory and predictive resources of the reduced theory. . . .

. . . it is to be expected that existing conceptual frameworks will eventually be reduced or displaced by new and better ones, and those in turn by frameworks better still; for who will be so brash as to assert that the feeble conceptual achievements of our adolescent species comprise an exhaustive account of anything at all? If we put aside this conceit, then the only alternatives to intertheoretic reduction are epistemic stagnation or the outright elimination of old frameworks as wholly false and illusory.

II. Theoretical Change and Perceptual Change

Esoteric properties and arcane theoretical frameworks are not the only things that occasionally enjoy intertheoretic reduction. Observable properties and common-sense conceptual frameworks can also enjoy smooth reduction. Thus, being a middle-A sound is identical with being an oscillation in air pressure at 440 hz; being red is identical with having a certain triplet of electromagnetic reflectance efficiencies; being warm is identical with having a certain mean level of microscopically embodied energies, and so forth.

Moreover, the relevant reducing theory is capable of replacing the old framework not just in contexts of calculation and inference. *It should be appreciated that the reducing theory can displace the old framework in all its observational contexts as well.* Given the reality of the property identities just listed, it is quite open to us to begin framing our spontaneous perceptual reports in the language of the more sophisticated reducing theory. It is even desirable that we begin doing this, since the new vocabulary observes distinctions that are in fact within the discriminatory reach of our native perceptual systems, though those objective distinctions go unmarked and unnoticed from within the old framework. We can thus make more penetrating use of our native perceptual equipment. Such displacement is also desirable for a second reason: the greater inferential or computational power of the new conceptual framework. We can thus make better inferential *use* of our new perceptual judgments than we made of our old ones.

It is difficult to convey in words the vastness of such perceptual transformations and the naturalness of the new conceptual regime, once established. A nonscientific example may help to get the initial point across.

Consider the enormous increase in discriminatory skill that spans the gap between an untrained child's auditory apprehension of a symphony and the same person's apprehension of the same symphony forty years later, heard in his capacity as conductor of the orchestra performing it. What was before a seamless voice is now a mosaic of distinguishable elements. What was before a dimly apprehended tune is now a rationally structured sequence of distinguishable and identifiable chords supporting an appropriately related melody line. The matured musician hears an entire world of structured detail, concerning which the child is both dumb and deaf.

Other modalities provide comparable examples. Consider the practiced and chemically sophisticated wine taster, for whom the "red wine" classification used by most of us divides into a network of fifteen or twenty distinguishable elements: ethanol, glycol, fructose, sucrose, tannin, acid, carbon dioxide, and so forth, whose relative concentrations he can estimate with accuracy.

Or consider the astronomer, for whom the speckled black dome of her youth has become a visible abyss, scattering nearby planets, yellow dwarf stars, blue and red giants, distant globular clusters, and even a remote galaxy or two, all discriminable as such and locatable in three-dimensional space with her unaided (repeat: *unaided*) eye.

In each of these cases, what is finally mastered is a conceptual framework—whether musical, chemical, or astronomical—a framework that embodies far more wisdom about the relevant sensory domain than is immediately apparent to untutored discrimination. Such frameworks are characteristically a cultural heritage, pieced together over many generations, and their mastery supplies a richness and penetration to our sensory lives that would be impossible in their absence.[2]

Our *introspective* lives are already the extensive beneficiaries of this phenomenon. The introspective discriminations we make are for the most part learned; they are acquired with practice and experience, often quite slowly. And the specific discriminations we learn to make are those it is useful for us to make. Generally, those are the discriminations that others are already making, the discriminations embodied in the psychological vocabulary of the language we learn. The conceptual framework for psychological states that is embedded in ordinary language is a modestly sophisticated theoretical achievement in its own right, and it shapes our matured introspection profoundly. If it embodied substantially *less* wisdom in its categories and connecting generalizations, our introspective apprehension of our internal states and activities would be much diminished, though our native discriminatory mechanisms remain the same. Correlatively, if folk psychology embodied substantially *more* wisdom about our inner nature than it actually does, our introspective discrimination and recognition could be very much *greater* than it is, though our native discriminatory mechanisms remain unchanged.

This brings me to the central positive suggestion of this paper. Consider now the possibility of learning to describe, conceive, and introspectively apprehend the teeming intricacies of our inner lives within the conceptual framework of a matured neuroscience, a neuroscience that successfully reduces, either smoothly or roughly, our common-sense folk psychology. Suppose we trained our native mechanisms to make a new and more detailed set of discriminations, a set that corresponded not to the primitive psychological taxonomy of ordinary language, but to some more penetrating taxonomy of states drawn from a completed neuroscience. And suppose we trained ourselves to respond to that reconfigured discriminative activity with judgments that were framed, as a matter of course, in the appropriate concepts from neuroscience.[3]

If the examples of the symphony conductor (who can hear the A*m7* chords), the oenologist (who can see and taste the glycol), and the astronomer (who can see the temperature of a blue giant star) provide a fair parallel, then the enhancement in our introspective vision could approximate a revelation. Dopamine levels in the limbic system, the spiking frequencies in specific neural pathways, resonances in the nth layer of the occipital cortex, inhibitory feedback to the lateral geniculate nucleus, and countless other neurophysical niceties could be moved into the objective focus of our introspective discrimination, just as G*m7* chords and A*dim* chords are moved into the objective focus of a trained musician's auditory discrimination. We will of course have to *learn* the conceptual framework of a matured neuroscience in order to pull this off. And we will have to *practice* its noninferential application. But that seems a small price to pay for the quantum leap in self-apprehension.

All of this suggests that there is no problem at all in conceiving the eventual reduction of mental states and properties to neurophysiological states and properties. A matured and successful neuroscience need only include, or prove able to define, a taxonomy of kinds with a set of embedding laws that faithfully mimics the taxonomy and causal generalizations of *folk* psychology. Whether future neuroscientific theories will prove able to do this is a wholly empirical question, not to be settled a priori. The evidence for a positive answer is substantial and familiar, centering on the growing explanatory success of the several neurosciences.

But there is negative evidence as well: I have even urged some of it myself ("Eliminative Materialism and the Propositional Attitudes," *op. cit.*). My negative arguments there center on the explanatory and predictive poverty of folk psy-

chology, and they question whether it has the categorical integrity to *merit* the reductive preservation of its familiar ontology. That line suggests substantial revision or outright elimination as the eventual fate of our mentalistic ontology. The qualia-based arguments of Nagel, Jackson, and Robinson, however, take a quite different line. They find no fault with folk psychology. Their concern is with the explanatory and descriptive poverty of any possible *neuroscience*, and their line suggests that emergence is the correct story for our mentalistic ontology. Let us now examine their arguments.

III. Thomas Nagel's Arguments

For Thomas Nagel, it is the phenomenological features of our experiences, the properties or *qualia* displayed by our sensations, that constitute a problem for the reductive aspirations of any materialistic neuroscience. In his classic position paper (*op. cit.*) I find three distinct arguments in support of the view that such properties will never find any plausible or adequate reduction within the framework of a matured neuroscience. All three arguments are beguiling, but all three, I shall argue, are unsound.

First Argument: What makes the proposed reduction of mental phenomena different from reductions elsewhere in science, says Nagel, is that

> It is impossible to exclude the phenomenological features of experience from a reduction, in the same way that one excludes the phenomenal features of an ordinary substance from a physical or chemical reduction of it — namely, by explaining them as effects on the minds of human observers (437).

The reason it is impossible to exclude them, continues Nagel, is that the phenomenological features are essential to experience and to the subjective point of view. But this is not what interests me about this argument. What interests me is the claim that reductions of various substances elsewhere in science *exclude the phenomenal features of the substance.*

This is simply false, and the point is extremely important. The phenomenal features at issue are those such as the objective redness of an apple, the warmth of a coffee cup, and the pitch of a sound. These properties are not excluded from our reductions. Redness, an objective phenomenal property of apples, is identical with a certain wavelength triplet of electromagnetic reflectance efficiencies. Warmth, an objective phenomenal property of objects, is identical with the mean level of the objects' microscopically embodied energies. Pitch, an objective phenomenal property of a sound, is identical with its oscillatory frequency. These electromagnetic and micromechanical properties, out there in the objective world, are genuine phenomenal properties. Despite widespread ignorance of their dynamical and microphysical details, it is these objective physical properties to which everyone's perceptual mechanisms are keyed.

The reductions whose existence Nagel denies are in fact so complete that one can already displace entirely large chunks of our common-sense vocabulary for observable properties and learn to frame one's perceptual judgments directly in terms of the reducing theory. The mean KE of the molecules in this room, for example, is currently about . . . 6.2×10^{-21} joules. The oscillatory frequency of this sound (I here whistle C one octave above middle C) is about 524 hz. And the three critical electromagnetic reflectance efficiencies (at .45, .53, and .63 μm) of this (white) piece of paper are all above 80 per cent. These microphysical and electromagnetic properties can be felt, heard, and seen, respectively. Our native sensory mechanisms can easily discriminate such properties, one from another, and their presence from their absence. They have been doing so for millennia. The "resolution" of these mechanisms is inadequate, of course, to reveal the microphysical details and the extended causal roles of the properties thus discriminated. But they are abundantly adequate to permit the reliable discrimination of the properties at issue.[4]

On this view, the standard perceptual properties are not "secondary" properties at all, in the standard sense which implies that they have no real existence save *inside* the minds of human observers. On the contrary, they are as objective as you please, with a wide variety of objective causal properties. Moreover, it would be a mistake even to try to "kick the phenomenal properties inwards," since that would only postpone the problem of reckoning their place in nature. We would only confront them again later, as we address the place in nature of mental phenomena. And, as Nagel correctly points out, the relocation dodge is no longer open to us, once the problematic properties are already located within the mind.

Nagel concludes from this that subjective qualia are unique in being immune from the sort of reductions found elsewhere in science. I draw a very different conclusion. The *objective* qualia (redness, warmth, etc.) should never have been "kicked inwards to the minds of observers" in the first place. They should be confronted squarely, and they should be reduced where they stand: *out*-side the human observer. As we saw, this can and has in fact been done. If objective phenomenal properties are so treated, then *subjective* qualia can be confronted with parallel forthrightness, and can be reduced where *they* stand: *in*side the human observer. So far then, the external and the internal case are not different: they are parallel after all.

Second Argument: A second argument urges the point that the intrinsic character of experiences, the qualia of sensations, are essentially accessible from only a single point of view, the subjective point of view of the experiencing subject. The properties of physical brain states, by contrast, are accessible from a variety of entirely objective points of view. We cannot hope adequately to account for the former, therefore, in terms of properties appropriate to the latter domain (cf. Nagel, 442–444).

This somewhat diffuse argument appears to be an instance of the following argument:

1. The qualia of my sensations are directly known by me, by introspection, as elements of my conscious self.

2. The properties of my brain states are *not* directly known by me, by introspection as elements of my conscious self.

∴ 3. The qualia of my sensations ≠ the properties of my brain states.

And perhaps there is a second argument here as well, a complement to the first:

1. The properties of my brain states are known-by-the-various-external-senses, as having such-and-such physical properties.
2. The qualia of my sensations are *not* known-by-the-various-external-senses, as having such-and-such physical properties.

∴ 3. The qualia of my sensations ≠ the properties of my brain states. . . .

. . . The fallacy committed in both cases is amply illustrated in the following parallel arguments.

1. Hitler is widely recognized as a mass murderer.
2. Adolf Schicklgruber is *not* widely recognized as a mass murderer.

∴ 3. Hitler ≠ Adolf Schicklgruber.

or

1. Aspirin is known by John to be a pain reliever.
2. Acetylsalicylic acid is *not* known by John to be a pain reliever.

∴ 3. Aspirin ≠ acetylsalicylic acid.

or, to cite an example very close to the case at issue,

1. Temperature is known by me, by tactile sensing, as a feature of material objects.
2. Mean molecular kinetic energy is *not* known by me, by tactile sensing, as a feature of material objects.

∴ 3. Temperature ≠ mean molecular kinetic energy.

The problem with all these arguments is that the "property" ascribed in premise 1 and withheld in premise 2 consists only in the subject item's being *recognized, perceived,* or *known* as something, *under some specific description or other.*

Such apprehension is not a genuine feature of the item itself, fit for divining identities, since one and the same subject may be successfully recognized under one description (e.g., "qualia of my mental state"), and yet fail to be recognized under another, equally accurate, coreferential description (e.g., "property of my brain state"). . . .

Third Argument: The last argument here is the one most widely associated with Nagel's paper. The leading example is the (mooted) character of the experiences enjoyed by an alien creature such as a bat. The claim is that, no matter how much one knew about the bat's neurophysiology and its interaction with the physical world, one could still not know, nor perhaps even imagine, what it is like to be a bat. Even total knowledge of the physical details still leaves something out. The lesson drawn is that the reductive aspirations of neurophysiology are doomed to dash themselves, unrealized, against the impenetrable keep of subjective qualia (cf. Nagel, 438 ff.).

This argument is almost identical with an argument put forward in a recent paper by Frank Jackson.[5] Since Jackson's version deals directly with humans, I shall confront the problem as he formulates it.

IV. Jackson's Knowledge Argument

Imagine a brilliant neuroscientist named Mary, who has lived her entire life in a room that is rigorously controlled to display only various shades of black, white, and grey. She learns about the outside world by means of a black/white television monitor, and, being brilliant, she manages to transcend these obstacles. She becomes the world's greatest neuroscientist, all from within this room. In particular, she comes to know everything there is to know about the physical structure and activity of the brain and its visual system, of its actual and possible states.

But there would still be something she did *not* know, and could not even imagine, about the actual experiences of all the other people who live outside her black/white room, and about her possible experiences were she finally to leave her room: the nature of the experience of seeing a ripe tomato, what it is like to see red or have a sensation-of-red. Therefore, complete knowledge of the physical facts of visual perception and its related brain activity *still leaves something out*. Therefore, materialism cannot give an adequate reductionist account of all mental phenomena.

To give a conveniently tightened version of this argument:

1. Mary knows everything there is to know about brain states and their properties.
2. It is not the case that Mary knows everything there is to know about sensations and their properties.

Therefore, by Leibniz's law,

3. Sensations and their properties ≠ brain states and their properties. . . .

. . . We can, I think, find at least two . . . shortcomings in this sort of argument.

The First Shortcoming: This defect is simplicity itself. 'Knows about' . . . is not *univocal* in both premises. . . . Jackson's argument is valid only if 'knows about' is univocal in both premises. But the kind of knowledge addressed in premise 1 seems pretty clearly to be different from the kind of knowledge addressed in (2). Knowledge in (1) seems to be a matter of having mastered a set of sentences or propositions, the kind one finds written in neuroscience texts, whereas knowledge in (2) seems to be a matter of having a representation of redness in some prelinguistic or sublinguistic medium of representation for sensory variables, or to be a matter of being able to *make* certain sensory discriminations, or something along these lines. . . .

. . . the difference between a person who knows all about the visual cortex but has never enjoyed a sensation of red, and a person who knows no neuroscience but knows well the sensation of red, may reside not in *what* is respectively known by each (brain states by the former, qualia by the latter), but rather in the different *type* of knowledge each has *of exactly the same thing*. The difference is in the manner of the knowing, not in the nature of the thing(s) known. . . .

. . . In sum, there are pretty clearly more ways of "having knowledge" than having mastered a set of sentences. And nothing in materialism precludes this. The materialist can freely admit that one has "knowledge" of one's sensations in a way that is independent of the scientific theories one has learned. This does not mean that sensations are beyond the reach of physical science. *It just means that the brain uses more modes and media of representation than the simple storage of sentences.* And this proposition is pretty obviously true: almost certainly the brain uses a considerable variety of modes and media of representation, perhaps hundreds of them. Jackson's argument, and Nagel's, exploit this variety illegitimately: both arguments equivocate on 'knows about.'

This criticism is supported by the observation that, if Jackson's form of argument were sound, it would prove far too much. Suppose that Jackson were arguing, not against materialism, but against dualism: against the view that there exists a nonmaterial substance — call it "ectoplasm" — whose hidden constitution and nomic intricacies ground all mental phenomena. Let our cloistered Mary be an "ectoplasmologist" this time, and let her know$_1$ everything there is to know about the ectoplasmic processes underlying vision. There would still be something she did not know$_2$: what it is like to see red. Dualism is therefore inadequate to account for all mental phenomena!

This argument is as plausible as Jackson's, and for the same reason: it exploits the same equivocation. But the truth is, such arguments show nothing, one way or the other, about how mental phenomena might be accounted for.

The Second Shortcoming: There is a further short-coming with Jackson's argument, one of profound importance for understanding one of the most exciting consequences to be expected from a successful neuroscientific account of mind. I draw your attention to the assumption that even a utopian knowledge of neuroscience *must* leave Mary hopelessly in the dark about the subjective qualitative nature of sensations not-yet-enjoyed. It is true, of course, that no sentence of the form "*x* is a sensation-of-red" will be deducible from premises restricted to the language of neuro-science. But this is no point against the reducibility of phenomenological properties. As we saw in section I, direct deducibility is an intolerably strong demand on reduction, and if this is all the objection comes to, then there is no objection worth addressing. What the defender of emergent qualia must have in mind here, I think, is the claim that Mary could not even *imagine* what the relevant experience would be like, despite her exhaustive neuroscientific knowledge, and hence must still be missing certain crucial information.

This claim, however, is simply false. Given the truth of premise 1, premise 2 seems plausible to Jackson, Nagel, and Robinson only because none of these philosophers has adequately considered how much one might know if, as premise 1 asserts, one knew *everything* there is to know about the physical brain and nervous system. In particular, none of these philosophers has even begun to consider the changes in our introspective apprehension of our internal states that could follow upon a wholesale revision in our conceptual framework for our internal states.

The fact is, we can indeed imagine how neuro-scientific information would give Mary detailed information about the qualia of various sensations. Recall our earlier discussion of the transformation of perception through the systematic reconceptualization of the relevant perceptual domain. In particular, suppose that Mary has learned to conceptualize her inner life, even in introspection, in terms of the completed neuro-science we are to imagine. So she does not identify her visual sensations crudely as "a sensation-of-black," "a sensation-of-grey," or "a sensation-of-white"; rather she identifies them more revealingly as various spiking frequencies in the *n*th layer of the occipital cortex (or whatever). If Mary has the relevant neuroscientific concepts for the sensational states at issue (viz., sensations-of-*red*), but has never yet been *in* those states, she may well be able to imagine being in the relevant cortical state, and imagine it with substantial success, even in advance of receiving external stimuli that would actually produce it.

One test of her ability in this regard would be to give her a stimulus that would (finally) produce in her the relevant state (viz., a spiking frequency of 90 hz in the gamma network: a "sensation-of-red" to us), and see whether she can identify it correctly *on introspective grounds alone*, as "a spiking frequency of 90 hz: the kind a tomato would cause." It does not seem to me to be impossible that she should succeed in this, and do so regularly on similar tests for other states, conceptualized clearly by her, but not previously enjoyed.

This may seem to some an outlandish suggestion, but the following will show that it is not. Musical chords are auditory phenomena that the young and unpracticed ear hears as undivided wholes, discriminable one from another, but without elements or internal structure. A musical education changes this, and one comes to hear chords as groups of discriminable notes. If one is sufficiently practiced to have absolute pitch, one can even name the notes of an apprehended chord. And the reverse is also true: if a set of notes is specified verbally, a trained pianist or guitarist can identify the chord and recall its sound in auditory imagination. Moreover, a really skilled individual can construct, in auditory imagination, the sound of a chord he may never have heard before, and certainly does not remember. Specify for him a relatively unusual one — an F ♯ 9th*add*13th for example — and let him brood for a bit. Then play for him three or four chords, one of which is the target, and see whether he can pick it out as the sound that meets the description. Skilled musicians can do this. Why is a similar skill beyond all possibility for Mary?

"Ah," it is tempting to reply, "musicians can do this only because chords are audibly structured sets of elements. Sensations of color are not."

But neither did chords seem, initially, to be structured sets of elements. They also seemed to be undifferentiated wholes. Why should it be unthinkable that sensations of color possess a comparable internal structure, unnoticed so far, but awaiting our determined and informed inspection? Jackson's argument, to be successful, must rule this possibility out, and it is difficult to see how he can do this *a priori*. Especially since there has recently emerged excellent empirical evidence to suggest that *our sensations of color are indeed structured sets of elements*. . . .

I do not mean to suggest, of course, that there will be no limits to what Mary can imagine. Her brain is finite, and its specific anatomy will have specific limitations. For example, if a bat's brain includes computational machinery that the human brain simply lacks (which seems likely), then the subjective character of *some* of the bat's internal states may well be beyond human imagination. Clearly, however, the elusiveness of the bat's inner life here stems not from the metaphysical "emergence" of its internal qualia, but only from the finite capacities of our idiosyncratically human brains. Within those sheerly structural limitations, our imaginations may soar far beyond what Jackson, Nagel, and Robinson suspect, if we possess a neuroscientific conceptual framework that is at last adequate to the intricate phenomena at issue.

I suggest then, that those of us who prize the flux and content of our subjective phenomenological experience need not view the advance of materialistic neuroscience with fear and foreboding. Quite the contrary. The genuine arrival of a materialist kinematics and dynamics for psychological state and cognitive processes will constitute not a gloom in which our inner life is suppressed or eclipsed, but rather a dawning, in which its marvelous intricacies are finally *revealed* — most notably, if we apply ourselves, in direct self-conscious introspection.

NOTES

1. Ernest Nagel, *The Structures of Science* (New York: Harcourt, Brace & World, 1961), ch. 11.

2. The role of theory in perception, and the systematic enhancement of perception through theoretical progress, are examined at length in my *Scientific Realism and the Plasticity of Mind, op. cit.* secs. 1–6.

3. I believe it was Paul K. Feyerabend and Richard Rorty who first identified and explored this suggestion. See Feyerabend, "Materialism and the Mind-Body Problem," *Review of Metaphysics*, XVIII.1, 65 (September 1963): 49–66; and Rorty, "Mind-Body Identity, Privacy, and Categories," *ibid.* XIX.1, 73 (September 1965): 24–54. This occurred in a theoretical environment prepared largely by Wilfrid Sellars in "Empiricism and the Philosophy of Mind," in Herbert Feigl and Michael Scriven, eds., *Minnesota Studies in the Philosophy of Mind*, vol. I (Minneapolis: University of Minnesota Press, 1956): secs. 45–63. The idea has been explored more recently in my "Eliminative Materialism and the Propositional Attitudes," this JOURNAL, LXXVIII, 2 (February 1981): 67–90.

4. See again my *Scientific Realism and the Plasticity of Mind, op. cit.*, secs. 2–6. See also Paul and Patricia Churchland, "Functionalism, Qualia, and Intentionality," *Philosophical Topics*, XII, 1 (October 1981): 121–145. Reprinted in J. I. Biro and R. W. Shahan, eds., in *Mind, Brain, and Function* (Norman: U of Oklahoma Press, 1982): 121–145.

5. "Epiphenomenal Qualia," *op. cit.* Howard Robinson runs a very similar argument in *Matter and Sense, op. cit.*, p. 4.

Further Questions

1. Churchland thinks we should drop our familiar vocabulary for describing our experiences and start describing them in the language of neuroscience. Why? Do you agree?

2. Which is the more plausible view of consciousness — reductionism or anti-reductionism?

Further Readings

Hofstadter, Douglas, and Daniel Dennett, eds. *The Mind's I*. New York: Basic Books, 1981. A mind-jolting collection. Interdisciplinary, including some excellent fiction.

McGinn, Colin. *The Character of Mind*. New York: Oxford University Press, 1982. A good, concise introduction.

Subjectivity

PAUL TELLER

Paul Teller teaches philosophy at the University of Illinois at Chicago and writes primarily on the philosophy of quantum theory. In this selection he attempts to further support the reductionist arguments presented by Churchland in the preceding selection. Teller agrees with Churchland that when Mary (the Mary of Jackson's example) first experiences colors, she does not learn anything that counts against physicalism. What Teller adds to Churchland's arguments is an explanation, congenial to physicalism, of why Mary *seems* to learn something that counts against physicalism.

Reading Questions

1. Teller concedes that the color-blind person (of his example) does not know what it is like to have the sensation of seeing something red, and hence that the color-blind person lacks something that the normally sighted person has. What?

2. Why, in Teller's view, doesn't the color-blind person's lacking this thing count against physicalism?

3. Why does Teller think the "subjectivity of experience is perfectly real, but redundant"?

4. What is the main reason descriptions fail to account fully for experience?

MARY, THE NEUROSCIENTIST with only black and white visual stimuli, learns something new when she first sees a ripe tomato. All parties agree that we can describe this learned new element as "learning what the experience of seeing something red is like." But what does this new knowledge involve?

In what is called the "knowledge argument," anti-physicalists insist that we are dealing with new knowledge of an emergent fact, transcending all objective physical facts which can be expressed in language or which can be known from a variety of "points of view." But physicalists, such as Nemirow [1980] and Lewis [1983], sug-

This essay was written expressly for this volume.

gest that what Mary learns is not a new fact. They suggest that Mary does not learn *that* anything at all. Instead, Mary learns *how* to do something — what she gains is an ability. In having the experience of seeing something red, she learns such things as how to recognize red by looking and how to imagine the experience. Often we gain such abilities only by having the experience, though Churchland [1985] shows that there can be alternative ways to such learning.

Pointing to abilities gained shows that, although we agree that Mary has learned something new, we have an alternative to saying that Mary has learned some new (nonphysical) fact. But this defense of physicalism does not yet convince because it does not show us why what is learned *seems* to involve a new fact. The ability defense does not address the intuited "subjective" or "qualitative" aspect of experience in which the nonphysical aspect of experience is supposed to lie.

What we call the subjectivity of experience is perfectly real, but, I suggest that the impression that it involves special facts arises from a confusion. Suppose we are in an advanced state of science which provides us with all the (Jackson) "physical" or (Nagel) "objective" facts. Suppose now that we arrange for a normally sighted person and a color-blind person to look at a clearly lit bright red patch. Lab assistants use cerebroscopes and other devices to collect all the relevant physical/objective facts, which they then communicate to the two subjects. According to the knowledge argument, the color-blind subject is still missing something that the normally sighted subject has — there is something that all this factual information leaves out. The color-blind subject still does not know "what it is like" to see something red. All the objective facts fail to communicate the experiences's "subjective element." Without yet knowing what the missing element is, must we not agree that the color-blind person misses something which the normally sighted person has?

Yes, of course! When all the facts have been communicated, the color-blind person still will not have the sensation of seeing something red. He will not be in that state. No matter what information we pass on, we will not thereby produce the neurological or other physical state which constitutes having the sensation. I submit that herein lies the alleged "missing subjective element." Put bluntly, I think people conflate the *having* of the experience with some occult further fact about the experience, about the straightforwardly objective state of the body which constitutes the experiential state.

If I am right, the so-called subjectivity of experience is perfectly real, but also redundant. The subjectivity of experience is nothing more than the having of an experience, the being in that state. The idea that experience must involve some kind of "subjective element" that goes beyond physical/objective facts is an illusion that arises because we can successfully communicate all the facts (the objective facts — there is no other kind) about a state to a person without thereby inducing that person to be in that state. But this circumstance should occasion no surprise. All the facts about a state are one thing. The state itself is quite another.

I suspect that this simple point was the one Einstein wanted to make when he said (so I've been told) that science cannot give you the taste of chicken soup.

Descriptions fall short of experience, trivially, because they are not the experience described. But what about the knowing what seeing red is like which the color-blind subject never has but which the normally sighted subject retains even when we take the red patch away and her sensation ceases? Here is where the ability analysis plays an essential role. The normally sighted person, unlike the color-blind one, can at will conjure up a memory of the sensation — she can imagine the experience. But the memory or imaging state is plausibly thought to be somewhat analogous to the full blown color sensing state. (People differ in how closely their imagining states resemble the full blown versions.) Insofar as "knowing what it's like" to have an experience goes beyond simply being in the relevant state, this knowledge constitutes the ability to get oneself into another state, relevantly like the original, which thereby counts as imagining the original, and which comes with its own "subjective element," its own "what it's like," amounting to nothing other than simply being in the state in question.

NOTE

The ideas presented here are discussed in more detail in Paul Teller, "Subjectivity and Knowing What It's Like," forthcoming.

References

Churchland, Paul. "Reduction, Qualia, and the Direct Introspection of Brain States," *Journal of Philosophy*, 82(1985)8–28.

Lewis, David. "Postscript to 'Mad Pain and Martian Pain,'" *Philosophical Papers*, Vol. I, Oxford University Press.

Nemirov, Laurence. "Review: Thomas Nagel, *Mortal Questions*," *Philosophical Review*, 89(1980)373–377.

Further Questions

1. Teller agrees that there is more to visual experience than meets the eye. This extra something is just the firing of neurons in the brain. But if Teller is right, shouldn't the subjective aspect of having an experience be fully describable by a scientific account of this neural activity? Is it?

2. Is it possible that subjectivistic descriptions can convey something not conveyed by scientific descriptions even though both describe exactly the same things? If so, in learning that the subjectivistic description is true, aren't we learning something new? A new fact? One that counts against physicalism?

Further Readings

Dennett, Daniel. *Brainstorms*. Montgomery, VT: Bradford Books, 1978. Sophisticated yet accessible essays by a well-known reductionist.

Fodor, J. *Representations*. Cambridge: M.I.T. Press, 1981. Ideas represent reality. How can neural activity *represent* anything? An answer from a leading philosopher of mind.

Part X

Nothingness

THE PHILOSOPHER JEAN-PAUL SARTRE WROTE, "Nothingness lies coiled in the heart of being, like a worm."

We may think we understand what it is to be. But how can we understand what it is to be if we don't understand what it is to *not* be?

We understand emptiness. Emptiness is not nothingness. Emptiness is the hollow core of something. Nothingness is wholly other. But what? It is not *to be*. It is to *not* be.

To *not be*? That is the question.

The Problem of Being

WILLIAM JAMES

Here William James argues that the problem of why anything at all exists is fundamental and inescapable. Either you have to assume a big unknown, all at once, or you must assume a bunch of little unknowns piecemeal. What is remarkable about this selection, aside from its clarity and precision, is that it was written years before the debate between the Big Bang and Steady State cosmological theorists. According to the first, the entire universe just pops into existence from nothing. According to the second, the universe is infinitely old and matter pops in out of nothing one electron at a time.

A biographical sketch of James appears on page 176–177.

Reading Questions

1. By "the world," James (like most philosophers) means not the planet earth but "the universe as a whole." He is asking you to think about why and how the universe came to be, why anything at all exists rather than nothing. This is probably one of the biggest Big Questions of all time. Have you ever thought about it? When, and why? What happens when you think about it? How does it make you feel?

2. What does James mean by "philosophic wonder" turning into "a sad astonishment"?

3. Do you think anyone will ever find an answer to the ultimate question? James says "we are all beggars here." What does he mean? Do you agree? Do you know of anyone, or of any group, that claims *not* to be a beggar on this point, but to have an answer?

4. What is the distinction between rationalist and empiricist treatments of the problem?

Schopenhauer on the Origin of the Problem

HOW COMES THE WORLD TO BE here at all instead of the nonentity which might be imagined in its place? Schopenhauer's remarks on this question may be considered classical. 'Apart from man,' he says, 'no being wonders at its own existence. When man first becomes conscious, he takes himself for granted, as something needing no explanation. But not for long; for, with the rise of the first reflection, that wonder begins which is the mother of metaphysics, and which made Aristotle say that men now and always seek to philosophize because of wonder — The lower a man stands in intellectual respects the less of a riddle does existence seem to him . . . but, the clearer his consciousness becomes the more the problem grasps him in its greatness. In fact the unrest which keeps the never stopping clock of metaphysics going is the thought that the non-existence of this world is just as possible as its existence. Nay more, we soon conceive the world as something the non-existence of which not only is conceivable but would indeed be preferable to its existence; so that our wonder passes easily into a brooding over that fatality which nevertheless could call such a world into being, and mislaid the immense force that could produce and preserve it into an activity so hostile to its own interests. The philosophic wonder thus becomes a sad astonishment, and like the overture to Don Giovanni, philosophy begins with a minor chord.'[1]

One need only shut oneself in a closet and begin to think of the fact of one's being there, of one's queer bodily shape in the darkness (a thing to make children scream at, as Stevenson says), of

one's fantastic character and all, to have the wonder steal over the detail as much as over the general fact of being, and to see that it is only familiarity that blunts it. Not only that *anything* should be, but that *this* very thing should be, is mysterious! Philosophy stares, but brings no reasoned solution, for from nothing to being there is no logical bridge.

Various Treatments of the Problem

Attempts are sometimes made to banish the question rather than to give it an answer. Those who ask it, we are told, extend illegitimately to the whole of being the contrast to a supposed alternative non-being which only particular beings possess. These, indeed, were not, and now are. But being in general, or in some shape, always was, and you cannot rightly bring the whole of it into relation with a primordial nonentity. Whether as God or as material atoms, it is itself primal and eternal. But if you call any being whatever eternal, some philosophers have always been ready to taunt you with the paradox inherent in the assumption. Is past eternity completed? they ask: If so, they go on, it must have had a beginning; for whether your imagination traverses it forwards or backwards, it offers an identical content or stuff to be measured; and if the amount comes to an end in one way, it ought to come to an end in the other. In other words, since we now witness its end, some past movement must have witnessed its beginning. If, however, it had a beginning, when was that, and why?

You are up against the previous nothing, and do not see how it ever passed into being. This dilemma, of having to choose between a regress

Chapter 3 from Some Problems of Philosophy, *by William James, Longmans, Green and Co., 1911.*

which, although called infinite, has nevertheless come to a termination, and an absolute first, has played a great part in philosophy's history.

Other attempts still are made at exorcising the question. Non-being is not, said Parmenides and Zeno; only being is. Hence what is, is necessarily being — being, in short, is necessary. Others, calling the idea of nonentity no real idea, have said that on the absence of an idea can no genuine problem be founded. More curtly still, the whole ontological wonder has been called diseased, a case of *Grübelsucht* like asking, 'Why am I myself?' or 'Why is a triangle a triangle?'

Rationalist and Empiricist Treatments

Rationalistic minds here and there have sought to reduce the mystery. Some forms of being have been deemed more natural, so to say, or more inevitable and necessary than others. Empiricists of the evolutionary type — Herbert Spencer seems a good example — have assumed that whatever had the least of reality, was weakest, faintest, most imperceptible, most nascent, might come easiest first, and be the earliest successor to nonentity. Little by little the fuller grades of being might have added themselves in the same gradual way until the whole universe grew up.

To others not the minimum, but the maximum of being has seemed the earliest First for the intellect to accept. 'The perfection of a thing does not keep it from existing,' Spinoza said, 'on the contrary, it founds its existence.'[2] It is mere prejudice to assume that it is harder for the great than for the little to be, and that easiest of all it is to be nothing. What makes things difficult in any line is the alien obstructions that are met with, and the smaller and weaker the thing the more powerful over it these become. Some things are so great and inclusive that to be is implied in their very nature. The anselmian or ontological proof of God's existence, sometimes called the cartesian proof, criticised by Saint Thomas, rejected by Kant, re-defended by Hegel, follows this line of thought. What is conceived as imperfect may lack being among its other lacks, but if God, who is expressly defined as *Ens perfectissimum*, lacked anything whatever, he would contradict his own definition. . . .

Hegel in his lordly way says: 'It would be strange if God were not rich enough to embrace so poor a category as Being, the poorest and most abstract of all.' This is somewhat in line with Kant's saying that a real dollar does not contain one cent more than an imaginary dollar. At the beginning of his logic Hegel seeks in another way to mediate nonentity with being. Since 'being' in the abstract, mere being, means nothing in particular, it is indistinguishable from 'nothing'; and he seems dimly to think that this constitutes an identity between the two notions, of which some use may be made in getting from one to the other. Other still queerer attempts show well the rationalist temper. Mathematically you can deduce 1 from 0 by the following process: $\frac{0}{0} = \frac{1-1}{1-1} = 1$. Or physically if all being has (as it seems to have) a 'polar' construction, so that every positive part of it has its negative, we get the simple equation: $+1-1=0$, *plus* and *minus* being the signs of polarity in physics.

The Same Amount of Existence Must Be Begged by All

It is not probable that the reader will be satisfied with any of these solutions, and contemporary philosophers, even rationalistically minded ones, have on the whole agreed that no one has intelligibly banished the mystery of *fact*. Whether the original nothing burst into God and vanished, as night vanishes in day, while God thereupon became the creative principle of all lesser beings; or whether all things have foisted or shaped themselves imperceptibly into existence, the same amount of existence has in the end to be assumed and begged by the philosopher. To comminute the difficulty is not to quench it. . . . you are the same beggar whatever you may pretend. You leave the logical riddle untouched, of how the coming of whatever is, came it all at once, or came it piecemeal, can be intellectually understood.[3]

Conservation vs. Creation

If being gradually *grew*, its quantity was of course not always the same, and may not be the same hereafter. To most philosophers this view has seemed absurd, neither God, nor primordial matter, nor energy being supposed to admit of increase or decrease. The orthodox opinion is that the quantity of reality must at all costs be conserved, and the waxing and waning of our phenomenal experiences must be treated as surface appearances which leave the deeps untouched.

Nevertheless, within experience, phenomena come and go. There are novelties; there are losses. The world seems, on the concrete and proximate level at least, really to grow. So the question recurs: How do our finite experiences come into being from moment to moment? By inertia? By perpetual creation? Do the new ones come at the call of the old ones? Why do not they all go out like a candle?

Who can tell off-hand? The question of being is the darkest in all philosophy. All of us are beggars here, and no school can speak disdainfully of another or give itself superior airs. For all of us alike, Fact forms a datum . . . which we cannot burrow under, explain or get behind. It makes itself somehow, and our business is far more with its What than with its Whence or Why.

NOTES

1. *The World as Will and Representation:* Appendix 17, 'On the metaphysical need of man,' abridged.
2. *Ethics*, part i, prop. xi, scholium.
3. In more technical language, one may say that fact or being is 'contingent,' or matter of 'chance,' so far as our intellect is concerned. The conditions of its appearance are uncertain, unforeseeable, when future, and when past, elusive.

Further Questions

1. James writes, "The question of being is the darkest in all philosophy." Why? Do you agree?
2. Do you think the best way to approach the problem would be through religion? Through science? Can you state how a *philosophical* approach might differ from both of these?

Further Readings

Heidegger, Martin. *An Introduction to Metaphysics.* New York: Anchor Books, 1961. This entire little book, sometimes beautifully clear and sometimes beautifully unclear, is devoted to the question, "Why is there something rather than nothing?"

Nozick, Robert. *Philosophical Explanations.* Cambridge: Harvard University Press, 1981, Chapter Two, "Why Is There Something Rather Than Nothing?" A prominent contemporary philosopher gives his views on "explaining everything" and "mystical experience."

Schopenhauer, Arthur. *The World As Will and Representation*, translated by E. F. J. Payne. New York: Dover, 1966, Vol. II, Ch. XVII, "On Man's Need for Metaphysics." Contains the passages quoted by James.

Is the Universe a Free Lunch?

PAUL DAVIES

Traditionally, the problem of the creation of the universe has been a religious, not a scientific, question. As you are about to see, over the last two decades this has changed dramatically. In the selection that follows, physicist Paul Davies (his biography appears on page 82) takes you to the very beginning of the universe — to the Big Bang *and beyond* —

Reading Questions

1. What strikes you about the way cosmologists reason about the origin of the universe? How would you describe their method? What do you think is good about it? Can you think of any shortcomings?

2. A "singularity" is what physicists call regions of the universe where the known physical laws break down. In that sense, the creation of the universe from nothing, the Big Bang, is a singularity. How, then, can physicists reason *beyond* the Big Bang?

3. The singularity, writes Davies, "is the one place in the universe where there is room, even for the most hard-nosed materialist, to admit God." Do you agree? Why?

4. How do you react to the "ultimate answers" that science provides to the ultimate question? Do you prefer religion's "ultimate answers"? Why, or why not? Which is better? Why? In what ways are they similar? In what ways are they different?

'Nothing can be created out of nothing.'

LUCRETIUS

WE CAN NOW DRAW TOGETHER all the strands of our investigation to construct a cosmic scenario that reveals the astonishing scope of the new physics to explain the physical world. I am not suggesting the scenario should be taken too seriously (though it is being discussed seriously by physicists). It does, however, illustrate the sort of ideas that modern physics has thrown up — ideas which cannot be ignored in our search for God.

. . . I posed what I called the challenge of the Big Four questions of existence: 'Why are the laws of nature what they are? Why does the universe consist of the things it does? How did those things arise? How did the universe achieve its organization?'

The new physics has gone a long way to provide answers for these questions. To take them in reverse order, we have seen how an initially chaotic state can evolve into a more orderly one provided there is a supply of negative entropy. We have also seen how that negative entropy can be generated by the expansion of the universe, so that there is no longer any need to assume, as did the scientists of earlier generations, that the universe was somehow created in a highly organized, specially arranged state. The present organization is consistent with a universe that began accidentally in a random state.

The question of the origin of physical things has been discussed in detail in the early chapters. Objects such as stars and planets are known to have formed from the primeval gases, while the cosmic material itself was evidently created in the big bang. Recent discoveries in particle physics have suggested mechanisms whereby matter can be created in empty space by the cosmic gravitational field, which only leaves the origin of spacetime itself as a mystery. But even here there are some indications that space and time could have sprung into existence spontaneously without violating the laws of physics. The reason for this bizarre possibility concerns the quantum theory.

We have seen how the quantum factor permits events to occur without causes in the subatomic world. Particles, for example, can appear out of nowhere without specific causation. When the quantum theory is extended to gravity, it involves the behaviour of spacetime itself. Although there is still no satisfactory theory of quantum gravity, physicists have a good idea of the broad features that would be entailed in such a theory. It would, for example, endow space and time with the same sort of fuzzy unpredictability that characterizes quantum matter. In particular, it would allow spacetime to be created and destroyed spontaneously and uncaused in the same way that particles are created and destroyed spontaneously and uncaused. The theory would entail a certain mathematically determined probability that, for instance, a blob of space would appear where none existed before. Thus, spacetime could pop out of nothingness as the result of a causeless quantum transition.

On general grounds the abrupt appearance of spacetime by a quantum mechanism might be expected to occur solely on an ultramicroscopic scale, because quantum processes usually apply only to microscopic phenomena. Indeed, the spontaneously created space might typically be only 10^{-33} cm in size. This finite blob of space need have no edges, however: it could be closed into a hypersphere. . . . Probably such a mini-universe would rapidly disappear again by another, reverse, quantum fluctuation. Nevertheless, there is a chance that, rather than fading away, the newly created blob of space will suddenly begin to inflate like a balloon.

The origin of this behaviour would lie with other quantum processes associated, not with gravity, but with the remaining forces of nature. . . . I briefly described the so-called 'inflationary universe scenario' in which the 'grand unified force' causes the nascent universe to become unstable and embark upon a phase of runaway exponential expansion. In this way the quantum microworld could swell to cosmic proportions in a minute fraction of a second. The energy accumulated in this big bang would, at the abrupt termination of the inflationary phase, become converted into matter and radiation, and the universe would then proceed according to conventional understanding.

In this remarkable scenario, the entire cosmos simply comes out of nowhere, completely in accordance with the laws of quantum physics, and creates along the way all the matter and energy needed to build the universe we now see. It thus incorporates the creation of all physical things, including space and time. Rather than postulate an unknowable singularity to start the universe off . . . the quantum spacetime model attempts to explain everything entirely within the context of the laws of physics. It is an awesome claim. We are used to the idea of 'putting something in and getting something out,' but getting something for nothing (or out of nothing) is alien. Yet the world of quantum physics routinely produces something for nothing. Quantum gravity suggests we might get everything for nothing. Discussing this scenario, the physicist Alan Guth remarked: 'It is often said that there is no such thing as a free lunch. The universe, however, is a free lunch.'

Does such a universe model have any need for God? . . . We saw how one traditional cosmological argument for God proceeded on the assumption that everything must have a cause. Quantum physics has confounded this claim. But what of the remaining two questions? Why does the universe possess the things and the laws it does? Can science provide an answer?

. . . It was explained how the goal of the so-called supergravity theory is to provide a mathematical description for all the forces of nature and all the fundamental particles of matter. If successful, this theory would reduce the remaining two questions to one. The 'things' of which the world is composed — protons, neutrons, mesons, electrons, and so on — would be accounted for within the framework of the supergravity theory. At present, the status of the physical laws is rather different. We generally know how an electron or a proton behaves once we have it, but we have no real idea of why there *are* electrons or protons and not particles of quite different properties. If supergravity is fully successful, it will tell us not only why there are the particles that exist, but also why they have the masses, charges and other properties that they do.

All of this will follow from a magnificent mathematical theory that will encompass all of physics (in the reductionist sense) in one superlaw. But we come back still to the question: why *that* superlaw?

We have thus reached the ultimate question of existence. Physics can perhaps explain the content, origin and organization of the physical universe, but not the laws (or superlaw) of physics itself. Traditionally, God is credited with having invented the laws of nature and created the things (spacetime, atoms, people, among others) on which those laws operate. The 'free lunch' scenario claims that all you need are the laws — the universe can take care of itself, including its own creation.

But what of the laws? They have to be 'there' to start with so that the universe can come into being. Quantum physics has to exist (in some sense) so that a quantum transition can generate the cosmos in the first place. Many scientists believe that the question of why the laws of physics are what they are is meaningless, or at least cannot be answered scientifically. Others have argued 'anthropically,' maintaining that the laws must be such as to admit observers. But there is a further possibility. Perhaps the laws — or the ultimate superlaw — will emerge to be the only *logically* possible physical principle. . . .

Further Questions

1. All the information about the universe that modern astronomers and astrophysicists have collected with their telescopes in 100 years is deduced from an amount of light that is equivalent to the energy of one snowflake hitting the surface of the earth. Relate this to the Problem of Induction raised by Bertrand Russell in the selection titled "Perception, Knowledge, and Induction." How do you suppose a physicist would respond? Better yet, ask one.

2. When you picture the creation of the universe as science envisions it, what does it look like? What does the nothingness that preceded it look like? How does it make you feel to push your imagination to such limits?

3. In the end, Davies suggests that the ultimate bottom line of everything is the underlying physical laws. But why these laws, rather than no laws? Has the ultimate question of existence really been answered? Do you think it ever will be?

Further Readings

Those who have had some physics, and certainly physics or astronomy or general science majors, should look up the following articles that explore what Davies calls "the less bold" theories — that the universe is a vacuum fluctuation from empty, flat spacetime.

Atkatz, D. and H. Pagels. "Origin of the Universe as a Quantum Tunneling Event." *Physical Review D 25*, 2065 (1982).

Brout, R., F. Englert, and E. Gunzig. "The Creation of the Universe as a Quantum Phenomenon." *Annals of Physics 115*, 78 (1978).

Tryon, E. P. "Is the Universe a Vacuum Fluctuation?" in *Nature 246*, 396 (1973).

For a sample of what Davies calls "the bolder versions," where the universe is a vacuum fluctuation *from nothing at all*, see the following.

Grishchuk, L. P. and Ya. B. Zeldovich. "Complete Cosmological Theories," in *The Quantum Theory of Space and Time*. M. J. Duff and C. J. Isham, eds. Cambridge: Cambridge University Press, 1982.

Vilenkin, A. "Creation of the Universe from Nothing." *Physics Letters B117*, 15 (1982).

For less technical and easy-to-read versions, see any of the fine books by Paul Davies, especially the following:

Davies, Paul. *The Edge of Infinity: Where the Universe Came From and How It Will End*. New York: Simon & Schuster, 1981.

——*God and the New Physics*. New York: Simon & Schuster, 1983.

——*Superforce*. New York: Touchstone, 1984.

For more on the Anthropic Principle, the best and most up-to-date book thus far written on the subject is:

Barrow, John, and Frank Tipler. *The Anthropic Cosmological Principle*. Oxford: Oxford University Press, 1986.

Part XI

Death

WHEREVER YOU GO, WHATEVER YOU DO, an armed assassin walks behind you. The nozzle presses cold against your neck. The gun is cocked, the bullet ready to shatter you forever.

You have no place to run, nowhere to hide. No one can help you. The assassin's finger is always on the trigger. Always.

Why doesn't he blow you away? Not yet. But soon. At any moment. Maybe now as you're reading this. Maybe you won't finish this page, this paragraph, this sentence, this word.

How do you feel?

Probably, you say to yourself there is no assassin. No gun. No bullet. But the truth is this: the bullet has already been fired. The bullet will find you. The bullet goes through walls, beliefs, schemes — it pierces everything in its relentless journey. Your death is on its way to you. Now.

Assassins are superfluous. Murder is superfluous. Suicide is superfluous. Life itself is all these things and then some. Death never misses. No one gets out alive.

What does death mean? *Your* death, something you can do nothing about yet which you must face and face alone, unarmed, defenseless, utterly naked. It waits for you: the ultimate unknown.

The Wine Is in the Glass

DANIEL KOLAK

In this short story a man sits alone in a restaurant. While waiting for his food to arrive, he ruminates.

A biography of Daniel Kolak appears on page 330.

Reading Questions

1. How often do you eat alone, without a book or magazine or television to distract you? Does it make you uncomfortable to sit and eat by yourself in a restaurant? Why?

2. What do you think about this man? Would you like to join him? What would you ask him? How might he respond?

THE WINE IS IN THE GLASS.

There is a man looking at the wine, thinking: there is wine in the glass and it is true that there is wine in the glass. I am the man looking at the glass, thinking: what is in the man, in me?

The man picks up the glass, raises the rim to his lips, purses his lips and, slowly, takes a sip. He swal-lows. He puts the glass back down onto the table.

There is now a little less wine in the glass. But now there is a little wine in the man, who thinks: the wine is still wine, it is in me. Soon it will change from wine to blood. It will become me. The wine becomes my blood. He smiles, and thinks: I don't know how to turn blood into wine but I know how to turn wine into blood. Actually, I don't. I couldn't do it outside me. Inside me, I just do it. Automatically. Without effort or thought. This is not a miracle. This is digestion. He burps (quietly, under his breath, to himself).

There are creases in the white tablecloth. He straightens them and wonders why, what the significance of it is. He concludes there is no significance. To the act of removing creases from a tablecloth, that is. Why, then, did he do it? He doesn't know. But he cares that he doesn't know. And, it bothers him that he cares. It also bothers him, now that he has reflected upon it, that he can't quite remove the creases. They have been ironed in. It wouldn't take much to do the ironing right. Whoever was ironing the tablecloth was in a hurry, or perhaps careless. If whoever ironed the tablecloth had been more attentive to the tablecloth now he, an ordinary man in a rather expensive restaurant passing time with ordinary thoughts while waiting to order his hopefully extraordinary dinner, would not be trying to straighten out the creases and thinking about it and also at the same time wondering why he was thinking about an inconsequential crease in an inconsequential tablecloth. He would be doing something else, thinking about something else or maybe not thinking about anything.

The man smiles to himself. To acknowledge that it is only to himself that he smiled he lowers his eyes to the crease on the tablecloth and shakes his head a little just in case anyone else is looking. Why did he do that? He does not know anybody in this restaurant. Nobody knows him. What does he care? But he does. How strange, he thinks, that he should be so self-conscious. He glances around the restaurant. No one is looking at him. Back to the crease in the tablecloth. Then to the wine in the glass. His image is in the wine.

The waiter, who noticed the man looking, rushes over.

"Ready to order, sir?"

"I'll have the blackened grouper."

"Baked potato or cottage fries?"

"What are cottage fries? Never mind. Baked potato."

"Like chips. Sliced."

"I'll have the baked."

"Salad or cole slaw?"

"Cole slaw. No. Make that salad."

"What kind of dressing would you like, sir?"

"What have you got?"

"We've got —"

"Italian?"

"Is creamy all right?"

"You don't have, ah, regular?"

"Our house is vinaigrette."

"Oh."

"Would you like that?"

"Fine."

The man stares at his image staring back at him from the wine in the glass while the waiter rushes off toward the kitchen. The man picks up the glass and then, changing his mind, puts it back down. His image stares back at him. He forgot to ask about bread. He would like some bread with his wine before the salad comes. He looks up but the waiter is gone.

The man thinks: what should I think about? I am by myself in a restaurant waiting for my food and I have time to think. But there is nothing in particular he wants to think about. Yet he feels anxious — only slightly — feeling as if he wants something only he doesn't quite know what. The food, ordered, would be coming. He would eat it and enjoy it and then walk to his car and drive home. Laughing (to himself) he shakes his head again. Why is he anticipating going home after the restaurant? Where else but home would he go? Translucent and dim little pictures flash through his consciousness, superimposed over his field of vision but so very dimly that he knows it is too much to think of them as actual pictures. They are like shadows of pictures. A bit like interference from another channel on a television set, only dimmer. The future, perhaps, inter-fearing with the present? He laughs at the pun. Inter-fearing. A possible future, perhaps. How strange, he thinks, that such thoughts run through his head. Thoughts paying attention to thoughts (inter-fearing with themselves) and thinking about why this is happening and then remarking — to whom, themselves? — that they are aware of what they (the thoughts) are doing —

The waiter comes with the salad and, the man is glad to see, a basket with fresh-baked bread. He remembers the time his girlfriend brought a basket, similar to this one, from Mexico as a present for his parents and there had been, hidden in it, some tiny eggs that had hatched into bugs. They discovered the bugs because the freshly hatched bugs made strange noises inside the wicker and so they put it out on the balcony in the snow. The bugs died. They threw the basket away anyway, just in case there were some eggs left in the basket.

"Here you go, sir."

"Is that baked here?"

"No, sir." The waiter takes the wine from the cooler and fills the glass. "We get it. Enjoy."

"Thank you."

The crust is nice and thick, dark, and the bread is still warm. The butter is whipped. The man breaks off a piece of bread, butters it, takes several bites. While still chewing he lifts the glass to his lips and soaks the bread and butter in his mouth with the wine.

"Mmmmm," he says aloud, but softly, only to himself.

The wine is very white and very dry and the tartness of it is delicious with the sweetness of the butter and the saltiness of the rich, wholewheat bread.

His thoughts are just running now, he is not paying attention to them — so that if someone interrupted him right now and asked, "What are you thinking about?" the man would more than likely look up, surprised, and say, with a full mouth, "Hm?" then quickly swallow and add, "Oh, I don't know. I was daydreaming," and he probably couldn't say what he was daydreaming about. But he was daydreaming about his girlfriend.

The salad is a bit soggy, he thinks, but very good. Very green. He thinks: I am turning food into thought, and then, thinks: why am I thinking about turning food into thought (into myself)? Is that what is happening? Is that what digestion is — turning food into thought and, among other things, into things like fingernails, liver cells, and blood? How do you get thoughts out of wine and bread?

Now, if something else were happening — say, a beautiful woman had walked into the restaurant, alone, and had sat within eyesight — he would be involved in this something else, whatever it would have happened to be. He would not be thinking about his own thoughts and the puzzling question of why he is thinking about his own thoughts. Rather, he would be looking, admiring her, undressing her in his mind, wondering what it would be like to do something sexual and preferably obscene with her — What a thought, he thought, while chewing on your salad! There is not even a suitable woman around who fits appropriately into his (only remotely realized) fantasy. An elderly couple sits several tables away and anyway the old woman has her back to him. Not very suitable. But perhaps they have a daughter. He begins laughing, until suddenly a piece of salad goes down the wrong way and he chokes. It is a big piece, too big, he knows (even though this is the one thing his mother had never particularly nagged him about) he didn't chew it properly, and he thinks: I just inhaled salad! What if I die?

Unable to breathe, he takes several gulps of wine to try and wash the green leaf down but it doesn't go down either, he can't even get the wine into his throat. It dribbles, rejected, down his chin. The salad gets lodged even deeper. Gasping loudly now, he tries hitting himself on the back but this only makes him panic more. Nothing is working. He sees the elderly couple looking.

The old man asks, "You all right?"

Like a fool (he thinks this to himself — "What a fool I am for nodding"), he nods. But he is not all right, he can't talk or breathe and his heart is pounding. He will pass out (he thinks, and his thinking is correct) if he doesn't get some oxygen soon.

The old man stands up, his napkin in his wrinkled hands held over his lap like a loin cloth. "Help? Some help? Do you need help?"

The old woman brings her scrunched napkin to her mouth, covering the lower part of her face like a veil. "What's the matter? Are you choking?"

Veils? Loin cloths? Why am I thinking like this, in analogies, he wonders? I might be dying!

The waiter does not hear the noise, he is in the kitchen on the telephone, taking a reservation.

"I say, are you all right?" shouts the old man.

He can't answer, he is dead. (You think this is too sudden. People don't just die like that. But maybe a piece of plaque got loose in the arteries around his heart. Or maybe you just don't like it when the hero of the story dies. But this guy was not a hero. He was just an ordinary guy in a restaurant thinking about his thoughts when the salad did him in. You don't even know his name or what he does [used to do] for a living or anything.)

The wine, undrunk, is in the glass. It is made from fermented grapes which (before they are crushed) grow in vineyards where seeds feed on water and sunlight and earth and whatever else seeds can use to turn earth into fruit — for instance corpses like the one the man has just become. (Look, even if it would have taken a little longer, what's the difference?) Soon, waiters (who are not called "waiters") dressed in black (just like the waiter in the kitchen who has just gotten off the phone but will be back on the

phone shortly, only blacker) will deliver the man — with a pompous ceremony even more formal than the one that would have delivered the blackened grouper (and which now the cook will himself gladly eat) — to the seeds and animals none of whom has ever paid a bill. The bill for this future ceremony (with music, there will be very sad ethnic music from the Mediterranean region, the man himself specified it), gratuities included, has been paid, well in advance, by the man who will soon be (if he isn't already) in the coffin. To be served, like the white wine in the glass, well chilled.

At home on the man's desk lies a letter the man had composed but not yet sent to his girlfriend:

> I want to make love to you. I want to touch you so that I can feel the texture of what you are. I want my feeling you to make you feel. The feeling of feeling you is the feeling of ecstasy. I want to make you stop, then go. Then stop, then go. To get so close that the dizzyness of the distance between us becomes a whirlpool of madness, danger, desire. When I look without looking I see my seeing and there you are: a mystery that moves. Into you I ascend into myself and forget that I too am no one. The veil of the world is the veil between us. Soft and transparent and warm like gauze. To love you is to be wounded. Sorrow is the joy of knowing the unknown. I don't want a looking-back but a looking-at: I want to know you now or not at all. Now is the place for knowing, touching, feeling, seeing. Now is now. My now is yours, forever.

Nice letter. Really, he was quite an extraordinary man. Oh, well. I could go on. But what would be the point? The man is dead.

Further Questions

1. What is this story about? What feelings does it evoke?

2. What is the significance of the letter? Do you see any importance in the fact that it was never mailed?

3. It seems to be a fact of life that we, the living, must feed on the dead. And it seems to be a fact of physics that nature recycles *everything* — that under ordinary circumstances matter and energy can neither be created nor destroyed. Relate these ideas to the themes and images of the story as you interpret them.

Further Readings

De Assis, Machado. *Epitaph of a Small Winner*. New York: Avon, 1978, William Grossman, translator. A novel "written by a deceased writer."

Donnely, John. "Death and Ivan Ilych." In John Donnely, ed., *Language, Metaphysics, and Death*. Bronx, NY: Fordham University Press, 1978, pp. 116–130.

Romains, Jules. *The Death of a Nobody*. New York: H. Fertig, 1976. An explicitly nonexistentialist view of death, the subject of which is not a man but, says the author, "an event."

Two of Leo Tolstoy's works evoke some of the most profound and meaningful sentiments ever written about death.

Tolstoy, Leo. *Memoirs of a Madman*. Originally published in 1884. A mystical treatment of the despair of death.

——*The Death of Ivan Ilych*. Originally published in 1886. About a symbolic Everyman who discovers the meaning of life only when confronted by death.

What Is Death?

J. KRISHNAMURTI

Can death, the unknown, become something known? That is the question to which Krishnamurti now turns.

A brief biography of Krishnamurti appears on page 35.

Reading Questions

1. Why are we afraid of the unknown?
2. Why, according to Krishnamurti, is death something the mind cannot "grasp" or "conceive of"?
3. What, according to Krishnamurti, is the function of death?
4. Do you agree with what he says about security, fragmentation, and aloneness?

. . . LIVING IS A PROCESS of continuity in memory, conscious as well as unconscious, with its various struggles, quarrels, incidents, experiences and so on. All that is what we call life; in opposition to that there is death, which is putting an end to all that. . . . we proceed to look for the relationship between life and death; if we can bridge the gap with some explanation, with belief in continuity, in the hereafter, we are satisfied. We believe in reincarnation or in some other form of continuity of thought and then we try to establish a relationship between the known and the unknown. We try to bridge the known and the unknown and thereby try to find the relationship between the past and the future. . . . We want to know how to bridge the living and the ending—that is our fundamental desire.

Now, can the end, which is death, be known while living? If we can know what death is while we are living, then we shall have no problem. It is because we cannot experience the unknown while we are living that we are afraid of it. Our struggle is to establish a relationship between ourselves, which is the result of the known, and the unknown which we call death. Can there be a relationship between the past and something which the mind cannot conceive, which we call death? Why do we separate the two? Is it not because our mind can function only within the field of the known, within the field of the continuous? One only knows oneself as a thinker, as an actor with certain memories of misery, of pleasure, of love, affection, of various kinds of experience; one only knows oneself as being continuous—otherwise one would have no recollection of oneself as being something. Now when that something comes to the end, which we call death, there is fear of the unknown; so we want to draw the unknown into the known and our whole effort is to give continuity to the unknown. That is, we do not want to know life, which includes death, but we want to know how to continue and not come to an end. We do not want to know life and death, we only want to know how to continue without ending. . . .

Now is it possible, while living, to die—which means coming to an end, being as nothing? Is it possible, while living in this world where everything is becoming more and more or becoming less and less, where everything is a process of climbing, achieving, succeeding, is it possible, in such a world, to know death? Is it possible to end all memories—not the memory of facts, the way to your house and so on, but the inward attachment through memory to psychological security, the memories that one has accumulated, stored up, and in which one seeks security, happiness? Is

it possible to put an end to all that—which means dying every day so that there may be a renewal to-morrow? It is only then that one knows death while living. . . .

*   *   *

What Is Death?*

ONE HAS KNOWN OF THOUSANDS OF DEATHS —the death of someone very close or the death of masses through the atomic bomb—Hiroshima and all the horrors that man has perpetrated on other human beings in the name of peace and in the pursuit of ideologies. So, without any ideology, without any conclusion, one asks: What is death? What is the thing that dies—that terminates? One sees that if there is something that is continuous it becomes mechanical. If there is an ending to everything there is a new beginning. If one is afraid then one cannot possibly find out what this immense thing called death is. It must be the most extraordinary thing. To find out what death is one must also enquire into what life is before death. One never does that. One never enquires what living is. Death is inevitable; but what is living? Is this living, this enormous suffering, fear, anxiety, sorrow, and all the rest of it—is this living? Clinging to that one is afraid of death. If one does not know what living is one cannot know what death is—they go together. If one can find out what the full meaning of living is, the totality of living, the wholeness of living, then one is capable of understanding the wholeness of death. But one usually enquires into the meaning of death without enquiring into the meaning of life. . . .

Death comes and with that one cannot argue; one cannot say: "Wait a few minutes more"—it is there. . . . [C]an the mind meet the end of everything while one is living, while one has vitality and energy, while one is full of life? When one's life is not wasted in conflicts and worries one is full of energy, clarity. Death means the ending of all that one knows, of all one's attachments, of one's bank accounts, of all one's attainments — there is a complete ending. Can the mind, while living, meet such a state? Then one will understand the full meaning of what death is. If one clings to the idea of 'me,' that me which one believes must continue, the me that is put together by thought, including the me in which one believes there is the higher consciousness, the supreme consciousness, then one will not understand what death is in life.

Thought lives in the known; it is the outcome of the known; if there is not freedom from the known one cannot possibly find out what death is, which is the ending of everything, the physical organism with all its ingrained habits, the identification with the body, with the name, with all the memories it has acquired. One cannot carry it all over when one goes to death. One cannot carry there all one's money; so, in the same way one has to end in life everything that one knows. That means there is absolute aloneness; not loneliness but aloneness, in the sense there is nothing else but that state of mind that is completely whole. Aloneness means all one.

Further Questions

1. How does Krishnamurti think we can achieve knowledge of death — knowledge of the unknown — while living? Do you agree? Why?

2. Do you agree that one must "end in life everything that one knows"? Why?

3. Krishnamurti seems to be suggesting that there is some positive value to be gained from the fact of death. Can you connect this with the other readings in this section? Has your overall view of death changed in any way? Why?

Further Readings

Chögyam, Trungpa, *Cutting Through Spiritual Materialism*. Boulder, CO: Shambhala Publications, 1973. A Buddhist perspective, obscurantist, sometimes unclear but often illuminating.

Krishnamurti, J. *Freedom from the Known*. New York: Harper & Row, 1969. Clear and concise.

Suzuki, Shunryu. *Zen Mind, Beginner's Mind*. San Francisco: Weatherhill, Inc., 1980. The Zen perspective, charmingly and amusingly written.

The Myth of Immortality

CLARENCE DARROW

Born in Kinsman, Ohio in 1857, Clarence Darrow became one of the most celebrated lawyers of all time. Among his famous cases were the defense in 1924 of Loeb and Leopold for the murder of a 14-year-old boy, and the Scopes "Monkey" trial, 1925, in which Darrow defended a Tennessee schoolteacher accused by religious and political leaders of the crime of teaching the Darwinian theory of evolution. His writings include *Crime, Its Cause and Treatment* (1925), *An Eye for an Eye* (1905), and *The Story of My Life* (1932). For an excellent anthology of his speeches, see *Attorney for the Damned*, Arthur Weinberg, ed., 1957.

In the following selection Darrow argues that the belief in life after death is unfounded, claiming that there is no good reason to believe in either the existence of an immaterial soul or in the Christian doctrine of the resurrection of the body. He thinks it would be better for everyone if we dropped such false beliefs, that doing so would make us better human beings.

Reading Questions

1. What does Darrow illustrate with his trip to Goofville story?
2. What are his arguments against the existence of an immaterial soul? What are his arguments against the resurrection of the body?
3. What do you think Darrow's motive is in saying what he says?

THERE IS, PERHAPS, no more striking example of the credulity of man than the widespread belief in immortality. This idea includes not only the belief that death is not the end of what we call life, but that personal identity involving memory persists beyond the grave. So determined is the ordinary individual to hold fast to this belief that, as a rule, he refuses to read or to think upon the subject lest it cast doubt upon his cherished dream. Of those who may chance to look at this contribution, many will do so with the determination not to be convinced, and will refuse even to consider the manifold reasons that might weaken their faith. I know that this is true, for I know the reluctance with which I long approached the subject and my firm determination not to give up my hope. Thus the myth will stand in the way of a sensible adjustment to facts.

Even many of those who claim to believe in immortality still tell themselves and others that neither side of the question is susceptible of proof. Just what can these hopeful ones believe that the word "proof" involves? The evidence against the persistence of personal consciousness is as strong as the evidence for gravitation, and much more obvious. It is as convincing and unassailable as the proof of the destruction of wood or coal by fire. If it is not certain that death ends personal identity and memory, then almost nothing that man accepts as true is susceptible of proof.

The beliefs of the race and its individuals are relics of the past. Without careful examination, no one can begin to understand how many of man's cherished opinions have no foundation in fact. The common experience of all men should teach them how easy it is to believe what they wish to accept. Experienced psychologists know perfectly well that if they desire to convince a man of some idea, they must first make him *want* to believe it. There are so many hopes, so many strong yearnings and desires attached to the doctrine of immortality that it is practically impossible to create in any mind the wish to be mortal. Still, in spite of strong desires, millions of people are filled with doubts and fears that will not down. After all, is it not better to look the question squarely in the face and find out whether we are harboring a delusion?

It is customary to speak of a "belief in immortality." First, then, let us see what is meant by the

Originally published in Forum 80 *(Oct. 1928).*

word "belief." If I take a train in Chicago at noon, bound for New York, I believe I will reach that city the next morning. I believe it because I have been to New York. I have read about the city. I have known many other people who have been there, and their stories are not inconsistent with any known facts in my own experience. I have even examined the timetables, and I know just how I will go and how long the trip will take. In other words, when I board the train for New York I believe I will reach that city because I have *reason* to believe it.

But if I am told that next week I shall start on a trip to Goofville; that I shall not take my body with me; that I shall stay for all eternity: can I find a single fact connected with my journey—the way I shall go, the part of me that is to go, the time of the journey, the country I shall reach, its location in space, the way I shall live there—or anything that would lead to a rational belief that I shall really make the trip? Have I ever known anyone who has made the journey and returned? If I am really to believe, I must try to get some information about all these important facts.

But people hesitate to ask questions about life after death. They do not ask, for they know that only silence comes out of the eternal darkness of endless space. If people really believed in a beautiful, happy glorious land waiting to receive them when they died; if they believed that their friends would be waiting to meet them; if they believed that all pain and suffering would be left behind: why should they live through weeks, months, and even years of pain and torture while a cancer eats its way to the vital parts of the body? Why should one fight off death? Because he does *not* believe in any real sense: He only hopes. Everyone knows that there is no real evidence of any such state of bliss; so we are told not to search for proof. We are to accept through faith alone. But every thinking person knows that faith can only come through belief. Belief implies a condition of mind that accepts a certain idea. This condition can be brought about only by evidence. True, the evidence may be simply the unsupported statement of your grandmother; it may be

wholly insufficient for reasoning men; but, good or bad, it must be enough for the believer or he could not believe.

Upon what evidence, then, are we asked to believe in immortality? There is no evidence. One is told to rely on faith, and no doubt this serves the purpose so long as one can believe blindly whatever he is told. . . .

The idea of continued life after death is very old. It doubtless had its roots back in the childhood of the race. In view of the limited knowledge of primitive man, it was not unreasonable. His dead friends and relatives visited him in dreams and visions and were present in his feeling and imagination until they were forgotten. Therefore the lifeless body did not raise the question of dissolution, but rather of duality. It was thought that man was a dual being possessing a body and a soul as separate entities, and that when a man died, his soul was released from his body to continue its life apart. Consequently, food and drink were placed upon the graves of the dead to be used in the long journey into the unknown. In modified forms, this belief in the duality of man persists to the present day.

But primitive man had no conception of life as having a beginning and an end. In this he was like the rest of the animals. Today everyone of ordinary intelligence knows how life begins, and to examine the beginnings of life leads to inevitable conclusions about the way life ends. If man has a soul, it must creep in somewhere during the period of gestation and growth.

All the higher forms of animal life grow from a single cell. Before the individual life can begin its development, it must be fertilized by union with another cell; then the cell divides and multiplies until it takes the form and pattern of its kind. At a certain regular time the being emerges into the world. During its term of life millions of cells in its body are born, die, and are replaced until, through age, disease, or some catastrophe, the cells fall apart and the individual life is ended.

It is obvious that but for the fertilization of the cell under right conditions, the being would not have lived. It is idle to say that the initial cell has a soul. In one sense it has life; but even that is precarious and depends for its continued life upon union with another cell of the proper kind. The human mother is the bearer of probably ten thousand of one kind of cell, and the human father of countless billions of the other kind. Only a very small fraction of these result in human life. If the unfertilized cells of the female and the unused cells of the male are human beings possessed of souls, then the population of the world is infinitely greater than has ever been dreamed. Of course no such idea as belief in the immortality of the germ cells could satisfy the yearnings of the individual for a survival of life after death.

If that which is called a "soul" is a separate entity apart from the body, when, then, and where and how was this soul placed in the human structure? The individual began with the union of two cells, neither of which had a soul. How could these two soulless cells produce a soul? I must leave this search to the metaphysicians. When they have found the answer, I hope they will tell me, for I should really like to know.

We know that a baby may live and fully develop in its mother's womb and then, through some shock at birth, may be born without life. In the past these babies were promptly buried. But now we know that in many cases, where the bodily structure is complete, the machine may be set to work by artificial respiration or electricity. Then it will run like any other human body through its allotted term of years. We also know that in many cases of drowning, or when some mishap virtually destroys life without hopelessly impairing the body, artificial means may set it in motion once more, so that it will complete its term of existence until the final catastrophe comes. Are we to believe that somewhere around the stillborn child and somewhere in the vicinity of the drowned man there hovers a detached soul waiting to be summoned back into the body by a pulmotor? This, too, must be left to the metaphysicians.

The beginnings of life yield no evidence of the beginnings of a soul. It is idle to say that the something in the human being which we call "life" is

the soul itself, for the soul is generally taken to distinguish human beings from other forms of life. There is life in all animals and plants, and at least potential life in inorganic matter. This potential life is simply unreleased force and matter —the great storehouse from which all forms of life emerge and are constantly replenished. It is impossible to draw the line between inorganic matter and the simpler forms of plant life, and equally impossible to draw the line between plant life and animal life, or between other forms of animal life and what we human beings are pleased to call the highest form. If the thing which we call "life" is itself the soul, then cows have souls; and, in the very nature of things, we must allow souls to all forms of life and to inorganic matter as well.

Life itself is something very real, as distinguished from the soul. Every man knows that his life had a beginning. Can one imagine an organism that has a beginning and no end? If I did not exist in the infinite past, why should I, or could I, exist in the infinite future? "But," say some, "your consciousness, your memory may exist even after you are dead. This is what we mean by the soul." Let us examine this point a little.

I have no remembrance of the months that I lay in my mother's womb. I cannot recall the day of my birth nor the time when I first opened my eyes to the light of the sun. I cannot remember when I was an infant, or when I began to creep on the floor, or when I was taught to walk, or anything before I was five or six years old. Still, all of these events were important, wonderful, and strange in a new life. What I call my "consciousness," for lack of a better word and a better understanding, developed with my growth and the crowding experiences I met at every turn. I have a hazy recollection of the burial of a boy soldier who was shot toward the end of the Civil War. He was buried near the schoolhouse when I was seven years old. But I have no remembrance of the assassination of Abraham Lincoln, although I must then have been eight years old. I must have known about it at the time, for my family and my community idolized Lincoln, and all America was in mourning at his death. Why do I remember the dead boy soldier who was buried a year before? Perhaps because I knew him well. Perhaps because his family was close to my childish life. Possibly because it came to me as my first knowledge of death. At all events, it made so deep an impression that I recall it now.

"Ah, yes," say the believers in the soul, "what you say confirms our own belief. You certainly existed when these early experiences took place. You were conscious of them at the time, even though you are not aware of it now. In the same way, may not your consciousness persist after you die, even though you are not now aware of the fact?"

On the contrary, my fading memory of the events that filled the early years of my life leads me to the opposite conclusion. So far as these incidents are concerned, the mind and consciousness of the boy are already dead. Even now, am I fully alive? I am seventy-one years old. I often fail to recollect the names of some of those I knew full well. Many events do not make the lasting impression that they once did. I know that it will be only a few years, even if my body still survives decay, when few important matters will even register in my mind. I know how it is with the old. I know that physical life can persist beyond the time when the mind can fully function. I know that if I live to an extreme old age, my mind will fail. I shall eat and drink and go to my bed in an automatic way. Memory—which is all that binds me to the past—will already be dead. All that will remain will be a vegetative existence; I shall sit and doze in the chimney corner, and my body will function in a measure even though the ego will already be practically dead. I am sure that if I die of what is called "old age," my consciousness will gradually slip away with my failing emotions; I shall no more be aware of the near approach of final dissolution than is the dying tree.

In primitive times, before men knew anything about the human body or the universe of which it is a part, it was not unreasonable to believe in spirits, ghosts, and the duality of man. For one thing, celestial geography was much simpler then. Just above the earth was a firmament in which the stars were set, and above the firmament was heaven. The place was easy of access, and in dreams the angels were seen going up and coming down on a ladder. But now we have a slightly more adequate conception of space and the infinite universe of which we are so small a part. Our great telescopes reveal countless worlds and planetary systems which make our own sink into utter insignificance in comparison. We have every reason to think that beyond our sight there is endless space filled with still more planets, so infinite in size and number that no brain has the smallest conception of their extent. Is there any reason to think that in this universe, with its myriads of worlds, there is no other life so important as our own? Is it possible that the inhabitants of the earth have been singled out for special favor . . . ?

Some of those who profess to believe in the immortality of man — whether it be of his soul or his body — have drawn what comfort they could from the modern scientific doctrine of the indestructibility of matter and force. This doctrine, they say, only confirms in scientific language what they have always believed. This, however, is pure sophistry. It is probably true that no matter or force has ever been or ever can be destroyed. But it is likewise true that there is no connection whatever between the notion that personal consciousness and memory persist after death and the scientific theory that matter and force are indestructible. For the scientific theory carries with it a corollary, that the forms of matter and energy are constantly changing through an endless cycle of new combinations. Of what possible use would it be, then, to have a consciousness that was immortal, but which, from the moment of death, was dispersed into new combinations so that no two parts of the original identity could ever be reunited again?

These natural processes of change, which in the human being take the forms of growth, disease, senility, death, and decay, are essentially the same as the process by which a lump of coal is disintegrated in burning. One may watch the lump of coal burning in the grate until nothing but ashes remains. Part of the coal goes up the chimney in the form of smoke; part of it radiates through the house as heat; the residue lies in the ashes on the hearth. So it is with human life. In all forms of life nature is engaged in combining, breaking down, and recombining her store of energy and matter into new forms. The thing we call "life" is nothing other than a state of equilibrium which endures for a short span of years between the two opposing tendencies of nature — the one that builds up and the one that tears down. In old age, the tearing-down process has already gained the ascendancy, and when death intervenes, the equilibrium is finally upset by the complete stoppage of the building-up process, so that nothing remains but complete disintegration. The energy thus released may be converted into grass or trees or animal life; or it may lie dormant until caught up again in the crucible of nature's laboratory. But whatever happens, the man — the *You* and the *I* — like the lump of coal that has been burned, is gone, irrevocably dispersed. All the King's horses and all the King's men cannot restore it to its former unity.

The idea that man is a being set apart, distinct from all the rest of nature, is born of man's emotions, of his loves and hates, of his hopes and fears, and of the primitive conceptions of undeveloped minds. The *You* or the *I* which is known to our friends does not consist of an immaterial something called a "soul" which cannot be conceived. We know perfectly well what we mean when we talk about this *You* and this *Me*: and it is equally plain that the whole fabric that makes up our separate personalities is destroyed, dispersed, disintegrated beyond repair by what we call "death."

Those who refuse to give up the idea of immortality declare that nature never creates a desire without providing the means for its satisfaction. They likewise insist that all people, from the rudest to the most civilized, yearn for another life. As a matter of fact, nature creates many desires which she does not satisfy; most of the wishes of men meet no fruition. But nature does not create any emotion demanding a future life. The only yearning that the individual has is to keep on living — which is a very different thing. This urge is found in every animal, in every plant. It is simply the momentum of a living structure: or, as Schopenhauer put it, "the will to live." What we long for is a continuation of our present state of existence, not an uncertain reincarnation in a mysterious world of which we know nothing.

All men recognize the hopelessness of finding any evidence that the individual will persist beyond the grave. As a last resort, we are told that it is better that the doctrine be believed even if it is not true. We are assured that without this faith, life is only desolation and despair. However that may be, it remains that many of the conclusions of logic are not pleasant to contemplate; still, so long as men think and feel, at least some of them will use their faculties as best they can. For if we are to believe things that are not true, who is to write our creed? Is it safe to leave it to any man or organization to pick out the errors that we must accept? The whole history of the world has answered this question in a way that cannot be mistaken.

And after all, is the belief in immortality necessary or even desirable for man? Millions of men and women have no such faith; they go on with their daily tasks and feel joy and sorrow without the lure of immortal life. The things that really affect the happiness of the individual are the matters of daily living. They are the companionship of friends, the games and contemplations. They are misunderstandings and cruel judgments, false friends and debts, poverty and disease. They are our joys in our living companions and our sorrows over those who die. Whatever our faith, we mainly live in the present — in the here and now. Those who hold the view that man is mortal are never troubled by metaphysical problems. At the end of the day's labor we are glad to lose our consciousness in sleep; and intellectually, at least, we look forward to the long rest from the stresses and storms that are always incidental to existence.

When we fully understand the brevity of life, its fleeting joys and unavoidable pains; when we accept the fact that all men and women are approaching an inevitable doom: the consciousness of it should make us more kindly and considerate of each other. This feeling should make men and women use their best efforts to help their fellow travellers on the road, to make the path brighter and easier as we journey on. It should bring a closer kinship, a better understanding, and a deeper sympathy for the wayfarer who must live a common life and die a common death.

Further Questions

1. Why does Darrow think giving up a belief in the afterlife would make us better? If he is right, why are people encouraged to hold on to a belief in the afterlife?

2. If we all believed that this life is all there is, how do you think our lives would change? Would they become worse or better? Why?

Further Readings

James, William. *Human Immortality*. New York: Houghton Mifflin, 1917. A defense of the idea that we survive bodily death.
Lamont, Corliss. *The Illusion of Immortality*. New York: Wisdom Library, 1959.
Penelhum, T. *Survival and Disembodied Existence*. New York: Humanities Press, 1969. Attacks both the idea of immortality and mind-body dualism.

Death

ROBERT NOZICK

Most of us assume that death presents a major problem for our lives. This seems almost too obvious to question. But trying to pin down exactly why death is bad is more difficult than one might think, as you are about to see.

A brief biography of Nozick appears on page 337.

Reading Questions

1. Why does Victor Frankl think there is a connection between the fact of death and the meaning of life? Does Nozick agree with him? Do you?

2. Would you want to live forever without growing old? Why or why not?

3. Nozick talks about the need to leave one's "traces" in the world, in the form of children, accomplishments, and so on. What kind of "traces" would you like to leave, and why?

IT IS OFTEN ASSUMED that there is a problem about the meaning of life because of our mortality. Why does the fact that all people die create a special problem? (If life were to go on forever, would there then be no problem about its meaning?) One opposite view has been proposed that welcomes the fact of death and makes a virtue of its apparently grim necessity. Victor Frankl writes that "death itself is what makes life meaningful," arguing for this startling view as follows. "What would our lives be like if they were not finite in time, but infinite? If we were immortal, we could legitimately postpone every action forever. It would be of no consequence whether or not we did a thing now; every act might just as well be done tomorrow or the day after or a year from now or ten years hence. But in the face of death as absolute *finis* to our future and boundary to our possibilities, we are under the imperative of utilizing our lifetimes to the utmost, not letting the singular opportunities—whose 'finite' sum constitutes the whole of life—pass by unused." It would appear, then, that persons who were or could become immortal should choose to set a temporal limit to their lives in order to escape meaninglessness; scientists who discovered some way to avoid natural death should suppress their discoveries.[1]

Frankl assumes our only desire is to have done certain things, to put certain things somewhere on our record. Because we shall die, if we are to have done these things by the end of our lives, we had better get on with them. However, we may desire to do things; our desire need not be merely to have done them. Moreover, if we had an infinite life, we might view it as a whole, as something to organize, shape and do something with. (Will this require us to be tolerant of very long gaps?) Persons who are immortal need not be limited to the desires and designs of mortals; they might well think up new plans that, in Parkinsonian fashion, expand to fill the available time. Despite his clear sympathy for religious thought, Frankl seems never to wonder or worry whether unlimited existence presents a problem of meaningfulness for God.

Whatever appeal Frankl's view has depends upon the more general assumption that certain limits, certain preexisting structures into which things can be poured, are necessary for meaningful organization. Similar things often are said in discussions of particular art forms, such as the sonnet and the sonata. Even were this general assumption true, though, death constitutes only one kind of structural limitation: finiteness in time. Other kinds are possible too, and we well might welcome these others somewhat more. The dual assumption that some limitation is necessary for meaning, and limitation in time is the only one that can serve, is surely too ill established to convince anyone that mortality is good for him—unless he is willing to grasp at any straw. If we are going to grasp at things, let them not be straws.[2]

Granting that our life ending in death is in tension, at least, with our existence having meaning, we have not yet isolated why this is so. We can pursue this issue by considering a puzzle raised by Lucretius, which runs as follows. No one is disturbed by there being a time before which they did not exist, before their birth or conception, although if the past is infinite, there was an infinite amount of time before you were born when you didn't exist. So why should you be disturbed by the fact that after you are dead, there also will be an infinite amount of time when you will not exist? What creates the asymmetry between the time before we were born and the time after we die, leading us to different attitudes toward these two periods?

Is it that death is bad because it makes our lives finite in duration? We can sharpen this issue with an extreme supposition. Imagine that the past is infinite and that you have existed throughout all of it, having forgotten most. If death, even in this case, would disturb you, this is not because it makes you merely finite, since you are not, we are supposing, merely finite in the past direction. What then is so especially distressing about a finite future? Is it that an extended future gives you a chance for further improvement and growth, the opportunity to build from what you are now, whereas an infinite past that culminates only in what you now are might seem puny indeed? We can test whether this accounts for any difference in our attitudes toward infinite future and infinite past by imagining two cases that are mirror images. The infinite future of one is the mirror image of the other's infinite past; each has heights to match the heights of the other. If we had existed infinitely long until now, done all and seen all (though now the memory is dim), would we be disturbed at dying? Perhaps not, perhaps then the asymmetry between past and future would disappear. Nevertheless, this view does not explain why there is an asymmetry between the past and future for finite beings. Why don't we bemoan our late (relative to the infinite past) birth, just as we bemoan our early death? Is the answer that we take the past as given and fixed already, and since, at the present juncture, it is what will happen that settles our fate, we therefore focus upon this?

In the mirror image situation, however, if we were satisfied with the life whose future was finite, that need not be simply because it contained an infinite past existence. That past existence must be specified as one in which we had done

all, seen all, known all, been all. An infinite but monotonous past would not make death welcome, except perhaps as a deserved closing. Is the crucial fact about death not that it makes us finite or limits our future, but that it limits the possibilities (of those we would choose) that we can realize? On this view, death's sting lies not in its destroying or obliterating our personality, but in thwarting it. Nonetheless, underneath many phenomena there seems to lurk not simply the desire to realize other possibilities, but the desire and the hope to endure beyond death, perhaps forever.

Traces

Death wipes you out. Dead, you are no longer around — around *here* at any rate — and if there is nowhere else where you'll be (heaven, hell, with the white light) then all that will be left of you is your effects, leavings, traces. People do seem to think it important to continue to be around somehow. The root notion seems to be this one: it shouldn't *ever* be as if you had never existed at all. A significant life leaves its mark on the world. A significant life is, in some sense, permanent; it makes a permanent difference to the world — it leaves traces. To be wiped out completely, traces and all, goes a long way toward destroying the meaning of one's life. Endurance, however, even if a necessary condition for a meaningful life, is certainly not sufficient. We shall have to ask what kind of trace is important, and why that kind is not important even when very evanescent. First, though, let us explore some of the ramifications of the notion that it shouldn't ever be as if one had never lived or existed at all.

People sometimes speak of achieving immortality through their children. (Will this include achieving immortality through a child, himself childless, who achieves it in some other way? Did Kant's parents do so by siring Kant?) It is puzzling that people speak of achieving immortality by leaving descendants, since they do not believe that their chain of descendants, although perhaps very extended, is going to be infinite. So how do descendants bring immortality rather than a somewhat extended mortality? Perhaps the situation is this: while infinite continuation is best, any continuation is better than none. When a ninety-year-old's only child dies childless at the age of sixty-eight, we feel sad for this parent who now will not be leaving behind that (expected) trace.

There are many manifestations of the desire not to sink completely into oblivion. Artists often strive to leave behind permanent masterpieces, thereby achieving what is called immortality — a goal rejected by the dadaists in their temporary "art-for-a-day." People erect tombstones for others, and some make that provision for themselves. Tombstones are continuing marks upon the world; through them people know where your remains are, and remember you — hence, they are called *memorials*.

When funeral orators say, "he will live in our hearts," the assumption is not that the listeners will live forever, thereby immortalizing the dead person. Nor is it assumed that "living on in the hearts of" is a transitive relation, so that the dead person will continue to live on in the further hearts where the listeners themselves will live on. Permanent survival is not involved here, but neither is it sufficient merely to continue on somewhat, however little. Imagine that the funeral orator had said, "he will continue on in our minds until we leave this building whereupon we all promptly will forget him."

Another phrase sometimes heard is: "as long as people survive, this man will not be forgotten, his achievements and memory will live on." Presumably, one would want to add the proviso that people *will* live on for a long time. This, perhaps, is as close to immortality as a person can get. Some people are disturbed by the thought that life will go on for others, yet without themselves in any way. They are forgotten, and left out; those who follow later will live as if you never had. Here, permanent survival is not the goal, only survival as long as life goes on. More modest reference groups than all of humanity might be picked; you can hope to be remembered as long

as your relations, friends, and acquaintances survive. In these cases it is not temporal enduringness that is crucial, but rather a certain sort of enduringness as shown in relationships to others.

When people desire to leave a trace behind, they want to leave a certain kind of trace. We all do leave traces, causal effects reverberate down: our voices move molecules which have their effects, we feed the worms, and so on. The kind of trace one wishes to leave is one that people know of in particular and that they know is due to you, one due (people know) to some action, choice, plan of yours, that expresses something you take to be important about the kind of person you are, such that people respect or positively evaluate both the trace and that aspect of yourself. We want somehow to live on, but not as an object lesson for others. Notice also that wanting to live on by leaving appropriate traces need not involve wanting continuous existence; you want there to be some time after which you continue to leave a mark, but this time needn't be precisely at your death. Artists as well as those who anticipate resurrection are quite willing to contemplate and tolerate a gap.

Why are traces important? There are several possibilities. First, the importance of traces might lie not in themselves but (only) in what they indicate. Traces indicate that a person's life had a certain meaning or importance, but they are not infallible signs of this — there may be traces without meaning, or meaning without traces. For instance, to "live on" in the memory of others indicates one's effect on these others. It is the effect that matters; even if each of them happened to die first, there still would have been that effect. On this first view, it is a mistake to scrutinize traces in an attempt to understand how life has or can have meaning, for at best traces are a symptom of a life's meaning. Second, traces might be an expression of something important about a life, but it might be important and valuable in addition that this be expressed.

Third, it might be thought that the leaving of traces is intrinsically important. A philosophical tradition going back to Plato holds that the permanent and unchanging is more valuable by virtue of being permanent and unchanging. For Plato, the changing objects of our ordinary everyday world were less valuable and less real than the unchanging permanent Forms or Ideas. These latter not only served an explanatory purpose, they were to be valued, respected, and even venerated. Therefore, when Socrates is asked whether distinct Forms correspond to "such things as hair, mud, dirt, or anything else which is vile and paltry," he is unwilling to say they do. Forms of such things do not seem very exalted, valuable or important, in contrast to the Forms of the Good, the Just, and the Beautiful. Some mathematicians have this attitude toward the permanent and unchanging mathematical objects and structures they study, investigate, and explore. (Other mathematicians, in contrast, think they have created this realm, or are engaged merely in the combinatorial manipulation of meaningless marks on paper or blackboard.)

Despite the pedigree of the tradition, it is difficult to discover why the more permanent is the more valuable or meaningful, why permanence or long-lastingness, why duration in itself, should be important. Consider those things people speak of as permanent or eternal. These include (apart from God) numbers, sets, abstract ideas, spacetime itself. Would it be better to be one of these things? The question is bizarre; how could a concrete person become an abstract object? Still, would anyone wish they *could* become the number 14 or the Form of Justice, or the null set? Is anyone pining to lead a setly existence?

Yet, it cannot be denied that some are gripped by the notion of traces continuing forever. Hence, we find some people disturbed over thermodynamics, worrying that millions of years from now the universe will run down into a state of maximum entropy, with no trace remaining of us or of what we have done. In their view, this eventuality makes human existence absurd; the eventual obliteration of all our traces also obliterates or undermines the meaningfulness of our existence. An account or theory of the meaning of life should find a place for this feeling, showing what facet of meaning it gets a grip upon; an adequate theory should explain the force of this feeling, even if it does not endorse or justify it.

NOTES

1. For a firm statement of the opposite view, see Alan Harrington, *The Immortalist* (Random House, New York, 1969). Frankl might avoid the consequences drawn in the text, by saying that though immortality would involve a sacrifice of meaningfulness, the other things gained might be even more important and so justify that sacrifice. Nevertheless, Frankl makes some parochial assumptions, and limits his vision of human possibilities. Even on his own terms, perhaps, you do best thinking you are mortal and very long-lived (having no good idea of approximately when the end would come, whether after 200 or 2,000 or 20,000 years), while in fact being immortal.

2. There seems to be no limit to the flimsiness of what philosophers will grasp at to disarm the fact of death. It has been argued that if death is bad, bad because it ends life, that can only be because what it ends is good. It cannot be that life, because it ends in death, is bad, for if it were bad then death, ending a bad thing, itself would be good and not bad. The argument concludes that the badness of death presupposes the goodness of the life that it ends. (See Paul Edwards, "Life, Meaning and Value of," *Encyclopedia of Philosophy*, Macmillan, New York, 1967, Vol. 4, pp. 469–470.)

Why think that the badness of death resides in and depends upon the goodness of what it ends rather than in the goodness of what it prevents? When an infant dies three minutes after delivery, is its death bad because of the goodness of those three minutes that it ends, or because of the goodness of the longer life which it prevents? Similarly, suppose that only an infinite life could be good; death then would be bad because it prevented this. It would not follow or be presupposed that the finite portion itself was good. I do not say here that only an infinite life can be good, merely that this argument, purporting to show that the badness of death presupposes the goodness of a finite life, fails.

Even stranger arguments about death have been produced. We find Epicurus saying, "Death is nothing to us . . . it does not concern either the living or the dead, since for the former it is not, and the latter are no more." Epicurus asks who death is bad for, and answers that it is not bad for anyone — not for anyone alive, for that person is not dead, and not for anyone dead, for dead people do not exist any more, and something can be bad only for someone who exists. Since there is no one for whom death is bad, Epicurus concludes, why should we fear it or even view it unfavorably? We shall not pause to unravel this argument, but note that it does have a limited point: if we believe death obliterates us, we should not fear it as if it were a bad *experience*.

Further Questions

1. Do you agree with the view that if ultimately the universe will be completely annihilated, leaving no trace of anything, then life is therefore absurd? Why or why not?

2. Woody Allen was once asked if he hoped to achieve immortality in the sense of living on forever in his movies. He responded that no, he would prefer to achieve immortality by living on forever in his New York apartment. Which would you prefer—forty years of great fame and great wealth or eighty years of moderate income and relative obscurity? How much value do you give to "longevity"? How much to "leaving something behind?" How did these values originate in you? What function do they serve?

3. A common argument for continuing to smoke cigarettes (or drink coffee, or abuse drugs, or drive fast) is that "a short happy life is better than a long, boring one." Do you agree? Why or why not?

Further Readings

Ducasse, Curt. *A Critical Examination of the Belief in Life after Death*. New York: Thomas, 1961.

Flew, Antony. *Body, Mind, and Death*. New York: Macmillan, 1964. Views from Hippocrates to Ryle.

Nozick, Robert. "R.S.V.P.—A Story." *Commentary*, Vol. 53, No. 3, March 1972, pp. 66–68. More on the subject of "traces."

Toynbee, Arnold, et al. *Man's Concern with Death*. New York: McGraw-Hill, 1968.

Williams, Bernard. "The Makropulos Case: Reflections on the Tedium of Immortality," in his *Problems of the Self*. Cambridge: Cambridge University Press, 1973, pp. 82–100. Reprinted in *Language, Metaphysics and Death*, John Donnely, ed. Bronx, NY: Fordham University Press, 1978, pp. 228–242.

Death

THOMAS NAGEL

We would all like to know what happens when we die. But there is another, important question: namely, what does death mean while we are still alive? In the following selection, Nagel explores "what it means to look forward to our own deaths," and why this is an important concern, by trying to bring together the objective and subjective points of view on death.

A brief biography of Thomas Nagel appears on page 390.

Reading Questions

1. By speaking about death in "phenomenological" terms, Nagel is asking whether it is possible to conceive of experiencing your own death "from the inside." What, if anything, do you think experiencing the ending of experience would be *like*?

2. What, according to Nagel, is the importance of being able to look *forward* to your death? Is this possible? Why, or why not?

3. How does Nagel try to bring together the objective and subjective points of view on death? Does he succeed?

4. What does Nagel mean by the "past-future asymmetry" of our view about death? What is the significance of it?

THE DESIRE TO GO ON LIVING, which is one of our strongest, is essentially first-personal: it is not the desire that a particular, publicly identifiable human being survive, though its fulfillment of course requires the survival of someone like that, and therefore it collides with objective indifference about the survival of anyone in particular. Your relation to your own death is unique, and here if anywhere the subjective standpoint holds a dominant position. By the same token, the internal standpoint will be vicariously dominant in your attitude toward the deaths of those to whom you are so close that you see the world through their eyes.

Some people believe in an afterlife. I do not; what I say will be based on the assumption that death is nothing, and final. I believe there is little to be said for it: it is a great curse, and if we truly face it nothing can make it palatable except the knowledge that by dying we can prevent an even greater evil. Otherwise, given the simple choice between living for another week and dying in five minutes I would always choose to live for another week; and by a version of mathematical induction I conclude that I would be glad to live forever.

Perhaps I shall eventually tire of life, but at the moment I can't imagine it, nor can I understand those many distinguished and otherwise reasonable persons who sincerely assert that they don't regard their own mortality as a misfortune.[1]

I can't take the kind of metaphysical consolation offered by Parfit (who observes that his view has parallels with Buddhism). By breaking down the metaphysical boundaries between himself and other persons, and loosening the metaphysical bonds that connect him now with his future self, he claims to have become less depressed about his own death, among other things. His death will be the termination of a certain connected sequence of activities and experiences, but not the annihilation of a unique underlying self. "Instead of saying, 'I shall be dead,' I should say, 'There will be no future experiences that will be related, in certain ways, to these present experiences.' Because it reminds me what this fact involves, this redescription makes this fact less depressing" (Parfit (2), p. 281). . . . I can't accept the metaphysical revision, but I'm not sure that if I did, I'd find the conclusion less depressing. I actually find Parfit's picture of *survival* depressing—but that of course is by comparison with what *I* take survival to be. By comparison with Parfitian survival, Parfitian death may not seem so depressing; but that may owe as much to the deficiencies of the former as to the advantages of the latter. . . .

I am not going to concentrate here on explaining why death is a bad thing. Life can be wonderful, but even if it isn't, death is usually much worse. If it cuts off the possibility of more future goods than future evils for the victim, it is a loss no matter how long he has lived when it happens. And in truth, as Richard Wollheim says, death is a misfortune even when life is no longer worth living (p. 267). But here I want to say something about what it means to look forward to our own deaths, and how, if at all, we can bring the inner and outer views together. The best I can hope to offer is a phenomenological account. I hope it is not simply idiosyncratic. Like the contingency of our birth, the inevitability of our death is easy to grasp objectively, but hard to grasp from within. Everyone dies; I am someone, so I will die. But it isn't just that TN will be killed in a plane crash or a holdup, have a stroke or a heart attack or lung cancer, the clothes going to the Salvation Army, the books to the library, some bits of the body to the organ bank and the rest to the crematorium. In addition to these mundane objective transitions, my world will come to an end, as yours will when you die. That's what's hard to get hold of: the internal fact that one day this consciousness will black out for good and subjective time will simply stop. My death as an event in the world is easy to think about; the end of my world is not.

One of the difficulties is that the appropriate form of a subjective attitude toward my own future is expectation, but in this case there is nothing to expect. How can I expect nothing *as such*? It seems that the best I can do is to expect its complement, a finite but indeterminate amount of something—or a determinate amount, if I am under definite sentence of death. Now a good deal could be said about the consequences of the finiteness of my future, but that is relatively banal

and something most of us automatically allow for, particularly after reaching the age of forty. I am concerned with the adequate recognition of my eventual annihilation itself. There will be a last day, a last hour, a last minute of consciousness, and that will be it. Off the edge.

To grasp this it isn't enough to think only of a particular stream of consciousness coming to an end. The external view of death is psychological as well as physical: it includes the idea that the person who you are will have no more thoughts, experiences, memories, intentions, desires, etc. That inner life will be finished. But the recognition that the life of a particular person in the world will come to an end is not what I am talking about. To grasp your own death from within you must try to look *forward* to it—to see it as a *prospect*.

Is this possible? It might seem that there could be no form of thought about your own death except either an external view, in which the world is pictured as continuing after your life stops, or an internal view that sees only this side of death—that includes only the finitude of your expected future consciousness. But this is not true. There is also something that can be called the expectation of nothingness, and though the mind tends to veer away from it, it is an unmistakable experience, always startling, often frightening, and very different from the familiar recognition that your life will go on for only a limited time—that you probably have less than thirty years and certainly less than a hundred. The positive prospect of the end of subjective time, though it is logically inseparable from these limits, is something distinct.

What is the specific object of this feeling? In part, it is the idea of the objective world and objective time continuing without me in it. We are so accustomed to the parallel progress of subjective and objective time that there is some shock in the realization that the world will go calmly on without me after I disappear. It is the ultimate form of abandonment.

But the special feeling I am talking about does not depend only on this, for it would be there even if solipsism were true — even if my death brought with it the end of the only world there was! Or even if, reversing the direction of dependence, my death was going to occur *in consequence* of the end of the world. (Suppose I came to believe a crackpot scientific theory that as the result of a spectacular and inexorable rise in matter/antimatter collisions, the universe was going to annihilate itself completely six months from now.) It is the prospect of nothingness itself, not the prospect that the world will go on after I cease to exist, that has to be understood.

It hardly needs saying that we are accustomed to our own existence. Each of us has been around for as long as he can remember; it seems the only natural condition of things, and to look forward to its end feels like the denial of something which is more than a mere possibility. It is true that various of my possibilities — things I might do or experience — will remain unrealized as a result of my death. But more fundamental is the fact that they will then cease even to be possibilities — when I as a subject of possibilities as well as of actualities cease to exist. That is why the expectation of complete unconsciousness is so different from the expectation of death. Unconsciousness includes the continued possibility of experience, and therefore doesn't obliterate the here and now as death does.

The internal awareness of my own existence carries with it a particularly strong sense of its own future, and of its possible continuation beyond any future that may actually be reached. It is stronger than the sense of future possibility attaching to the existence of any particular thing in the world objectively conceived — perhaps of a strength surpassed only by the sense of possible continuation we have about the world itself.

The explanation may be this. In our objective conception of the world, particular things can come to an end because the possibility of their nonexistence is allowed for. The possibility of both the existence and the nonexistence of a particular object, artefact, organism, or person is given by actualities which underlie either possibility and coexist with both of them. Thus the existence of certain elements and the truth of the laws of chemistry underlie the possibility of synthesizing a particular chemical compound, or of decomposing it. Such possibilities rest on actualities.

But some possibilities seem themselves to be basic features of the world and not to depend on more deep-seated actualities. For example the number of possible permutations of m things taken n at a time, or the number of possible Euclidean regular solids, are possibilities whose existence is not contingent on anything.

Now the various possibilities some of which make up my life, and many of which I will never realize, are contingent on my existence. My existence is the actuality on which all these possibilities depend. (They also depend on the existence of things outside me which I can encounter, but let me leave that aside for the moment.) The problem is that when I think of myself from the inside, there seems to be nothing still more basic which reveals the actuality of my existence as in turn the realization of a possibility of existence which is correlative with a possibility of nonexistence based on the same foundation. In other words the possibilities which define the subjective conditions of my life seem not to be explainable in turn, within a subjective view, as the contingent realization of deeper possibilities. Nothing is subjectively related to them as the existence of the elements is related to the possibility of a compound.

To explain them we have to go outside of the subjective view for an objective account of why TN exists and has the characteristics that determine his subjective possibilities. They rest on an external actuality.

But this gives rise to an illusion when we think about our lives from inside. We can't really make these external conditions part of the subjective view; in fact we have no idea how they generate our subjective possibilities on any view. It is as if the possible contents of my experience, as opposed to the actualities, themselves constituted a

universe, a domain within which things can occur but which is not itself contingent on anything. The thought of the annihilation of this
universe of possibilities cannot then be thought
of as the realization of yet another possibility already given by an underlying subjective actuality.
The subjective view does not allow for its own
annihilation, for it does not conceive of its existence as the realization of a possibility. This is the
element of truth in the common falsehood that it
is impossible to conceive of one's own death.

All this is fairly obvious, but I think it explains
something. The sense each person has of himself
from inside is partly insulated from the external
view of the person who he is, and it projects itself
into the future autonomously, so to speak. My
existence seems in this light to be a universe of
possibilities that stands by itself, and therefore
stands in need of nothing else in order to continue. It comes as a rude shock, then, when this
partly buried self-conception collides with the
plain fact that TN will die and I with him. This is
a very strong form of nothingness, the disappearance of an inner world that had not been
thought of as a contingent manifestation at all
and whose absence is therefore not the realization of a possibility already contained in the conception of it. It turns out that I am not the sort of
thing I was unconsciously tempted to think I
was: a set of ungrounded possibilities as opposed
to a set of possibilities grounded in a contingent
actuality. The subjective view projects into the future its sense of unconditional possibilities, and
the world denies them. It isn't just that they
won't be actualized—they will *vanish*.

This is not just a realization about the future.
The submerged illusion it destroys is implicit in
the subjective view of the present. In a way it's as
if I were dead already, or had never really existed.
I am told that the fear of flying typically has as its
object not just the possibility of crashing, but flying itself: hurtling along in a smallish vehicle
miles above the surface of the earth. It's a bit like
that, only in this case it's something you can repeatedly forget and rediscover: all along you have

been thinking you were safely on the ground and
suddenly you look down and notice that you're
standing on a narrow girder a thousand feet
above the pavement.

I have said nothing so far about the most perplexing feature of our attitude toward death: the
asymmetry between our attitudes to past and future nonexistence. We do not regard the period
before we were born in the same way that we regard the prospect of death. Yet most of the things
that can be said about the latter are equally true of
the former. Lucretius thought this showed it was
a mistake to regard death as an evil. But I believe
it is an example of a more general future-past
asymmetry which is inseparable from the subjective view.

Parfit has explored the asymmetry in connection with other values such as pleasure and pain.
The fact that a pain (of ours) is in prospect rather
than in the past has a very great effect on our
attitude toward it, and this effect cannot be regarded as irrational (Parfit (3), sec. 64).

While I have no explanation of the asymmetry,
I believe it must be admitted as an independent
factor in the subjective attitude toward our own
death. In other words it can't be accounted for in
terms of some other difference between past and
future nonexistence, any more than the asymmetry in the case of pain can be accounted for in
terms of some other difference between past and
future pains, which makes the latter worse than
the former.

It is a fact perhaps too deep for explanation
that the cutting off of future possibilities, both
their nonactualization and their obliteration even
as possibilities, evokes in us a very different reaction from any parallel nonrealization or nonexistence of possibilities in the past. As things are, we
couldn't have come into existence earlier than we
did, but even if we could, we wouldn't think of
prenatal nonexistence as the same kind of deprivation as death. And even though our nonexistence two hundred years ago faces us with the
fact that our subjective existence is the realization
of a possibility grounded in objective facts about

the world, this does not affect us as the prospect of our annihilation does. The sense of subjective possibility does not project itself into the past with the same imaginative reality with which it faces the future. Death is the negation of something the possibility of whose negation seems not to exist in advance.

The incongruity between this and the objective view of death is clear: much of what was said about birth and the meaning of life applies here and need not be repeated. My death, like any other, is an event in the objective order, and when I think of it that way, detachment seems natural: the vanishing of this individual from the world is no more remarkable or important than his highly accidental appearance in it. That applies both to the full inner life of the individual and to the objective standpoint itself. Granted that the death of something that exists seems worse than its not coming into existence, it still seems not a matter of great seriousness, considered as part of the general cosmic flux.

Another reason to regard death without too much concern is that everyone's mortality is part of the general cycle of biological renewal which is an inseparable part of organic life. Particular deaths may be horrible or premature, but human death itself is a given which, like the fact that hawks eat mice, it makes no sense to deplore. This is no more consoling to someone about to die than it would be to a mouse about to be eaten by a hawk, but it is another obstacle to closing the subjective-objective gap.

One could try to close it in the opposite direction by arguing that the impersonal standpoint should take its view of each death from the attitude of the one whose death it is. If for each person his own death is awful, then every death should be regarded objectively as awful. Detached indifference would then be in a form of blindness to what is clear from an internal perspective—and not the only example of such blindness.

There is something right about this; certainly it would be a good thing if some people took death more seriously than they do.[2] But if we try to do justice to the fact that death is the ultimate loss for everybody, it isn't clear what the objective standpoint has to do with the thought of this perpetual cataract of catastrophe in which the world comes to an end hundreds of thousands of times a day. We cannot regard all those deaths with the interest with which their subjects regard them: sheer emotional overload prevents it, as anyone who has tried to summon a feeling adequate to an enormous massacre knows. The objective standpoint simply cannot accommodate at its full subjective value the fact that everyone, oneself included, inevitably dies. There really is no way to eliminate the radical clash of standpoints in relation to death.

None of this means one can't subordinate one's life to other things—sometimes it would be indecent not to. People are willing to die for what is external to themselves: values, causes, other people. Anyone incapable of caring enough about something outside himself to sacrifice his life for it is seriously limited. Moreover such external concerns, while they may require the loss of life, often have the effect of diminishing that loss and can even be cultivated for the purpose. The more you care about people and things outside your own life, the less by comparison will be the loss from death, and you can, to a degree, reduce the evil of death by externalizing your interests as it approaches: concentrating on the welfare of those who will survive you and on the success of projects or causes that you care about independently of whether you will be around to see what happens. We see this kind of disinvestment in mortal, individual life all the time—and more ambiguously in the personal desire for posthumous fame, influence, or recognition.

But the effect of these measures should not be exaggerated. There is no way to achieve a fully integrated attitude no matter how much you expand your objective or posthumous interests. The objectively unremarkable death of this creature will terminate both its stream of conscious experience and the particular objective conception of reality in which its death is included. Of course from the objective standpoint the existence or nonexistence of any particular objective self, including this one, is unimportant. But that is a limited consolation. The objective standpoint may try to cultivate an indifference to its own annihilation, but there will be something false about it: the individual attachment to life will force its way back even at this level. Here, for once, the objective self is not in a position of safety. We may see more clearly, but we cannot rise above death by occupying a vantage point that death will destroy.

The objective standpoint can't really be domesticated. Not only does it threaten to leave us behind, but it gives us more than we can take on in real life. When we acknowledge our containment in the world, it becomes clear that we are incapable of living in the full light of that acknowledgment. Our problem has in this sense no solution, but to recognize that is to come as near as we can to living in light of the truth.

NOTES

1. For example Williams (3), ch. 6, "The Makropulos Case; Reflections on the Tedium of Immortality." Can it be that he is more easily bored than I?

2. The widespread willingness to rely on thermonuclear bombs as the ultimate weapon displays a cavalier attitude toward death that has always puzzled me. My impression is that whatever they may say, most of the defenders of these weapons are not suitably horrified at the possibility of a war in which hundreds of millions of people would be killed. This may be due to monumental lack of imagination, or perhaps to a peculiar attitude toward risk which leads to the discounting of probabilities of disaster substantially below 50 percent. Or it may be a mechanism of defensive irrationality that appears in circumstances of aggressive conflict. But I suspect that an important factor may be belief in an afterlife, and that the proportion of those who think that death is not the end is much higher among partisans of the bomb than among its opponents.

Further Questions

1. To what problem is Nagel referring in the final sentence when he says there is no solution? Why does he think the recognition that this problem is unsolvable will bring us "as near as we can to living in light of the truth"? Do you agree? Why?

2. Nagel does not offer any explanation of why we view the time *after* our lives differently, usually with much greater fear, than the time *before* we were born. Can you think of any reasons why we do?

3. Compare Nagel's views with those of Nozick in the previous selection. What do they have in common? Where do they differ?

Further Readings

Hick, John. *Death and Eternal Life*. New York: Harper & Row, 1977.

Hofstadter, Douglas. "A Conversation with Einstein's Brain," in *The Mind's I*. New York: Basic Books, 1981. A superb piece on the puzzling question of what it means to have an experience "from the inside"; Einstein's brain is encoded into a fully "functional" book, replete with memories and psychology, at the time of death, and the book "talks." Has Einstein survived?

Phillips, D. Z. *Death and Immortality*. New York: Macmillan, 1970.

Wollheim, Richard. *The Thread of Life*. Cambridge: Harvard University Press, 1984.

Part XII

Meaning

MANY HAVE CLAIMED TO KNOW the meaning of life. Probably more answers have been given on this topic than on any other. Yet, in spite of all the answers, the meaning of life is not understood. Why?

Perhaps because there is no meaning: life is absurd.

Perhaps because the answers up to now have not been good enough: we need a new, bigger and better answer.

Perhaps because the answer is not an answer: we should look, instead, for a big, colorful question mark, hanging suspended by nothing amidst a blinding abyss of unknowing.

My Confession

LEO TOLSTOY

Count Leo Tolstoy (1828–1910) was born, educated, and lived almost all of his life in Russia. At the age of 50, after writing some of the greatest novels ever written, including *War and Peace* and *Anna Karenin*, Tolstoy experienced a religious crisis, described in the following selection, in which he sought the meaning of life and found it in faith. Tolstoy's discovery led him to advocate humility, nonviolence, vegetarianism, the moral value of manual labor, the avoidance of luxury, and sexual abstinence. After his conversion, he continued to write prolifically and produced *The Death of Ivan Ilyich* during this latter period of his life.

Reading Questions

1. What is the "strange thing" that began to happen to Tolstoy?
2. What perplexity is he evoking with the phrase, "Why? Well, and then?"
3. Why does he feel as if somebody had played a mean trick on him by creating him?
4. What is the "cruel truth" of life?
5. What are the two drops of honey in Tolstoy's life, and why are they no longer sweet to him?

6. When Tolstoy says that he can no longer keep himself from seeing the truth, "and the truth is death," what does he mean? Is he just making the mistake of supposing that to be valuable at all, something must last forever? Or is he trying to convey a deeper insight?

7. How did Tolstoy resolve his crisis? Did he resolve it by taking refuge in a system of beliefs that he accepted on faith, or did he solve it by having a genuine insight he had previously overlooked? (Or are these two the same?)

ALTHOUGH I REGARDED AUTHORSHIP as a waste of time, I continued to write during those fifteen years. I had tasted of the seduction of authorship, of the seduction of enormous monetary remunerations and applauses for my insignificant labour, and so I submitted to it, as being a means for improving my material condition and for stifling in my soul all questions about the meaning of my life and life in general.

In my writings I advocated, what to me was the only truth, that it was necessary to live in such a way as to derive the greatest comfort for oneself and one's family.

Thus I proceeded to live, but five years ago something very strange began to happen with me: I was overcome by minutes at first of perplexity and then of an arrest of life, as though I did not know how to live or what to do, and I lost myself and was dejected. But that passed, and I continued to live as before. Then those minutes of perplexity were repeated oftener and oftener, and always in one and the same form. These arrests of life found their expression in ever the same questions: "Why? Well, and then?"

At first I thought that those were simply aimless, inappropriate questions. It seemed to me that that was all well known and that if I ever wanted to busy myself with their solution, it would not cost me much labour, — that now I had no time to attend to them, but that if I wanted to I should find the proper answers. But the questions began to repeat themselves oftener and oftener, answers were demanded more and more persistently, and, like dots that fall on the same spot, these questions, without any answers, thickened into one black blotch.

There happened what happens with any person who falls ill with a mortal internal disease. At first there appear insignificant symptoms of indisposition, to which the patient pays no attention; then these symptoms are repeated more and more frequently and blend into one temporally indivisible suffering. The suffering keeps growing, and before the patient has had time to look around, he becomes conscious that what he took for an indisposition is the most significant thing in the world to him, — is death.

The same happened with me. I understood that it was not a passing indisposition, but something very important, and that, if the questions were going to repeat themselves, it would be necessary to find an answer for them. And I tried to answer them. The questions seemed to be so foolish, simple, and childish. But the moment I touched them and tried to solve them, I became convinced, in the first place, that they were not childish and foolish, but very important and profound questions in life, and, in the second, that, no matter how much I might try, I should not be able to answer them. Before attending to my Samára estate, to my son's education, or to the writing of a book, I ought to know why I should do that. So long as I did not know why, I could not do anything. I could not live. Amidst my thoughts of farming, which interested me very much during that time, there would suddenly pass through my head a question like this: "All right, you are going to have six thousand de-

From My Confession *by Leo Tolstoy. Trans. Leo Wiener (Dent, 1905).*

syatínas of land in the Government of Samára, and three hundred horses, — and then?" And I completely lost my senses and did not know what to think farther. Or, when I thought of the education of my children, I said to myself: "Why?" Or, reflecting on the manner in which the masses might obtain their welfare, I suddenly said to myself: "What is that to me?" Or, thinking of the fame which my works would get me, I said to myself: "All right, you will be more famous than Gógol, Púshkin, Shakespeare, Molière, and all the writers in the world, — what of it?" And I was absolutely unable to make any reply. The questions were not waiting, and I had to answer them at once; if I did not answer them, I could not live. . . .

All that happened with me when I was on every side surrounded by what is considered to be complete happiness. I had a good, loving, and beloved wife, good children, and a large estate, which grew and increased without any labour on my part. I was respected by my neighbours and friends, more than ever before, was praised by strangers, and, without any self-deception, could consider my name famous. With all that, I was not deranged or mentally unsound, — on the contrary, I was in full command of my mental and physical powers, such as I had rarely met with in people of my age: physically I could work in a field, mowing, without falling behind a peasant; mentally I could work from eight to ten hours in succession, without experiencing any consequences from the strain. And while in such condition I arrived at the conclusion that I could not live, and, fearing death, I had to use cunning against myself, in order that I might not take my life.

This mental condition expressed itself to me in this form: my life is a stupid, mean trick played on me by somebody. Although I did not recognize that "somebody" as having created me, the form of the conception that some one had played a mean, stupid trick on me by bringing me into the world was the most natural one that presented itself to me.

Involuntarily I imagined that there, somewhere, there was somebody who was now having fun as he looked down upon me and saw me, who had lived for thirty or forty years, learning, developing, growing in body and mind, now that I had become strengthened in mind and had reached that summit of life from which it lay all before me, standing as a complete fool on that summit and seeing clearly that there was nothing in life and never would be. And that was fun to him —

But whether there was or was not that somebody who made fun of me, did not make it easier for me. I could not ascribe any sensible meaning to a single act, or to my whole life. I was only surprised that I had not understood that from the start. All that had long ago been known to everybody. Sooner or later there would come diseases and death (they had come already) to my dear ones and to me, and there would be nothing left but stench and worms. All my affairs, no matter what they might be, would sooner or later be forgotten, and I myself should not exist. So why should I worry about all these things? How could a man fail to see that and live, — that was surprising! A person could live only so long as he was drunk; but the moment he sobered up, he could not help seeing that all that was only a deception, and a stupid deception at that! Really, there was nothing funny and ingenious about it, but only something cruel and stupid.

Long ago has been told the Eastern story about the traveller who in the steppe is overtaken by an infuriated beast. Trying to save himself from the animal, the traveller jumps into a waterless well, but at its bottom he sees a dragon who opens his jaws in order to swallow him. And the unfortunate man does not dare climb out, lest he perish from the infuriated beast, and does not dare jump down to the bottom of the well, lest he be devoured by the dragon, and so clutches the twig of a wild bush growing in the cleft of the well and holds on to it. His hands grow weak and he feels that soon he shall have to surrender to the peril which awaits him at either side; but he still holds on and sees two mice, one white, the other black, in even measure making a circle around the main trunk of the bush to which he is clinging, and nibbling at it on all sides. Now, at any moment, the bush will break and tear off, and he will fall into the dragon's jaws. The traveller sees that and knows that he will inevitably perish; but while he is still clinging, he sees some drops of honey hanging on the leaves of the bush, and so reaches out for them with his tongue and licks the leaves. Just so I hold on to the branch of life, knowing that the dragon of death is waiting inevitably for me, ready to tear me to pieces, and I cannot understand why I have fallen on such suffering. And I try to lick that honey which used to give me pleasure; but now it no longer gives me joy, and the white and the black mouse day and night nibble at the branch to which I am holding on. I clearly see the dragon, and the honey is no longer sweet to me. I see only the inevitable dragon and the mice, and am unable to turn my glance away from them. That is not a fable, but a veritable, indisputable, comprehensible truth.

The former deception of the pleasures of life, which stifled the terror of the dragon, no longer deceives me. No matter how much one should say to me, "You cannot understand the meaning of life, do not think, live!" I am unable to do so, because I have been doing it too long before. Now I cannot help seeing day and night, which run and lead me up to death. I see that alone, because that alone is the truth. Everything else is a lie.

The two drops of honey that have longest turned my eyes away from the cruel truth, the love of family and of authorship, which I have called an art, are no longer sweet to me.

"My family —" I said to myself, "but my family, my wife and children, they are also human beings. They are in precisely the same condition that I am in: they must either live in the lie or see the terrible truth. Why should they live? Why should I love them, why guard, raise, and watch them? Is it for the same despair which is in me, or for dullness of perception? Since I love them, I cannot conceal the truth from them, — every step in cognition leads them up to this truth. And the truth is death."

"Art, poetry?" For a long time, under the influence of the success of human praise, I tried to persuade myself that that was a thing which could be done, even though death should come and destroy everything, my deeds, as well as my memory of them; but soon I came to see that that, too, was a deception. It was clear to me that art was an adornment of life, a decoy of life. But life lost all its attractiveness for me. How, then, could I entrap others? So long as I did not live my own life, and a strange life bore me on its waves; so long as I believed that life had some sense, although I was not able to express it, — the reflections of life of every description in poetry and in the arts afforded me pleasure, and I was delighted to look at life through this little mirror of art; but when I began to look for the meaning of life, when I experienced the necessity of living myself, that little mirror became either useless, superfluous, and ridiculous, or painful to me. I could no longer console myself with what I saw in the mirror, namely, that my situation was stupid and desperate. . . .

By abandoning myself to the bright side of knowledge I saw that I only turned my eyes away from the question. No matter how enticing and clear the horizons were that were disclosed to me, no matter how enticing it was to bury myself in the infinitude of this knowledge, I comprehended that these sciences were the more clear, the less I needed them, the less they answered my question.

"Well, I know," I said to myself, "all which science wants so persistently to know, but there is no answer to the question about the meaning of my life." But in the speculative sphere I saw that, in spite of the fact that the aim of the knowledge was directed straight to the answer of my question, or because of that fact, there could be no other answer than what I was giving to myself: "What is the meaning of my life?" — "None." Or, "What will come of my life?" — "Nothing." Or,

"Why does everything which exists exist, and why do I exist?" — "Because it exists."

Putting the question to the one side of human knowledge, I received an endless quantity of exact answers about what I did not ask: about the chemical composition of the stars, about the movement of the sun toward the constellation of Hercules, about the origin of species and of man, about the forms of infinitely small, imponderable particles of ether; but the answer in this sphere of knowledge to my question what the meaning of my life was, was always: "You are what you call your life; you are a temporal, accidental conglomeration of particles. The interrelation, the change of these particles, produces in you that which you call life. This congeries will last for some time; then the interaction of these particles will cease, and that which you call life and all your questions will come to an end. You are an accidentally cohering globule of something. The globule is fermenting. This fermentation the globule calls its life. The globule falls to pieces, and all fermentation and all questions will come to an end." Thus the clear side of knowledge answers, and it cannot say anything else, if only it strictly follows its principles.

With such an answer it appears that the answer is not a reply to the question. I want to know the meaning of my life, but the fact that it is a particle of the infinite not only gives it no meaning, but even destroys every possible meaning. . . .

I lived for a long time in this madness, which, not in words, but in deeds, is particularly characteristic of us, the most liberal and learned of men. But, thanks either to my strange, physical love for the real working class, which made me understand it and see that it is not so stupid as we suppose, or to the sincerity of my conviction, which was that I could know nothing and that the best that I could do was to hang myself, — I felt that if I wanted to live and understand the meaning of life, I ought naturally to look for it, not among those who had lost the meaning of life and wanted to kill themselves, but among those billions departed and living men who had been carrying their own lives and ours upon their shoulders. And I looked around at the enormous masses of deceased and living men, — not learned and wealthy, but simple men, — and I saw something quite different. I saw that all these billions of men that lived or had lived, all, with rare exceptions, did not fit into my subdivisions, and that I could not recognize them as not understanding the question, because they themselves put it and answered it with surprising clearness. Nor could I recognize them as Epicureans, because their lives were composed rather of privations and suffering than of enjoyment. Still less could I recognize them as senselessly living out their meaningless lives, because every act of theirs and death itself was explained by them. They regarded it as the greatest evil to kill themselves. It appeared, then, that all humanity was in possession of a knowledge of the meaning of life, which I did not recognize and which I condemned. It turned out that rational knowledge did not give any meaning to life, excluded life, while the meaning which by billions of people, by all humanity, was ascribed to life was based on some despised, false knowledge.

The rational knowledge in the person of the learned and the wise denied the meaning of life, but the enormous masses of men, all humanity, recognized this meaning in an irrational knowledge. This irrational knowledge was faith, the same that I could not help but reject. That was God as one and three, the creation in six days, devils and angels, and all that which I could not accept so long as I had not lost my senses.

My situation was a terrible one. I knew that I should not find anything on the path of rational knowledge but the negation of life, and there, in faith, nothing but the negation of reason, which was still more impossible than the negation of life. From the rational knowledge it followed that life was an evil and men knew it, — it depended on men whether they should cease living, and yet they lived and continued to live, and I myself lived, though I had known long ago that life was meaningless and an evil. From faith it followed that, in order to understand life, I must renounce reason, for which alone a meaning was needed.

There resulted a contradiction, from which there were two ways out: either what I called rational was not so rational as I had thought; or that which to me appeared irrational was not so irrational as I had thought. And I began to verify the train of thoughts of my rational knowledge.

In verifying the train of thoughts of my rational knowledge, I found that it was quite correct. The deduction that life was nothing was inevitable; but I saw a mistake. The mistake was that I had not reasoned in conformity with the question put by me. The question was, "Why should I live?" that is, "What real, indestructible essence will come from my phantasmal, destructible life? What meaning has my finite existence in this infinite world?" And in order to answer this question, I studied life.

The solutions of all possible questions of life apparently could not satisfy me, because my question, no matter how simple it appeared in the beginning, included the necessity of explaining the finite through the infinite, and vice versa.

I asked, "What is the extra-temporal, extra-causal, extra-spatial meaning of life?" But I gave an answer to the question, "What is the temporal, causal, spatial meaning of my life?" The result was that after a long labour of mind I answered, "None." . . .

When I saw that [. . . for philosophy the solution remains insoluble] I understood that it was not right for me to look for an answer to my question in rational knowledge, and that the answer given by rational knowledge was only an indication that the answer might be got if the question were differently put, but only when into the discussion of the question should be introduced the question of the relation of the finite to the infinite. I also understood that, no matter how irrational and monstrous the answers might be that faith gave, they had this advantage that they introduced into each answer the relation of the finite to the infinite, without which there could be no answer.

No matter how I may put the question, "How must I live?" the answer is, "According to God's law." "What real result will there be from my life?" — "Eternal torment or eternal bliss." "What is the meaning which is not destroyed by death?" — "The union with infinite God, paradise."

Thus, outside the rational knowledge, which had to me appeared as the only one, I was inevitably led to recognize that all living humanity had a certain other irrational knowledge, faith, which made it possible to live.

All the irrationality of faith remained the same for me, but I could not help recognizing that it alone gave to humanity answers to the questions of life, and, in consequence of them, the possibility of living.

The rational knowledge brought me to the recognition that life was meaningless, — my life stopped, and I wanted to destroy myself. When I looked around at people, at all humanity, I saw that people lived and asserted that they knew the meaning of life. I looked back at myself: I lived so long as I knew the meaning of life. As to other people, so even to me, did faith give the meaning of life and the possibility of living.

Looking again at the people of other countries, contemporaries of mine and those passed away, I saw again the same. Where life had been, there faith, ever since humanity had existed, had given the possibility of living, and the chief features of faith were everywhere one and the same.

No matter what answers faith may give, its every answer gives to the finite existence of man the sense of the infinite, — a sense which is not destroyed by suffering, privation, and death. Consequently in faith alone could we find the meaning and possibility of life. What, then, was faith? I understood that faith was not merely an evidence of things not seen, and so forth, not revelation (that is only the description of one of the symptoms of faith), not the relation of man to man (faith has to be defined, and then God, and not first God, and faith through him), not merely an agreement with what a man was told, as faith was generally understood, — that faith was the knowledge of the meaning of human life, in consequence of which man did not destroy himself, but lived. Faith is the power of life. If a man lives he believes in something. If he did not believe that he ought to live for some purpose, he would not live. If he does not see and understand the phantasm of the finite, he believes in that finite; if he understands the phantasm of the finite, he must believe in the infinite. Without faith one cannot live. . . .

In order that all humanity may be able to live, in order that they may continue living, giving a meaning to life, they, those billions, must have another, a real knowledge of faith, for not the fact that I, with Solomon and Schopenhauer, did not kill myself convinced me of the existence of faith, but that these billions had lived and had borne us, me and Solomon, on the waves of life.

Then I began to cultivate the acquaintance of the believers from among the poor, the simple and unlettered folk, of pilgrims, monks, dissenters, peasants. The doctrine of these people from among the masses was also the Christian doctrine that the quasi-believers of our circle professed. With the Christian truths were also mixed in very many superstitions, but there was this difference: the superstitions of our circle were quite unnecessary to them, had no connection with their lives, were only a kind of an Epicurean amusement, while the superstitions of the believers from among the labouring classes were to such an extent blended with their life that it would have been impossible to imagine it without these superstitions, — it was a necessary condition of that life. I began to examine closely the lives and beliefs of these people, and the more I examined them, the more did I become convinced that they had the real faith, that their faith was necessary for them, and that it alone gave them a meaning and possibility of life. In contradistinction to what I saw in our circle, where life without faith was possible, and where hardly one in a thousand professed to be a believer, among them there was hardly one in a thousand who was not a believer. In contradistinction to what I saw

in our circle, where all life passed in idleness, amusements, and tedium of life, I saw that the whole life of these people was passed in hard work, and that they were satisfied with life. In contradistinction to the people of our circle, who struggled and murmured against fate because of their privations and their suffering, these people accepted diseases and sorrows without any perplexity or opposition, but with the calm and firm conviction that it was all for good. In contradistinction to the fact that the more intelligent we are, the less do we understand the meaning of life and the more do we see a kind of a bad joke in our suffering and death, these people live, suffer, and approach death, and suffer in peace and more often in joy. In contradistinction to the fact that a calm death, a death without terror or despair, is the greatest exception in our circle, a restless, insubmissive, joyless death is one of the greatest exceptions among the masses. And of such people, who are deprived of everything which for Solomon and for me constitutes the only good of life, and who withal experience the greatest happiness, there is an enormous number. I cast a broader glance about me. I examined the life of past and present vast masses of men, and I saw people who in like manner had understood the meaning of life, who had known how to live and die, not two, not three, not ten, but hundreds, thousands, millions. All of them, infinitely diversified as to habits, intellect, culture, situation, all equally and quite contrary to my ignorance knew the meaning of life and of death, worked calmly, bore privations and suffering, lived and died, seeing in that not vanity, but good.

I began to love those people. The more I penetrated into their life, the life of the men now living, and the life of men departed, of whom I had read and heard, the more did I love them, and the easier it became for me to live. Thus I lived for about two years, and within me took place a transformation, which had long been working within me, and the germ of which had always been in me. What happened with me was that the life of our circle, — of the rich and the learned, —

not only disgusted me, but even lost all its meaning. All our acts, reflections, sciences, arts, — all that appeared to me in a new light. I saw that all that was mere pampering of the appetites, and that no meaning could be found in it; but the life of all the working masses, of all humanity, which created life, presented itself to me in its real significance. I saw that that was life itself and that the meaning given to this life was truth, and I accepted it.

Further Questions

1. It is hard to read Tolstoy's account without being moved. If you were moved, *what* moved you? His beliefs, or the beautiful way he expresses them, or the simple humanity with which he lived his life? Did you like best those parts of his account that agree with what you already believe? Or were you led to see something that you hadn't seen before? If the latter, what? If you were charmed by Tolstoy, was it by the beautiful way he expressed himself or by what he expressed?

2. When you read an essay like this one, do you look for new insight or merely a beautiful expression of what you already believe? What can you learn about yourself from the way you answer these questions? Can you learn whether you are searching for truth or just for confirmation?

Further Readings

Frankl, Victor. *Man's Search for Meaning*. Boston: Beacon Press, 1963. A noted psychologist looks at some of the issues that troubled Tolstoy.

Rolston, III, Holmes. *Science and Religion*. New York: Random House, 1987. A thorough, easy-to-read attempt to explore the interface between science and religion.

The Myth of Sisyphus

ALBERT CAMUS

French essayist, novelist, and playwright Albert Camus was born in Algeria in 1913. After studying philosophy at the University of Algiers, he worked as a meteorologist, stockbroker's agent, civil servant, journalist, and actor and director in an amateur theatrical company. During World War II he joined the French resistance movement. As a journalist he often got into trouble with authorities by campaigning for economic and social reforms on behalf of Algerians. He died in an automobile accident in 1960.

Camus expressed his theme of the absurd and irrational nature of the world in various forms. Among his best: a collection of essays, *The Myth of Sisyphus* (1942); the novels, *The Stranger* (1946), *The Plague* (1948), and *The Fall* (1957); and the play, *Caligula* (1944). He won the Nobel Prize for literature in 1957.

Reading Questions

1. Why does Camus think the world is absurd? What does he mean by this? Do you agree?
2. Is there room for freedom in an absurd world? Why?
3. Camus seems to suggest that while the world does not have any meaning, your individual life *can* have meaning. How?
4. Why does Camus think the question of the meaning of life is the most important one? How does the question of suicide enter into it?
5. What does he mean in saying that we perceive the world to be "dense"?
6. How do human beings "secrete the inhuman"?
7. What are the facts from which he cannot separate himself?

An Absurd Reasoning

ABSURDITY AND SUICIDE

THERE IS BUT ONE TRULY SERIOUS philosophical problem, and that is suicide. Judging whether life is or is not worth living amounts to answering the fundamental question of philosophy. All the rest—whether or not the world has three dimensions, whether the mind has nine or twelve categories—comes afterwards. These are games; one must first answer. And if it is true, as Nietzsche claims, that a philosopher, to deserve our respect, must preach by example, you can appreciate the importance of that reply, for it will precede the definitive act. These are facts the heart can feel; yet they call for careful study before they become clear to the intellect.

If I ask myself how to judge that this question is more urgent than that, I reply that one judges by the actions it entails. I have never seen anyone die for the ontological argument. Galileo, who held a scientific truth of great importance, abjured it with the greatest ease as soon as it endangered his life. In a certain sense, he did right.[1] That truth was not worth the stake. Whether the earth or the sun revolves around the other is a matter of profound indifference. To tell the truth, it is a futile question. On the other hand, I see

many people die because they judge that life is not worth living. I see others paradoxically getting killed for the ideas or illusions that give them a reason for living (what is called a reason for living is also an excellent reason for dying). I therefore conclude that the meaning of life is the most urgent of questions. How to answer it? On all essential problems (I mean thereby those that run the risk of leading to death or those that intensify the passion of living) there are probably but two methods of thought: the method of La Palisse and the method of Don Quixote. Solely the balance between evidence and lyricism can allow us to achieve simultaneously emotion and lucidity. In a subject at once so humble and so heavy with emotion, the learned and classical dialectic must yield, one can see, to a more modest attitude of mind deriving at one and the same time from common sense and understanding. . . .

All great deeds and all great thoughts have a ridiculous beginning. Great works are often born on a streetcorner or in a restaurant's revolving door. So it is with absurdity. The absurd world more than others derives its nobility from that abject birth. In certain situations, replying "nothing" when asked what one is thinking about may be pretense in a man. Those who are loved are well aware of this. But if that reply is sincere, if it symbolizes that odd state of soul in which the void becomes eloquent, in which the chain of daily gestures is broken, in which the heart vainly seeks the link that will connect it again, then it is as it were the first sign of absurdity.

It happens that the stage sets collapse. Rising, streetcar, four hours in the office or the factory, meal, streetcar, four hours of work, meal, sleep, and Monday Tuesday Wednesday Thursday Friday and Saturday according to the same rhythm — this path is easily followed most of the time. But one day the "why" arises and everything begins in that weariness tinged with amazement. "Begins" — this is important. Weariness comes at the end of the acts of a mechanical life, but at the same time it inaugurates the impulse of consciousness. It awakens consciousness and provokes what follows. What follows is the gradual return into the chain or it is the definitive awakening. At the end of the awakening comes, in time, the consequence: suicide or recovery. In itself weariness has something sickening about it. Here, I must conclude that it is good. For everything begins with consciousness and nothing is worth anything except through it. There is nothing original about these remarks. But they are obvious; that is enough for a while, during a sketchy reconnaissance in the origins of the absurd. Mere "anxiety," as Heidegger says, is at the source of everything.

Likewise and during every day of an unillustrious life, time carries us. But a moment always comes when we have to carry it. We live on the future: "tomorrow," "later on," "when you have made your way," "you will understand when you are old enough." Such irrelevancies are wonderful, for, after all, it's a matter of dying. Yet a day comes when a man notices or says that he is thirty. Thus he asserts his youth. But simultaneously he situates himself in relation to time. He takes his place in it. He admits that he stands at a certain point on a curve that he acknowledges having to travel to its end. He belongs to time, and by the horror that seizes him, he recognizes his worst enemy. Tomorrow, he was longing for

tomorrow, whereas everything in him ought to reject it. That revolt of the flesh is the absurd.[2]

A step lower and strangeness creeps in: perceiving that the world is "dense," sensing to what a degree a stone is foreign and irreducible to us, with what intensity nature or a landscape can negate us. At the heart of all beauty lies something inhuman, and these hills, the softness of the sky, the outline of these trees at this very minute lose the illusory meaning with which we had clothed them, henceforth more remote than a lost paradise. The primitive hostility of the world rises up to face us across millennia. For a second we cease to understand it because for centuries we have understood in it solely the images and designs that we had attributed to it beforehand, because henceforth we lack the power to make use of that artifice. The world evades us because it becomes itself again. That stage scenery masked by habit becomes again what it is. It withdraws at a distance from us. Just as there are days when under the familiar face of a woman, we see as a stranger her we have loved months or years ago, perhaps we shall come even to desire what suddenly leaves us so alone. But the time has not yet come. Just one thing: that denseness and that strangeness of the world is the absurd.

Men, too, secrete the inhuman. At certain moments of lucidity, the mechanical aspect of their gestures, their meaningless pantomime makes silly everything that surrounds them. A man is talking on the telephone behind a glass partition; you cannot hear him, but you see his incomprehensible dumb show: you wonder why he is alive. This discomfort in the face of man's own inhumanity, this incalculable tumble before the image of what we are, this "nausea," as a writer of today calls it, is also the absurd. Likewise the stranger who at certain seconds comes to meet us in a mirror, the familiar and yet alarming brother we encounter in our own photographs is also the absurd.

I come at last to death and to the attitude we have toward it. On this point everything has been said and it is only proper to avoid pathos. Yet one will never be sufficiently surprised that everyone lives as if no one "knew." This is because in reality there is no experience of death. Properly speaking, nothing has been experienced but what has been lived and made conscious. Here, it is barely possible to speak of the experience of others' deaths. It is a substitute, an illusion, and it never quite convinces us. That melancholy convention cannot be persuasive. The horror comes in reality from the mathematical aspect of the event. If time frightens us, this is because it works out the problem and the solution comes afterward. All the pretty speeches about the soul will have their contrary convincingly proved, at least for a time. From this inert body on which a slap makes no mark the soul has disappeared. This elementary and definitive aspect of the adventure constitutes the absurd feeling. Under the fatal lighting of that destiny, its uselessness becomes evident. No code of ethics and no effort are justifiable *a priori* in the face of the cruel mathematics that command our condition.

Let me repeat: all this has been said over and over. I am limiting myself here to making a rapid classification and to pointing out these obvious themes. They run through all literatures and all philosophies. Everyday conversation feeds on them. There is no question of reinventing them. But it is essential to be sure of these facts in order to be able to question oneself subsequently on the primordial question. I am interested — let me repeat again — not so much in absurd discoveries as in their consequences. If one is assured of these facts, what is one to conclude, how far is one to go to elude nothing? Is one to die voluntarily or to hope in spite of everything? . . .

Of whom and of what indeed can I say: "I know that!" This heart within me I can feel, and I judge that it exists. This world I can touch, and I likewise judge that it exists. There ends all my knowledge, and the rest is construction. For if I try to seize this self of which I feel sure, if I try to define and to summarize it, it is nothing but water slipping through my fingers. I can sketch one by one all the aspects it is able to assume, all those likewise that have been attributed to it, this upbringing, this origin, this ardor or these silences, this nobility or this vileness. But aspects cannot

be added up. This very heart which is mine will forever remain indefinable to me. Between the certainty I have of my existence and the content I try to give to that assurance, the gap will never be filled. Forever I shall be a stranger to myself. In psychology as in logic, there are truths but no truth. Socrates' "Know thyself" has as much value as the "Be virtuous" of our confessionals. They reveal a nostalgia at the same time as an ignorance. They are sterile exercises on great subjects. They are legitimate only in precisely so far as they are approximate.

And here are trees and I know their gnarled surface, water and I feel its taste. These scents of grass and stars at night, certain evenings when the heart relaxes — how shall I negate this world whose power and strength I feel? Yet all the knowledge on earth will give me nothing to assure me that this world is mine. You describe it to me and you teach me to classify it. You enumerate its laws and in my thirst for knowledge I admit that they are true. You take apart its mechanism and my hope increases. As the final stage you teach me that this wondrous and multicolored universe can be reduced to the atom and that the atom itself can be reduced to the electron. All this is good and I wait for you to continue. But you tell me of an invisible planetary system in which electrons gravitate around a nucleus. You explain this world to me with an image. I realize then that you have been reduced to poetry: I shall never know. Have I the time to become indignant? You have already changed theories. So that science that was to teach me everything ends up in a hypothesis, that lucidity founders in metaphor, that uncertainty is resolved in a work of art. What need had I of so many efforts? The soft lines of these hills and the hand of evening on this troubled heart teach me much more. I have returned to my beginning. I realize that if through science I can see phenomena and enumerate them, I cannot, for all that, apprehend the world. Were I to trace its entire relief with my finger, I should not know any more. And you give me the choice between a description that is sure but that teaches me nothing and hypotheses that claim to teach me but that are not sure. A stranger to my-self and to the world, armed solely with a thought that negates itself as soon as it asserts, what is this condition in which I can have peace only by refusing to know and to live, in which the appetite for conquest bumps into walls that defy its assaults? To will is to stir up paradoxes. Every-thing is ordered in such a way as to bring into being that poisoned peace produced by thought-lessness, lack of heart, or fatal renunciations.

Hence the intelligence, too, tells me in its way that this world is absurd. Its contrary, blind rea-son, may well claim that all is clear; I was waiting for proof and longing for it to be right. But de-spite so many pretentious centuries and over the heads of so many eloquent and persuasive men, I know that is false. On this plane, at least, there is no happiness if I cannot know. That universal reason, practical or ethical, that determinism, those categories that explain everything are enough to make a decent man laugh. They have nothing to do with the mind. They negate its profound truth, which is to be enchained. In this unintelligible and limited universe, man's fate henceforth assumes its meaning. A horde of irra-tionals has sprung up and surrounds him until his ultimate end. In his recovered and now studied lucidity, the feeling of the absurd becomes clear and definite. I said that the world is absurd, but I was too hasty. This world in itself is not reason-able, that is all that can be said. But what is ab-surd is the confrontation of this irrational and the wild longing for clarity whose call echoes in the human heart. The absurd depends as much on man as on the world. For the moment it is all that links them together. It binds them one to the other as only hatred can weld two creatures together. . . .

ABSURD FREEDOM

Now the main thing is done, I hold certain facts from which I cannot separate. What I know, what is certain, what I cannot deny, what I can-not reject — this is what counts. I can negate ev-erything of that part of me that lives on vague nostalgias, except this desire for unity, this long-

ing to solve, this need for clarity and cohesion. I can refute everything in this world surrounding me that offends or enraptures me, except this chaos, this sovereign chance and this divine equivalence which springs from anarchy. I don't know whether this world has a meaning that transcends it. But I know that I do not know that meaning and that it is impossible for me just now to know it. What can a meaning outside my con-dition mean to me? I can understand only in hu-man terms. What I touch, what resists me — that is what I understand. And these two certainties — my appetite for the absolute and for unity and the impossibility of reducing this world to a ra-tional and reasonable principle — I also know that I cannot reconcile them. What other truth can I admit without lying, without bringing in a hope I lack and which means nothing within the limits of my condition?

If I were a tree among trees, a cat among ani-mals, this life would have a meaning, or rather this problem would not arise, for I should belong to this world. I should *be* this world to which I am now opposed by my whole consciousness and my whole insistence upon familiarity. This ridic-ulous reason is what sets me in opposition to all creation. I cannot cross it out with a stroke of the pen. What I believe to be true I must therefore preserve. What seems to me so obvious, even against me, I must support. And what constitutes the basis of that conflict, of that break between the world and my mind, but the awareness of it? If therefore I want to preserve it, I can through a constant awareness, ever revived, ever alert. This is what, for the moment, I must remember. At this moment the absurd, so obvious and yet so hard to win, returns to a man's life and finds its home there. At this moment too, the mind can leave the arid, dried-up path of lucid effort. That path now emerges in daily life. It encounters the world of the anonymous impersonal pronoun "one," but henceforth man enters in with his re-volt and his lucidity. He has forgotten how to hope. This hell of the present is his Kingdom at last. All problems recover their sharp edge. Ab-stract evidence retreats before the poetry of forms and colors. Spiritual conflicts become embodied and return to the abject and magnificent shelter of man's heart. None of them is settled. But all are transfigured. Is one going to die, escape by the leap, rebuild a mansion of ideas and forms to one's own scale? Is one, on the contrary, going to take up the heart-rending and marvelous wager of the absurd? Let's make a final effort in this regard and draw all our conclusions. The body, affection, creation, action, human nobility will then resume their places in this mad world. At last man will again find there the wine of the absurd and the bread of indifference on which he feeds his greatness.

Let us insist again on the method: it is a matter of persisting. At a certain point on his path the absurd man is tempted. History is not lacking in either religions or prophets, even without gods. He is asked to leap. All he can reply is that he doesn't fully understand, that it is not obvious. Indeed, he does not want to do anything but what he fully understands. He is assured that this is the sin of pride, but he does not understand the notion of sin; that perhaps hell is in store, but he has not enough imagination to visualize that strange future; that he is losing immortal life, but that seems to him an idle consideration. An attempt is made to get him to admit his guilt. He feels innocent. To tell the truth, that is all he feels — his irreparable innocence. This is what allows him everything. Hence, what he demands of himself is to live *solely* with what he knows, to accommodate himself to what is, and to bring in nothing that is not certain. He is told that nothing is. But this at least is a certainty. And it is with this that he is concerned: he wants to find out if it is possible to live *without appeal*. . . .

Now I can broach the notion of suicide. It has already been felt what solution might be given. At this point the problem is reversed. It was previously a question of finding out whether or not life had to have a meaning to be lived. It now becomes clear, on the contrary, that it will be lived all the better if it has no meaning. Living an experience, a particular fate, is accepting it fully. Now, no one will live this fate, knowing it to be absurd, unless he does everything to keep before him that absurd brought to light by consciousness. Negating one of the terms of the opposition on which he lives amounts to escaping it. To abolish conscious revolt is to elude the problem. The theme of permanent revolution is thus carried into individual experience. Living is keeping the absurd alive. Keeping it alive is, above all, contemplating it. Unlike Eurydice, the absurd dies only when we turn away from it. One of the only coherent philosophical positions is thus revolt. It is a constant confrontation between man and his own obscurity. It is an insistence upon an impossible transparency. It challenges the world anew every second. Just as danger provided man the unique opportunity of seizing awareness, so metaphysical revolt extends awareness to the whole of experience. It is that constant presence of man in his own eyes. It is not aspiration, for it is devoid of hope. That revolt is the certainty of a crushing fate, without the resignation that ought to accompany it.

This is where it is seen to what a degree absurd experience is remote from suicide. It may be thought that suicide follows revolt — but wrongly. For it does not represent the logical outcome of revolt. It is just the contrary by the consent it presupposes. Suicide, like the leap, is acceptance at its extreme. Everything is over and man returns to his essential history. His future, his unique and dreadful future — he sees and rushes toward it. In its way, suicide settles the absurd. It engulfs the absurd in the same death. But I know that in order to keep alive, the absurd cannot be settled. It escapes suicide to the extent that it is simultaneously awareness and rejection of death. It is, at the extreme limit of the condemned man's last thought, that shoelace that despite everything he sees a few yards away, on the very brink of his dizzying fall. The contrary of suicide, in fact, is the man condemned to death.

That revolt gives life its value. Spread out over the whole length of a life, it restores its majesty to that life. To a man devoid of blinders, there is no finer sight than that of the intelligence at grips with a reality that transcends it. The sight of human pride is unequaled. No disparagement is of any use. That discipline that the mind imposes on itself, that will conjured up out of nothing, that face-to-face struggle have something exceptional about them. To impoverish that reality whose inhumanity constitutes man's majesty is tantamount to impoverishing him himself. I understand then why the doctrines that explain everything to me also debilitate me at the same time. They relieve me of the weight of my own life, and yet I must carry it alone. At this juncture, I cannot conceive that a skeptical metaphysics can be joined to an ethics of renunciation.

Consciousness and revolt, these rejections are the contrary of renunciation. Everything that is indomitable and passionate in a human heart quickens them, on the contrary, with its own life. It is essential to die unreconciled and not of one's own free will. Suicide is a repudiation. The absurd man can only drain everything to the bitter end, and deplete himself. The absurd is his extreme tension, which he maintains constantly by solitary effort, for he knows that in that consciousness and in that day-to-day revolt he gives proof of his only truth, which is defiance. This is a first consequence. . . .

The Myth of Sisyphus

The gods had condemned Sisyphus to ceaselessly rolling a rock to the top of a mountain, whence the stone would fall back of its own weight. They had thought with some reason that there is no more dreadful punishment than futile and hopeless labor.

If one believes Homer, Sisyphus was the wisest and most prudent of mortals. According to another tradition, however, he was disposed to practice the profession of highwayman. I see no contradiction in this. Opinions differ as to the reasons why he became the futile laborer of the underworld. To begin with, he is accused of a certain levity in regard to the gods. He stole their secrets. Ægina, the daughter of Æsopus, was carried off by Jupiter. The father was shocked by that disappearance and complained to Sisyphus. He, who knew of the abduction, offered to tell

about it on condition that Æsopus would give water to the citadel of Corinth. To the celestial thunderbolts he preferred the benediction of water. He was punished for this in the underworld. Homer tells us also that Sisyphus had put Death in chains. Pluto could not endure the sight of his deserted, silent empire. He dispatched the god of war, who liberated Death from the hands of her conqueror.

It is said also that Sisyphus, being near to death, rashly wanted to test his wife's love. He ordered her to cast his unburied body into the middle of the public square. Sisyphus woke up in the underworld. And there, annoyed by an obedience so contrary to human love, he obtained from Pluto permission to return to earth in order to chastise his wife. But when he had seen again the face of this world, enjoyed water and sun, warm stones and the sea, he no longer wanted to go back to the infernal darkness. Recalls, signs of anger, warnings were of no avail. Many years more he lived facing the curve of the gulf, the sparkling sea, and the smiles of earth. A decree of the gods was necessary. Mercury came and seized the impudent man by the collar and, snatching him from his joys, led him forcibly back to the underworld, where his rock was ready for him.

You have already grasped that Sisyphus is the absurd hero. He *is*, as much through his passions as through his torture. His scorn of the gods, his hatred of death, and his passion for life won him that unspeakable penalty in which the whole being is exerted toward accomplishing nothing. This is the price that must be paid for the passions of this earth. Nothing is told us about Sisyphus in the underworld. Myths are made for the imagination to breathe life into them. As for this myth, one sees merely the whole effort of a body straining to raise the huge stone, to roll it and push it up a slope a hundred times over; one sees the face screwed up, the cheek tight against the stone, the shoulder bracing the clay-covered mass, the foot wedging it, the fresh start with arms outstretched, the wholly human security of two earth-clotted hands. At the very end of his long effort measured by skyless space and time without depth, the purpose is achieved. Then

Sisyphus watches the stone rush down in a few moments toward that lower world whence he will have to push it up again toward the summit. He goes back down to the plain.

It is during that return, that pause, that Sisyphus interests me. A face that toils so close to stones is already stone itself! I see that man going back down with a heavy yet measured step toward the torment of which he will never know the end. That hour like a breathing-space which returns as surely as his suffering, that is the hour of consciousness. At each of those moments when he leaves the heights and gradually sinks toward the lairs of the gods, he is superior to his fate. He is stronger than his rock.

If this myth is tragic, that is because its hero is conscious. Where would his torture be, indeed, if at every step the hope of succeeding upheld him? The workman of today works every day in his life at the same tasks, and this fate is no less absurd. But it is tragic only at the rare moments when it becomes conscious. Sisyphus, proletarian of the gods, powerless and rebellious, knows the whole extent of his wretched condition: it is what he thinks of during his descent. The lucidity that was to constitute his torture at the same time crowns his victory. There is no fate that cannot be surmounted by scorn. . . .

If the descent is thus sometimes performed in sorrow, it can also take place in joy. This word is not too much. Again I fancy Sisyphus returning toward his rock, and the sorrow was in the beginning. When the images of earth cling too tightly to memory, when the call of happiness becomes too insistent, it happens that melancholy rises in man's heart: this is the rock's victory, this is the rock itself. The boundless grief is too heavy to bear. These are our nights of Gethsemane. But crushing truths perish from being acknowledged. Thus, Œdipus at the outset obeys fate without knowing it. But from the moment he knows, his tragedy begins. Yet at the same moment, blind and desperate, he realizes that the only bond linking him to the world is the cool hand of a girl. Then a tremendous remark rings out: "Despite so many ordeals, my advanced age

and the nobility of my soul make me conclude that all is well." Sophocles' Œdipus, like Dostoevsky's Kirilov, thus gives the recipe for the absurd victory. Ancient wisdom confirms modern heroism.

One does not discover the absurd without being tempted to write a manual of happiness. "What! by such narrow ways—?" There is but one world, however. Happiness and the absurd are two sons of the same earth. They are inseparable. It would be a mistake to say that happiness necessarily springs from the absurd discovery. It happens as well that the feeling of the absurd springs from happiness. "I conclude that all is well," says Œdipus, and that remark is sacred. It echoes in the wild and limited universe of man. It teaches that all is not, has not been, exhausted. It drives out of this world a god who had come into it with dissatisfaction and a preference for futile sufferings. It makes of fate a human matter, which must be settled among men.

All Sisyphus' silent joy is contained therein. His fate belongs to him. His rock is his thing. Likewise, the absurd man, when he contemplates his torment, silences all the idols. In the universe suddenly restored to its silence, the myriad wondering little voices of the earth rise up. Unconscious, secret calls, invitations from all the faces, they are the necessary reverse and price of victory. There is no sun without shadow, and it is essential to know the night. The absurd man says yes and his effort will henceforth be unceasing. If there is a personal fate, there is no higher destiny, or at least there is but one which he concludes is inevitable and despicable. For the rest, he knows himself to be the master of his days. At that subtle moment when man glances backward over his life, Sisyphus returning toward his rock, in that slight pivoting he contemplates that series of unrelated actions which becomes his fate, created by him, combined under his memory's eye and soon sealed by his death. Thus, convinced of the wholly human origin of all that is human, a blind man eager to see who knows that the night has no end, he is still on the go. The rock is still rolling.

I leave Sisyphus at the foot of the mountain! One always finds one's burden again. But Sisyphus teaches the higher fidelity that negates the gods and raises rocks. He too concludes that all is well. This universe henceforth without a master seems to him neither sterile nor futile. Each atom of that stone, each mineral flake of that night-filled mountain, in itself forms a world. The struggle itself toward the heights is enough to fill a man's heart. One must imagine Sisyphus happy.

NOTES

1. From the point of view of the relative value of truth. On the other hand, from the point of view of virile behavior, this scholar's fragility may well make us smile. [Albert Camus.]

2. But not in the proper sense. This is not a definition, but rather an *enumeration* of the feelings that may admit of the absurd. Still, the enumeration finished, the absurd has nevertheless not been exhausted. [Albert Camus.]

Further Questions

1. In what sense are we like Sisyphus? In what sense are we different?
2. Why, according to Camus, must we imagine Sisyphus happy? Do you agree? Why?
3. Nearly everyone, at one time or another, has thought about suicide. Have you? When? Why does Camus consider suicide as the one truly serious philosophical problem? Do you agree? Why?

Further Readings

The views of two well-known "philosophical" psychologists are of particular interest for a psychological perspective:

Frankl, Victor. *Man's Search for Meaning*. Boston: Beacon, 1963.
May, Rollo. *Man's Search for Himself*. New York: W. W. Norton, 1953.

Other suggested readings are:

Klemke, E. D. *The Meaning of Life*. New York: Oxford University Press, 1981. Presents religious, atheistic, and philosophical perspectives on the meaning of life.
Kluge, Eike-Henner W. *The Practice of Death*. New Haven: Yale University Press, 1975. Contains philosophical arguments for and against suicide.
Perlin, Seymour. *A Handbook for the Study of Suicide*. New York: Oxford University Press, 1975. See, especially, the article by Richard Brandt, "The Morality and Rationality of Suicide," pp. 61–76.

Is Life Meaningful?

RICHARD TAYLOR

A brief biography of Taylor appears on p. 185. In this selection, from Taylor's *Good and Evil* (1984), he claims that life *is* meaningful and gives his response to the challenge to meaningfulness posed by "The Myth of Sisyphus."

Reading Questions

1. Do any of the ways Taylor modifies the story of Sisyphus affect the meaning of Sisyphus's life?
2. Do you agree with Taylor that meaninglessness is essentially endless pointlessness? Do you agree that our lives resemble such pointlessness?
3. What is the "little afterthought" of the gods with regard to Sisyphus that is both "perverse" and "merciful," and why?
4. What same "spectacle" do all living things present?
5. How does Taylor think we should look at all of life?

THE QUESTION OF WHETHER LIFE has any meaning is difficult to interpret, and the more one concentrates his critical faculty on it the more it seems to elude him, or to evaporate as any intelligible question. One wants to turn it aside, as a source of embarrassment, as something that, if it cannot be abolished, should at least be decently covered. And yet I think any reflective person recognizes that the question it raises is important, and that it ought to have a significant answer.

If the idea of meaningfulness is difficult to grasp in this context, so that we are unsure what sort of thing would amount to answering the question, the idea of meaninglessness is perhaps less so. If, then, we can bring before our minds a clear image of meaningless existence, then perhaps we can take a step toward coping with our original question by seeing to what extent our lives, as we actually find them, resemble that image, and draw such lessons as we are able to from the comparison.

Meaningless Existence

A perfect image of meaninglessness, of the kind we are seeking, is found in the ancient myth of Sisyphus. Sisyphus, it will be remembered, betrayed divine secrets to mortals, and for this he was condemned by the gods to roll a stone to the top of a hill, the stone then immediately to roll back down, again to be pushed to the top by Sisyphus, to roll down once more, and so on again and again, *forever*. Now in this we have the picture of meaningless, pointless toil, of a meaningless existence that is absolutely *never* redeemed. It is not even redeemed by a death that, if it were to accomplish nothing more, would at least bring this idiotic cycle to a close. If we were invited to imagine Sisyphus struggling for awhile and accomplishing nothing, perhaps eventually falling from exhaustion, so that we might suppose him then eventually turning to something having some sort of promise, then the meaninglessness of that chapter of his life would not be so stark. It would be a dark and dreadful dream, from which he eventually awakens to sunlight and reality. But he does not awaken, for there is nothing for him to awaken to. His repetitive toil is his life and reality, and it goes on forever, and it is without any meaning whatever. Nothing ever comes out of what he is doing, except simply, more of the same. Not by one step, nor by a thousand, nor by ten thousand does he even expiate by the smallest token the sin against the gods that led him into his fate. Nothing comes of it, nothing at all.

This ancient myth has always enchanted men, for countless meanings can be read into it. Some of the ancients apparently thought it symbolized the perpetual rising and setting of the sun, and others the repetitious crashing of the waves upon the shore. Probably the commonest interpretation is that it symbolizes man's eternal struggle and unquenchable spirit, his determination always to try once more in the face of overwhelming discouragement. This interpretation is further supported by that version of the myth according to which Sisyphus was commanded to roll the stone *over* the hill, so that it would finally roll down the other side, but was never quite able to make it.

I am not concerned with rendering or defending any interpretation of this myth, however. I have cited it only for the one element it does unmistakably contain, namely, that of a repetitious, cyclic activity that never comes to anything. We could contrive other images of this that would serve just as well, and no myth-makers are needed to supply the materials of it. Thus, we can imagine two persons transporting a stone — or even a precious gem, it does not matter — back and forth, relay style. One carries it to a near or distant point where it is received by the other; it is returned to its starting point, there to be recovered by the first, and the process is repeated over and over. Except in this relay nothing counts as winning, and nothing brings the contest to any close, each step only leads to a repetition of itself. Or we can imagine two groups of prisoners, one of them engaged in digging a prodigious hole in the ground that is no sooner finished than it is filled in again by the other group, the latter then digging a new hole that is at once filled in by the first group, and so on and on endlessly.

Now what stands out in all such pictures as oppressive and dejecting is not that the beings who enact these roles suffer any torture or pain, for it need not be assumed that they do. Nor is it that their labors are great, for they are no greater than the labors commonly undertaken by most men most of the time. According to the original myth, the stone is so large that Sisyphus never quite gets it to the top and must groan under every step, so that his enormous labor is all for nought. But this is not what appalls. It is not that his great struggle comes to nothing, but that his existence itself is without meaning. Even if we suppose, for example, that the stone is but a pebble that can be carried effortlessly, or that the holes dug by the prisoners are but small ones, not the slightest meaning is introduced into their lives. The stone that Sisyphus moves to the top of the hill, whether we think of it as large or small, still rolls back every time, and the process is repeated forever. Nothing comes of it, and the work is simply pointless. That is the element of the myth that I wish to capture.

Again, it is not the fact that the labors of Sisyphus continue forever that deprives them of meaning. It is, rather, the implication of this: that they come to nothing. The image would not be changed by our supposing him to push a different stone up every time, each to roll down again. But if we supposed that these stones, instead of rolling back to their places as if they had never been moved, were assembled at the top of the hill and there incorporated, say, in a beautiful and enduring temple, then the aspect of meaninglessness would disappear. His labors would then have a point, something would come of them all, and although one could perhaps still say it was not worth it, one could not say that the life of Sisyphus was devoid of meaning altogether. Meaningfulness would at least have made an appearance, and we could see what it was.

That point will need remembering. But in the meantime, let us note another way in which the image of meaninglessness can be altered by making only a very slight change. Let us suppose that the gods, while condemning Sisyphus to the fate just described, at the same time, as an afterthought, waxed perversely merciful by implanting in him a strange and irrational impulse; namely a compulsive impulse to roll stones. We may if we like, to make this more graphic, suppose they accomplish this by implanting in him some substance that has this effect on his character and drives. I call this perverse, because from our point of view there is clearly no reason why anyone should have a persistent and insatiable desire to do something so pointless as that. Nevertheless, suppose that is Sisyphus' condition. He has but one obsession, which is to roll stones, and it is an obsession that is only for the moment appeased by his rolling them — he no sooner gets a stone rolled to the top of the hill than he is restless to roll up another.

Now it can be seen why this little afterthought of the gods, which I called perverse, was also in fact merciful. For they have by this device managed to give Sisyphus precisely what he wants — by making him want precisely what they inflict on him. However it may appear to us, Sisyphus' fate now does not appear to him as a condemnation, but the very reverse. His one desire in life is to roll stones, and he is absolutely guaranteed its endless fulfillment. Where otherwise he might profoundly have wished surcease, and even welcomed the quiet of death to release him from endless boredom and meaninglessness, his life is now filled with mission and meaning, and he seems to himself to have been given an entry to heaven. Nor need he even fear death, for the gods have promised him an endless opportunity to indulge his single purpose, without concern or frustration. He will be able to roll stones *forever*.

What we need to mark most carefully at this point is that the picture with which we began has not really been changed in the least by adding this supposition. Exactly the same things happen as before. The only change is in Sisyphus' view of them. The picture before was the image of meaningless activity and existence. It was created precisely to be an image of that. It has not lost that meaninglessness, it has now gained not the least shred of meaningfulness. The stones still roll back as before, each phase of Sisyphus' life still exactly resembles all the others, the task is never completed, nothing comes of it, no temple ever begins to rise, and all this cycle of the same pointless thing over and over goes on forever in this picture as in the other. The *only* thing that has happened is this: Sisyphus has been reconciled to it, and indeed more, he has been led to embrace it. Not, however, by reason or persuasion, but by nothing more rational than the potency of a new substance in his veins.

The Meaninglessness of Life

I believe the foregoing provides a fairly clear content to the idea of meaninglessness and, through it, some hint of what meaningfulness, in this sense, might be. Meaninglessness is essentially endless pointlessness, and meaningfulness is therefore the opposite. Activity, and even long, drawn-out and repetitive activity, has a meaning if it has some significant culmination, some more or less lasting end that can be considered to have been the direction and purpose of the activity. But the descriptions so far also provide something else; namely, the suggestion of how an existence that is objectively meaningless, in this sense, can nevertheless acquire a meaning for him whose existence it is.

Now let us ask: Which of these pictures does life in fact resemble? And let us not begin with our own lives, for here both our prejudices and wishes are great, but with the life in general that we share with the rest of creation. We shall find, I think, that it all has a certain pattern, and that this pattern is by now easily recognized.

We can begin anywhere, only saving human existence for our last consideration. We can, for example, begin with any animal. It does not matter where we begin, because the result is going to be exactly the same.

Thus, for example, there are caves in New Zealand, deep and dark, whose floors are quiet pools and whose walls and ceilings are covered with soft light. As one gazes in wonder in the stillness of these caves it seems that the Creator has reproduced there in microcosm the heavens themselves, until one scarcely remembers the enclosing presence of the walls. As one looks more closely, however, the scene is explained. Each dot of light identifies an ugly worm, whose luminous tail is meant to attract insects from the surrounding darkness. As from time to time one of these insects draws near it becomes entangled in a sticky thread lowered by the worm, and is eaten. This goes on month after month, the blind worm lying there in the barren stillness waiting to entrap an occasional bit of nourishment that will only sustain it to another bit of nourishment until. . . . Until what? What great thing awaits all this long and repetitious effort and makes it worthwhile? Really nothing. The larva just transforms itself finally to a tiny winged adult that lacks even mouth parts to feed and lives only a day or two. These adults, as soon as they have mated and laid eggs, are themselves caught in the threads and are devoured by the cannibalist worms, often without having ventured into the day, the only point to their existence having now been fulfilled. This has been going on for millions of years, and to no end other than that the same meaningless cycle may continue for another millions of years.

All living things present essentially the same spectacle. The larva of a certain cicada burrows in the darkness of the earth for seventeen years, through season after season, to emerge finally into the daylight for a brief flight, lay its eggs, and die — this all to repeat itself during the next seventeen years, and so on to eternity. We have already noted, in another connection, the struggles of fish, made only that others may do the same after them and that this cycle, having no other point than itself, may never cease. Some birds span an entire side of the globe each year and then return, only to insure that others may follow the same incredibly long path again and again. One is led to wonder what the point of it all is, with what great triumph this ceaseless effort, repeating itself through millions of years, might finally culminate, and why it should go on and on for so long, accomplishing nothing, getting nowhere. But then one realizes that there is no point to it at all, that it really culminates in nothing, that each of these cycles, so filled with toil, is to be followed only by more of the same. The point of any living thing's life is, evidently, nothing but life itself.

This life of the world thus presents itself to our eyes as a vast machine, feeding on itself, running on and on forever to nothing. And we are part of that life. To be sure, we are not just the same, but the differences are not so great as we like to think; many are merely invented, and none really cancels the kind of meaninglessness that we found in Sisyphus and that we find all around, wherever anything lives. We are conscious of our activity. Our goals, whether in any significant sense we choose them or not, are things of which we are at least partly aware and can therefore in some sense appraise. More significantly, perhaps, men have a history, as other animals do not, such that each generation does not precisely resemble all those before. Still, if we can in imagination disengage our wills from our lives and disregard the deep interest each man has in his own existence, we shall find that they do not so little resemble the existence of Sisyphus. We toil after goals, most of them — indeed every single one of them — of transitory significance and, having gained one of them, we immediately set forth for the next, as if that one had never been, with this next one being essentially more of the same. Look at a busy street any day, and observe the throng going hither and thither. To what? Some office or shop, where the same things will be done today as were done yesterday, and are done now so they may be repeated tomorrow. And if we think that, unlike Sisyphus, these labors do have a point, that they culminate in something lasting and, independently of our own deep interests in them, very worthwhile, then we simply have not considered the thing closely enough. Most such effort is directed only to the establishment and perpetuation of home and family; that is, to the begetting of others who will follow in our steps to do more of the same. Each man's life thus resembles one of Sisyphus' climbs to the summit of his hill, and each day of it one of his steps; the difference is that whereas Sisyphus himself returns to push the stone up again, we leave this to our children. We at one point imagined that the labors of Sisyphus finally culminated in the creation of a temple, but for this to make any difference it had to be a temple that would at least endure, adding beauty to the world for the remainder of time. Our achievements, even though they are often beautiful, are mostly bubbles; and those that do last, like the sand-swept pyramids, soon become mere curiosities while around them the rest of mankind continues its perpetual toting of rocks, only to see them roll down. Nations are built upon the bones of their founders and pioneers, but only to decay and crumble before long, their rubble then becoming the foundation for others directed to

[margin note: We always want more.]

exactly the same fate. The picture of Sisyphus is the picture of existence of the individual man, great or unknown, of nations, of the race of men, and of the very life of the world.

On a country road one sometimes comes upon the ruined hulks of a house and once extensive buildings, all in collapse and spread over with weeds. A curious eye can in imagination reconstruct from what is left a once warm and thriving life, filled with purpose. There was the hearth, where a family once talked, sang, and made plans; there were the rooms, where people loved, and babes were born to a rejoicing mother; there are the musty remains of a sofa, infested with bugs, once bought at a dear price to enhance an ever-growing comfort, beauty, and warmth. Every small piece of junk fills the mind with what once, not long ago, was utterly real, with children's voices, plans made, and enterprises embarked upon. That is how these stones of Sisyphus were rolled up, and that is how they became incorporated into a beautiful temple, and that temple is what now lies before you. Meanwhile other buildings, institutions, nations, and civilizations spring up all around, only to share the same fate before long. And if the question "What for?" is now asked, the answer is clear: so that just this may go on forever.

The two pictures — of Sisyphus and of our own lives, if we look at them from a distance — are in outline the same and convey to the mind the same image. It is not surprising, then, that men invent ways of denying it, their religions proclaiming a heaven that does not crumble, their hymnals and prayer books declaring a significance to life of which our eyes provide no hint whatever.[1] Even our philosophies portray some permanent and lasting good at which all may aim, from the changeless forms invented by Plato to the beatific vision of St. Thomas and the ideals

of permanence contrived by the moderns. When these fail to convince, then earthly ideals such as universal justice and brotherhood are conjured up to take their places and give meaning to man's seemingly endless pilgrimage, some final state that will be ushered in when the last obstacle is removed and the last stone pushed to the hilltop. No one believes, of course, that any such state will be final, or even wants it to be in case it means that human existence would then cease to be a struggle; but in the meantime such ideas serve a very real need.

The Meaning of Life

We noted that Sisyphus' existence would have meaning if there were some point to his labors, if his efforts ever culminated in something that was not just an occasion for fresh labors of the same kind. But that is precisely the meaning it lacks. And human existence resembles his in that respect. Men do achieve things — they scale their towers and raise their stones to their hilltops — but every such accomplishment fades, providing only an occasion for renewed labors of the same kind.

But here we need to note something else that has been mentioned, but its significance not explored, and that is the state of mind and feeling with which such labors are undertaken. We noted that if Sisyphus had a keen and unappeasable desire to be doing just what he found himself doing, then, although his life would in no way be changed, it would nevertheless have a meaning for him. It would be an irrational one, no doubt, because the desire itself would be only the product of the substance in his veins, and not any that reason could discover, but a meaning nevertheless.

And would it not, in fact, be a meaning incomparably better than the other? For let us examine again the first kind of meaning it could have. Let us suppose that, without having any interest in rolling stones, as such, and finding this, in fact, a galling toil, Sisyphus did nevertheless have a deep interest in raising a temple, one that would be beautiful and lasting. And let us suppose he succeeded in this, that after ages of

---

1. A popular Christian hymn, sung often at funerals and typical of many hymns, expresses this thought:

> Swift to its close ebbs out life's little day;
> Earth's joys grow dim, its glories pass away;
> Change and decay in all around I see:
> O thou who changest not, abide with me.

dreadful toil, all directed at this final result, he did at last complete his temple, such that now he could say his work was done, and he could rest and forever enjoy the result. Now what? What picture now presents itself to our minds? It is precisely the picture of infinite boredom! Of Sisyphus doing nothing ever again, but contemplating what he has already wrought and can no longer add anything to, and contemplating it for an eternity! Now in this picture we have a meaning for Sisyphus' existence, a point for his prodigious labor, because we have put it there; yet, at the same time, that which is really worthwhile seems to have slipped away entirely. Where before we were presented with the nightmare of eternal and pointless activity, we are now confronted with the hell of its eternal absence.

Our second picture, then, wherein we imagined Sisyphus to have had inflicted on him the irrational desire to be doing just what he found himself doing, should not have been dismissed so abruptly. The meaning that picture lacked was no meaning that he or anyone could crave, and the strange meaning it had was perhaps just what we were seeking.

At this point, then, we can reintroduce what has been until now, it is hoped, resolutely pushed aside in an effort to view our lives and human existence with objectivity; namely, our own wills, our deep interest in what we find ourselves doing. If we do this we find that our lives do indeed still resemble that of Sisyphus, but that the meaningfulness they thus lack is precisely the meaningfulness of infinite boredom. At the same time, the strange meaningfulness they possess is that of the inner compulsion to be doing just what we were put here to do, and to go on doing it forever. This is the nearest we may hope to get to heaven, but the redeeming side of that fact is that we do thereby avoid a genuine hell.

If the builders of a great and flourishing ancient civilization could somehow return now to see archaeologists unearthing the trivial remnants of what they had once accomplished with such effort—see the fragments of pots and vases, a few broken statues, and such tokens of another age and greatness—they could indeed ask themselves what the point of it all was, if this is all it finally came to. Yet, it did not seem so to them then, for it was just the building, and not what was finally built, that gave their life meaning. Similarly, if the builders of the ruined home and farm that I described a short while ago could be brought back to see what is left, they would have the same feelings. What we construct in our imaginations as we look over these decayed and rustling pieces would reconstruct itself in their very memories, and certainly with unspeakable sadness. The piece of a sled at our feet would revive in them a warm Christmas. And what rich memories would there be in the broken crib? And the weed-covered remains of a fence would reproduce the scene of a great herd of livestock, so laboriously built up over so many years. What was it all worth, if this is the final result? Yet, again, it did not seem so to them through those many years of struggle and toil, and they did not imagine they were building a Gibraltar. The things to which they bent their backs day after day, realizing one by one their ephemeral plans, were precisely the things in which their wills were deeply involved, precisely the things in which their interests lay, and there was no need then to ask questions. There is no more need of them now—the day was sufficient to itself, and so was the life.

This is surely the way to look at all of life—at one's own life, and each day and moment it contains; of the life of a nation; of the species; of the life of the world; and of everything that breathes. Even the glow worms I described, whose cycles of existence over the millions of years seem so pointless when looked at by us, will seem entirely different to us if we can somehow try to view their existence from within. Their endless activity, which gets nowhere, is just what it is their will to pursue. This is its whole justification and meaning. Nor would it be any salvation to the birds who span the globe every year, back and forth, to have a home made for them in a cage with plenty of food and protection, so that they would not have to migrate any more. It would be their condemnation, for it is the doing that counts for them, and not what they hope to win by it. Flying these prodigious distances, never ending, is what it is in their veins to do, exactly as it was in Sisyphus' veins to roll stones, without end, after the gods had waxed merciful and implanted this in him.

A human being no sooner draws his first breath than he responds to the will that is in him to live. He no more asks whether it will be worthwhile, or whether anything of significance will come of it, than the worms and the birds. The point of his living is simply to be living, in the manner that it is his nature to be living. He goes through his life building his castles, each of these beginning to fade into time as the next is begun; yet, it would be no salvation to rest from all this.

It would be a condemnation, and one that would in no way be redeemed were he able to gaze upon the things he has done, even if these were beautiful and absolutely permanent, as they never are. What counts is that one should be able to begin a new task, a new castle, a new bubble. It counts only because it is there to be done and he has the will to do it. The same will be the life of his children, and of theirs; and if the philosopher is apt to see in this a pattern similar to the unending cycles of the existence of Sisyphus, and to despair, then it is indeed because the meaning and point he is seeking is not there — but mercifully so. The meaning of life is from within us, it is not bestowed from without, and it far exceeds in both its beauty and permanence any heaven of which men have ever dreamed or yearned for.

Further Questions

1. In the end, Taylor tries to snatch meaningfulness (for our lives) from the jaws of meaninglessness. Did he convince you?

2. Compare Tolstoy's and Taylor's accounts of what makes life meaningful. Do they have anything in common? How do they differ? Which, if either, is more plausible to you?

Further Readings

Russell, Bertrand. *The Conquest of Happiness*. New York: New American Library, 1930. Russell's account of bouts with meaninglessness.

Sanders, Steven, and David Cheney, eds. *The Meaning of Life*. Englewood Cliffs, NJ: Prentice-Hall, 1980. A good anthology.

Meaning

THOMAS NAGEL

In this selection Thomas Nagel argues that the problem of the meaning of life is due to a clash between two perspectives we can take on our lives: an internal, subjective perspective, the standpoint from which we ordinarily live our lives, and an external, objective perspective. Each of us has the capacity for both perspectives, and even though these perspectives cannot be reconciled, neither perspective can be shed. The external, objective perspective is an expression of our wish for transcendence, but it leads easily to alienation and a sense of loss of meaning.

A brief biography of Nagel appears on page 390.

Reading Questions

1. Explain and illustrate the main difference between the two perspectives Nagel distinguishes.

2. Why, according to Nagel, is our capacity for adopting these two perspectives a problem?

3. What are Nagel's reasons for rejecting the suggestions that we either reconcile the two perspectives or shed one of them?

4. Does Nagel have a solution of his own to the problem of the meaning of life?

5. Compare what Nagel says about seeing our lives from the outside with what Taylor says about seeing our lives from the inside.

6. How does Nagel distinguish particular problems about the meaning of life that arise from within it, from general ones about the meaning of life as a whole? Why are the philosophical problems not the same in both cases? At what point does absurdity come in?

7. In what ways is the human drama like watching a Little League baseball game?

8. Why doesn't an impersonal perspective necessarily lead to nihilism?

9. What is the "global view"?

10. Does Nagel think there is some way of eliminating the "inner conflict"?

11. What is his argument that the absurd is part of human life?

12. What is the cause of the "civil wars" of the self?

IN SEEING OURSELVES FROM OUTSIDE we find it difficult to take our lives seriously. This loss of conviction, and the attempt to regain it, is the problem of the meaning of life.

I should say at the outset that some people are more susceptible to this problem than others, and even those who are susceptible to it vary over time in the degree to which it grips them. Clearly there are temperamental and circumstantial factors at work. Still, it is a genuine problem which we cannot ignore. The capacity for transcendence brings with it a liability to alienation, and the wish to escape this condition and to find a larger meaning can lead to even greater absurdity. Yet we can't abandon the external standpoint be-

cause it is our own. The aim of reaching some kind of harmony with the universe is part of the aim of living in harmony with ourselves.

To the subjective view, the conditions that determine whether life makes sense are simply given, as part of the package. They are determined by the possibilities of good and evil, happiness and unhappiness, achievement and failure, love and isolation that come with being human, and more specifically with being the particular person you are in the particular social and historical setting in which you find yourself. From inside no justification can coherently be sought for trying to live a good and meaningful life by those standards; and if it were needed, it couldn't be found.

Serious problems about the meaning of a life can arise entirely within it, and these should be distinguished from the completely general philosophical problem of the meaning of life, which arises from the threat of objective detachment. A life may be absurd, and felt to be absurd, because it is permeated by trivia or dominated by a neurotic obsession or by the constant need to react to external threats, pressures, or controls. A life in which human possibilities for autonomy and development are largely unrealized and untested will seem deficient in meaning; someone faced with such a life may lack the significant will to live as a purely internal matter, not because of any objective detachment. But all these forms of meaninglessness are compatible with the possibility of meaning, had things gone differently.

The philosophical problem is not the same, for it threatens human life even at its subjective best with objective meaninglessness, and with absurdity if it cannot stop taking itself seriously. This problem is the emotional counterpart of that sense of arbitrariness which the objective self feels at being someone in particular.

Each of us finds himself with a life to lead. While we have a certain amount of control over it, the basic conditions of success and failure, our basic motives and needs, and the social circumstances that define our possibilities are simply given. Shortly after birth we have to start running just to keep from falling down, and there is only limited choice as to what will matter to us. We worry about a bad haircut or a bad review, we try to improve our income, our character, and our sensitivity to other people's feelings, we raise children, watch Johnny Carson, argue about Alfred Hitchcock or Chairman Mao, worry about getting promoted, getting pregnant, or becoming impotent — in short we lead highly specific lives within the parameters of our place, time, species, and culture. What could be more natural?

Yet there is a point of view from which none of it seems to matter. When you look at your struggle as if from a great height, in abstraction from the engagement you have with this life because it is yours — perhaps even in abstraction from your

identification with the human race — you may feel a certain sympathy for the poor beggar, a pale pleasure in his triumphs and a mild concern for his disappointments. And of course given that this person exists, there is little he can do but keep going till he dies, and try to accomplish something by the standards internal to his form of life. But it wouldn't matter all that much if he failed, and it would matter perhaps even less if he didn't exist at all. The clash of standpoints is not absolute, but the disparity is very great.

This kind of detachment is certainly possible for us, but the question is whether *it* matters. What am I doing out there, pretending to be a visitor from outer space — looking at my life from a great height in abstraction from the fact that it is mine, or that I am human and a member of this culture? How can the unimportance of my life from that point of view have any importance for *me*? Perhaps the problem is a purely philosophical artefact, and not real.

I'll return to this objective later, but first let me pose another: Even if the problem can't be dismissed as unreal, it may have a simple solution. Is it so certain that the attitudes really conflict as they appear to? Since the two judgments arise from different perspectives, why isn't their content appropriately relativized to those perspectives, rendering the conflict illusory? If that were true, it would be no more problematic that the course of my life should matter from inside but not from outside than that a large mouse should be a small animal, or that something should look round from one direction and oval from another.

I do not believe this solution is available, logical as it may seem. The trouble is that the two attitudes have to coexist in a single person who is actually leading the life toward which he is simultaneously engaged and detached. This person does not occupy a third standpoint from which he can make two relativized judgments about his life. If all he had were two relativized judgments, they would leave him with no attitude toward his life at all — only information about the appropriate attitude from two points of view, neither of which was his. But in fact he occupies both of the conflicting points of view and his attitudes derive from them both.

The real problem is with the external point of view, which cannot remain a mere spectator once the self has expanded to accommodate it. It has to join in with the rest and lead this life from which it is disengaged. As a result the person becomes in significant part detached from what he is doing. The objective self is dragged along by the unavoidable engagement of the whole person in the living of a life whose form it recognizes as arbitrary. It generates a demand for justification which it at the same time guarantees to be unsatisfiable, because the only available justification depends on the view from inside.

Some philosophers have held that the soul is trapped in the body. To Plato this meant not just that the soul is housed in the body, but that the needs of the body invade and compromise the soul, threatening it with domination by its basest portion, the appetites. I am talking about something different but analogous, the inevitable engagement of the objective self in a particular contingent life, whose consequence is not depravity but absurdity. It isn't so much the animal aspects of life which generate the absurd, for no judgment of importance need attach to an instinctive effort to survive. The problem comes especially with those more developed human projects that pretend to significance and without which life would not be human. It is heightened by the equally human involvement we all have with our *own* lives and ambitions.

This invites a quick solution to the problem. Perhaps we can avoid the absurd if we devote ourselves to providing only for the basic needs of everyone. There is a great deal of misery in the world, and many of us could easily spend our lives trying to eradicate it—wiping out starvation, disease, and torture.

Such aims do indeed seem to give life a meaning that is hard to question. But while they are certainly worthy and perhaps imperative goals, they cannot eliminate the problem. Granted, one advantage of living in a world as bad as this one is that it offers the opportunity for many activities whose importance can't be questioned. But how could the main point of human life be the elimination of evil? Misery, deprivation, and injustice prevent people from pursuing the positive goods which life is assumed to make possible. If all such goods were pointless and the only thing that really mattered was the elimination of misery, that really *would* be absurd. The same could be said of the idea that helping others is the only thing that really gives meaning to life. If no one's life has any meaning in itself, how can it acquire meaning through devotion to the meaningless lives of others?

No, even if the problem of meaning can be postponed until all misery is wiped out, it will not go away permanently. In any case, most of us face it in our own lives. Some of us have bigger egos than others, and a dominant obsession with personal standing or success is recognized as absurd even without the benefit of philosophy. But everyone who is not either mystically transformed or hopelessly lacking in self-esteem regards his life and his projects as important, and not just to him.

From outside we do indeed tend to see most of our pursuits as important only relatively. Watching the human drama is a bit like watching a Little League baseball game: the excitement of the participants is perfectly understandable but one can't really enter into it. At the same time, since one *is* one of the participants, one is caught up in the game directly, in a way that cannot include an admission of relativity. When you are considering a career, marriage, children, or even whether to go on a diet, review a book, or buy a car, the external standpoint is excluded and you face the matter directly, from the internal standpoint of ordinary life. The detached external view just has to come along, and accommodate itself to the unqualified concerns that it can't internalize. At the same time there is a temptation to resist this detachment by inflating the sense of objective importance inside one's life, either by overvaluing one's own significance or by attributing a wider significance to one's pursuits.

It is the same phenomenon we have discussed in other connections—in epistemology, for example.

The internal view resists the reduction to a subjective interpretation of its contents which the external view tries to force on it. But this puts the objective standpoint in conflict with itself. Finding my life objectively insignificant, I am nevertheless unable to extricate myself from an unqualified commitment to it — to my aspirations and ambitions, my wishes for fulfillment, recognition, understanding, and so forth. The sense of the absurd is the result of this juxtaposition.

This is not an artificial problem created by a philosophical misstep, any more than epistemological skepticism is. Just as we can't evade skepticism by denying the pretensions of our beliefs about the world and interpreting them as entirely relative to a subjective or personal point of view, so we can't evade the impact of objective detachment by denying the objective pretensions of our dominant aims in life. This would simply falsify the situation. The problem of the meaning of life is in fact a form of skepticism at the level of motivation. We can no more abandon our unqualified commitments at will than we can abandon our beliefs about the world in response to skeptical arguments, however persuasive we may find them, as Hume famously observed. Nor, I believe, can we avoid either problem by refusing to take that step outside ourselves which calls the ordinary view into question.

Several routes might be attempted out of this impasse. I don't believe there is a way out, though there are adjustments we can make to live with the conflict. But it is worth considering what would be required to eliminate it entirely. I'll discuss two proposals which try to meet the problem head-on and one which tries to dissolve it.

The first solution to consider is the most Draconian: to deny the claims of the subjective view, withdraw from the specifics of individual human life as much as possible, minimize the area of one's local contact with the world and concentrate on the universal. Contemplation, meditation, withdrawal from the demands of the body and of society, abandonment of exclusive personal ties and worldly ambition — all this gives the objective standpoint less to be disengaged from, less to regard as vain. I gather this response is recommended by certain traditions, though I don't know enough to be sure that it isn't a caricature: the loss of self in the individual sense is thought to be required by the revelations of an impersonal view, which takes precedence over the view from here. And apparently it is possible for some individuals to achieve this withering away of the ego, so that personal life continues only as vehicle for the transcendent self, not as an end in itself.[1]

I cannot speak from experience, but it seems to me a high price to pay for spiritual harmony. The amputation of so much of oneself to secure the unequivocal affirmation of the rest seems a waste of consciousness. I would rather lead an absurd life engaged in the particular than a seamless transcendental life immersed in the universal. Perhaps those who have tried both would laugh inscrutably at this preference. It reflects the belief that the absurdity of human life is not such a bad thing. There are limits to what we should be prepared to do to escape it — apart from the point that some of these cures may be more absurd than the disease.

The second solution is the opposite of the first — a denial of the objective unimportance of our lives, which will justify full engagement from the objective standpoint. While this response to detachment has some merit, the truth in it is not enough to resolve the conflict.

. . . An impersonal perspective doesn't necessarily lead to nihilism. It may fail to discover *independent* reasons to care about what subjectively concerns us, but much that is of value and significance in the world can be understood directly only from within the perspective of a particular form of life, and this can be recognized from an external standpoint. The fact that the point of something can't be understood from the objective standpoint alone doesn't mean it must be regarded objectively as pointless, any more than the fact that the value of music is not directly comprehensible to someone deaf from birth means he has to judge it worthless. His knowledge of its value must depend on others. And the objective standpoint can recognize the authority of particular points of view with regard to worth as it can with regard to essentially perspectival facts. This includes recognizing the worth of what is of value only to a particular creature—who may be oneself. We might say that absolute value is revealed to the objective view through the evidence available to particular perspectives, including one's own. So even if there is no externally appreciable reason for the existence of any particular form of life, including my own, at least some of the values, positive and negative, that are defined by reference to it can be externally acknowledged. Playing in a Little League baseball game, making pancakes, or applying a coat of nail polish are perfectly good things to do. Their value is not necessarily canceled by the fact that they lack external justification.

This is not enough, however, to harmonize the two standpoints, because it doesn't warrant a particular objective interest in the individual life that happens to be mine, or even in the general form of human life of which it is an instance. These things have been handed to me and they demand my full attention. But to the external view, many different actual and possible subjective values must be acknowledged. Those arising within my life may evoke sympathy, but that is not the same as true objective engagement. My life is one of countlessly many, in a civilization that is also not unique, and my natural devotion to it is quite out of proportion to the importance I can reasonably accord it from outside.

From there I can accord it no more importance than it merits in a global view which includes all possible forms of life and their value on an equal footing. It is true that my life is the one among all these that I am in the best position to devote attention to, and it could be argued that the traditional principle of division of labor warrants my concentrating on it in the usual way as the best method of contributing to the cosmic pool. But while there is something in this, it should not be exaggerated. The argument would not really justify us in engaging fully with our personal aims from an objective standpoint, and

such engagement as it warranted would be on sufferance from an objective concern for the whole of which we were a part. This is at best a method of partial reconciliation between inner and outer views; we can try to avoid assigning ourselves a personal importance grotesquely out of line with our objective value, but we can't realistically hope to close the gap completely. So while the acknowledgment of objective worth inside human life may make the conflict of standpoints less extreme, it doesn't eliminate it.

The third candidate solution I want to discuss can be thought of as an argument that the problem is unreal. The objection is that to identify with the objective self and find its detachment disturbing is to forget who you are. There is something deranged in looking at one's existence from so far outside that one can ask why it matters. If we were actually detached spirits about to be thrown into the world by embodiment in a particular creature whose form of life had so far been only externally observed by us, it would be different: we might well feel a threat of impending captivity. But it isn't like that. We are first of all and essentially individual human beings. Our objectivity is simply a development of our humanity and doesn't allow us to break free of it. It must serve our humanity and to the extent that it does not we can forget about it.

The point here is to force withdrawal of the external demand which gives rise to the problem. This is a natural and in some ways appealing response, but as a conclusive argument it will not work. Objectivity is not content to remain a servant of the individual perspective and its values. It has a life of its own and an aspiration for transcendence that will not be quieted in response to the call to reassume our true identity. This shows itself not only in the permanent disaffection from individual life that is the sense of the absurd, but in the demands for objective justification which we sometimes *can* meet, as in the development of ethics. The external standpoint plays an important positive role in human motivation as well as a negative one, and the two cannot be separated. Both depend on the independence of the external view and the pressure it puts us under to bring it into our lives. The sense of the absurd is just a perception of the limits of this effort, reached when we ascend higher on the transcendental ladder than our merely human individuality can follow, even with the help of considerable readjustment. The objective self is a vital part of us, and to ignore its quasi-independent operation is to be cut off from oneself as much as if one were to abandon one's subjective individuality. There is no escape from alienation or conflict of one kind or another.

In sum, I believe there is no credible way of eliminating the inner conflict. Nonetheless, we have a motive for reducing it, and it is possible to promote a degree of harmony between the two standpoints without taking drastic measures. The attitude toward one's own life is inevitably dominated by the fact that it, unlike all those others, is one's own. But the domination should not be so complete that the objective standpoint treats the values defined by that life as ultimate. While objective reason does naturally fall into the service of the subjective passions, it can retain its recognition, however sympathetic, that they are the passions of a particular individual and whatever importance they may have derives from that. So objectivity itself is split into spectator and participant. It devotes itself to the interests and the ambitions, including the competitive ambitions, of one person while at the same time recognizing that he is no more important than anyone else and that the human form of life is not the embodiment of all value.

One of the devices by which these two attitudes are combined is morality, which seeks a way to live as an individual that affirms the equal worth of other individuals and is therefore externally acceptable. Morality is a form of objective reengagement. It permits the objective assertion of subjective values to the extent that this is compatible with the corresponding claims of others. It can take various forms, some of which I have discussed. All of them involve, to one degree or another, occupying a position far enough outside your own life to reduce the importance of the difference between yourself and other people, yet not so far outside that all human values vanish in a nihilistic blackout.

But there is more to integration than that. The most general effect of the objective stance ought to be a form of humility: the recognition that you are no more important than you are, and that the fact that something is of importance to you, or that it would be good or bad if you did or suffered something, is a fact of purely local significance. Such humility may seem incompatible with full immersion in one's life and in the pursuit of those enjoyments and goods that it makes possible. It may sound like a form of deadening self-consciousness, or self-denigration, or asceticism: but I don't think it has to be.

It does not create self-consciousness but simply gives it content. Our capacity for taking an external view of ourselves poses the problem; we cannot get rid of it, and we must find some attitude or other that reckons with it. Humility falls between nihilistic detachment and blind self-importance. It doesn't require reflection on the cosmic arbitrariness of the sense of taste every time you eat a hamburger. But we can try to avoid the familiar excesses of envy, vanity, conceit, competitiveness, and pride — including pride in our culture, in our nation, and in the achievements of humanity as a species. The human race has a strong disposition to adore itself, in spite of its record. But it is possible to live a complete life of the kind one has been given without overvaluing it hopelessly. We can even resist the tendency to overvalue the historical present, both positively and negatively; what is going on in the world right now is not for that reason especially important. The present is where we are, and we cannot see it only in timeless perspective. But we can forget about it now and then, even if it won't forget about us.

Finally, there is an attitude which cuts through the opposition between transcendent universality and parochial self-absorption, and that is the attitude of nonegocentric respect for the particular.[2] It is conspicuous as an element in aesthetic response, but it can be directed to all kinds of things, including aspects of one's own life. One can simply look hard at a ketchup bottle, and the question of significance from different standpoints will disappear. Particular things can have a noncompetitive completeness which is transparent to all aspects of the self. This also helps explain why the experience of great beauty tends to unify the self: the object engages us immediately and totally in a way that makes distinctions among points of view irrelevant.

It is hard to know whether one could sustain such an attitude consistently toward the elements of everyday life. It would require an immediacy of feeling and attention to what is present that doesn't blend well with the complex, forward-looking pursuits of a civilized creature. Perhaps it would require a radical change in what one did, and that would raise the question whether the simplification was worth it.

Apart from this, the possibilities for most of us are limited. Some people are genuinely unworldly, but if it doesn't come naturally, the attempt to achieve this condition is likely to be an exercise in dishonesty and self-distortion. Most of us care a great deal about forms of individual success that we can see from an impersonal standpoint to be much less significant than we cannot help taking them to be from inside our lives. Our constitutional self-absorption together with our capacity to recognize its excessiveness make us ir-

reducibly absurd even if we achieve a measure of subjective-objective integration by bringing the two standpoints closer together. The gap is too wide to be closed entirely, for anyone who is fully human.

So the absurd is part of human life. I do not think this can be basically regretted, because it is a consequence of our existence as particular creatures with a capacity for objectivity. Some philosophers, such as Plato, have been unhappy that the higher self was trapped in a particular human life, and others, such as Nietzsche, have denigrated the role of the objective standpoint; but I believe the significant diminution of either of them in force or importance would lessen us and is not a reasonable aim. Repression can operate effectively and damagingly not just against the instincts but against the objective intelligence. These civil wars of the self result in an impoverished life. It is better to be simultaneously engaged and detached, and therefore absurd, for this is the opposite of self-denial and the result of full awareness. . . .

NOTES

1. Or perhaps alternatively, each particular element, whatever its character, is seen as a manifestation of the universal.

2. I am grateful to Jacob Adler for making me see this.

Further Questions

1. There is a voluminous literature on the question of whether life is meaningful. There is almost no discussion of why we should *care* whether life is meaningful. Do *you* care? Why?

2. Nagel claims that the problem of the meaning of life is due to a clash between two perspectives that we can take on our lives. What about conflicting ideas of the source of the problem—for instance, the old idea (see, for example, Tolstoy) that the problem is due to death?

3. Nagel tries to distinguish between a philosophical problem of the meaning of life and various psychological problems. He claims that the philosophical problem is different because it threatens human life with objective meaninglessness even when life is at its subjective best. But Nagel admits that the philosophical problem doesn't bother everyone, and even those who are bothered aren't bothered all the time. So perhaps the so-called philosophical problems are largely just psychological problems. What do you think?

Further Readings

Gilman, Charlotte Perkins. "The Yellow Wallpaper," in Ann Lane, ed. *The Charlotte Perkins Gilman Reader*. New York: Pantheon, 1980, pp. 3–20. A beautiful story, written in the 1890s, about a sensitive woman who goes mad for lack of meaningful work and an environment in which she can find her own identity.

Klemke, E. D., ed. *The Meaning of Life*. New York: Oxford University Press, 1981. Perhaps the best anthology on the topic. Includes a select bibliography.

A Fast Car and a Good Woman

RAYMOND MARTIN

In this selection Raymond Martin questions the psychological validity of philosophical worries about the meaning of life. He suggests that as often as not such worries merely mask a deep, underlying problem: our inability to stay satisfied.

A brief biography of Martin appears on pages 125–126.

Reading Questions

1. Martin distinguishes between the problem of the meaning of life and the problem of life. How?

2. Martin criticizes Tolstoy, Nagel, and Taylor. What are his criticisms of each?

3. Martin claims that, at least this side of enlightenment, there is no fully satisfying solution to the problem of life. Why?

4. What connection does he see between there being no solution to the problem of life and the fact that many people feel that death challenges the meaning of their lives?

POVERTY, SICKNESS, LONELINESS, alienation, feelings of inferiority, an inability to give and receive love. Such problems can challenge the meaning of our lives. There is no puzzle about why. When we are afflicted with them, we suffer. If our suffering is bad enough and seemingly intractable, we may lose the sense that our lives are worth living.

Such problems are practically, but not philosophically, challenging. When they cause suffering that is avoidable, the important question is how to avoid it. When they cause suffering that is inevitable, the question is how to accept it. Learning how to avoid suffering when we can and accept it when we must are not part of the problem of the meaning of life. They are part of the problem of life.

Death also challenges the meaning of our lives. But in the case of death, unlike in the cases of the other problems mentioned, it is not clear why. What does the fact that our lives will come to an end have to do with whether they are worth living? There seems to be no connection. I shall suggest a partial answer.

The problem of the meaning of life is the philosophical question of how, if at all, our lives can be worth living. It concerns, for instance, such speculative questions as whether there is an overriding purpose or pattern for human life as a whole that confers meaning on our individual lives, and whether there is an objective source of value for our lives. The problem of life, on the other hand, is the practical question of how to live our lives so that they are as worth living as they can be. Clearly the problem of life is more important. In fact, it can seem so much more important that it is a tenet of practical wisdom that if we take proper care of our lives, questions of meaning will take care of themselves. That's good advice, unless you are the sort of person who *has* to address questions of meaning to take proper care of your life. Not everyone does, and even among those who do, questions of meaning will seem more important at some times than at others.

Tolstoy is the classic example of someone for whom questions of meaning can be urgent.

> . . . I was overcome by minutes at first of perplexity and then of an arrest of life, as though I did not know how to live or what to do, and I lost myself and was dejected. But that passed and I continued to live as before. Then those minutes of perplexity were repeated oftener and oftener, and always in one and the same form. These arrests of life found their expression in ever the same questions: "Why? Well, and then?"

> At first I thought that those were simply aimless, inappropriate questions . . . [But they] began to repeat themselves oftener and oftener, answers were demanded more and more persistently, and, like dots that fall on the same spot, these questions, without any answers, thickened into one black blotch.

> . . . And I was absolutely unable to make any reply. The questions were not waiting and I had to answer them at once; if I did not answer them, I could not live.[1]

Empathizing with Tolstoy's existential anguish can unravel our familiar everyday rationalizations and expose a secret need for understanding we keep buried deep within. Stripped of our pretensions, we look freshly—at our own lives, at the lives of those around us, at the lives of everyone who has ever lived—and we ask: Why? There is no answer. Just the silent, anxious echo of our question. And sometimes a nagging doubt.

There is something fishy about existential anguish. Even when it comes wrapped in the paper of respectable philosophical questioning, it often smells suspiciously like a rationalization of unmentioned problems. Tolstoy, for instance, portrays himself as one who would be happy, except for worries about the meaning of life. But is it really worries about the meaning of his life that keep dragging him down? There are questions he can ask about the meaning of his life, doubts to be raised. But questions and doubts can be raised about anything. Questions are not necessarily problems. They can be. We can make a psychological problem out of almost anything. But how often are philosophical questions genuine psychological problems? When it seems that our philosophical questions give rise to existential anguish, should we marvel at the depth of our insight or suspect self-deception?

There is one familiar way philosophy can give rise to psychological problems. The naive person whose sense of security is built on a foundation of unquestioned beliefs can have those beliefs suddenly swept out from under him or her by philosophical questioning. Consider, for instance, a person whose sense of security rests on religious beliefs that suddenly become subject to doubt. The resulting turmoil can be so painfully confusing as to call into question the meaning of life.

Without minimizing this sort of problem, I wish to set it aside. The philosophical questioning which induces it usually directly challenges only the beliefs we depend on for security, not the meaning of our lives per se. The suffering comes not from some insoluble philosophical problem but from the sudden realization that our personal ideologies rest on dubious assumptions.

Most people get over this realization quickly enough (usually too quickly), either by forgetting or ignoring their doubts or else by finding a new basis for security. I am asking whether there is a deeper and more direct philosophical challenge to the meaning of our lives which is at least as psychologically valid as the one that depends on philosophical naiveté, yet is not so easily set aside or outgrown.

In sum, I have distinguished three challenges to the meaning of our lives: bad times, death, and philosophical doubts of a sort that can arise even when our lives are going quite well. My concern, now, is with the third of these challenges. Putting aside problems caused by the realization that our personal ideologies rest on dubious assumptions, I am asking whether challenges of this third sort—that is, philosophical doubts about the meaning of our lives that can arise even when our lives are going quite well—are psychologically genuine. I don't deny that when our lives are going quite well, psychological problems can arise. I'm asking how likely it is that philosophical questions are the explanation. I admit they may sometimes be the explanation. I'm asking whether there isn't usually some deeper explanation, a source of anxiety and despair we may not be facing if we allow ourselves to become preoccupied with philosophy.

Thomas Nagel sets aside as unphilosophical those challenges to the meaning of life that arise because things go wrong and "are compatible with the possibility of meaning had things gone differently." Philosophical challenges to meaning, in his view, threaten human life with "objective meaninglessness" even when it is "at its subjective best." And he seems to think that philosophical challenges to meaning are a chronic source of deep psychological problems.

> In seeing ourselves from outside we find it difficult to take our lives seriously. This loss of conviction, and the attempt to regain it, is the problem of the meaning of life.
>
> . . . it is a genuine problem which we cannot ignore. The capacity for transcendence brings

with it a liability to alienation. . . . Yet we can't abandon the external standpoint because it is our own.

It is our own, Nagel says, because the objective self is such a vital part of us that "to ignore its quasi-independent operation is to be cut off from oneself as much as if one were to abandon one's subjective individuality." So, in Nagel's view, there is no escape from this sort of alienation—"no credible way of eliminating the inner conflict"—and, hence, no solution to the philosophical problem of the meaning of life.

But there is help, Nagel thinks, and it comes from two sources:

> [Morality] permits the objective assertion of subjective values to the extent that this is compatible with the corresponding claims of others. It . . . [involves] occupying a position far enough outside your own life to reduce the importance of the difference between yourself and other people, yet not so far outside that all human values vanish in a nihilistic blackout. . . .
>
> . . . Humility falls between nihilistic detachment and blind self-importance. . . . The human race has a strong disposition to adore itself, in spite of its record. But it is possible to live a complete life of the kind one has been given without overvaluing it hopelessly.[2]

Even so, Nagel thinks that "the gap is too wide to be closed entirely, for anyone who is fully human." So, although morality and humility help, the problem is insoluble. Serious internal conflict remains. In sum, Nagel agrees with Tolstoy, though for different reasons, that philosophical challenges to the meaning of life are an important source of psychological problems.

If Nagel and Tolstoy are right, practical wisdom is wrong. Questions of meaning do not take care of themselves. If you are intellectually sensitive, then to take proper care of your life, you have to attend to questions about meaning. Tolstoy's self-portrait seems to show that these questions *can* bring you down. Nagel's view is that if you think honestly and correctly about questions of meaning, they *will* bring you down.

Tolstoy solved his problem by embracing Christianity. Nagel claims there is no honest solution. Nagel's analysis of the philosophical issues is elegant. Yet his account, like Tolstoy's, is psychologically suspect.

To see why, think about a time when your life *was* at its subjective best. Maybe you were young and had just fallen deeply in love with someone who had just fallen deeply in love with you. Perhaps you were in the throes of sexual ecstasy or enveloped in mystical bliss. Or you may have played some instrument, or danced, or acted, or wrote much better than you ever thought you could. Perhaps you were simply drawn out of yourself by the muted texture of an autumn day or the vibrant sting of cold rain against your face.

Whatever your peak experiences, were you worried then about the meaning of life? Did *questions* about meaning *bother* you, that is, were they *problems* for you? Of course not. If your life really was at its subjective best, then probably it was sufficient: you lacked nothing. Because you had solved the problem of life, at least temporarily, questions about the meaning of life did not even arise. If such questions had been raised, you would have regarded them as an entertainment or, more likely, dismissed them as irrelevant. Perhaps, then, practical wisdom is right after all: how to live well is the only psychologically valid issue.

When we are happy, *questions* about the meaning of our lives rarely ever become *problems*. The solution to the *problem* of the meaning of life, then, is simple: be happy. The really important question is: how? Life is too short to try out many paths to happiness. We have to take our chances. And we have to take some of our most important chances when we are young and relatively inexperienced. Through ignorance or bad luck, people often choose the wrong paths to happiness and, as a consequence, suffer. Such bad choices are obviously an important source of suffering, particularly for people in circumstances sufficiently advantaged that they have the luxury of choice. But the fact that people make bad choices about how to be happy does not in and of

itself give rise to *philosophical* problems about the meaning of our lives.

Like Nagel, Richard Taylor locates *philosophical* questions about the meaning of our lives in the tension between objective meaninglessness —for him, "endless pointlessness"—and subjective meaning. His view is that our lives are objectively meaningless, but not meaningless per se.

> At this point, then, we can reintroduce . . . our own wills, our deep interest in what we find ourselves doing. If we do this we find that our lives do indeed still resemble that of Sisyphus, but . . . the strange meaningfulness they possess is that of the inner compulsion to be doing just what we were put here to do, and to go on doing it forever.

In other words, the tasks people set for themselves, the things to which

> they bent their backs day after day, realizing one by one their ephemeral plans, were precisely the things in which their wills were deeply involved, precisely the things in which their interests lay, and there was no need then to ask questions. There is no more need of them now—the day was sufficient to itself, and so was the life. This is surely the way to look at all of life. . . .

So, in Taylor's view, subjective meaningfulness resides in activity in which our wills are involved.

> A human being no sooner draws his first breath than he responds to the will that is in him to live. He no more asks whether it will be worthwhile, or whether anything of significance will come of it, than the worms and the birds. The point of his living is simply to be living, in the manner that it is his nature to be living. . . . What counts is that one should be able to begin a new task, a new castle, a new bubble. It counts only because it is there to be done and he has the will to do it. . . . The meaning of life is from within us, it is not bestowed from without, and it far exceeds in both its beauty and permanence any heaven of which men have ever dreamed or yearned for.[3]

Taylor's view, in sum, is that the value derived from activity in which our wills are involved is enough to sustain the meaning of our lives, indeed, is as much as we can rationally hope for.

Is it? Looking around, we see people *willfully* building their castles and bubbles, so to speak, just as Taylor says they do, but not as *meaningfully* as he claims. Surely Thoreau was not all wrong when he observed that most people live in quiet desperation.

Taylor finds meaning everywhere. Nagel finds it nowhere. The saccharine sweetness of Taylor's conclusion makes Nagel's pessimism look appealing. But neither account feels psychologically valid. Taylor's is too romantic and makes meaning too easy. Nagel's is too intellectual and makes meaning too hard.

It is worth exploring the middle ground. A plausible view suggested by Taylor's discussion is that people have meaningful lives not when they are doing what they *will* to do but when they are doing what they *love* to do. Such a view seems to leave a place for meaningfulness without romanticizing human life. For most people are not doing what they love to do but, rather, what they have to do, or what they feel they have to do. The human spectacle is not a scene of yeoman farmers toiling happily in their fields. It includes a fair proportion of tired, unhappy people, resigned to their painful, dreary lives, trying desperately to distract and anesthetize themselves.

Meaning, then, on this criterion, is neither impossible nor inevitable. Nor is it all or nothing. It is a matter of degree. Is the answer, then, not that your life is or is not inherently meaningful but, rather, that it can be meaningful, and is meaningful largely to the degree that you are doing what you love to do? That seems a more likely hypothesis than the ones already considered. Yet, in its implicit suggestion that the main problem of meaning is the practical problem of finding out what you love to do and then doing it, this view too may be hopelessly romantic.

Oscar Wilde once remarked that there are only two problems in life: not getting what you want, and getting it. If Wilde is right, then what many people think is the whole problem — not getting what you want (or doing what you want to do) — is really only part of the problem. Ironically, the rest of the problem is what these same people think is the solution. It is hard to quarrel with that much of Wilde's observation. Getting what you want *can* be problematic. Wilde's remark also *suggests*, however, that getting what you want not only *can be* but *will be* problematic. If that's true, then our lives are an insoluble problem.

It is easy to see how not getting what you want can be a problem. And, if you want the wrong things — say, the pleasures of an unhealthy lifestyle — it's also easy to see how getting what you want can be a problem. But what if you want the right things — things that are not only good in themselves but also good for you. How could wanting the right things be a problem?

Think back to those times when your life was at its subjective best. Granted, at those moments you were not bothered by questions about the meaning of life. But were you completely satisfied? That's a loaded question. How could you ever know that you couldn't have been even more satisfied? So far as you could tell, then, were you completely satisfied? Probably you were. If you were, then it must be possible to be so happy that, so far as you can tell, you have all of your unsatisfied wants driven out of you — at least all of them that detract from your happiness. That may or may not be complete satisfaction. But it's close enough for most of us. And we sometimes get it. In and of itself, it's a solution, not a problem. But it inevitably leads to a problem, the real problem: *it doesn't last*.

Life is a tease. It promises more lasting satisfactions than it delivers. No matter how good it gets, eventually we always find ourselves wanting more. If we lose what was satisfying us completely, we want it back. If we keep it, we want more of it or else we want something else. And we will want in a way that detracts from our happiness. That's a psychological truth you can bet the farm on. Whatever you think is going to satisfy you completely, it is not going to satisfy you completely for long. It may for a while. If you are clever, you may even distract yourself from noticing that the itch of unsatisfied desire has returned. But if you look closely, you will see that what you wanted, what you may have thought would be enough, what you were sure would satisfy you completely, does not really do it.

Most of us have the dubious luxury of thinking that we would be happy if only we had something we cannot have, or we were doing something we cannot do. Our deprivation nourishes the illusion that complete satisfaction—that lasts—is attainable, if only the external circumstances of our lives were better. Tolstoy did not have the luxury of that illusion. He had everything he wanted—wealth, fame, a loving family—and was doing what he wanted to do. Yet still he wasn't satisfied. He had so much that he couldn't imagine what more he wanted—unless perhaps it was answers. So he embraced answers, and then—so he would have us believe—he was happy. That is his story: that it was lack of answers that brought him down in the first place, and that it was his subsequent conviction that he had answers—his "irrational knowledge"—that made everything right again.

Perhaps. But another possibility is that Tolstoy's lack of answers was at most a symptom of the problem, not the real problem. Since he had everything and was doing what he wanted to be doing, what, then, could his real problem have been? It *could* have been simply that even with everything, Tolstoy's life did not stay at its subjective best: satisfied, he could not stay satisfied. The problem could have been that Tolstoy wanted his life to be at its subjective best but could not keep it there. So, when he came down, as inevitably he did, he wanted more, even though, as we say, "he had everything." In other words, the problem could have been simply that while life allowed him to taste complete satisfaction, it didn't last.

If not getting what you want (or not doing what you want to do) won't satisfy you completely, and getting what you want (or doing what you want to do) won't satisfy you completely either, it's worth thinking briefly about the extreme alternative: don't want. That's the essence of the Buddha Gautama's contribution to solving the problem of life. It may or may not be the right solution. We don't really have to decide. For even if it is the right solution, it is the Buddha's solution, not ours. We may give lip service to that solution, but few of us really see it as a realistic option for ourselves. If we did, we'd be off somewhere, perhaps meditating in a monastery in Burma, not taking college courses or reading essays like this one on the meaning of life. We may say we're on the "path." And we may be. But even on the path we still spend most of our waking time trying to get what we want. Except that on the path, in addition to all of the usual wants—security, sex, love, power, glory—we now have an unusual want: not wanting. The path is crowded with spiritual materialists.[4]

We're back to a realistic pessimism. The answer to the problem of the meaning of life may simply be that we're stuck with a life of fleeting satisfactions and unsatisfied desires. Whatever the value of morality and humility, they are precious little help in solving this problem. Doing what you love to do is a great help, probably the most important contribution you can make to the meaningfulness of your life. Ironically, doing what you love to do may even be a critical part of the most important contribution you can make to the lives of those around you. Even so, at least this side of enlightenment, there may be no fully satisfying solution to the problem of life.

Since satisfaction doesn't last, then either we have to continually resatisfy ourselves or successfully and pleasantly distract ourselves from the fact that we haven't. That seems to be our fate, and if we're reasonably good at these two tasks, it's not such a bad fate. But neither is it a fully satisfying solution to the problem of life. In other words, what I am suggesting is that the root psychological problem, the one that keeps arising even when our lives are going quite well, may simply be that we cannot satisfy ourselves completely for long. That is why even among people whose lives are going quite well, almost everyone is chronically unsatisfied. Acknowledging that this is the problem can bring us down from our philosophical heights. Back on earth, we can redirect our energies toward solving the problem of life. To do that, we follow our individual recipes for happiness: a fast car and a good woman, or whatever you think will do it for you.

The acknowledgment that there is no fully satisfying solution to the problem of life can quash our hopes that we will ever get the complete and lasting satisfaction we crave. That is one of the deepest and most emotionally significant hopes we have. True, that hope may never have survived rational scrutiny anyway, but that doesn't stop us from secretly nourishing it. It comes as a profound disappointment to finally admit, not just verbally, but completely, that whether we get what we want or not we will never stay satisfied for long.

And then there is death. Death has always been a puzzle for philosophers. Not what it is, but why we have some of the attitudes toward it we do. For present purposes, we can ignore most of these famous enigmas. Our question is this: Why does death threaten the meaning of our lives? Surely part of the answer is the familiar observation that we fear we may vanish without leaving a significant trace — that our lives will not have made a positive difference. But, of course, that should not be a problem for people, such as Tolstoy, whose lives have gone as well as possible and, hence, who have made a positive difference. There must be more than that to the challenge to meaning that death poses. The analysis just given suggests part of the answer.

Death threatens the meaningfulness of our lives partly because it ends our struggle for satisfaction. Because death kills us, the prospect that death is near kills the unspoken and irrational hope that if only we had a little more time, we might satisfy our need for psychological closure — for complete satisfaction. If we have already given up that hope, we will fear death less. We may even welcome it as a merciful release from a struggle we cannot help throwing ourselves into even though we know we shall never win it. In any case, death challenges the meaningfulness of our lives partly because the prospect that death is near makes it painfully obvious that we will lose the struggle for satisfaction. Death is a major symbol of defeat.

Return once again to those moments when your life was at its subjective best. Those moments brought complete satisfaction. And complete satisfaction is a kind of victory over death. A person, for instance, can be so much in love, so deeply satisfied, she feels that she could die and it wouldn't matter. When our experience gets that good, we have won the battle for satisfaction, and death holds no terror. The problem is that our victory is only temporary. Death is a persistent foe, and desire its ally. Satisfied, we cannot stay satisfied. The itch of desire returns, the struggle resumes. Until death ends the struggle — perhaps forever.[5]

NOTES

1. Leo Tolstoy's reflections on the meaning of life are contained in his book, *My Confession*, translated by Leo Wiener, Dent and Sons, 1905.

2. Thomas Nagel's thoughts on the meaning of life were published originally in his essay, "The Absurd," *The Journal of Philosophy*, v. 63, 1971, pp. 716–727. The passages quoted are taken from that portion of Nagel's *The View from Nowhere*, Oxford University Press, 1986, 214–223, that is reprinted in the present volume.

3. Richard Taylor's views are from his book, *Good and Evil*, Macmillan, 1970, and they are also reprinted in the present volume.

4. I have borrowed the notion of "spiritual materialism" from Chögyam Trungpa, *Cutting Through Spiritual Materialism*, Boulder, Colorado: Shambhala Publications, 1973.

5. Ramakrishna Puligandla, Jeanne Ann Whittington, Michael Slote, Daniel Kolak, and Kate Wheeler commented perceptively on an earlier draft of the original version of this paper, which was written for a symposium on the meaning of life, sponsored by the Society for Asian and Comparative Philosophy, at the Central Division meetings of the American Philosophical Association, Chicago, April 1989, and then included in the first edition of *The Experience of Philosophy*. The paper has been revised for the second edition of *The Experience of Philosophy*.

Further Questions

1. Which is more important for you: the problem of the meaning of life or the problem of life? Must you solve the former to solve the latter?

2. What is your personal solution to the problem of life?

3. Is being completely satisfied compatible with having unsatisfied desires? If it is, does this fact undermine Martin's argument?

Further Readings

Lao Tzu. *The Way of Life*. Witter Bynner translation. New York: Perigee Books, 1944, 1972. The Taoist classic on how to live well. One of the best translations for Americans.

Sujata. *Beginning to See*. San Francisco: Apple Pie Books, 1983. Marvelous epigrams (and cartoons) on the problem of life.

Walpola, Rahula. *What the Buddha Taught*. 2nd ed. New York: Grove, 1974. The Buddha's views on suffering.

Part XIII

Ethics

N ATURE HAS NO RESPECT FOR MORALITY. Nature kills indiscriminately. Rocks, animals, insects, and plants know nothing of morality. We do. Isn't our moral sense part of what makes us special?

Perhaps. But we kill far more efficiently than either nature or any of its creatures. In this century alone, more than fifty million human beings have been slaughtered in war, and today we're in danger of destroying not only the rest of humanity but all life on this planet. Meanwhile, we continue to ravage the earth, enslave other animals, and pollute our environment. We rape and pillage and murder one another, often without provocation. That is almost a distinction in itself. However, there is at least one other animal that murders its own kind without provocation: rats.

Many claim morality can save us from ourselves. Others say we must save ourselves from morality. But what does it mean to be moral? Is morality objective? Subjective? An expression of self-interest? A way of keeping self-interest in check? Who is to determine what is right and what is wrong? Are there moral truths and, if so, how can we know them? How can we settle moral disagreements?

We might not know the answers to any of these questions. But, unlike all other known creatures, we can at least ask them.

The Categorical Imperative

IMMANUEL KANT

The great German philosopher Immanuel Kant (1724–1804) was born in East Prussia, where his grandfather had emigrated from Scotland. Kant was the first modern philosopher who earned his living as a university professor. But instead of having his salary set and paid by an administration, he collected his money directly from the students! His most famous and influential works are *The Critique of Pure Reason* (1781) and *Groundwork of the Metaphysics of Morals* (1785). He got in a lot of trouble with the king, Frederick William II, for the "distortion and depreciation of many leading and fundamental doctrines of holy writ and Christianity," and was ordered not to lecture or write further on religious subjects. Kant dutifully obeyed, until the king died; then he dutifully resumed.

Kant argued for the objectivity of morals. He is one of the best representatives of the view that moral laws are binding on everyone and always without any qualification — hence "categorical."

Reading Questions

1. What distinguishes the *hypothetical* from the *categorical* imperative?
2. Kant believed morality could be summed up, like scientific laws, in one ultimate principle. What is that principle?

3. By "maxim," Kant means "rule." By "universal law," he means something that is binding upon everyone, always. Thus, he says, "Act only according to that maxim by which you can at the same time will that it should become a universal law." But what, according to Kant, is supposed to guide your *will*?

4. What makes the categorical imperative categorical, and how can you know it is categorical rather than hypothetical?

5. Why does Kant think that human beings are ends in themselves?

6. What does he mean by human "will"?

7. Why does Kant think that duty is a categorical imperative?

NOTHING CAN POSSIBLY BE CONCEIVED in the world, or even out of it, which can be called good without qualification, except a *good will*. Intelligence, wit, judgment, and other *talents* of the mind, however they may be named, or courage, resolution, perseverance, as qualities of temperament, are undoubtedly good and desirable in many respects; but these gifts of nature may also become extremely bad and mischievous if the will which is to make use of them, and which, therefore, constitutes what is called *character*, is not good. It is the same with the *gifts of fortune*. Power, riches, honor, even health, and the general well-being and contentment with one's condition which is called *happiness*, inspire pride, and often presumption, if there is not a good will to correct the influence of these on the mind, and with this also to rectify the whole principle of acting, and adapt it to its end. The sight of a being who is not adorned with a single feature of a pure and good will, enjoying unbroken prosperity, can never give pleasure to an impartial rational spectator. Thus a good will appears to constitute the indispensable condition even of being worthy of happiness.

There are even some qualities which are of service to this good will itself, and may facilitate its action, yet which have no intrinsic unconditional value, but always presuppose a good will, and this qualifies the esteem that we justly have for them, and does not permit us to regard them as absolutely good. Moderation in the affections and passions, self-control, and calm deliberation are not only good in many respects, but even seem to constitute part of the intrinsic worth of the person; but they are far from deserving to be called good without qualification, although they have been so unconditionally praised by the ancients. For without the principles of a good will, they may become extremely bad; and the coolness of a villain not only makes him far more dangerous, but also directly makes him more abominable in our eyes than he would have been without it.

A good will is good not because of what it performs or effects, not by its aptness for the attainment of some proposed end, but simply by virtue of the volition — that is, it is good in itself, and considered by itself is to be esteemed much higher than all that can be brought about by it in favor of any inclination, nay, even of the sum-total of all inclinations. Even if it should happen that, owing to special disfavor of fortune, or the niggardly provision of a stepmotherly nature, this will should wholly lack power to accomplish its purpose, if with its greatest efforts it should yet achieve nothing, and there should remain only the good will (not, to be sure, a mere wish, but the summoning of all means in our power), then, like a jewel, it would still shine by its own light, as a thing which has its whole value in itself. Its usefulness or fruitlessness can neither add to nor take away anything from this value. It would be, as it were, only the setting to enable us to

From Immanuel Kant, The Fundamental Principles of the Metaphysics of Morals. *Translated by Thomas K. Abbott, 1889.*

handle it the more conveniently in common commerce, or to attract to it the attention of those who are not yet connoisseurs, but not to recommend it to true connoisseurs, or to determine its value. . . .

Everything in nature works according to laws. Rational beings alone have the faculty of acting according *to the conception* of laws, that is according to principles, *i.e.* have a *will*. Since the deduction of actions from principles requires *reason*, the will is nothing but practical reason. . . . the relation of the objective laws to a will that is not thoroughly good is conceived as the determination of the will of a rational being by principles of reason, but which the will from its nature does not of necessity follow.

The conception of an objective principle, in so far as it is obligatory for a will, is called a command (of reason), and the formula of the command is called an Imperative. . . .

Now all *imperatives* command either *hypothetically* or *categorically*. . . .

. . . If now the action is good only as a means *to something else*, then the imperative is *hypothetical*; if it is conceived as good *in itself* and consequently as being necessarily the principle of a will which of itself conforms to reason, then it is *categorical*. . . .

When I conceive of a hypothetical imperative, in general I do not know beforehand what it will contain until I am given the condition. But when I conceive a categorical imperative, I know at once what it contains. For as the imperative contains besides the law only the necessity that the maxims shall conform to this law, while the law contains no conditions restricting it, there remains nothing but the general statement that the maxim of the action should conform to a universal law, and it is this conformity alone that the imperative properly represents as necessary.

There is . . . but one categorical imperative, namely, this: *Act only on that maxim whereby thou canst at the same time will that it should become a universal law.*

Now if all imperatives of duty can be deduced from this one imperative as from their principle, then, although it should remain undecided whether what is called duty is not merely a vain notion, yet at least we shall be able to show what we understand by it and what this notion means.

Since the universality of the law according to which effects are produced constitutes what is properly called *nature* in the most general sense (as to form), that is the existence of things so far as it is determined by general laws, the imperative of duty may be expressed thus: *Act as if the maxim of thy action were to become by thy will a universal law of nature.*

We will now enumerate a few duties, adopting the usual division of them into duties to ourselves and to others, and into perfect and imperfect duties.

1. A man reduced to despair by a series of misfortunes feels wearied of life, but is still so far in possession of his reason that he can ask himself whether it would not be contrary to his duty to himself to take his own life. Now he inquires whether the maxim of his action could become a universal law of nature. His maxim is: From self-love I adopt it as a principle to shorten my life when its longer duration is likely to bring more evil than satisfaction. It is asked then simply whether this principle founded on self-love can become a universal law of nature. Now we see at once that a system of nature of which it should be a law to destroy life by means of the very feeling whose special nature it is to impel to the improvement of life would contradict itself, and therefore could not exist as a system of nature; hence that maxim cannot possibly exist as a universal law of nature, and consequently would be wholly inconsistent with the supreme principle of all duty.

2. Another finds himself forced by necessity to borrow money. He knows that he will not be able to repay it, but sees also that nothing will be lent to him, unless he promises stoutly to repay it in a definite time. He desires to make this promise,

but he has still so much conscience as to ask himself: Is it not unlawful and inconsistent with duty to get out of a difficulty in this way? Suppose, however, that he resolves to do so, then the maxim of his action would be expressed thus: When I think myself in want of money, I will borrow money and promise to repay it, although I know that I never can do so. Now this principle of self-love or of one's own advantage may perhaps be consistent with my whole future welfare; but the question now is, Is it right? I change then the suggestion of self-love into a universal law, and state the question thus: How would it be if my maxim were a universal law? Then I see at once that it could never hold as a universal law of nature, but would necessarily contradict itself. For supposing it to be a universal law that everyone when he thinks himself in a difficulty should be able to promise whatever he pleases, with the purpose of not keeping his promise, the promise itself would become impossible, as well as the end that one might have in view in it, since no one would consider that anything was promised to him, but would ridicule all such statements as vain pretences.

3. A third finds in himself a talent which with the help of some culture might make him a useful man in many respects. But he finds himself in comfortable circumstances, and prefers to indulge in pleasure rather than to take pains in enlarging and improving his happy natural capacities. He asks, however, whether his maxim of neglect of his natural gifts, besides agreeing with his inclination to indulgence, agrees also with what is called duty. He sees then that a system of nature could indeed subsist with such a universal law although men (like the South Sea islanders) should let their talents rest, and resolve to devote their lives merely to idleness, amusement, and propagation of their species — in a word, to enjoyment; but he cannot possibly *will* that this should be a universal law of nature, or be implanted in us as such by a natural instinct. For, as a rational being, he necessarily wills that his facul-

ties be developed, since they serve him, and have been given him, for all sorts of possible purposes.

4. A fourth, who is in prosperity, while he sees that others have to contend with great wretchedness and that he could help them, thinks: What concern is it of mine? Let everyone be as happy as Heaven pleases, or as he can make himself; I will take nothing from him nor even envy him, only I do not wish to contribute anything to his welfare or to his assistance in distress! Now no doubt if such a mode of thinking were a universal law, the human race might very well subsist, and doubtless even better than in a state in which everyone talks of sympathy and good-will, or even takes care occasionally to put it into practice, but, on the other side, also cheats when he can, betrays the rights of men, or otherwise violates them. But although it is possible that a universal law of nature might exist in accordance with that maxim, it is impossible to *will* that such a principle should have the universal validity of a law of nature. For a will which resolved this would contradict itself, inasmuch as many cases might occur in which one would have the need of the love and sympathy of others, and in which, by such a law of nature, sprung from his own will, he would deprive himself of all hope of the aid he desires. . . .

We have thus established at least this much, that if duty is a conception which is to have any import and real legislative authority for our actions, it can only be expressed in categorical, and not at all in hypothetical imperatives. We have also, which is of great importance, exhibited clearly and definitely for every practical application the content of the categorical imperative, which must contain the principle of all duty if there is such a thing at all. We have not yet, however, advanced so far as to prove *a priori* that there actually is such an imperative, that there is a practical law which commands absolutely of itself, and without any other impulse, and that the following of this law is duty. . . .

Now I say: man and generally any rational being *exists* as an end in himself, *not merely as a means* to be arbitrarily used by this or that will, but in all his actions, whether they concern himself or other rational beings, must be always regarded at the same time as an end. All objects of the inclinations have only a conditional worth; for if the inclinations and the wants founded on them did not exist, then their object would be without value. But the inclinations themselves being sources of want are so far from having an absolute worth for which they should be desired, that, on the contrary, it must be the universal wish of every rational being to be wholly free from them. Thus the worth of any object which is *to be acquired* by our action is always conditional. Beings whose existence depends not on our will but on nature's, have nevertheless, if they are rational beings, only a relative value as means, and are therefore called *things*; rational beings, on the contrary, are called *persons*, because their very nature points them out as ends in themselves, that is as something which must not be used merely as means, and so far therefore restricts freedom of action (and is an object of respect). These, therefore, are not merely subjective ends whose existence as a worth *for us* as an effort of our action, but *objective ends*, that is things whose existence is an end in itself: an end moreover for which no other can be substituted, which they should subserve *merely* as means, for otherwise nothing whatever would possess *absolute worth*; but if all worth were conditioned and therefore contingent, then there would be no supreme practical principle of reason whatever.

If then there is a supreme practical principle or, in respect of the human will, a categorical imperative, it must be one which, being drawn from the conception of that which is necessarily an end for everyone because it is *an end in itself,* constitutes an *objective* principle of will, and can therefore serve as a universal practical law. The foundation of this principle is: *rational nature exists as an end in itself.* Man necessarily conceives his own existence as being so: so far then this is a *subjective* principle of human action. But every other rational being regards its existence similarly, just on the same rational principle, that holds for me: so that it is at the same time an objective principle, from which as a supreme practical law all laws of the will must be capable of being deduced. Accordingly the practical imperative will be as follows: *So act as to treat humanity, whether in thine own person or in that of any other, in every case as an end withal, never as means only. . . .*

The conception of every rational being as one which must consider itself as giving all the maxims of its will universal laws, so as to judge itself and its actions from this point of view — this conception leads to another which depends on it and is very fruitful, namely, that of a *kingdom of ends*.

By a *kingdom* I understand the union of different rational beings in a system by common laws. Now since it is by laws that ends are determined as regards their universal validity, hence, if we abstract from the personal differences of rational beings, and likewise from all the content of their private ends, we shall be able to conceive all ends combined in a systematic whole (including both rational beings as ends in themselves, and also the special ends which each may propose to himself), that is to say, we can conceive a kingdom of ends, which on the preceding principle is possible.

Further Questions

1. Kant believed that lying is always forbidden by the categorical imperative. Suppose, however, that your neighbor comes over looking for her husband, whom she plans to kill. Unbeknownst to her, he is hiding in your basement. Do you point the way? How do you think Kant would respond? [In "On a Supposed Right to Lie from Altruistic Motives," in his *Critique of Practical Reason and Other Writings in Moral Philosophy*, translated by Lewis White Beck (University of Chicago Press, 1949), Kant *does* respond.]

2. What do you think of Kant's maxim to always treat others as an end, never only as a means? What is the relation between this maxim and the categorical imperative?

Further Readings

The two best translations of Kant's ethical writings are by Lewis White Beck:

Beck, Lewis White. *Critique of Practical Reason*. Indianapolis, IN: Bobbs-Merrill, 1959.

——*Foundations of the Metaphysics of Morals*. Indianapolis, IN: Bobbs-Merrill, 1959.

Other works by Kant:

Kant, Immanuel. *Lectures on Ethics*. Louis Infield, Trans. Methuen, 1930.

——*The Moral Law, or Kant's Groundwork of the Metaphysics of Morals*. H. J. Paton, Trans. London: Hutchinson's University Library, 1948.

For secondary sources, see:

Acton, H. B. *Kant's Moral Philosophy*. New York: Macmillan, 1970.

Ross, W. D. *Kant's Ethical Theory*. Oxford: Oxford University Press, 1954.

Utilitarianism

JOHN STUART MILL

John Stuart Mill (1806–1873) was born in London. Educated by his father, a prominent historian, economist, and philosopher, Mill began to study Greek at age 3 and by the time he was 8 he had read major works of Plato in the original and began the study of Latin, Euclid, and algebra. By 12 he had read Aristotle's logical treatises. By 14 he has mastered logic, mathematics, and all of world history. At 19 he had a nervous breakdown.

Raised by his father on the utilitarian doctrines of Jeremy Bentham and the "philosophical radicals," Mill ended up revolutionizing their ideas in one of the most influential books on ethics ever written, *Utilitarianism* (1863). In his *On Liberty* (1859), he argued that the greatest happiness of the greatest number would best be achieved by allowing people as much freedom of thought and action as possible. In *The Subjection of Women* (1861), he argued for the then-radical idea that women should be allowed to vote and have careers. He spoke out on the discrimination against women, helped found the first women's suffrage society, and was one of the first advocates of birth control. In his *System of Logic* (1843), he argued that all knowledge comes from experience. In *Considerations on Representative Government* (1861), he argued that representative government is preferable to constitutional monarchy and enlightened aristocracy.

Reading Questions

1. What is the principle on which Mill wants to base morality?
2. What does he mean by "happiness"?
3. Why does Mill think that if an act produces the greatest amount of happiness, that act is right?
4. How does he distinguish "higher" from "lower" pleasures? What role does moral obligation play? Do you agree?
5. What does Mill mean by "utility"?
6. What is the "Greatest Happiness Principle"?

THE CREED WHICH ACCEPTS [utility] as the foundation of morals, or the Greatest Happiness Principle, holds that actions are right in proportion as they tend to promote happiness, wrong as they tend to produce the reverse of happiness. By happiness is intended pleasure, and the absence of pain; by unhappiness, pain, and the privation of pleasure. To give a clear view of the moral standard set up by the theory, much more requires to be said; in particular, what things it includes in the ideas of pain and pleasure; and to what extent this is left an open question. But these supplementary explanations do not affect the theory of life on which this theory of morality is grounded —namely, that pleasure, and freedom from pain, are the only things desirable as ends; and that all desirable things (which are as numerous in the utilitarian as in any other scheme) are desirable either for the pleasure inherent in themselves, or as means to the promotion of pleasure and the prevention of pain.

Now, such a theory of life excites in many minds, and among them in some of the most estimable in feeling and purpose, inveterate dislike. To suppose that life has (as they express it) no higher end than pleasure—no better and nobler object of desire and pursuit—they designate as utterly mean and grovelling; as a doctrine worthy only of swine, . . .

. . . the accusation supposes human beings to be capable of no pleasures except those of which swine are capable. If this supposition were true,

the charge could not be gainsaid, but would then be no longer an imputation; for if the sources of pleasure were precisely the same to human beings and to swine, the rule of life which is good enough for the one would be good enough for the other. The comparison of the Epicurean life to that of beasts is felt as degrading, precisely because a beast's pleasures do not satisfy a human being's conceptions of happiness. Human beings have faculties more elevated than the animal appetites, and when once made conscious of them, do not regard anything as happiness which does not include their gratification. I do not, indeed, consider the Epicureans to have been by any means faultless in drawing out their scheme of consequences from the utilitarian principle. To do this in any sufficient manner, many Stoic, as well as Christian elements require to be included. But there is no known Epicurean theory of life which does not assign to the pleasures of the intellect, of the feelings and imagination, and of the moral sentiments, a much higher value as pleasures than to those of mere sensation. It must be admitted, however, that utilitarian writers in general have placed the superiority of mental over bodily pleasures chiefly in the greater permanency, safety, uncostliness, etc., of the former— that is, in their circumstantial advantages rather than in their intrinsic nature. And on all these points utilitarians have fully proved their case; but they might have taken the other, and, as it may be called, higher ground, with entire consis-

From J. S. Mill, Utilitarianism. First published in 1863.

tency. It is quite compatible with the principle of utility to recognise the fact, that some *kinds* of pleasure are more desirable and more valuable than others. It would be absurd that while, in estimating all other things, quality is considered as well as quantity, the estimation of pleasures should be supposed to depend on quantity alone.

If I am asked, what I mean by difference of quality in pleasures, or what makes one pleasure more valuable than another, merely as a pleasure, except its being greater in amount, there is but one possible answer. Of two pleasures, if there be one to which all or almost all who have experience of both give a decided preference, irrespective of any feeling of moral obligation to prefer it, that is the more desirable pleasure. If one of the two is, by those who are competently acquainted with both, placed so far above the other that they prefer it, even though knowing it to be attended with a greater amount of discontent, and would not resign it for any quantity of the other pleasure which their nature is capable of, we are justified in ascribing to the preferred enjoyment a superiority in quality, so far outweighing quantity as to render it, in comparison, of small account.

Now it is an unquestionable fact that those who are equally acquainted with, and equally capable of appreciating and enjoying, both, do give a most marked preference to the manner of existence which employs their higher facilities. Few human creatures would consent to be changed into any of the lower animals, for a promise of the fullest allowance of a beast's pleasures; no intelligent human being would consent to be a fool, no instructed person would be an ignoramus, no person of feeling and conscience would be selfish and base, even though they should be persuaded that the fool, the dunce, or the rascal is better satisfied with his lot than they are with theirs. They would not resign what they possess more than he for the most complete satisfaction of all the desires which they have in common with him. If they ever fancy they would, it is only in cases of unhappiness so extreme, that to escape from it they would exchange their lot for almost any

other, however undesirable in their own eyes. A being of higher faculties requires more to make him happy, is capable probably of more acute suffering, and certainly accessible to it at more points, than one of an inferior type; but in spite of these liabilities, he can never really wish to sink into what he feels to be a lower grade of existence. We may give what explanation we please of this unwillingness; we may attribute it to pride, a name which is given indiscriminately to some of the most and to some of the least estimable feelings of which mankind are capable: we may refer it to the love of liberty and personal independence, an appeal to which was with the Stoics one of the most effective means for the inculcation of it; to the love of power, or to the love of excitement, both of which do really enter into and contribute to it: but its most appropriate appellation is a sense of dignity, which all human beings possess in one form or other, and in some, though by no means in exact, proportion to their higher faculties, and which is so essential a part of the happiness of those in whom it is strong, that nothing which conflicts with it could be, otherwise than momentarily, an object of desire to them. Whoever supposes that this preference takes place at a sacrifice of happiness—that the superior being, in anything like equal circumstances, is not happier than the inferior—confounds the two very different ideas, of happiness, and content. It is indisputable that the being whose capacities of enjoyment are low, has the greatest chance of having them fully satisfied; and a highly endowed being will always feel that any happiness which he can look for, as the world is constituted, is imperfect. But he can learn to bear its imperfections, if they are at all bearable; and they will not make him envy the being who is indeed unconscious of the imperfections, but only because he feels not at all the good which those imperfections qualify. It is better to be a human being dissatisfied than a pig satisfied; better to be Socrates dissatisfied than a fool satisfied. And if the fool, or the pig, are of a different opinion, it is because they only know their own side of the question. The other party to the comparison knows both sides.

not true

It may be objected, that many who are capable of the higher pleasures, occasionally, under the influence of temptation, postpone them to the lower. But this is quite compatible with a full appreciation of the intrinsic superiority of the higher. Men often, from infirmity of character, make their election for the nearer good, though they know it to be the less valuable; and this no less when the choice is between two bodily pleasures, than when it is between bodily and mental. They pursue sensual indulgences to the injury of health, though perfectly aware that health is the greater good. It may be further objected, that many who begin with youthful enthusiasm for everything noble, as they advance in years sink into indolence and selfishness. But I do not believe that those who undergo this very common change, voluntarily choose the lower description of pleasures in preference to the higher. I believe that before they devote themselves exclusively to the one, they have already become incapable of the other. Capacity for the nobler feelings is in most natures a very tender plant, easily killed, not only by hostile influences, but by mere want of substance; and in the majority of young persons it speedily dies away if the occupations to which their position in life has devoted them, and the society into which it has thrown them, are not favourable to keeping that higher capacity in exercise. Men lose their high aspirations as they lose their intellectual tastes, because they have not time or opportunity for indulging them; and they addict themselves to inferior pleasures, not because they deliberately prefer them, but because they are either the only ones to which they have access, or the only ones which they are any longer capable of enjoying. It may be questioned whether any one who has remained equally susceptible to both classes of pleasures, ever knowingly and calmly preferred the lower, though many, in all ages, have broken down in an ineffectual attempt to combine both.

From this verdict of the only competent judges, I apprehend there can be no appeal. On a question which is the best worth having of two pleasures, or which of two modes of existence is the most grateful to the feelings, apart from its moral attributes and from its consequences, the judgment of those who are qualified by knowledge of both, or, if they differ, that of the majority among them, must be admitted as final. And there needs be the less hesitation to accept this judgment respecting the quality of pleasures, since there is no other tribunal to be referred to even on the question of quantity. What means are there of determining which is the acutest of two pains, or the intensest of two pleasurable sensations, except the general suffrage of those who are familiar with both? Neither pains nor pleasures are homogeneous, and pain is always heterogeneous with pleasure. What is there to decide whether a particular pleasure is worth purchasing at the cost of a particular pain, except the feelings and judgment of the experienced? When, therefore, those feelings and judgment declare the pleasures derived from the higher faculties to be preferable *in kind*, apart from the question of intensity, to those of which the animal nature, disjoined from the higher faculties, is susceptible, they are entitled on this subject to the same regard.

I have dwelt on this point, as being a necessary part of a perfectly just conception of Utility or Happiness, considered as the directive rule of human conduct. But it is by no means an indispensable condition to the acceptance of the utilitarian standard; for that standard is not the agent's own greatest happiness, but the greatest amount of happiness altogether; and if it may possibly be doubted whether a noble character is always the happier for its nobleness, there can be no doubt that it makes other people happier, and that the world in general is immensely a gainer by it. Utilitarianism, therefore, could only attain its end by the general cultivation of nobleness of character, even if each individual were only benefited by the nobleness of others, and his own, so far as happiness is concerned, were a sheer deduction from the benefit. But the bare enunciation of such an absurdity as this last, renders refutation superfluous.

According to the Greatest Happiness Principle, as above explained, the ultimate end, with reference to and for the sake of which all other things are desirable (whether we are considering our own good or that of other people), is an existence exempt as far as possible from pain, and as rich as possible in enjoyments, both in point of quantity and quality; the test of quality, and the rule for measuring it against quantity, being the preference felt by those who in their opportunities of experience, to which must be added their habits of self-consciousness and self-observation, are best furnished with the means of comparison. This, being, according to the utilitarian opinion, the end of human action, is necessarily also the standard of morality; which may accordingly be defined, the rules and precepts for human conduct, by the observance of which an existence such as has been described might be, to the greatest extent possible, secured to all mankind; and not to them only, but, so far as the nature of things admits, to the whole sentient creation. . . .

. . . the happiness which forms the utilitarian standard of what is right in conduct, is not the agent's own happiness, but that of all concerned. As between his own happiness and that of others, utilitarianism requires him to be as strictly impartial as a disinterested and benevolent spectator. In the golden rule of Jesus of Nazareth, we read the complete spirit of the ethics of utility. To do as you would be done by, and to love your neighbour as yourself, constitute the ideal perfection of utilitarian morality.

Further Questions

1. Utilitarianism has been accused of being a "godless doctrine." Can you see any reason why?
2. Why does Mill want you to increase the happiness of everyone concerned, not just your own? Do you agree?
3. What do you think Kant would say about Mill's Greatest Happiness Principle? Who do you side with, and why?
4. What do you suppose Mill's stand would be on drugs? Pornography?

Further Readings

Gorovitz, Samuel, ed. *John Stuart Mill: Utilitarianism*. Indianapolis, IN: Bobbs-Merrill, 1971. One of the best and most complete collections on the subject.

Hearn, Thomas, ed. *Studies in Utilitarianism*. New York: Appleton-Century-Crofts, 1971.

Ross, W. D. *The Right and the Good*. Oxford: Oxford University Press, 1930. One of the strongest attacks on utilitarianism.

Schneewind, J. B., ed. *Mill's Ethical Writings*. New York: Collier, 1965. See Mill's essay on his predecessor, Jeremy Bentham.

Smart, J. J. C. and Bernard Williams. *Utilitarianism: For and Against*. Cambridge: Cambridge University Press, 1973.

Thomas, William. *Mill*. New York: Oxford University Press, 1985. A brief overview of Mill's life and his major ideas.

Beyond Good and Evil

FRIEDRICH NIETZSCHE

Born in Roeken, Germany into a puritanical, religious family, Friedrich Nietzsche (1844–1900), the son of a minister, became one of the most influential and outspoken critics of religion, particularly of Christianity, and he mounted one of the greatest attacks ever on traditional morality.

After studying at the University of Bonn and the University of Leipzig, he became a professor of philosophy at the University of Basel. Among his many important and provocative works are *Thus Spake Zarathustra* (1884), *Beyond Good and Evil* (1886), *The Genealogy of Morals* (1887), *The Antichrist* (1888), and *The Will to Power* (1906).

From Nietzsche comes the famous slogan, "God is dead." The English-speaking world (George Bernard Shaw and H. L. Mencken are two notable exceptions) has tended to underplay the value of his writings, often discounting them on the psychological level as mere reaction to his childhood, whereas in Germany and France many of the most important philosophers, psychologists, theologians, novelists, and poets have been influenced by him. These include Thomas Mann, Hermann Hesse, Karl Jaspers, Martin Heidegger, Sigmund Freud, and Jean-Paul Sartre.

Reading Questions

1. What strikes you about Nietzsche's style? How do you react to it? Why?
2. Why does Nietzsche hope that the study of morals, which he considers "tedious," never becomes interesting?
3. He says, "Is moralising not — immoral?" Why? Do you agree?
4. He calls Christianity "the most fatal and seductive lie that has ever yet existed" and urges you to declare open war with it. Why? For what purpose? What bothers him so about Christianity? Do you agree? Why?
5. What does he think is the "will to the denial of life" under disguise?
6. What does he say is the *fundamental fact* of all history?
7. Why does he think that only by denying God can people save the world?
8. Why are Christians "little lying abortions of bigotry"?
9. Why does Nietzsche think Christians should be incarcerated in lunatic asylums?
10. Why does he think Jews led a parasitic existence?
11. What is the "soil" of Judaism out of which Christianity grew?
12. What is the "moral idiosyncrasy" by which psychologists have been corrupted?

I HOPE TO BE FORGIVEN for discovering that all moral philosophy hitherto has been tedious and has belonged to the soporific appliances — and that "virtue," in my opinion, has been more injured by the *tediousness* of its advocates than by anything else; at the same time, however, I would not wish to overlook their general usefulness. It is desirable that as few people as possible should reflect upon morals, and consequently it is *very* desirable that morals should not some day become interesting! But let us not be afraid! Things still remain today as they have always been: I see no one in Europe who has (or discloses) an idea of the fact that philosophising concerning morals might be conducted in a dangerous, captious, and ensnaring manner — that *calamity* might be involved therein. . . . No new thought, nothing of the nature of a finer turning or better expression of an old thought, not even a proper history of what has been previously thought on the subject: an *impossible* literature, taking it all in all unless one knows how to leaven it with some mischief. In effect, the old English vice called *cant*, which is *moral Tartuffism*, has insinuated itself also into these moralists (whom one must certainly read with an eye to their motives if one *must* read them), concealed this time under the new form of the scientific spirit; moreover, there is not absent from them a secret struggle with the pangs of conscience, from which a race of former Puritans must naturally suffer, in all their scientific tinkering with morals. (Is not a moralist the opposite of a Puritan? That is to say, as a thinker who regards morality as questionable, as worthy of interrogation, in short, as a problem? Is moralising not — immoral?) In the end, they all want *English* morality to be recognised as authoritative, inasmuch as mankind, or the "general utility," or "the happiness of the greatest number," — no! the happiness of *England*, will be best served thereby.

They would like, by all means, to convince themselves that the striving after *English* happiness, I mean after *comfort* and *fashion* (and in the highest instance, a seat in Parliament), is at the same time the true path of virtue; in fact, that in so far as there has been virtue in the world hitherto, it has just consisted in such striving. Not one of those ponderous, conscience-stricken herding-animals (who undertake to advocate the cause of egoism as conducive to the general welfare) wants to have any knowledge or inkling of the facts that the "general welfare" is no ideal, no goal, no notion that can be at all grasped, but is only a nostrum, — that what is fair to one *may not* at all be fair to another, that the requirement of one morality for all is really a detriment to higher men, in short, that there is a *distinction of rank* between man and man, and consequently between morality and morality. They are an unassuming and fundamentally mediocre species of men, these utilitarian Englishmen, . . . Every elevation of the type "man," has hitherto been the work of an aristocratic society — and so will it always be — a society believing in a long scale of gradations of rank and differences of worth among human beings, and requiring slavery in some form or other. Without the *pathos of distance*, such as grows out of the incarnated difference of classes, out of the constant outlooking and downlooking of the ruling caste on subordinates and instruments, and out of their equally constant practice of obeying and commanding, of keeping down and keeping at a distance — that other more mysterious pathos could never have arisen, the longing for an ever new widening of distance within the soul itself, the formation of ever higher, rarer, further, more extended, more comprehensive states, in short, just the elevation of the type "man," the continued "self-surmounting of man," to use a moral formula in a supermoral sense. To be sure, one

From Nietzsche, Beyond Good and Evil, *translated by Helen Zimmern*, The Twilight of the Idols *and* The Will to Power, *translated by A. M. Ludovici*, in The Complete Works of Friedrich Nietzsche, *translated under Oscar Levy (1909–1911)*.

must not resign oneself to any humanitarian illusions about the history of the origin of an aristocratic society (that is to say, of the preliminary condition for the elevation of the type "man"): the truth is hard. Let us acknowledge unprejudicedly how every higher civilisation hitherto has *originated*! Men with a still natural nature, barbarians in every terrible sense of the word, men of prey, still in possession of unbroken strength of will and desire for power, threw themselves upon weaker, more moral, more peaceful races (perhaps trading or cattle-rearing communities), or upon old mellow civilisations in which the final vital force was flickering out in brilliant fireworks of wit and depravity. At the commencement, the noble caste was always the barbarian caste: their superiority did not consist first of all in their physical, but in their psychical power—they were more *complete* men (which at every point also implies the same as "more complete beasts").

To refrain mutually from injury, from violence, from exploitation, and put one's will on a par with that of others: this may result in a certain rough sense in good conduct among individuals when the necessary conditions are given (namely, the actual similarity of the individuals in amount of force and degree of worth, and their co-relation within one organisation). As soon, however, as one wished to take this principle more generally, and if possible even as *the fundamental principle of society*, it would immediately disclose what it really is—namely, a Will to the *denial* of life, a principle of dissolution and decay. Here one must think profoundly to the very basis and resist all sentimental weakness: life itself is essentially appropriation, injury, conquest of the strange and weak, suppression, severity, obtrusion of peculiar forms, incorporation, and at the least, putting it mildest, exploitation;—but why should one for ever use precisely these words on which for ages a disparaging purpose has been stamped? Even the organisation within which, as was previously supposed, the individuals treat each other as equal—it takes place in every

healthy aristocracy—must itself, if it be a living and not a dying organisation, do all that towards other bodies, which the individuals within it refrain from doing to each other: it will have to be the incarnated Will to Power, it will endeavour to grow, to gain ground, attract to itself and acquire ascendency—not owing to any morality or immorality, but because it *lives*, and because life *is* precisely Will to Power. On no point, however, is the ordinary consciousness of Europeans more unwilling to be corrected than on this matter; people now rave everywhere, even under the guise of science, about coming conditions of society in which "the exploiting character" is to be absent:—that sounds to my ears as if they promised to invent a mode of life which should refrain from all organic functions. "Exploitation" does not belong to a depraved, or imperfect and primitive society: it belongs to the *nature* of the living being as a primary organic function; it is a consequence of the intrinsic Will to Power, which is precisely the Will to Life.—Granting that as a theory this is a novelty—as a reality it is the *fundamental fact* of all history: let us be so far honest towards ourselves!

In a tour through the many finer and coarser moralities which have hitherto prevailed or still prevail on the earth, I found certain traits recurring regularly together and connected with one another, until finally two primary types revealed themselves to me, and a radical distinction was brought to light. There is *master*-morality and *slave*-morality;—I would at once add, however, that in all higher and mixed civilisations, there are also attempts at the reconciliation of the two moralities; but one finds still oftener the confusion and mutual misunderstanding of them, indeed, sometimes their close juxtaposition—even in the same man, within one soul. The distinctions of moral values have either originated in a ruling caste, pleasantly conscious of being different from the ruled—or among the ruled class, the slaves and dependents of all sorts. In the first case, when it is the rulers who determine the conception "good," it is the exalted, proud disposition which is regarded as the distinguishing feature, and that which determines the order of rank. The noble type of man separates from himself the beings in whom the opposite of this exalted, proud disposition displays itself: he despises them. Let it at once be noted that in this first kind of morality the antithesis "good" and "bad" means practically the same as "noble" and "despicable";—the antithesis "good" and "*evil*" is of a different origin. The cowardly, the timid, the insignificant, and those thinking merely of narrow utility are despised; moreover, also, the distrustful, with their constrained glances, the self-abasing, the dog-like kind of men who let themselves be abused, the mendicant flatterers, and above all the liars:—it is a fundamental belief of all aristocrats that the common people are untruthful. "We truthful ones"—the nobility in ancient Greece called themselves. It is obvious that everywhere the designations of moral value were at first applied to *men*, and were only derivatively and at a later period applied to *actions*; it is a gross mistake, therefore, when historians of morals start with questions like, "Why have sympathetic actions been praised?" The noble type of man regards himself as a determiner of values; he does not require to be approved of; he passes the judgment: "What is injurious to me is injurious in itself"; he knows that it is he himself only who confers honour on things; he is a creator of values. He honours whatever he recognises in himself: such morality is self-glorification. In the foreground there is the feeling of plenitude, of power, which seeks to overflow, the happiness of high tension, the consciousness of a wealth which would fain give and bestow:—the noble man also helps the unfortunate, but not—or scarcely—out of pity, but rather from an impulse generated by the super-abundance of power. The noble man honours in himself the powerful one, him also who has power over himself, who knows how to speak and how to keep silence, who takes pleasure in subjecting himself to severity and hardness, and has reverence for all that is severe and hard. "Wotan placed a hard heart in

my breast," says an Old Scandinavian Saga: it is thus rightly expressed from the soul of a proud Viking. Such a type of man is even proud of *not* being made for sympathy; the hero of the Saga therefore adds warningly: "He who has not a hard heart when young, will never have one." The noble and brave who think thus are the furthest removed from the morality which sees precisely in sympathy, or in acting for the good of others, or in *désintéressement*, the characteristic of the moral; faith in oneself, pride in oneself, a radical enmity and irony towards "selflessness," belong as definitely to noble morality, as do a careless scorn and precaution in presence of sympathy and the "warm heart."—It is the powerful who *know* how to honour, it is their art, their domain for invention. The profound reverence for age and for tradition—all law rests on this double reverence,—the belief and prejudice in favour of ancestors and unfavourable to newcomers, is typical in the morality of the powerful; and if, reversely, men of "modern ideas" believe almost instinctively in "progress" and the "future," and are more and more lacking in respect for old age, the ignoble origin of these "ideas" has complacently betrayed itself thereby. A morality of the ruling class, however, is more especially foreign and irritating to present-day taste in the sternness of its principle that one has duties only to one's equals; that one may act towards beings of a lower rank, towards all that is foreign, just as seems good to one, or "as the heart desires," and in any case "beyond good and evil": it is here that sympathy and similar sentiments can have a place. The ability and obligation to exercise prolonged gratitude and prolonged revenge—both only within the circle of equals,—artfulness in retaliation, *raffinement* of the idea in friendship, a certain necessity to have enemies (as outlets for the emotions of envy, quarrelsomeness, arrogance—in fact, in order to be a good *friend*): all these are typical characteristics of the noble morality, which, as has been pointed out, is not the morality of "modern ideas," and is therefore at present difficult to realise, and also to unearth and disclose.

— It is otherwise with the second type of morality, *slave-morality*. Supposing that the abused, the oppressed, the suffering, the unemancipated, the weary, and those uncertain of themselves, should moralise, what will be the common element in their moral estimates? Probably a pessimistic suspicion with regard to the entire situation of man will find expression, perhaps a condemnation of man, together with his situation. The slave has an unfavourable eye for the virtues of the powerful; he has a scepticism and distrust, a *refinement* of distrust of everything "good" that is there honoured — he would fain persuade himself that the very happiness there is not genuine. On the other hand, *those* qualities which serve to alleviate the existence of sufferers are brought into prominence and flooded with light; it is here that sympathy, the kind, helping hand, the warm heart, patience, diligence, humility, and friendliness attain to honour; for here these are the most useful qualities, and almost the only means of supporting the burden of existence. Slave-morality is essentially the morality of utility. Here is the seat of the origin of the famous antithesis "good" and "evil": — power and dangerousness are assumed to reside in the evil, a certain dreadfulness, subtlety, and strength, which do not admit of being despised. According to slave-morality, therefore, the "evil" man arouses fear: according to master-morality, it is precisely the "good" man who arouses fear and seeks to arouse it, while the bad man is regarded as the despicable being. The contrast attains its maximum when, in accordance with the logical consequences of slave-morality, a shade of depreciation — it may be slight and well-intentioned — at last attaches itself even to the "good" man of this morality; because, according to the servile mode of thought, the good man must in any case be the *safe* man: he is good-natured, easily deceived, perhaps a little stupid, *un bonhomme*. Everywhere that slave-morality gains the ascendency, language shows a tendency to approximate the significance of the words "good" and "stupid." . . .

* * *

What then, alone, can our teaching be? — That no one gives man his qualities, either God, society, his parents, his ancestors, nor himself. . . . No one is responsible for the fact that he exists at all, that he is constituted as he is, and that he happens to be in certain circumstances and in a particular environment. The fatality of his being cannot be divorced from the fatality of all that which has been and will be. This is not the result of an individual attention, of a will, of an aim, there is no attempt at attaining to any "ideal man," or "ideal happiness" or "ideal morality" with him — it is absurd to wish him to be careering towards some sort of purpose. *We* invented the concept "purpose"; in reality purpose is altogether lacking. One is necessary, one is a piece of fate, one belongs to the whole, one is in the whole — there is nothing that could judge, measure, compare, and condemn our existence, for that would mean judging, measuring, comparing and condemning the whole. *But there is nothing outside the whole!* The fact that no one shall any longer be made responsible, that the nature of existence may not be traced to a *causa prima*, that the world is an entity neither as a sensorium nor as a spirit — *this alone is the great deliverance* — thus alone is the innocence of Becoming restored. . . . The concept "God" has been the greatest objection to existence hitherto. . . . We deny God, we deny responsibility in God: thus alone do we save the world.

* * *

I regard Christianity as the most fatal and seductive lie that has ever yet existed — as the greatest and most *impious* lie: I can discern the last sprouts and branches of its ideal beneath every form of disguise, I decline to enter into any compromise or false position in reference to it — I urge people to declare open war with it.

The morality of paltry people as the measure of all things: this is the most repugnant kind of degeneracy that civilisation has ever yet brought into existence. And this *kind of ideal* is hanging still, under the name of "God," over men's heads!!

However modest one's demands may be concerning intellectual cleanliness, when one touches the New Testament one cannot help experiencing a sort of inexpressible feeling of discomfort; for the unbounded cheek with which the least qualified people will have their say in its pages, in regard to the greatest problems of existence, and claim to sit in judgment on such matters, exceeds all limits. The impudent levity with which the most unwieldy problems are spoken of here (life, the world, God, the purpose of life), as if they were not problems at all, but the most simple things which these little bigots *know all about!!!*

This was the most fatal form of insanity that has ever yet existed on earth: — when these little lying abortions of bigotry begin laying claim to the words "God," "last judgment," "truth," "love," "wisdom," "Holy Spirit," and thereby distinguishing themselves from the rest of the world; when such men begin to transvalue values to suit themselves, as though they were the sense, the salt, the standard, and the measure of all things; then all that one should do is this: build lunatic asylums for their incarceration. To *persecute* them was an egregious act of antique folly: this was taking them too seriously; it was making them serious. . . .

The *law*, which is the fundamentally realistic formula of certain self-preservative measures of a community, forbids certain actions that have a definite tendency to jeopardise the welfare of that community: it does *not* forbid the attitude of mind which gives rise to these actions — for in the pursuit of other ends the community requires these forbidden actions, namely, when it is a matter of opposing its *enemies*. The moral idealist now steps forward and says: "God sees into men's hearts: the action itself counts for nothing; the reprehensible attitude of mind from which it proceeds must be extirpated. . . ." In normal conditions men laugh at such things; it is only in exceptional cases, when a community lives *quite* beyond the need of waging war in order to maintain itself, that an ear is lent to such things. Any attitude of mind is abandoned, the utility of which cannot be conceived.

This was the case, for example, when Buddha appeared among a people that was both peaceable and afflicted with great intellectual weariness.

This was also the case in regard to the first Christian community (as also the Jewish), the primary condition of which was the absolutely *unpolitical* Jewish society. Christianity could grow only upon the soil of Judaism — that is to say, among a people that had already renounced the political life, and which led a sort of parasitic existence within the Roman sphere of government. Christianity goes a step *farther*: it allows men to "emasculate" themselves even more; the circumstances actually favour their doing so. — *Nature* is *expelled* from morality when it is said, "Love ye your enemies": for *Nature's* injunction, "Ye shall *love* your neighbour and *hate* your enemy," has now become senseless in the law (in instinct); now, even *the love a man feels for his neighbour* must first be based upon something (*a sort of love of God*). *God* is introduced everywhere, and *utility* is withdrawn; the natural *origin* of morality is denied everywhere: the *veneration of Nature*, which lies in *acknowledging a natural morality*, is *destroyed* to the roots. . . .

Whence comes the *seductive charm* of this emasculate ideal of man? Why are we not *disgusted* by it, just as we are disgusted at the thought of a eunuch? . . . The answer is obvious: it is not the voice of the eunuch that revolts us, despite the cruel mutilation of which it is the result; for, as a matter of fact, it has grown sweeter. . . . And owing to the very fact that the "male organ" has been amputated from virtue, its voice now has a feminine ring, which, formerly, was not to be discerned.

On the other hand, we have only to think of the terrible hardness, dangers, and accidents to which a life of manly virtues leads . . . to perceive how the most robust type of man was fascinated and moved by the voluptuous ring of this "goodness" and "purity." . . .

The *Astuteness of moral castration.* — How is war waged against the virile passions and valuations? No violent physical means are available;

the war must therefore be one of ruses, spells, and lies — in short, a "spiritual war."

First recipe: One appropriates virtue in general, and makes it the main feature of one's ideal; the older ideal is denied and declared to be *the reverse of all ideals*. Slander has to be carried to a fine art for this purpose.

Second recipe: One's own type is set up as a general *standard*; and this is projected into all things, behind all things, and behind the destiny of all things — as God.

Third recipe: The opponents of one's ideal are declared to be the opponents of God; one arrogates to oneself a *right* to great pathos, to power, and a right to curse and to bless.

Fourth recipe: All suffering, all gruesome, terrible, and fatal things are declared to be the results of opposition to *one's* ideal — all suffering is *punishment* even in the case of one's adherents (except it be a trial, etc.).

Fifth recipe: One goes so far as to regard Nature as the reverse of one's ideal, and the lengthy sojourn amid natural conditions is considered a great trial of patience — a sort of martyrdom; one studies contempt, both in one's attitudes and one's looks towards all "natural things."

Sixth recipe: The triumph of anti-naturalism and ideal castration, the triumph of the world of the pure, good, sinless, and blessed, is projected into the future as the consummation, the finale, the great hope, and the "Coming of the Kingdom of God."

I hope that one may still be allowed to laugh at this artificial hoisting up of a small species of man to the position of an absolute standard of all things?

To what extent psychologists have been corrupted by the moral idiosyncrasy! — Not one of the ancient philosophers had the courage to advance the theory of the non-free will (that is to say, the theory that denies morality); — not one had the courage to identify the typical feature of happiness, of every kind of happiness ("pleasure"), with the will to power: for the pleasure of power was considered immoral; — not one had the courage to regard virtue as a *result of immorality* (as a result of a will to power) in the service of a species (or of a race, or of a *polis*); for the will to power was considered immoral.

In the whole of moral evolution, there is no sign of truth: all the conceptual elements which come into play are fictions; all the psychological tenets are false; all the forms of logic employed in this department of prevarication are sophisms. The chief feature of all moral philosophers is their total lack of intellectual cleanliness and self-control: they regard "fine feelings" as arguments: their heaving breasts seem to them the bellows of godliness. . . .

This "virtue" made wholly abstract was the highest form of seduction; to make oneself abstract means to *turn one's back on the world*.

The moment is a very remarkable one: the Sophists are within sight of the first *criticism* of morality, the first *knowledge* of morality: — they classify the majority of moral valuations (in view of their dependence upon local conditions) together; — they lead one to understand that every form of morality is capable of being upheld dialectically: that is to say, they guessed that all the fundamental principles of a morality must be *sophistical* — a proposition which was afterwards proved in the grandest possible style by the ancient philosophers from Plato onwards (up to Kant); — they postulate the primary truth that there is no such thing as a "moral *per se*," a "good *per se*," and that it is madness to talk of "truth" in this respect.

Further Questions

1. Specifically, and in your own words, what do you suppose Nietzsche would say about the preceding two selections? Do you agree? How might Kant and Mill respond? How might

Nietzsche respond to their responses? Who is right, and why? Also, *who is to say* who is right, and on what grounds?

2. Distinguish between and explain Nietzsche's notions of *slave morality* and *master morality*. How might you apply these concepts to present society?

Further Readings

The first three editions in the list, translated and edited by Walter Kaufmann, are the best place to begin a study of Nietzsche:
Kaufmann, Walter. *The Portable Nietzsche*. New York: Viking, 1954.
——*Basic Writings of Nietzsche*. New York: Modern Library, 1967.
——*Genealogy of Morals*. New York: Random House, 1967.

Other suggested readings are:
Kaufmann, Walter. *Nietzsche: Philosopher, Psychologist, Antichrist*. New York: Doubleday, 1960. Revised edition.
Mencken, H. L. *The Philosophy of Friedrich Nietzsche*. New York: Luce & Co., 1913.
Morgan, George. *What Nietzsche Means*. Cambridge: Harvard University Press, 1941.

The Conscience of Huckleberry Finn

JONATHAN BENNETT

Jonathan Bennett was born in Greymouth, New Zealand. He teaches philosophy at Syracuse University in New York. His books include *Kant's Analytic* (1966), *Kant's Dialectic* (1974), *Locke, Berkeley, Hume* (1971), and *A Study of Spinoza's Ethics* (1984). In this provocative selection he argues against the commonly accepted idea that we should always let our conscience and our personal feelings guide our actions.

Reading Questions

1. Heinrich Himmler, head of the Nazi S.S., was instrumental in exterminating millions of people. Jonathan Edwards was an American theologian in the eighteenth century. Huck Finn is the famous Mark Twain character. How and why does Bennett use these three personas to make his point?

2. According to one type of moral theory, an act is right only if it produces good consequences; according to another, an act is right only if it is in accordance with some rule or principle. Which do you think Bennett would advocate, and why?

3. How, according to Bennett, should the relation between one's moral conscience and one's moral principles be guided? Do you agree? Can you think of any objections? How might Bennett respond?

4. Does Himmler follow his moral principles? Does Huck Finn? Who do you think is the better person, and why?

IN THIS PAPER, I SHALL PRESENT not just the conscience of Huckleberry Finn but two others as well. One of them is the conscience of Heinrich Himmler. He became a Nazi in 1923; he served drably and quietly, but well, and was rewarded with increasing responsibility and power. At the peak of his career he held many offices and commands, of which the most powerful was that of leader of the S.S. — the principal police force of the Nazi regime. In this capacity, Himmler commanded the whole concentration-camp system, and was responsible for the execution of the so-called 'final solution of the Jewish problem.' It is important for my purposes that this piece of social engineering should be thought of not abstractly but in concrete terms of Jewish families being marched to what they think are bathhouses, to the accompaniment of loud-speaker renditions of extracts from *The Merry Widow* and *Tales of Hoffman*, there to be choked to death by poisonous gases. Altogether, Himmler succeeded in murdering about four and a half million of them, as well as several million gentiles, mainly Poles and Russians.

The other conscience to be discussed is that of the Calvinist theologian and philosopher Jonathan Edwards. He lived in the first half of the eighteenth century, and has a good claim to be considered America's first serious and considerable philosophical thinker. He was for many years a widely-renowned preacher and Congregationalist minister in New England; in 1748 a dispute with his congregation led him to resign (he couldn't accept their view that unbelievers

should be admitted to the Lord's Supper in the hope that it would convert them); for some years after that he worked as a missionary, preaching to Indians through an interpreter; then in 1758 he accepted the presidency of what is now Princeton University, and within two months died from a smallpox inoculation. Along the way he wrote some first-rate philosophy: his book attacking the notion of free will is still sometimes read. Why I should be interested in Edwards' *conscience* will be explained in due course.

I shall use Heinrich Himmler, Jonathan Edwards and Huckleberry Finn to illustrate different aspects of a single theme, namely the relationship between *sympathy* on the one hand and *bad morality* on the other.

* * *

All that I can mean by a 'bad morality' is a morality whose principles I deeply disapprove of. When I call a morality bad, I cannot prove that mine is better; but when I here call any morality bad, I think you will agree with me that it is bad; and that is all I need.

There could be dispute as to whether the springs of someone's actions constitute a *morality*. I think, though, that we must admit that someone who acts in ways which conflict grossly with our morality may nevertheless have a morality of his own — a set of principles of action which he sincerely assents to, so that for him the problem of acting well or rightly or in obedience to conscience is the problem of conforming to *those* principles. The problem of conscientiousness can

"The Conscience of Huckleberry Finn" by Jonathan Bennett, Philosophy, *Vol. 49 (1974), pp. 123–143.*
Reprinted with the permission of Cambridge University Press and the author.

arise as acutely for a bad morality as for any other: rotten principles may be as difficult to keep as decent ones.

As for 'sympathy': I use this term to cover every sort of fellow-feeling, as when one feels pity over someone's loneliness, or horrified compassion over his pain, and when one feels a shrinking reluctance to act in a way which will bring misfortune to someone else. These *feelings* must not be confused with *moral judgments*. My sympathy for someone in distress may lead me to help him, or even to think that I ought to help him; but in itself it is not a judgment about what I ought to do but just a *feeling* for him in his plight. We shall get some light on the difference between feelings and moral judgments when we consider Huckleberry Finn.

Obviously, feelings can impel one to action, and so can moral judgments; and in a particular case sympathy and morality may pull in opposite directions. This can happen not just with bad moralities, but also with good ones like yours and mine. For example, a small child, sick and miserable, clings tightly to his mother and screams in terror when she tries to pass him over to the doctor to be examined. If the mother gave way to her sympathy, that is to her feeling for the child's misery and fright, she would hold it close and not let the doctor come near; but don't we agree that it might be wrong for her to act on such a feeling? Quite generally, then, anyone's moral principles may apply to a particular situation in a way which runs contrary to the particular thrusts of fellow-feeling that he has in that situation. My immediate concern is with sympathy in relation to bad morality, but not because such conflicts occur only when the morality is bad.

Now, suppose that someone who accepts a bad morality is struggling to make himself act in accordance with it in a particular situation where his sympathies pull him another way. He sees the struggle as one between doing the right, conscientious thing, and acting wrongly and weakly, like the mother who won't let the doctor come

near her sick, frightened baby. Since we don't accept this person's morality, we may see the situation very differently, thoroughly disapproving of the action he regards as the right one, and endorsing the action which from his point of view constitutes weakness and backsliding.

Conflicts between sympathy and bad morality won't always be like this, for we won't disagree with every single dictate of a bad morality. Still, it can happen in the way I have described, with the agent's right action being our wrong one, and vice versa. That is just what happens in a certain episode in chapter 16 of *The Adventures of Huckleberry Finn*, an episode which brilliantly illustrates how fiction can be instructive about real life.

* * *

Huck Finn has been helping his slave friend Jim to run away from Miss Watson, who is Jim's owner. In their raft-journey down the Mississippi river, they are near to the place at which Jim will become legally free. Now let Huck take over the story:

> Jim said it made him all over trembly and feverish to be so close to freedom. Well, I can tell you it made me all over trembly and feverish, too, to hear him, because I begun to get it through my head that he *was* most free—and who was to blame for it? Why, *me*. I couldn't get that out of my conscience, no how nor no way. . . . It hadn't ever come home to me, before, what this thing was that I was doing. But now it did; and it stayed with me, and scorched me more and more. I tried to make out to myself that *I* warn't to blame, because *I* didn't run Jim off from his rightful owner; but it warn't no use, conscience up and say, every time: 'But you knowed he was running for his freedom, and you could a paddled ashore and told somebody.' That was so—I couldn't get around that, no way. That was where it pinched. Conscience says to me: 'What had poor Miss Watson done to you, that you could see her nigger go off right under your eyes and never say one single word? What did that poor old woman do to you, that

you could treat her so mean? . . ?' I got to feeling so mean and so miserable I most wished I was dead.

Jim speaks of his plan to save up to buy his wife, and then his children, out of slavery; and he adds that if the children cannot be bought he will arrange to steal them. Huck is horrified:

> Thinks I, this is what comes of my not thinking. Here was this nigger which I had as good as helped to run away, coming right out flat-footed and saying he would steal his children — children that belonged to a man I didn't even know; a man that hadn't ever done me no harm.
>
> I was sorry to hear Jim say that, it was such a lowering of him. My conscience got to stirring me up hotter than ever, until at last I says to it: 'Let up on me — it ain't too late, yet — I'll paddle ashore at first light, and tell.' I felt easy, and happy, and light as a feather, right off. All my troubles was gone.

This is bad morality all right. In his earliest years Huck wasn't taught any principles, and the only ones he has encountered since then are those of rural Missouri, in which slave-owning is just one kind of ownership and is not subject to critical pressure. It hasn't occurred to Huck to question those principles. So the action, to us abhorrent, of turning Jim in to the authorities presents itself *clearly* to Huck as the right thing to do.

For us, morality and sympathy would both dictate helping Jim to escape. If we felt any conflict, it would have both these on one side and something else on the other — greed for a reward, or fear of punishment. But Huck's morality conflicts with his sympathy, that is, with his un-argued, natural feeling for his friend. The conflict starts when Huck sets off in the canoe towards the shore, pretending that he is going to reconnoitre, but really planning to turn Jim in:

> As I shoved off, [Jim] says: 'Pooty soon I'll be a-shout'n for joy, en I'll say, it's all on accounts o' Huck I's a free man . . . Jim won't ever forget you, Huck; you's de bes' fren' Jim's ever had; en you's de *only* fren' old Jim's got now.'

I was paddling off, all in a sweat to tell on him; but when he says this, it seemed to kind of take the tuck all out of me. I went along slow then, and I warn't right down certain whether I was glad I started or whether I warn't. When I was fifty yards off, Jim says:

> 'Dah you goes, de ole true Huck; de on'y white genlman dat ever kep' his promise to old Jim.' Well, I just felt sick. But I says, I *got* to do it — I can't get *out* of it.

In the upshot, sympathy wins over morality. Huck hasn't the strength of will to do what he sincerely thinks he ought to do. Two men hunting for runaway slaves ask him whether the man on his raft is black or white:

> I didn't answer up prompt. I tried to, but the words wouldn't come. I tried, for a second or two, to brace up and out with it, but I warn't man enough — hadn't the spunk of a rabbit. I see I was weakening; so I just give up trying, and up and says: 'He's white.'

So Huck enables Jim to escape, thus acting weakly and wickedly — he thinks. In this conflict between sympathy and morality, sympathy wins.

One critic has cited this episode in support of the statement that Huck suffers 'excruciating moments of wavering between honesty and respectability.' That is hopelessly wrong, and I agree with the perceptive comment on it by another critic, who says:

> The conflict waged in Huck is much more serious: he scarcely cares for respectability and never hesitates to relinquish it, but he does care for honesty and gratitude — and both honesty and gratitude require that he should give Jim up. It is not, in Huck, honesty at war with respectability but love and compassion for Jim struggling against his conscience. His decision is for Jim and hell: a right decision made in the mental chains that Huck never breaks. His concern for Jim is and remains *irrational*. Huck finds many reasons for giving Jim up and none for stealing him. To the end Huck sees his compassion for Jim as a weak, ignorant, and wicked felony.[1]

This is precisely correct — and it can have that virtue only because Mark Twain wrote the episode with such unerring precision. The crucial point concerns *reasons*, which all occur on one side of the conflict. On the side of conscience we have principles, arguments, considerations, ways of looking at things:

'It hadn't ever come home to me before what I was doing'

'I tried to make out that I warn't to blame'

'Conscience said "But you knowed . . ." — I couldn't get around that'

'What had poor Miss Watson done to you?'

'This is what comes of my not thinking'

'. . . children that belonged to a man I didn't even know.'

On the other side, the side of feeling, we get nothing like that. When Jim rejoices in Huck, as his only friend, Huck doesn't consider the claims of friendship or have the situation 'come home' to him in a different light. All that happens is: 'When he says this, it seemed to kind of take the tuck all out of me. I went along slow then, and I warn't right down certain whether I was glad I started or whether I warn't.' Again, Jim's words about Huck's 'promise' to him don't give Huck any *reason* for changing his plan: in his morality promises to slaves probably don't count. Their effect on him is of a different kind: 'Well, I just felt sick.' And when the moment for final decision comes, Huck doesn't weigh up pros and cons: he simply *fails* to do what he believes to be right — he isn't strong enough, hasn't 'the spunk of a rabbit.' This passage in the novel is notable not just for its finely wrought irony, with Huck's weakness of will leading him to do the right thing, but also for its masterly handling of the difference between general moral principles and particular unreasoned emotional pulls.

* * *

Consider now another case of bad morality in conflict with human sympathy, the case of the odious Himmler. Here, from a speech he made to some S.S. generals, is an indication of the content of his morality:

What happens to a Russian, to a Czech, does not interest me in the slightest. What the nations can offer in the way of good blood of our type, we will take, if necessary by kidnapping their children and raising them here with us. Whether nations live in prosperity or starve to death like cattle interests me only in so far as we need them as slaves to our *Kultur*; otherwise it is of no interest to me. Whether 10,000 Russian females fall down from exhaustion while digging an antitank ditch interests me only in so far as the antitank ditch for Germany is finished.[2]

But has this a moral basis at all? And if it has, was there in Himmler's own mind any conflict between morality and sympathy? Yes there was. Here is more from the same speech:

. . . I also want to talk to you quite frankly on a very grave matter . . . I mean . . . the extermination of the Jewish race. . . . Most of you must know what it means when 100 corpses are lying side by side, or 500, or 1,000. To have stuck it out and at the same time — apart from exceptions caused by human weakness — to have remained decent fellows, that is what has made us hard. This is a page of glory in our history which has never been written and is never to be written.

Himmler saw his policies as being hard to implement while still retaining one's human sympathies — while still remaining a 'decent fellow.' He is saying that only the weak take the easy way out and just squelch their sympathies, and is praising the stronger and more glorious course of retaining one's sympathies while acting in violation of them. In the same spirit, he ordered that when executions were carried out in concentration camps, those responsible 'are to be influenced in such a way as to suffer no ill effect in their character and mental attitude.' A year later he boasted that the S.S. had wiped out the Jews

without our leaders and their men suffering any damage in their minds and souls. The danger was considerable, for there was only a narrow path between the Scylla of their becoming heartless ruffians unable any longer to treasure life, and the Charybdis of their becoming soft and suffering nervous breakdowns.

And there really can't be any doubt that the basis of Himmler's policies was a set of principles which constituted his morality—a sick, bad, wicked *morality*. He described himself as caught in 'the old tragic conflict between will and obligation.' And when his physician Kersten protested at the intention to destroy the Jews, saying that the suffering involved was 'not to be contemplated,' Kersten reports that Himmler replied:

> He knew that it would mean much suffering for the Jews. . . . 'It is the curse of greatness that it must step over dead bodies to create new life. Yet we must . . . cleanse the soil or it will never bear fruit. It will be a great burden for me to bear.'

This, I submit, is the language of morality.

So in this case, tragically, bad morality won out over sympathy. I am sure that many of Himmler's killers did extinguish their sympathies, becoming 'heartless ruffians' rather than 'decent fellows'; but not Himmler himself. Although his policies ran against the human grain to a horrible degree, he did not sandpaper down his emotional surfaces so that there was no grain there, allowing his actions to slide along smoothly and easily. He did, after all, bear his hideous burden, and even paid a price for it. He suffered a variety of nervous and physical disabilities, including nausea and stomach-convulsions, and Kersten was doubtless right in saying that these were 'the expression of a psychic division which extended over his whole life.'

This same division must have been present in some of those officials of the Church who ordered heretics to be tortured so as to change their theological opinions. Along with the brutes and the cold careerists, there must have been some

who cared, and who suffered from the conflict between the sympathies and their bad morality.

* * *

In the conflict between sympathy and bad morality, then, the victory may go to sympathy as in the case of Huck Finn, or to morality as in the case of Himmler.

Another possibility is that the conflict may be avoided by giving up, or not ever having, those sympathies which might interfere with one's principles. That seems to have been the case with Jonathan Edwards. I am afraid that I shall be doing an injustice to Edwards' many virtues, and to his great intellectual energy and inventiveness; for my concern is only with the worst thing about him—namely his morality, which was worse than Himmler's.

According to Edwards, God condemns some men to an eternity of unimaginably awful pain, though he arbitrarily spares others—'arbitrarily' because none deserve to be spared:

> Natural men are held in the hand of God over the pit of hell; they have deserved the fiery pit, and are already sentenced to it; and God is dreadfully provoked, his anger is as great towards them as to those that are actually suffering the executions of the fierceness of his wrath in hell . . . ; the devil is waiting for them, hell is gaping for them, the flames gather and flash about them, and would fain lay hold on them . . . ; and . . . there are no means within reach that can be any security to them. . . . All that preserves them is the mere arbitrary will, and uncovenanted unobliged forebearance of an incensed God.[3]

Notice that he says 'they have deserved the fiery pit.' Edwards insists that men *ought* to be condemned to eternal pain; and his position isn't that this is right because God wants it, but rather that God wants it because it is right. For him, moral standards exist independently of God, and God can be assessed in the light of them (and of course found to be perfect). For example, he says:

They deserve to be cast into hell; so that . . . justice never stands in the way, it makes no objection against God's using his power at any moment to destroy them. Yea, on the contrary, justice calls aloud for an infinite punishment of their sins.

Elsewhere, he gives elaborate arguments to show that God is acting justly in damning sinners. For example, he argues that a punishment should be exactly as bad as the crime being punished; God is infinitely excellent; so any crime against him infinitely bad; and so eternal damnation is exactly right as a punishment—it is infinite, but, as Edwards is careful also to say, it is 'no more than infinite.'

Of course, Edwards himself didn't torment the damned; but the question still arises of whether his sympathies didn't conflict with his *approval* of eternal torment. Didn't he find it painful to contemplate any fellow-human's being tortured for ever? Apparently not:

The God that holds you over the pit of hell, much as one holds a spider or some loathsome insect over the fire, abhors you, and is dreadfully provoked; . . . he is of purer eyes than to bear to have you in his sight; you are ten thousand times so abominable in his eyes as the most hateful venomous serpent is in ours.

When God is presented as being as misanthropic as that, one suspects misanthropy in the theologian. This suspicion is increased when Edwards claims that 'the saints in glory will . . . understand how terrible the sufferings of the damned are; yet . . . will not be sorry for [them].'[4] He bases this partly on a view of human nature whose ugliness he seems not to notice:

The seeing of the calamities of others tends to heighten the sense of our own enjoyments. When the saints in glory, therefore, shall see the doleful state of the damned, how will this heighten their sense of the blessedness of their own state. . . . When they shall see how miserable others of their fellow-creatures are . . . ;

when they shall see the smoke of their torment, . . . and hear their dolorous shrieks and cries, and consider that they in the mean time are in the most blissful state, and shall surely be in it to all eternity; how they will rejoice!

I hope this is less than the whole truth! His other main point about why the saints will rejoice to see the torments of the damned is that it is *right* that they should do so:

The heavenly inhabitants . . . will have no love nor pity to the damned. . . . [This will not show] a want of a spirit of love in them . . . ; for the heavenly inhabitants will know that it is not fit that they should love [the damned] because they will know then, that God has no love to them, nor pity for them.

The implication that *of course* one can adjust one's feelings of pity so that they conform to the dictates of some authority—doesn't this suggest that ordinary human sympathies played only a small part in Edwards' life?

* * *

Huck Finn, whose sympathies are wide and deep, could never avoid the conflict in that way; but he is determined to avoid it, and so he opts for the only other alternative he can see—to give up morality altogether. After he has tricked the slave-hunters, he returns to the raft and undergoes a peculiar crisis:

I got aboard the raft, feeling bad and low, because I knowed very well I had done wrong, and I see it warn't no use for me to try to learn to do right; a body that don't get *started* right when he's little, ain't got no show—when the pinch comes there ain't nothing to back him up and keep him to his work, and so he gets beat. Then I thought a minute, and says to myself, hold on—s'pose you'd a done right and give Jim up; would you feel better than what you do now? No, says I, I'd feel bad—I'd feel just the same way I do now. Well, then, says I, what's the use you learning to do right, when it's troublesome to do right and ain't no trouble to do wrong, and the wages is just the same? I was stuck. I couldn't answer that. So I reckoned I wouldn't bother no more about it, but after this always do whichever come handiest at the time.

Huck clearly cannot conceive of having any morality except the one he has learned — too late, he thinks — from his society. He is not entirely a prisoner of that morality, because he does after all reject it; but for him that is a decision to relinquish morality as such; he cannot envisage revising his morality, altering its content in face of the various pressures to which it is subject, including pressures from his sympathies. For example, he does not begin to approach the thought that slavery should be rejected on moral grounds, or the thought that what he is doing is not theft because a person cannot be owned and therefore cannot be stolen.

The basic trouble is that he cannot or will not engage in abstract intellectual operations of any sort. In chapter 33 he finds himself 'feeling to blame, somehow' for something he knows he had no hand in; he assumes that this feeling is a deliverance of conscience; and this confirms him in his belief that conscience shouldn't be listened to:

> It don't make no difference whether you do right or wrong, a person's conscience ain't got no sense, and just goes for him *anyway*. If I had a yaller dog that didn't know no more than a person's conscience does, I would pison him. It takes up more room than all the rest of a person's insides, and yet ain't no good, nohow.

That brisk, incurious dismissiveness fits well with the comprehensive rejection of morality back on the raft. But this is a digression.

On the raft, Huck decides not to live by principles, but just to do whatever 'comes handiest at the time' — always acting according to the mood of the moment. Since the morality he is rejecting is narrow and cruel, and his sympathies are broad and kind, the results will be good. But moral principles are good to have, because they help to protect one from acting badly at moments when one's sympathies happen to be in abeyance. On the highest possible estimate of the role one's sympathies should have, one can still allow for principles as embodiments of one's best feelings, one's broadest and keenest sympathies. On that view, principles can help one across intervals when one's feelings are at less than their best, i.e. through periods of misanthropy or meanness or self-centredness or depression or anger.

What Huck didn't see is that one can live by principles and yet have ultimate control over their content. And one way such control can be exercised is by checking of one's principles in the light of one's sympathies. This is sometimes a pretty straightforward matter. It can happen that a certain moral principle becomes untenable — meaning literally that one cannot hold it any longer — because it conflicts intolerably with the pity or revulsion or whatever that one feels when one sees what the principle leads to. One's experience may play a large part here: experiences evoke feelings, and feelings force one to modify principles. Something like this happened to the English poet Wilfred Owen, whose experiences in the First World War transformed him from an enthusiastic soldier into a virtual pacifist. I can't document his change of conscience in detail; but I want to present something which he wrote about the way experience can put pressure on morality.

The Latin poet Horace wrote that it is sweet and fitting (or right) to die for one's country — *dulce et decorum est pro patria mori* — and Owen wrote a fine poem about how experience could lead one to relinquish that particular moral principle.[5] He describes a man who is too slow donning his gas mask during a gas attack — 'As under a green sea I saw him drowning,' Owen says. The poem ends like this:

> In all my dreams before my helpless sight
> He plunges at me, guttering, choking, drowning
> If in some smothering dreams, you too could pace
> Behind the wagon that we flung him in,
> And watch the white eyes writhing in his face,
> His hanging face, like a devil's sick of sin;

If you could hear, at every jolt, the blood
Come gargling from the froth-corrupted lungs,
Bitter as the cud
Of vile, incurable sores on innocent tongues, —
My friend, you would not tell with such high
   zest
To children ardent for some desperate glory,
The old Lie: Dulce et decorum est
   pro patria mori.

*   *   *

There is a difficulty about drawing from all this a moral for ourselves. I imagine that we agree in our rejection of slavery, eternal damnation, genocide, and uncritical patriotic self-abnegation; so we shall agree that Huck Finn, Jonathan Edwards, Heinrich Himmler, and the poet Horace would all have done well to bring certain of their principles under severe pressure from ordinary human sympathies. But then we can say this because we can say that all those are bad moralities, whereas we cannot look at our own moralities and declare them bad. This is not arrogance: it is obviously incoherent for someone to declare the system of moral principles that he *accepts* to be *bad*, just as one cannot coherently say of anything that one *believes* it but it is *false*.

Still, although I can't point to any of my beliefs and say 'That is false', I don't doubt that some of my beliefs *are* false; and so I should try to remain open to correction. Similarly, I accept every single item in my morality — that is inevitable — but I am sure that my morality could be improved, which is to say that it could undergo changes which I should be glad of once I had made them. So I must try to keep my morality open to revision, exposing it to whatever valid pressures there are — including pressures from my sympathies.

I don't give my sympathies a blank cheque in advance. In a conflict between principle and sympathy, principles ought sometimes to win. For example, I think it was right to take part in the Second World War on the allied side; there were many ghastly individual incidents which might have led someone to doubt the rightness of his participation in that war; and I think it would have been right for such a person to keep his sympathies in a subordinate place on those occasions, not allowing them to modify his principles in such a way as to make a pacifist of him.

Still, one's sympathies should be kept as sharp and sensitive and aware as possible, and not only because they can sometimes affect one's principles or one's conduct or both. Owen, at any rate, says that feelings and sympathies are vital even when they can do nothing but bring pain and distress. In another poem he speaks of the blessings of being numb in one's feelings: 'Happy are the men who yet before they are killed/Can let their veins run cold', he says. These are the ones who do not suffer from any compassion which, as Owen puts it, 'makes their feet/Sore on the alleys cobbled with their brothers.' He contrasts these 'happy' ones, who 'lose all imagination,' with himself and others 'who with a thought besmirch/Blood over all our soul.' Yet the poem's verdict goes against the 'happy' ones. Owen does not say that they will act worse than the others whose souls are besmirched with blood because of their keen awareness of human suffering. He merely says that they are the losers because they have cut themselves off from the human condition:

By choice they made themselves immune
To pity and whatever moans in man
Before the last sea and the hapless stars;
Whatever mourns when many leave these shores;
Whatever shares
The eternal reciprocity of tears.[6]

NOTES

1. M.J. Sidnell, 'Huck Finn and Jim', *The Cambridge Quarterly*, vol. 2, pp. 205–206.
2. Quoted in William L. Shirer, *The Rise and Fall of the Third Reich* (New York, 1960), pp. 937–938. Next quotation: Ibid., p. 966. All further quotations relating to Himmler are from Roger Manwell and Heinrich Fraenkel, *Heinrich Himmler* (London, 1965), pp. 132, 197, 184 (twice), 187.
3. Vergilius Ferm (ed.), *Puritan Sage: Collected Writings of Jonathan Edwards* (New York, 1953),

p. 370. Next three quotations: Ibid, p. 366, p. 294 ('no more than infinite'), p. 372.

4. This and the next two quotations are from 'The End of the Wicked Contemplated by the Righteous: or, The Torments of the Wicked in Hell, no Occasion of Grief to the Saints in Heaven', from *The Works of President Edwards* (London, 1817), vol. IV, pp. 507–508, 511–512, and 509 respectively.

5. I am grateful to the Executors of the Estate of Harold Owen, and to Chatto and Windus Ltd., for permission to quote from Wilfred Owen's 'Dulce et Decorum Est' and 'Insensibility.'

6. This paper began life as the Potter Memorial Lecture, given at Washington State University in Pullman, Washington, in 1972.

Further Question

1. How does Bennett resolve the difficulties he raises? Do you agree? Why? Would you resolve them any differently?

Further Readings

Brandt, Richard. *Value and Obligation*. New York: Harcourt, Brace & World, 1961.
Hospers, John. *Human Conduct*. New York: Harcourt, Brace & World, 1961.
Taylor, Paul. *Problems of Moral Philosophy*. Belmont, CA: Wadsworth, 1978.

Science and Ethics

BERTRAND RUSSELL

In this selection Bertrand Russell argues that ethical values are subjective. Sentences, such as, "Beauty is good," which express ethical values do not assert anything and hence are not capable of being either true or false. "Beauty is good," for instance, is roughly equivalent to, "Would that everyone loved the beautiful." Such sentences may express desires, but they assert nothing. Thus, when people disagree about a question of values, we may be able to persuade them to change their minds, but we cannot do so by appeal to relevant evidence—because there is none.

A brief biography of Russell appears on page 217.

Reading Questions

1. Russell claims values are subjective. Why, then, does he say that the framing of moral rules, so long as the good is known, is a matter for science?

2. When Russell says that ethics is an attempt to give universal, and not merely personal, importance to our desires, what does he mean?

3. What is the difference between a sentence and an assertion? Why, on Russell's view, can scientific sentences, but not ethical ones, be used to make assertions?

... THE FRAMING OF MORAL RULES, so long as the ultimate Good is supposed known, is a matter for science. For example: should capital punishment be inflicted for theft, or only for murder, or not at all? Jeremy Bentham, who considered pleasure to be the Good, devoted himself to working out what criminal code would most promote pleasure, and concluded that it ought to be much less severe than that prevailing in his day. All this, except the proposition that pleasure is the Good, comes within the sphere of science.

But when we try to be definite as to what we mean when we say that this or that is "the Good," we find ourselves involved in very great difficulties. Bentham's creed that pleasure is the Good roused furious opposition, and was said to be a pig's philosophy. Neither he nor his opponents could advance any argument. In a scientific question, evidence can be adduced on both sides, and in the end one side is seen to have the better case — or, if this does not happen, the question is left undecided. But in a question as to whether this or that is the ultimate Good, there is no evidence either way; each disputant can only appeal to his own emotions, and employ such rhetorical devices as shall rouse similar emotions in others.

Take, for example, a question which has come to be important in practical politics. Bentham held that one man's pleasure has the same ethical importance as another man's, provided the quantities are equal; and on this ground he was led to advocate democracy. Nietzsche, on the contrary, held that only the great man can be regarded as important on his own account, and that the bulk of mankind are only means to his well-being. He viewed ordinary men as many people view animals: he thought it justifiable to make use of them, not for their own good, but for that of the superman, and this view has since been adopted to justify the abandonment of democracy. We have here a sharp disagreement of great practical importance, but we have absolutely no means, of a scientific or intellectual kind, by which to persuade either party that the other is in the right. There are, it is true, ways of altering men's opinions on such subjects, but they are all emotional, not intellectual.

Questions as to "values" — that is to say, as to what is good or bad on its own account, independently of its effects — lie outside the domain of science, as the defenders of religion emphatically assert. I think that in this they are right, but I draw the further conclusion, which they do not draw, that questions as to "values" lie wholly outside the domain of knowledge. That is to say, when we assert that this or that has "value," we are giving expressions to our own emotions, not to a fact which would still be true if our personal feelings were different. To make this clear, we must try to analyze the conception of the Good.

It is obvious, to begin with, that the whole idea of good and bad has some connection with desire. *Prima facie*, anything that we all desire is "good," and anything that we all dread is "bad." If we all agreed in our desires, the matter could be left there, but unfortunately our desires conflict. If I say "what I want is good," my neighbor will say "No, what I want." Ethics is an attempt—

Excerpt from Bertrand Russell, Religion and Science, *Oxford University Press, 1935. Reprinted by permission of Oxford University Press.*

though not, I think, a successful one — to escape from this subjectivity. I shall naturally try to show, in my dispute with my neighbor, that my desires have some quality which makes them more worthy of respect than his. If I want to preserve a right of way, I shall appeal to the landless inhabitants of the district; but he, on his side, will appeal to the landowners. I shall say: "What use is the beauty of the countryside if no one sees it?" He will retort: "What beauty will be left if trippers are allowed to spread devastation?" Each tries to enlist allies by showing that his own desires harmonize with those of other people. When this is obviously impossible, as in the case of a burglar, the man is condemned by public opinion, and his ethical status is that of a sinner.

Ethics is thus closely related to politics: it is an attempt to bring the collective desires of a group to bear upon individuals; or, conversely, it is an attempt by an individual to cause his desires to become those of his group. This latter is, of course, only possible if his desires are not obviously opposed to the general interest: the burglar will hardly attempt to persuade people that he is doing them good, though plutocrats make similar attempts, and often succeed. When our desires are for things which all can enjoy in common, it seems not unreasonable to hope that others may concur; thus the philosopher who values Truth, Goodness and Beauty seems, to himself, to be not merely expressing his own desires, but pointing the way to the welfare of all mankind. Unlike the burglar, he is able to believe that his desires are for something that has value in an impersonal sense.

Ethics is an attempt to give universal, and not merely personal, importance to certain of our desires. I say "certain" of our desires, because in regard to some of them this is obviously impossible, as we saw in the case of the burglar. The man who makes money on the Stock Exchange by means of some secret knowledge does not wish others to be equally well informed: Truth (in so far as he values it) is for him a private possession,

not the general human good that it is for the philosopher. . . .

. . . Every attempt to persuade people that something is good (or bad) in itself, and not merely in its effects, depends upon the art of rousing feelings, not upon an appeal to evidence. In every case the preacher's skill consists in creating in others emotions similar to his own — or dissimilar, if he is a hypocrite. I am not saying this as a criticism of the preacher, but as an analysis of the essential character of his activity.

When a man says "this is good in itself," he seems to be making a statement, just as much as if he said "this is square" or "this is sweet." I believe this to be a mistake. I think that what the man really means is: "I wish everybody to desire this," or rather "Would that everybody desired this." If what he says is interpreted as a statement, it is merely an affirmation of his own personal wish; if, on the other hand, it is interpreted in a general way, it states nothing, but merely desires something. The wish, as an occurrence, is personal, but what it desires is universal. It is, I think, this curious interlocking of the particular and the universal which has caused so much confusion in ethics.

The matter may perhaps become clearer by contrasting an ethical sentence with one which makes a statement. If I say "all Chinese are Buddhists," I can be refuted by the production of a Chinese Christian or Mohammedan. If I say "I believe that all Chinese are Buddhists," I cannot be refuted by any evidence from China, but only by evidence that I do not believe what I say; for what I am asserting is only something about my own state of mind. If, now, a philosopher says "Beauty is Good," I may interpret him as meaning either "Would that everybody loved the beautiful" (which corresponds to "all Chinese are Buddhists") or "I wish that everybody loved the beautiful" (which corresponds to "I believe that all Chinese are Buddhists"). The first of these makes no assertion, but expresses a wish; since it affirms nothing, it is logically impossible that there should be evidence for or against it, or for it to possess either truth or falsehood. The second sentence, instead of being merely optative, does make a statement, but is one about the philosopher's state of mind, and it could only be refuted by evidence that he does not have the wish that he says he has. This second sentence does not belong to ethics, but to psychology or biography. The first sentence, which does belong to ethics, expresses a desire for something, but asserts nothing.

Ethics, if the above analysis is correct, contains no statements, whether true or false, but consists of desires of a certain general kind, namely such as are concerned with the desires of mankind in general—and of gods, angels, and devils, if they exist. Science can discuss the causes of desires, and the means for realizing them, but it cannot contain any genuinely ethical sentences, because it is concerned with what is true or false.

The theory which I have been advocating is a form of the doctrine which is called the "subjectivity" of values. This doctrine consists in maintaining that, if two men differ about values, there is not a disagreement as to any kind of truth, but a difference of taste. If one man says "oysters are good" and another says "I think they are bad," we recognize that there is nothing to argue about. The theory in question holds that all differences as to values are of this sort, although we do not naturally think them so when we are dealing with matters that seem to us more exalted than oysters. The chief ground for adopting this view is the complete impossibility of finding any arguments to prove that this or that has intrinsic value. If we all agreed, we might hold that we know values by intuition. We cannot prove, to a color-blind man, that grass is green and not red. But there are various ways of proving to him that he lacks a power of discrimination which most men possess, whereas in the case of values there are no such ways, and disagreements are much more frequent than in the case of colors. Since no way can be even imagined for deciding a difference as to

values, the conclusion is forced upon us that the difference is one of tastes, not one as to any objective truth.

The consequences of this doctrine are considerable. In the first place, there can be no such thing as "sin" in any absolute sense; what one man calls "sin" another may call "virtue," and though they may dislike each other on account of this difference, neither can convict the other of intellectual error. Punishment cannot be justified on the ground that the criminal is "wicked," but only on the ground that he has behaved in a way which others wish to discourage. Hell, as a place of punishment for sinners, becomes quite irrational.

In the second place, it is impossible to uphold the way of speaking about values which is common among those who believe in Cosmic Purpose. Their argument is that certain things which have been evolved are "good," and therefore the world must have had a purpose which was ethically admirable. In the language of subjective values, this argument becomes: "Some things in the world are to our liking, and therefore they must have been created by a Being with our tastes, Whom, therefore, we also like, and Who, consequently, is good." Now it seems fairly evident that, if creatures having likes and dislikes were to exist at all, they were pretty sure to like some things in their environment, since otherwise they would find life intolerable. Our values have been evolved along with the rest of our constitution, and nothing as to any original purpose can be inferred from the fact that they are what they are.

Those who believe in "objective" values often contend that the view which I have been advocating has immoral consequences. This seems to me to be due to faulty reasoning. There are, as has already been said, certain ethical consequences of the doctrine of subjective values, of which the most important is the rejection of vindictive punishment and the notion of "sin." But the more general consequences which are feared, such as the decay of all sense of moral obligation, are not to be logically deduced. Moral obligation, if it is to influence conduct, must consist not merely of a belief, but of a desire. The desire, I may be told, is the desire to be "good" in a sense which I no longer allow. But when we analyze the desire to be "good" it generally resolves itself into a desire to be approved, or, alternatively, to act so as to bring about certain general consequences which we desire. We have wishes which are not purely personal, and, if we had not, no amount of ethical teaching would influence our conduct except through fear of disapproval. The sort of life that most of us admire is one which is guided by large impersonal desires; now such desires can, no doubt, be encouraged by example, education, and knowledge, but they can hardly be created by the mere abstract belief that they are good, nor discouraged by an analysis of what is meant by the word "good."

When we contemplate the human race, we may desire that it should be happy, or healthy, or intelligent, or warlike, and so on. Any one of these desires, if it is strong, will produce its own morality; but if we have no such general desires, our conduct, whatever our ethic may be, will only serve social purposes in so far as self-interest and the interests of society are in harmony. It is the business of wise institutions to create such harmony as far as possible, and for the rest, whatever may be our theoretical definition of value, we must depend upon the existence of impersonal desires. When you meet a man with whom you have a fundamental ethical disagreement—

for example, if you think that all men count equally, while he selects a class as alone important—you will find yourself no better able to cope with him if you believe in objective values than if you do not. In either case, you can only influence his conduct through influencing his desires: if you succeed in that, his ethic will change, and if not, not.

Some people feel that if a general desire, say for the happiness of mankind, has not the sanction of absolute good, it is in some way "irrational." This is due to a lingering belief in objective values. A desire cannot, in itself, be either rational or irrational. It may conflict with other desires, and therefore lead to unhappiness; it may rouse opposition in others, and therefore be incapable of gratification. But it cannot be considered "irrational" merely because no reason can be given for feeling it. We may desire A because it is a means to B, but in the end, when we have done with mere means, we must come to something which we desire for no reason, but not on that account "irrationally." All systems of ethics embody the desires of those who advocate them, but this fact is concealed in a mist of words. Our desires are, in fact, more general and less purely selfish than most moralists imagine; if it were not so, no theory of ethics would make moral improvement possible. It is, in fact, not by ethical theory, but by the cultivation of large and generous desires through intelligence, happiness, and freedom from fear, that men can be brought to act more than they do at present in a manner that is consistent with the general happiness of mankind. . . .

Further Questions

1. When two people have a moral disagreement, say, about the conditions, if any, under which abortion is morally justified, they can sometimes argue for hours over who is right, each side often acknowledging the relevance of considerations brought up by the other. Nothing like that ever happens over whether chocolate ice cream tastes better than vanilla—something we all acknowledge is simply a matter of taste. But if Russell is right about ethics, aren't both disputes ultimately of the same sort? Why then do they seem so different?

2. Some people — because of their greater intelligence or knowledge or practical wisdom — seem better judges of values than others. Imagine that all of the people most competent to judge values — all "ideal observers" — agreed about what was good and what was bad. Would that show that values are objective? But, if values could be objective, doesn't that show that sentences expressing those values at least make assertions?

Further Readings

Frankena, William. *Ethics*. Englewood Cliffs, NJ: Prentice Hall, 1963. A clear, short introduction.
Pojman, Louis, ed. *Ethical Theory*. Belmont, CA: Wadsworth, 1989. An excellent anthology.

Amoralism

RICHARD GARNER

Richard Garner teaches philosophy at Ohio State University. He has recently combined his work in ethics, the philosophy of language, and Asian philosophy in a book, *Beyond Morality* (Temple University Press, 1993). In this selection, which includes some sections from his book, Garner introduces a position he calls "amoralism." He argues that amoralism is a more plausible stance than forms of moralism that rely on the notion of intrinsic value or objective obligation. He then criticizes Thomas Nagel's attempt to use the badness of pain to establish the objectivity of value. Garner concludes by suggesting that informed, compassionate amoralism is capable of guiding us to a very satisfactory existence, without the deception and the rhetoric that are the hallmark of moralism.

Reading Questions

1. Explain Garner's distinction between the moralist and the amoralist.
2. How does Garner understand the claim that something is "intrinsically valuable"?
3. What is the relevance of the badness of pain to the dispute between the moralist and the amoralist?
4. Explain Nagel's distinction between external value, agent-relative value, and agent-neutral value.
5. What, according to Garner, is wrong with morality? What reasons does he give for claiming that we might be better off without it? Do you agree with this claim?

1. The Threat of Amoralism

Moral judgment belongs, as does religious judgment, to a level of ignorance at which even the concept of the real, the distinction between the real and the imaginary, is lacking. (Nietzsche, *Twilight of the Idols*, p. 55).

But whatsoever is the object of any man's appetite or desire, that is it which he for his part calls *good*; and the object of his hate and aversion, *evil*; and of his contempt, *vile* and *inconsiderable*. For these words of *good*, *evil*, and *contemptible* are ever used with relation to the person that uses them, there being nothing simply and absolutely so, nor any common rule of good and evil to be taken from the nature of the objects themselves. . . . (Hobbes, *Leviathan*, 53)

Subhuti, though we speak of 'goodness' the Tathagata [Buddha] declares that there is no goodness, such is merely a name. (The Buddha, *The Diamond Sutra*, Section 23, in Price and Wong, 1969)

WHAT IF NIETZSCHE, HOBBES, and the Buddha are right? What if nothing is good or bad, right or wrong, permitted or forbidden? What if there are no rights, no obligations, no virtues or vices? What if our valueless world is filled with valueless beings acting from their ignorance and their desires, and subject to morality only because they have not seen that it is a convenient fiction, a noble lie, a paternalistic deception?

The problem with such a categorical denial of morality and value is that almost no one believes it. 'Goodness' may be only a "name," but it is a powerful and a useful one. Perhaps, then, we should not say that nothing is good, but only that nothing is good *in itself*, or good independent of some relation to human desires and standards. Rather than flat-out denying morality, we might try to affirm it, with the acknowledgement that it is a conventional human creation. "Things are good and bad, right and wrong, permitted and forbidden," we might say, "but only because *people* prefer, command, permit, and forbid them." Moral rules and rights are genuine, but they are genuine *artifacts* — things we create and then embody in our cultures and our language.

Sensible as this might be, this humanized and relativized way of looking at value and obligation will never replace the original. When morality is taken to be a human artifact, it loses its ability to bind anyone who chooses not to be bound, or to motivate anyone who wishes to resist. If duty is merely the command of our group, it is too easy to ask what gives *them* the right to make commands, and what gives *us* the duty to obey. If all "You ought to" amounts to is "I (or we) want you to," then you can just say "So what?"

So, both a strong form of amoralism (nothing is good or bad, right or wrong) and a milder form of relativistic morality (things are good or bad, right or wrong, relative to desires, agreements, standards, etc.) will alarm anyone who wants morality to provide more than an optional guide to conduct. And this, I would say, includes most people. We live in a sea of moral concepts, distinctions, slogans, assumptions, principles, dogmas, and guilt. We assume that any competent adult knows the difference between right and wrong. We also assume that there is a difference between right and wrong. This belief is so strong and so widespread that moral philosophers use sentences like *Hitler was evil, It is wrong to incinerate cats, kick dogs,* or *knowingly and willingly torture innocents,* as starting points, not conclusions, of their arguments. Nobody, they assume, could reasonably doubt any of these things.

And yet there *are* amoralists, and a careful amoralist may prefer not to say that it is wrong to kick dogs or that Hitler was evil. Anyone who really believes that nothing is "really evil" has to believe that Hitler was "not really evil." The problem with saying this, and with saying that Hitler was "really not evil," is that in an environment

This selection was written especially for this volume and is included by kind permission of the author.

where the normal (evaluative) use of 'evil' is in place, these ways of putting things can express a lack of disapproval of Hitler. The amoralist, who may disapprove of Hitler as much as anyone, just doesn't want to use the word 'evil' with its standard objectivist implications.

When Hobbes tells us that 'good' is just a word we use of things which we desire, and that there is no "common rule of good and evil to be taken from the nature of the objects themselves," he seems to be going against common sense and a legion of philosophers who will insist that we dislike pain because it is bad, and not the other way around.

Moralists take *morality* seriously and consider themselves and others bound by its requirements. Amoralists think that if we are bound, it can only be because we bind ourselves. Moralists take *value* seriously and say that our admiration does not make a good thing good. Amoralists think that at best goodness is relative to some unjustifiable standard, and at worst, the idea is incoherent.

2. *Moral Discussions*

How could amoralists have come to a conclusion that goes so against everything we hear from our parents, preachers, professors, and peers? Well, perhaps they have noticed what happens when people argue about moral issues. The idea that rational beings have reasons for their actions and beliefs influences many of the conventions that govern our interactions. It opens the way for discussion, persuasion, debate, criticism, and compromise. Also, the idea that rational beings will or should have reasons for their moral judgments makes it easy to support a convention that allows us to ask our fellow rational beings for their reasons.

The surprising thing about the demand for reasons in the ease with which it can be satisfied. When we make a moral judgment in public we are usually ready with argument-fragments, slo-gans, and information to offer in defense of our claim. If we take the trouble, we can even come up with a moral defense for actions we think are morally wrong.

Why are we so good at this? Why are we so rarely at a loss for words when it is time to defend moral judgments? It may be because we have learned to expect those who do not agree with us to ask for reasons. Knowing this, we are prepared. Fortunately, the reason we produce doesn't have to be a super-reason, powerful enough to convince any rational being. Almost anything not obviously false or irrelevant will do for a start. If we associate with people who share our moral beliefs and pay attention to what they say, we will develop an arsenal of reasons that will see us through most challenges.

There are many issues that have attracted the attention of moralists, moral philosophers, and concerned citizens — abortion, capital punishment, sexual morality, human rights, the treatment of animals, and all the problems flowing from our attempts to distribute the benefits and burdens of society. Around each of these issues there has developed a pattern of disputation involving everything from one-line slogans to complex and subtle arguments. Many of these slogans are insulting in their simplicity (abortion is murder, an eye for an eye), and many of the arguments play fast and loose with language and hidden assumptions. But the one-liners sink in, and the arguments will be similar enough to standard patterns of rational debate to satisfy the minimal demands made upon those who wish to hold a moral position.

Arguments about moral issues can develop in many directions. Some degenerate into theological disputes and others come to an impasse over some difficult or abstract problem in ethics or in philosophy (What is the nature of goodness? What is a person?). Sometimes moral arguments evolve into disputes about meaning (the meaning of 'life,' or of 'rights,' or of 'humane'), and often they come to a standstill over some factual claim that neither side can prove or disprove (Does capital punishment decrease the number of offenses or only the number of offenders?).

When we move from the question of whether it is wrong to eat animals to the question of what a person is, or from the question of whether or not abortion is wrong to the question of when human life begins, we have replaced a difficult question about morality with a certifiably unanswerable philosophical question. This does not bring the argument any closer to a resolution. Usually it turns out that our theory of human life or of personhood takes the shape it must to bolster our more personal and practical beliefs about diet and abortion. This shift to a more "basic" question will usually guarantee that the protagonists will arrive at an impasse—the natural end-state of a philosophical dispute.

Of course those involved in disputes about values, moral beliefs, and related philosophical questions are not trying to arrive at an impasse—they are trying to convince some opponent (real or imagined) whose beliefs and attitudes differ from theirs. Since value disputes often concern our behavior or character, when a cool, impartial, rational approach doesn't budge our opponent, we may be tempted to resort to more questionable methods. Then we try to gain an advantage by giving new meanings to words, by claiming that our favorite moral principles need no defense, or that they are true by definition. We presuppose, but do not mention, principles or facts we rely on to help establish our conclusion. In our eagerness to be declared blameless or even justified, we imply that anyone would have to be insane, stupid, or evil to disagree with us. When our initial efforts fail, we often resort to techniques designed to make our opponents angry and/or confused—we become insulting and nasty, domineering, rude, or even obscene. When those who are arguing are unevenly matched in skill, experience, energy, information, or eloquence, it is usual for the apparent loser to feel that the apparent winner has capitalized on an unfair advantage. The ritualistic, hypocritical, and rhetorical nature of our public arguments about morality helps explain the fact that after discussing an issue like abortion for hours, the only change in the minds of the antagonists may be in their estimation of the intelligence or the sincerity of the opposition.

While the sorry state of moral "discussions" should lead us to wonder about the objectivity of morality, it does not prove anything. I suggest, however, that if we look more closely at the character of moral judgments themselves, at what they are, and at what they are supposed to do, we will find other reason to suspect that Nietzsche, Hobbes, and the Buddha are right, and that "moral judgments agree with religious ones in believing in realities which are no realities."

3. Intrinsic Value

Kant said that a "good will" is not good because of its effects, it is good in itself. "When it is considered in itself, then it is to be esteemed very much higher than anything which it might ever bring about merely in order to favor some inclination, or even the sum total of all inclinations." Even if a good will is powerless to attain its end, it would "like a jewel, still shine by its own light as something which has its full value in itself." (Kant, 394)

We use the expressions 'intrinsically good,' 'good in itself,' and 'good as an end' almost interchangeably. Intrinsic goodness is a kind of goodness a thing has apart from its relation to other things. A thing is *intrinsically good* if it is good no matter what else is true and no matter how people feel about it. A thing is *good in itself* when it is good just because of the kind of thing it is—its goodness is, presumably, part of its nature. Finally, a thing is *good as an end* when it is worth choosing apart from any consequences that might flow from choosing it, or use to which it might be put.

This might "explain" the intrinsic part, but it doesn't explain the goodness. Nor is it clear what would — which is why some have taken goodness to be unanalysable. But what needs to be explained is what can be explained, and what can be explained is our use of moral language, and our habit of thinking of things as good and bad. We did not learn to use the words 'good' and 'bad' in isolation, but as a part of learning a language and a set of social practices, standards, rules, and exceptions. We begin by believing what we are told, and by accepting any value that does not cause us immediate and intense discomfort — and some that do. Our common language and system of values unites us and provides a setting for our individuality, and our socialization makes us human, so these things are not to be scorned. But we can understand and participate in most conventional ways of using 'good' and 'bad' without becoming involved with the concept of "intrinsic value." Since we all want to live and to be healthy and happy, we can (and do) says that "good food" and "good habits" are food and habits that promote health and happiness, and that bad food and habits accomplish the reverse.

But what do we say when someone asks us what makes health and happiness good? It is not easy to say what happiness is good *for*, and if we do think of something, we will soon find ourselves facing the further question of what *that* is good for, and so on till we run out of answers or time. The claim that something is *intrinsically good* is designed to stop this game by heading off further questions. If a thing is intrinsically good, it is good, period, and nobody gets to ask "What makes it good?" or "What is it good for?"

But even if that is how it is supposed to work, how are we to understand this question-stopper? Since we learned to use 'good' to evaluate actual items according to familiar (if implicit) standards and purposes, why should we think we can extend it to encompass such an abstract notion as intrinsic goodness? When there are established standards it is natural to rank things on the basis of those standards. Something is a good apple if it is tart, large, unmarked, and wormless. A car that does not break down and is fast (or easy on gas, or impressive) is a good car. Bill is a good plumber and Bob is a good friend. But what is it for a thing to be, not a good X, and not "good-for Y" or "good as Z," but just good, period — good-in-itself? If someone were to speak up for the "intrinsically useful," that which is useful in itself, useful as an end, we would see the joke. Why do we not see it when we speak of intrinsic value?

4. *Crazy Objectivity*

We all have preferences and standards, and it is a common belief that we prefer things because they are preferable and like things because they are good. The idea that we *give* value to things by valuing them, that values are "conventional" or "subjective," makes it impossible to see the difference between the desired and the desirable. Wisely or foolishly, what we want is objective value — value that exists apart from what we have come to desire, value that does not depend on changing conventions and individual whims, value that commands our respect and requires our support.

Some think that we can resolve the question of whether or not anything has objective value by turning our attention to pain and pleasure. If pain can be shown to be objectively bad, or pleasure objectively good, then the claims of those who say that values have at most a subjective existence, and the claims of those who say that they have no existence at all, can be resisted.

Thomas Nagel has his eye on this controversy when he proposes to defend the objectivity of ethics in his chapter on value in *The View from Nowhere*. He tries to show that there are objective values by showing that "sensory pleasure is good and pain bad, no matter whose they are." (Nagel [3], 156–57) He confesses to thinking it is "self-evident" that pleasure is good and pain bad

(Nagel [3], 160), but since not everyone shares this intuition, he offers to provide an argument to show that "there is no plausibility in the zero position, that pleasure and pain have no value of any kind that can be objectively recognized." (Nagel [3], 157)

The "zero-position" that pain is not objectively bad will never win a popularity contest. The badness of pain is such a common example of what is obvious that it is easy to see why someone would think it self-evident. In the face of serious pain and human nastiness we find ourselves tempted to adopt a kind of fundamentalism about values that I call *crazy objectivity*. Crazy objectivists take the phenomenology of moral experience *very* seriously, and this leads them to say that values are discovered not invented, that they are independent of our beliefs and preferences, perhaps even of our existence.

When John Mackie argued that values are not objective, not part of the "fabric of the world," he was attacking crazy objectivity. (Mackie, 15) Objective values, he said, would have to be "entities or qualities or relations of a very strange sort, utterly different from anything else in the universe," and any awareness of them "would have to be by some special faculty of moral perception or intuition, utterly different from our ordinary way of knowing everything else." (Mackie, 38) What makes crazy objectivity really crazy is the belief in what Mackie called objective prescriptivity. If judgments of value and obligation were objectively prescriptive, then something about the way things are would "require" us to do or to choose some things; in Mackie's words, some situations would have a kind of "ought-to-be-ness" or "ought-not-to-be-ness" about them.

Crazy objectivity is difficult to understand, easy to criticize, and widely believed. Mackie is convincing when he argues against it, but many recent defenders of objective value deny that their form of realism requires any "queer" metaphysical properties or epistemological miracles. They aspire to be realists about value without at the same time embracing any seriously crazy species of objectivity. This is certainly what Nagel aims for when he treats objectivity as a relative notion, and offers to explain objective values in terms of reasons.

5. *The Relativity of Objectivity*

Objectivity is relative because we have the capacity to be more or less objective: "to acquire a more objective understanding of some aspect of life or the world, we step back from our initial view of it and form a new conception which has that view and its relation to the world as its object." (Nagel [3], 4) It is clear that on this interpretation we never attain complete objectivity, but it is not clear how objective we can become or how many directions there are in which we can step.

We can easily get to what can be called "Level One" objectivity, where we "see" that a quantity of pain is equally pain and equally bad wherever it occurs. Here it makes no difference whether it is your pain or my pain, pain now or pain tomorrow — anything bad here and now is bad everywhere and always.

At Level One we universalize, but why stop there? We can, from an even more objective vista, "Level Two," observe the making of the value judgment, record a Level One willingness to universalize, and then simply hold back from making the value judgment. We can just register the pain — without value, but no less painful for that. This is not as unusual as it may at first seem: we regularly manage to experience minor and moderate pains and scrapes without the slightest thought that they are anything more than painful and inconvenient. We waste no time assigning them a value.

When speaking with others about our pain, we don't even use the word 'bad' in its normal evaluative way. When we say that our pain is "bad" we typically mean that it is intense; and when we say it is "not bad" we mean that it doesn't hurt very much — that it could be worse. To say that some pain is "really" bad is to say that it is extremely painful, not that it has negative intrinsic value. When we want to cancel this non-evaluative quantitative use we can insert the word 'objectively' (or imagine it is there). If pain is "objectively bad," it is not just painful, and not just very painful, it has "badness."[1]

Those who think that pain is "objectively" bad will say that anyone who experiences pain as *simply* painful is blind to one of its real features, and they may add that someone who is unaware of the badness of pain will be less motivated to help others who suffer. But this is not so. Whether a person who has attained the second level of objectivity will be motivated to act in a certain way is a function of the motivational structures that survive the journey. There is no reason why an aversion to pain (one's own or that of another) should not survive a journey to Level Two value-neutral objectivity. If values *are* projections of desires and aversions, then when the values are stripped away, the desires and aversions remain, strong as ever and ready to motivate.

An aversion to pain is not the same thing as the belief that pain is bad. We can have either without the other. But if we can step back from the judgment that pain is bad, can we step back from the aversion as well? Can we reach "Level Three," where we experience pain or see someone else experiencing it, but have no aversion to either situation? To some extent we can, but it is not as easy to do this as it is to reach Level Two objectivity. To step back from the belief that pain is bad we simply suspend the making of certain evaluative judgments.[2] To step back from the aversion, we must cultivate the sort of calm neutrality we sometimes achieve when we put mer-thiolate on a cut, "play through the pain," or eat hot peppers. How far are we able to carry this out depends on our inner resolve, on how "bad" (that is, how intense) the pain becomes, and on whether it is our own pain or that of someone else. One can attain the second level of objectivity

(value neutrality) completely, but the third (affective neutrality) only up to a point.

6. *Reasons and Pain*

So far I have argued that someone who manages to think of pain as evaluatively neutral might still be motivated to avoid it because of a natural aversion that can never be completely transcended. But perhaps the really important question isn't about motivation at all. Perhaps what should be asked is whether, from this place where pain is seen as devoid of badness, people will *have a reason* to alleviate pain — whether or not they are then motivated to do anything. The answer to *this* question, of course, depends on what it is to have a reason.

In this way we are led to the second aspect of Nagel's attempt to give us a non-crazy form of objectivity, his explanation of objective value in terms of reasons. Fundamental to this account is a distinction between "agent-relative" and "agent-neutral" value. "An objective judgment that some kind of thing has agent-relative value," he says, "commits us only to believing that someone has reason to want and pursue it if it is related to him in the right way (being in his interest, for example)." (Nagel [3], 154) By contrast, if something has agent-neutral (positive) value, then "*anyone* has reason to want it to exist — and that includes someone considering the world in detachment from the perspective of any particular person within it." (Nagel [3], 153)

Nagel also distinguishes between "internal" reasons (or values), which depend on the interests of sentient beings, and "external" ones, which do not. He is willing to admit that there is some evidence that things "have an intrinsic value which is not merely a function of the satisfaction that people may derive from them or of the fact that anyone wants them — a value which is not reducible to their value *for* anyone." (Nagel [3], 153) Such a value would be external value, and external reasons would appeal to it rather than to anything about the interests or other states of sentient beings. External value sounds very much like the sort of value embraced by the crazy objectivist. But Nagel manages to avoid crazy objectivity by choosing not to discuss external values, and by confessing that he does not know how to establish whether there are any such values.[3]

If the question of external value is to be put to one side, we are forced to focus on internal value, value based on interests. So if pain is "objectively" bad, it will be either because it has agent-relative (negative) value or because it has agent-neutral (negative) value.

Nagel says that if "pleasure and pain have no value of any kind that can be objectively recognized," then "I have no reason to take aspirin for a severe headache . . . and that looking at it from outside, you couldn't even say that someone has a reason not to put his hand on a hot stove, just because of the pain." (Nagel [3], 157) Of course these conclusions must be rejected. Nagel does have a reason to take the aspirin and we all have a reason not to put our hands on hot stoves — if he doesn't take the aspirin the pain will continue, and if we put our hands on a hot stove it will hurt like hell. So pleasure and pain have agent-relative value that can be objectively recognized.

According to Nagel, if that is the only kind of value things have, then the knowledge that someone *else* is feeling pain, or is about to, gives *me* no reason to do anything. In that case, someone with a headache "will have to say that though he has a reason to want an analgesic, there is no reason for him to have one, or for anyone else who happens to be around to give him one." (Nagel [3], 160) But if pain has *agent-neutral* value, then "anyone has a reason to want any pain to stop, whether or not it is his." (Nagel [3], 159)

Nagel once thought he had a general argument from agent-relative to agent-neutral value, but in *The View from Nowhere* he abandons this claim for the more modest claim that the inference does go through in the special case of pains and pleasures. (Nagel [3], 159)[4] He says that

"the pain, though it comes attached to a person and his individual perspective, is just as clearly hateful to the objective self as to the subjective individual." (Nagel [3], 160) If I have a pain and then step back and "observe" myself feeling the pain, my (more) objective self is in no way insulated from that pain. The claim that the pain is "as hateful to the objective self" must mean that, from the more objective point of view, the pain hurts as much as it did before I took the step, and that I am as averse to it now as I was then.

When I step back and observe myself feeling the pain, it is not hard to attain Level One objectivity, where it is clear that there is no relevant difference between my pain and your pain. I feel the pain, I want it to be gone, and I believe that your pain feels as bad to you as mine does to me. If I call my pain hateful, dreadful, or even objectively bad, I will have to say the same of yours. "The pain," says Nagel, "can be detached in thought from the fact that it is mine without losing any of its dreadfulness. It has, so to speak, a life of its own. That is why it is natural to ascribe to it a value of its own." (Nagel [3], 160)

But pain has no "life of its own" apart from some suffering being, and while we might think it "unnatural" not to regard another's intense pain as dreadful, it is possible to remain unmoved by it. Further, even if the contemplation of pain as such leads some to ascribe pain a *value* of its own, it does not lead everyone in this direction. The fact that someone is feeling dreadful pain does not automatically give me, and everyone else as well, a reason for acting to prevent or end that pain.

And yet Nagel thinks that everyone does have such a reason. He asks: "From the objective standpoint, can I stop with an endorsement of the sufferer's efforts to avoid or alleviate it [the pain], without going on to acknowledge an impersonal reason to want it to go away?" (Nagel [3], 161) His answer is that we cannot stop there because to do so would overrule "the clearest authority present in the situation" — the sufferer:

We are thinking from no particular point of view about how to regard a world which contains points of view. What exists inside those points of view can be considered from outside to have some sort of value simply as part of what is happening in the world, and the value assigned to it should be that which it overwhelmingly appears to have from the inside. (Nagel [3], 161)

If we are resting at Level Two, value-neutral objectivity, we will not be inclined to adopt the claim of "the sufferer" that his pain, or pain in general, is objectively bad. Standing where we do, we are never forced to take on the values we would accept if we were standing somewhere else — and wherever we stand, we need not grant the very curious claim that everything has value "simply as part of what is happening in the world." Indeed, if we are outside a point of view, we usually refrain from assigning things the features they "overwhelmingly" appear to have from inside. Otherwise, what is the difference?

Nagel says that someone who is suffering intense pain does not stop with the thought that he himself has a reason for wanting the pain to be gone, but advances to the thought that "it [the pain] is bad and should be got rid of." This thought, he says, does not even bring in a reference to the person whose pain it is. "The desire to be rid of pain has only the pain as its object." (Nagel [3], 161) This may or may not be correct phenomenology, but when I hurt, it is *my* pain I want to be rid of; and even someone who has managed to refrain from thinking of his pain as *his*, can still want to be rid of it without advancing to the thought that it is *bad*, or that it *should* be got rid of. One need not allow pain itself to push one into realism about value.

Not everyone motivated to work against pain harbors strong evaluative concepts. If we have, as Marcus Aurelius advised, "silenced our assessor," we may be richly aware of the pain of others, and we may (for our own agent-relative reasons) work actively for its reduction, all without saying or thinking that it is bad, awful, horrible, or dreadful. My reason for wanting the pain of others to stop can be *the fact that it hurts, and I know it*. Is that fact not as good a *reason* as the fact (which may not be enough of a *fact*) that it is bad? To be sure, the nonevaluative fact lacks the authority and the universality with which objective moral facts are traditionally imbued, but we may just have to learn to live with that. The anti-realist's non-evaluative reason ("because it hurts") is capable of leading sympathetic people to immediate action; the evaluative reason ("because it is bad"), on the other hand, invites skepticism and distracting philosophical quibbles, and really won't move anyone who isn't already disposed to be moved by the suffering itself.[5]

If pain had *external* value (intrinsic badness), then there would be a reason for everyone to want all of it to stop. Nagel wisely refrained from resting his case on such a dubious notion, but now it is beginning to appear that his substitute, agent-neutral badness, cannot be ascribed to all pain. Not everyone does have a reason to want all pain to be gone, though most people have (agent-relative) reasons for wanting their own pain and the pain of some others to be gone, reasons based on a natural and adjustable aversion to pain. The only way we could guarantee that everyone has a reason for wanting all pain to be gone is to revert back to external value — which, as we shall see in the next and final section, is more or less what Nagel does when he claims that the reason everyone has for wanting all pain to be gone is its badness.

7. The Bad-Reason Circle

Nagel tried to give us objective value without crazy objectivity by explaining objective value in terms of reasons. In an attempt to escape from Mackie's argument from queerness he said that the "objective badness" of pain "is not some mysterious further property that all pains have, but just the fact that there is reason for anyone capable of viewing the world objectively to want it to stop." (Nagel [3], 144) Now if the agent-relative badness of X's pain is the fact that X has a reason for wanting it to stop, and the agent-neutral badness of anyone's pain is the fact that anyone has a reason for wanting it to stop, we may well wonder what that reason is.[6] It looks as if Nagel's answer is that the reason we all have for wanting all pain to stop is the fact that pain is bad, horrible, and awful. He says that we should accept the conclusion that "suffering is a bad thing, period, and not just for the sufferer," and that if he is suffering great pain "there's a reason for me to be given morphine which is independent of the fact that the pain is mine — namely that it's awful." (Nagel [3], 162) In the earlier Tanner lectures he says that his reason for wanting his neighbor's pain to cease "is just that it's awful, and I know it." (Nagel [2], 110)[7]

This is where the trouble looms. Even if we do have a reason for wanting all pain to stop, *Nagel* can't give the badness of pain as that reason. He has just told us that the badness of pain is not some "mysterious further property that all pains have, but just the fact that there is reason for anyone capable of viewing the world objectively to want it to stop." So, if Nagel now says that the reason people have for wanting pain to stop is its badness, he will be caught in a very tight circle: the reason people have for wanting pain to stop is the fact that it is bad, and what it is for it to be bad is that people have a reason for wanting it to stop.

Perhaps Nagel's error, if indeed it is an error, can be explained by his belief in the self-evidence of pain's badness. Arguments for a sure thing tend to look good from the reflected glory of their conclusions. Nagel is right to emphasize the relativity of objectivity and the importance of agent-relative value, and to warn us against a kind of over-objectification which only acknowledges impersonal reasons — reasons from no point of view. But I think he has underestimated the power of projectivism to explain the "phenomenological fact" that we (I would say "some of us")

seem to apprehend what seem to be normative truths (Nagel, 179), and overestimated the strength of his argument against the anti-realist, who has attained the "second level" of objectivity (value neutrality) and sees no reason to return to former realist habits.

8. Attacks on Amoralism

When we look closely at what I have described as the ritualistic, hypocritical, and rhetorical nature of our arguments about morality, we may be led to take the amoralist position more seriously. And when we think carefully about what the moralist is actually saying, about what the world would have to be like for morality to be objectively prescriptive, for values to be a part of the "fabric of the universe," amoralism may be even more tempting. But it is not easy to be an amoralist in a sea of moralists. The amoralist comes forward with a view of things that makes much of what others say false or nonsense. This is not a position to occupy lightly. But it is a position that can be defended, a position that the amoralist believes fits in better with *everything* else we know than any form of moralism ever invented.

Amoralism, the rejection of the characteristic claims of moralists, is neither a philosophy of life nor a guide to conduct. But neither is moralism, as such. Everything depends on which moral principles a given moralist holds, and then on how closely those principles are followed and on how loosely they are interpreted. I believe that we can easily do without morality if we can supplement our amoralism with *compassion, a desire to know what is going on, and a disposition to be non-duplicitous*. By 'doing without morality' I do not mean doing without kindness or turning ourselves into sociopathic predators. I simply mean rejecting the idea that there are intrinsic values, non-conventional obligations, objective duties, natural rights, or any of the other peremptory items moralists cherish. To reject morality is to reject these beliefs, but this is something very few people have ever been willing to do. The automatic first impulse is to attack amoralism, which is fair enough if the attack is fair, which it usually isn't.

Bernard Williams opens his book *Morality* with an attempt to answer "the amoralist," who is "supposedly immune to moral considerations." We can't expect philosophers under the influence of moralism to wear themselves out constructing a coherent external challenge to their own pre-suppositions. But their responses to their external opponents are typically directed against weak versions of foolish positions, against those who violate (or promote the violation of) conventional moral standards, and against selfishness and heartless misanthropy. Amoralists are imagined to be inconsiderate monsters, as when Williams suggests that the amoralist may not even be "recognizably human."

A. THE AMORALIST AS AN IMMORAL, HEARTLESS, SELFISH JERK WHO DENIES THE OBVIOUS

Amoralism has been criticized for contributing to immoral behavior—behavior that violates conventional morality. Maybe it does and maybe it doesn't. There are moralists who lie, cheat, steal, and despise humanity; and amoralists who tell the truth, play fair, and treat others with respect. Given that one can always concoct a moral rationalization for violating conventional morality, it is not easy to judge how much positive effect a belief in objectively binding moral principles will have on a person's behavior.

Some critics confuse the amoralist with the pathological egoist. They say that amoralists are necessarily selfish and either lack compassion or feel it arbitrarily and sporadically. But what we believe about morality is independent of how much we care about others and of how many of them we care about. When Williams says that the amoralist "in his pure form" is "immune to moral considerations," he means that the amoralist is totally unmoved by the suffering of others. This

amoralist has no "inclination to tell the truth or keep promises if it does not suit him to do so." By way of contrast, when *I* say that amoralists are "immune to moral considerations," I mean that while they may actively and regularly promote the welfare of others, they aren't led to do this by moral beliefs. My amoralists may be moved by the suffering of others, but not by being told that suffering is intrinsically bad, or that others have a moral right to help.

We are right to worry about people who are unmoved by the pain of others. We understand Williams when he calls them psychopaths and monsters. But they aren't psychopaths and monsters because they "reject morality," they are psychopaths and monsters because they don't care about the suffering of others. Someone bound only by the dictates of some morality and utterly without affection, sympathy or kindness would be a monster too—a moral monster.

Sometimes amoralists are presented as denying some obvious truth, or asserting something too horrible to be accepted. Gilbert Harman says that extreme nihilism (the belief that "nothing is ever right or wrong, just or unjust, good or bad") implies

> that there are no moral constraints—that everything is permitted. As Dostoevsky observes, it implies that there is nothing wrong with murdering your father. It also implies that slavery was not unjust and that Hitler's extermination camps were not immoral. These are not easy conclusions to accept. (Harman, 11)

Whatever extreme nihilists might mean by saying that nothing is right or wrong, just or unjust, good or bad, they will not want to deny that there are conventional moral constraints, and that law, custom, other people, and our own rules forbid many things.

The amoralist is not denying that we have a conventional morality, and the moralist is saying more than that we have created sets of conventional rules and rights. The moralist insists that the immorality of death camps and slavery does not depend on what people happen to think, want, believe, buy into, or choose. The amoralist can join with the moralist in this rejection of subjectivism, but must demur when the moralist adds that death camps and slavery are *really* wrong, not just unacceptable by conventions we adopt from our society or inherit from our genes.

Amoralists who do not want to misrepresent themselves will not say that the extermination camps were immoral, however much they may detest them. But they will also hesitate to say that the camps were "not immoral" because those who hear this may take them to accept the institution of morality and to be giving not unfavorable marks to extermination camps. If we do not want to be mistaken for moralists, we must avoid moralist ways of expressing ourselves. We can be sure that plenty of amoralists give in to the temptation to exploit the power of moral language. Those who do are fair game for anyone who wants to score a point for moralism by exposing an amoralist committing morality. But when this happens, the problem is with the amoralist, not with amoralism.

B. WHAT TO DO ABOUT AMORALISM AND AMORALISTS?

Those who believe the amoralist is likely to exhibit antisocial behavior may try to think up techniques to make amoralists change their ways. Others are content to try to change amoralists' beliefs about morality, or at least to make amoralists acknowledge that they cannot rationally reject certain moral principles or values.

(1) Argument. In *Morality*, Bernard Williams looks for an answer to the "amoralist" he identifies as a psychopathic monster. Williams knows that *this* amoralist will not be moved by arguments, and that "the idea of arguing him into morality is surely idiotic." (Williams, 8) Accordingly, he supplies us with a less extreme amoralist—one it is, presumably, not idiotic to try to argue into morality. His example is the stereo-

type from a gangster movie (the mobster), "who cares about his mother, his child, even his mistress." He helps people, but only when he feels like it: he considers the interests of others, but not consistently or on any regular basis. Williams says that if "morality can be got off the ground rationally," we ought to be able to get it off the ground in an argument with someone like this. (Williams, 2)

The mobster cares about his close associates, but there is a wide gap between this feeling and the belief that he *ought* to care about people he doesn't even know, and yet another gap between that belief and any actual caring-behavior. The only thing the moralist can do is catch the mobster making some moral judgment of his own and then try to convince him that unless he makes similar judgments about relevantly similar cases he will have to add inconsistency to his list of crimes. If, however, the mobster knows how to argue, he knows enough to deny that the cases are relevantly similar, to withdraw his moral judgment, or to tell the moralist to get lost.

If I am right about morality, arguments will never get their hooks into someone, however rational and moral, who wishes to resist them. Even if one has been roundly trounced and forced to admit in public that justice is the greatest of all goods, that has no necessary connection with what one subsequently believes or does. One can treat the discussion as part of the entertainment.

(2) Persuasion. It is not hard to persuade attentive, open-minded, non-defensive people to treat others with more consideration. We can describe suffering in detail and paint in unattractive colors the life of the person who profits from the misery of others. We can document the effects of crack addiction, state torture, death squads, and slaughterhouses.

Merely knowing that there are such things as death squads is very different from fully realizing that there are. To "realize" what the death squads do is to go well beyond the words "There are death squads" and allow our imaginations and our memories to supply some horrible details. Because we are so often insulated by ignorance from the effects of what we do, or cause to be done, Peter Singer's few pictures of animals in labs and factory farms in his book *Animal Liberation* probably did more for animal welfare than all his arguments. But just as our arguments won't take hold unless our victim has the right principles, persuasion only works when we can appeal to desires or attitudes, some compassion, pity, or spark of good will that already exists. Fortunately this is not a serious problem because few humans lack all such desires and feelings.

(3) Coercion. When argument and persuasion fail, we can either give up trying to control the offending behavior, or we can turn to force or fraud. Moralists who identify the amoralist with the pathological egoist, and then observe that arguments and pleas are useless with such a monster, sometimes conclude that we have no choice but to threaten him, and if necessary to isolate him, or even hunt him down and kill him. Needless to say, these extreme remedies are unnecessary to cope with the average amoralist, who probably has as many kind and generous impulses as the next person, or some informed and compassionate amoralist, who has more. Amoralists will not believe that laws can be given a moral justification, but they are not likely to want to live without them. Coercion by laws falls equally on the heads of moralists and amoralists, and both can be glad there are penalties for murder and for dumping toxic waste in the river.

(4) Denial. One way to combat amoralism is to show that some form of moralism is true, another is to attack amoralism, and a third is to deny that amoralism is a possible position. One way to argue for the third option is to say that to desire something is to value it, and that to value it is to think it is valuable. If this is so, then it will turn out that no one with desires can deny the reality of value. Similarly, someone might try to argue that the mere fact that we choose one course of action over another is enough to establish that we have moral principles.

Only sophistical tricks can help the moralist here because just as there is no non-fallacious path from the desired to the desirable, there is none from the fact that I desire or choose something to the fact that I think it is desirable. This is not to say that people who desire things do not think the things they desire are worthy of desiring. Often they do. It is just to remain sensitive to the fact that sometimes people realize that what they desire doesn't deserve to be desired.

Some moralists point not to the desires and choices of amoralists, but to their deeds. If "amoralists" behave as if they subscribe to moral principles, then why not conclude that they do, perhaps without realizing it? Amoralists who are fair can be accused of believing in justice, and amoralists who tell the truth and help others can be charged with holding the moral principles of truthfulness and beneficence.

But these accusations are easily answered. There is a respect in which amoralists do subscribe to moral principles, and a more important respect in which they do not. The non-duplicitous amoralist subscribes to a principle (non-duplicity) moralists might call a moral principle. But amoralists who adhere to non-duplicity as a policy will not subscribe to that policy as moralists do, because they will not see it as objectively binding. Amoralists who allow their principles of action to be called "moral principles" run the risk of giving the impression that they subscribe to the moralist assumptions that lie behind their moralist way of talking.

It makes more sense for an amoralist to resist the idea that the principle of non-duplicity is a moral principle, acknowledging only that others interpret it that way. If I have adopted some such principle as a non-moral and non-binding guideline, then I will be prepared to explain how I understand it, why I have adopted it, and why I recommend it to others, when I do. I am not prepared to give it a moral justification and neither, I suspect, is the moralist. Friendly and compassionate amoralists are helpful, truthful, and respectful without once thinking this practice is required by anything other than the way of acting they have chosen or accepted.

Moralists, who would rather have the obligations and values dictated from a more objective source, may complain that the choice of these friendly policies is arbitrary and that there is nothing to stop the amoralist from selecting some harsher alternative. But this is misleading. It is not as if amoralists arrive at their ways of coping with others carelessly or at random—our ways of interacting result from a lifetime of experience, reflection, and indoctrination. We do not adopt a way of dealing with others as we might adopt a dog from the pound. Our "way of interacting" is part of who we are, formed over the decades, warped and straightened by our successes and failures. So the charge of being arbitrary doesn't amount to much. It is true that the amoralist has no unquestionable moral principles on which to base choices, but as it turns out, neither does the moralist. The difference is that the amoralist doesn't think, or pretend to think, that someday such principles might emerge from hiding.

9. What Is Wrong with Morality?

The conventions of morality are based on the widely held but mistaken assumption that the demands of morality are objectively authoritative, categorical, rational, justifiable, and sometimes universal. People are taught and encouraged to think of moral judgments as expressing such demands, and this teaching is reinforced by the presuppositions underlying the use of moral language. Nearly everyone assumes it would be dangerous not to have an objective morality, so even Mackie, who sees through the pretenses of the moral realists, spends the second half of his book trying to "invent right and wrong."

My suggestion is that we do not need morality. If morality requires objective prescriptivity

and there is no such thing, then when we realize this we either have to abandon morality or agree to participate in a conspiracy to promote it as something we know it is not. It is risky, unnecessary, and more difficult than we think to control others by misleading them about the true character of the world, but this is exactly what we do when we continue to use moral language in a way that implies things we do not accept. Hence, as we have seen, the honest amoralist who despises Nazi atrocities will not even say that the Nazis were evil, or that they were morally wrong to do what they did.

The questions of morality are so controversial, so related to even more controversial questions in philosophy, and so interwoven with personal interest and self-esteem, that it would be naive to think that even the simplest of them is going to be resolved by philosophers engaging in cool, rational deliberation and discussion. If the devil can quote scripture, more human monsters can construct (or hire moral philosophers to construct) a moral defense for anything they want to do.

Moralists claim that morality beats compassion and kindness, since these feelings come and go. But morality only beats compassion and kindness if it makes good on its own ground, which it can't, and if it actually is capable of influencing behavior, which can be debated. Compassion, on the other hand, is a direct motivator, and it doesn't have to be justified. It is a way of looking, and a disposition to help. If you care about somebody, if you want them to be happy, there is nothing to prove and no problem about motivation. If you merely think it is your duty to help them, then it will always be possible to dig up some excuse for not doing anything.

So what is wrong with morality? It isn't what people think it is, and if they saw it for what it is, it wouldn't work. It encourages deception and even self-deception. Anything can be given a moral defense by a clever sophist, but no moral judgment can be conclusively established, no moral debate resolved once and for all. Morality can be (and has been) used to defend cruelty, selfishness, exploitation and neglect. By itself morality is insufficient for motivation, and its actual contribution to any decision is far from clear. It is not necessary for the kind of behavior it is thought to be a device to promote, and since people can be conventionally good without believing in the objectivity of morality, it makes sense to consider some alternatives. *The* alternative is, and always has been (in one form or another), expanded sympathies, increased concern for others.

I believe that if we could establish this "informed compassionate amoralism" we could leave morality, with its lies and its guilt, with its bogus heteronomy, its capacity for exploitation and rationalization, its unresolvable arguments, and its perpetual flirtation with religion, behind us. Freud was probably right when he called religion a childhood neurosis, but what he didn't say (because he didn't believe it) was that morality is an adolescent one.

Works Cited

Harman, Gilbert. *The Nature of Morality*. New York: Oxford University Press, 1977.

Hobbes, Thomas. *Leviathan*. Indianapolis: Bobbs-Merrill Company, 1958.

Kant, Immanuel. *Grounding for the Metaphysics of Morals*, trans. James Ellington. Indianapolis: Hackett Publishing Company, 1981.

Mackie, J. L. *Ethics: Inventing Right and Wrong*. Harmondsworth: Penguin, 1977.

Nagel, Thomas. [1] *The Possibility of Altruism*. Oxford: Oxford University Press, 1970. [2] "The Limits of Objectivity," in *The Tanner Lectures on Human Values*, Vol. 1 (edited by Sterling M. McMurrin). Salt Lake City: University of Utah Press, 1980. [3] *The View from Nowhere*. Oxford: Oxford University Press, 1986.

Nietzsche, Friedrich. *Twilight of the Idols*. R. J. Hollingdale trans. Harmondsworth: Penguin, 1968.

Price, A. F. and Wong Mou-Lam (trans.). *The Diamond Sutra and The Sutra of Hui Neng*. Boulder: Shambhala, 1969.

Williams, Bernard. *Morality: An Introduction to Ethics*, New York: Harper Touchbook, 1972.

Wong, David B. *Moral Relativity*. Berkeley: University of California Press, 1984.

NOTES

1. I will usually adhere to the philosophical usage in what I write here. When I write that pain is (or is not) "bad" I mean 'bad' in the evaluative and not the neutral quantitative way.

2. I am not saying that it is easy to stop making value judgments, just that it is easier to do that than it is to eliminate our aversion and attraction.

3. In his Tanner Lectures, Nagel said that he is "not sure whether there are such values." (Nagel [2], 107)

4. This argument is developed in Chapters 11 and 12 of *The Possibility of Altruism*.

5. David B. Wong makes a similar point in *Moral Relativity* when he says that "it is generally true that the more real people are to us, the more we are moved to act in their welfare; but this is made true by the way we understand others and by sympathy, not by the existence of objective reasons." (Wong, 85)

6. Someone might object that I have assumed that there is no difference between "there is (or someone has) reason to want something" and "there is (or someone has) *a* reason to want something." I am not sure there is *much* of a difference, but I am sure that Nagel uses both sorts of expression, and does not exploit any distinction between them in his argument. In one place, for example, he says that "if the relief of pain has neutral value as well, then anyone has a reason to want any pain to stop, whether or not it is his." (Nagel [3], 159). In another, he says that if something has agent-neutral value, then "*anyone* has reason to want it to exist — and that includes someone considering the world in detachment from the perspective of any particular person within it." (Nagel [3], 153).

7. Nagel goes on to say that the question, "How can *his* pain give *me* or anyone else looking at it from outside a reason [to want him to be given an analgesic]?" is a "crazy" question, but adds that the obvious answer to the question is that "pain is awful." "The pain of the man groaning in the next bed," he says, "is just as awful as yours. That's the reason to want him to have an analgesic." (Nagel [2], 110). I am assuming that "being awful" is just an extreme case of "being bad," and that Nagel is not just saying that we have a reason to want the genuinely awful (i.e., intense and prolonged) pain to stop, but that we have a reason to want it all to stop. It's being bad is bad enough.

Further Questions

1. Observe some actual moral discussions among your friends and associates. Do you think that Garner's characterization of the dismal state of moral argumentation is accurate?
2. Is it correct to say that the average person subscribes to some form of crazy objectivity?
3. What reasons, if any, do you have for wanting the pain of others to stop?
4. What would it take to make a world without morality livable?

Further Readings

Garner, Richard. *Beyond Morality*. Philadelphia: Temple University Press, 1993. An extremely accessible and insightful argument for amoralism. Highly recommended.

Mackie, J. L. *Ethics: Inventing Right and Wrong*. Harmondsworth: Penguin, 1977. An earlier version of a view like Garner's.

Taylor, Richard. *Good and Evil*. Buffalo, N.Y.: Prometheus Books, 1984. A readable and lively introduction to ethics.

Part XIV

Values

IMAGINE MAKING A PERFECT VERSION OF YOURSELF. No flaws!
What would you choose to keep the same and what would you choose to change, from the way you are now?

Most of us value things like money, fame, health, happiness, and so on. But these are things we *have*, not things we *are*. What do we value about ourselves?

In dealing with others, things like honesty, openness, and sincerity tend to be high on our lists. Do we value these things as highly in ourselves?

Suppose you were *completely* honest, open, sincere — always, with everyone. What would your life be like? Would you like that version of yourself? That is the question to which we now turn.

Existentialism

JEAN-PAUL SARTRE

French philosopher, playwright, and novelist Jean-Paul Sartre was born in Paris in 1905, the son of a naval officer; his mother was the cousin of the famous theologian and jungle doctor, Albert Schweitzer. Orphaned at a young age, Sartre was raised by his grandfather and educated in Paris. During World War II he joined the French Army where he behaved like an anarchist and also used the time to work on a novel, typing it in front of his commanding officers. He became a German prisoner of war for eight months during which time he "sings, writes, puts on plays, acts, composes, lectures, teachers, plays the fool, and, finally, escapes with false papers" (*Sartre: A Life* by Annie Cohen-Solal. Pantheon, 1987, p. 151).

Although he did not invent existentialism, Sartre is certainly one of its most famous and evocative exponents. Among his famous and enduring works are the novel *Nausea* (1938), the plays *No Exit* (1944), *The Flies* (1946), and *The Condemned of Altona* (1960), and the massive philosophical work *Being and Nothingness* (1943). In 1964 he refused to accept the Nobel Prize in Literature that was awarded him, calling the prize a political tool of the East-West struggle. In the following selection, Sartre gives a lucid and simple explanation of the meaning of existentialism.

Reading Questions

1. Sartre distinguishes himself from "religious" existentialists. Why? What makes his brand of existentialism "atheistic"?
2. What is the significance of the paper-cutter example?
3. What does Sartre mean by, "existence precedes essence"? Does this apply to everything?
4. He gives two meanings of "subjectivism." Which is the "essential meaning of existentialism," and why?
5. What is the point of the story of Abraham?
6. What does Sartre mean by saying that we are all "condemned to be free"?
7. What does Sartre mean by "human nature"? Why does he think that there is no such thing?

. . . WHAT IS MEANT by the term *existentialism?*

Most people who use the word would be rather embarrassed if they had to explain it, since, now that the word is all the rage, even the work of a musician or a painter is being called existentialist. A gossip columnist in *Clartés* signs himself *The Existentialist*, so that by this time the word has been so stretched and has taken on so broad a meaning, that it no longer means anything at all. It seems that for want of an advance-guard doctrine analogous to surrealism, the kind of people who are eager for scandal and flurry turn to this philosophy which in other respects does not at all serve their purposes in this sphere.

Actually, it is the least scandalous, the most austere of doctrines. It is intended strictly for specialists and philosophers. Yet it can be defined easily. What complicates matters is that there are two kinds of existentialist; first, those who are Christian, among whom I would include Jaspers and Gabriel Marcel, both Catholic; and on the other hand the atheistic existentialists, among whom I class Heidegger, and then the French existentialists and myself. What they have in common is that they think that existence precedes essence, or, if you prefer, that subjectivity must be the starting point.

Just what does that mean? Let us consider some object that is manufactured, for example, a book or a paper-cutter: here is an object which has been made by an artisan whose inspiration came from a concept. He referred to the concept of what a paper-cutter is and likewise to a known method of production, which is part of the concept, something which is, by and large, a routine. Thus, the paper-cutter is at once an object produced in a certain way and, on the other hand, one having a specific use; and one can not postulate a man who produces a paper-cutter but does not know what it is used for. Therefore, let us say that, for the paper-cutter, essence — that is, the ensemble of both the production routines and the properties which enable it to be both produced and defined — precedes existence. Thus, the presence of the paper-cutter or book in front of me is determined. Therefore, we have here a technical view of the world whereby it can be said that production precedes existence.

When we conceive God as the Creator, He is generally thought of as a superior sort of artisan. Whatever doctrine we may be considering, whether one like that of Descartes or that of Leibnitz, we always grant that will more or less follows understanding or, at the very least,

From Existentialism *by Jean-Paul Sartre, Philosophical Library Publishers, 1957. Reprinted by permission of the publisher.*

accompanies it, and that when God creates He knows exactly what He is creating. Thus, the concept of man in the mind of God is comparable to the concept of paper-cutter in the mind of the manufacturer, and, following certain techniques and a conception, God produces man, just as the artisan, following a definition and a technique, makes a paper-cutter. Thus, the individual man is the realization of a certain concept in the divine intelligence.

In the eighteenth century, the atheism of the *philosophies* discarded the idea of God, but not so much for the notion that essence precedes existence. To a certain extent, this idea is found everywhere; we find it in Diderot, in Voltaire, and even in Kant. Man has a human nature; this human nature, which is the concept of the human, is found in all men, which means that each man is a particular example of a universal concept, man. In Kant, the result of this universality is that the wild-man, the natural man, as well as the bourgeois, are circumscribed by the same definition and have the same basic qualities. Thus, here too the essence of man precedes the historical existence that we find in nature.

Atheistic existentialism, which I represent, is more coherent. It states that if God does not exist, there is at least one being in whom existence precedes essence, a being who exists before he can be defined by any concept, and that this being is man, or, as Heidegger says, human reality. What is meant here by saying that existence precedes essence? It means that, first of all, man exists, turns up, appears on the scene, and, only afterwards, defines himself. If man, as the existentialist conceives him, is indefinable, it is because at first he is nothing. Only afterward will he be something, and he himself will have made what he will be. Thus, there is no human nature, since there is no God to conceive it. Not only is man what he conceives himself to be, but he is also only what he wills himself to be after this thrust toward existence.

Man is nothing else but what he makes of himself. Such is the first principle of existentialism. It is also what is called subjectivity, the name we are labeled with when charges are brought against us. But what do we mean by this, if not that man has a greater dignity than a stone or table? For we mean that man first exists, that is, that man first of all is the being who hurls himself toward a future and who is conscious of imagining himself as being in the future. Man is at the start a plan which is aware of itself, rather than a patch of moss, a piece of garbage, or a cauliflower; nothing exists prior to this plan; there is nothing in heaven; man will be what he will have planned to be. Not what he will want to be. Because by the word "will" we generally mean a conscious decision, which is subsequent to what we have already made of ourselves. I may want to belong to a political party, write a book, get married; but all that is only a manifestation of an earlier, more spontaneous choice that is called "will." But if existence really does precede essence, man is responsible for what he is. Thus, existentialism's first move is to make every man aware of what he is and to make the full responsibility of his existence rest on him. And when we say that a man is responsible for himself, we do not only mean that he is responsible for his own individuality, but that he is responsible for all men.

The word subjectivism has two meanings, and our opponents play on the two. Subjectivism means, on the one hand, that an individual chooses and makes himself; and, on the other, that it is impossible for man to transcend human subjectivity. The second of these is the essential meaning of existentialism. When we say that man chooses his own self, we mean that every one of us does likewise; but we also mean by that that in making this choice he also chooses all men. In fact, in creating the man that we want to be, there is not a single one of our acts which does not at the same time create an image of man as we think he ought to be. To choose to be this or that is to affirm at the same time the value of what we choose, because we can never choose evil. We always choose the good, and nothing can be good for us without being good for all.

If, on the other hand, existence precedes essence, and if we grant that we exist and fashion our image at one and the same time, the image is valid for everybody and for our whole age. Thus, our responsibility is much greater than we might have supposed, because it involves all mankind. If I am a workingman and choose to join a Christian trade-union rather than be a communist, and if by being a member I want to show that the best thing for man is resignation, that the kingdom of man is not of this world, I am not only involving my own case—I want to be resigned for everyone. As a result, my action has involved all humanity. To take a more individual matter, if I want to marry, to have children; even if this marriage depends solely on my own circumstances or passion or wish, I am involving all humanity in monogamy and not merely myself. Therefore, I am responsible for myself and for everyone else. I am creating a certain image of man of my own choosing. In choosing myself, I choose man.

This helps us understand what the actual content is of such rather grandiloquent words as anguish, forlornness, despair. As you will see, it's all quite simple.

First, what is meant by anguish? The existentialists say at once that man is anguish. What that means is this: the man who involves himself and who realizes that he is not only the person he chooses to be, but also a lawmaker who is, at the same time, choosing all mankind as well as himself, can not help escape the feeling of his total and deep responsibility. Of course, there are many people who are not anxious; but we claim that they are hiding their anxiety, that they are fleeing from it. Certainly, many people believe that when they do something, they themselves are the only ones involved, and when someone says to them, "What if everyone acted that way?" they shrug their shoulders and answer, "Everyone doesn't act that way." But really, one should always ask himself, "What would happen if everybody looked at things that way?" There is no escaping this disturbing thought except by a kind of double-dealing. A man who lies and makes excuses for himself by saying "not everybody does that," is someone with an uneasy conscience, because the act of lying implies that a universal value is conferred upon the lie.

Anguish is evident even when it conceals itself. This is the anguish that Kierkegaard called the anguish of Abraham. You know the story: an angel has ordered Abraham to sacrifice his son; if it really were an angel who has come and said, "You are Abraham, you shall sacrifice your son," everything would be all right. But everyone might first wonder, "Is it really an angel, and am I really Abraham? What proof do I have?"

There was a madwoman who had hallucinations; someone used to speak to her on the telephone and give her orders. Her doctor asked her, "Who is it who talks to you?" She answered, "He says it's God." What proof did she really have that it was God? If an angel comes to me, what proof is there that it's an angel? And if I hear voices, what proof is there that they come from heaven and not from hell, or from the subconscious, or a pathological condition? What proves that they are addressed to me? What proof is there that I have been appointed to impose my choice and my conception of man on humanity? I'll never find any proof or sign to convince me of that. If a voice addresses me, it is always for me to decide that this is the angel's voice; if I consider that such an act is a good one, it is I who will choose to say that it is good rather than bad.

Now, I'm not being singled out as an Abraham, and yet at every moment I'm obliged to perform exemplary acts. For every man, everything happens as if all mankind had its eyes fixed on him and were guiding itself by what he does. And every man ought so say to himself, "Am I really the kind of man who has the right to act in such a way that humanity might guide itself by my actions?" And if he does not say that to himself, he is masking his anguish.

There is no question here of the kind of anguish which would lead to quietism, to inaction. It is a matter of a simple sort of anguish that anybody who has had responsibilities is familiar with. For example, when a military officer takes the responsibility for an attack and sends a certain number of men to death, he chooses to do so, and in the main he alone makes the choice. Doubtless, orders come from above, but they are too broad; he interprets them, and on this interpretation depend the lives of ten or fourteen or twenty men. In making a decision he can not help having a certain anguish. All leaders know this anguish. That doesn't keep them from acting; on the contrary, it is the very condition of their action. For it implies that they envisage a number of possibilities, and when they choose one, they realize that it has value only because it is chosen. We shall see that this kind of anguish, which is the kind that existentialism describes, is explained, in addition, by a direct responsibility to the other men whom it involves. It is not a curtain separating us from action, but is part of action itself.

When we speak of forlornness, a term Heidegger was fond of, we mean only that God does not exist and that we have to face all the consequences of this. The existentialist is strongly opposed to a certain kind of secular ethics which would like to abolish God with the least possible expense. About 1880, some French teachers tried to set up a secular ethics which went something like this: God is a useless and costly hypothesis; we are discarding it; but, meanwhile, in order for there to be an ethics, a society, a civilization, it is essential that certain values be taken seriously and that they be considered as having an *a priori* existence. It must be obligatory, *a priori*, to be honest, not to lie, not to beat your wife, to have children, etc., etc. So we're going to try a little device which will make it possible to show that values exist all the same, inscribed in a heaven of ideas, though otherwise God does not exist. In other words — and this, I believe, is the tendency of everything called reformism in France — nothing will be changed if God does not exist. We shall find ourselves with the same norms of honesty, progress, and humanism, and we shall have made

of God an outdated hypothesis which will peacefully die off by itself.

The existentialist, on the contrary, thinks it very distressing that God does not exist, because all possibility of finding values in a heaven of ideas disappears along with Him; there can no longer be an *a priori* Good, since there is no infinite and perfect consciousness to think it. Nowhere is it written that the Good exists, that we must be honest, that we must not lie; because the fact is we are on a plane where there are only men. Dostoievsky said, "If God didn't exist, everything would be possible." That is the very starting point of existentialism. Indeed, everything is permissible if God does not exist, and as a result man is forlorn, because neither within him nor without does he find anything to cling to. He can't start making excuses for himself.

If existence really does precede essence, there is no explaining things away by reference to a fixed and given human nature. In other words, there is no determinism, man is free, man is freedom. On the other hand, if God does not exist, we find no values or commands to turn to which legitimize our conduct. So, in the bright realm of values, we have no excuse behind us, nor justification before us. We are alone, with no excuses.

That is the idea I shall try to convey when I say that man is condemned to be free. Condemned, because he did not create himself, yet, in other respects is free; because, once thrown into the world, he is responsible for everything he does. The existentialist does not believe in the power of passion. He will never agree that a sweeping passion is a ravaging torrent which fatally leads a man to certain acts and is therefore an excuse. He thinks that man is responsible for his passion.

The existentialist does not think that man is going to help himself by finding in the world some omen by which to orient himself. Because he thinks that man will interpret the omen to suit himself. Therefore, he thinks that man, with no support and no aid, is condemned every moment to invent man. Ponge, in a very fine article, has said, "Man is the future of man." That's exactly it. But if it is taken to mean that this future is recorded in heaven, that God sees it, then it is false, because it would really no longer be a future. If it is taken to mean that, whatever a man may be, there is a future to be forged, a virgin future before him, then this remark is sound. But then we are forlorn.

To give you an example which will enable you to understand forlornness better, I shall cite the case of one of my students who came to see me under the following circumstances: his father was on bad terms with his mother, and, moreover, was inclined to be a collaborationist; his older brother had been killed in the German offensive of 1940, and the young man, with somewhat immature but generous feelings, wanted to avenge him. His mother lived alone with him, very much upset by the half-treason of her husband and the death of her older son; the boy was her only consolation.

The boy was faced with the choice of leaving for England and joining the Free French Forces — that is, leaving his mother behind — or remaining with his mother and helping her to carry on. He was fully aware that the woman lived only for him and that his going-off — and perhaps his death — would plunge her into despair. He was also aware that every act that he did for his mother's sake was a sure thing, in the sense that it was helping her to carry on, whereas every effort he made toward going off and fighting was an uncertain move which might run aground and prove completely useless; for example, on his way to England he might, while passing through Spain, be detained indefinitely in a Spanish camp; he might reach England or Algiers and be stuck in an office at a desk job. As a result, he was faced with two very different kinds of action: one, concrete, immediate, but concerning only one individual; the other concerned incomparably vaster group, a national collectivity, but for that very reason was dubious, and might be interrupted en route. And, at the same time, he was wavering between two kinds of ethics. On the one hand, an ethics of sympathy, of personal devotion; on the other, a broader ethics, but one whose efficacy was more dubious. He had to choose between the two.

Who could help him choose? Christian doctrine? No. Christian doctrine says, "Be charitable, love your neighbor, take the more rugged path, etc., etc." But which is the more rugged path? Whom should he love as a brother? The fighting man or his mother? Which does the greater good, the vague act of fighting in a group, or the concrete one of helping a particular human being to go on living? Who can decide *a priori*? Nobody. No book of ethics can tell him. The Kantian ethics says, "Never treat any person as a means, but as an end." Very well, if I stay with my mother, I'll treat her as an end and not as a means; but by virtue of this very fact, I'm running the risk of treating the people around me who are fighting, as means; and, conversely, if I go to join those who are fighting, I'll be treating them as an end, and, by doing that, I run the risk of treating my mother as a means.

If values are vague, and if they are always too broad for the concrete and specific case that we are considering, the only thing left for us is to trust our instincts. That's what this young man tried to do; and when I saw him, he said, "In the end, feeling is what counts. I ought to choose whichever pushes me in one direction. If I feel that I love my mother enough to sacrifice everything else for her — my desire for vengeance, for action, for adventure — then I'll stay with her. If, on the contrary, I feel that my love for my mother isn't enough, I'll leave."

But how is the value of a feeling determined? What gives his feeling for his mother value? Precisely the fact that he remained with her. I may say that I like so-and-so well enough to sacrifice a certain amount of money for him, but I may say so only if I've done it. I may say "I love my mother well enough to remain with her" if I have remained with her. The only way to determine the value of this affection is, precisely, to perform an act which confirms and defines it. But, since I require this affection to justify my act, I find myself caught in a vicious circle.

On the other hand, Gide has well said that a mock feeling and a true feeling are almost indistinguishable; to decide that I love my mother and will remain with her, or to remain with her by putting on an act, amount somewhat to the same thing. In other words, the feeling is formed by the acts one performs; so, I can not refer to it in order to act upon it. Which means that I can neither seek within myself the true condition which will impel me to act, nor apply to a system of ethics for concepts which will permit me to act. You will say, "At least, he did go to a teacher for advice." But if you seek advice from a priest, for example, you have chosen this priest; you already knew, more or less, just about what advice he was going to give you. In other words, choosing your adviser is involving yourself. The proof of this is that if you are a Christian, you will say, "Consult a priest." But some priests are collaborating, some are just marking time, some are resisting. Which to choose? If the young man chooses a priest who is resisting or collaborating, he has already decided on the kind of advice he's going to get. Therefore, in coming to see me he knew the answer I was going to give him, and I had only one answer to give: "You're free, choose, that is, invent." No general ethics can show you what is to be done; there are no omens in the world. The Catholics will reply, "But there are." Granted — but, in any case, I myself choose the meaning they have.

When I was a prisoner, I knew a rather remarkable young man who was a Jesuit. He had entered the Jesuit order in the following way: he had had a number of very bad breaks; in childhood, his father died, leaving him in poverty, and he was a scholarship student at a religious institution where he was constantly made to feel that he was being kept out of charity; then, he failed to get any of the honors and distinctions that children like; later on, at about eighteen, he bungled a love affair; finally, at twenty-two, he failed in military training, a childish enough matter, but it was the last straw.

This young fellow might well have felt that he had botched everything. It was a sign of something, but of what? He might have taken refuge in bitterness or despair. But he very wisely looked upon all this as a sign that he was not made for secular triumphs, and that only the triumphs of religion, holiness, and faith were open to him. He saw the hand of God in all this, and so entered the order. Who can help seeing that he alone decided what the sign meant?

Some other interpretation might have been drawn from this series of setbacks; for example, that he might have done better to turn carpenter or revolutionist. Therefore, he is fully responsible for the interpretation. Forlornness implies that we ourselves choose our being. Forlornness and anguish go together.

As for despair, the term has a very simple meaning. It means that we shall confine ourselves to reckoning only with what depends upon our will, or on the ensemble of probabilities which make our action possible. When we want something, we always have to reckon with probabilities. I may be counting on the arrival of a friend. The friend is coming by rail or street-car; this supposes that the train will arrive on schedule, or that the street-car will not jump the track. I am left in the realm of possibility; but possibilities are to be reckoned with only to the point where my action comports with the ensemble of these possibilities, and no further. The moment the possibilities I am considering are not rigorously involved by my action, I ought to disengage myself from them, because no God, no scheme, can adapt the world and its possibilities to my will. When Descartes said, "Conquer yourself rather than the world," he meant essentially the same thing.

Further Questions

1. Sartre, like Nietzsche, denies the existence of God. Why does he find it so distressing that God does not exist? Do you agree? Why?

2. What does the story about his student who comes seeking advice about whether to join the Free French illustrate? How does he use this example to criticize Kantian and Christian ethics? What does the example suggest about those seeking the advice of authority?

3. What are Sartre's views on responsibility?

Further Readings

The two main philosophical influences on Sartre were Edmund Husserl and Martin Heidegger, and so an introductory understanding of them can help one to understand Sartre. Two good places to start are:

Krell, David Farrell, ed. *Martin Heidegger: Basic Writings*. New York: Harper & Row, 1977.

Lauer, Quentin, *Phenomenology: Its Genesis and Prospects*. New York: Harper & Row, 1958. Provides a background on Husserl.

Other good sources are:

Barrett, William. *Irrational Man: A Study in Existential Philosophy*. New York: Doubleday, 1958. An excellent general overview.

Blackman, H. J. *Six Existentialist Thinkers*. London: Routledge & Kegan Paul, 1952. Kierkegaard, Nietzsche, Jaspers, Marcel, Heidegger, and Sartre.

Cohen-Solal, Annie. *Sartre: A Life*. New York: Pantheon, 1987. Anna Concogni, trans. The best and most complete biography of Sartre's life.

Sartre, Jean-Paul. *Words*. New York: Vintage Books, 1981. A moving biography of his childhood, beautifully written.

Sheridan, James. *The Radical Conversion*. Athens, OH: Ohio University Press, 1969.

Warnock, Mary. *The Philosophy of Sartre*. London: Hutchinson, 1966.

On Being Normal

RUTH BENEDICT

Ruth Fulton Benedict (1887–1948), one of the most distinguished anthropologists of the first half of the twentieth century, taught at Columbia University. Although she did much field work on Native American cultures, she is best known for her theoretical writings. A member of the Bureau of Overseas Intelligence during World War II, in 1946 she also published a book on Japanese culture. In the following selection, she argues that notions of normality, abnormality, deviance, and so on are culturally defined.

Reading Questions

1. Benedict thinks that what we regard as normality is culturally defined. What does she mean? Why does she think this?

2. Benedict claims that "we do not any longer make the mistake of deriving the morality of our own locality and decade directly from the inevitable constitution of human nature." Can you think of any actual examples in which people do try to do this?

MODERN SOCIAL ANTHROPOLOGY HAS BECOME more and more a study of the varieties and common elements of cultural environment and the consequences of these in human behavior. For such a study of diverse social orders primitive peoples fortunately provide a laboratory not yet entirely vitiated by the spread of a standardized world-wide civilization. Dyaks and Hopis, Fijians and Yakuts are significant for psychological and sociological study because only among these simpler peoples has there been sufficient isolation to give opportunity for the development of localized social forms. In the higher cultures the standardization of custom and belief over a couple of continents has given a false sense of the inevitability of the particular forms that have gained currency, and we need to turn to a wider survey in order to check the conclusions we hastily base upon this near-universality of familiar customs. Most of the simpler cultures did not gain the wide currency of the one which, out of our experience, we identify with human nature, but this was for various historical reasons, and certainly not for any that gives us as its carriers a monopoly of social good or of social sanity. Modern civilization, from this point of view, becomes not a necessary pinnacle of human achievement but one entry in a long series of possible adjustments.

These adjustments, whether they are in mannerisms like the ways of showing anger, or joy, or grief in any society, or in major human drives like those of sex, prove to be far more variable than experience in any one culture would suggest. In certain fields, such as that of religion or of formal marriage arrangements, these wide limits of variability are well known and can be fairly described. In others it is not yet possible to give a generalized account, but that does not absolve us of the task of indicating the significance of the work that has been done and of the problems that have arisen.

One of these problems relates to the customary modern normal-abnormal categories and our conclusions regarding them. In how far are such categories culturally determined, or in how far can we with assurance regard them as absolute? In how far can we regard inability to function socially as diagnostic of abnormality, or in how far is it necessary to regard this as a function of the culture?

As a matter of fact, one of the most striking facts that emerge from a study of widely varying cultures is the ease with which our abnormals function in other cultures. It does not matter what kind of "abnormality" we choose for illustration, those which indicate extreme instability, or those which are more in the nature of character traits like sadism or delusions of grandeur or of persecution, there are well-described cultures in which these abnormals function at ease and with honor, and apparently without danger or difficulty to the society.

The most notorious of these is trance and catalepsy. Even a very mild mystic is aberrant in our culture. But most peoples have regarded even extreme psychic manifestations not only as normal and desirable, but even as characteristic of highly

From Ruth Benedict: "Anthropology and the Abnormal" in The Journal of General Psychology, *X (1934), pp. 59–82. Reprinted by permission of The Helen Dwight Reid Educational Foundation. Published by Heldref Publications, 1319 Eighteenth St., NW, Washington, D.C. 20036-1802. Copyright 1934.*

valued and gifted individuals. . . . It is hard for us, born and brought up in a culture that makes no use of the experience, to realize how important a rôle it may play and how many individuals are capable of it, once it has been given an honorable place in any society. . . .

The most spectacular illustrations of the extent to which normality may be culturally defined are those cultures where an abnormality of our culture is the cornerstone of their social structure. It is not possible to do justice to these possibilities in a short discussion. A recent study of an island of northwest Melanesia by Fortune [*Sorcerers of Dobu*] describes a society built upon traits which we regard as beyond the border of paranoia. In this tribe the exogamic groups look upon each other as prime manipulators of black magic, so that one marries always into an enemy group which remains for life one's deadly and unappeasable foes. They look upon a good garden crop as a confession of theft, for everyone is engaged in making magic to induce into his garden the productiveness of his neighbors'; therefore no secrecy in the island is so rigidly insisted upon as the secrecy of a man's harvesting of his yams. Their polite phrase at the acceptance of a gift is, "And if you now poison me, how shall I repay you this gift?" Their preoccupation with poisoning is constant; no woman ever leaves her cooking pot for a moment unattended. Even the great final economic exchanges that are characteristic of this Melanesian culture area are quite altered in Dobu since they are incompatible with this fear and distrust that pervades the culture. They go farther and people the whole world outside their own quarters with such malignant spirits that all-night feasts and ceremonials simply do not occur here. They have even rigorous religiously enforced customs that forbid the sharing of seed even in one family group. Anyone else's food is deadly poison to you, so that communality of stores is out of the question. For some months before harvest the whole society is on the verge of starvation, but if one falls to the temptation and eats up one's seed yams, one is an outcast and a beachcomber for life. There is no coming back. It involves, as a matter of course, divorce and the breaking of all social ties.

Now in this society where no one may work with another and no one may share with another, Fortune describes the individual who was regarded by all his fellows as crazy. He was not one of those who periodically ran amok and, beside himself and frothing at the mouth, fell with a knife upon anyone he could reach. Such behavior they did not regard as putting anyone outside the pale. They did not even put the individuals who were known to be liable to these attacks under any kind of control. They merely fled when they saw the attack coming on and kept out of the way. "He would be all right tomorrow." But there was one man of sunny, kindly disposition who liked work and liked to be helpful. The compulsion was too strong for him to repress it in favor of the opposite tendencies of his culture. Men and women never spoke of him without laughing; he was silly and simple and definitely crazy. Nevertheless, to the ethnologist used to a culture that has, in Christianity, made his type the model of all virtue, he seemed a pleasant fellow.

An even more extreme example, because it is of a culture that has built itself upon a more complex abnormality, is that of the North Pacific Coast of North America. The civilization of the Kwakiutl, at the time when it was first recorded in the last decades of the nineteenth century, was one of the most vigorous in North America. It was built up on an ample economic supply of goods, the fish which furnished their food staple being practically inexhaustible and obtainable with comparatively small labor, and the wood which furnished the material for their houses, their furnishings, and their arts being, with however much labor, always procurable. They lived in coastal villages that compared favorably in size with those of any other American Indians and they kept up constant communication by means of sea-going dug-out canoes.

It was one of the most vigorous and zestful of the aboriginal cultures of North America, with complex crafts and ceremonials, and elaborate and striking arts. It certainly had none of the earmarks of a sick civilization. The tribes of the Northwest Coast had wealth, and exactly in our terms. That is, they had not only a surplus of economic goods, but they made a game of the manipulation of wealth. It was by no means a mere direct transcription of economic needs and the filling of those needs. It involved the idea of capital, of interest, and of conspicuous waste. It was a game with all the binding rules of a game, and a person entered it as a child. His father distributed wealth for him, according to his ability, at a small feast or potlatch, and each gift the receiver was obliged to accept and to return after a short interval with interest that ran to about 100 per cent a year. By the time the child was grown, therefore, he was well launched, a larger potlatch had been given for him on various occasions of exploit or initiation, and he had wealth either out at usury or in his own possession. Nothing in the civilization could be enjoyed without validating it by the distribution of this wealth. Everything that was valued, names and songs as well as material objects, were passed down in family lines, but they were always publicly assumed with accompanying sufficient distributions of property. It was the game of validating and exercising all the privileges one could accumulate from one's various forbears, or by gift, or by marriage, that made the chief interest of the culture. Everyone in his degree took part in it, but many, of course, mainly as spectators. In its highest form it was played out between rival chiefs representing not only themselves and their family lines but their communities, and the object of the contest was to glorify oneself and to humiliate one's opponent. On this level of greatness the property involved was no longer represented by blankets, so many thousand of them to a potlatch, but by higher units of value. These higher units were like our bank notes. They were incised copper tablets, each of them named, and having a value that depended upon their illustrious history. This was as high as ten thousand blankets, and to possess one of

them, still more to enhance its value at a great potlatch, was one of the greatest glories within the compass of the chiefs of the Northwest Coast.

The details of this manipulation of wealth are in many ways a parody on our own economic arrangements, but it is with the motivations that were recognized in this contest that we are concerned in this discussion. The drives were those which in our own culture we should call megalomaniac. There was an uncensored self-glorification and ridicule of the opponent that it is hard to equal in other cultures outside of the monologues of the abnormal. . . . All of existence was seen in terms of insult. Not only derogatory acts performed by a neighbor or an enemy, but all untoward events, like a cut when one's axe slipped, or a ducking when one's canoe overturned, were insults. All alike threatened first and foremost one's ego security, and the first thought one was allowed was how to get even, how to wipe out the insult. . . .

In their behavior at great bereavements this set of the culture comes out most strongly. Among the Kwakiutl it did not matter whether a relative had died in bed of disease, or by the hand of an enemy, in either case death was an affront to be wiped out by the death of another person. The fact that one had been caused to mourn was proof that one had been put upon. A chief's sister and her daughter had gone up to Victoria, and either because they drank bad whiskey or because their boat capsized they never came back. The chief called together his warriors. "Now I ask you, tribes, who shall wail? Shall I do it or shall another?" The spokesman answered, of course, "Not you, Chief. Let some other of the tribes." Immediately they set up the war pole to announce their intention of wiping out the injury, and gathered a war party. They set out, and found seven men and two children asleep and killed them. "Then they felt good when they arrived at Sebaa in the evening."

The point which is of interest to us is that in our society those who on that occasion would feel good when they arrived at Sebaa that evening would be the definitely abnormal. There would be some, even in our society, but it is not a recognized and approved mood under the circumstances. On the Northwest Coast those are favored and fortunate to whom that mood under those circumstances is congenial, and those to whom it is repugnant are unlucky. This latter minority can register in their own culture only by doing violence to their congenial responses and acquiring others that are difficult for them. The person, for instance, who, like a Plains Indian whose wife has been taken from him, is too proud to fight, can deal with the Northwest Coast civilization only be ignoring its strongest bents. If he cannot achieve it, he is the deviant in that culture, their instance of abnormality. . . .

Behavior honored upon the Northwest Coast is one which is recognized as abnormal in our civilization, and yet it is sufficiently close to the attitudes of our own culture to be intelligible to us and to have a definite vocabulary with which we may discuss it. The megalomaniac paranoid trend is a definite danger in our society. It is encouraged by some of our major preoccupations, and it confronts us with a choice of two possible attitudes. One is to brand it as abnormal and reprehensible, and is the attitude we have chosen in our civilization. The other is to make it an essential attribute of ideal man, and this is the solution in the culture of the Northwest Coast.

These illustrations, which it has been possible to indicate only in the briefest manner, force upon us the fact that normality is culturally defined. An adult shaped to the drives and standards of either of these cultures, if he were transported into our civilization would fall into our categories of abnormality. He would be faced with the psychic dilemmas of the socially unavailable. In his own culture, however, he is the pillar of society, the end result of socially inculcated mores, and the problem of personal instability in his case simply does not arise.

No one civilization can possibly utilize in its mores the whole potential range of human behavior. Just as there are great numbers of possible phonetic articulations, and the possibility of language depends on a selection and standardization of a few of these in order that speech communication may be possible at all, so the possibility of organized behavior of every sort, from the fashions of local dress and houses to the dicta of a people's ethics and religion, depends upon a similar selection among the possible behavior traits. In the field of recognized economic obligations or sex tabus this selection is as non-rational and subconscious a process as it is in the field of phonetics. It is a process which goes on in the group for long periods of time and is historically conditioned by innumerable accidents of isolation or of contact of peoples. In any comprehensive study of psychology, the selection that different cultures have made in the course of history within the great circumference of potential behavior is of great significance.

Every society, beginning with some slight inclination in one direction or another, carries its preference farther and farther, integrating itself more and more completely upon its chosen basis, and discarding those types of behavior that are uncongenial. Most of those organizations of personality that seem to us most incontrovertibly abnormal have been used by different civilizations in the very foundations of their institutional life. Conversely the most valued traits of our normal individuals have been looked on in differently organized cultures as aberrant. Normality, in short, within a very wide range, is culturally defined. It is primarily a term for the socially elaborated segment of human behavior in any culture; and abnormality, a term for the segment that that particular civilization does not use. The very eyes with which we see the problem are conditioned by the long traditional habits of our own society.

It is a point that has been made more often in relation to ethics than in relation to psychiatry. We do not any longer make the mistake of deriving the morality of our own locality and decade directly from the inevitable constitution of human nature. We do not elevate it to the dignity of a first principle. We recognize that morality differs in every society, and is a convenient term for socially approved habits. Mankind has always preferred to say, "It is morally good," rather than "It is habitual," and the fact of this preference is matter enough for a critical science of ethics. But historically the two phrases are synonymous.

The concept of the normal is properly a variant of the concept of the good. It is that which society has approved. A normal action is one which falls well within the limits of expected behavior for a particular society. Its variability among different peoples is essentially a function of the variability of the behavior patterns that different societies have created for themselves, and can never be wholly divorced from a consideration of culturally institutionalized types of behavior.

Each culture is a more or less elaborate working-out of the potentialities of the segment it has chosen. In so far as a civilization is well integrated and consistent within itself, it will tend to carry farther and farther, according to its nature, its initial impulse toward a particular type of action, and from the point of view of any other culture those elaborations will include more and more extreme and aberrant traits.

Each of these traits, in proportion as it reinforces the chosen behavior patterns of that culture, is for that culture normal. Those individuals to whom it is congenial either congenitally, or as the result of childhood sets, are accorded prestige in that culture, and are not visited with the social contempt or disapproval which their traits would call down upon them in a society that was differently organized. On the other hand, those individuals whose characteristics are not congenial to the selected type of human behavior in that community are the deviants, no matter how valued their personality traits may be in a contrasted civilization.

The Dobuan who is not easily susceptible to fear of treachery, who enjoys work and likes to be helpful, is their neurotic and regarded as silly. On the Northwest Coast the person who finds it difficult to read life in terms of an insult contest will be the person upon whom fall all the difficulties of the culturally unprovided for. The person who does not find it easy to humiliate a neighbor, nor to see humiliation in his own experience, who is genial and loving, may, of course, find some unstandardized way of achieving satisfactions in his society, but not in the major patterned responses that his culture requires of him. If he is born to play an important rôle in a family with many hereditary privileges, he can succeed only by doing violence to his whole personality. If he does not succeed, he has betrayed his culture; that is, he is abnormal.

I have spoken of individuals as having sets toward certain types of behavior, and of these sets as running sometimes counter to the types of behavior which are institutionalized in the culture to which they belong. From all that we know of contrasting cultures it seems clear that differences of temperament occur in every society. The matter has never been made the subject of investigation, but from the available material it would appear that these temperament types are very likely of universal recurrence. That is, there is an ascertainable range of human behavior that is found wherever a sufficiently large series of individuals is observed. But the proportion in which behavior types stand to one another in different societies is not universal. The vast majority of the individuals in any group are shaped to the fashion of that culture. In other words, most individuals are plastic to the moulding force of the society into which they are born. In a society that values trance, as in India, they will have supernormal experience. In a society that institutionalizes homosexuality, they will be homosexual. In a society that sets the gathering of possessions as the chief human objective, they will amass property. The deviants, whatever the type of behavior the culture has institutionalized, will remain few in number, and there seems no more difficulty in moulding the vast malleable majority to the "normality" of what we consider an aberrant trait than to the normality of such accepted behavior patterns as acquisitiveness. The small proportion of the number of the deviants in any culture is not a function of the sure instinct with which that society has built itself upon the fundamental sani-ties, but of the universal fact that, happily, the majority of mankind quite readily take any shape that is presented to them.

Further Questions

1. Construct the best argument you can *against* the last sentence in Benedict's paper. How could Benedict best respond to your argument?

2. Are the differences of opinion people have about how one should behave *evidence* that how one actually should behave is relative to one's culture? Are they evidence that there is no truth of the matter about how one actually should behave?

Further Readings

"Anthropology and Ethics." *The Monist*, June, 1963. A good collection of philosophical essays on relativism.

Gifford, N. *When in Rome*. A lucid, elementary discussion.

Krausz, M., and J. Meiland, eds. *Relativism: Cognitive and Moral*. Notre Dame: University of Notre Dame Press, 1982. Advanced readings.

Honesty

ADRIENNE RICH

Adrienne Rich, poet and essayist, is one of the most profound and provocative feminists writing today. Educated at Radcliffe, she has taught at various women's colleges and Women's Studies programs across the country. She writes, "I am not suggesting that you imitate male loyalties; . . . I believe that the bonding of women must be utterly different and for an utterly different end; not the misering of resources and power, but the release, in each other, of the yet unexplored resources and transformative power of women, so long despised, confined, and wasted. Get all the knowledge and skill you can in whatever professions you enter; but remember that most of your education must be self-education, in learning the things women need to know and in calling up the voices we need to hear within ourselves." Two of the best places to begin reading her work are *Blood, Bread, and Poetry: Selected Prose 1979–1985* (New York: W. W. Norton, 1986, preceding quote pp. 9–10) and *On Lies, Secrets, and Silence: Selected Prose, 1966–1978* (W. W. Norton, 1979), from which the following selection is taken.

Reading Questions

1. What does Rich mean by "the void"?
2. How does she distinguish male from female ideas of honor? Do you agree? What is the relationship between honor and lying?
3. Why, according to Rich, do liars lie? When you lie, is that why *you* lie?
4. Why does she compare "truth" to the pattern of a carpet?
5. "In lying to others," she writes, "we end up lying to ourselves." Do you agree?
6. How, according to Rich, have women been forced to lie, for their survival, to men? Do you agree? Why?

THESE NOTES ARE CONCERNED WITH relationships between and among women. When "personal relationship" is referred to, I mean a relationship between two women. (It will be clear in what follows when I am talking about women's relationships with men.)

The old, male idea of honor. A man's "word" sufficed — to other men — without guarantee.

"Our Land Free, Our Men Honest, Our Women Fruitful" — a popular colonial toast in America.

Male honor also having something to do with killing: *I could not love thee, Dear, so much/Lov'd I not Honour more*, ("To Lucasta, On Going to the Wars"). Male honor as something needing to be avenged: hence, the duel.

Women's honor, something altogether else: Virginity, chastity, fidelity to a husband. Honesty in women has not been considered important. We have been depicted as generically whimsical, deceitful, subtle, vacillating. And we have been rewarded for lying.

Men have been expected to tell the truth about facts, not about feelings. They have not been expected to talk about feelings at all.

Yet even about facts they have continually lied.

We assume that politicians are without honor. We read their statements trying to crack the code. The scandals of their politics: not that men in high places lie, only that they do so with such indifference, so endlessly, still expecting to be be-lieved. We are accustomed to the contempt inherent in the political lie.

* * *

To discover that one has been lied to in a personal relationship, however, leads one to feel a little crazy.

* * *

Lying is done with words, and also with silence.

The woman who tells lies in her personal relationships may or may not plan or invent her lying. She may not even think of what she is doing in a calculated way.

A subject is raised which the liar wishes buried. She has to go downstairs, her parking meter will have run out. Or, there is a telephone call she ought to have made an hour ago.

She is asked, point-blank, a question which may lead into painful talk: "How do you feel about what is happening between us?" Instead of trying to describe her feelings in their ambiguity and confusion, she asks, "How do *you* feel?" The other, because she is trying to establish a ground of openness and trust, begins describing her own feelings. Thus the liar learns more than she tells.

And she may also tell herself a lie: that she is concerned with the other's feelings, not with her own.

But the liar is concerned with her own feelings.

The liar lives in fear of losing control. She cannot even desire a relationship without manipulation, since to be vulnerable to another person means for her the loss of control.

The liar has many friends, and leads an existence of great loneliness.

* * *

The liar often suffers from amnesia. Amnesia is the silence of the unconscious.

To lie habitually, as a way of life, is to lose contact with the unconscious. It is like taking sleeping pills, which confer sleep but blot out dreaming. The unconscious wants truth. It ceases to speak to those who want something else more than truth.

In speaking of lies, we come inevitably to the subject of truth. There is nothing simple or easy about this idea. There is no "the truth," "a truth" —truth is not one thing, or even a system. It is an increasing complexity. The pattern of the carpet is a surface. When we look closely, or when we become weavers, we learn of the tiny multiple threads unseen in the overall pattern, the knots on the underside of the carpet.

This is why the effort to speak honestly is so important. Lies are usually attempts to make everything simpler—for the liar—than it really is, or ought to be.

In lying to others we end up lying to ourselves. We deny the importance of an event, or a person, and thus deprive ourselves of a part of our lives. Or we use one piece of the past or present to screen out another. Thus we lose faith even with our own lives.

The unconscious wants truth, as the body does. The complexity and fecundity of dreams comes from the complexity and fecundity of the unconscious struggling to fulfill that desire. The complexity and fecundity of poetry come from the same struggle.

* * *

An honorable human relationship—that is, one in which two people have the right to use the word "love"—is a process, delicate, violent, often terrifying to both persons involved, a process of refining the truths they can tell each other.

It is important to do this because it breaks down human self-delusion and isolation.

It is important to do this because in so doing we do justice to our own complexity.

It is important to do this because we can count on so few people to go that hard way with us.

* * *

I come back to the questions of women's honor. Truthfulness has not been considered important for women, as long as we have remained physically faithful to a man, or chaste.

We have been expected to lie with our bodies: to bleach, redden, unkink or curl our hair, pluck eyebrows, shave armpits, wear padding in various places or lace ourselves, take little steps, glaze finger and toe nails, wear clothes that emphasized our helplessness.

We have been required to tell different lies at different times, depending on what the men of the time needed to hear. The Victorian wife or the white southern lady, who were expected to have no sensuality, to "lie still"; the twentieth-century "free" woman who is expected to fake orgasms.

We have had the truth of our bodies withheld from us or distorted; we have been kept in ignorance of our most intimate places. Our instincts have been punished: clitoridectomies for "lustful" nuns or for "difficult" wives. It has been difficult, too, to know the lies of our complicity from the lies we believed.

The lie of the "happy marriage," of domesticity—we have been complicit, have acted out the fiction of a well-lived life, until the day we testify in court of rapes, beatings, psychic cruelties, public and private humiliations.

Patriarchal lying has manipulated women both through falsehood and through silence. Facts we needed have been withheld from us. False witness has been borne against us.

And so we must take seriously the question of truthfulness between women, truthfulness among women. As we cease to lie with our bodies, as we cease to take on faith what men have said about us, is a truly womanly idea of honor in the making?

*   *   *

Women have been forced to lie, for survival, to men. How to unlearn this among other women?

"Women have always lied to each other."

"Women have always whispered the truth to each other."

Both of these axioms are true.

"Women have always been divided against each other."

"Women have always been in secret collusion."

Both of these axioms are true.

In the struggle for survival we tell lies. To bosses, to prison guards, the police, men who have power over us, who legally own us and our children, lovers who need us as proof of their manhood.

There is a danger run by all powerless people: that we forget we are lying, or that lying becomes a weapon we carry over into relationships with people who do not have power over us.

*   *   *

I want to reiterate that when we talk about women and honor, or women and lying, we speak within the context of male lying, the lies of the powerful, the lie as false source of power.

Women have to think whether we want, in our relationships with each other, the kind of power that can be obtained through lying.

Women have been driven mad, "gaslighted," for centuries by the refutation of our experience and our instincts in a culture which validates only male experience. The truth of our bodies and our minds has been mystified to us. We therefore have a primary obligation to each other: not to undermine each others' sense of reality for the sake of expediency; not to gaslight each other.

Women have often felt insane when cleaving to the truth of our experience. Our future depends on the sanity of each of us, and we have a profound stake, beyond the personal, in the proj-

ect of describing our reality as candidly and fully as we can to each other.

*   *   *

There are phrases which help us not to admit we are lying: "my privacy," "nobody's business but my own." The choices that underlie these phrases may indeed be justified; but we ought to think about the full meaning and consequences of such language.

Women's love for women has been represented almost entirely through silence and lies. The institution of heterosexuality has forced the lesbian to dissemble, or be labeled a pervert, a criminal, a sick or dangerous woman, etc., etc. The lesbian, then, has often been forced to lie, like the prostitute or the married woman.

Does a life "in the closet"—lying, perhaps of necessity, about ourselves to bosses, landlords, clients, colleagues, family, because the law and public opinion are founded on a lie—does this, can it, spread into private life, so that lying (described as *discretion*) becomes an easy way to avoid conflict or complication? can it become a strategy so ingrained that it is used even with close friends and lovers?

Heterosexuality as an institution has also drowned in silence the erotic feelings between women. I myself lived half a lifetime in the lie of that denial. That silence makes us all, to some degree, into liars.

When a woman tells the truth she is creating the possibility for more truth around her.

*   *   *

The liar leads an existence of unutterable loneliness.

The liar is afraid.

But we are all afraid: without fear we become manic, hubristic, self-destructive. What is this particular fear that possesses the liar?

She is afraid that her own truths are not good enough.

She is afraid, not so much of prison guards or bosses, but of something unnamed within her.

The liar fears the void.

The void is not something created by patriarchy, or racism, or capitalism. It will not fade away with any of them. It is part of every woman.

"The dark core," Virginia Woolf named it, writing of her mother. The dark core. It is beyond personality; beyond who loves us or hates us.

We begin out of the void, out of darkness and emptiness. It is part of the cycle understood by the old pagan religions, that materialism denies. Out of death, rebirth; out of nothing, something.

The void is the creatrix, the matrix. It is not mere hollowness and anarchy. But in women it has been identified with lovelessness, barrenness, sterility. We have been urged to fill our "emptiness" with children. We are not supposed to go down into the darkness of the core.

Yet, if we can risk it, the something born of that nothing is the beginning of our truth.

The liar in her terror wants to fill up the void, with anything. Her lies are a denial of her fear; a way of maintaining control.

* * *

Why do we feel slightly crazy when we realize we have been lied to in a relationship?

We take so much of the universe on trust. You tell me: "In 1950 I lived on the north side of Beacon Street in Somerville." You tell me: "She and I were lovers, but for months now we have only been good friends." You tell me: "It is seventy degrees outside and the sun is shining." Because I love you, because there is not even a question of lying between us, I take these accounts of the universe on trust: your address twenty-five years ago, your relationship with someone I know only by sight, this morning's weather. I fling unconscious tendrils of belief, like slender green threads, across statements such as these, statements made so unequivocally, which have no tone or shadow of tentativeness. I build them into the mosaic of my world. I allow my universe to change in minute, significant ways, on the basis of things you have said to me, of my trust in you.

I also have faith that you are telling me things it is important I should know; that you do not conceal facts from me in an effort to spare me, or yourself, pain.

Or, at the very least, that you will say, "There are things I am not telling you."

When we discover that someone we trusted can be trusted no longer, it forces us to reexamine the universe, to question the whole instinct and concept of trust. For awhile, we are thrust back onto some bleak, jutting ledge, in a dark pierced by sheets of fire, swept by sheets of rain, in a world before kinship, or naming, or tenderness exist; we are brought close to formlessness.

* * *

The liar may resist confrontation, denying that she lied. Or she may use other language: forgetfulness, privacy, the protection of someone else. Or, she may bravely declare herself a coward. This allows her to go on lying, since that is what cowards do. She does not say, *I was afraid*, since this would open the question of other ways of handling her fear. It would open the question of what is actually feared.

She may say, *I didn't want to cause pain*. What she really did not want is to have to deal with the other's pain. The lie is a short-cut through another's personality.

* * *

Truthfulness, honor, is not something which springs ablaze of itself; it has to be created between people.

This is true in political situations. The quality and depth of the politics evolving from a group depends in very large part on their understanding of honor.

Much of what is narrowly termed "politics" seems to rest on a longing for certainty even at the cost of honesty, for an analysis which, once given, need not be reexamined. Such is the dead-endedness — for women — of Marxism in our time.

Truthfulness anywhere means a heightened complexity. But it is a movement into evolution.

Women are only beginning to uncover our own truths; many of us would be grateful for some rest in that struggle, would be glad just to lie down with the sherds we have painfully unearthed, and be satisfied with those. Often I feel this like an exhaustion in my own body.

The politics worth having, the relationships worth having, demand that we delve still deeper.

* * *

The possibilities that exist between two people, or among a group of people, are a kind of alchemy. They are the most interesting thing in life. The liar is someone who keeps losing sight of these possibilities.

When relationships are determined by manipulation, by the need for control, they may possess a dreary, bickering kind of drama, but they cease to be interesting. They are repetitious; the shock of human possibilities has ceased to reverberate through them.

When someone tells me a piece of the truth which has been withheld from me, and which I needed in order to see my life more clearly, it may bring acute pain, but it can also flood me with a cold, sea-sharp wash of relief. Often such truths come by accident, or from strangers.

It isn't that to have an honorable relationship with you, I have to understand everything, or tell you everything at once, or that I can know, beforehand, everything I need to tell you.

It means that most of the time I am eager, longing for the possibility of telling you. That these possibilities may seem frightening, but not destructive, to me. That I feel strong enough to hear your tentative and groping words. That we both know we are trying, all the time, to extend the possibilities of truth between us.

The possibility of life between us.

Further Questions

1. How would you describe Adrienne Rich's writing style? What does it evoke in you? Which of the other selections that you've read in this book is it most like? From which ones does it differ most? Do you see any philosophical significance in these differences and similarities?

2. Why does she think it so important for women to express their feelings, to break the silence that has been imposed on them?

3. You would think that those closest to us would be our greatest source of truth about ourselves. But Rich claims that such truths often "come by accident, or from strangers." Do you agree? Why?

Further Readings

For general works on feminism, see:

De Beauvoir, Simone. *The Second Sex*. New York: Penguin, 1976. By the life-long friend and companion of Jean-Paul Sartre.

Kelley, Joan. *Women, History, and Theory*. Chicago: University of Chicago Press, 1984.

Millett, Kate. *Sexual Politics*. New York: Doubleday, 1970. Rich calls it a "landmark book."

Roberts, Joan, ed. *Beyond Intellectual Sexism; A New Woman, A New Reality*. New York: David McKay, 1976.

Openness

JONATHAN GLOVER

Jonathan Glover teaches philosophy at Oxford University and writes primarily in the areas of ethics and philosophy of mind. In this selection, he considers how our lives would be affected if we were more transparent to each other and whether that would be a good thing.

Reading Questions

1. How important is mental privacy? Under what circumstances would you be willing to relinquish yours? Are there any circumstances under which you would relinquish it completely?

2. Do you think your intimate relationships would improve if you and those you love were completely transparent to each other?

A remote radio-communications system using belt transceivers is presently undergoing prototype testing. Systems of this type can monitor geographical location and psychophysiological variables, as well as permit two-way coded communication with people in their natural social environment. Probable subjects include individuals susceptible to emergency medical conditions that occasionally preclude calling for help (e.g. epilepsy, diabetes, myocardial infarctions), geriatric or psychiatric outpatients, and parolees. It is conceivable, for example, that convicts might be given the option of incarceration or parole with mandatory electronic surveillance. (Robert L. Schwitzgebel: *Emotions and Machines: A Commentary on the Context and Strategy Of Psychotechnology*)

During the last few years, methodology has been developed to stimulate and record the electrical activity of the brain in completely unrestrained monkeys and chimpanzees. This procedure should be of considerable clinical interest because it permits exploration of the brain for unlimited periods in patients without disturbing their rest or normal spontaneous activities. (José M. R. Delgado: *Journal of Nervous and Mental Disease* 1968)

THE DEVELOPMENT OF ELECTRONIC monitoring devices makes it possible for us to keep people under surveillance without locking them up in prison. We could largely replace prison by a system of keeping track of convicted criminals without restricting their movements. This thought can arouse both anxiety and optimism. The anxiety (when not about the effectiveness of such a system in restraining criminal activity) is about the invasion of privacy involved in such monitoring. The optimism comes from the thought that submitting to a monitoring system might be much less terrible than going to prison.

Advocates of monitoring systems use the argument that they would be more humane, and would be no more an invasion of privacy than prison. They suggest that we should try out monitoring for its effectiveness in preventing crime. If these systems turn out to be no more ineffective than prisons, it may seem that their supporters will have won the argument.

But it is a bit more complicated than this. Monitoring systems, just because they are less horrible to submit to than prison, may be resorted to more readily. Periods of monitoring might be much longer than prison sentences, and many more people might be monitored than are now sent to prison. We would then live in a society in which many had lost a lot of privacy. Perhaps social gains, such as a reduced crime rate and the abolition of prisons, would be thought great enough to outweigh this loss. But the issue is not a simple one, and the ways in which monitoring techniques could be developed and used have to be taken into account.

One obvious development is to monitor, not merely where people are, but also various of their physical states. Dr. Schwitzgebel mentions some useful applications of this internal monitoring in the cases of people with conditions dangerous to themselves. The extension to sex offenders, and to people liable to do harm when drunk or in fits of rage, can easily be imagined. And, as techniques for recording the electrical and chemical activity of the brain grow more sophisticated, we can expect it to become possible to monitor physical and psychological states with increasing precision.

When we think of more finely tuned monitoring, which would cross the blurred boundary between physical and psychological states, we are likely to feel increasing anxiety at the potential for invasion of privacy. To many people it will seem obvious that any extension of monitoring to psychological states should be resisted. But it is worth scrutinizing what is often taken for granted, and asking what the reasons are for valuing privacy as we do. Would it really be so terrible if our feelings and thoughts could be monitored by other people? What would be lost in a world without privacy?

To pose this issue in its sharpest form, let us consider the extreme case, in which the neurosciences have developed to the point where, by monitoring the activity of a person's brain, others could know in some detail the contents of his mind.

1. Monitoring Thoughts

The idea that we could monitor thoughts in this way presupposes that different mental states are correlated with different states of the brain. This is the working assumption of much psychology and neurophysiology, but it is controversial. We cannot be certain what future scientific work will show, and we are probably in for many surprises before the brain is fully understood. Yet there is already much suggestive work showing that electrical stimulation of particular points of the cortex can evoke highly specific memories, or that seeing particular patterns involves the firing of specific neurons in the cortex. In the scientific context, the working assumption, even if by no means impregnable, seems plausible.

Some philosophers have argued that there could not exist comprehensive and detailed psychophysical laws, while others disagree. These arguments will not be gone into here. The plan is to consider the implications of a technology based on monitoring brain activity, with deliberate casualness about current opinions as to which way the neurosciences will develop.

But there is a question which cannot be shelved here. What does it mean to talk of monitoring someone's thoughts and feelings? In a way, we all know what it is to have thoughts, and in most cases it seems absurd to suggest that someone does not know what thought he is having. Yet, despite this, there is a real problem in saying what having a thought consists in. And this problem causes difficulty for the idea of monitoring thoughts.

What is the problem about thoughts? Some thinking is in words, but sometimes we have a thought not formulated in words, where, if we are aware of anything, it is perhaps only some image. When I am struck by the thought that I have forgotten to telephone for a taxi, it may be that no words cross my mind. Perhaps I simply have a mental picture of a taxi. In such cases, images do not just come to mind on their own, but come with an interpretation. If I tell someone else that I have a mental picture of a taxi, he will not know what thought I am having, though I may be in no doubt at all that my thought is about the phone call. This process of interpretation, which applies to words as well as images, is something we know almost nothing about. This is why psychological studies of thinking, which can tell us so much about the strategies people use for solving problems, have so far told us so little about what our ordinary 'background' stream of consciousness consists in.

Because the process of interpretation is so important, even where the thought has embodiment in words or images, someone monitoring simply those words or images passing through my mind will have an incomplete knowledge of what I am thinking about. We can imagine a device that would decode the brain's activity and project on to a screen images corresponding to those in the person's mind. (We might need two screens: one for experiences involved in seeing, and one for visual imagination.) Thoughts which take place in words could be reproduced on a soundtrack, and images which are not visual or auditory could be reproduced by similar devices. But it is much less clear what it would be to give public embodiment to the process of interpreting these words and images. For this reason it seems better to discuss monitoring only words and images. It has to be recognized that a technology letting us do this would not give us perfect knowledge of people's mental lives.

Let us suppose that these devices are developed, and that they are produced in conveniently portable form. You come into the room holding what looks like a small portable television. The next thing I know is that I hear coming from it the words that are running through my mind,

and see my accompanying visual images on the screen. This technology will make people's minds largely transparent. Despite the problems about interpreting words and images, we will often have a fairly good idea of what others are thinking.

Will this be the end of privacy? In one way, the answer is clearly 'yes'. For, as the onion layers of privacy are peeled away, if there is a centre it must surely be the contents of the mind. But the machines so far described will leave us with an intermittent privacy of a kind. For, while the contents of a mind would always in principle be open to inspection, for much of the time it would not be under scrutiny. This is because of our limited powers of attention. Even with several thought-reading machines going at once, I could only attend to the thoughts of one or two people at a time. Some television enthusiasts have more than one set, so that they can watch programmes on different channels at the same time. The limitations on how far this could go are obvious. And, apart from problems of limited attention, most of us would want to spend most of the time doing other things, or thinking our own thoughts, and would probably not spend long tuned in to the minds of others. (Though artists and writers might find their thoughts constantly monitored by people doing courses about creativity.)

A society or a government determined to eliminate privacy could overcome these difficulties by developing a central monitor and memory store, where everyone's thoughts could be recorded and stored, so that they would be available for scrutiny when desired. At this point, systematic thought policing would be possible.

In our present world, governments and other organizations can destroy or hamper the freedom to express thoughts, but at least thought itself is always free. The introduction of thought-policing would make many people's lives scarcely worth living. It would also give governments complete power to block new ideas and social change, if only by killing or locking up people as soon as they had the ideas. Thought-policing is so appalling that there is a lot to be said for the view that work on developing thought-reading machines is immoral, merely because it helps to make it possible.

2. Transparency in a Free Community

Much of the horror of devices to make our minds transparent to others has to do with their uses in an authoritarian society. We are surely right to fear these potential uses, but some of our deepest anxieties about privacy come from other sources. This can be seen by a thought experiment in which we eliminate misuse by the authorities. Imagine a community of free and equal people. (It is not clear what this comes to, but imagine the nearest we can get in practice to an anarchist utopia.) Even here, the general availability of thought-reading machines can be seen as a terrible threat.

Why should we be disturbed if our thoughts become transparent to others? Some explanations that come to mind involve particular projects, or particular kinds of thought, which generate their own reasons for secrecy. If we are trying to give someone a surprise, bargaining with him, or trying to swindle or cheat him, the project will collapse if our thoughts are publicly available. A society transparent in this way will be one in which bargaining and swindling are impossible, which will no doubt have repercussions on our economy. But most of us will see little reason for being appalled. More personal anxieties are stronger. Some of our thoughts would seem discreditable, or at least embarrassing. Feelings of jealousy or resentment, sexual fantasies, or Walter Mitty daydreams of a self-flattering kind would all be sources of embarrassment. And, less selfishly, we are glad to keep some thoughts about other people secret so that we do not hurt them.

But these reasons, although psychologically powerful, may not go the heart of the matter. They concern particular kinds of thoughts and feelings. We can imagine a society in which bargaining and swindling did not exist, and in which daydreams and sexual fantasies were no longer a matter for embarrassment. In that society, people might still feel a resistance to their mental lives being made transparent to others. There is a case for saying that the value of privacy depends on something deeper than the embarrassing or hurtful aspects of particular thoughts and feelings. It may be bound up with the nature of relationships, and with our sense of our own identity.

3. Relationships

On one view, the fact that we have an area of privacy is more important than which particular activities or thoughts are included in it. (This is suggested in a particularly perceptive discussion of these issues by Charles Fried.[1]) The claim is that privacy is necessary for different kinds of relationships. We choose how far to admit people to friendship or other relationships with us partly by controlling how much of what is private we reveal to them. As Fried puts it,

> Love or friendship can be partially expressed by the gift of other rights—gifts of property or of service. But these gifts, without the intimacy of shared private information, cannot alone constitute love or friendship. The man who is generous with his possessions, but not with himself, can hardly be a friend, nor—and this more clearly shows the necessity of privacy for love—can the man who, voluntarily or involuntarily, shares everything about himself with the world indiscriminately.

But is it certain that gradations of intimacy are necessary for differences of relationship? In a world of transparent relationships, there would still be room for people being generous with themselves to different degrees. We would continue to give people different amounts of our concern and our time. We would respond to people with varying degrees of warmth, and this would be more obvious than it is now. Close relationships would consist in choosing to be together, and in the way people would feel about each other. There would no longer be the mutual lowering of the barriers of privacy. Closeness would be different from now, but not so different as to be non-existent.

It does seem that some of the pleasures of relationships involve talking about things that otherwise would be private. We like to do things together and to talk about our responses. (Part of the appeal of films and, especially, novels is that they often portray people from the inside, and so give us comparisons to use in trying to capture and articulate our own fugitive private experiences.) In talking to each other, and so learning to express (and sharpen) our experiences, we are doing something similar to what a novelist does. If we were transparent to each other, some of the things we now say would not need to be said. But it does not follow that all such conversation would be eliminated. This is because our conversation does not just report responses, but shapes them. We often only get clear about our *own* thoughts and feelings by trying to express them to someone else, and by listening to their thoughts in return. So transparency would not destroy conversation, though we might just think together without having to talk.

But another aspect of relationships might be threatened by transparency. In our present state, privacy gives a special quality to the times when it is waived. Other people can seem like medieval fortified towns. We can climb the hill and walk round outside their walls. But if they open the gate and let us in, we have the pleasures of exploration, seeing squares and houses and churches, sometimes like those we know and sometimes quite different. And while you are showing me round your town, I am showing you round mine, so that we are each at the same time explorer and host. A world without privacy would be a world in which the gates of all towns would always be open, so the excitement of the first admission would be less.

If these changes in relationships are for the worse, they provide a reason for rejecting, not only the thought-reading machine, but also any *voluntary* general lowering of the barriers which protect privacy. The changes are equally likely whether our privacy is invaded from outside or whether it is given away freely.

But the value placed on gradations of intimacy need not be a reason against a much greater degree of transparency than we have now. We hide behind so many different layers of defences. There are barriers created by context: you can't mention that here. And there are barriers of manner and style, created perhaps because we feel threatened, signalling that we are unapproachable about this, or will not talk about that. Sometimes the threat turns out to be imaginary. Tolstoy describes this in *Anna Karenin*:

> Levin had often noticed in discussions between the most intelligent people that after enormous efforts, and endless logical subtleties and talk, the disputants finally became aware that what they had been at such pains to prove to one another had long ago, from the beginning of the argument, been known to both, but that they liked different things, and would not define what they liked for fear of its being attacked. He had often had the experience of suddenly in the middle of a discussion grasping what it was the other liked and at once liking it too, and immediately he found himself agreeing, and then all arguments fell away useless. Sometimes the reverse happened: he at last expressed what he liked himself, which he had been arguing to defend and, chancing to express it well and genuinely, had found the person he was disputing with suddenly agree.[2]

When we do not feel threatened, we are more willing to take down the barriers, and less timid people sometimes take them down even when they do feel threatened.

It may be that already, as the result of innumerable individual decisions, we are moving towards greater transparency. These things are hard to establish, and no doubt vary from culture to culture. But it seems to me that in our century, there has been a strong trend towards greater honesty in relationships, with greater openness about things which used to be private, and that this is part of a beneficial transformation of our consciousness and social life. (If taking down the barriers is starting to transform us, the obstruction of this process is another charge, to add to the familiar ones, against political systems where people fear the authorities, and so need the barriers.) This change could go a long way further, and still leave us room for different degrees of privacy and intimacy.

The effects of transparency on relationships would be in several ways beneficial. Deception, with its resulting erosion of love and friendship, would be impossible. And relationships now are obscured, not only by deception, but also by our limited ability to express our thoughts and feelings, and by our lack of perception about other people. The thought-reading machine, because of the problems about interpretation, would not abolish these limitations, but it would greatly reduce their obscuring effects. As we understood more about each other's mental lives, we would form more realistic pictures of each other, and it seems plausible that this would make relationships better rather than worse. And a stronger sense of community might result from the barriers of privacy coming down, together with the ending of a sense of loneliness and isolation which some people feel because of their inability to share their experiences.

Sometimes a society of transparent relationships is held up as an ideal. In a fine interview on his seventieth birthday,[3] Jean-Paul Sartre was asked, 'Does it bother you when I ask you about yourself?' He replied:

No, why? I believe that everyone should be able to speak of his innermost being to an interviewer. I think that what spoils relations among people is that each keeps something hidden from the other, something secret, not necessarily from everyone, but from whomever he is speaking to at the moment. I think transparency should always be substituted for what is secret, and I can quite well imagine the day when two men will no longer have secrets from each other, because no one will have any more secrets from anyone, because subjective life, as well as objec-

tive life, will be completely offered up, given . . . There is an as-for-myself (*quant-à-soi*), born of distrust, ignorance, and fear, which keeps me from being confidential with another, or not confidential enough. Personally, moreover, I do not express myself on all points with the people I meet, but I try to be as translucent as possible, because I feel that this dark region that we have within ourselves, which is at once dark for us and dark for others, can only be illuminated for ourselves in trying to illuminate it for others . . . One can't say everything, you know that well. But I think that later, that is, after my death, and perhaps after yours, people will talk about themselves more and more and that this will produce a great change. Moreover, I think that this change is linked to a real revolution. A man's existence must be entirely visible to his neighbour, whose own existence must in turn be entirely visible to him, in order for true social harmony to be established.

There is obviously a big difference between Sartre's ideal and the world of the thought-reading machine. Sartre envisages people voluntarily abandoning their own secrecy of thought, rather than having the power to invade that of others. His transition period would involve no loss of autonomy, and might involve relatively little distress. The introduction of the thought-reading machine would not respect people's autonomy, but would strip them of secrecy against their will. It is hard to see how the process could fail to cause great unhappiness, both to those losing protective secrecy and to those who would be hurt by the thoughts of others. Resistance would be so strong that there might develop an arms race of offensive and defensive technology: devices to jam the thought-reading machines, devices to jam the jammers, and so on. But if, after the horrors of the transition period, the world of the thought-reading machine became established, the effect on relationships might be much the same as that of voluntarily lowering the barriers. And it is not obvious that transparent relationships would be worse than opaque ones.

4. *Identity and Individuality*

In our present world, the sort of people we are is to some extent the result of our own choices. (The question of the extent to which our choices could have been different raises the problems about determinism and free will, which will not be discussed here. But, whatever the solution to those problems, most of us prefer to have our identity modifiable by our decisions.) It may be that privacy contributes to this control. Charles Fried has said that we often have thoughts we do not express, and that only when we choose to express them do we adopt them as part of ourselves. If the end of privacy is the end of any distinction between thoughts being endorsed and merely being entertained, then we may lose some control over our identity. It may have been some view of this kind which led Justices Warren and Brandeis to argue that a legal right to privacy is independent of more general property rights: 'The principle which protects personal writings and all other personal productions, not against theft and physical appropriation, but against publication in any form, is in reality not the principle of private property, but that of an inviolate personality'.[4]

In suggestions of this kind, there is something obscure about the idea of personality or identity. For what a person is depends on all his features, including those concealed from others. A sufficiently subtle thought-reading machine would detect the difference between thoughts merely coming to mind and thoughts being endorsed. All that would be lost is concealment of thoughts only entertained. But it is part of me that I do entertain these thoughts, and my identity is not changed because this aspect of it comes to light. So when people say that transparency might threaten our freedom to choose our identity, they may not have in mind 'identity' in the sense of being a particular kind of person, but 'identity' in a sense closer to 'images of ourselves projected to other people'. It is obviously true that the abolition of privacy will reduce the control we have over the pictures other people have of us. But this seems more of a threat to our reputation than to our identity. Our freedom to define ourselves, when not just a matter of manipulation of image, is our freedom to choose between beliefs and attitudes, and to opt for some kinds of actions and ways of life rather than others. And this is not destroyed by others knowing what different ideas we have also considered.

Perhaps the threat posed by transparency is more oblique. It may be that public scrutiny of my mind does not in itself change my identity, but rather has effects which will inhibit the development of individuality. You will know when I am contemplating the ideas and actions you disapprove of, and I will know at once of your attitude. This may create very strong pressures to conform. John Stuart Mill wrote in 1859 of the social pressures towards respectability and conformity: 'In our times, from the highest class of society down to the lowest, everyone lives as under the eye of a hostile and dreaded censorship'.[5] One result of transparency might be to extend the social censorship inwards, so that there would be the same pressures for conformity of thought and feeling as there are for conformity of behaviour. We have only partial control over our thoughts and feelings, but the social censorship might persuade us to turn away from lines of thought which we knew might lead us into dangerous areas, as well as not to act on ideas arousing disapproval.

Privacy is necessary if we are not to be stifled by other people. Even in our present world, without the thought-reading machine, being permanently observed, as in some prisons, can destroy individuality. (Sartre, in an earlier phase, talked in *Being and Nothingness* with an almost neurotic horror of being observed by other people, and vividly presented the awfulness of permanent scrutiny in *Huis Clos*, where hell for three people is being locked for ever in a room together.) To be observed by other people can build up a feeling of pressure to justify what we are doing and how we are doing it, or to justify doing nothing. For many people, happiness, and perhaps creativity and originality, flourish where there are long stretches free from critical appraisal.

Perhaps we have the potential to grow more robust, and in a world of transparent relationships we might grow stronger in our resistance to pressures to conform. But it is hard to see how the extra pressures could be avoided, with their obvious threat to individuality.

5. The Two Perspectives

I have suggested that transparency would not in itself threaten our identity, and that its effects on relationships might, after a transition period, be beneficial. But it is plausible that it would allow new and powerful social pressures for conformity. If this account is accepted, our view of any proposed steps towards the transparent world will depend on how we weigh these different gains and losses. Any appraisal is difficult because it is hard to imagine relationships so transformed. If the threat to individuality seems much more clear than the benefits to relationships, many of us will be very cautious in our attitude to the dismantling of the barriers of privacy.

Yet it may be that our horror at the thought of entering the transparent world is nothing to the horror with which people in the transparent world will look back at our lives. They may think of us as hiding behind barriers of mutual pretense, like the inhabitants of a suburban street hiding behind fences and hedges. They might be far more concerned to avoid the reinstatement of the barriers of privacy than we are to avoid them being dismantled. The conflict between their perspective and ours, which will reappear in other contexts, raises a deep theoretical difficulty in deciding what sort of world we should aim for.

NOTES

1. *An Anatomy of Values*, Harvard, 1970, chapter 9.
2. *Anna Karenin*, translated by Rosemary Edmonds, Harmondsworth, 1954, p. 421.
3. 'Sartre at Seventy: An Interview,' *New York Review of Books*, August 1975.
4. 'The Right to Privacy,' *Harvard Law Review* 1890.
5. *On Liberty*, chapter 3.

Further Questions

1. What differences are there, if any, between honesty and openness?
2. Do you think that honesty and openness are a good thing generally, or only under certain conditions? What conditions?

Further Readings

Goffman, Erving. *The Presentation of Self in Everyday Life*. New York: Doubleday, 1959. A classic account of how we project our "image" to the world.
Weil, Simone. "Friendship," in *Waiting for God*. Emma Crauford, trans. New York: Harper & Row, 1973. A noted mystic looks at the intimacy of friendship.

Sincerity

JEAN-PAUL SARTRE

In his classic, *Being and Nothingness* (1956), the French existentialist Jean-Paul Sartre claims that we are radically free to choose what we are. But we fear our freedom. Fearing our freedom, we try to shield ourselves from it by pretending that we have a fixed nature that limits it. In this selection Sartre examines the related phenomena of "bad faith" and "sincerity," and he argues that both are ways of refusing to face the fact that we have no fixed natures.

A brief biography of Sartre appears on page 548.

Reading Questions

1. What is "bad faith"? What is "sincerity"?

2. Sartre thinks the woman in the first example tries to hide her freedom by pretending that she is a thing. Do you agree? If so, explain how she does this.

3. Does the advice, "Be yourself," make any sense? What does Sartre think? What do you think? Explain your answers by reference to the example of the waiter.

4. Is sincerity an escape from the bad faith exhibited in the examples of the woman and the waiter? Or is it just another version of bad faith? Explain your answer by reference to the example of the homosexual.

. . . TAKE THE EXAMPLE OF A WOMAN who has consented to go out with a particular man for the first time. She knows very well the intentions which the man who is speaking to her cherishes regarding her. She knows also that it will be necessary sooner or later for her to make a decision. But she does not want to realize the urgency; she concerns herself only with what is respectful and discreet in the attitude of her companion. She does not apprehend this conduct as an attempt to achieve what we call "the first approach"; that is, she does not want to see possibilities of temporal development which his conduct presents. She restricts this behavior to what is in the present; she does not wish to read in the phrases which he addresses to her anything other than their explicit meaning. If he says to her, "I find you so attractive!" she disarms this phrase of its sexual background; she attaches to the conversation and to the behavior of the speaker, the immediate meanings, which she imagines as objective qualities. The man who is speaking to her appears to her sincere and respectful as the table is round or square, as the wall coloring is blue or gray. The qualities thus attached to the person she is listening to are in this way fixed in a permanence like that of things, which is no other than the projection of the strict present of the qualities into the temporal flux. This is because she does not quite know what she wants. She is profoundly aware of the desire which she inspires, but the desire cruel and naked would humiliate and horrify her. Yet she would find no charm in a respect which would be only respect. In order to satisfy her, there must be a feeling which is addressed wholly to her *personality—i.e.,* to her full freedom—and which would be a recognition of her freedom. But at the same time this feeling must be wholly desire; that is, it must address itself to her body as object. This time then she refuses to apprehend the desire for what it is; she does not even give it a name; she recognizes it only to the extent that it transcends itself toward admiration, esteem, respect and that it is wholly absorbed in the more refined forms which it produces, to the extent of no longer figuring anymore as a sort of warmth and density. But then suppose he takes her hand. This act of her companion risks changing the situation by calling for an immediate decision. To leave the hand there is to consent in herself to flirt, to engage herself. To withdraw it is to break the troubled and unstable harmony which gives the hour its charm. The aim is to postpone the moment of decision as long as possible. We know what happens next: the young woman leaves her hand there, but she *does not notice* that she is leaving it. She does not notice because it happens by chance that she is at this moment all intellect. She draws her companion up to the most lofty regions of sentimental speculation; she speaks of Life, of her life, she shows herself in her essential aspect—a personality, a consciousness. And during this time the divorce of the body from the soul is accomplished; the hand rests inert between the warm hands of her companion—neither consenting nor resisting—a thing.

We shall say that this woman is in bad faith. But we see immediately that she uses various procedures in order to maintain herself in this bad faith. She has disarmed the actions of her companion by reducing them to being only what they are; that is, to existing in the mode of the in-itself. But she permits herself to enjoy his desire, to the extent that she will apprehend it as not being

what it is, will recognize its transcendence. Finally while sensing profoundly the presence of her own body—to the point of being aroused, perhaps—she realizes herself as *not being* her own body, and she contemplates it as though from above as a passive object to which events can *happen* but which can neither provoke them nor avoid them because all its possibilities are outside of it. What unity do we find in these various aspects of bad faith? It is a certain art of forming contradictory concepts which unite in themselves both an idea and the negation of that idea. The basic concept which is thus engendered utilizes the double property of the human being, who is at once a *facticity* and a *transcendence*. These two aspects of human reality are and ought to be capable of a valid coordination. But bad faith does not which either to coordinate them or to surmount them in a synthesis. Bad faith seeks to affirm their identity while preserving their differences. It must affirm facticity as *being* transcendence and transcendence as *being* facticity, in such a way that at the instant when a person apprehends the one, he can find himself abruptly faced with the other. . . .

If a man is what he is, bad faith is forever impossible and candor ceases to be his ideal and becomes instead his being. But is man what he is? And more generally, how can he *be* what he is when he exists as consciousness of being? If candor or sincerity is a universal value, it is evident that the maxim "one must be what one is" does not serve solely as a regulating principle for judgments and concepts by which I express what I am. It posits not merely an ideal of knowing but an ideal of *being*; it proposes for us an absolute equivalence of being with itself as a prototype of being. In this sense it is necessary that we *make ourselves* what we are. But what *are we* then if we have the constant obligation to make ourselves what we are, if our mode of being is having the obligation to be what we are?

Let us consider this waiter in the café. His movement is quick and forward, a little too precise, a little too rapid. He comes toward the patrons with a step a little too quick. He bends forward a little too eagerly; his voice, his eyes express an interest a little too solicitous for the order of the customer. Finally there he returns, trying to imitate in his walk the inflexible stiffness of some kind of automaton while carrying his tray with the recklessness of a tight-rope-walker by putting it in a perpetually unstable, perpetually broken equilibrium which he perpetually re-establishes by a light movement of the arm and hand. All his behavior seems to us a game. He applies himself to chaining his movements as if they were mechanisms, the one regulating the other; his gestures and even his voice seem to be mechanisms; he gives himself the quickness and pitiless rapidity of things. He is playing, he is amusing himself. But what is he playing? We need not watch long before we can explain it: he is playing at *being* a waiter in a café. There is nothing there to surprise us. The game is a kind of marking out and investigation. The child plays with his body in order to explore it, to take inventory of it; the waiter in the café plays with his condition in order to *realize* it. This obligation is not different from that which is imposed on all tradesmen. Their condition is wholly one of ceremony. The public demands of them that they realize it as a ceremony; there is the dance of the grocer, of the tailor, of the auctioneer, by which they endeavor to persuade their clientele that they are nothing but a grocer, an auctioneer, a tailor. A grocer who dreams is offensive to the buyer, because such a grocer is not wholly a grocer. Society demands that he limit himself to his function as a grocer, just as the soldier at attention makes himself into a soldier-thing with a direct regard which does not see at all, which is no longer meant to see, since it is the rule and not the interest of the moment which determines the point he must fix his eyes on (the sight "fixed at ten paces"). There are indeed many precautions to imprison a man in what he is, as if we lived in perpetual fear that he might escape from it, that he might break away and suddenly elude his condition.

In a parallel situation, from within, the waiter in the café can not be immediately a café waiter in the sense that this inkwell *is* an inkwell, or the glass is a glass. It is by no means that he can not form reflective judgments or concepts concerning his condition. He knows well what it "means": the obligation of getting up at five o'clock, of sweeping the floor of the shop before the restaurant opens, of starting the coffee pot going, *etc.* He knows the rights which it allows: the right to the tips, the right to belong to a union, *etc.* But all these concepts, all these judgments refer to the transcendent. It is a matter of abstract possibilities, of rights and duties conferred on a "person possessing rights." And it is precisely this person *who I have to be* (if I am the waiter in question) and who I am not. It is not that I do not wish to be this person or that I want this person to be different. But rather there is no common measure between his being and mine. It is a "representation" for others and for myself, which means that I can be he only in *representation*. But if I represent myself as him, I am not he; I am separated from him as the object from the subject, separated *by nothing*, but this nothing isolates me from him. I can not be he, I can only play *at being* him; that is, imagine to myself that I am he. And thereby I affect him with nothingness. In vain do I fulfill the functions of a café waiter. I can be he only in the neutralized mode, as the actor is Hamlet, by mechanically making the *typical gestures* of my state and by aiming at myself as an imaginary café waiter through those gestures taken as an "analogue." What I attempt to realize is a being-in-itself of the café waiter, as if it were not just in my power to confer their value and their urgency upon my duties and the right of my position, as if it were not my free choice to get up each morning at five o'clock or to remain in bed, even though it meant getting fired. As if from the very fact that I sustain this role in existence I did not transcend it on every side, as if I did not constitute myself as one *beyond* my condition. Yet there is no doubt that I *am* in a sense a café waiter — otherwise could I not just as well call myself a diplomat or a reporter? But if I am one, this can not be in the mode of being-in-itself. I am a waiter in the mode of *being what I am not*. . . .

Let us take an example: A homosexual frequently has an intolerable feeling of guilt, and his whole existence is determined in relation to this feeling. One will readily foresee that he is in bad faith. In fact it frequently happens that this man, while recognizing his homosexual inclination, while avowing each and every particular misdeed which he has committed, refuses with all his strength to consider himself "*a paederast*." His case is always "different," peculiar; there enters into it something of a game, of chance, of bad luck; the mistakes are all in the past; they are explained by a certain conception of the beautiful which women can not satisfy; we should see in them the results of a restless search, rather than the manifestations of a deeply rooted tendency, *etc., etc.* Here is assuredly a man in bad faith who borders on the comic since, acknowledging all the facts which are imputed to him, he refuses to draw from them the conclusion which they impose. His friend, who is his most severe critic, becomes irritated with this duplicity. The critic asks only one thing — and perhaps then he will show himself indulgent: that the guilty one recognize himself as guilty, that the homosexual declare frankly — whether humbly or boastfully matters little — "I am a paederast." We ask here: Who is in bad faith? The homosexual or the champion of sincerity?

The homosexual recognizes his faults, but he struggles with all his strength against the crushing view that his mistakes constitute for him a *destiny*. He does not wish to let himself be considered as a thing. He has an obscure but strong feeling that a homosexual is not a homosexual as this table is a table or as this red-haired man is red-haired. It seems to him that he has escaped from each mistake as soon as he has posited it and recognized it; he even feels that the psychic duration by itself cleanses him from each misdeed, constitutes for him an undertermined future, causes him to be born anew. Is he wrong? Does he not recognize in himself the peculiar, irreducible character of human reality? His attitude includes then an undeniable comprehension of truth. But at the same time he needs this perpetual rebirth, this constant escape in order to live; he must constantly put himself beyond reach in order to avoid the terrible judgment of collectivity. Thus he plays on the word *being*. He would be right actually if he understood the phrase "I am not a paederast" in the sense of "I am not what I am." That is, if he declared to himself, "To the extent that a pattern of conduct is defined as the conduct of a paederast and to the extent that I have adopted this conduct, I am a paederast. But to the extent that human reality can not be finally defined by patterns of conduct, I am not one." But instead he slides surreptitiously toward a different connotation of the word "being." He understands "not being" in the sense of "not-being-in-itself." He lays claim to "not being a paederast" in the sense in which this table *is not* an inkwell. He is in bad faith.

But the champion of sincerity is not ignorant of the transcendence of human reality, and he knows how at need to appeal to it for his own advantage. He makes use of it even and brings it up in the present argument. Does he not wish, first in the name of sincerity, then of freedom, that the homosexual reflect on himself and acknowledge himself as a homosexual? Does he not let the other understand that such a confession will win indulgence for him? What does this mean if not that the man who will acknowledge himself as a homosexual will no longer be *the same* as the homosexual whom he acknowledges being and that he will escape into the region of freedom and of good will? The critic asks the man then to be what he is in order no longer to be what he is. It is the profound meaning of the saying, "A sin confessed is half pardoned." The critic demands of the guilty one that he constitute himself as a thing, precisely in order no longer to treat him as a thing. And this contradiction is constitutive of the demand of sincerity. Who can not see how offensive to the Other and how reassuring for me is a statement such as, "He's just a paederast," which removes a disturbing freedom from a trait and which aims at henceforth constituting all the acts of the Other as consequences following strictly from his essence. That is actually what the critic is demanding of his victim —that he constitute himself as a thing, that he should entrust his freedom to his friend as a fief, in order that the friend should return it to him subsequently—like a suzerain to his vassal. The champion of sincerity is in bad faith to the degree that in order to reassure himself, he pretends to judge, to the extent that he demands that freedom as freedom constitute itself as a thing. We have here only one episode in that battle to the

death of consciousness which Hegel calls "the relation of the master and the slave." A person appeals to another and demands that in the name of his nature as consciousness he should radically destroy himself as consciousness, but while making this appeal he leads the other to hope for a rebirth beyond this destruction. . . .

Thus the essential structure of sincerity does not differ from that of bad faith . . . Total, constant sincerity as a constant effort to adhere to oneself is by nature a constant effort to dissociate oneself from oneself. . . .

Further Questions

1. Can you think of any ways in which you or your friends try to define yourselves, thus putting limits on your freedom? If so, why do you think you do this?

2. "We can talk truthfully about what we have been, but not about what we are, because not being things, there is nothing that we are. Everything is possible for us." Discuss.

Further Readings

Bergmann, Frithjof. *On Being Free*. South Bend, IN: University of Notre Dame Press, 1977. An attempt to work out a theory of freedom along Sartrean lines.

Davidson, Donald. "Deception and Division," in Jon Elster, ed., *The Multiple Self*. Cambridge: Cambridge University Press, 1985, pp. 79–92. A short but sophisticated paper on self-deception by a noted philosopher.

Fingarette, Herbert. *Self Deception*. New York: Humanities Press, 1969. A classic exploration of the process of self definition.

Haight, Mary. *A Study of Self-Deception*. New York: Humanities Press, 1980. A British philosopher criticizes Fingarette and suggests an alternative theory.

Human Life

DANIEL MAGUIRE

Daniel Maguire is a Catholic theologian who teaches Moral Theology at Marquette University. He has been an outspoken advocate of women's rights and is a member of Catholics of Free Choice. Among his books are *The Moral Choice* (Doubleday, 1978),

The New Subversives: Anti-Americanism of the Religious Right (Continuum, 1982), and *A New American Justice* (Doubleday, 1980). In the following selection, he questions the motives and values that lie behind the "right-to-life" movement.

Reading Questions

1. Before you being reading, you might think about your own stand on abortion. Write down the main *reasons* you have for your position.
2. Why is Maguire critical of anti-abortionist's allusions to the Nazi Holocaust?
3. What impressed Maguire most about holding in his hands a metal cup with a recently aborted fetus in it?

I SHOULD NOT HAVE BEEN NERVOUS the first day I drove to the abortion clinic. After all, I wasn't pregnant. There would be no abortions done this day. I would see no patients and no picketers. And yet tremors from a Catholic boyhood wrenched my usually imperturbable stomach. I was filled with dread and foreboding.

What was it that brought this Philadelphia Irish-Catholic male moral theologian to the clinic door? Abortion has not been my academic obsession. My wife and I have had no personal experience with abortion, although it once loomed as a possible choice in our lives. Our first son, Danny, was diagnosed as terminally ill with Hunter's syndrome when Margie was three months pregnant with our second child. However, amniocentesis revealed that the fetus, now Tommy, was normal.

The stimulus for my visit was the woman who agonized with Margie and me over the decision she had rather conclusively made, and asked us, as ethicists, to ponder with her all the pro's and con's. She was almost six weeks pregnant. Her life situation was seriously incompatible with parenting and she could not bear the thought of adoption. After her abortion, she told us she had made the right decision, but she paid the price in tears and trauma.

More generally, I was drawn to this uneasy experience by women. I have often discussed abortion with women in recent years, been struck by how differently they viewed it. I experienced their resentment at the treatment of the subject by the male club of moral theologians. One woman, an author and professor at a Chicago seminary, wrote me after reading my first article on abortion ("Abortion: A Question of Catholic Honesty," *The Christian Century*, September 14–21, 1983) thanking me and surprising me. She said she found it difficult to use the American bishops' pastoral letter on nuclear war because these *men* could agonize so long over the problems of *men* who might decide to end the world, but had not a sympathetic minute for the moral concerns of a woman who judges that she cannot bring her pregnancy to term.

I knew that my visit would not give me a woman's understanding of the abortion decision, but I hoped it might assist me, in the phrase of French novelist Jean Sulivan, to "lie less" when I write about this subject and to offend less those women who come this way in pain.

Those who write on liberation theology go to Latin America to learn; those who write on abortion stay at their desks. Until recently, all churchly writing on abortion has been done by desk-bound celibate males. If experience is the plasma of theory, the experience obtained in a clinic three blocks from Marquette, where I teach and have done research on abortion, could only enhance my theological ministry.

Meeting the Clinic Staff

One day last May, I called the Milwaukee Women's Health Organization and spoke to its director, Elinor Yeo, an ordained minister of the United Church of Christ. I was afraid she would find my request to spend time at her clinic unseemly and out of order. She said she would call back when she finished an interview with a patient and spoke to her staff. She called later to tell me that the staff was enthusiastic about my prospective visits, adding the ironic note that the patient she was interviewing when I first called was a Marquette University undergraduate.

The clinic door still had traces of red paint from a recent attack. The door was buzzed open only after I was identified. A sign inside read: PLEASE HELP OUR GUARD. WE MAY NEED WITNESSES IF THE PICKETS GET OUT OF CONTROL. YOU CAN HELP BY OBSERVING AND LETTING HIM/HER KNOW IF YOU SEE TROUBLE. I realized that these people live and work in fear of "pro-life" violence. In the first half of this year there have been 58 reported incidents of criminal violence at clinics, including bombing, arson, shootings, and vandalism.

Elinor Yeo sat with me for more than an hour describing the clinic's activities. Half of its patients are teenagers; half, Catholics; and 20 percent, black. Of the 14 patients seen on a single day the previous week, one was 13 years old; one, 14; and, one 15. Nationally, most abortions are performed within eight weeks of conception, at which point the *conceptus* is still properly called an embryo; 91 percent are within 12 weeks. At this clinic, too, most abortions are performed in the first two months. Most of the patients are poor; the clinic is busiest at the time when welfare checks come in. The normal cost for an abortion

here is $185. For those on public assistance, it is $100.

I asked Elinor about the right-to-lifers' claim that most women who have abortions are rich. She replied: "The typical age of an abortion patient at this clinic is 19 years." In what sense is a 19-year-old woman with an unwanted pregnancy rich?

I asked about the charge that doing abortions makes doctors rich. She assured me that, given their budget, all the doctors who work for them would make more if they remained in their offices. The doctors are also sometimes subject to harassment and picketing at their homes. Their care of patients is excellent, and they often end up delivering babies for these same women at some later date.

Each patient is given private counseling. About half want their male partners with them for these sessions. If there is an indication that the man is more anxious for the abortion than the woman, private counseling is carefully arranged. Every interested woman is offered the opportunity to study charts on embryonic and fetal development, and all women are informed of alternatives to abortion. The consent form, to be signed at the end of the interview and counseling sessions, includes the words: "I have been informed of agencies and services available to assist me to carry my pregnancy to term should I desire. . . . The nature and purposes of an abortion, the alternatives to pregnancy termination, the risks involved, and the possibility of complications have been fully explained to me."

All counselors stress reproductive responsibility. Two of the counselors have worked with Elinor for 14 years. One is the mother of five children, the other, of three. Free follow-up advice on contraception is made available. It is the explicit goal of the counselors not to have the woman return for another abortion. According to Yeo, those most likely to have repeat abortions are women who reject contraceptive information and say they will never have sex again until they are married. It became ironically clear to me that the women working in this abortion clinic prevent more abortions than the zealous pickets demonstrating outside.

Yeo says that only 5 percent of the patients have evey seriously considered adoption as an alternative. *Abortion* or *keeping* are the two options considered by these young women. (Ninety-five percent of teenagers who deliver babies keep them, according to Elinor Yeo.)

Adoption is, of course, the facile recommendation of the bumper-sticker level of this debate. One patient I spoke to at a subsequent visit to the clinic told me how unbearable the prospect was of going to term and then giving up the born baby. For impressive reasons she found herself in no condition to have a baby. Yet she had begun to take vitamins to nourish the embryo in case she changed her mind. "If I continued this nurture for nine months, how could I hand over to someone else what would then be my baby?" It struck me forcefully how aloof and misogynist it is not to see that the adoption path is full of pain. Here is one more instance of male moralists prescribing the heroic for women as though it were simply moral and mandatory.

The surgery lasts some 5 to 15 minutes. General anesthesia is not needed in these early abortions. Most women are in and out of the clinic in two and one half-hours. They return in two weeks for a checkup. These early abortions are done by suction. I was shown the suction tube that is used and was surprised to find that it is only about twice the width of a drinking straw. This was early empirical information for me as to *what* it is that is aborted at this stage.

All patients are warned about pregnancy aftermath groups that advertise and offer support but actually attempt to play on guilt and recruit these women in their campaign to outlaw all abortions, even those performed for reasons of health. One fundamentalist Protestant group in Milwaukee advertises free pregnancy testing. When the woman arrives, they subject her to grisly slides on abortions of well-developed fetuses. They take

the woman's address and phone number and tell her they will contact her in two weeks at home. The effects of this are intimidating and violative of privacy and often lead to delayed abortions of more developed fetuses.

Meeting the Women

My second visit was on a Saturday when the clinic was busy, I arrived at 8:30 in the morning. The picketers were already there, all men, except for one woman with a boy of 10. A patient was in the waiting room, alone. We greeted each other, and I sat down and busied myself with some papers, wondering what was going on in her mind. I was later to learn that she was five to six weeks pregnant. I was told that she was under psychiatric care for manic-depression, and receiving high doses of lithium to keep her mood swings under control. However, lithium in high doses may be injurious to the formation of the heart in embryos and early fetuses.

Pro-life? Pro-choice? How vacuous the slogans seemed in the face of this living dilemma. What life options were open to this woman? Only at the expense of her emotional well-being could a reasonably formed fetus come to term. This woman had driven alone a long distance that morning to get to the clinic and she would have to return home alone afterward. She had to walk to the door past demonstrators showing her pictures of fully formed fetuses and begging her: "Don't kill your baby! Don't do it." However well-intentioned they may be, in what meaningful moral sense were those picketers in this instance pro-life?

As I watched this woman I thought of one of my colleagues who had recently made a confident assertion that there could be no plausible reason for abortion except to save the physical life of the woman or if the fetus was anencephalic. This woman's physical life was not at risk and the embryo would develop a brain. But saving *life* involves more than cardiopulmonary continuity. How is it that in speaking of women we so easily reduce human life to physical life? What certitudes persuade theologians that there are only two marginal reasons to justify abortion? Why is the Vatican comparably sure that while there may be *just* wars with incredible slaughter, there can be no *just* abortions? Both need to listen to the woman on lithium as she testifies that life does not always confine itself within the ridges of our theories.

With permission I sat in on some of the initial interviews with patients. The first two were poor teenagers, each with an infant at home, and each trying to finish high school. One was out of work. Elinor Yeo let her know that they were now hiring at "Wendy's." I was impressed that the full human plight of the patients was of constant concern to the staff. The other young woman had just gotten a job after two years and would lose it through pregnancy. One woman counted out her $100 and said: "I hate to give this up; I need it so much."

The staff told me about the various causes of unwanted pregnancies. One staff member said that it would seem that most young men have "scorn for condoms." "Making love" does not describe those sexual invasions. For these hostile inseminators nothing is allowed to interfere with their pleasure. Often there is contraceptive failure. One recent case involved a failed vasectomy. Sometimes conception is admittedly alcohol- and drug-related. A few women concede that they were "testing the relationship." Often it is a case of a broken relationship where the woman, suddenly alone, feels unable to bring up a child. Economic causes were most common. Lack of job, lack of insurance, a desire to stay in school and break out of poverty.

I wondered how many "pro-lifers" voted for Ronald Reagan because of his antiabortion noises, even though Reaganomics decreased the income of the lowest fifth of society's families by 8 percent while increasing the income of the rich. More of this could only be more poverty, more ruin, more social chaos, more unwanted pregnancies, and more women at clinic doors.

Meeting the Picketers

The picketers are a scary lot. Because of them a guard has to be on duty to escort the patients from their cars. Before the clinic leased the adjacent parking lot — making it their private property — some picketers used to attack the cars of the women, screaming and shaking the car. The guard told me he was once knocked down by a picketer. Without the guard, some of the demonstrators surround an unescorted woman and force her to see and hear their message. Other picketers simply carry placards and pray. One day, 20 boys from Libertyville, Illinois, were bused in to picket. They were not passive. They had been taught to shout at the women as they arrived. One staff member commented: "Statistically, one quarter to one third of these boys will face abortion situations in their lives. I wonder how this experience will serve them then."

A reporter from the Milwaukee *Journal* arrived, and I followed her when she went out to interview the picketers. Two picketers recognized me. Since I have been quoted in the press in ways that did not please, I am a persona non grata to this group. I had a chance to feel what the women patients endure. "You're in the right place, Maguire. In there, where they murder the babies." I decided they were not ripe for dialogue, so I remained silent and listened in on the interview.

I learned that some of these men had been coming to demonstrate every Saturday for nine years. Their language was filled with allusions to the Nazi Holocaust. Clearly, they imagine themselves at the ovens of Auschwitz, standing in noble protest as innocent *persons* are led to their death. There could hardly be any higher drama in their lives. They seem not to know that the Nazis were antiabortion too — for Aryans. They miss the anti-Semitism and insult in this use of Holocaust imagery. The 6 million murdered Jews and more than 3 million Poles, Gypsies, and homosexuals were actual, not potential, persons who were killed. Comparing their human dignity to that of prepersonal embryos is no tribute to the Holocaust dead.

Sexism too is in bold relief among the picketers. Their references to "these women" coming here to "kill their babies" are dripping with hatred. It struck me that for all their avowed commitment to life, these are the successors of the witch-hunters.

Meeting the Embryos

On my third visit to the clinic, I made bold to ask to see the products of some abortions. I asked in such a way as to make refusal easy, but my request was granted. The aborted matter is placed in small cloth bags and put in jars awaiting disposal. I asked to see the contents of one of the bags of a typical abortion—a six- to nine-week pregnancy—and it was opened and placed in a small metal cup for examination. I held the cup in my hands and saw a small amount of unidentifiable fleshy matter in the bottom of the cup. The quantity was so little that I could have hidden it if I had taken it into my hand and made a fist.

It was impressive to realize that I was holding in the cup what many people think to be the legal and moral peer of a woman, if not, indeed, her superior. I thought too of the Human Life Amendment that would describe what I was seeing as a citizen of the United States with rights of preservation that would countermand the good of the woman bearer. I have held babies in my hands and now I held this embryo. I know the difference.

Conclusions

• My visits to the clinic made me more anxious to maintain the legality of abortions for women who judge they need them. There are no moral grounds for political consensus against this freedom on an issue where good experts and good people disagree. It also made me anxious to work to reduce the need for abortion by fighting the causes of unwanted pregnancies; *sexism* en-

forced by the institutions of church, synagogue, and state that diminishes a woman's sense of autonomy; *poverty* induced by skewed budgets; *antisexual* bias that leads to eruptive sex; and the other *macro* causes of these micro tragedies.

• I came to understand that abortion can be the *least* violent option facing a woman. It is brutally insensitive to pretend that for women who resort to abortion, death is the only extremity they face.

• I came away from the clinic with a new longing for a moratorium on self-righteousness and sanctimonious utterances from Catholic bishops on the subject of abortion. An adequate Catholic theology of abortion has not yet been written. But the bishops sally forth as though this complex topic were sealed in a simple negative. Bishops like New York's John O'Connor, who use tradition as though it were an oracle instead of an unfinished challenge, are not helping at all. A position like O'Connor's has two yields: (a) it insults the Catholic intellectual tradition by making it look simplistic, and (b) it makes the bishops the allies of a right wing that has been using its newfound love of embryos as an ideological hideaway for many who resist the bishops' call for peace and social justice.

• Finally, I come from the abortion clinic with an appeal to my colleagues in Catholic moral theology. Many theologians (especially clerics) avoid this issue or behave weirdly or skittishly when they touch it. How do Catholic theologians justify their grand silence when they are allowing physicalism, crude historical distortions, and fundamentalistic notions of "Church teaching" to parade as "the Catholic position"? Why are ethical errors that are thoroughly lambasted in the birth-control debate tolerated when the topic is abortion? Geraldine Ferraro and Governor Mario Cuomo of New York are taking the heat and trying to do the theology on this subject. Their debts to American Catholic theologians are minuscule. What service do we Church teachers give when errors, already corrected in theology, are allowed to roam unchallenged in the pastoral and political spheres? Why are nonexperts, church hierarchy or not, allowed to set the *theological* terms of this debate? What service is it to ecumenism to refuse serious dialogue not only with women but with mainline Jewish and Protestant theologians on this issue? Vatican II said that "ecumenical dialogue could start with discussions concerning the application of the gospel to moral questions." That dialogue has not happened on abortion, and our brothers and sisters from other communions are waiting for it.

I realize, as do my colleagues in Catholic ethics, that abortion is not a pleasant topic. At its best, abortion is a negative value, unlike the positive values of feeding the poor and working for civil rights. On top of that it has become the litmus test of orthodoxy, and that spells danger in the Catholic academe. But, beyond all this, we in the Catholic family have been conditioned against an objective and empathic understanding of abortion. We are more sensitized to embryos than to the women who bear them. I claim no infallibility on this subject, but I do insist that until we open our affections to enlightenment here, we will none of us be wise.

Further Questions

1. Do you agree with Maguire's conclusions? Why?
2. Can you think of any other political "movements," past or present, that might be suspect in the same way that Maguire suggests the anti-abortion movement is suspect?

Further Readings

Feinberg, Joel, ed. *The Problem of Abortion*. Belmont, CA: Wadsworth, 1984. One of the best collections of philosophy articles on the subject.

Rachels, James. "Does Morality Depend on Religion," in his *The Elements of Moral Philosophy*. New York: Random House, 1986. An excellent overall introduction.

Tooley, Michael. *Abortion and Infanticide*. Oxford: Clarendon Press, 1983.

Sex Roles: The Argument from Nature

JOYCE TREBILCOT

Joyce Trebilcot is professor of philosophy at Washington University in St. Louis, where she co-founded and has been coordinator, for many years, of the Women's Studies program. Her main areas of research are in feminist and lesbian-feminist philosophy. In the following selection, she considers the question of whether, in an ideal society, there should be any differences in the roles that are assigned to women and men.

Reading Questions

1. What does Trebilcot mean by "sex role"?

2. Trebilcot responds to three attempts to show that natural psychological differences between the sexes imply that there should be sex roles: the arguments from inevitability, from well-being, and from efficiency. Explain in your own words what each of these three arguments involves, how Trebilcot responds to each, and whether, in your view, her response is adequate.

I AM CONCERNED HERE with the normative question of whether, in an ideal society, certain roles should be assigned to females and others to males. In discussions of this issue, a great deal of attention is given to the claim that there are natural psychological differences between the sexes. Those who hold that at least some roles should be sex roles generally base their view primarily on an appeal to such natural differences, while many of those advocating a society without sex roles argue either that the sexes do not differ in innate psychological traits or that there is no evidence that they do.[1] In this paper I argue that whether there are natural psychological differences between females and males has little bearing on the issue of whether society should reserve certain roles for females and others for males.

Let me begin by saying something about the claim that there are natural psychological differences between the sexes. The issue we are dealing with arises, of course, because there are biological differences among human beings which are bases for designating some as females and others as males. Now it is held by some that, in addition to biological differences between the sexes, there are also natural differences in temperament, interests, abilities, and the like. In this paper I am concerned only with arguments which appeal to these psychological differences as bases of sex roles. Thus I exclude, for example, arguments

that the role of jockey should be female because women are smaller than men or that boxers should be male because men are more muscular than women. Nor do I discuss arguments which appeal directly to the reproductive functions peculiar to each sex. If the physiological processes of gestation or of depositing sperm in a vagina are, apart from any psychological correlates they may have, bases for sex roles, these roles are outside the scope of the present discussion.

It should be noted, however, that virtually all those who hold that there are natural psychological differences between the sexes assume that these differences are determined primarily by differences in biology. According to one hypothesis, natural psychological differences between the sexes are due at least in part to differences between female and male nervous systems. As the male fetus develops in the womb, the testes secrete a hormone which is held to influence the growth of the central nervous system. The female fetus does not produce this hormone, nor is there an analogous female hormone which is significant at this stage. Hence it is suggested that female and male brains differ in structure, that this difference is due to the prenatal influence of testicular hormone, and that the difference in brains is the basis of some later differences in behavior.[2]

A second view about the origin of allegedly natural psychological differences between the

From Joyce Trebilcot, "Sex Roles: The Argument From Nature," Ethics vol. 85, no. 3 (April 1975), pp. 249–255. Published by the University of Chicago Press and reprinted with their permission and with the permission of the author. Copyright © 1975 by The University of Chicago Press.

An earlier version of this paper was read for the meeting of the American Philosophical Association, Western Division, April 1974.

sexes, a view not incompatible with the first, is psychoanalytical. It conceives of feminine or masculine behavior as, in part, the individual's response to bodily structure. On this view, one's more or less unconscious experience of one's own body (and in some versions, of the bodies of others) is a major factor in producing sex-specific personality traits. The classic theories of this kind are, of course, Freud's: penis envy and the castration complex are supposed to arise largely from perceptions of differences between female and male bodies. Other writers make much of the analogies between genitals and genders: the uterus is passive and receptive, and so are females; penises are active and penetrating, and so are males.[3] But here we are concerned not with the etiology of allegedly natural differences between the sexes but rather with the question of whether such differences, if they exist, are grounds for holding that there should be sex roles.

That a certain psychological disposition is natural only to one sex is generally taken to mean in part that members of that sex are more likely to have the disposition, or to have it to a greater degree, than persons of the other sex. The situation is thought to be similar to that of height. In a given population, females are on the average shorter than males, but some females are taller than some males. . . . The shortest members of the population are all females, and the tallest are all males, but there is an area of overlap. For psychological traits, it is usually assumed that there is some degree of overlap and that the degree of overlap is different for different characteristics. Because of the difficulty of identifying natural psychological characteristics, we have of course little or no data as to the actual distribution of such traits.

I shall not undertake here to define the concept of role, but examples include voter, librarian, wife, president. . . . A sex role is a role performed only or primarily by persons of a particular sex. Now if this is all we mean by "sex role," the problem of whether there should be sex roles must be dealt with as two separate issues: "Are sex roles a good thing?" and "Should society enforce sex roles?" One might argue, for example, that sex roles have value but that, even so, the demands of individual autonomy and freedom are such that societal institutions and practices should not enforce correlations between roles and sex. But the debate over sex roles is of course mainly a discussion about the second question, whether society should enforce these correlations. The judgment that there should be sex roles is generally taken to mean not just that exclusive roles are a good thing, but that society should promote such exclusivity.

In view of this, I use the term "sex role" in such a way that to ask whether there should be sex roles is to ask whether society should direct women into certain roles and away from others, and similarly for men. A role is a sex role then (or perhaps an "institutionalized sex role") only if it is performed exclusively or primarily by persons of a particular sex *and* societal factors tend to encourage this correlation. These factors may be of various kinds. Parents guide children into what are taken to be sex-appropriate roles. Schools direct students into occupations according to sex. Marriage customs prescribe different roles for females and males. Employers and unions may refuse to consider applications from persons of the "wrong" sex. The media carry tales of the happiness of those who conform and the suffering of the others. The law sometimes penalizes deviators. Individuals may ridicule and condemn role crossing and smile on conformity. Societal sanctions such as these are essential to the notion of sex role employed here.

I turn now to a discussion of the three major ways the claim that there are natural psychological differences between the sexes is held to be relevant to the issue of whether there should be sex roles.

1. Inevitability

It is sometimes held that if there are innate psychological differences between females and males, sex roles are inevitable. The point of this argument is not, of course, to urge that there should be sex roles, but rather to show that the normative question is out of place, that there will be sex roles, whatever we decide. The argument assumes first that the alleged natural differences between the sexes are inevitable; but if such differences are inevitable, differences in behavior are inevitable; and if differences in behavior are inevitable, society will inevitably be structured so as to enforce role differences according to sex. Thus, sex roles are inevitable.

For the purpose of this discussion, let us accept the claim that natural psychological differences are inevitable. . . . Does it follow that there must be sex roles, that is, that the institutions and practices of society must enforce correlations between roles and sex?

Surely not. Indeed, such sanctions would be pointless. Why bother to direct women into some roles and men into others if the pattern occurs regardless of the nature of society? Mill makes the point elegantly in *The Subjection of Women:* "The anxiety of mankind to interfere in behalf of nature, for fear lest nature should not succeed in effecting its purpose, is an altogether unnecessary solicitude."[4]

It may be objected that if correlations between sex and roles are inevitable, societal sanctions enforcing these correlations will develop because people will expect the sexes to perform different roles and these expectations will lead to behavior which encourages their fulfillment. This can happen, of course, but it is surely not inevitable. One need not act so as to bring about what one expects.

Indeed, there could be a society in which it is held that there are inevitable correlations between roles and sex but institutionalization of these correlations is deliberately avoided. What is inevitable is presumably not, for example, that every woman will perform a certain role and no man will perform it, but rather that most women will perform the role and most men will not. For any individual, then, a particular role may not be inevitable. Now suppose it is a value in the soci-

ety in question that people should be free to choose roles according to their individual needs and interests. But then there should not be sanctions enforcing correlations between roles and sex, for such sanctions tend to force some individuals into roles for which they have no natural inclination and which they might otherwise choose against.

I conclude then that, even granting the assumptions that natural psychological differences, and therefore role differences, between the sexes are inevitable, it does not follow that there must be sanctions enforcing correlations between roles and sex. Indeed, if individual freedom is valued, those who vary from the statistical norm should not be required to conform to it.

2. Well-Being

The argument from well-being begins with the claim that, because of natural psychological differences between the sexes, members of each sex are happier in certain roles than in others, and the roles which tend to promote happiness are different for each sex. It is also held that if all roles are equally available to everyone regardless of sex, some individuals will choose against their own well-being. Hence, the argument concludes, for the sake of maximizing well-being there should be sex roles: society should encourage individuals to make "correct" role choices.

Suppose that women, on the average, are more compassionate than men. Suppose also that there are two sets of roles, "female" and "male," and that because of the natural compassion of women, women are happier in female than in male roles. Now if females and males overlap with respect to compassion, some men have as much natural compassion as some women, so they too will be happier in female than in male roles. Thus, the first premise of the argument from well-being should read: Suppose that, because of natural psychological differences between the sexes, *most* women are happier in female roles and *most* men in male roles. The argument continues: If all roles are equally available to everyone, some of the women who would be happier in female roles will choose against their own well-being, and similarly for men.

Now if the conclusion that there should be sex roles is to be based on these premises, another assumption must be added—that the loss of potential well-being resulting from societally produced adoption of unsuitable roles by individuals in the overlapping areas of the distribution is *less* than the loss that would result from "mistaken" free choices if there were no sex roles. With sex roles, some individuals who would be happier in roles assigned to the other sex perform roles assigned to their own sex, and so there is a loss of potential happiness. Without sex roles, some individuals, we assume, [would] choose against their own well-being. But surely we are not now in a position to compare the two systems with respect to the number of mismatches produced. Hence, the additional premise required for the argument, that overall well-being is greater with sex roles than without them, is entirely unsupported.

Even if we grant, then, that because of innate psychological differences between the sexes members of each sex achieve greater well-being in some roles than in others, the argument from well-being does not support the conclusion that there should be sex roles. In our present state of knowledge, there is no reason to suppose that a sex role system which makes no discriminations within a sex would produce fewer mismatches between individuals and roles than a system in which all roles are open equally to both sexes.

3. Efficiency

If there are natural differences between the sexes in the capacity to perform socially valuable tasks, then, it is sometimes argued, efficiency is served if these tasks are assigned to the sex with the greatest innate ability for them. Suppose, for example, that females are naturally better than males at learning foreign languages. This means that, if everything else is equal and females and males are given the same training in a foreign language, females, on the average, will achieve a higher level of skill than males. Now suppose that society needs interpreters and translators and that in order to have such a job one must complete a special training program whose only purpose is to provide persons for these roles. Clearly, efficiency is served if only individuals with a good deal of natural ability are selected for training, for the time and effort required to bring them to a given level of proficiency is less than that required for the less talented. But suppose that the innate ability in question is normally distributed within each sex and that the sexes overlap. . . . If we assume that a sufficient number of candidates can be recruited by considering only persons in the shaded area, they are the only ones who should be eligible. There are no men in this group. Hence, although screening is necessary in order to exclude nontalented women, it would be inefficient even to consider men, for it is known that no man is as talented as the talented women. In the interest of efficiency, then, the occupational roles of interpreter and translator should be sex roles: men should be denied access to these roles but women who are interested in them, especially talented women, should be encouraged to pursue them.

This argument is sound. That is, if we grant the factual assumptions and suppose also that efficiency for the society we are concerned with has some value, the argument from efficiency provides one reason for holding that some roles should be sex roles. This conclusion of course is only prima facie. In order to determine whether there should be sex roles, one would have to weigh efficiency, together with other reasons for such roles, against reasons for holding that there should not be sex roles. The reasons against sex roles are very strong. They are couched in terms of individual rights—in terms of liberty, justice, equality of opportunity. Efficiency by itself does not outweigh these moral values. Nevertheless, the appeal to nature, if true, combined with an appeal to the value of efficiency, does provide one reason for the view that there should be sex roles.

The arguments I have discussed here are not the only ones which appeal to natural psychological differences between the sexes in defense of sex roles, but these three arguments — from inevitability, well-being, and efficiency — are, I believe, the most common and the most plausible ones. The argument from efficiency alone, among them, provides a reason — albeit a rather weak reason — for thinking that there should be sex roles. I suggest, therefore, that the issue of natural psychological differences between women and men does not deserve the central place it is given, both traditionally and currently, in the literature on this topic.

It is frequently pointed out that the argument from nature functions as a cover, as a myth to make patriarchy palatable to both women and men. Insofar as this is so, it is surely worthwhile exploring and exposing the myth. But of course most of those who use the argument from nature take it seriously and literally, and this is the spirit in which I have dealt with it. Considering the argument in this way, I conclude that whether there should be sex roles does not depend primarily on whether there are innate psychological differences between the sexes. The question is, after all, not what women and men naturally are, but what kind of society is morally justifiable. In order to answer this question, we must appeal to the notions of justice, equality, and liberty. It is these moral concepts, not the empirical issue of sex differences, which should have pride of place in the philosophical discussion of sex roles.

NOTES

1. For support of sex roles, see, for example, Aristotle, *Politics*, book 1: and Erik Erikson, "Womanhood and the Inner Space," *Identity: Youth and Crisis* (New York: W. W. Norton & Co., 1968). Arguments against sex roles may be found, for example, in J. S. Mill, "The Subjection of Women," in *Essays on Sex Equality: John Stuart Mill and Harriet Taylor Mill*, ed. Alice S. Rossi (Chicago: University of Chicago Press, 1970); and Naomi Weisstein, "Psychology Constructs the Female," in *Women in Sexist Society*, ed. Vivian Gornick and Barbara K. Moran (New York: Basic Books, 1971).

2. See John Money and Anke A. Ehrhardt, *Man and Woman, Boy and Girl* (Baltimore: Johns Hopkins Press, 1972).

3. For Freud, see, for example, "some Psychological Consequences of the Anatomical Distinction between the Sexes," in *Sigmund Freud: Collected Papers*, ed. James Strachey (New York: Basic Books, 1959), 5:186–97. See also Karl Stern, *The Flight from Woman* (New York: Farrar, Straus & Giroux, 1965), chap. 2; and Erikson.

4. Mill, p. 154.

Further Questions

1. Should women in the military be used in combat roles? What do you think Trebilcot's view would be? What is your view?

2. It is sometimes said that if heads of state were women, there would be fewer wars. Assume, for the sake of argument, that this is true and that war is the greatest evil. Would we then have a good reason for prohibiting men from being heads of state? How do you think Trebilcot would answer? How do you answer?

Further Readings

De Beauvoir, Simone. *The Second Sex*. New York: Penguin, 1976. A classic of feminist thought.

Millett, Kate. *Sexual Politics*. New York: Doubleday, 1970. An important contribution.

Pearsall, Marilyn. *Woman and Values*. Belmont, Calif.: Wadsworth, 1986. Feminism, ethics, and values; a timely anthology.

The Value of Philosophy

BERTRAND RUSSELL

This selection is the final chapter of Russell's short, classic introduction to philosophy, *The Problems of Philosophy*, which, although written in 1912, is still often used as an introductory text in philosophy courses. In it, Russell claims that philosophy is valuable not because it produces goods or knowledge but, rather, because it can have a mind-expanding and liberating effect upon those who study it.

A brief biography of Russell appears on page 217.

Reading Questions

1. How does Russell describe the practical person, and what are the practical person's prejudices from which we must free ourselves?
2. How does he describe the instinctive person?
3. Explain how, in Russell's view, "the self" enlarges itself.
4. How is philosophical thinking related to the practical world of action and justice?
5. How does Russell's "instinctive man" view philosophical questioning or speculation? Do you know any such people? Why do they view philosophy that way? Were you ever such a person? If so, and you changed, what got you to change?
6. Some students feel that philosophy is worthless because it does not yield definite results. How would Russell respond?
7. Russell says the value of philosophy is in its uncertainty. What does he mean? Do you agree?
8. What, in Russell's view, is the value of philosophy?

HAVING NOW COME TO THE END of our brief and very incomplete review of the problems of philosophy, it will be well to consider, in conclusion, what is the value of philosophy and why it ought to be studied. It is the more necessary to consider this question, in view of the fact that many men, under the influence of science or of practical affairs, are inclined to doubt whether philosophy is anything better than innocent but useless trifling, hair-splitting distinctions, and controversies on matters concerning which knowledge is impossible.

"The Value of Philosophy" from The Problems of Philosophy *by Bertrand Russell (1912).*

This view of philosophy appears to result, partly from a wrong conception of the ends of life, partly from a wrong conception of the kind of goods which philosophy strives to achieve. Physical science, through the medium of inventions, is useful to innumerable people who are wholly ignorant of it; thus the study of physical science is to be recommended, not only, or primarily, because of the effect on the student, but rather because of the effect on mankind in general. Thus utility does not belong to philosophy. If the study of philosophy has any value at all for others than students of philosophy, it must be only indirectly, through its effects upon the lives of those who study it. It is in these effects, therefore, if anywhere, that the value of philosophy must be primarily sought.

But further, if we are not to fail in our endeavour to determine the value of philosophy, we must first free our minds from the prejudices of what are wrongly called 'practical' men. The 'practical' man, as this word is often used, is one who recognizes only material needs, who realizes that men must have food for the body, but is oblivious of the necessity of providing food for the mind. If all men were well off, if poverty and disease had been reduced to their lowest possible point, there would still remain much to be done to produce a valuable society; and even in the existing world the goods of the mind are at least as important as the goods of the body. It is exclusively among the goods of the mind that the value of philosophy is to be found; and only those who are not indifferent to these goods can be persuaded that the study of philosophy is not a waste of time.

Philosophy, like all other studies, aims primarily at knowledge. The knowledge it aims at is the kind of knowledge which gives unity and system to the body of the sciences, and the kind which results from a critical examination of the grounds of our convictions, prejudices, and beliefs. But it cannot be maintained that philosophy has had any very great measure of success in its attempts to provide definite answers to its questions. If you ask a mathematician, a mineralogist, a historian, or any other man of learning, what definite body of truths has been ascertained by his science, his answer will last as long as you are willing to listen. But if you put the same question to a philosopher, he will, if he is candid, have to confess that his study has not achieved positive results such as have been achieved by other sciences. It is true that this is partly accounted for by the fact that, as soon as definite knowledge concerning any subject becomes possible, this subject ceases to be called philosophy, and becomes a separate science. The whole study of the heavens, which now belongs to astronomy, was once included in philosophy; Newton's great work was called 'the mathematical principles of natural philosophy.' Similarly, the study of the human mind, which was a part of philosophy, has now been separated from philosophy and has become the science of psychology. Thus, to a great extent, the uncertainty of philosophy is more apparent than real: those questions which are already capable of definite answers are placed in the sciences, while those only to which, at present, no definite answer can be given, remain to form the residue which is called philosophy.

This is, however, only a part of the truth concerning the uncertainty of philosophy. There are many questions — and among them those that are of the profoundest interest to our spiritual life — which, so far as we can see, must remain insoluble to the human intellect unless its powers become of quite a different order from what they are now. . . . Has the universe any unity of plan or purpose, or is it a fortuitous concourse of atoms? Is consciousness a permanent part of the universe, giving hope of indefinite growth in wisdom, or is it a transitory accident on a small planet on which life must ultimately become impossible? Are good and evil of importance to the universe or only to man? Such questions are asked by philosophy, and variously answered by various philosophers. But it would seem that, whether answers be otherwise discoverable or not, the answers suggested by philosophy are none of them demonstrably true. Yet, however slight may be the hope of discovering an answer, it is part of the business of philosophy to continue the consideration of such questions, to make us aware of their importance, to examine all the approaches to them, and to keep alive that speculative interest in the universe which is apt to be killed by confining ourselves to definitely ascertainable knowledge.

Many philosophers, it is true, have held that philosophy could establish the truth of certain answers to such fundamental questions. They have supposed that what is of most importance in religious beliefs could be proved by strict demonstration to be true. In order to judge of such attempts, it is necessary to take a survey of human knowledge, and to form an opinion as to its methods and its limitations. On such a subject it would be unwise to pronounce dogmatically; but if the investigations of our previous chapters have not led us astray, we shall be compelled to renounce the hope of finding philosophical proofs of religious beliefs. We cannot, therefore, include as part of the value of philosophy any definite set of answers to such questions. Hence, once more, the value of philosophy must not depend upon any supposed body of definitely ascertainable knowledge to be acquired by those who study it.

The value of philosophy is, in fact, to be sought largely in its very uncertainty. The man who has no tincture of philosophy goes through life imprisoned in the prejudices derived from common sense, from the habitual beliefs of his age or his nation, and from convictions which have grown up in his mind without the co-operation or consent of his deliberate reason. To such a man the world tends to become definite, finite, obvious; common objects rouse no questions, and unfamiliar possibilities are contemptuously rejected. As soon as we begin to philosophize, on the contrary, we find . . . that even the most everyday things lead to problems to which only very incomplete answers can be given. Philosophy, though unable to tell us with certainty what is the true answer to the doubts which it raises, is able to suggest many possibilities which enlarge our thoughts and free them from the tyranny of custom. Thus, while diminishing our feeling of certainty as to what things are, it greatly increases our knowledge as to what they may be; it removes the somewhat arrogant dogmatism of those who have never travelled into the region of liberating doubt, and it keeps alive our sense of wonder by showing familiar things in an unfamiliar aspect.

Apart from its utility in showing unsuspected possibilities, philosophy has a value — perhaps its chief value — through the greatness of the objects which it contemplates, and the freedom from narrow and personal aims resulting from this contemplation. The life of the instinctive man is shut up within the circle of his private interests: family and friends may be included, but the outer world is not regarded except as it may help or hinder what comes within the circle of instinctive wishes. In such a life there is something feverish and confined, in comparison with which the philosophic life is calm and free. The private world of instinctive interest is a small one, set in the midst of a great and powerful world which must, sooner or later, lay our private world in ruins. Unless we can so enlarge our interests as to include the whole outer world, we remain like a garrison in a beleaguered fortress, knowing that the enemy prevents escape and that ultimate surrender is inevitable. In such a life there is no peace, but a constant strife between the insistence of desire and the powerlessness of will. In one way or another, if our life is to be great and free, we must escape this prison and this strife.

One way of escape is by philosophic contemplation. Philosophic contemplation does not, in its widest survey, divide the universe into two hostile camps — friends and foes, helpful and hostile, good and bad — it views the whole impartially. Philosophic contemplation, when it is unalloyed, does not aim at proving that the rest of the universe is akin to man. All acquisition of knowledge is an enlargement of the Self, but this enlargement is best attained when it is not directly sought. It is best obtained when the desire for knowledge is alone operative, by a study which does not wish in advance that its objects should have this or that character, but adapts the Self to the characters which it finds in its objects. This enlargement of Self is not obtained when, taking the Self as it is, we try to show that the world is so similar to this Self that knowledge of it is possible without any admission of what seems alien. The desire to prove this is a form of self-assertion and, like all self-assertion, it is an obstacle to the growth of Self which it desires, and of which the Self knows that it is capable. Self-assertion, in philosophic speculation as elsewhere, views the world as a means to its own ends; thus it makes the world of less account than Self, and the Self sets bounds to the greatness of its goods. In contemplation, on the contrary, we start from the non-Self, and through its greatness the boundaries of Self are enlarged; through the infinity of the universe the mind which contemplates it achieves some share in infinity.

For this reason greatness of soul is not fostered by those philosophies which assimilate the universe to Man. Knowledge is a form of union of Self and not-Self; like all union, it is impaired by dominion, and therefore by any attempt to force the universe into conformity with what we find in ourselves. There is a widespread philosophical tendency towards the view which tells us that Man is the measure of all things, that truth is man-made, that space and time and the world of universals are properties of the mind, and that, if there be anything not created by the mind, it is unknowable and of no account for us. This view . . . is untrue; but in addition to being untrue, it has the effect of robbing philosophic contemplation of all that gives it value, since it fetters contemplation to Self. What it calls knowledge is not a union with the not-Self, but a set of prejudices, habits, and desires, making an impenetrable veil between us and the world beyond. The man who finds pleasure in such a theory of knowledge is like the man who never leaves the domestic circle for fear his word might not be law.

The true philosophic contemplation, on the contrary, finds its satisfaction in every enlargement of the not-Self, in everything that magnifies the objects contemplated, and thereby the subject contemplating. Everything, in contemplation, that is personal or private, everything that depends upon habit, self-interest, or desire, distorts the object, and hence impairs the union which the intellect seeks. By thus making a barrier between subject and object, such personal and private things become a prison to the intellect. The free intellect will see as God might see, without a *here* and *now*, without hopes and fears, without the trammels of customary beliefs and traditional prejudices, calmly, dispassionately, in the sole and exclusive desire of knowledge — knowledge as impersonal, as purely contemplative, as it is possible for man to attain. Hence also the free intellect will value more the abstract and universal knowledge into which the accidents of private history do not enter, than the knowledge brought by the senses, and dependent, as such knowledge must be, upon an exclusive and personal point of view and a body whose sense-organs distort as much as they reveal.

The mind which has become accustomed to the freedom and impartiality of philosophic contemplation will preserve something of the same freedom and impartiality in the world of action and emotion. It will view its purposes and desires as parts of the whole, with the absence of insistence that results from seeing them as infinitesimal fragments in a world of which all the rest is unaffected by any one man's deeds. The impartiality which, in contemplation, is the unalloyed desire for truth, is the very same quality of mind which, in action, is justice, and in emotion is that universal love which can be given to all, and not only to those who are judged useful or admirable. Thus contemplation enlarges not only the objects of our thoughts, but also the objects of our actions and our affections: it makes us citizens of the universe, not only of one walled city at war with all the rest. In this citizenship of the universe consists man's true freedom, and his liberation from the thraldom of narrow hopes and fears.

Thus, to sum up our discussion of the value of philosophy; Philosophy is to be studied, not for the sake of any definite answers to its questions, since no definite answers can, as a rule, be known to be true, but rather for the sake of the questions themselves; because these questions enlarge our conception of what is possible, enrich our intellectual imagination and diminish the dogmatic assurance which closes the mind against speculation; but above all because, through the greatness of the universe which philosophy contemplates, the mind also is rendered great, and becomes capable of that union with the universe which constitutes its highest good.

Further Questions

1. Russell says philosophy aims at knowledge. Other than knowledge about who said what, did you achieve any knowledge from your study of philosophy? What? Of the things you learned, what is most valuable to you? Why?

2. Russell says the person who has most profited from philosophy "will see as God might see, without a here and now, without hopes and fears . . ." There are alternative views of the value of philosophy. Karl Marx, for instance, who in this respect is at the other extreme from Russell, said the point of philosophy is not to understand the world, but to change it. What would you say the main value of philosophy has been for you?

Further Readings

Nietzsche, Friedrich. *The Portable Nietzsche*. New York: Viking Press, 1954. Philosophy and power.

Suzuki, D. *Zen Mind, Beginner's Mind*. San Francisco: Weatherhill, 1970. A classic of meditation literature. On the value of not thinking.

Philosophy

FREEMAN DYSON

Freeman Dyson is a professor of physics at the Institute for Advanced Study in Princeton. Besides his work in theoretical physics, he has written popular meditations on the problems of war, the human condition, nuclear weapons, and the universe in *Disturbing the Universe* (Harper & Row, 1979), *Weapons and Hope* (Harper & Row, 1984), and *Infinite in All Directions* (Harper & Row, 1985). The following excerpt is from a letter Dyson wrote about his longtime friend and fellow physicist, Richard Feynman, who won a Nobel Prize for his work in particle physics.

April 9, 1981

DEAR _____,

I just spent a marvelous three days with Dick Feynman and wished you had been there to share him with us. Sixty years and a big cancer operation have not blunted him. He is still the same Feynman that we knew in the old days at Cornell.

We were together at a small meeting of physicists organized by John Wheeler at the University of Texas. For some reason Wheeler decided to hold the meeting at a grotesque place called World of Tennis, a country club where Texas oil-millionaires go to relax. So there we were. We all grumbled at the high prices and the extravagant ugliness of our rooms. But there was nowhere else to go. Or so we thought. But Dick thought otherwise. Dick just said: "To hell with it. I am not going to sleep in this place," picked up his suitcase and walked off alone into the woods. In the morning he reappeared, looking none the worse for his night under the stars. He said he did not sleep much, but it was worth it.

We had many conversations about science and history, just like in the old days. But now he had something new to talk about, his children. He said: "I always thought I would be a specially good father because I wouldn't try to push my kids into any particular direction. I wouldn't try to turn them into scientists or intellectuals if they didn't want it. I would be just as happy with them if they decided to be truck-drivers or guitar-players. In fact I would even like it better if they went out in the world and did something real instead of being professors like me. But they always find a way to hit back at you. My boy Carl for instance. There he is in his second year at MIT, and all he wants to do with his life is to become a god-damned philosopher!" . . .

Further Questions

1. Philosophy is often regarded, especially by the parents of students who would like to major in it, as one of the most impractical of disciplines. Do you think the figures in the table on pages 597 and 598 have any bearing on whether studying philosophy at the university actually is that impractical?

2. "Being a philosopher is not a question of what your major at the university happens to be or what you may do for a living. Rather, it simply means being disposed to think critically about the most basic assumptions we make in our attempts to understand the world and act effectively in it, and also being disposed to imagine reasonable alternatives to these assumptions. For a thinking person, there is no alternative to being a philosopher." Based on your study of philosophy, would you agree?

From the personal correspondence of Freeman Dyson. Used by permission of the author.

How Undergraduates Perform on Graduate Admissions Tests*

Percentages above and below the mean score of U.S. citizens who took the tests in 1981–82

Graduate Record Examination

Verbal		Quantitative	
Philosophy	+ 17.6%	Physics	+ 29.5%
Anthropology	+ 16.4%	Mathematics	+ 26.3%
English	+ 14.5%	Engineering	+ 25.1%
History	+ 10.8%	Computer Science	+ 22.9%
Foreign Languages	+ 7.9%	Chemistry	+ 18.3%
Humanities (Misc.)	+ 7.3%	Science (Misc.)	+ 14.5%
Physics	+ 6.6%	Economics	+ 12.4%
Journalism	+ 5.7%	Biological Science	+ 8.0%
Biological Science	+ 5.4%	Philosophy	+ 4.6%
Political Science	+ 3.5%	Anthropology	− 1.7%
Science (Misc.)	+ 3.5%	Business Administr.	− 2.3%
Psychology	+ 3.1%	Psychology	− 4.0%
Mathematics	+ 2.7%	Foreign Languages	− 4.2%
Chemistry	+ 2.1%	Political Science	− 5.0%
Arts and Music	+ 1.7%	Humanities (Misc.)	− 5.0%
Economics	+ .8%	History	− 5.5%
Social Sci. (Misc.)	− .4%	English	− 5.7%
Computer Science	− 1.5%	Social Sci. (Misc.)	− 7.2%
Sociology	− 5.0%	Arts and Music	− 8.4%
Speech	− 6.0%	Journalism	− 8.6%
Engineering	− 7.3%	Speech	− 14.3%
Business Administr.	− 9.1%	Sociology	− 15.0%
Social Work	− 9.1%	Education	− 15.8%
Education	− 10.4%	Social Work	− 20.8%

(Continued)

*These figures are taken from *The Standardized Test Scores of College Graduates, 1964–1982,* prepared for The Study Group on the Conditions of Excellence in American Higher Education by Clifford Adelman, Senior Associate, National Institute of Education (August 1985).

(Continued)

Law School Adm. Test		Grad. Manag't Adm. Test	
Mathematics	+ 12.8%	Mathematics	+ 13.3%
Economics	+ 9.6%	Philosophy	+ 11.0%
Philosophy	+ 8.7%	Engineering	+ 10.0%
Engineering	+ 8.0%	Chemistry	+ 7.5%
Chemistry	+ 7.6%	Economics	+ 7.3%
Foreign Languages	+ 5.7%	Computer Science	+ 5.4%
English	+ 5.6%	Government	+ 4.6%
Humanities (Misc.)	+ 4.7%	History	+ 4.6%
Anthropology	+ 4.0%	English	+ 4.1%
Biological Science	+ 4.0%	Biological Science	+ 3.3%
Accounting	+ 3.4%	Foreign Languages	+ 3.3%
Finance	+ 3.4%	Humanities (Misc.)	+ 1.8%
Government	+ 3.3%	Psychology	+ .8%
History	+ 2.9%	Science (Misc.)	+ .8%
Science (Misc.)	+ 2.8%	Political Science	+ .6%
Psychology	+ .9%	Social Sci. (Misc.)	+ .3%
Journalism	+ .7%	Finance	− .8%
Arts and Music	− .5%	Arts and Music	− 1.2%
Business (Misc.)	− .9%	Accounting	− 1.5%
Social Sci. (Misc.)	− .9%	Education	− 4.2%
Political Science	− 1.6%	Business (Misc.)	− 5.0%
Speech	− 2.7%	Sociology	− 5.0%
Business Administr.	− 4.5%	Management and In-	
Management and In-		dustr. Management	− 7.7%
dustr. Management	− 5.4%	Marketing	− 8.1%
Sociology	− 7.0%		
Education	− 8.7%		
Social Work	− 10.1%		

Glossary

Ad hoc. One's defense of a theory in response to an objection is *ad hoc* if one defends the theory by modifying it artificially, simply changing it enough to avoid the objection but without explaining why the change is natural or necessary quite apart from the objection. Usually, when one says that someone else's defense of a theory is ad hoc, the implication is that if the person cannot do better in defending the theory he or she ought to admit that it is wrong.

Ad hominem objection. Instead of objecting to what another says by showing that what he or she says is false, one irrelevantly attacks the person instead. For instance, Jones: "The minimum wage should be raised since one cannot live decently, in many parts of the country, on minimum wages." Smith: "Jones is a Communist, and his opinion, which is typical Commie tripe, should be disregarded."

Affirming the consequent. An incorrect mode of reasoning in which one infers from the fact that the consequent of a conditional (what follows the "then" in an "if . . . , then . . ." statement) is true, that the antecedent of the condition (what follows the "if") is true. For instance, one affirms the consequent if one argues as follows: If Jones is a Communist, then Jones is an atheist. Jones is an atheist. Therefore, Jones is a Communist.

A fortiori. With even stronger reason. For instance, "If it is unlikely that Senator Blowhard will win the election even in his own state, then, a fortiori, it is unlikely that he will win it in the country as a whole."

Agent. Someone who performs an action.

Agent causation. Usually it is thought that causes and effects must be events. But some philosophers have claimed that the cause of an action may be, rather than any event, simply the agent who performed the action. This is usually said as a way of defending freedom of the will against the theories of determinists.

Agnosticism. See *atheism.*

Analytic statement/synthetic statement. A statement is analytic if it cannot be false because its denial is self-contradictory, a condition that will obtain when a statement is true merely because of the meaning of the words used to formulate it, as in the statement that all bachelors are unmarried, or because of its logical form, as in the statement that either pigs can fly or it's not the case that pigs can fly. An analytic statement that is true because of its logical form is said to be *tautology.* Statements that are not analytic are synthetic. The denial of a synthetic statement is not self-contradictory.

A posteriori. A statement is *a posteriori* if one has to appeal to experience to determine whether it is true. For example, the statement "All swans are white," which most Europeans believed at the beginning of the nineteenth century, is both *a posteriori* and also false (since there are black swans). An *a posteriori* statement is contingent, rather than necessary, in that even if it is true, it is the sort of statement (unlike, say, "A rose is a rose") that, if the facts had been different, could have been false. See *analytic.*

A priori. A statement is *a priori* if one can determine whether it is true without appealing to experience. For example, "If there are more than four people in the room, then there are more than two people in the room." An *a priori* statement is necessary, rather than contingent, in that if it is true, it could not have been false, and if it is false, it could not have been true.

Argument. In ordinary usage, an argument is a debate between two or more people, often a heated debate. Philosophers also use the word "argument" to mean a set of statements consisting of a conclusion and one or more premises that are said to provide grounds or reasons for the conclusion. In the philosophical sense of "argument," words such as "for," "since," "due to," and "because" often precede statements intended to be premises, while words such as "thus," "so," "hence," "therefore," "it follows that," and "then" often precede statements intended to be conclusions.

Artificial intelligence (abbreviated AI). An area of study in computer science and psychology that involves writing computer programs that simulate, or mimic, certain "intelligent" human activities, such as playing chess or carrying on a conversation.

Atheism/theism/agnosticism. Atheism is the view that God does not exist; theism, the view that God does exist; and agnosticism, the view that no one (or, alternatively, the person who calls himself or herself an agnostic) knows whether God exists.

Behaviorism. There are two main forms. *Methodological* behaviorism is the view that only external behavior should be investigated by the science of psychology. B. F. Skinner is the best known methodological behaviorist. *Analytic* (or *philosophical*) behaviorism is the view that when we use mentalistic language to apparently refer to private mental episodes what we are actually talking about is external behavior.

Burden of proof. In a disagreement, sometimes one side is expected to prove its case, and if it can't, the other side wins. In such a situation, the side that is expected to prove its case is said to have the burden of proof.

Conditional. An "if . . . , then . . ." statement. For instance, if Jones wins the lottery, then he will be a rich man.

Confirmation/disconfirmation/verification/falsification. A statement or theory has been confirmed (or verified) when there is evidence for it that is strong enough to entitle us to believe that the statement or theory is true. It is disconfirmed (or falsified) when the evidence against it entitles us to believe that the statement or theory is false.

Contradiction/self-contradiction. One or more statements that both affirm that something is the case and also deny it. The joint affirmation and denial may be explicit or implicit. It is always the case that contradictory statements are false. When two or more statements are jointly contradictory, it is always the case that at least one of them is false.

Deductive argument/deduction/inductive argument/induction. A correct deductive argument is an argument such that if we assume its premises are true, then its conclusion must be true; that is, an argument such that it would be self-contradictory to affirm its premises while also denying its conclusion. Correct deductive arguments provide absolutely conclusive evidence for their conclusions. Correct inductive arguments, on the other hand, support their conclusions by showing only that they are probably true.

Descriptive. See *normative*.

Disconfirmation. See *confirmation*.

Dualism. See *substance*.

Equivocation. See *verbal dispute*.

Falsification. See *confirmation*.

Idealism. See *substance*.

Inductive argument. See *deductive argument*.

Law of nature. A lawlike universal statement of the form, "All *A*s are *B*," or "If *X*, then *Y*," or "Whenever *X*, then *Y*", which is empirically testable or an essential part of a theory that is empirically testable. Lawlike statements, when true, are not true accidentally but must be true because of the way the world is constituted. For instance, the universal statement that all the marbles in the jar are black, even if it were true, is not lawlike, since one could have made it false simply by putting a white marble in the jar. The universal statements that formulate laws in physics, on the other hand, are lawlike since one could not, even if one tried, do something to make them false.

Materialism. See *substance*.

Necessary condition/sufficient condition. Generally, something, *X*, is a *necessary* condition for something else, *Y*, just in case *Y* without *X* is impossible; and something, *X*, is a *sufficient* condition for something else, *Y*, just in case *X* without *Y* is impossible. For example, the presence of oxygen is a necessary condition for fire, since it is impossible for there to be a fire unless oxygen is present. On the other hand, the fire is a sufficient condition for the presence of oxygen, since if there is a fire, oxygen must be present.

Normative/descriptive. A statement is normative when it expresses a value, for instance, when it says how people ought to behave or what is good and what is bad. A statement is descriptive, on the other hand, when it merely states the facts without expressing any values.

Ontology. The study of being, that is, of what basic kinds of things exist. See *substance*.

Physicalism. See *substance*.

Proposition. An assertion that is either true or false.

Self-contradiction. See *contradiction*.

Sound deductive argument. A correct (or valid) deductive argument all of the premises of which are true. That is, a deductive argument all of the premises of which are true and which satisfies the following condition: its premises cannot be affirmed and its conclusion denied without self-contradiction. (Inductive arguments, by contrast, are neither sound nor unsound, valid nor invalid; instead, we say of inductive arguments that they are either good or bad, reasonable or unreasonable, acceptable or unacceptable, and so on.)

Statement. See *proposition*.

Straw-man. A bad form of arguing in which one tries to refute a position by arguing against a much weaker version of it than other versions that are known to be available.

Substance. The stuff of which things are made. Dualists, for instance, believe there are two basic kinds of substances: physical (material, corporeal) and mental. Idealists believe there is only one basic kind of substance: mental. Physicalists (materialists) also believe there is only one basic substance: physical.

Sufficient condition. See *necessary condition*.

Synthetic statement. See *analytic statement*.

Tautology. Strictly speaking, a statement that is necessarily true merely by virtue of its logical form. For instance, any so-called "identity statement," such as "A rose is a rose." More loosely, any analytic statement. See *analytic statement*.

Theism. See *atheism*.

Theodicy. A theory the point of which is to explain how God's knowledge, power, and goodness are compatible with the existence of evil (or apparently unnecessary suffering) in the world.

Token. See *type*.

Truth of language. An analytic statement, such as "All bachelors are unmarried," including such tautologies as, "A rose is a rose." See *analytic statement*.

Turing machine. A simple kind of computer, thought up by the mathematician A. M. Turing, that reads symbols on a tape, causing changes in the computer's internal states, which in turn cause the computer to erase and print symbols on the tape. It is often debatable what the capacities and limits of such a machine may be. Computer scientists, psychologists, and philosophers of mind have often thought it of great theoretical significance how such debates are resolved.

Type/token. Two (or more) things of the same sort, or general kind, are said to be tokens of the same type. For instance, two cats are two tokens of the type *cat*.

Vacuous. Literally, empty. In philosophy, sometimes a term of abuse, as when one says that someone else's claim is vacuous as a way of saying that the claim is not the least bit informative. For instance, the statement "God is good, but in a sense of 'good' that is utterly and completely beyond human comprehension" might be said by a critic to be vacuous. However, the word *vacuous* also has a more technical meaning in logic, as when certain universal statements, such as "All unicorns are friendly," may be said to be vacuously true because they are true merely in virtue of being about things that do not exist.

Valid deductive argument. See *sound deductive argument*.

Verbal dispute. A dispute that may appear to be genuine but actually is not because the people disputing are using key words in different senses. Such disputes are sometimes said to depend on an *equivocation*. When one person's argument is undermined by his or her using a key term in more than one sense, the argument is said to depend on an *equivocation*.

Verification. See *confirmation*.

Weltanschauung. A German word meaning "world-view." A very general theory of the way things are; an overview that provides a framework for more specific views and beliefs.

Yoga. Certain exercise and meditative techniques, usually derived from Hinduism, that are designed to calm the mind and/or bring about enlightenment.